The Methodists and
Revolutionary America,
1760 – 1800

The Methodists and Revolutionary America, 1760–1800

THE SHAPING OF AN EVANGELICAL CULTURE

DEE E. ANDREWS

PRINCETON UNIVERSITY PRESS

PRINCETON, NEW JERSEY

Library of Congress Cataloging-in-Publication Data

Andrews, Dee
The Methodists and revolutionary America, 1760–1800: the shaping
of an evangical culture / Dee E. Andrews.
p. cm.
Includes bibliographical references and index.
ISBN 0–691–00958–9 (alk. paper)
1. Methodist Church—United States—History—18th century.
2. United States—Church history—18th century,   3. Methodism—
History—18th century. I. Title
BX8236.A53   2000   287' .0973'09033—dc21   99–37485

This book has been composed in Times Roman typeface

The paper used in this publication meets the minimum requirements
of ANSI / NISO Z39.48-1992 (R1997) (*Permanence of Paper*)

http://pup.princeton.edu

Printed in the United States of America

2 3 4 5 6 7 8 9 10

FOR MY PARENTS

JAMES ANDREWS, JR.
ELISABETT BARDSLEY ANDREWS

WITH LOVE

CONTENTS

ILLUSTRATIONS

FOR HISTORIANS of the American Revolution, there can be few more compelling questions than how a republic forged in the image of enlightened rationalism and shaped by the rejection of state-sponsored church coercion should come to be marked by a powerful and widely accepted religiosity. So much so that less than sixty-five years after Independence Alexis de Tocqueville could famously declaim on the fundamental influence of Christianity on the American mind, and Americans' responses to issues as diverse as abolition, Nativism, and temperance would derive from religious sources. While there is no disputing that the American colonies and the new United States of 1776 were already home to myriad churches, sects, and religious seekers, many of them interpreting the conflict with Great Britain in millennial terms, the rising dominance of religious, especially evangelical, culture throughout the nation after 1800 is equally manifest.

Not least among these changes was the rising popular influence of John Wesley's Methodists. Coming of age in the heated and unpredictable years of the Revolutionary struggle—the only American church that can make this claim—the Methodists were literally the children of the Revolutionary era. Yet while the ranks of American religious historians include Methodist or Wesleyan scholars of the first order—among them William Warren Sweet, Timothy L. Smith, Donald G. Mathews, and Russell E. Richey (author of the cogent *Early American Methodism*)—the ascent of Wesley's movement remains largely unfamiliar terrain to students of American history and is as good as invisible in narratives of the American Revolution itself.

Methodism's virtual absence from American social and political historiography stands in marked contrast to the extensively employed Puritan paradigm and, conversely, to Methodism's central place in contemporary work on English state and society. For while American historians continue to hark back to a model of Puritan influence on American society during and well after the Revolutionary years, despite the rising rather than declining influence of British political and cultural example, scholars of eighteenth-century England have long treated Methodism as one of the leading social phenomena of the period. The terms of the debate regarding the English movement were established long ago by French historian Elie Halévy in his essay "The Birth of Methodism in England," first published in 1906. Wesleyanism, Halévy argued, co-opted popular radicalism in mid-eighteenth-century England and made possible the oddly mystical character of Victorian liberalism, fusing the values of liberty and piety in wholly new ways.

My interest in Wesley's Methodists was sparked by somewhat different concerns. As an undergraduate I was familiar with E. P. Thompson's impassioned polemic on the baleful influence of Methodism on working-class culture in industrializing Britain, the most compelling reinterpretation of the Halévy thesis. But the Methodists did not reenter my consciousness until the start of graduate work at the University of Pennsylvania several years later. At this time, when claims to the uniquely American character of the Great Awakening were perhaps at an all-time high, I was puzzled as to why the Great Awakener himself—George Whitefield—was rarely identified as a Methodist, and his formal status as an ordained Anglican minister rarely cited. Even more mysterious was the transformation of Whitefield's Methodism from an American Calvinist phenomenon to a Wesleyan one within the short span of the Revolutionary War, a metamorphosis that harbingered the supplanting of covenantal Puritanism by the Finneyite, indeed, Wesleyan-style, revivalism of the Second Great Awakening.

I first researched the Methodists from the "bottom up" in a graduate anthropology paper on Philadelphia's African Methodists. Here further questions arose: If Methodism was as stifling of laboring-class autonomy as E. P. Thompson insisted, why had so many slaves and free blacks flooded into the American movement? In claiming their African identity, what were black Methodists—among them the first members of Richard Allen's "African Methodist Episcopal Church," their names inscribed on a list that I unearthed in the basement archives of Philadelphia's Old St. George's Church—to gain from this profoundly "Anglo" movement? And what of the place of women in the Wesleyan ranks, those like George Eliot's Dinah Morris, the English Methodist lay preacher who won the heart of the evangelical hero in Eliot's novel *Adam Bede*? They found little or no place in the burgeoning field of American women's history. Labor historians, it appeared, were especially averse to acknowledging the impact of religion, for better *or* worse, on America's nascent working classes. And the existence of numerous Methodists among the new republic's rising entrepreneurs, many of them former artisans, and especially among Maryland's rural and urban elite, appeared to have been unknown, or at least of little interest to urban historians and scholars of early American capitalism.

When I turned to Methodist spiritual journals—expecting from early excursions into Francis Asbury's writings to find tightly rendered descriptions of circuit riding, quarterly meetings, and disciplinary control—I was astonished to discover a world of fantastic religious voyaging, well stocked with prophetic dreams, visionary trances, and other ecstatic states so familiar in anthropological treatments of religion and magic. Through the work of David Hall, Jon Butler, and Christine Heyrman, early Americans' popular religious passions are now well known. Yet the "interior" journey of the revival meeting—its essentially ritualistic character and the awakened believer's difficult crossing from the revival's seductive circle to the Methodist society's demanding conformity—remained unexplored landscape.

As I worked to reshape my dissertation on Middle Atlantic Methodism into this book, other themes fairly leaped from the sources: the fundamental role of missionaries, the prevalence of grassroots household organizing, the multiple ethnic forces underlying even the most English of movements in the Revolutionary era, the youth of many Methodist converts, and the process by which a movement of British origin was Americanized over these same years. Methodism, it seemed, was both of the Revolution and apart from it, a religious event that perhaps more than any other demonstrated the degree to which the religious cast of the new nation was not an automatic product of national character or nationalist-millennial destiny but constructed from the missionary labors of evangelical preachers and coaxed out of the convictions of their followers. Wesleyan values, furthermore, while a product of many of the same cultural forces that produced the patriot movement—the declaring of independence from the deadweight of the past, the liberal redefinition of the role of the church in society, a passion for reform, the raising up of common men, and a collective sense of destiny—as often as not were in conflict rather than in confluence with the larger political drama the revolutionaries savored so thoroughly. While the Methodist narrative mirrors the path of Revolutionary change, from the interwar years of the 1760s to the triumph of the Democratic Republicans in the election of 1800, Wesley's evangelical followers surveyed an alternative route to happiness. It was one that increasing numbers of Americans were to pursue with each passing year.

● ● ●

I have long anticipated the pleasure of repaying the many debts incurred while completing this study. My first work on the Methodists was completed as a doctoral dissertation under Richard S. Dunn. He has read more versions of this manuscript than he probably cares to count, and while my discussion of Wesley's movement has undergone numerous transformations since I left Penn, its narrative shape, empirical grounding, and social historical ethos are all of Richard Dunn's inspiration. No graduate student or working historian could ask for a more compassionate or perspicacious teacher. He warned me many years ago that the study of history is an all-consuming affair. I have demonstrated the truth of this maxim perhaps all too well.

   I am solely responsible for the idiosyncrasies and errors remaining, but numerous scholars have attempted to keep me from grief along the way. Jon Butler provided singular and wholly spontaneous assistance as mentor, reader, letter writer, and, through his work, guide extraordinaire through the thickets of early American religion. This book would not have been completed without his example and his unflagging encouragement. Michael Zuckerman rendered the best of all possible gifts: an unsparing reading of the manuscript in its last stages. Jean Soderlund and Jackie Reinier each critiqued the manuscript with their customary precision and wisdom. Edith Gelles, Richard Godbeer, Will Gravely, Glenna Matthews, Russell Richey, Nancy Thompson, and Steve Whitman furnished expert readings of individual chapters, and Ann Braude at the Pew Fellows Conference in 1996 pointed out the pitfalls of depending too much on preachers. In earlier stages of this work I also collected insights from Richard Beeman, Ruth Bloch, Rupert Davies, Mary Dunn, David Jaffee, Hugh McLeod, Reid Mitchell, Gary Nash, Roy Ritchie, and Steve Rosswurm. Patricia Bonomi supplied an especially astute assessment of the first version of the manuscript for Princeton University Press, and without Gail Ullmann's early championing, the book might never have come to light. Deborah Malmud has since provided expert editorial guidance, and Lauren Lepow has rendered superb copyediting. Methodist scholars Will Gravely, Russell Richey, Kenneth Rowe, Edwin Schell, and William Williams were indispensable resources when I was a graduate student researcher, and have maintained their interest in my work in the years since. Two Methodist editorial projects eased my labors no end: Francis Asbury's *Journal and Letters*, three note-packed volumes published jointly by Epworth Press and Abingdon Press in 1958, and John Wesley's *Works*, superbly edited by Frank Baker, Richard Heitzenrater, and a host of other Methodist scholars, with volumes still forthcoming from Abingdon Press. Frank Baker may in some respects be held accountable for the detailed referencing in what follows, since at a lunch at Duke University he once gave me advice on research that I have never forgotten: one must look everywhere.

Looking, if not everywhere, at as many Methodist collections and relevant archives as possible to retrieve from obscurity the more than plentiful but widely scattered manuscript sources, I found superb keepers of Methodist and other collections. Ken Rowe at Drew University and Edwin Schell at the United Methodist Historical Society in Baltimore supplied expert guidance, as did David Himrod at the United Library at Garrett Evangelical–Seabury Western Seminaries in Evanston, Illinois; Phebe Jacobsen at the Maryland State Archives in Annapolis; F. Garner Ranney at the Maryland Diocesan Archives of the Protestant Episcopal Church in Baltimore; Jennifer Bryan and Francis O'Neill at the Maryland Historical Society; Brian McCloskey at Old St. George's Church in Philadelphia; Margaret Heilbrun at the New-York Historical Society; Philip Lapsansky at the Library Company of Philadelphia; Linda Stanley at the Historical Society of Pennsylvania; Anne Verplanck at Independence National Historical Park; Constance Cooper at the Historical Society of Delaware; and my graduate school ally and friend Ellen Gartrell at Duke University Library. Through visits and correspondence, I was well served by the staffs at collections cited throughout the source notes. Nancy Richards of Cliveden in Germantown generously shared her knowledge of the Benjamin Chew Papers, and Lynne Dakin Hastings at Hampton Historic Site brought to my attention the contrasting portraits of the two mistresses of the Ridgely estate, one in her preconversion finery, the other as plain as a Quaker. The book benefited especially from the uncomplaining assistance of the Interlibrary Loan Service at the California State University, Hayward (CSUH) University Library and the attentive staff at the lifesaving Graduate Theological Union Library in Berkeley.

I have also had the good fortune to receive substantial fellowship support for travel to collections and for writing. During graduate studies, my research was sustained by a Charlotte W. Newcombe Dissertation Fellowship from the Woodrow Wilson National Fellowship Foundation, a Mellon Fellowship with the Philadelphia (now McNeil) Center for Early American Studies, and an Albert J. Beveridge Award for Research in American History from the American Historical Association. In subsequent years I have been awarded a research grant from the American Philosophical Society, a Summer Stipend from the National Endowment for the Humanities, several faculty development grants and a Research, Scholarship, and Creative Activity Award from CSUH, and, most essential for completion of the project, a Faculty Fellowship with the Pew Program in Religion and American History, under the stewardship of Jon Butler and Harry Stout at Yale University. Participation in the annual conference of Pew Fellows at Yale and several earlier meetings—especially the History Workshop on Religion and Society in London, the Methodist Bicentennial Conference at Drew University, two seminars with the Philadelphia Center for Early American Studies, and a gathering with the Bay Area Seminar in Early American History and Culture in Berkeley—helped shape my thinking on the Methodists in vital ways.

Finally, this project also would not have been concluded without the kind support of good friends, colleagues, and family. Sarah Andrews Brown, Susan Schnare, Glenna Matthews, Jackie Reinier, Barry Bergen, Alan Karras, Susan Godfrey, Robin Brickman, Marge George, Jane Berendsen-Hill, along with Hank Reichman, Judy Stanley, Dan Gilliard, and Dick Orsi, were infinitely emboldening. Armando Gonzales at CSUH made my year with the Pew Fellowship possible. Gary McBride interpreted the mysteries of double-entry bookkeeping in Methodist account books, and Amy Molinelli furnished last-minute fact-checking. Above all, my student and good friend Lynne Goodman performed tireless yeowoman service checking the accuracy of the several thousand quoted words and passages in the manuscript, reading the manuscript not once but several times, and supplying critical direction at difficult crossroads. She has marvelously demonstrated the axiom, familiar from a certain Broadway tune of my childhood, that when one becomes a teacher by your students you'll be taught.

Last but never least, the love and intellectual companionship of my parents helped to inspire all aspects of this study. My father, to my sorrow, did not live to see it in print, but his lifelong affectionate presence and his passion for history, religion, and politics, together with my mother's gentle irreverence, political and literary discernment, and love of eighteenth-century things, inform whatever interpretive intuition I may possess. My sisters and brothers, Sue, Eric, Billy, and Barbara, and sisters- and brother-in-law, Brenda, Lois, and John, each living felicitously close to a major research library, put me up as well as put up with me as I cut short yet another visit to go in search of Methodists. None of us is a Methodist, nor were any of our forebears, but coming to terms with a religious culture other than my own is a pilgrimage I'm glad to have traveled, and with such good company along the way.

San Francisco
December 1998

The Methodists and
Revolutionary America,
1760 – 1800

Figure 1. *Frontispiece.* Thomas Pownall, *A Map of the Middle British Colonies in North America,* 1776, after Lewis Evans. Courtesy of the Rudy L. Ruggles Collection, The Newberry Library, Chicago.

How American was Early American Methodism?

JOHN WESLEY, founder of the most successful religious movement in eighteenth-century Britain, began his missionary career in 1735, an employee of the Society for the Propagation of the Gospel in Foreign Parts, bound for General James Oglethorpe's Georgia colony. Here on the precarious southeastern edge of British America, wedged between South Carolina and Spanish Florida, the colony's frontier dissolving into an interior controlled by powerful southeastern woodlands tribes, Wesley was directed by the SPG to serve as parish priest for Georgia's heterogeneous settler population and to convert the Chickasaws. Instead, with the support of his younger brother Charles, the colony's secretary of Indian affairs, Wesley first experimented with what would become the essential ingredients of his religious movement: the introduction of intensive prayer meetings, the resorting to female church officers, the practices of hymn singing, itinerating, preaching out-of-doors, and ministering to the poor and outcast, including African slaves. Before he left the colony in late 1737, less than two years later, Wesley had published the first Methodist psalmbook and begun the process of formulating his own peculiar brand of Arminian theology, one that would stress the free will of the believer, the universal availability of salvation, and the palpability of religious conversion. Shortly after their return to Britain, Wesley and his brother Charles founded the Methodist movement, comprising a "connexion" of itinerant preachers and a network of "united societies." By the end of the 1740s, Methodism would expand into a realmwide phenomenon, sustained by increasing numbers of lay itinerants, by the Wesley brothers' massive literary output, and by John Wesley's lifelong charismatic leadership.

In time Methodism would flourish in the American setting as it did in Britain, but this was unforeseen by its founder. John Wesley considered his Georgia mission a failure. Stymied by his parishioners' recalcitrance, his own rigid attachment to Anglican ceremony, and his inability to attract more than the Chickasaws' token interest in Anglicanism, Wesley had given up trying to convert the colonies. Instead, the first Americans called "Methodists" were followers of George Whitefield, the Wesleys' evangelical comrade and Calvinist competitor, who dominated American Methodism until the arrival of Wesley's itinerants in the Middle Colonies in 1769. The coming of the Revolutionary War and Independence, futhermore, presented numerous difficulties for the first Wesleyans. Preaching their freewill evangelicalism, so unpalatable to Calvinists, Old and New Light alike, and intruding on Anglican authority as they moved from Philadelphia and New York City into Maryland and points further south, the Wesleyan itinerants were sullied by John Wesley's repeated public attacks on the patriot movement. The itinerants interfered with the rising tide of republicanism in more concrete ways as well, by not only attracting a devoted following among women and blacks—often outsiders to the Revolutionary agitation—but also turning potential militia and Continental Army recruits into pacifist noncombatants.

After the Revolutionary War, the remaining American preachers faced the further dilemma of establishing themselves as a legitimate church under their English-born leader, Francis Asbury. The Methodist Episcopal Church (MEC) was founded successfully, if not uncontroversially, in 1784, but in a climate inhospitable to churches and clergymen. John Wesley died in 1791; yet the American Methodist Church was not free from the presumption of British influence until the last American tour of Asbury's British cosuperintendent, Thomas Coke, in 1804. Following the lead of the English movement and despite a potentially huge southern and southwestern white membership, many of the American itinerants were also active opponents of slavery. Throughout the colonies and the new states, they were perceived as parvenus, or worse, magicians capable of seducing young and old into their cultlike revivalist societies and class meetings.

Despite these obstacles and the repeated portrayal of Methodists as enemies to the American cause and to a conflict that would establish a newly defined American republican identity, Methodist itinerants, inheritors of the Wesleys' missionary system, continued to expand their networks throughout the United States, so widely that by 1800 they had put in place the foundation of an evangelical federation extending from the Atlantic seaboard to the Ohio River Valley and from New England to Natchez. The Methodist Church encompassed itinerants' circuits, local societies, and evangelical households in every part of the new nation, with a membership of 64,000 and climbing.[1] Thousands more had been exposed to Methodist preaching supplied by mostly young traveling ministers at every opportunity and in every possible venue. Indians, the original object of Wesley's mission, rarely numbered among these converts, but conversion of the "heathen" remained a historical subtext of much of the Methodist missionary drive. The church indisputably depended on a substantial female following and, with the exception of the Baptists, the MEC incorporated a greater African American membership than any other church or American institution. By the eve of the Civil War, Methodist churches as a whole, although subject to schism and divided into Northern and Southern halves, accounted for an estimated one-third of American church membership; the most encompassing denomination in the country, they boasted close to 20,000 places of worship, 8,000 more than the Baptists, their closest competitors.[2]

The rise of American Methodism, then, is a paradox, one that should attract the interest of a broad spectrum of religious, social, and Revolutionary scholars. Yet, until recently, Methodism's compelling traits have sparked the curiosity of relatively few historians of religion and even fewer Revolutionary historians. As Nathan Hatch has stressed, while Methodism "remains the most powerful religious movement in American history, its growth a central feature in the emergence of the United States as a republic," historians have consistently discussed its success "blandly and uninspiringly as a component of the western phase of the Second Great Awakening."[3]

For Hatch, American historians' failure to understand Methodism as one of the shaping forces in the new republic may be attributed to a number of factors: the overemphasis on the study of religion as intellectual history; denominational scholars' tendency to "sanitize" the history of religion by focusing on its respectable aspects to the exclusion of the "enthusiasm" of groups like the Methodists; and the stigma borne by Methodism for its lower-middle-class origins. "Perhaps," Hatch suggests, "historians ignore Methodism because Wesleyans are too quintessentially American."[4]

A closer look at the origins of the American Methodist movement through the years of the Revolution and after, however, suggests other reasons for the Wesleyans' low profile in American historiography. For while it is true, as Hatch asserts, that Methodism was to become the American religion, its origins lie in the much wider British imperial setting, and for most of its first generation the movement had little that was distinctly "American" about it. The paradox of Methodism concerns not so much why historians have shown so little interest in this mass movement as why Americans joined it in the first place and how a British missionary society became America's church.

Methodism's broad-ranging appeal derived from many sources, but four interrelated developments account for the peculiar shape the movement took and the energy that propelled it forward. First, Wesleyan Methodism arose in a period of substantial change in British and American religion, beginning with the redefinition of the relationship between church and state at the end of the seventeenth century. The "church," John Locke wrote, severing the ancient tie between church and polity, was "a free society of men" joined together to worship God in whatever way they deemed proper. In this reformulation, the church was "absolutely separate" from the civil realm.[5] The product of England's "Century of Revolution," when religious sects proliferated in unprecedented numbers, the enlightened reconceptualization of the relationship of church to state provided both a theoretical justification for toleration and the moral foundations of denominationalism.

Recognition of the need for churches and religious movements to live with each other's differences came none too soon. The Wesley brothers lived in a religiously and ethnically diverse world. Their London was peopled not only by Anglicans and English folk, but by an array of English and European churches and religious "colonies," from Quakers, Baptists, Congregationalists, and Presbyterians, to Huguenot, Moravian, Flemish, and Palatine refugees from European wars, as well as small communities of Roman Catholics and Sephardic Jews. In British America—the larger British universe—and particularly in the emerging socioeconomic powerhouse of the greater Middle Colonies, Anglicans and their Congregational offspring were the minority religions in a smorgasbord of Quakers, Baptists, Presbyterians, German and Scandinavian Lutherans, German and Dutch Reformed, Huguenots, Catholics, Jews, and various sectarians who pass fleetingly through the historical record. Methodists, admirers of the eclecticism of early Christianity—the "Primitive Church"—accepted the diversity of this religious world as a matter of fact. For this reason, Wesley specifically invited members of all churches and sects to join the Methodists, to seek what Wesley called "holiness" whatever their formal church affiliation.[6]

The invitation came in the form of the second important ingredient of the Methodist system: missionary preaching. Missionizing, as it will be called here, and aggressive outreach followed on the multiplication of denominations competing for British and colonial recruits at the end of the seventeenth century as well as the growth of an increasingly unchurched population in Britain and America. As often as not, missionizing was directed at those on the margins of society—mariners, miners, and other poor folk—and especially those on the margins of Britain's imperial influence in North America, as evidenced by the numbers of Anglican and other ministers who started out their American careers as ministers to one or another Indian tribe.

But by the 1730s, evangelical missionaries' scope encompassed all "hearers" within listening distance, and "heathens" were defined as those who had not yet converted to evangelical-style Christianity. At the same time, by the end of the century, Methodist preachers were at work not only in England and the United States, but also in Wales, Scotland, Ireland, Canada, and the West Indies, soon to expand into Africa and India, among an extraordinary array of European, African, Native American, and Asian populations. As a missionary religion, Methodism displayed its most essential features: it was all-encompassing, ambitious, and "catholic," seeking a universal and inclusive membership and dispensing with stringent tests of faith common among the more exclusivist and frequently community-based Reformed churches and Quaker meetings. It was as a missionary religion that Methodists, as their American opponents put it, "relished the manumitting Subject"[7] and began to attract thousands of Africans and their children into their American societies.

Throughout these relentless journeyings, Methodist preachers sought to propagate the third important aspect of the movement, what they called "the one thing needful": religious experience. Recruits came to the Wesley brothers' particular brand of popular religious culture through the widespread fascination with religious experimentation in eighteenth-century Britain and America. In the 1730s and 1740s, the years of the great revivals in Britain and the Great Awakening in America, colonists' involvement in experimental religious communities ran high, and "emotional" or "enthusiastic" responses to evangelical preaching were increasingly accepted, indeed encouraged. Wesleyan revivalism, forged in these years and incorporating all varieties of oral culture, synthesized the central features of Anglican worship with a sonic ritual that gave shape and often tangible reality to otherwise abstruse theological doctrines.[8] Religious "seekers" with little initial knowledge of theological dispute or denominational history moved from denomination to denomination. In this climate, Wesleyan itinerants provided a discourse of religious affections and "heart-religion" that served as a guide to the new believer attempting to make sense of an often baffling personal transformation.

These new recruits were then incorporated into the fourth important ingredient of the movement: formal congregations known simply as the Methodist societies.

Starting as a cottage meeting or otherwise private gathering, the Methodist religious society was a fluid entity, not dissimilar to the clubs and committees that propagated many features of the American resistance to British rule. Even after the raising of chapel walls, Methodist prayer groups, called classes, regularly convened in private households. Most converts, furthermore, experienced the depths and heights of their religious crises within their own households or those of their masters and mistresses—rather than, as is commonly assumed, in the throes of the revival meeting. It is perhaps not surprising that many of the itinerants' chief supporters were women and many others were servants and slaves who often first came into contact with a Methodist preacher when he arrived at the front or back door. At the same time, the drive to raise chapel buildings was powerful, and in time Methodist chapels, constructed in meetinghouse plain style, provided the metaphorical scaffolding for community building among the new republic's young, mobile, and increasingly diverse population, as well as the setting for some of the movement's most telling schisms.[9]

The transformation of the Methodist movement itself, from offspring of John Wesley to the American phenomenon it was to become in the years after 1800, is the larger subject of this study. For much of the Revolutionary period, widespread acceptance of Methodism among Americans hardly seemed possible. Riven by disputes among preachers before and after the Revolutionary War, ridiculed by the major churches for their preachers' lack of academic training, and divided through the 1780s and 1790s by conflicts among the itinerants that challenged Francis Asbury's command of his missionary organization, the MEC seemed to survive *despite* rather than because of the break with Britain. Early American Methodists fought over the future of their church—providing compelling evidence of the roads not taken by Asbury and the other leading preachers. And like many other churches after the Revolutionary War, the Methodists were uncertain of the course ahead for religious institutions in the new republic. Christianity seemed assaulted on all sides, and republicanism, one itinerant bluntly stated, "eats [religion] out of many hearts."[10]

Emerging at a critical juncture in American history, the Methodist movement was nevertheless to benefit enormously from the changes wrought by the Revolution, as John Wesley's Primitive Christianity supplied a popular evangelical alternative to traditional forms of religious community, patriarchal family relations, and the rough-and-tumble, largely masculine, world of Revolutionary-era politics. Focusing instead on the missionary call, a knee-bending, vocal revival ritual, and the formation of voluntary "societies" comprising numerous, multivarious, and assertive rank and file, the Methodist movement reshaped the Revolution's republican legacy.

• • •

Regarding the geographical context of much of this narrative: Beyond its British origins, Methodism first came into American popularity in the greater Middle Atlantic, the region ranging from the Atlantic coastline on the east to the Appalachians on the edge of the western continental frontier, and from the Hudson River

Valley on the north to the Potomac River separating Maryland from Virginia on the south.[11] In addition to serving as Methodism's American birthplace, the greater Middle Atlantic was the new nation's most complex region and hence provides ideal conditions for coming to some understanding of the Methodists' tribulations and triumphs in their first generation of expansion.

Within its boundaries, the greater Middle Atlantic contained many of the significant social, economic, and cultural features of Revolutionary America. Rural and urban, distinguished by old and new settlements and a violent western frontier, the region was also home to the new republic's most heterogeneous population, including native-born and immigrant, slave and free, Protestant and Catholic, rich and poor, urban-dwelling and rural-dwelling, and the numerous categories in between: first generation Americans, free blacks, indentured servants, the unchurched, and the middling classes, among others.

For the Methodists, the area remained critical throughout their first generation of growth. The earliest Methodist immigrants arrived here in 1760, and a number pursued the Wesleyan mission well beyond Wesley's control. The first American Methodist societies were also established here. The traveling preachers found some of their most receptive audiences in Delaware and Maryland's Eastern Shore well into the nineteenth century, and promoted some of their first frontier revivals in western New York, Pennsylvania, and Maryland. The Middle Atlantic cities of New York, Philadelphia, and Baltimore were communication centers for the Methodists, just as they were for the American patriots, as well as the location of several key Methodist chapels. Among these were the thousand-member-strong Baltimore City congregation—forming the core of Methodism's "capital city"— as well as the Strawberry Alley Chapel on Fell's Point in the same town, the John Street Chapel in New York, St. George's Chapel in Philadelphia, and Richard Allen's African Methodist society, also in Philadelphia.

The Middle Atlantic city societies, furthermore—the focus of close examination in Part II—provide rare insight into the composition and operation of eighteenth-century Methodist congregations. Most important, they reveal the extraordinary mélange of Americans who sought out Methodist preaching. Many were workingmen; others were part of a burgeoning mercantile and entrepreneurial elite reshaping the Middle Atlantic economy; still others were servants and slaves; and the majority were women breaking with family tradition to join the Methodists on their own or in the company of other women. The city societies were also links in a chain of Methodist meetings to which the first itinerants made frequent visits and where they established early classes: in Brooklyn and Newtown on Long Island, and New Rochelle on the Long Island Sound; in Elizabethtown, Newark, Trenton, and Burlington in New Jersey; in Wilmington, New Castle, and Dover in Delaware; in Annapolis on the northern Chesapeake Bay; and in Georgetown and Alexandria on the Potomac. By 1800, the thoroughfares connecting these towns and cities had been trodden by Methodist itinerants for close to forty years.

The number and array of Methodist adherents revealed by these cities' records calls into question the frequent assumption that Methodism was, as English scholars have described it, an exclusively working-class event; or, as American historians are inclined to assume, a largely rural, western, or southern story.

This study will not dispute the primary geographical locus—South and West—of Methodism as it was to develop in the boom years of the early nineteenth century. Expansion into America's hinterlands was indeed the major goal of American Methodism's first leader, Francis Asbury. The bishop envisioned a church that would claim the allegiance of settlers throughout the largely agricultural states. He considered farming and frontiersmanship to be the ideal callings for the ideal Methodist, free of the many temptations of city life and the dangers of political controversy. Like many Americans then and now, Asbury subscribed to the often mistaken belief that city folk were richer than country folk and hence less likely to adhere to Christian piety. Despite the central role of urban leaders in his movement, Asbury lamented the ill effects of city living on his itinerants: "We have had few city preachers," he wrote, "but what have been spoiled for a poor man's preachers."[12] The sizable revivals in Hanover County, Virginia, in the 1770s, sponsored by the indefatigable American preachers working their way through the Revolutionary landscape, confirmed Asbury's hunch that American Methodism—in contrast to its English parent—was a religion well suited to an expansive agrarian nation.

I will argue, however, that Methodism's social complexity defies typecasting. From one end of Revolutionary America to the other, this critical religious and social movement was transformed from European import into American original. Understanding how this change came about is the larger goal of this study.

PART I

Origins

CHAPTER ONE

Raising Religious Affections

THE ANGLICAN SOCIETIES, THE WESLEYS, AND GEORGIA

At the end of the seventeenth century, the Church of England, winner of more than a century and a half of religious conflict, faced an unprecedented dilemma. While the Anglican Church remained established by law, and the numbers of subjects belonging to dissenting churches in England, Wales, and Ireland were relatively few, the church's old rivals, the Congregationalists and Presbyterians, and new contestants, the Baptists and Quakers, had survived the turmoil of the English Revolution and its aftermath, with chapels and meetinghouses in every county of the realm. Whigs and Tories alike believed that Catholic power was in reascendance, while London filled with German and French Protestant refugees from the religious wars in Europe. The universities, the church's intellectual well-springs, were as absorbed with the revelations of the Scientific Revolution as they were with the training of Anglican ministers. In Ireland, Anglican influence was manifestly weak among the general population. Anglican clergy and their wealthy supporters were convinced that vice—gambling, drunkenness, and prostitution—was on the rise.[1]

In the American colonies the religious landscape was, if anything, more complex. With the expansion of mercantile networks into new territories after 1660, Britain's North American empire—from the English West Indies to Nova Scotia and the Appalachian foothills on the continental western frontier—loomed as an enormous but strangely undaunting challenge for ambitious Europeans, religious and otherwise. The English conquest of these territories, in process in the Anglo-French wars, opened up entire new areas for the exercise of Anglican authority over the European, African, and Indian inhabitants. Yet, to the frustration of their Anglican opponents, in 1700 Congregationalists, Quakers, even the Dutch Reformed, and others, exercised as great authority in America as did Britain's official church—if not more.[2]

As at no time in its past, the church faced the prospect of a permanent splintering of its flock. Worse yet, it confronted the possibility of an irreversible reduction of its power in society. The new attitude of many "enlightened" English observers at the end of the seventeenth century was summed up in John Locke's liberal code: a church, any church, Locke wrote, is "a free society of men, joining together of their own accord for the public worship of God in such manner as they believe will be acceptable to the Deity for the salvation of their souls." Regarding the place of an established church in civil society, he added, "the church itself is absolutely separate and distinct from the commonwealth and civil affairs." In

Locke's radical redefinition of church and state, the Anglican Church was one among equals.[3]

In this social and intellectual context, a dual development occurred for British religious institutions. First, while Parliament continued to regulate the Dissenters and discriminate against Roman Catholics, Jews, Muslims, Unitarians, and atheists, it now granted dissenting churches two things: the right to exist, as set out by the provisions of the Toleration Act; and temporary membership in the Anglican Church for politically ambitious Dissenters, as set out by the Occasional Conformity Act. In essence these statutes guaranteed automatic status as a legal Christian to any British subject espousing belief in the Trinity. Hence Nonconformists were no longer perceived by the Anglican majority as dangerous schismatics separated from the one true church, but as Christians called by a particular name in legal distinction from the established church. English religion, that is, was denominationalized.[4]

At the same time, the Anglican Church—traditionally the purveyor of sacred ritual, arbiter of social morality, and protector of the poor in Britain and its colonies—began to compete with the dissenting churches in the propagation of the gospel at home and in America. They did so by forming missionary societies, the first, the Society for the Reformation of Manners, organized in 1691 by a cohort of clergymen and pious merchants and professionals. In 1698 and 1699, Dr. Thomas Bray, Anglican commissary for Maryland, established two further missionary spin-offs, Dr. Bray's Associates and the Society for the Promotion of Christian Knowledge (SPCK), to support gospel work in the colonies, provide libraries to parishes in England and abroad, and educate poor children. The agency most pertinent to this study, the Society for the Propagation of the Gospel in Foreign Parts (SPG), was organized by Dr. Bray and a board of lay and clerical advocates in 1701 to command the work of Anglican evangelization abroad. From these groups a series of religious societies for the encouragement of virtue and the discouragement of vice proliferated throughout England, so that by the 1730s some thirty to forty reforming societies existed in London alone.[5] These clublike groups were bolstered by growing support for toleration and the historical conviction that the Anglican Church was at long last fulfilling the mandate of Primitive Christianity as the chief among multiple churches or "administrations" bound together in Christian charity. Thus one such persuaded Anglican wrote: "In the Primitive Ages of Christianity they say, there was, under Variety of Administrations, an illustrious Union of Affections; Light and Love were not so disjoined; Humility made them willing to stoop mutually to one another. . . ."[6] As large sections of the church splintered into myriad parts, the original Primitive mission would survive, and members of the Anglican societies would emulate the first Christians by ministering to the unchurched and heathens, in Britain and abroad. Hence the chief task of the representatives of the religious societies and the church in America was to promote religious commitment not only among parishioners but among potential parishioners, slaves, and, wherever possible, Indians.

The SPG missionaries and their counterparts around the world, however few in number, served as models of religious inspiration for many pious Anglicans.

Not least of these were the members of one Anglican household that was to have an enormous influence on the evolution of English evangelicalism, the Wesleys of Epworth, Lincolnshire. The paternal head of the Wesleys, the Reverend Samuel Wesley, son of a dissenting minister, was educated at Newington Green, a Congregational school in London where he was a schoolmate of Daniel Defoe. Wesley had returned to the Anglican faith as a young man, matriculated at Oxford, and, for a time, considered a career as a missionary in India.[7] Susanna Wesley, also the child of Puritans—her father, Samuel Annesley, was the pastor of a large and distinguished London congregation—had likewise returned to her family's ancestral Anglicanism, a decision she confirmed by marrying Samuel in about 1689. At the Epworth rectory the Wesleys raised a family of nine offspring. In their mother's words, the Wesley children "were always put into a regular method of living, in such things as they were capable of, from their birth." In the manner of a religious order, the Wesley children were trained to eat, nap, take medicine, and ask assistance of the servants by means of a regimen superintended by their mother. The aim, as Susanna herself stressed, was to "conquer their will, and bring them to an obedient temper."[8] Samuel's missionary interests were satisfied by his founding of a small religious society, associated with the SPCK, for prayer and Scripture reading and for the translation of pious tracts from Dutch and German into the "vulgar tongue" for distribution among the English.[9]

In her experiments with behavior modification and family management, Samuel's wife Susanna sustained a strong Puritan strain, probably drawn from her own childhood, that would have been familiar to many New Englanders.[10] But by the birth of her later children, two other influences were equally important. Like many eighteenth-century Christians and members of the Anglican religious societies, Susanna evinced a fascination with the Primitive Church, both for the belief that revelation had played a direct role in the affairs of the early church and as a model of practical Christianity. In an extended dialogue composed for her daughter in 1711/12 and foreshadowing her son John's theological preoccupations, Susanna carefully set forth a proof of God and the necessity of both enlightened reason and revelation in Christian belief. "Christian religion," she wrote, "as distinguished from natural religion," that is, the religion of Adam in Paradise, "is a complete system of rules for faith and practice, calculated for the present state of mankind." "It is revelation," she continued, "has instructed us in the knowledge of our own condition [since Adam's fall]; how human nature became corrupted; and by what means it is capable of being restored to its primitive purity." In short, "our Saviour came, not to teach us a new, but to retrieve the old, natural religion, and to put us again under the conduct of right reason, by the direction and assistance of his Holy Spirit." The soul might be returned to its uncorrupted state by practical piety, a disciplined will, and openness to divine love.[11]

While her husband was away on business in London, Susanna Wesley began to convene her children for Sunday prayer and sermon readings, and she soon attracted members of the parish who crowded into the rectory to hear the minister's wife "preach." Samuel objected to the practice for its appearance of impropriety and because of what he called Susanna's "sex." Foreshadowing her son's later indifference to parochial rules, Susanna firmly replied and at some length: "[A]s I am a woman, so I am also mistress of a large family. And though the superior charge of the souls contained in it lies upon you, as head of the family, and as their minister; yet in your absence I cannot but look upon every soul you leave under my care as a talent committed to me, under a trust, by the great Lord of all the families of heaven and earth."[12]

One of the significant influences on Susanna's religious evolution at this time was the missionary tract, *Propagation of the Gospel in the East*, discovered by one of the Wesley children in Samuel Wesley's library. From this brief but colorful narrative, Susanna learned of the efforts of two Lutheran ministers to establish charity schools for the *"Training up of Children"* in Tranquebar on the southeastern coast of India. At the request of German settlers living in the area, they also initiated an "Exercise of Piety in our own House," which became so popular that the Danish church in Tranquebar permitted them to preach on its premises. Building a chapel on the outskirts of the settlement, the missionaries, in keeping with the new culture of toleration, invited everyone to attend, "let him be *Heathen, Mahometan, Papist*, or *Protestant*."[13] Susanna reported to her husband, "I was never, I think, more affected with anything than with the relation of their travels; and was exceeding pleased with the noble design they were engaged in." It now came to her that although she was "not a man nor a minister of the gospel, and so, cannot be employed in such a worthy employment as they were," there was evangelical work she could do. A missionary within her own household, Susanna initiated weekly meetings with each of her children to examine their spiritual state. She also began to speak "more freely and affectionately than before" with neighbors continuing to attend her impromptu meetings, their numbers growing to more than two hundred listeners at a time.[14]

Susanna Wesley's effortless application of missionary methods to household management reflected the degree to which devout members of the established church, not least importantly Anglican women, imbibed the changes transforming religious culture after the Glorious Revolution: the increasingly interdenominational inspiration for religious proselytizing (the Tranquebar missionaries, for one example, were German Lutherans rather than Anglican employees of the SPG), the appeal to the English of the "reformation of manners," the fascination with "heathens" on the peripheries of empire, and the understanding that the call to the unconverted might be made closer to home, in the household or cottage sphere, possibly by an amateur preacher, possibly by a woman.

The multiple inspirations that informed the imaginations of two of the Wesley children, John and Charles, born respectively in 1703 and 1707, may be discovered in their mother's household evangelizing. Beginning life as prototypes of young East Indians—unshaped and ripe for the gospel—the Wesley boys learned early that their mother's chief task in rearing them was to turn their wills, forcibly if necessary, to God. Her role, that is, was to convert them.[15] The Wesley brothers were to become the most ambitious and successful shapers of religious discourse in eighteenth-century Britain. But initially they were hardly distinguishable from other pious young men attracted to the Anglican reforming societies as they settled into comfortable collegiate careers at Oxford, their father's alma mater. In 1725, John was ordained deacon and, in 1726, elected a fellow at Lincoln College. The brothers enjoyed the life of gentlemen scholars until about February 1730, when John, inspired by the Pietist writings of William Law, joined Charles and two of Charles's fellow students at Merton College in the forming of their own religious society, one of several extraecclesiastical prayer groups at the university. Their stated aim was to aspire to the practice of "holy living," described by Law and set out in late medieval and English Reformation tracts like Thomas à Kempis's *Imitation of Christ* and Jeremy Taylor's *Holy Living* and *Holy Dying*. Among Charles's fellow undergraduates, the Merton College group came to be known by the sarcastic sobriquet "The Holy Club."[16]

The Holy Club attended Sunday services, paid punctilious attention to the rites of the church, fasted, and performed evangelical and educational labors among the inmates at the Oxford jail and prison, many of them women, children, and debtors. To avoid the onanistic temptations of lying late in bed, John Wesley began the lifelong habit of rising early, among other abstemious practices.[17] In short time, the Holy Club came to be known by further pejorative epithets, including the "Sacramentarians," the "Godly Club," and, simply, the "Enthusiasts." The "Methodists," the name that adhered, derived from as many as three different sources, among them the club's "custom of regulating their time and planning the business of the day every morning," as George Whitefield, a scholarship student and Holy Club member was to recall.[18] Altogether, these pursuits gave the group a High Church / Low Church identity at one and the same time, its members favoring the rites and rituals of Anglicanism on the one hand, while stressing austerity and self-denial, traits commonly associated with dissenting sects, on the other.[19]

Still moving in Oxford circles and following in his father's footsteps, John Wesley was ordained an Anglican priest and elected to the SPCK in 1728. In 1733 he published his first work, *A Collection of Forms of Prayer for every day of the week*, its title reflecting the earnest piety of the early Methodists.[20] On his father's death in April 1735, no longer a young man, John applied for the living at Epworth parish but was turned down. At this critical juncture, while they were still working under the aegis of the Anglican Church, the Wesley brothers' lives suddenly moved in a new direction, away from the cloistered comforts of British academe and parochial life and toward something less predictable. By the fall of 1735 they had signed on for the Georgia venture under the patronage of General James Oglethorpe, a family friend, with John assigned to serve as SPG missionary and Charles Wesley as secretary of Indian affairs. Another Oxford Methodist, Benjamin Ingham, joined the expedition, as did Charles Delamotte, the son of a British-Huguenot sugar merchant, to serve as John Wesley's lay assistant.[21]

John Wesley's charge in Georgia was to provide religious instruction and services for the Anglican colonists and to serve as Christian catechizer to the Chickasaws, a southeastern tribe allied with the British against the Spanish enemy in Florida. Altogether, the Oxford Methodists may have found the Georgia venture especially fitting since its intended beneficiaries were those whom Oglethorpe called "the honest and unfortunate" debtors, like those subject to the Holy Club's ministrations at the Oxford jail. Wesley was to discover further that his work included ministering to German and Scottish settlers and cooperating with August Spangenberg, the missionary-pastor of the Moravians, another group taking their chances in Georgia.[22] Reflecting a spiritual crisis ongoing since his Oxford years, Wesley's "chief motive" in traveling to the new colony, however, was "the hope of saving my own soul," an ambition he tied specifically to working among the Indians.[23]

Disembarking at Savannah in February 1736, a settlement literally cut out of the American forest, the Methodists set about the various duties of their appointments. John Wesley undertook to persuade the Georgia pioneers to systematize their religious life, with emphasis on regular observation of the sacraments of baptism and communion. He and Benjamin Ingham made contact with the Chickasaws. In his capacity as secretary of Indian affairs, Charles Wesley issued licenses to Georgia's Indian traders. Charles Delamotte served as the colony's schoolmaster.[24]

Unfortunately for the Methodists, relations between the first Georgia settlers and their superserious clergy quickly degenerated into a morass of ill will and recrimination. A quarrel between Oglethorpe and Charles Wesley drove the latter back to England just four and a half months after his arrival. Benjamin Ingham had also departed by early 1737.[25] John Wesley at first achieved more success at the Savannah settlement. But soon after Oglethorpe's return to England in November 1736, Wesley's authority was challenged by the colony's chief magistrate, Oglethorpe's deputy, with whose niece, Sophey Hopkey, Wesley had engaged in an awkward and unsuccessful courtship. Now engaged to another settler, Hopkey, with the aid of her future husband, procured Wesley's arrest for allegedly defaming her reputation and refusing her communion. Wesley was tried by a grand jury for ecclesiastical innovations, charges that he in part denied and in part attempted to justify. The indictment was rejected by the Anglican commissary in South Carolina, who reported back to London that the "chief Magistrate is now [John Wesley's] Enemy, & so, of course, [Wesley] is quite naught: a Setter forth of strange Doctrine, a Jesuit, a spiritual Tyrant, a Mover of Sedition, &c." Further defending the SPG missionary, the commissary noted that two-thirds of the grand jury was composed of settlers dependent on the magistrate's store.[26]

Equally disappointing was Wesley's work among the Chickasaws. Like many missionaries Wesley planned to learn the language of the tribe with whom he was attempting to communicate. In addition to his evangelical inspiration, Wesley brought with him the increasingly beneficent European view of eastern woodlands tribal culture, holding that the Georgia Indians possessed "no vain philosophy to corrupt [the Bible], no luxurious, sensual, covetous, ambitious expounders to soften its unpleasing truths." Echoing his mother's early association of household proselytizing with East Indian evangelization, Wesley added that the American Indians were "as little children, humble, willing to learn, and eager to do, the will of God."[27] His exchanges with the tribe, later published in the *Gentleman's Magazine*, reveal more persuasively the Chickasaws' fear of annihilation by the

Spanish, the English, and the rival Choctaws than Wesley's missionary efficacy.[28] In September 1737 Wesley observed realistically, "The reason for which I left [England] had now no force, there being no possibility as yet of instructing the Indians; neither had I as yet found or heard of any Indians on the continent of America who had the least desire of being instructed." In December 1737, arrested in a second suit connected with the Hopkey case, Wesley fled on foot to Charleston. He sailed for England near the end of December 1737. Charles Delamotte, waiting for the arrival of the colony's new missionary, George Whitefield, returned to England the following June.[29]

The Invention of Wesleyan Methodism

Despite the multiple embarrassments of John Wesley's one and only sojourn with the SPG and his only American journey, the Georgia experiment was not an entirely unproductive one for the future of Wesley's system. Wesley's biographer Frank Baker has pointed out that the Oxford-educated cleric's instincts for innovation and literary popularization were already in force in Georgia, if not yet joined with an understanding of how best to communicate these to his audience. In Savannah, Wesley formed extraecclesiastical prayer groups directed by lay leaders, much like popular holy clubs and foreshadowing Methodist classes. He appointed deaconesses, drawing women into a formal role in assisting the ministry. The informal state of religion in the colony prompted him and Benjamin Ingham to rely on extempory prayer and extensive traveling, mostly on foot, to the settlements around Savannah, as well as some open-air preaching. Influenced by his reading of Primitive Christianity, Wesley favored early morning services, and in imitation of German pietistic practice he introduced hymn singing at Sunday services and communion. In 1737 Huguenot printer Lewis Timothy published Wesley's first hymnbook, *A Collection of Psalms and Hymns*, in Charleston: an anthology of seventy hymns by various authors, including George Herbert, Isaac Watts, and anonymous German composers. Wesley also preached to Georgia's poorest settlers, African slaves, gaining some understanding of the conditions of slavery upon which he would draw years later. And he experimented with gathering the settlers in Moravian-style single-sex prayer meetings called bands.[30]

The grand jury charges leveled against Wesley, furthermore, while likely arising from the heated conflict with Oglethorpe's deputy, reveal the extent to which Wesley was already perceived as a clerical innovator. Among the charges were assertions that Wesley had changed the order of the liturgy, introduced new and unauthorized psalms and hymns, confined communion to a select group of congregants, and employed spies to invade the private affairs of the colony's settlers. Perhaps most alarming to the men in Georgia, Wesley was said to have taught "wives and servants that they ought absolutely to follow the course of mortifications, fastings, and diets, and two sets of prayers prescribed by him, without any regard to the interests of their private families, or the commands of their respective

husbands and masters." This not far-fetched accusation that the Methodists undermined family order was to dog Wesley's itinerants through the rest of the century.[31]

On his return to London, John Wesley's spiritual crisis, begun at Oxford, became more pronounced. Almost immediately the Wesley brothers and a number
of the other Oxford Methodists became involved with the European religious
immigrant and refugee communities living in the city, including the Moravians—
already familiar from the Georgia experience—French Prophets, and Huguenots.
A sectarian movement of medieval origin, the Moravians, known formally as
Unitas Fratrum (Unity of the Brethren), had survived as a "Hidden Seed" in
Counter-Reformation Europe. In the 1720s they came under the shaping influence
of Count Nikolaus Ludwig von Zinzendorf at whose Saxony estate the sect had
established the communal settlement of Herrnhut.[32] Similar to the Oxford Methodists, the Moravians emulated Primitive Christianity, particularly the mandates
of holy living and practical piety. Various features of their worship appealed to
the Georgia Methodists (Ingham and Delamotte were both to convert to Moravianism), including midnight vigils called watch nights, quasi-sacramental meals
called love feasts, and the division of Moravian communities into bands or groups
of men and women, segregated by sex and marital status and hearing one another's
confessions.[33] Despite their semimonastic living arrangements, Moravians believed that members might join their sect and remain communicants in their state
or sectarian churches. Like the SPG, they sponsored a traveling ministry to sustain
their "diaspora"—their role in revitalizing existing churches—so that by the
1730s Moravian missionaries were working across an extraordinary geographical
expanse: as far afield as Greenland, the West Indies, Surinam, the Gold Coast,
South Africa, and Ceylon. The missionaries' accomplishments were communi-
cated to the faithful back in Europe at "Gemeintag" or letter days. In London, the
Moravian colony had established its own religious society, among whose attenders was General Oglethorpe.[34]

Through their Huguenot and Moravian connections, the Wesley brothers were
also attracted to the more flamboyant refugee sect of the Camisards, or "French
Prophets." The Prophets had fled to Britain in 1706 following the suppression of
their millennially inspired uprising in the southern French province of Languedoc.
Known for public exhibitions of entrancement and speaking in tongues, especially
by their female inspirées, the Prophets had been objects of study for British religious experimentalists since the turn of the century.[35] The influences of Moravian
quietism and Camisard ecstaticism, soon to prove contradictory, converged for
John Wesley when, shortly after returning from Georgia, he met the Moravian
leader Peter Böhler at the residence of French Prophet supporter Francis
Wynantz.[36]

Although, as Richard Heitzenrater has shown, Wesley was to discover before
long that the German and English Moravian communities differed on various
particulars, Peter Böhler pressed upon Wesley the twofold doctrine of conversion
espoused by the English branch of the United Brethren: that conversion—the
knowledge that Christ had died for one's sins—occurred instantaneously and, if
authentic, was invariably accompanied by perfection, the assurance that the con-

vert had been made "perfect" or sinless by the Holy Spirit. This latter doctrine—also called "sanctification," or simply "holiness"—was to play a major role in Methodist theology and experience. At this early stage, however, Wesley was more interested in Böhler's scriptural and experiential proofs for religious transformation through faith.[37] In a short time, Böhler persuaded the Wesley brothers that they were only partially justified, that is, "awakened" rather than fully converted, and criticized them for their undue emphasis on good works. "Of faith in Jesus they have no other idea than the generality of people have," Böhler wrote to Count Zinzendorf. "They justify themselves," he continued, by assuming that their worldly works were proof of their salvation.[38]

Under Moravian guidance, the Wesley brothers now set off on a whole new spiritual quest. At the beginning of May 1738 John Wesley and James Hutton, a London printer-bookseller and Moravian sympathizer, organized a religious society that first convened at Hutton's house and then in Fetter Lane above Fleet Street. The group welcomed Anglicans and Moravians alike and subscribed to a set of rules combining the practices of the Anglican societies with those of the Brethren, including the use of bands and love feasts. A second group, also admitting Moravians, was founded by Hutton in Aldersgate Street.[39] At two subsequent meetings of these assemblies, first Charles and then John Wesley experienced a calming but palpable spiritual assurance, John's on the evening of May 24 at the Aldersgate society during the reading of Luther's "Preface to the Epistle to the Romans." Of this moment Wesley wrote, in the language of heart-religion that was soon to be encoded into eighteenth-century religious discourse, "About a quarter before nine, while [the society's reader] was describing the change which God works in the heart through faith in Christ, I felt my heart strangely warmed." He continued, "I did trust in Christ, Christ alone for salvation, and an assurance was given me that he had taken away *my* sins, even *mine*, and saved *me* from the law of sin and death."[40]

Within days Wesley had begun to exhort his fellow society-members on the subject of conversion, with not altogether happy results. James Hutton's wife reported to the Wesleys' older brother that John had announced that "five days before he was not a Christian, and this he was as well assured of as that five days before he was not in that room, and the way for them all to be Christians was to believe, and own, that they were not now Christians." Mrs. Hutton complained of the impact of the Wesleys' paired conversions on their London audiences: "Now it is a most melancholy thing to have not only our children, but many others, to disregard all teaching, but by such a spirit as comes to some in dreams, to others in such visions as will surprise you to hear of."[41] In the summer of 1738 Wesley traveled to the Moravians' settlement at Herrnhut where he spent two weeks viewing the communal living arrangements at first hand and listening to Christian David, the Bohemian refugee leader and mechanic preacher, expound on the Scriptures.[42] On his return to Britain, Wesley and his brother Charles were received by the bishop of London, head of the SPG, who reprimanded them for heterodoxy, gently this time, less so later. In December Wesley published the

Rules of the Band Societies, a summary of personal questions for the bands at Fetter Lane and Aldersgate Street, adopted from the Herrnhut United Brethren.[43]

By all appearances, the Wesleys were moving in the direction, formerly favored by the Puritans, of linking religious conversion with religious association and practical piety. Had this been all there was to the "new" Methodism, it would likely have remained a small neo-Puritan sect, rapidly to splinter from the established church as yet another form of exclusionist dissenting organization. Instead, two key ingredients became central to and ultimately dominant in Wesley's Methodism. One was the missionary zeal that Wesley had exhibited in Georgia and was now to direct toward the large and increasingly unchurched population of England, Ireland, and Wales—the "heathen" population of Britain. The other was his embracing of enthusiastic religious experience. Wesley became a people's preacher, speaking and publishing in terms accessible to his frequently unchurched, poor, and laboring-class "hearers."

As a popular preacher, Wesley (and his brother Charles, his hymn-composing collaborator) had a potentially enormous audience in Britain. Despite the efforts of reform-minded individuals within the various Anglican societies, as Michael Watts has shown, the Anglican establishment was remarkably unresponsive to the large-scale socioeconomic changes underway in eighteenth-century Britain; in short, the church's parochial structure had been "rendered obsolete" in the new industrial centers of the North, Midlands, and Southwest. At the start of the century Newcastle-upon-Tyne, for one example, was peopled with 18,000 inhabitants and contained just four parish churches. In the 1710s, Manchester and Liverpool each possessed just two parish churches for 8,000 and 12,500 inhabitants respectively, and Bolton just one for 5,500 inhabitants. By the 1730s, Nottingham relied on two Anglican churches for a population of 8,000, as did Taunton in Somerset for 9,000. Sheffield contained just one Anglican church for a population nearing 10,000. In the early 1740s, Halifax was the largest parish in England, encompassing 124 square miles and comprising 6,200 households, or approximately 28,000 people; of these, 160 took communion.[44] While in the cities the middling classes filled the dissenting churches, English and Welsh rural folk, cottagers, and day laborers were left to compete for seats, if they could or sought to, in small and aging structures designed for medieval villages.[45]

The state of many English parishes provided rich raw material for clerics willing to break a few rules, a proclivity Wesley had already exhibited in Georgia. There Wesley had traveled under difficult conditions to the settlements in the colony where for lack of church buildings he had also early engaged in outdoor preaching. He continued to travel in England as he had in Georgia, preaching to various congregations and at religious societies in Oxford, London, and other locations. At one stop, in Faversham, he saw "a few of those who were called Christians but were indeed more savage in their behavior than the wildest Indians I have yet met with."[46] In February 1739, Wesley's younger colleague, George Whitefield, brought the Georgia experience home when he preached to about two hundred mine workers in Kingswood on the outskirts of Bristol, Britain's dissenting capital. In April 1739, at Whitefield's urging, Wesley for the first time since Georgia experimented with preaching in the fields, also near Bristol.[47]

Wesley accounted for these innovations by invoking a relatively vague but all-encompassing scriptural allusion, distinguishing between what he perceived as divine and secular commandments. "[O]n scriptural principles I do not think it hard to justify whatever I do," he wrote. "God in Scripture commands me, according to my power, to instruct the ignorant, reform the wicked, confirm the virtuous. Man forbids me to do this in another's parish." Wesley contended that since "I have now no parish of my own, nor probably ever shall," he had no other choice than to preach out-of-doors. "I look upon *all the world* as *my parish*," so that "in whatever part of it I am, I judge it meet, right, and my bounden duty, to declare unto all that are willing to hear the glad tidings of salvation."[48] He espoused, that is, the missionary's credo: conversion of the lapsed and heathen alike, in and outside of formal parochial and congregational structures, at home and abroad. Over the next fifty years, Wesley preached as many as 40,000 sermons and traveled as many as 250,000 miles, chiefly in England, Wales, and Ireland. In assuming this popular mantle, as Albert Outler has suggested, Wesley at last reached the resolution of his long spiritual crisis.[49]

As the harbinger of "good news" to any among the thousands of the British populace willing to listen, Wesley also entered into a dialectic with his hearers and came to a reassessment of the operation of the Holy Spirit on the common believer: the second important feature that prevailed in his religious unorthodoxy. While retaining sanctification as a distinctive Methodist doctrine, Wesley moved away from Peter Böhler's narrow description of the "instantaneous" conversion to stress instead the palpability of the conversion experience, even if manifested in ecstatic form.

Despite the impact of Wesley's Aldersgate experience on his religious consciousness, the embracing of religious enthusiasm was an unlikely posture for Wesley, the Oxford graduate and devout Anglican priest. Like eighteenth-century Whig reformers, Wesley and his brother were initially suspicious of the over-zealous attachment to religious experience that enthusiasm was believed to signify. Wesley reported of an ecstatic participant at a meeting of French Prophets in January 1739: "Two or three of our company were much affected and believed she spoke by the Spirit of God. But this was in no wise clear to me." Such reactions, Wesley continued, "might be either hysterical or artificial. And the same words any person of a good understanding and well versed in the Scriptures might have spoken." In spring 1739, he supported his brother's successful efforts to expel followers of the Prophets from the Fetter Lane Society.[50] But soon after his conversion, John Wesley was described by even close associates as "an enthusiast, a seducer, and a setter-forth of new doctrines." And although he remained dubious of the ecstatic outbursts attending the Camisards' meetings, Wesley recorded these with anthropological objectivity in his soon-to-be published journals.[51]

Wesley began to change his mind about religious enthusiasm upon reading *A Faithful Narrative of the Surprising Work of God, in the Conversion of many hundred Souls in Northampton* by the New England divine Jonathan Edwards.

Edwards's approving rendition of his congregants' heightened response to his preaching in the first years of New England's Great Awakening persuaded Wesley that the vocal outbursts and episodes of entrancement and even possession that multiplied in religious society meetings and at outdoor preaching, in Bristol and in London, were legitimate expressions of the working of the Holy Spirit.[52] In June 1739, he observed a variety of ecstatic responses to prayer at a meeting in Wapping. "I have seen many hysterical and many epileptic fits," he commented, "but none of them were like these. . . ."[53] To the argument made that God did not work miracles in the modern world, Wesley now responded, paraphrasing Scripture, "I have heard these things with my own ears and seen them with my eyes." Participants in the Methodist meetings, he argued, were undergoing "sensible inspiration," the experience of grace palpably accessible to the believer through his or her physical senses.[54] The dual conversion of justification (the assurance of Christ's pardon for one's sins) and sanctification (the assurance that one had reached a state of sinless perfection) did not necessarily occur instantaneously or simultaneously, as Peter Böhler had insisted. Rather, the transformation of the "heart" might take myriad outward forms, from quietist to enthusiast, depending on the spiritual receptivity of the seeker. As long as they were sensibly felt, the two manifestations of conversion could be considered real experiences essential to the individual's salvation.[55]

Coupling the Anglican Arminian doctrine which taught that salvation was universal, that is, available to all who sought it, with the conviction that "the bulk of mankind . . . are competent judges of those truths which are necessary to present and future happiness," Wesley had now cut the pattern for the Methodist revival.[56] While many observers were increasingly alarmed by the rise of what in short time was condemned as Methodist enthusiasm, and Methodist itinerants were to be greeted with hostility by a host of adversaries throughout Britain and Ireland, revival partisans believed they were experiencing the initial stages of the "New Birth" or Christian awakening, as the phrase "great awakening" later came to imply. In this way, Wesley and his supporters achieved their unique combining of Anglican efforts at religious reform with the religious strenuosity favored by Nonconformists. Raising "religious affections," to use Jonathan Edwards's phrase,[57] became the goal of the new religious missions.

WESLEY VERSUS WHITEFIELD

The Wesleys and their advocates were not the only Methodists remaining from the Oxford Holy Club, however. George Whitefield also adopted the term "Methodist" for himself and his followers through the rest of his preaching career. And although unsympathetic contemporaries frequently saw little difference between the two, Wesleyan Methodism and Whitefieldian Methodism were notably divergent from the start.

Ten years John Wesley's junior and significantly beneath the Wesley brothers in social rank, George Whitefield was born in Bristol in 1714, the son of an innkeeper. As his recent biographer Harry Stout writes, Whitefield resolved his "love/hate relationship with the world, status and achievement" through an "all-compelling sense of personal destiny." His religious career, like Wesley's, was promoted by his mother, although for reasons of social rather than religious advancement. Whitefield evinced an earlier attraction to the theater, but once at Oxford, he joined the "methodist subculture." After his stint as Wesley's successor in Georgia, Whitefield began a lifelong progress as a spectacular public performer devoted to proselytizing for the New Birth.[58]

Wesley and Whitefield began as allies. Most important, it was through Whitefield's example as a field-preacher to the coal-miners of Kingswood that Wesley made "all the world" his parish. Within several months, however, the two missionaries-turned-evangelists had fallen into a theological dispute that divided each from the other for the rest of their life's work. Like the Welsh field-preacher Howell Harris, George Whitefield was an unusual hybrid, an Anglican Calvinist with a firm belief in the doctrines of ineluctable election and the irreversible salvation of sanctified Christians, the Protestant version of "saints."[59] Wesley, by contrast, continued to espouse Anglican Arminianism, emphasizing the potentiality of universal salvation as promised by Christ as well as the dangers of a fall from grace by those already converted. In April 1739, Wesley published the sermon "Free Grace," in which he set forth his theological views but chiefly launched an attack on predestinarians, whom he condemned as blasphemers. John Fletcher, Wesley's theological point man, was later to summarize the Wesleyan position regarding the Calvinist "error." Christians who overstressed "the difficulties of keeping Christ's laws," he wrote, whether intentionally or not, have "Calvinistically traduced the equity of our gracious God, and inadvertently encouraged the Antinomian delusions." After these initial controversies, Whitefield and Wesley were to resume their correspondence, but neither strayed from his original theological stance.[60]

The systems sponsored by these two Anglican clerics differed in other ways as well, however. Whitefield, a performer at heart, also exhibited a notable lack of zeal for organization and administration. As Wesley was later to write, Whitefield's American followers had "no shadow of discipline; nothing of the kind. They were formed into no societies."[61] By contrast, within several short years of his conversion, Wesley had placed in operation a network of Methodist congregations, a connection of itinerant preachers, and a publishing program that were to become critical factors in the expansion of his movement.

The first of these innovations, the Wesleyan Methodist societies, evolved from the Wesley brothers' original contact with the Moravians. By the summer of 1739, it was apparent that the Moravians' model of a religious society was too restrictive for the Wesley brothers' purposes, ill-fitting the catholic mold from which their new sense of religious mission was cast.[62] Rather than rejecting the dependence on religious meetings for the recruiting of followers, however, Wesley redefined the religious society: from a top-down Anglican association designed for the edification of the poor, or, alternatively, the exclusive, gathered church of the Puritan elect or Moravian sect, to a meeting open to all seekers. In July, he authorized the building of the first Methodist chapel or preaching house in Bristol, called simply "The Room." At the end of 1739, the Methodists also began to meet in the Foundery, an abandoned government ironworks in Moorfields outside London. In July 1740, John and Charles Wesley broke with the Moravians and the Fetter Lane Society to constitute their own reforming congregation, called the "United Society," or, reflecting more accurately the numbers of meetings involved, the "United Societies."[63]

Adapting the enlightened redefinition of the church as a voluntary association to his own purposes, Wesley asserted, paraphrasing Scripture, that the only condition required of members of the Methodists' congregations was "a desire to flee from the wrath to come, and to be saved from their sins." The Methodist organization, Wesley insisted, was founded "without any previous design," and "afterwards called a *Society*—a very innocent name, and very common in London for any number of people *associating* themselves together."[64] As Frederick Dreyer has shown, the Wesleyan societies were held together by an implicit contract between Wesley and his followers. And like a kind of religious club, the United Society was neither sect nor church, thus enabling Wesley to evade charges of separation from the Church of England.[65]

The United Societies maintained a number of Moravian features, including band meetings, watch nights, love feasts, and letter days. Wherever preaching houses were built, men and women sat separately, divided by a rail.[66] At the same time, Wesley quickly modified the often intense same-sex meetings of the bands with the introduction of class meetings, initially organized to raise money for the preaching house debt in Bristol, but soon converted into informal confessional sessions, often in the homes of the faithful. The Methodists in this way assumed yet another aspect of sectarian religious movements—the household meeting— with which John Wesley was familiar from his childhood. The first Wesleyans also adopted what they understood to be some of the features of the Primitive Church, in some cases to the point of the sharing of property.[67] Women in particular were attracted to the Methodist societies as to a celibate sect, devoting themselves to worship to the exclusion of their familial and maternal obligations. The Methodist clubs became substitute families, where members addressed each other as "brother" and "sister," and class meetings provided the safe confines within which the newly faithful bore witness to each other's conversions.[68]

The monastic tendencies of early Methodism are also apparent in Wesley's recruitment of a company of lay preachers called the "Methodist Connexion." Initiated in 1741 by Wesley's appointment of Thomas Maxfield as his official assistant, Wesley's itinerant connection was formally organized at the first Methodist conference, held at the Foundery in 1744 and attended by John and Charles Wesley, four sympathetic Anglican clergymen, and four unordained laymen. The number of licensed preachers rose rapidly thereafter, and at each of the subsequent conferences these were appointed to travel on assigned circuits in pairs. The lay preachers were under Wesley's straightforwardly authoritarian rule and were prohibited from administering sacraments or ordaining fellow preachers.[69] But the formation of a Methodist connection set in motion processes not entirely under

Wesley's control. Hence while women were excluded from the itinerancy, a striking number of female converts—including Mary Bosanquet (author of the proto-feminist religious tract *Jesus, Altogether Lovely* and, later, wife of John Fletcher), Grace Bennett, and Ann Gilbert— crossed the boundaries between the household sphere and public preaching, in some cases journeying in the faith over great distances. Sarah Crosby, among the best known of Wesleyan female preachers, exhorted to hundreds of listeners at a time and traveled widely through the Midlands and Yorkshire, occasionally as Wesley's informal assistant.[70] The local societies also spawned another important cadre of Methodist actors, other laymen called local preachers. Several of these men were to have greater initial impact on the American scene than Wesley's licensed itinerants.[71]

In keeping with Wesley's popular goals, the Methodist preachers worked in some of Britain's newest and poorest industrial centers, particularly in Lincolnshire, Cornwall, and the West Riding of Yorkshire. Contemporaries derided them as "a ragged legion of preaching barbers, cobblers, tinkers, scavengers, draymen and chimney sweepers," mechanic itinerants little different from the religious radicals who had turned England upside down during the English Revolution.[72] Through the 1740s, Wesley's middling- and laboring-class followers were objects of abuse by anti-Methodist mobs, who often collected among the poor or were fostered by magistrates and local grandees. John Walsh writes that the "resentment of gentry and clergy is not hard to explain. They feared [Methodism] as a challenge to public order and to the authority of their class." The Methodist societies, Walsh continues, "were tended by itinerant agents, whose origins were unknown, whose persons were obscure, and who appeared to have no formal authorisation whatever." Fears of these leveling agents, combined with memories of the religious conflicts of the previous century, and the characterization of the itinerants as "insolent boys"—a charge that would carry over into the American context—go far to account for the frequently virulent attacks on Wesley's preachers.[73] Despite this often intense opposition, by 1746 (the first year in which circuits were recorded in the conference minutes), the Wesleyans had divided England and Wales into the seven itinerant districts of London, Bristol, Evesham, Yorkshire, Newcastle, Wales, and Cornwall.[74] In 1747, in a move important for the future of the movement in America, Wesley also traveled to Ireland in the first of at least twenty-one visits. Here a Methodist society had been gathered in Dublin by an English local preacher, and the newly arriving licensed itinerants attracted large audiences as well as hostile assailants encouraged by the Anglican-dominated government.[75]

Unlike Whitefield, finally, Wesley primed his followers' appetite for preachers' lives, accounts of travel to the margins of Christendom, and "remarkable" conversions with a steady stream of popular publications. Volumes of sermons, letters, journals, controversial tracts, Christian histories, magazines, popular treatises, advice books, and hymnbooks poured forth from the presses of the Wesleys' publishers. Always Wesley was conscious of the plebeian origins of the vast majority of his followers. Thus *Primitive Physic*, his guide to domestic medicine, was, he claimed, based upon "Experience, Common Sense, and the common Inter-

Figure 2. Robert Pranker after John Griffiths, *Enthusiasm Displayed*, 1755.
A mixed crowdin Upper Moorfields, London, gathers to hear a weeping Methodist
preacher. © copyright The British Museum.

est of mankind" and designed to replace medical tomes "too dear for poor men
to buy, and too hard for plain men to understand."[76] Methodists could learn the
rules of the Wesleyan way of life from the strict social dicipline code set out in
The Nature, Design, and General Rules of the United Societies, or the *General
Rules* for short, published yearly.[77] And members imbibed the essentials of what
the Wesley brothers called "Social Holiness" in the literally thousands of hymns
composed by Charles Wesley and published in numerous anthologies that also
contained the work of other writers. Charles Wesley's hymns expressed succinctly
the ingredients of the Methodist message—part Moravian mysticism, part impassioned evangelicalism—embodying the main ingredients of the Methodist "heart-
religion."[78] As a whole, the Methodist publishing program revealed Wesley's gifts
as a "retailer" of popular publications designed to introduce his audience to fundamental Christian teachings and the elements of a pious life.[79]

   Thus Wesley and Whitefield pursued their increasingly divergent paths to evangelizing the British public, pursued even to markedly different geographical lo-

Figure 3. *John Wesley*, by Robert Hunter, 1765. With kind permission of the Trustees of the Leysian Mission, Wesley's Chapel, London.

cales. While Wesley spent the remainder of his career traveling in England, Scotland, and Ireland, Whitefield completed a total of six tours of the American colonies between 1738 and 1770. Here he received a warm reception among the colonies' neo-Calvinist clergy, including Jonathan Edwards, and the Tennent family who had already welcomed him into their religious meetings in Scotland.[80] Wherever possible, Whitefield took especial advantage of the diverse religious culture of the greater Middle Atlantic, where some form of religious toleration had been written into three of the colonial charters (in Maryland, New Jersey, and Pennsylvania along with the three lower counties of Delaware) before the same policy was adopted in Britain in 1689. The church-attending population was divided into myriad denominations and sects representing virtually every European Protestant group, as well as Catholics and Jews. Whitefield's audiences also included large numbers of African slaves, whenever permitted by their masters to witness the powers of the great evangelist.[81]

Here as in England Whitefield took advantage of Anglican weakness, particularly the lack of clergy. By the time of Whitefield's Great Awakening tour of 1739–1741, Anglican efforts at missionary outreach had gone a long way to establish the Church of England as a religious force in the colonies. A full-scale "Anglican renaissance," to use Jon Butler's phrase, was well underway by the 1720s. The church was established by law in New York City and surrounding counties, as well as in the Chesapeake and the Carolinas. New parishes were being surveyed throughout Maryland and the South. By the 1740s, the rebuilding of Philadelphia's Christ Church in stately Georgian style, reflecting the American Anglicans' episcopal ambitions for the colonies, was nearing completion. Smaller but equally refined Anglican structures were raised in parishes throughout the provincial countryside. These new sacred spaces drew in an array of worshipers, but especially an aspiring colonial elite.[82]

For the most part, however, throughout the first half of the century, the Anglican ministry, like other colonial clerics, continued to struggle with the often punishing conditions of a colonial living. Responsible for vast expanses of territory—the colonial equivalent of overpopulated parishes in Britain—the SPG had achieved minimal success in attracting communicants, for which they were regularly criticized by their evangelical rivals. A typical parish in Maryland, designed to serve a dispersed population, ranged between twenty and fifty miles in length and extended to as much as two hundred square miles in area. While the SPG missionaries reported healthy attendance at their services, their answers to the bishop of London's queries of 1724 revealed that their churches were understaffed and undersupplied, their incomes dependent on the vagaries of the tobacco market, and their houses in disrepair, with parish vestries providing little or no support for schooling or libraries.[83] The ministers had given up on converting the few Indians still living nearby. As one respondent bluntly declared, "No means used to convert the Indians; their language unknown to us."[84] The missionaries were also blocked by slaveholders from working among the African population. His parishioners, one minister on the Eastern Shore reported, were "generally so brutish that they would not suffer their Negroes to be instructed, catechized, or baptized."[85]

The Anglican renaissance was thus deeply threatened by George Whitefield's arrival. A harsh, sometimes reckless critic of the church and of his former employer, the SPG, Whitefield wielded tremendous popular influence as he swept down the Atlantic coastline attracting the curious, faithful, previously indifferent, and knowingly sophisticated of all backgrounds. Throughout these travels, Whitefield, as Harry Stout and Frank Lambert have both shown, relied on his well-documented rhetorical genius, a powerful understanding of religious theater, and a well-developed sense of the commercial potentialities of evangelization.[86] Along the way he garnered cross-denominational support from friends and allies, established letter-writing networks, and encouraged the more or less spontaneous formation of religious meetings.[87]

Despite negative reactions to his presence, Whitefield was able to attract a healthy representation of colonial society to his meetings. In Philadelphia, Benjamin Franklin became an unlikely ally and observed that Whitefield's preaching drew in "Multitudes of all Sects and Denominations." In 1739, Whitefield's supporters in the city, including Franklin, built the evangelist a preaching hall, paid for by subscribers from various churches. Revealing the now widespread fascination with the missionary life that had so appealed to Susanna Wesley, Franklin reported, "Both House and Ground were vested in Trustees, expressly for the Use of any Preacher of any religious Persuasion who might desire to say something to the People of Philadelphia, the Design in building not being to accommodate any particular Sect, but the Inhabitants in general, so that even if the Mufti of Constantinople were to send a Missionary to preach Mahometanism to us, he would find a Pulpit at his Service."[88] Whitefield might not have been so ecumenical, but he maintained strong ties with American Calvinist leaders ordinarily perceived as Anglican adversaries. As he wrote to Wesley regarding the latter's possible return to the continent: "I dread your coming over to America because the work of God is carried on here (and that in a glorious manner) by doctrines quite opposite to those you hold."[89]

In this way Whitefield dominated American evangelical networks for a period of thirty years, from the Great Awakening in the 1740s to his death in 1770, effectively excluding Wesleyan influence and preserving a distinctly Calvinist tone to the American revivals. Except on the occasions when an overwrought Anglican establishment feared the return of the Wesley brothers, "Methodism" in the colonies was associated with the Calvinist evangelist.[90] In this process, Whitefield was increasingly "Americanized," perhaps in no more telling way than in his conviction that the Anglican Church was among those British authorities conspiring to deprive the Americans of their liberties.[91] By contrast, when John Wesley was known at all, it was through the handful of his publications that were pirated by American printers in Philadelphia and New York, or when Anglican observers confused the two men.[92]

As a celebrity-evangelical, however, Whitefield's fame and influence were susceptible to the passage of time and his own demise. Thus while Whitefield set the tone for the evangelical style in America—with pronounced charismatic, dramaturgical, and commercial elements—the structure and, to a large extent, the content of future evangelical movements would be shaped by the other Methodists, John Wesley's followers. The first of the "new" Methodists were to migrate to the American provinces at the start of the 1760s. They formed the unlikely beginnings of a new movement.

WESLEYAN MIGRATION TO BRITISH AMERICA

In his massive study of the migration to British America after the French and Indian War, Bernard Bailyn has estimated that a population of approximately 221,500 Europeans and Africans flooded into the mainland colonies between the years 1760 and 1775, among them 125,000 English, Scotch, and Irish Protestants, 12,000 German-speaking immigrants, and 84,500 slaves. By Bailyn's count, three-fifths of the Europeans (British, Irish, and German) entered the Middle Atlantic colonies of New York, Pennsylvania, and Maryland, to remain or move on to the frontier.[93] These colonies' population and that of their main port towns, Philadelphia and New York, surged over the following fifteen years as the new arrivals settled in ethnically and religiously distinctive enclaves, worked as servants and day laborers on tobacco and wheat farms, or pressed on to Indian territory, producing a self-regulated, sometimes violent political culture far removed from the metropolitan center in Westminster.[94]

The first Wesleyans, arriving in America in the 1760s, formed a small part of this population movement. Economic migrants from Ireland, none were formal members of Wesley's itinerant connection, and only one among them, Robert Strawbridge, appears to have intended to evangelize the Americans. But the imperatives of Wesleyan Methodism—its missionary drive, cross-denominational appeal, enthusiastic preaching, and household recruitment of followers—eventually produced a critical mass of Wesleyan classes and societies in the colonies, and the early makings of an American Methodist itinerancy.

The most numerous of the first American Wesleyans were part of an Irish community whose refugee ancestors, about 4,000 in number, had fled the German Palatinate during the War of Spanish Succession in the early part of the century and settled in county Limerick. The "Irish Palatines" were quickly reduced in number by the voluntary return of more than 500 families to England, but the remaining settlers enjoyed modest privileges as tenants with extended leases on Lord Southwell's estate near Rathkeale and Ballingrane, supporting themselves by the raising of flax for linen manufacturing. Many joined the Anglican Church while continuing to educate their children in German. They were also susceptible to Wesleyan preaching. It is likely that several of the future American Methodists—among them Philip Embury, a carpenter and local preacher, and his cousin Barbara Ruckle (later Heck)—converted sometime after hearing Wesley preach in Limerick in 1752. By the late 1750s, a substantial contingent worshiped at the Methodist preaching house in the village of Courtmatrix.[95]

At the end of the 1750s, the Irish Palatines' protected status evaporated as their leases came to an end and rents were sharply raised. In 1760 as the latest war between Britain and France was concluded, a small group—including Embury, Heck, and a number of Wesleyan men who had organized into a linen and hempen manufacturing company—emigrated to the province of New York. Disembarking at New York City on 11 August, the migrants moved a short distance into the cottages that skirted the city barracks at the base of Manhattan Island. While the linen company repeatedly petitioned the provincial government for acreage in the Hudson River Valley suitable for raising flax, Philip Embury supported his family by teaching school. Probably attracted by the large German congregation, the Emburys and Hecks baptized their children at Trinity Lutheran Church. The group began to move away from their Wesleyan persuasion, a tendency accentuated by the arrival of a second group from Rathkeale, including Barbara Heck's brother Paul, in August 1765.[96]

In September or October 1766, according to Methodist oral tradition, as the men among the new migrants settled into a card game at one or another of the Palatine hearthsides, Heck interrupted the game, sweeping the playing cards into her apron and heaving them into the fire. She then pressed Embury, by all accounts a reticent recruit, to undertake preaching anew.[97] The resulting Methodist class, comprising the Emburys, the Hecks, the Hecks' servant man John Lawrence, and their black servant woman Betty, first gathered at the Emburys' cottage residence.[98] As attendance grew, the new Wesleyan class moved to larger quarters at an "upper room" adjoining the barracks. New attendants included musicians from the Sixteenth Regiment, members of a local family named Parks, one of the inmates of the city poorhouse, and eventually the master of the poorhouse, Billy Littlewood himself.[99]

Unknown to the New Yorkers, more extensive Wesleyan networks were under cultivation in Maryland through the work of another Irish migrant and local preacher, Robert Strawbridge. The son of a prosperous farmer in Drummersnave (now Drumsna), county Leitrim, Strawbridge was rumored to be a follower of Lawrence Coughlan, who was to be expelled from the Wesleyan connection for receiving irregular ordination.[100] Strawbridge, like the group from county Limerick, left Ireland for economic reasons, but judging by his rapid move into itinerant preaching in America and his peculiar resistance to Methodist authority thereafter, he was well prepared to travel as an independent missionary.[101]

The Strawbridges—Robert, his wife, Elizabeth Piper (also a devout Methodist), and probably a niece and nephew—arrived in America sometime in 1760 or 1761 and settled on a tenantry near Sam's Creek in Frederick County, Maryland. While Elizabeth Strawbridge exhorted the surrounding families, converting farmer John Evans and forming a Methodist class, Robert set out on a remarkably wide preaching circuit through Frederick, Baltimore, and Harford Counties, and to the edge of the Eastern Shore.[102] A poor man whose growing family relied on the generosity of neighbors during his long absences, Strawbridge nevertheless attracted the attention of a variety of listeners wherever he went, drawn to his charismatic presence and melodious singing voice. By the mid-1760s, he had converted members of the Bond family of Bethesda near Fallston, the Dallams near Aberdeen, and the Watters on Deer Creek, members of Harford County's lesser gentry and leading actors in the Methodist movement in Maryland thereafter.[103] Sometime early in his unofficial ministry, with the encouragement of, and possible ordination by, German preacher Benedict Schwope (future cofounder with Martin Boehm of the German Brethren), Strawbridge expanded his powers by baptizing the young son of a family at Sam's Creek.[104] In about 1764 he built a small log preaching house adjoining his tenantry. The size of the house scarcely reflected Strawbridge's influence. By the late 1760s his followers were to be found throughout the area, ranging from Jacob Toogood, a slave and the first known black Wesleyan preacher in America, to the Strawbridges' Quaker landlord, and members of the Anglican gentry in Garrison Forest outside Baltimore.[105]

The New York and Maryland Wesleyan populations grew separately through the 1760s, with no apparent contact. They were of little interest to the Anglican authorities, who continued to identify Methodism with George Whitefield and other errant Anglican Calvinists. Among the latter was William McClenachan, a Northern Irish minister, briefly missionary among the Maine Indians, who had divided the parish in Mount Holly, New Jersey, over the New Birth, and whose followers built St. Paul's Church in Philadelphia.[106] In New York in 1764, according to SPG Minister Hugh Neill, Methodist sympathizers were pressing to have the vacancy at Trinity Church filled by a "sound Whitfilian." Observing that vestries were regularly composed of seven members, Neill alerted the Anglican authorities: "It is easy to get six or seven Methodists [that is, Whitefieldians], Laymen and Ministers in every city who will be glad of an opportunity to give a guinea a piece to have the ruling of the Church in North America."[107]

But among the "Whitefieldians" there were also hundreds of potential Wesleyan converts—religious seekers attracted to the promise of the New Birth but raised as or near the influence of Anglicans, Quakers, Mennonites, or Freewill Baptists rather than Congregationalists and Presbyterians, or from among Whitefield's growing black following. Edward Evans is a case in point. An Irish shoemaker who emigrated to the colonies in the 1730s, Evans was converted by Whitefield during the revivals of the 1740s. As he was to write to Wesley years later, he had known of the Wesley brothers by reputation but had been discouraged from corresponding by both Whitefield and Peter Böhler, whom Evans had met on one of the latter's American visits. In due time Evans determined that Whitefield was "a weak and vain man" who had "sunk entirely into what is called Calvin opinion." Consequently Evans determined to join one of the Moravian communities, probably at Bethlehem, Pennsylvania. For twelve years the United Brethren "fully engaged [his] time and attention," but Evans was to leave the Moravians as well, disillusioned with their "Jesuitical evasion[s]" and Count Zinzendorf's "absolute rule and direction" over Moravian affairs. The count's teachings, Evans complained to Wesley, were "observed and followed as the Bulls or Decretals of the Pope." "[S]ick of disappointment," Evans determined to spend the rest of his days "in a separated way, and cleave to Jesus only."[108] He began to travel and preach independently and by the late 1760s was the leader of a small prayer group in Philadelphia.[109]

Neither Anglican nor Moravian, Calvinist nor Quaker, Evans's religious sensibilities paralleled those of many Americans in the wake of Whitefield's well-publicized, highly attended progresses. Moving from church to church, these Americans were a "people prepared" for religious transformation, but their readiness was based more on the efficacy of religious experience itself than on the persuasiveness of religious disputation.[110] Evans finally fell in with the Wesleyans but not in any way recognizable to outside observers, that is, by any kind of formal membership. By 1770 he was preaching at the interdenominational chapel he helped build in Greenwich, New Jersey, where one of the Swedish pastors described him as "a good old simple minded man who had not been ordained, nor of any particular religion."[111]

As increasing numbers of British migrants poured into North America in the late 1760s, it was only a matter of time before an aspiring British Wesleyan "discovered" the various classes and societies now meeting in Wesley's name or otherwise primed for ties back to the British movement. The discoverer, Captain Thomas Webb, was an ideal candidate for the task.[112] A veteran of the Seven Years War, Webb possessed the combined characteristics of a military man, at once steady and flamboyant, and eager to engage in projects and campaigns. In 1759, he had published a military treatise and, before the Proclamation of 1763 brought an end to his plans, had attempted to found a colony called "New Wales" west of the Appalachians. After rapid-fire conversions to Moravianism and then to Methodism in England in 1764, he applied his organizational talents, and enthusiastic tendencies, to an informal itinerant vocation allied with Wesley's connection.[113] Charles Wesley, less tolerant of Methodist ecstaticism than his brother, described Webb as "a strange man, and very much of an enthusiast," and urged that Webb "keep his abundance of visions and revelations to himself."[114] But Webb's patriarchal style, heightened by his appearance in regimental uniform, a signature green patch shielding his war-injured right eye, matched the popular notion of what an Old Testament orator ought to look like.[115] On his return to America, Webb retired at age thirty-nine, retaining the courtesy title "Captain," and married into the Arding family of Jamaica, Long Island. Now a man of property, Webb was in a good position to contribute substantially to the Methodist societies that he stumbled across or otherwise pulled together in the course of his travels.[116]

Sometime in 1766, Webb encountered Embury's society in New York City and brought several new members into the group, including war veteran William Lupton from his former regiment, as well as other new English and Irish arrivals to the city. In 1767, the society moved their meetings to a rigging loft in Horse and Cart (later William) Street, a space sufficiently large to hold an attentive audience.[117] Webb also proselytized in the neighborhood of his wife's family on Long Island, and organized a Wesleyan class in Brooklyn comprising equal numbers of blacks and whites.[118] In 1767 or 1768, extending his preaching circuit south, he found Evans's group in Philadelphia, composed of an assortment of tradesmen and disillusioned members of St. Paul's Church. As the Philadelphia society grew in size, it also moved to a sail rigging loft, located near the waterfront in Dock Street, and then to the "Pott-house" in Loxley Court.[119] Over the next several years Webb was to be instrumental in converting followers in and around Newtown, Long Island; in New Mills, Trenton, and Burlington, New Jersey; in Wilmington, Delaware; and possibly as far south as northern Maryland: the full range of the Middle Atlantic coastline.[120]

But Webb's most important role stemmed from his interest in connecting the American Wesleyans with their English parent. It was probably under Webb's influence that the New Yorkers undertook two dramatic steps: to build their own preaching house and to tell John Wesley about it. The vehicle for this communication was Thomas Taylor, an English Methodist then living in the city.

Taylor wrote to Wesley in April 1768, recounting the rise of the New York society, which he attributed to George Whitefield's influence on the "state of religion" in New York City and to Captain Webb's preaching to the congregation in his "scarlet coat." The numbers in attendance increased so fast, in fact, "that our house for this six weeks past would not contain the half of the people."[121]

By this time, the society had accepted the offer of a supporter to acquire two lots on John Street "on good security" from Mary Barclay, widow of the Anglican rector Henry Barclay, pending the purchase price of £600 that the society was expected to fund.[122] "[M]any ministers have cursed us in the name of the Lord," Taylor wrote, "and laboured with all their might to shut up their congregations from assisting us." But the group, supported by Webb and William Lupton, had already collected or borrowed close to £400. They now hoped that the balance needed to secure the lots and construct a house might be raised in Britain. Perhaps, Taylor urged upon Wesley, "if you would intimate our circumstances to particular persons of ability," such donors might find it in their hearts to "contribute to the first preaching-house on the original Methodist plan in all America. . . ." It was hoped that Wesley would send over "an able, experienced preacher—one who has both gifts and graces necessary for the work." Taylor believed that "the progress of the gospel here depends much on the qualifications of the preachers." The New Yorkers "would sell our coats and shirts" to pay the passage.[123]

The New York society collected the necessary funds for purchasing the John Street lots through a public subscription, probably still in circulation when Taylor forwarded his letter to Wesley. Identifying its authors as Wesleyan followers whose aim it was to "build a small house," the subscription paper emphasized that the chapel would be one "where the Gospel of Jesus Christ might be preached without distinction of sects or parties." Like Wesley's United Society, in other words, the John Street Chapel, also called Wesley Chapel, would support a religious society without denominational affiliation.[124]

Despite Taylor's observation that a number of New Yorkers opposed the Wesleyans' pretensions, the appeal raised more than £400 from 250 contributors, representing a notable cross section of the city's inhabitants. Chief among the Wesleyans were Webb and Lupton as well as Charles White and Richard Sause, both master artisans from Dublin; James Jarvis, a hat manufacturer from Newtown, Long Island; and future postwar leaders in the society, Paul Hick and John and Mary Staples.[125] Thirty-six of the contributors were women; and several at this early date were slaves. Reflecting the evangelical vogue among the city's elite, other contributors included Philip Livingston, the Presbyterian merchant and political Whig; James De Lancey and Oliver De Lancey, the Livingstons' political adversaries; and a number of vestrymen from Trinity Church. Donations from three Anglican ministers—Samuel Auchmuty (Barclay's successor at Trinity Church), John Ogilvie (a former missionary to the Mohawks), and Charles Inglis—further suggest the popularity of evangelicalism among the city's Anglicans that SPG minister Hugh Neill had predicted.[126] The preaching house, a simple stone structure with backless seats and a gallery reached by a ladder, was built

Figure 4. *John Street* [New York City], *1768*, by Joseph B. Smith, ca. 1817. The artist depicts the newly built John Street Chapel flanked by cottages similar to those inhabited by New York's first Wesleyans. Courtesy of the Museum of the City of New York, New York.

by society members. Embury preached the inaugural sermon from his family Bible in October 1768.[127]

In addition to the communication from Thomas Taylor, John Wesley was kept abreast of American developments by several friends and correspondents. In the same month that the John Street Chapel opened, Wesley dined with fellow evangelical Carl Magnus von Wrangel, provost of the Swedish church returning home from his Philadelphia appointment. The provost, Wesley observed, "seemed to be greatly united to the American Christians, and he strongly pleaded for our sending some of our preachers to help them, multitudes of whom are as sheep without a shepherd."[128] Another Wesleyan traveling in America, Thomas Bell, wrote back to England less optimistically regarding the future of the New York Methodists, whom he described as "very poor in this world." The Dutch Reformed minister, Bell reported, preached against the Methodists, and the Anglicans, upon whom the society sometimes relied for support, "have strayed from England into the wild woods here; and they are running wild after this world." In the wake of his campaigns, "[m]any of the people of America have been stirred up to seek the Lord, by Mr. Whitefield; but what his reason could be, for not forming them into classes, I do not know." Thomas Webb, maintaining close ties to Britain, undoubtedly wrote to Wesley as well. In 1768, a number of Robert Strawbridge's followers, furthermore, sent a "pressing Call" to England for preachers.[129]

Wesley's expressions of interest in the colonies, however, remained tepid at best. At the 1768 conference he circulated copies of Thomas Taylor's letter among the itinerants, but just one, Robert Williams, responded. In his journal, Wesley did not record his reaction to von Wrangel's recommendations that he send itinerants to America, but moved quickly on to other subjects: an essay on music he had recently read, travels through the West Country, a particularly good reception to preaching among "rich and poor" in Portsmouth.[130] The colonies, by comparison, were a long way off, far from Wesley's controlling oversight and reminiscent of an unpleasant past. By all appearances, Wesley, like most of his contemporaries, identified America as Whitefield's territory.[131]

Thus by the end of the 1760s, eight years after the first Wesleyan Methodists migrated to America, Wesleyan Methodism remained a diffuse force in the colonies, consisting of many household meetings but just a handful of societies and preaching houses from New York to northern Maryland. By contrast, in Pennsylvania alone the Lutherans were meeting in 142 churches, the Quakers in 64 meetinghouses, and the Anglicans in 24 parishes, and Presbyterian and German Reformed churches alike possessed substantial memberships.[132] In the late 1760s it may be assumed that when Americans heard the term "Methodist," they still thought of George Whitefield.

In the 1770s this balance would change dramatically as Whitefield's influence waned with his death, and Methodism became associated with a new, and for many Americans more troubling, force out of Britain. For the Anglicans, the Wesleyans were yet another manifestation of the challenge presented by Whitefield and his followers. For other Americans, the Wesleyans represented an unseemly and potentially seditious element in Revolutionary times. By the height of the war, Americans would associate John Wesley with Tory opposition to the common cause rather than as Whitefield's Anglican competitor. At the same time, increasing numbers of Americans from New York to North Carolina flocked to Wesleyan preaching and the new Methodist revivals.

CHAPTER TWO

The Wesleyan Connection

THE FIRST American Methodists' attachment to John Wesley, founder and self-anointed leader of the Methodist Connexion and United Societies, was not significantly different from that of their British counterparts. Although the vast majority of his American followers had never met him, Wesley became their chosen father-in-Christ, just as he was the paterfamilias of the Methodists remaining in Britain. The American Methodists believed that some form of dependence on Wesley's connection of preachers was both necessary and desirable. They expected material support—money, books, and preachers—from the British movement. And they hoped that, despite the three-thousand-mile Atlantic span that separated the British Wesleyans from the Americans, Wesley would tour North America as he had regularly traveled through England, Wales, Scotland, and Ireland. In the imperial context, loyalty to Wesley was in no way in contradiction with Methodists' attachment to their new American location.

Signs of missionary independence, however, and popular assertiveness were apparent in the early movement. By 1769, the Irish preacher Robert Strawbridge had been traveling through Maryland and the surrounding provinces for nine years, putting in place a network of Methodist household meetings that was to survive the crisis years of the Revolution, and attracting a long-lived following of lay preachers. Methodist followers in various Middle Atlantic venues—in New York City and on Long Island, in central Nw Jersey, in Philadelphia and Wilmington, and in the counties around Baltimore—had been organized without formal assistance from the British connection. And while many American Wesleyans, like their British counterparts, had been raised as Anglicans, evidence suggests that others came from a host of churches and sects of English, Scottish, Welsh, German, French, and Dutch origin, or were slaves only recently removed from indigenous West African cultures. The first official Wesleyan itinerants, arriving in Philadelphia in 1769, were to be fascinated by the colonies' diversity, as were other European travelers. The British preachers, among them a little-known Wesleyan assistant named Francis Asbury, recognized the potentially enormous challenges and opportunities for missionizing posed by the restless and often unchurched American population.

Under these circumstances, the escalating political crisis of the Revolution—beginning with the Stamp Act riots in the summer of 1765, followed rapidly by opposition to the Townshend Program of selective taxation, the deployment of the British army to quell unrest in Boston in 1767–1768, and renewed American patriot resistance with Parliament's passage of the Tea Act in 1773—had far-reaching implications for Wesley's small movement. Followers of an English cleric whose royalist views were widely known among American patriots, the

American Methodists found themselves in a singular position during the Revolutionary War. While Whig leaders struggled to develop a republican synthesis to
unite Americans against the British, the Methodists were sponsoring a movement
that pressed for closer British ties. And while the Continental Army and state
militias sought to recruit able-bodied men for the defense of the new nation,
Methodist itinerants were withdrawing from the defensive forces, preaching a
gospel of personal transformation that had little in common with tests of republican manhood.

Ultimately and remarkably, Methodism survived Independence. While Francis
Asbury was confined to Delaware through the course of the war, in virtual isola-
tion from the remaining itinerants, the ardent followers of Robert Strawbridge
as well as the American preachers recruited by Wesley's organization sustained
Wesleyan Methodism throughout the greater Middle Atlantic and the new circuits
in the South. The American itinerants emerged from the Revolutionary conflict
with the added allure of having passed through their own Christian sufferings. Out
of an often tense union of the American preachers' solidarity, Francis Asbury's
determination, and the missionary aspirations of another British preacher, Thomas
Coke, the Methodist Episcopal Church was ultimately and unexpectedly born.

THE WESLEYAN ITINERANTS IN AMERICA

In spring 1769, Robert Williams, a Welsh itinerant with Irish experience, was the
first licensed preacher to receive John Wesley's permission to travel in America.
Known as a maverick critic of the Anglican clergy, Williams failed to receive
conference support and relied instead on the patronage of Dublin merchant
Thomas Ashton for the cost of his passage. Arriving in the colonies sometime in
late August or early September, Ashton and Williams traveled their separate ways:
Ashton up the Hudson River Valley to found the Methodist community of Ash-
grove, near Cambridge, New York, where Philip Embury and a number of the
Irish Palatines finally settled in 1770;[1] and Williams to the Methodist societies in
New York and Philadelphia, supporting himself through the reprint and sale of
as many as ten of Wesley's publications, chiefly hymnbooks. Continuing on to
Maryland, he made friendly contact with Robert Strawbridge. Further south in
Virginia, he was to work successfully with the evangelical Anglican minister
Devereux Jarratt.[2]

Williams's Irish itinerating made him a suitable candidate for the American
scene, and he was soon to work effectively with Robert Strawbridge through the
Maryland countryside. But with word out of the American Methodists' pleas for
British help, licensed preachers were more easily recruited for what would be for
many the formative adventure of their lives. At the August 1769 conference Richard Boardman, a seasoned itinerant, and Joseph Pilmore, a young preacher just
returned from Wales, responded to Wesley's announcement seeking licensed
preachers for the colonies. The two men were duly appointed to the new American
circuit number 50. They set sail from Gravesend on the first of September with

books, £50 in cash, and little fanfare, disembarking in Gloucester Point, New Jersey, on 21 October.[3]

Crossing the Delaware River to Philadelphia, Boardman recorded that the itinerants "found a little Society" of approximately 100 members and "preached to a great number of people," a disparity between the size of formal society membership and public audiences that was to persist throughout the Methodists' early years. Several days later Boardman traveled to New York, where, according to his estimate, he was greeted by 1,700 listeners at the new chapel. Remarking on a singular characteristic of his new circuit, Boardman noted that the numbers of blacks in attendance "affects me much."[4] The two preachers now concentrated their energies on formalizing the Philadelphia and New York societies' connection with the United Society back in England. In the two cities, they introduced the Methodist discipline, including love feasts, watch nights, and public readings of Wesley's *General Rules*. In New York in particular they placed the new preaching house on the so-called Model Deed devised by Wesley to secure Methodist preaching houses for the use of his connection.[5] Pilmore also assisted the Philadelphia society, a growing group of men and women, in purchasing "a very large Shell of a Church" at Fourth and Race Streets from a bankrupt German Reformed congregation.[6] To ease the rising concerns of other churches regarding Wesleyan competition, Pilmore assured St. Paul's that Methodism was "never designed to make a Separation from the Church of England or be looked upon as a Church." Their chapel, called St. George's, was "intended for the benefit of all those of every Denomination. . . ."[7]

Boardman and Pilmore together, revealing congregational tendencies frowned upon by their missionary cohort, continued to concentrate on the New York and Philadelphia societies while leaving the bulk of traveling to more adventurous unlicensed itinerants: Thomas Webb, who organized new meetings in New Castle and Wilmington in Delaware and in Burlington, Trenton, and New Mills (now Pemberton) in New Jersey; and Robert Williams, who remained active in the South. John King, another English Wesleyan traveling without conference support, was licensed by Pilmore to preach in Baltimore City.[8] Pilmore himself soon developed a following in Philadelphia, where he preached "on Xtian *moderation*" and "the reasonableness of loving the people of God, though they may belong to different Societies, and hold different opinions," among other Anglican-inspired ecumenical themes.[9]

Pilmore especially surveyed the ecclesiastical landscape, frequenting the meetings of various congregations—Roman Catholic, Quaker, Jewish, Dutch Reformed, and Moravian—in and around Philadelphia and New York and exhorting audiences from a variety of pulpits, among them St. Paul's in Philadelphia, the Swedes Church in Kingsessing near Philadelphia, the Huguenot Church in New Rochelle, New York, and the Presbyterian preaching hall in Mount Holly, New Jersey, originally built for Indian missionary David Brainerd.[10] In a short time Pilmore came to believe that the colonies were ripe for evangelization. "It is not in America as it is in England," he wrote to a fellow Methodist in the old country, "for there is no Church that is one Establish'd more than another. All Sects have equal authority with the Church of England." Contradicting his earlier assurances to the listeners at St. Paul's, he now asserted that if the Methodists "should form a Church we should soon have the largest congregations in these two Cities. . . . [I]n many places they have not a Minister of any Denomination for forty or fifty miles." He added with some excitement, "What a field for Methodist preachers!"[11]

At the end of September, a little less than a year after Boardman and Pilmore's arrival, the American religious scene and the potential for Wesleyan Methodist expansion changed abruptly with the death of George Whitefield in Newburyport, Massachusetts. Pilmore mournfully recorded the "melancholy news of the Death of that excellent Saint of God, Mr. George Whitefield" in his journal.[12] While neither he nor Boardman had made contact with the Anglican evangelist, Whitefield's influence was manifest throughout the greater Middle Atlantic and would have been especially apparent to the Wesleyans. Writing to Wesley, Thomas Taylor had testified to Whitefield's impact on New York City in the last of his great campaigns through America. Whitefield converts might be counted among those belonging to Robert Strawbridge's society near Frederick, Maryland, at Bohemia Manor in Cecil County, Maryland, and in the Methodist congregations in Philadelphia and New Jersey. The first generation of Wesleyan converts probably included an appreciable number of children of former Whitefield acolytes.[13]

For the Wesleyans, nevertheless, Whitefield's death provided an unprecedented opportunity that Wesley, ever cautious about the American experiment but ever competitive, was not likely to ignore. On learning that Whitefield patroness Lady Huntingdon had appointed Charles Piercy, another Calvinist Anglican, as Whitefield's successor in America, Wesley's lieutenant John Fletcher hurriedly contacted Joseph Benson, once associated with the countess but now estranged from Calvinist evangelicalism, to urge him to travel to America. Informed of American developments by Thomas Webb, Fletcher stressed that there were "few men [in the colonies] capable of managing the difficult points of a controversy," typically the Calvinists' greatest strength.[14] Benson declined the appointment, but Wesley now exerted more energy to recruit preachers for circuit number 50. In late October 1771, the first of several bands of Wesleyan preachers traveled to America. The younger of the first pair, Richard Wright, soon returned to England, unprepared for the rigors of the American appointment.[15] The older, Francis Asbury, was to labor for the next forty-five years to unify and solidify the American movement.

More than forty years Wesley's junior, Asbury was born in Handsworth parish in the colliery district near Birmingham in August 1745. In his own words he was the son of "people in common life," his father, Joseph, a farmer and gentleman's gardener, and his mother, Elizabeth, a devout Welsh Christian. After the childhood death of Francis's older sister, Elizabeth Asbury retreated into intensive reading, imparting to her son the memory of her "poring over a book for hours together." The young Asbury was ridiculed by his schoolmates for his mother's piety and likely because he "abhorred fighting and quarrelling"—so much so that he acquired the nickname *Methodist Parson*" long before he had heard a Methodist preach. In early adolescence, finding his schoolmaster was "a great churl," he left school and went into service as an live-in apprentice, probably for the blacksmith and forge-owner Henry Foxall whose son of the same name would later emigrate to America and become a leading Methodist there.[16]

When Francis was an impressionable thirteen or fourteen years of age, Elizabeth Asbury invited a traveling Baptist shoemaker-preacher to lead a prayer meeting at her house. Francis was now "convinced there was some thing more in religion than I had ever been acquainted with." He began to attend Calvinist evangelical preaching at the parish church in West Bromwich, sponsored by the local nobleman, William Legge, the second earl of Dartmouth. A year later Asbury heard Wesley's deputy John Fletcher and Benjamin Ingham preach at Wednesbury, notorious for anti-Methodist agitation. Now fifteen, he experienced the religious passage of justification while praying with a group of friends in his father's barn. A year later, he was persuaded he was sanctified, or cleansed of sin. As he wrote in the reserved tone that was to characterize much of his journal, "About sixteen I experienced a marvellous display of the grace of God, which some might think was full sanctification, and was indeed very happy. . . ." The sublime effects of his religious experience soon passed, but Asbury was a changed youth and he avidly "turned" preacher, first as a prayer leader at his mother's all-female devotional group, and, moving up the ladder of Wesleyan advancement, as a seventeen-year-old exhorter, an eighteen-year-old Methodist local preacher, and a twenty-one-year-old licensed itinerant for Wesley's connection.[17]

Asbury's decision to go to America was a dramatic break—the women of one Hampshire prayer group wrote sympathetically to his parents, "[W]e can scarce believe he is so mad"—but it was also a logical extension of the continuum that had taken him from a tradesman's life to that of a Wesleyan missionary. In the opening passages of his journal, he examined his own motives for the journey in the question-and-response form of early Methodist discourse: "Whither am I going? To the New World. What to do? To gain honour? No, if I know my own heart. To get money? No: I am going to live to God, and to bring others so to do." Rejecting honor and wealth—the common objectives of the men he knew—Asbury instead focused, if at first tentatively, on his evangelical mandate. "The people God owns in England, are the Methodists," he reassured himself. "The doctrines they preach, and the discipline they enforce, are, I believe, the purest of any people now in the world." A loyal Englishman, he added, "If God does not acknowledge me in America, I will soon return to England."[18] But from the start he was convinced that the burden of converting "the continent" rested with the Methodists.

For many years both before and after the Revolutionary War, Asbury deferred to other more senior itinerants, not only to Wesley, but also to Thomas Rankin—shortly to be named American superintendent—and Thomas Coke, Asbury's future cosuperintendent in the American church. Possessed of good connections, grammar school educations, and, in the case of Wesley and Coke, university degrees and ordination powers, these men were born into the social ranks that produced Britain's professional and ruling elite, even among the popular and ecstatic Methodists. Through the first part of his career, Asbury, by contrast, was handicapped by his artisan background. The son of a gardener, educated at the primary level, and without formal training in ancient languages, he was unlikely to achieve the rank of minister with any ease. Although a lifelong reader, he was not as yet a published author, and in future years he relied on the better-educated members of the American church to edit and produce his one significant literary production, his journal. This he wrote in workmanlike prose with little of the felicity of expression or confidence of generalization typical of his mentor Wesley's writings.[19] He was, in short, a plebeian figure.

By Wesley's standards, just the same, the scruples that held Asbury to a subordinate position were the very traits that qualified him for exercising authority in America until more experienced itinerants arrived. Asbury unswervingly supported the "Methodist plan" or "old plan" of strict adherence to Wesley's discipline, including loyalty to the Anglican Church. From his first arrival Asbury opposed any hint of separation or independence in the American movement, in particular Robert Strawbridge's freelance ministry in Maryland.[20]

Despite objections from Americans accustomed to running their own prayer groups, Asbury labored to tie together the Methodist societies, first traveling circuit number 50 as originally defined between New York and Philadelphia and then moving out to Delaware, New Jersey, and Cecil County, Maryland. In the spring and fall of 1772, the new Methodist chapels in Greenwich and Trenton, New Jersey, the latter led by silversmith Joseph Toy, were added to the American circuit.[21] Under pressure from Asbury, the licensed itinerants now began to journey farther afield. In June 1772, Joseph Pilmore set out for Baltimore, where he preached to a Sunday crowd of about a thousand listeners on the city green and discovered a "little company" of seekers at the evangelical German Reformed Church. Here and at Fell's Point in East Baltimore, where "many English people are settled for the convenience of the shiping," the preacher set up new societies and read Wesley's *General Rules* to the new Methodists. Forty members were meeting in the Reformed Church by the following month. Methodism quickly took root in what would soon become its American capital.[22]

Before traveling on to Virginia, and eventually all the way to Savannah (Wesley's former missionary haunt), Pilmore also made contact with several of Robert Strawbridge's meetings in the rural hinterland outside Baltimore. He discovered thriving household meetings, classes, and societies, with chapels built at Bush Forest and Deer Creek in Harford County.[23] Together with their mentor, William Watters, Richard Owings, and Philip Gatch were already traveling "in little bands" through the surrounding neighborhoods, singing, praying, and reading Scripture. Under Strawbridge's influence it is likely that these preachers, only informally affiliated with the Wesleyans, had also administered the rites of baptism and possibly communion among their followers, a deviation from regular practice that Asbury strongly disapproved of.[24]

Rewarding his lieutenant's loyalty, Wesley appointed Asbury as his formal American assistant in October 1772, demoting Richard Boardman in the process. While hampered in his dealings with the other itinerants by an unpolished rigidity he was soon to shed, the new assistant now extended his influence further. He too made contact with the Maryland societies in extensive tours through Strawbridge's territory and established a lifelong alliance with Philip Wilhelm Otterbein, pastor of the evangelical German Reformed Church in Baltimore and one of the founders of the new German Brethren.[25] In November 1772, Asbury also met Strawbridge at the Sam's Creek society in Frederick County, the first of several encounters. On 23 December at a quarterly meeting in Aberdeen, Maryland, Asbury and the Irish preacher wrangled over the Maryland preachers' adoptions of sacramental powers. "[B]rother Strawbridge pleaded much for the ordinances," Asbury observed, "and so did the people, who appeared to be much biased by him." Several days later Asbury was convinced that Strawbridge had failed to advertise his preaching appointment at the Bush Forest Chapel in order to discourage attendance.[26] Despite these tensions, Asbury recruited supporters from among Strawbridge's converts, a number of them Irish immigrants, others American-born.[27] By the early 1770s, Methodists in the various societies in Pennsylvania, New Jersey, and New York were in regular contact with each other and provided support for the building of new chapels.[28]

Asbury's success in winning over many of the first American Methodists may be attributed in part to his relentless round of preaching and networking. Through these interwar years, the new superintendent adhered to as rigorous an itinerary as he demanded of his fellow preachers. In a typical month, whether in good health or bad, he was on the road one day out of two, preaching at each new settlement or household he came upon and revisiting old ones.[29] Like the first Methodists in Britain he sermonized to prisoners and attended their executions. Undeterred by his lack of formal education and gaining in confidence, he established ties with several of Methodism's future patrons. At Bohemia Manor in Cecil County, Maryland, the Bayard, Bassett, and Sluyter families, descendants of Labadists, a quietist sect, and former Whitefieldian Methodists, now adopted Wesleyan Methodism.[30] And especially important, Asbury gained access to the young commercial elite in Baltimore County, including Harry Dorsey Gough and his wife Prudence Carnan Gough, proprietors of Perry Hall on the outskirts of Baltimore City.[31] By early 1774 Asbury had turned Baltimore into an American Methodist center, with construction underway on Strawberry Alley Chapel in Fell's Point, and a subscription in circulation for a new building in Lovely Lane, south of Market (later Baltimore) Street.[32] In the same year, new chapels were built in Baltimore County, and new societies formed in Queen Annes County.[33]

Asbury nevertheless complained to Wesley of the difficulties he encountered in the American work, particularly Boardman and Pilmore's resistance to his discipline and their favoring of the New York and Philadelphia congregations. At the same time, Thomas Webb, ever the promoter of the Wesleyan cause and briefly living in England, attended the 1772 Leeds conference to back Wesley's call for more itinerants. Following the pattern of appointing two preachers at a time to a circuit, Wesley now designated Thomas Rankin, a thirty-five-year-old Scot, to replace Asbury as superintendent, with George Shadford, an Englishman, as his assistant.[34]

Rankin came to the colonies with extensive itinerant experience and an acerbic impression of Americans, the consequence of a year spent as a merchant's agent in Charleston, South Carolina, where the inhabitants appeared to him "a dissipated and thoughtless generation." He had an administrator's love of organization. "I now saw the whole economy of Methodism in the most favourable light," he wrote of his early admiration for John Wesley's system. "[T]he class and band meetings, meeting of the society, body-bands, lovefeasts, &c., I saw the great utility of, and it gave me the utmost pleasure to conform to every part."[35] Bolstered by the knowledge that Wesley "had been dissatisfied with the conduct of those who superintended the rising work there," Rankin was prepared to enforce discipline among the Americans so that the seeds of the Wesleyan system would more easily take root.[36]

Rankin and Shadford arrived in Philadelphia in June 1773. Rankin immediately convened the first itinerants' conference at St. George's in Philadelphia. The small group of preachers agreed to prohibit Robert Williams from publishing Wesley's books without permission and censured the Maryland preachers' occasional adoption of sacramental functions. An exception was made for Robert Strawbridge himself, a remarkable concession to this itinerant's popular appeal. Rankin reported back to Britain that the American Methodist population amounted to 1,160 members from New York to Virginia. With the exception of William Watters, now licensed as a traveler, each of the ten preachers working on the rising number of American circuits was either English, Irish, or Scottish. This preponderance of Britons appeared to trouble neither Rankin nor Asbury.[37]

Through the next several years, Rankin maintained the missionary profile of the movement among whites, blacks, and some Indians. He "found profit" in speaking not once but several times with John Brainerd, brother of David (the Indian missionary). In Philadephia he met with members of the Nanticoke tribe. In his journal, he commented repeatedly on slaves' responsiveness to Methodist preaching, including the seventy laborers working at the Gough plantation at Perry Hall in Baltimore County. Exhibiting another important characteristic of his generation of English evangelicals, he made contact with antislavery activists in America, befriending Quaker abolitionists Israel Pemberton and Anthony Benezet.[38] In the fall of 1775, he spoke privately with several members of the Continental Congress regarding "what a farce it was for them to contend for liberty when they themselves kept some hundreds of thousands of poor blacks in most cruel bondage."[39] And as the imperial crisis deepened, Rankin would attribute the impasse between Britain and America to their shared culpability for "the dreadful sin of buying and selling the souls and bodies of the poor Africans."[40]

At the second preachers' conference in May 1774, also in Philadelphia, Rankin and the itinerants "proceeded in all things on the same plan as in England which our minutes will declare." A resolution to pay the preachers a quarterly stipend of £6 in Pennsylvania currency and traveling expenses marked the beginning of a professional American Methodist ministry.[41] To solidify attachment to the British Wesleyans, Rankin bestowed formal certificates upon the itinerants and distributed copies of the minutes of the original Wesleyan conference of 1744, along with the proceedings of the latest British conferences and selected tracts by Wesley.[42] Each year Rankin dutifully reported the rising numbers of circuits, itinerants, and especially members—1,160 in 1773, 2,073 in 1774, 3,148 in 1775, 4,921 in 1776—back to England, tallies that did not include the sizable population of slaves attracted to Methodist preaching but prohibited by their masters from joining Methodist societies.[43] While some of the itinerants bridled under Rankin's regimen, so much so that Asbury himself complained of its severity, Wesley praised his superintendant and George Shadford for their devotion to the "good old Methodist discipline and doctrine."[44] With the arrival of James Dempster, Martin Rodda, and unlicensed itinerant William Glendinning in the fall of 1774, the ranks of British itinerants remained strong.[45]

In the early 1770s, even before Rankin's arrival, the Anglican clergy recognized that a shift was occurring among the American Methodists. In 1772, several clergy wrote to the bishop of London in favor of the ordination of William Stringer, the evangelical Anglican in charge of St. Paul's in Philadelphia. Referring to Whitefield's impact on his advocates at St. Paul's, they explained that "the former Heats have subsided" and the congregation was ready to rejoin with the Anglicans. "Had that People fallen into the hands of *Methodist* & other Strolling Preachers of the present day," the clergy added, "they would have been drawn still further on in their Irregularity, & at last totally lost to our Church."[46] Whitefieldian Methodists, several years after their charismatic leader's death, were now respectable. In their place, the plebeian Wesleyans had become objects of suspicion for the Anglican hierarchy and in short time would appear so to the patriot movement as well.

THE COMING OF THE WAR

The intensifying struggle between the Americans and the British Parliament in the 1760s and early 1770s received little attention from the bands of Wesleyan "strolling preachers" in the Middle Atlantic and southern provinces. Thomas Rankin reached America at the same time as word of the Tea Act, Parliament's effort to bolster the finances of the East India Company with the grant of a virtual monopoly on the American tea trade. Seven months later, when Boston patriots heaved ninety thousand pounds of the company's tea into Boston Harbor, Rankin makes no reference to this catalytic event or the "tea parties" in other American port towns.[47] Subsequent events occurring in rapid succession—Parliament's Coercive Acts, passed May 1774 in retaliation for the events in Boston; the impromptu congresses assembled by American Whigs to organize support for the New Englanders; the Virginia provincial congress's call for a continental (intercolonial) meeting to convene in Philadelphia the following fall—Rankin considered unworthy of mention in his itinerant journal.[48]

By the time of the convening of the Continental Congress in September 1774, many American patriots were moving rapidly toward a republican conception of the origins of political authority in America. Radicals like Thomas Jefferson now asserted that as "British Americans" the colonists possessed the same rights as British subjects, that the king of England was "no more than the chief officer of the people," and that the British Parliament had "no right to exercise authority over us."[49] The king's subjects were worthy of better or less government than Parliament provided, and Americans, male and female, were virtuous in ways that the British, absorbed in the attractions and temptations of commercial society and imperial power, had now forgotten. But it was not until October 1774 that Rankin alludes to the American crisis, remarking laconically, "From the first of my coming here, it has always been impressed on my mind, that God has a controversy with the inhabitants of the British Colonies."[50]

The British preachers' reluctance to record their political sentiments also reflected Wesley's early if temporary success at separating his movement from political controversy. In keeping with what he believed were his movement's strictly religious goals, Wesley had long advised his preachers to stay away from politics. "The *distinguishing marks* of a Methodist," he wrote in 1742, "are not his *opinions* of any sort. His assenting to this or that scheme of religion, his embracing any particular set of notions, his espousing the judgment of one man or another, are all quite wide of the point." Rather, Methodists were to follow "the plain, old Christianity that I teach, renouncing and detesting all other marks of distinction." In *Reasons against a Separation from the Church of England*, defending his movement against charges of rebellion against the church, Wesley wrote that Methodists "look upon *ourselves*, not as the authors or ringleaders of a particular sect or party . . . but as messengers of God to those who are Christians in name, but heathens in heart and in life. . . ."[51] Like the adherents of the Primitive Church, the true Methodist would cultivate a pacific relationship with both church and state and resist combining political with religious affairs. In March 1775, on the eve of the skirmishes at Lexington and Concord, Wesley wrote to his American preachers, "It is your part to be peace-makers, to be loving and tender to all, but to addict yourselves to no party."[52]

Yet, while he instructed his itinerants and followers to remain mute on political issues, Wesley, an educated cleric, never doubted the propriety of expressing his own opinions on affairs of state. What may have been more perplexing for his American followers was the position he ultimately chose. Given his own history, Wesley might well have been expected to come to the defense of Americans' liberties. Champion of the poor and a populist leader, Wesley shared many traits with the model Whig politician Americans admired, bestowing patronage based on merit, endowing chapels and schools, and dispensing literature to the people at large for improvement of their morals, minds, and manners. Throughout his writings, Wesley stressed the people's "common sense" and asserted the "plowman's" ability to judge affairs of the spirit.[53] Wesley's activities, furthermore, were subsidized in a businesslike fashion by Methodist society members, and his organizational ideas were distinctly reformist, jettisoning traditional forms of social dependence in favor of communities—religious societies—of mutual self-improvement.[54] Not unlike many colonial leaders, even Thomas Jefferson, Wesley

frequently conceived his authority as a form of management rather than as a fixture of social or political prerogative as in the Tory view.[55]

In keeping with these Whig proclivities, on learning of the outbreak of war in Massachusetts, Wesley wrote to the earl of Dartmouth, the Methodist patron and secretary of state for the American colonies: "I can not avoid thinking . . . That an oppressed People asked for nothing more than their Legal Rights." The war, Wesley wrote, would not be easily won, since the Americans were "Enthusiasts for Liberty," even if "calm, deliberate Enthusiasts," and men who fought "for their Wives, Children, Liberty!" would have an important advantage "over men who fight only for pay." Regarding the king's British subjects, he added, "As I travel four or five thousand miles every year, I have an opportunity of conversing freely with many persons of every denomination, than any one alive in the three kingdoms." He was thus familiar with the "Disposition of the people, English, Scots, and Irish," a "huge majority" of whom were "exasperated almost to madness." The precipitous decline in commerce brought on by the American conflict, combined with "Inflammatory Papers" now distributed "with the utmost diligence, in every corner of the land"—as they had been during the English Civil Wars in the 1640s—and the expense of provisions, incited the people dangerously against the king.[56]

But Wesley was also a new religious paternalist, and like most eighteenth-century clergy he favored a strong role for the church in society. Harking back to his parents' nonjuring sentiments following the Glorious Revolution, Wesley remained loyal to king and church in the country tradition, setting himself up as the conduit between those authorities and his Methodist "family."[57] Ultimately the American patriots' increasing resentment of imperial authority was far removed from Wesley's political instincts. Thus when in August 1775 the king declared the colonies to be in a state of rebellion and all those aiding and abetting the rebels to be traitors, Wesley, with no apparent sense of contradicting his advice to his preachers, took an aggressively pro-Tory stance. He did so especially in his deceptively titled first offering on the subject, *A Calm Address to Our American Colonies*, printed in Bristol in September 1775.

In keeping with contemporary practices of friendly plagiarism, *A Calm Address* was virtually a word-for-word copy of an anti-American polemic issued earlier by Samuel Johnson. Wesley made no effort to soften Johnson's outright rejection of the Americans' claims that they had retained their rights as British subjects upon emigration from Britain. On the contrary, the tract argued that the Americans had ceded their rights to life, liberty, and property to king and Parliament after the first generation of settlement. "You are the descendants of men who either had no votes, or resigned them by emigration," Wesley exclaimed through Johnson's words. "You have therefore exactly what your ancestors left you: not a vote in making laws, nor in chusing legislators, but the happiness of being protected by laws, and the duty of obeying them." As befitted Wesley's High Church principles, *A Calm Address* maintained that the colonies were similar to the vestry of a large parish, empowered with the authority to levy a tax on its inhabitants but regulated and subject to taxation by an external authority, as in the Anglican

Church's supervision of its parishes. The colonists were the unfortunate dupes of a conspiring crew of enemies of the monarchy who wanted nothing more than to erect "their grand idol, their dear [Puritan] Commonwealth upon its ruins."[58]

A Calm Address sold well, approximately forty thousand copies in three weeks' time on the British market. Wesley had tapped a popular sentiment, one increasingly unsympathetic toward the Americans. Compounding the offense to the American patriots, Wesley then proceeded to issue at least seven other royalist pamphlets or open letters.[59]

Despite Wesley's new role as royal apologist, most of the Methodist itinerants in America, British and native-born, attempted to follow their leader's advice to avoid political dispute or engagement in the rising tides of republicanism and loyalist reaction. In May 1775, a month after Lexington and Concord and a week after the Second Continental Congress convened in the statehouse in Philadelphia, the preachers met in conference at St. George's Chapel several blocks away. Here they called for a "General fast in all our Societies for the prosperity of the work of God & *peace* of America and great brittain," with no further editorial comment.[60] In December 1775, when the British government was preparing to send the largest British fleet ever assembled to suppress the American rebellion, Rankin, indulging in a correspondence with Lord Dartmouth, was still focusing on ways that harmony between the British and the Americans might be restored. His suggestions included a repeal of the offensive acts of Parliament, a pardon for those connected to the rebellion, the withdrawal of troops, the prompt reopening of the American ports, and an agreement by the king and Parliament to receive deputations from each of the colonies to settle their differences with the British government. In a postscript, Rankin assured Dartmouth that wherever he preached in New York, New Jersey, Pennsylvania, Maryland, and Virginia, the people expressed a detestation for republican government.[61]

Word of Wesley's public posturing on the conflict—heedlessly embodying so many features of British imperial arrogance, social condescension, and Anglican hegemonic ambition—soon reached an American audience, however, and alerted patriot leaders to the possibility of a Methodist menace. Asbury believed that had Wesley been an American subject, "no doubt but he would have been as zealous an advocate of the American cause." As it was, Wesley had done the opposite, and "some inconsiderate persons have taken occasion to censure the Methodists in America, on account of Mr. Wesley's political sentiments."[62]

These and related developments placed the American Methodists and their British itinerants in an untenable position. In Pennsylvania, where the war now accentuated long-standing tensions between merchants and artisans, the proprietary government and militia rank and file, and pacifists and activist patriots, claims to Tory authority were suddenly as repellent as they had been in New England since the Stamp Act.[63] Philadelphians were the first to read Thomas Paine's *Common Sense*, published in the city in January 1776 and reprinted repeatedly thereafter. In his lucid and impassioned argument, Paine called for the elimination of every remnant of hereditary privilege in America through an all-out war for independence. Providing a secular vision of the priesthood of all believers, Paine asserted

that the average plowman not only had the ability to judge affairs of state but had had this authority stolen from him by generations of robber kings.[64] By the summer of 1776, Pennsylvania's provincial leaders had been forced out of power, and radicals like Paine, David Rittenhouse, James Cannon, Christopher Marshall, Timothy Matlack, and James Wilson, many of them recent immigrants or ethnic outsiders, not unlike many Methodists, rushed in to fill the political vacuum left by the departing elite.[65]

Over the winter and summer of 1776, in the sphere of greatest concern to the Methodists, the Americans were also reconstructing the relationship of church and state. By the time the Continental Congress voted in favor of Independence in July 1776, the constitutional conventions in several new states had incorporated into their constitutions protections for religious freedom, although restricted to professors of Christianity or some form of Trinitarianism.[66] In New Jersey, Pennsylvania, and Delaware, the absence of a religious establishment was sustained. In New York, the Anglican Church was disestablished in the few counties where it had received tax support, and clergymen were prohibited from holding political office. In Maryland, the 1777 state bill of rights forbade the government to compel citizens to attend or support any one church and excluded clergymen from officeholding.[67] And in Virginia, where the Methodist preachers were increasingly popular, the Anglican Church remained established by default only when its supporters and opponents were unable to come to agreement on a church settlement. Jefferson's Statute for Religious Freedom, surpassing earlier legislative motions with a strict separation of religious and political spheres, was ultimately passed by Virginia's legislature in 1786. These Revolutionary changes virtually destroyed the Anglicans' missionary and hegemonic efforts underway since the earliest years of the SPG. Henceforth, the church would be like any other denomination, a precipitous decline in status that was to have an important impact on the Methodist movement at the end of the war.[68]

In this context, the Methodists, until now a set of little-known missionaries of chief concern to the Anglicans, were projected into unwanted prominence by their British origins, Wesley's notoriety, and yet another dangerous deviation from republican norms: the rising antislavery convictions of many of the preachers. Methodists, patriots reported, were proxies for their papist-style leader, sent to preach passive obedience to British authority or, worse, active and militant loyalist spies working against the common cause and fostering slave rebellion. Formerly a movement of small account espousing the apolitical teachings of an English religious reformer, the Methodists were now widely perceived as presumptuous outsiders bent on betraying American independence.

The patriots' sour impression of the Wesleyans was confirmed by the actions of a number of the British preachers. During Virginia's debates on the Anglican establishment in 1776, Rankin's assistant, George Shadford, circulated among the Virginia Methodists a petition opposing disestablishment. Speaking on behalf of "the whole Body of the people Commonly called Methodists in Virginia," Shadford pointed out that unlike the Baptists and Presbyterians, the Methodists "are not Dessenters, but a Religious Society in Communion with the Church of

England." They conceived that "very bad Consequences would arise from the abolishment of the establishment—We therefore pray that as the Church of England ever hath been, so it may continue to be Established."[69] Attacks on the establishment represented an attack on their mother church, Shadford believed, and a misjudgment of the church's commitment to religious freedom. Asbury agreed, observing of Silas Mercer, an antiestablishment Baptist patriot in Virginia: "His is republicanism run mad. Why afraid of religious establishments in these days of enlightened liberty?"[70]

It was probably the aggressive loyalism of Thomas Webb, the war veteran turned Methodist consolidator, that did most to hurt the Methodists' reputation among informed Whigs, however. Residing with his second wife, Englishwoman Grace Gilbert, in New Mills, New Jersey, Webb had continued to travel and preach since his return from Britain. In Philadelphia his oratory had attracted the attention of no less an observer than Continental Congressman John Adams, who pronounced "the old soldier" as "one of the most fluent, eloquent Men I ever heard." Webb also initiated a significant correspondence with Lord Dartmouth, the recipient of so much advice from the Methodist leadership. On the eve of the war, he reported to the secretary that the "New England people" planned to "overturn the [English] constitution, and if possible, establish a democracy upon its ruins." Webb claimed nevertheless that "if his Majesty's standard was to be hoisted, that three fourths of the people [i.e., those outside New England] would immediately join it." He went on to suggest that a massive shutdown of the American ports and exploitation of British manufacturers' and artisans' grievances following the loss of trade would force the British government to act against the rebellion. The "true cause of all the present disturbance, both in Great Britain and America," Webb concluded, "[is] namely that restless spirit of independency, which can never be happy under any government."[71]

By the end of 1776, as war spread into New Jersey, Webb was true to his word to provide any necessary assistance to the Crown and began to pass military intelligence about Washington's movements on to the British command. Traveling into Pennsylvania for more information, Webb later claimed that he had warned the British that the American commander was planning an attack on Trenton on Christmas Day, a tip that the British, to their regret, had failed to heed. Subsequently, they took more seriously Webb's other confidences regarding the American advance through the state, where the Webbs continued to live in this early part of the war.[72]

Throughout these months, Webb, a loyal veteran of the late war with France, also continued to behave as if he were exempt from American authority. When Washington issued a proclamation warning that all those who had refused to take an oath of allegiance to one of the states were required to move behind British lines within thirty days, Webb petitioned the New Jersey Council for a pass to New York City, occupied by the British. When ordered by Governor William Livingston to leave New Jersey, Webb instead traveled to Baltimore to settle his financial affairs and itinerate among the Maryland Methodists, undoubtedly good sources of information on the progress of the war. He rapidly came under the surveillance of Maryland officials, who reported to the American command that the itinerant was a spy and should not be permitted to travel to New York. "It is a certain truth," Samuel Purviance, Jr., reported to General Philip Schuyler, "that all the Denomination called Methodists almost to a man (with us [i.e., in Baltimore]) are enemies to our cause under the mask of religion, and are countenanced by the Tories."[73]

Purviance's generalization was not entirely accurate. While it was the case that a number of prominent Methodist patrons—including Delaware justice Thomas White, shortly to be Asbury's wartime protector, as well as supporters in New York—were known loyalists, numerous other Methodist laymen (in contradistinction to the noncombatant itinerants) were active patriots before and after Independence. In July 1775, several Methodists joined the Association of Free Men in Maryland, pledging to defend the state against the British by force.[74] Methodist patron Samuel Owings, Jr., of Baltimore County, although accused of Tory leanings, served on the Baltimore Committee of Correspondence and was a colonel in the Soldier's Delight Battalion of Militia.[75] In Harford County, Richard Dallam, converted by Strawbridge and newly allied with Asbury, was a member and then treasurer of the Committee of Observation in 1774 and 1775. In June 1775, he was a delegate to the Maryland Provincial Convention that issued the Association of the Freemen of Maryland, supporting the measures of the Continental Congress following Lexington and Concord. By November 1776, Dallam was enlisted in the Company of Harford County Rifles. Although he permitted Methodists to supply substitutes for their military service, by 1780 Dallam was in charge of capturing deserters from various Maryland regiments.[76] Jesse Hollingsworth, a Baltimore merchant and Methodist, was one of forty-nine Marylanders to operate privateers assisting the patriots during the war. He also undertook the rebuilding of ships for the Maryland Council of Safety and the purchase and delivery of food and arms to the patriot forces. Hollingsworth supplied the council with necessary intelligence regarding his brother Henry's skirmish with the British at Head of Elk, Maryland, and was himself wounded "by a stragling Party of the Enemy."[77] In New Jersey, Methodists John Fitch of Trenton, James Sterling of Burlington, and Thomas Ware of Mount Holly were known to be resolute patriots. Fitch, later the inventor of the American steamboat, served time on a British prison ship in New York harbor.[78]

For the American command, however, Thomas Webb was a dangerous man: a former military officer with extensive networks among an unreliable and possibly religiously deluded population. On 7 May 1777 after his return to New Jersey, where he sold his property in New Mills and moved his family to Burlington en route to loyalist New York, Webb was arrested and brought before the Continental Congress on charges of spying. To Webb's good fortune, the charges were dismissed on a technicality, and he was instead sent as a prisoner of war to the Moravian settlement at Bethlehem outside Philadelphia.[79] Here he remained until, after a personal appeal to General Washington by Grace Webb and repeated negotiations with the American command and the deputy commissary of prisoners for the British in New York (Daniel Chamier, husband of Achsah Chamier, a Baltimore Methodist patroness), he and his family were released to return permanently to Britain in October 1778.[80]

With or without Webb's meddling, the British Methodist preachers were in an unenviable position in America, and their problems only intensified as the war expanded into the areas surrounding Chesapeake and Delaware Bays in early 1777. Informed by Wesley not to expect any additional preachers from the British connection "till these troubles are at an end,"[81] Rankin presented a contingency plan for the future to the preachers' conference meeting at the Watters' Chapel in Deer Creek, Maryland, in May 1777. In the event that the "old preachers" were "constrain'd to return to great brittain," the Americans were to adhere to "Articles of agreement" until other preachers could be sent over. Taken virtually word for word from the loyalty oath sworn by the English preachers to Wesley since 1769, the articles were ultimately signed by twenty-five itinerants. A committee, comprising Daniel Ruff, William Watters, Philip Gatch, Edward Dromgoole, and William Glendinning—three Americans and just two Britons, a shift from the earlier dominance of British preachers and toward a preponderance of Strawbridge recruits—was appointed to act as a joint superintendency in the event of the British itinerants' departure.[82]

In the meantime, Rankin attempted to adhere to Wesley's rules of political disengagement.[83] But privately he scorned the patriots and defended those who favored the British. His true sentiments emerged during a dinner at the Perry Hall estate outside Baltimore attended by several of the local gentry and two Methodist preachers. Rankin's sympathy for the wife of a Maryland Tory evoked an impassioned response from Captain John Sterett, an American Whig, as observed by preacher John Littlejohn:

> The Capt flew into a voilent pass[io]n [and] told M^r R[ankin] after pushing away his plate I have as much Re[li]g[io]^n as you. M^r R[ankin] said perhaps you have [and] M^r S[terett] added, & I am as well prepared to die as you, [and] push^g back his chair, [he] unbuttoned his wastecoat, call^g M^r R[ankin] scoundrel Villian Tory &c. [Captain Sterett] s^d Mr Wesley had employ^d his Tongue & pen agst the States, & that every M[ethodist] P[reacher] were tools for [the] Gov^t [and] oug^t to be stopted travel^g & swore he wl^d resent it. M^r [Rankin] said you may do as you please M^r S [terett]. M^r S[terett] added I wish you would resent it, but you have no soul, you coward you are all a parcel of Villians, & I will take care of you if ever I meet you in Balt[im]o[re].

Rankin remained impervious to Sterett's threats, but "all was confusion" among the guests around him. On his return to England, he called the American Whigs "cruel and Bloody men."[84]

Other more serious developments condemned the British Methodists in American eyes. In August 1777, Martin Rodda, Rankin's assistant, was arrested for loyalist operations in Maryland, among them campaigning openly for the British and allegedly joining an armed force of some eighty men in a rebellion on the Eastern Shore. Rodda was threatened with execution by the American military, narrowly escaping through the aid of a Methodist householder.[85] When George Shadford and American loyalist Samuel Spraggs procured a joint pass from

General William Smallwood in Wilmington to travel to Philadelphia and from there to Great Britain, Smallwood chastised the preachers, "Now you have done us all the hurt you can, you want to go home." Shadford followed the appointed route to Philadelphia, but Spraggs crossed over to New York, where he, John Mann (a former Moravian), and James Dempster (another of Wesley's preacher emissaries) reaped the benefits of British protection in the occupied city and served as preachers at Wesley Chapel for the duration of the war.[86]

On Wesley's orders, Rankin pressed Asbury to return to Britain with the other British itinerants. Asbury, however, showed increasing signs of attachment to the American scene. In 1777, he wrote to Joseph Benson in England that he believed Rankin's object "was to sweep the continent of every preacher that Mr. Wesley sent to it and of every respectable traveling preacher of Europe who had graduated among us, whether English or Irish." Rankin had told the preachers, Asbury insisted, that if they returned to Britain, they would receive ordination so that they might renew their American ministry "with high respectability" when the war ended—a promise of professional advancement that Asbury, the plebeian itinerant, likely found difficult to believe.[87]

Briefly considering a move to Antigua as the next step in his missionary career, Asbury decided instead to seek sanctuary in Delaware.[88] In a remarkable misreading of his chief lieutenant's abilities and ambition, Rankin wrote to England that Asbury remained on the continent because he was "unwilling to leave a few Books behind." Rankin, Rodda, Shadford, Robert Lindsay (an Irish itinerant), and an unidentified black preacher departed for England from the Delaware Capes on 3 March 1778.[89] Of the over sixty American and British preachers who had joined the American connection since the preachers' conference in 1773, only twenty-eight, less than half, were still traveling. Of the Wesleyan licensed itinerants, just one—Francis Asbury—remained in patriot territory.[90] By all appearances, the Wesleyan connection had ceased to exist in America.

AMERICAN METHODISTS AND THE WAR EXPERIENCE

The war did not end the Methodist *movement* in the new states, however. While fewer in number than at the start of the war, the American itinerants continued to travel after the departure of the British preachers, and their adherents continued to open their households to preaching. The conditions of the war made the Methodist mission hazardous but not impossible, and while contact with Britain virtually ceased, a phalanx of young and eager preachers was in place, ready to propagate the Methodist gospel with or without the approval of the American authorities.

Twenty-eight new itinerants joined the connection in the war years from 1777 through 1779.[91] A number of the new or remaining American itinerants, such as John Dickins, John Littlejohn, Edward Dromgoole, and William Glendinning, had emigrated from England, Ireland, and Scotland. But many more were American-born, including William Watters, Philip Gatch, Daniel Ruff, Nathan Perigau, Sater Stephenson, and Freeborn Garrettson, all from Robert Strawbridge's sphere of influence.[92] Close to half of the ninety itinerants who joined the itinerancy between 1774 and 1784 were from Baltimore, Harford, and Anne Arundel Counties, Maryland, representing varying ethnic backgrounds. John Hagerty, fluent in German, preached regularly to German-speaking audiences in Maryland and Pennsylvania.[93] Unordained and for the most part informally educated, the preachers formed the first generation of what would become an enduring professional fraternity despite the impact of the war.[94]

Perhaps the hardest standard for the preachers to maintain in these years continued to be Wesley's proscription of partisanship. While the English leader had not required that his followers be pacifists—on the contrary, Methodism was as popular among soldiers as among other laboring-class folk in England and the colonies—the imperatives of Methodist conversion combined with Wesleyan teachings of passive nonresistance turned many men into noncombatants. Joseph Everett, a Maryland convert, was a case in point. Originally a "warm whig," he had volunteered for militia service during the war and attended every muster day for his troop until, on leaving camp one day in February 1778, he attended a revival meeting in his neighborhood. Without apparent premeditation or prior pacifist convictions, Everett suddenly became "weary" of what he called "evil company" while military matters "began to sink in my esteem."[95]

Consequently the American itinerants bore the brunt of the patriot leadership's suspicions that all Methodists were undercover loyalists, and despite proclamations of religious liberty by each of the states, the preachers were under frequent survelliance by the American authorities. As early as June 1775, John Littlejohn was reported to an Anne Arundel magistrate for traveling without a pass. The official insisted that "[t]he Preech⁵ are Tories sent by Wesley to preech passive obediance & nonresistance, I never let one of those fellows come into the neighbourh[ood]."[96] Beginning in 1776, Methodist preachers began to abstain from military service and were imprisoned and fined for noncompliance with militia drafts; these included eight of the Maryland preachers—William Duke, Edward Dromgoole, Freeborn Garrettson, Philip Gatch, Joseph Hartley, John Littlejohn, Jesse Lee, and William Watters—as well as Benjamin Abbott and his son David in New Jersey.[97] In December 1776, when Strawbridge's followers Nathan Perigau and Sater Stephenson were brought before the Baltimore County Committee of Observation as nonassociators and nonenrollers, they argued that as clergymen they were exempt from military service. Their case was referred to the Maryland Council of Safety, which was asked to determine whether the denominations without ordination—Methodists, Quakers, Mennonites, and Moravians—were protected by the clerical exemption. In this instance, the council was sympathetic, and the itinerants were released without fines.[98]

As the fighting encroached on Baltimore in August 1777, the patriot reaction to the itinerants and their followers grew harsher, however. Whatever their claims to pacifism, and often because of these, Methodist men especially were objects of deep suspicion and feared being dragged by horse into militia encampments for interrogation. By October, one itinerant reported that "native preechers cl⁴ not travel such persecution raged."[99] Further complicating the preachers' status, in

December 1777 the Maryland legislature, pressed by a militant lower house, passed an "Act for the better security of Government" requiring an oath or affirmation of allegiance to the state by free men over the age of eighteen. The Security Act barred noncompliers from political participation and from teaching, preaching, engaging in commerce, or practicing law, medicine, surgery, or apothecary.[100] Those defying the law were liable for a treble tax on every hundred pounds' worth of real or personal property. Less stringent laws, requiring oaths of allegiance without military service, were passed in Delaware and Pennsylvania.[101]

The Maryland act had an immediate impact on the Methodist itinerants. Shortly after its provisions went into effect, on 1 March 1778, Joseph Hartley was arrested in Queen Annes County on the Eastern Shore and then incarcerated in the Easton jail in Talbot County for illegal preaching. As the local Anglicans remembered bitterly nearly twenty years later, Hartley continued to attempt to recruit listeners by preaching through the jail windows. William Wrenn and Robert Wooster, both local preachers, were detained in Annapolis for the same infraction.[102] In October 1778, the General Court of the Western Shore indicted twenty itinerants and local preachers for preaching, among them Nathan Perigau and Sater Stephenson as well as John Littlejohn, William Duke, and Harry Dorsey Gough, the last serving as a local preacher and suspected of Tory leanings. William Moore, an Irish-born merchant who itinerated during the war, was indicted on ten counts, convicted of three, and fined £233.8 per count.[103] In February 1780, another American, Freeborn Garrettson, was arrested in Dorchester County on the Eastern Shore as a "Disaffected fugitive" from Delaware, where he had been traveling, and spent sixteen days in the Cambridge jail. He was released on a bond of £20,000 "common Money" (the currency much inflated by the war) provided by Thomas Hill Airey, a gentleman farmer and Methodist sympathizer.[104]

With the increasing pressure of prosecutions and other tensions resulting from the Methodist intrusion into the patriot sphere, it is not surprising that the American political and military leadership characterized the Wesleyan itinerants as a collective threat to public safety. Regarding Somerset and Worcester Counties on the lower Eastern Shore and Sussex and Kent Counties in Delaware, already popular Methodist centers, General William Smallwood believed there were "few circles of the like Extent in New York or the Jersey State which abound more in Disaffected people." Some religious adherents abjured sincerely, "yet by far the greater number conceal their true motives and make Religion a Cloak for their nefarious Designs."[105] Smallwood's convictions were confirmed by several loyalist uprisings on the Eastern Shore in the fall of 1777, led, it was rumored, "by some scoundrel Methodist preachers," including the British Wesleyan Martin Rodda.[106] The freelancing Toryism of lapsed Methodist local preacher Cheney Clow, who raised an armed force of approximately 150 loyalists in Kent County, Delaware, was perhaps the greatest source of anxiety. Although a denominational survey of the rebels ordered by Governor Caesar Rodney identified only two other Methodists among Clow's forces, the former preacher's antipatriot agitations did little to improve the Methodists' reputation.[107] "If a person was disposed to persecute a Methodist preacher," one Wesleyan observed, "it was only necessary to call him a *Tory*, and then they might treat him as cruelly as they pleased. For in many places the existing laws were little regarded."[108]

The American preachers' loyalties—torn between their political sentiments, their heart-religion, and the expectations of their gender—were severely tested by the war. At the start of the conflict, William Watters had responded to a Virginia minister's claims that the Methodists were Tories sent to America to preach passive obedience, retorting that all people are tempted by sin, including the British who oppressed the Americans and ministers who attacked other religious adherents. "I concluded by observing, that though I did not think politics ought to be introduced into the sacred pulpit on any occasion; yet I did most seriously deny that there was one drop of Tory blood flowing through my veins."[109] John Littlejohn, traveling in Baltimore County in spring 1777, felt "like a Fath'less child, abandoned by all my friends, because I was a poor Methodist boy" rather than a patriot volunteer. Yet, among Methodist nonpartisans in Maryland, Littlejohn was "much tempted agst the people & think they are so agst me, because they find I am in fav^r of the American cause." By August of the same year, Littlejohn had resolved his conflicts more satisfactorily: "I once thought it every Christ^n duty to fight for his country," he wrote in his journal, "& doubted ye sincerity of those who refused. I am now convinced, that Christians may & many are sincere in this point." Yet he thought that the Americans would rightfully win the war. Regarding those opposed to Independence, "I wish 'em safe out of the Country for w^t all their confidence in the British cause, I feel they will be mistaken, the [American] cause is Gods."[110]

Political conditions in Maryland, home to many of the American preachers, were especially challenging. John Littlejohn was informed of the Maryland loyalty oath by a local Methodist Whig, Col. Thomas Dorsey, who hoped he would subscribe to it. Instead, Littlejohn sent the colonel a draft of an oath he "tho^t any conscientious Man might take; & that a Preech^r of the Gospel might take w^t a good cons[cienc]^e whether he was an Englishor or a native citizean." This version likely resembled one that preacher Nelson Reed endorsed for himself, affirming he would honor the oath "as far as my conscience will allow (so help me God)."[111] Despite urgings from a number of his patriot friends, Littlejohn refused to conform and consequently found himself among the itinerants cited by the legislature for illegal preaching. Similarly, Jesse Lee "weighed the matter over and over again, but my mind was settled; as a Christian and as a preacher of the gospel I could not fight. I could not reconcile it to myself to bear arms, or to kill one of my fellow creatures. . . ." He was nonetheless recruited into the army in North Carolina and as a "friend to my country" was assigned alternative service as a wagon driver until his discharge in 1780. The cook for the same regiment was also a Methodist.[112]

Most profoundly, Methodist adherence tested the limits of the itinerants' determination to restrain their responses to assaults and other forms of physical and verbal abuse. Freeborn Garrettson's experience was representative of the preachers' sometimes narrow escapes from wartime violence. Traveling through Maryland and Delaware after the British preachers' return to England, Garrettson was threatened with crowd attack and with physical punishment by at least one local magistrate. Already persuaded by his prewar conversion to give up militia service and free his slaves, Garrettson had adopted the Methodist nonpartisan stance wholeheartedly.[113] In June or July 1778, while riding on a local thoroughfare in Queen Annes County, he was arrested by one John Brown, a former county justice, who commenced beating him without apparent provocation. Garrettson wrote of the confrontation:

> Not being far from his quarter, [Brown] called aloud for help. I saw several persons as I thought, with a rope, running to his assistance. Providentially, at this moment he let go my bridle; had not this been the case, it is probable they would have put an end to my life: for the beasts of the field seemed to be in the utmost rage. I thought the way was now open for my escape; and being on an excellent horse, I gave him the whip, and got a considerable distance before he [Brown] could mount; but he, knowing the way better than myself, took a nearer rout, and came in upon me with a full strain; and as he passed, struck at me with all his might; my horse immediately made a full stop, my saddle turned, and I fell with force upon the ground, with my face within an inch of a sharp log.[114]

Other Methodists were subject to similar rough treatment from both ends of the social hierarchy. On the Frederick circuit in western Maryland in 1775, Philip Gatch was partially blinded by a tar-and-feather mob. The "uprore was great," Gatch recollected, "some a swearing and some a crying."[115] In New Jersey around the same time, where Presbyterian support for the Revolution was strong, Benjamin Abbott escaped a beating when the leader of a posse pronounced his preaching the best he had heard since Robert Williams.[116] Through the intervention of the local magistrate in Elk Ridge, Maryland—in this instance supporting the Methodists—John Littlejohn was spared an attack "by some of the bett[r] sort, as they suppose they are."[117] The harassment came from all quarters, revealing the degree to which the Methodists continued to be disdained by the British authorities as much as by the Americans. The meetings at Wesley Chapel, thriving in loyalist-controlled New York, were nonetheless interrupted by roistering soldiers who dug a pit in front of the steps of the meetinghouse, causing hapless worshipers to fall in as they exited the building. The regimental players in *The Devil to Pay in the West Indies* later invaded the sanctuary decked out in full costume, the lead actor draped in a cowhide with red horns.[118]

For their part, the Methodists retaliated in a manner by turning militia musters into their own ritual events. On at least one occasion, Methodist preachers invited local women supporters and probably their black followers to attend preaching during militia exercises, a cacophony of competing voices that militia officers could not have welcomed.[119] "[A]ltogether adverse to shedding blood," as Freeborn Garrettson stated, and superseriously pious, the Methodist itinerants increasingly set themselves apart from these conventionally masculine displays of ribaldry and local mastery.[120]

Francis Asbury's wartime experience was less hazardous but perhaps more frustrating. In February 1778, just before the 1 March deadline for the Maryland loyalty oath, Asbury removed himself to Thomas and Mary White's plantation, fifteen miles south of Dover, near the Maryland border. As he later wrote: "From *March* 10, 1778, on conscientious principles I was a non-juror, and could not preach in the State of Maryland; and therefore withdrew to the Delaware State, where the clergy were not required to take the State oath."[121] His retreat did not protect him entirely from the war. Delaware was among the states most divided by the conflict, and its counties were continuously threatened by patriot and loyalist raids as well as British invasion along the coast. Despite his growing fellow feeling for the Americans—verified to the patriots when they intercepted a letter in which Asbury expressed sympathy for the American cause—Asbury's host was a Tory who in spring 1776 had participated in an aborted rebellion with another Methodist supporter, Richard Bassett, captain of the light horse, and John Clarke, a Kent County local justice of the peace. White was subsequently elected as a loyalist delegate to the Delaware Constitutional Convention. The following year, with the election of Caesar Rodney as governor, the Whigs came to power in the state, and in April 1778 White was arrested on order of the Continental Congress. Asbury fled to the Methodist community in Sudlersville, Maryland, hiding overnight in a marsh before reaching his destination. With White's release in early May, Asbury returned to Delaware, where he remained for two more years, becoming a Delaware citizen.[122]

Denied the daily routine and continuous travel by which he appears to have suppressed personal attachment to friends and family back in Britain, Asbury fell in and out of depression during these months. In addition to White's problems, he made note in his journal of the arrests of Methodist preachers in Maryland. When he attempted to ride a distance in May 1778, he was uncharacteristically fatigued. In September he wrote of "a day of peculiar temptations. . . . My usefulness appeared to be cut off; I saw myself pent up in a corner; my body in a manner worn out; my English brethren gone, so that I had no one to consult; and every surrounding object and circumstance wore a gloomy aspect."[123]

Methodist historian William Williams has observed that Asbury's Delaware sojourn was "particularly important for the long-term development of Methodism," as the English missionary "studied and thought a great deal about the future of Wesley's societies in America."[124] While he had little control over the remaining preachers, he maintained important contacts with Governor Rodney as well as Richard Bassett and the Reverend Samuel Magaw in Dover. "I went where I thought fit in every part of the state, frequently lodged in the houses of very reputable people of the world and we had a great work."[125] He continued to assert his authority—assigning circuits, sending emissaries to the annual conferences that he himself did not attend, and pronouncing on the marriage plans of preachers who traveled by various subterfuges through patriot-controlled territory to confer with him.[126]

But the survival of Methodism during the war depended as much on the freelance activities of the American preachers, and the several English itinerants remaining in New York, as it did on Asbury's exertions. The numbers of Methodist adherents multiplied in the war years in areas in and outside Asbury's control. In

1778, the official tally of members of the Methodist societies stood at 6,095, slightly lower than the previous year's but more than five times the count at the first conference of 1773. By 1779, 8,577 Americans were members of Methodist societies. By 1782 and the end of the war, the figure had risen to 11,785.[127] The majority of these new fellow travelers were to be found in the lower Middle Atlantic and the South. A revival in Virginia in 1775–1776, memorialized in an account by the Reverend Devereux Jarratt, turned the Brunswick circuit in Virginia into the largest Methodist district in the new states in 1776, with a total of 1,611 adherents.[128] Success continued to be striking in Virginia, where nearly half of the close to 7,000 American Methodists resided in 1777. Close to a third of Methodists—more than 2,000—were inhabitants of Delaware and Maryland, with 900 members in the Baltimore circuit (including city and county) alone.[129] While the Methodists in Philadelphia were ejected from St. George's Chapel, turned into a riding school for the British troops, the John Street society in New York, ministered by their three loyalist preachers, remained strong, with worshipers protected by the same British forces that from time to time harassed them.[130] Altogether, despite his troubles on the Eastern Shore in the late 1770s, Freeborn Garrettson preached "in more than a hundred new places" in the course of fifteen months, helping to spur attendance at Methodist revival meetings closer to Asbury's base. In August 1779, six or seven hundred people from Philadelphia, Delaware, and the Eastern Shore each day attended a quarterly meeting near Dover.[131] In a conflict that bore many features of a civil war, with patriots pitted against loyalists, radical activists against religious sectarians, and slaves against masters, the Methodists surged forward, a new dynamic force led by a remarkably resilient band of young preachers most of whom made no demands on Americans' political allegiance and rarely interfered with republican claims to political hegemony.

By the end of the war, the increasing popularity of the itinerants led to conflicts among local authorities with competing views of the Methodists' political reliability. In Oxford, Pennsylvania, a "Gentleman" from Lancaster—who believed "the Methodists to be Torify'd" and had "sent all the Methodist preachers he can catch to Lancaster G[ao]l"—threatened the commission of a local official who had permitted Methodists to preach at his house.[132] But as the war moved south, charges against the increasingly popular evangelists went unindicted by the general courts, or the itinerants were simply permitted to move on, although it was not until 1782 that Methodists were exempted from the penalties for nonjuring, a year after most other exemptions were enacted.[133]

The revivals continued as the fighting between the British and the Americans with their French allies came to an end in lower Virginia in 1781. In addition to their Virginia societies, the Methodists now boasted more than thirty-five regular meeting places—a mix of household venues and chapels—in Delaware and the Eastern Shore.[134] A number of itinerants had established themselves as heroic noncombatants despite the sobriquet "Wesleyan" attached to their preaching. Prominent Methodist laymen had served the patriots' cause, and prominent patriots shielded and even patronized the movement. At the same time, hundreds of households, many headed by women whose husbands had been long absent in militias or Washington's army, or who had fled across enemy lines, sustained the itinerants as they circulated in and out of revival areas. The size of the preachers' slave and free black following during the war is not known, but by 1786, when tallies of whites and blacks first appeared in the published minutes of Methodist conferences, blacks were counted as constituting 1,890 out of 20,681 Methodists, or close to 10 percent of the Methodist population. Of these many were slaves officially manumitted or otherwise promised freedom by their Methodist masters and mistresses, and beginning the long labor to pay for their freedom.[135]

By the end of the war, the Wesleyan Methodists had proven themselves survivors—and, most important, compatible with the new political order and in demand in strongly patriot territory. The shape survival would take was nonetheless uncertain when Francis Asbury set out to travel his old circuits in April 1780.

POSTWAR CONDITIONS, SEPARATION, AND THE MEC

"[H]ere begins the melinium," Philip Gatch recorded excitedly in his journal at the war's end, "Independancy is obtained. [T]he revolutionary War at an end and we freed from every oppression, only that of sin, and Satan, and theire is Jesus at the right hand of God ready to grant repentance and remission of sins both to Jew, and Gentile."[136] For the new evangelicals, the new republic was ripe for conversion, and religious seekers were now freer than ever to choose what form their conversions would take. Despite the troubles brought on by the conflict with Britain, missionary expansion, solidarity among the preachers who had survived the war, and greater revival triumphs were all foreseeable outcomes in a nation prizing a religious economy of freely competing churches.

The Methodists, however, were not like just any church. In fact, they were not a church at all. Rather they were the most successful of the Anglican reforming societies, the popular cousin of the SPG, the SPCK, and Dr. Bray's Associates, designed to revitalize Christianity in and outside the established church. Separation from the church into a separate denomination had been rejected by the Wesleys, John and Charles, from the start. As John Wesley had written in 1758, "Whether it be *lawful* or no . . . it is by no means *expedient* for us to separate from the established Church."[137]

By the end of the Revolutionary War, nevertheless, there were at least four reasons why it was not only lawful but also expedient for the Methodists to separate from the English church. First, there was the wartime deterioration of American Anglicanism, the reluctant host of the Methodist movement and the parent church of numerous Methodists. While recent work on Anglicanism and the Revolution has shown that the Anglicans were far from sliding into irreversible decline with Independence, the health of the church, like that of the Methodist societies, varied signficantly from region to region. The incidental deaths of incumbents accounted for a larger number of vacancies than did loyalism or depletion of parishioners in the Chesapeake region during the war.[138] At the same time, 63 out of 286 of the Anglican clergy as a whole, a significant number, were loyalists. The only Anglican churches in operation in Pennsylvania, New Jersey, New York, and Connecticut just four months after Independence were those in Philadelphia and New York City, one or two in rural Pennsylvania, and two in Connecticut. By the end of the war, only nine out of fifty Anglican ministers who had tended parishes in Pennsylvania, New York, and New England remained in the United States.[139] A series of contingencies, from disestablishment to the refusal of prominent High Church Anglicans to dispense with prayers for the king in religious services, the flight of loyalist ministers and SPG missionaries back to England, and the disintegration or destruction of parish buildings—particularly in war-torn Middle Atlantic states like New Jersey, where most of the loyalist Anglican clergy were concentrated—abased the dynamism of the church and virtually destroyed its vision of continental hegemony.[140]

The Anglicans' predicament presented a dilemma for the Methodists as well. Before the war, as in Britain, the itinerants had depended on the church for access to the sacraments—or ordinances, as the Methodists called them—of communion and baptism, administered by fully ordained, vestry-appointed Anglican clergy or SPG ministers. Despite the Anglican hierarchy's conviction that the preachers were raiding their churches and the tendency of other churches to expel members who joined the Methodists, many, likely most, Methodists were ongoing communicants of the Anglican Church or other denominations. Throughout the war, the preachers adhered to Wesley's standard policy of permitting society members to continue to receive the sacraments from a duly ordained Anglican minister or to otherwise remain attached to their original churches.[141]

With the coming of the Revolution, however, as American itinerant Jesse Lee later recounted, "our societies were deprived of the ordinances of *baptism, and the Lord's supper*: for the ministers of the church of England had mostly left their parishes: some of them were silenced, others left off preaching, because they could not procure a maintenance of it; and many more went into the British dominions."[142] Robert Strawbridge's experiments with unorthodox priestly powers now took on new relevance, as the British Wesleyan emissaries, under various clouds of political suspicion, returned to Britain, and the American itinerants, many of them Strawbridge's converts, were left to their own devices.

The emerging conflict among the American preachers over the adoption of these ministerial powers constituted the second significant development threatening the Methodists' connection with their Anglican parent. Beginning at the May 1777 preachers' conference in Deer Creek, Maryland, where Thomas Rankin turned down a petition from a number of preachers seeking to ordain an American presbytery before he was forced back to England, access to the sacraments was an increasingly rancorous issue. So much so that several of Robert Strawbridge's followers agreed to ignore the proscriptions of the British-run conference and when necessary to administer ordinances themselves. After Rankin's departure, the main body of the preachers meeting at Fluvanna, Virginia (thereafter called the "Fluvanna Conference"), in 1779 elected a "Presbetry" composed of Philip Gatch, James Foster, and Reuben Ellis (Le Roy Cole serving as backup) to administer communion, as well as baptism, "either Sprinkling or Plunging as the Parent or Adult shall choose." The last provision suggests that the Baptists were much on the preachers' minds. Most strikingly, the presbytery was empowered to ordain other preachers. Commenting on the state of the Anglicans that had especially driven the Fluvanna attenders to adopt these measures, Gatch wrote that "some of the Preachers undertook to administer the ordinances through necessity. [I]t was to keep our societies togather."[143] As a local preacher, Robert Strawbridge was not present in Fluvanna, but as Methodist scholar Frank Baker has stressed, "[t]here can be little question that his unseen hand was behind the southern preachers."[144]

The sacramental controversy—ostensibly a struggle over the powers of Methodist ministry but also a cultural contest between Strawbridge's democratic Irish Methodism and Asbury's loyalty to Wesley's authoritarian "old plan"—continued unsatisfactorily resolved for four years, prompting Asbury to declare upon Strawbridge's death in 1781, "[T]he Lord took him away in judgment, because he was in a way to do hurt to his cause."[145] But the Irish preacher's influence, born of nearly twenty years of evangelical work in Maryland, Virginia, and Pennsylvania, was irrefutable and inescapably raised the question of how association with the Anglican Church might further hamper Methodist expansion.

By the time the Treaty of Paris was signed in 1783, many Methodist adherents, "through fear, necessity, or choice," had already emigrated into "the back settlements" beyond the Appalachian frontier and called for the preachers to follow them, a dispersal of believers that posed a third problem for the Methodists. Richard Owings, a Strawbridge recruit, was the first to cross the Appalachians in search of converts.[146] Yet the Methodists were not in a good position to establish themselves in the old or new territories in North America. Asbury wrote to Wesley itemizing some of the difficulties posed by competition with other denominations in the new republic, stressing that he believed that "the Calvinists on the one hand, and the Universalians on the other, very much retard the work of God, especially in Pennsylvania and the Jerseys, for they both appear to keep people from seeking heart religion." While Maryland was relatively free of Calvinist influence, in "Virginia, North and South Carolina, and Georgia, the Baptists labour to stand by what they think is the good old cause." Ironically, among the Methodists' competitors were the revitalized Anglicans, poised to form a new Protestant Episcopal Church from the ruins of the colonial church and in a good position to siphon off the Methodist itinerants qualified to join holy orders. With the end of the war, some of the movement's more educated preachers were considering just such a move.[147]

Most Methodist itinerants, however, were not equipped to compete or join up with their experienced clerical counterparts among the Anglicans and other denominations, a limitation that constituted yet another difficulty after the war. The Methodist travelers, the bulk of impressionistic evidence suggests, were young, informally educated, and generally of middling status, or at most, sons of the lesser gentry. Asbury's task at the end of the war remained similar to Rankin's before the war: to bring order and discipline to a movement with few claims to the standard source of public respect: an educated and ordained clergy. Hence among other proposals agreed to at a preachers' meeting at Choptank, Delaware, in 1781 was the extension of the probationary period for preachers from one year to two, "considering the youth of [the] preachers & their small gifts."[148] Without formal church status, the Methodists had little or no ecclesiastical clout with American clergymen. "Humiliating indeed was our condition," one of the preachers recalled. "Not a man in holy orders among us; and against us formidable combinations were formed," among the clergy as much as the laity. "[D]enounced from the pulpit as illiterate, unsound in our principles, and enthusiastic in our spirit and practice—in a word, every way incompetent, and only to be despised— the multitude, men and women, were imboldened to attack us; and it was often a matter of diversion to witness how much they appeared to feel their own superiority."[149] Thus the Methodist itinerants might well lose whatever advantage they had as the clergy of the "old" denominations—the Anglicans, Congregationalists, and Presbyterians chief among them—recouped their losses from the war and reclaimed their place at the head of the American denominational order.

What then was the purpose, in the standard Wesleyan scheme of things, of attempting to "reform" the members of the existing churches? Thus Asbury wrote to Wesley in the fall of 1783: "Is Methodism intended for the benefit of all denominations of reformed Christians? Can a Quaker, as well as a member of any other church, be in Society, and hold his outward peculiarities, without being forced to receive the ordinances?" The Methodists now included former Presbyterians, Lutherans, Mennonites, German sectarians, and Baptists. "If we preach up [Anglican] ordinances to these people," Asbury pointed out, ". . . we shall drive them back to their old churches that have disowned them; and who will do all they can to separate them from us." Continued attachment to the Anglicans was likely to jeopardize the Methodists' hold on this diverse following.[150]

Instead of being poised to meet such demands, the Methodists remained in a suspended state, awaiting some sign from their English leader that would direct them toward an appropriate course of action. Wesley's instructions, as ever, reflected his great reluctance to lose control of the American movement. In October 1783, he reiterated his support for Asbury's authority, the need for the Americans to "abide by the Methodist doctrine and discipline," to beware of clerical imposters coming in from Britain and Ireland, as well as "perverse" theology, especially Calvinism. Still an Anglican cleric, Wesley remained opposed to separation from the Methodists' parent church.[151] By this time, however, the English founder, approaching age eighty and facing the prospect of the dissolution of his itinerant connection upon his death, had begun to develop a rationale for ordaining his own preachers, one that would be consistent with a historical interpretation of the Primitive Church, and that would ultimately serve his American "assistants" as well.

In Wesley's view, the Primitive Church had consisted of two ranks of clergy: a higher order of bishops and presbyters, endowed with the power to administer sacraments and ordain other clergy; and a lower order of ministers empowered to preach and perform baptisms. Wesley was of course a member of the upper rank. Together with at least two other "presbyters," he believed that he could legitimately ordain his itinerants. Like their Anglican counterparts, they then might exercise priestly powers over baptism and communion, but more important, initiate further ordinations to carry on Wesley's work long after his death.[152] Wesley continued loath to carry out such measures, but in February 1784 he set the process in motion when he agreed to a set of measures assuring the independence, if not precisely the separation, of the English connection. In particular he signed a "Deed of Declaration" with selected members of his connection endowing them with legal status as his heirs.[153]

At the same time, he began to develop plans for the Americans with the assistance of a new confidant, ordained priest and doctor of civil laws, Thomas Coke. An Oxford graduate and man of property, the Welsh-born Coke, two years younger than Francis Asbury, was an unusually urbane and courteous, if often voluable and unpredictable, member of Wesley's connection. Experiencing conversion in 1772, he appears to have attended his first Methodist conference in 1777. By the early 1780s, he had become Wesley's "right-hand man," rising to special prominence as the cosponsor of the Deed of Declaration. He was also an ambitious missionary, with aims to evangelize populations outside Britain. In 1784 he and another preacher published their plan to missionize the "Heathen Nations," otherwise unidentified, calling for a replication among populations well beyond British boundaries of the "amazing Change" the itinerants had brought about among the "Ignorant and uncivilized" in the United Kingdom.[154]

Around this time, Wesley began conferring with Coke about the possibility of ordaining the American preachers. In April 1784, Coke urged Wesley to authorize him to travel to the new states to gather "sufficient Information" on the "State of the Country and the [American] Societies." The following August, Coke, probably not for the first time, suggested that Wesley ordain him and two other well-seasoned itinerants, Richard Whatcoat and Thomas Vasey, for work in America. The creation of such a presbytery would be "the most scriptural way" to pursue ordination of preachers in America and "most agreeable to the practice of the primitive churches." It would also give Coke influence with Asbury, who, he had reason to believe, would otherwise resist his intrusions. "In short," Coke wrote, "it appears to me that everything should be prepared, and everything proper to be done, that can possibly be done, this side the water."[155] Through ordination of a select group of their preachers, Wesley would secure the Americans' attachment to the "old Methodist doctrine and discipline," thereby caging the specters of nonconformity and schism that his brother Charles was certain would stalk a separated Methodist Church.[156] Such work would also fit well into Coke's scheme to missionize the "Heathen Nations."

Wesley was persuaded, by Coke's points or by some other influence. At the end of the summer of 1784, now working with dispatch, he carried his theory of Primitive ordination into practical application. In a brief ceremony in Bristol on 1 September, Wesley, together with James Creighton, another evangelical Anglican priest, and Thomas Coke, styled themselves a Primitive presbytery and ordained Whatcoat and Vasey as deacons. The following day, Wesley and Creighton further ordained Whatcoat and Vasey as elders and Thomas Coke as superintendent, qualifying the three men to operate as a presbytery in America.[157] Wesley was careful not to publicize the full meaning of his actions. As he wrote in his published journal: "Being now clear in my own mind, I took a step which I had long weighed in my mind and appointed Mr. Whatcoat and Mr. Vasey to go and serve the desolate sheep in America." But in his private diary and on the certificate issued to Whatcoat and Vasey, he openly used the word "ordained" to describe this dramatic departure from former, long-standing deference to Anglican apostolic authority.[158]

The English leader elaborated on his actions in a pastoral letter to the Americans. Recognizing that "many of the Provinces of North America are totally disjoined from their Mother Country and erected into independent States," Wesley now abandoned his opposition to American Independence, stating that "the English Government has no authority over [the Provinces], either civil or ecclesiastical, any more than over the States of Holland." In America, moreover, there were no bishops and, technically speaking, until the pending reconstitution of the Anglican Church, no parish priests. "So that for some hundred miles together," Wesley asserted, emphasizing Anglican failure, "there is none either to baptize or to administer the Lord's supper. Here, therefore, my scruples [regarding ordination] are at an end; and I conceive myself at full liberty, as I violate no order and invade no man's right by appointing and sending labourers into the harvest." In a remarkable reversal of his wartime pronouncements, Wesley concluded:

> As our American brethren are now totally disentangled both from the State and from the English hierarchy, we dare not entangle them again either with the one or the other. They are now at full liberty simply to follow the Scriptures and the Primitive Church. And we judge it best that they should stand fast in that liberty wherewith God has so strangely made them free.[159]

In a stroke, Wesley cleared away all past objections to innovations in church-state relations and the political independence of Americans and resolved the sacramental conflict that had absorbed the American itinerants for seven years: the Methodists would simply administer their own sacraments. "Scriptures and the Primitive Church" were more important than political or national ties, and together these formed the imaginative driving forces behind Wesley's willingness as ever to break ecclesiastical rules.

Whether Wesley intended to create something called a Methodist Church is far less clear, however. Concerned that the American preachers might go the way of "Independents, & gathering Congregations each for himself; Or procuring Ordination in a *regular way*, & accepting Parochial cures," Wesley, writing to Asbury in October, left open "what Method will be most effectual, to fix the work on such a stable foundation as will not easily be overturned." He was concerned that the Americans move "slowly, step by step," and once the "plan with respect to the Provinces" was resolved, that they send missionaries to Antigua (where Methodism had been introduced to the slave population by Thomas Webb's brother-in-law, Nathaniel Gilbert) and Nova Scotia (where a large British and expatriate American Methodist population now resided). As to further help from England, the Methodists should not expect it but should rather "use yᵉ Means you have."[160]

Perhaps to clarify these points, Wesley had composed a "little sketch" of his plans for the American future. The sketch has not survived to confirm most historians' assumption that Wesley mandated the formation of a separate church. In no other surviving record does he direct Coke or Asbury to form a church, or denomination, or even sect. Rather, by all appearances he instructed the Americans to organize themselves into a missionary association with ordination powers derived from himself and his hastily devised presbytery, a preaching connection that would continue to serve as a revitalizing force for other churches and sects while gathering their own exclusive societies as well. Such a resolution would have been completely in keeping with his own lifelong work as a reforming missionary. Recognition that his actions as good as authorized a church represented perhaps too great a dissonance with his own espoused attachment to the mother church for Wesley to consciously admit.[161]

If not from Wesley's fertile imagination, then where did the explicit determination to organize an American church come from? A not far-fetched candidate is Thomas Coke, Wesley's trusted emissary. It is unlikely, however, that Coke came to such a decision arbitrarily. His progress, and the timing whereby "Wesley's" plan was revealed to the Americans, suggests something else.

Coke set sail with his two companions on 18 September 1784, armed with ordination certificates, Wesley's pastoral letter to the Americans, Wesley's "sketch of his plans," a printed *Sunday Service* (closely modeled on the Anglican liturgy), and a copy of the *Collection of Psalms and Hymns*. On shipboard, Coke spent much of his time reading on the history of church government, reflecting at one point that "religion is liable to be secularized and made the tool of sinister and ambitious men" when too closely associated with the state, evidence suggesting that Coke had arrived at a further rationale for breaking the Anglican link.[162]

Upon their arrival in New York on 3 November, the English emissaries were welcomed by the Methodist society with some anticipation. Coke here revealed what he called "Mr. *Wesley's* Plan" to John Dickins, the English-born stationed preacher. Dickins, Coke wrote, "highly approves of [the plan], says that all the Preachers most earnestly long for such a regulation, and that Mr. *Asbury* he is sure will agree to it." He urged Coke to publish it since "Mr. *Wesley* has determined the point," and hence the proposal was not to be questioned. Perhaps influenced by further conversations with Dickins, himself a former ally of Robert Strawbridge, Coke moved on to Philadelphia where he announced to the Methodist society what (in the American edition of his journal) he called "our new plan of Church Government," his first reference to such a design.[163] On 13 November, he and Richard Whatcoat then met with Freeborn Garrettson at Richard Bassett's house in Dover, Delaware. Garrettson wrote of the meeting, "I was somewhat surprised when I heard Mr. Wesley's new plan opened . . . [but] thought I would sit in silence." Since the introduction of ordination, on the heels of the Americans' own sacramental controversy, would not have been unwelcome, it is likely that what had become an announcement of separation into a wholly distinct church was what made Garrettson "sit in silence."[164] The evidence is too scanty for firm conclusions, but it is likely that beginning with his enthusiastic reception in New

York, followed by exposure to the Americans and their history of independence during the war, Coke was swiftly persuaded of the necessity and popularity of not simply a "regulation" for ordaining the preachers, but of a full-fledged "Church Government."

The degree to which "Wesley's" plan went beyond what the Americans expected and what Wesley himself had foreseen is further confirmed by Coke and Asbury's first meeting on 14 November at the newly erected Barratt's Chapel, near Frederica, Delaware. Here five to six hundred preachers and people alike, participants in a well-advertised quarterly meeting, awaited Wesley's deputy, undoubtedly bolstering the English Methodist's convictions that he was properly interpreting Wesley's mandate. Coke wrote of the occasion: "[A] plain, robust man came up to me in the pulpit, and kissed me: I thought it could be no other than Mr. *Asbury*."[165] By contrast, Asbury, now informed of the plan for complete independence from the Anglican Church, "was shocked when first informed of the intention of these my brethren in coming to this country."[166]

Ever sensitive to American sensibilities, Asbury had preconvened a "council" of preachers to discuss whatever Coke might tell them. This group now agreed to the calling of a conference in Baltimore at the end of December to ratify a fully developed version of the proposed church. Freeborn Garrettson was sent to announce the meeting to itinerants traveling through the South. Americans now began to refer explicitly to the formation of a separate church, assumed to be fully authorized by Wesley. Baltimore Methodist Adam Fonerden, writing to a correspondent just after the Frederica meeting, reported that a "Church" would be formed in keeping with Wesley's instructions; this was not to be "forced upon us, but left to our Choice" at a special preachers' conference. Asbury and Coke, Fonerden continued, were to act as joint superintendents, since Asbury would not act alone in a matter of such importance. Another itinerant, probably informed so by Garrettson, reported that Coke and his assistants had come to America "under authority from the Rev^d. M^r. John Wesley, for the purpose of forming the Societies into a Church."[167]

By the time the preachers were on their way to Baltimore, it was widely believed that Wesley had authorized every part of the new plan. American preacher Thomas Haskins commented in particular on the unusual haste with which the gathering was called "at this inclement season of the year" and the problems that separation, which he believed Wesley had sponsored, would bring to the Methodists' relations with their mother church. Joining several preachers riding to Baltimore, Haskins conversed "on this new plan proposed by Mr. John Wesley" to form the Methodists into a "separate independent Church." Considering his checkered reputation during the Revolutionary War, Haskins observed, Wesley had perhaps once again misjudged American affairs. "M^r. Wesley seems to be of Opinion that the matter will admit of no delay. I acknowledge M^r. W——y to be a great & good, judicious & sensible Man—But not infallible particularly with respect to the political, civil & religious affairs of America." Better to wait until the regularly scheduled preachers' conference the following June. In the meanwhile, "as generous & dutiful Sons of the Episcopal Church to whom we have from time to time publicly professed ourselves to be united," the Methodists ought to discuss Wesley's plans with "as many of her Clergy as possible." Otherwise, "how justly [shall we] . . . be stigmatized by the sober & judicious as hunters after power & disturbers of the peace & good order of the Church & State In which we live."[168]

The "good order of the Church & State" in which Americans lived had by now greatly changed, however. The Anglican Church was disestablished, and the relationship of Anglicans to Methodists no longer resembled that of a forbearing and worldly parent to a rebellious if righteous child, the postwar Methodists appearing rather as potentially devouring offspring. On the eve of the December conference, the Anglicans, aware of the Methodist threat, sent two Episcopal ministers, the Reverends William West and John Andrews, to forestall the organization of the church. They made Thomas Coke the remarkable offer of an American bishopric. Revealing their own understanding of the rising strength of the Methodists among the Americans, they also proposed the election of one bishop out of every two per state "from among the people called Methodists, so long as that distinction should be kept up among us." Coke, they reported back to the Anglican hierarchy, declined the offer, citing the primacy of Wesley's authority and the centrality of the itinerancy to the Methodist system. The ministers also discovered that Asbury, in attendance but proffered no clerical advancement, ardently believed that the Methodists "had always been treated by us [the Anglicans] with abundance of contempt." "*[T]hese gentlemen,*" Andrews wrote to William White, "*are not wholly free from resentment.*" Indeed, while the German Reformed minister Philip William Otterbein was to participate in Asbury's ordination as cohead of the new church, no Anglican clergy were invited to the December conference that created the Anglican Church's evangelical blood relation.[169]

The "Christmas Conference," as this preachers' convention came to be known, assembled at the Lovely Lane Chapel in Baltimore on Friday, 24 December 1784. It adjourned a little more than a week later, on Sunday, 2 January. By its conclusion, approximately sixty preachers, or three-quarters of the American connection, had participated. Predictably, the participants were young men, many raw recruits with three years' or less of traveling experience.[170] Thomas Haskins's record of the events of the meeting, complete with editorial comments, relays something of its pace:

Frid 24—Conference set—1. Question proposed was whether we shou'd have the ordinances administered among us & we shoud be erected into an independa[nt] church— Unanimously carried in the affirmative. 2. Whether our church shou'd be that of an Episcopal or Presbyterian Church—answered that of an Episcopal Church—called the Methodist Episcopal Church of America—3. How many orders of Ministers shall we have. Ans[r]. Three 1. Superintendant 2. Elders. 3. Deacons—4. That a superintendant shall have a negative voice in all ordinations. Conference have [power] to suspend or turn out a superintendant, on being found faulty, etc, etc, etc, etc.

On the Monday following the weekend:

> The preachers being generally come together, the proceedings on friday were unanimously agred to after a recapitulation. Tuesd. 28. Wed. 29. Thu. 30. Fri. 31. were spent in forming a government for our n[ew] Church & in Electing & ordaining superintendant[s] Elders & Decons. I was nominated for the Deconship but begged time for consideration.[171]

Asbury's description of the proceedings is equally perfunctory: "[I]t was agreed to form ourselves into an Episcopal Church, and to have superintendents, elders, and deacons." "When the conference was seated," he continues, "Dr. Coke and myself were unanimously elected to the superintendency of the Church, and my ordination followed, after being previously ordained deacon and elder. . . ."[172]

Historians have readily observed that the new American Methodist Church differed from the English connection in at least one fundamental way: all the important features of the Methodist Church were voted on. Deferring to the political mores of the new republic and the American preachers' long-held expectations of involvement in conference decisions, Asbury required that the choice of the superintendents, his own ordination, and that of the elders and deacons be determined by election. As one participant later recalled, "As well as I remember every thing or measure that was proposed was put to a vote, and a majority carried it."[173] Among the measures agreed to was that "[d]uring the Life of the Rev. Mr. Wesley, we acknowledge ourselves his Sons in the Gospel, ready in Matters belonging to Church-Government, to obey his Commands." As this was to be a new American church, however, the statement was duly qualified to emphasize that after Wesley's death the preachers would undertake "every Thing that we judge consistent with the Cause of Religion in *America* and the political Interests of these States." Overall, the American preachers exercised significantly greater power over their leaders than did the English preachers over Methodism's founder.[174]

But here and elsewhere Asbury also displayed a political acumen that was to serve him well in future years and the ability to not only shape but control Methodism's democratic centrifuge. With minor exceptions, the organizing conference elevated to eldership men who had formed the ranks of Asbury's steady supporters.[175] The conference's most striking decision—to incorporate a vigorous antislavery plank in its first discipline—had been supported by the preachers since their 1780 meeting. Potentially more difficult was the adoption of the episcopal church form and inclusion of the word "Episcopal" in the church's name. The maker of the motion appears to have been none other than John Dickins, the ardent supporter of ordination and, likely, the organization of a separate church, from the moment Coke arrived in New York.[176]

Perhaps more noteworthy than the use of elections, furthermore, a common practice in other churches, was the Methodists' new willingness to make a clean break with their Anglican past. Coke was unsentimental on the subject. Preaching to the Christmas Conference, he pronounced dead the Anglican order of church-and-state. As Coke told the young preachers, positioning them in their new history, before the Revolution the Church of England "did for many years groan in *America* under grievances of the heaviest kind. Subjected to a Hierarchy, which weighs every thing in the scales of politics, its most important interests were repeatedly sacrificed to the supposed advantages of *England*. The Churches were, in general, filled with the parasites and bottle-companions of the rich and the great." "Blessed be GOD," Coke continued, "and praised be his HOLY NAME, that the memorable Revolution has struck off these intolerable fetters, and broken the antichristian union which before subsisted between Church and State."[177] The stigmatizing of the American Anglicans as the church of hierarchy, privilege, and corruption had begun, initiated by their own evangelical offspring. The Methodists now represented themselves as the unabashed proponents of separation of church and state and the episcopal church of the future.

Similar to all American denominations in the decades after the Revolutionary War, the Methodists continued to struggle with the contradictory tensions of searching for an instrumental role for religion in the new republic while espousing disestablishment and freedom of religious choice. Unlike the Congregationalists and Presbyterians, however, the Methodists did not dwell on the millennial destiny of the republic or dream of an explicitly nationalist hegemony.[178] Instead, they remained first and foremost a popular missionary movement. "Every thing went on as it had before our organization," one preacher claimed. "Ordination was the only thing we had seemed to lack; and this lack was now supplied."[179]

By this means the Methodists believed they might accomplish their main goal with few distracting diversions into politics, clerical or secular: to expose every American within listening distance to the magnetic power of the religious rite at the heart of the movement, the Methodist revival meeting.

CHAPTER THREE

The Making of a Methodist

BY HIS OWN account, John Littlejohn was born in Penrith, Cumberland County, England, in December 1755, one of eight children. His parents were people of means and sent their son to a Latin school until "by various misfortunes" Littlejohn's father lost his business and moved to London to rebuild his wealth. John was removed to a trade school where he learned the artisan's skills of reading, writing, and arithmetic. Shortly thereafter he was apprenticed to a tin manufacturer in London. Within a year, one guinea and change in his pocket, Littlejohn had run away, setting out on foot for the 284 miles to his mother's house in Penrith. Here, as befitted his age and rebelliousness, he was reapprenticed to one Thomas Broomfield, a storekeeper in Port Tobacco, Maryland, in the North American colonies.

John Littlejohn's voyage to America began in Newcastle-on-Tyne, probably in 1767, where he embarked with Mr. Broomfield, a pious woman named Mrs. Small, sixty-five indentured servants, fourteen convicts, and the ship's crew. Over the course of the journey, sickness broke out, one or two of the servants died, a mariner fell overboard, and all were put on half-rations. Littlejohn consoled himself in conversations with Mrs. Small. The ship arrived at Saint Mary's River after a "boisterous passage" of twenty-one weeks, and Littlejohn began to work in Broomfield's store. Here, Littlejohn recalled, "I lost my veneration for the Sab^h day, f^m the example of the family who were part of the church of Engl^d, part Romans, [and] each party went to church or chapple on Sunday & generly spent the afternoons at Cards."

Littlejohn soon grew impatient with the confines of Broomfield's store and signed on to a third apprenticeship with English-born saddler Thomas Slack in Northumberland County, Virginia. Slack, an unmarried man, did not keep house, and his new apprentice boarded out. "Here I learn't to play at Cards, dice &c till all my religious Ideas were gone, which my good Moth[er]: had early impressed my mind w^t." Two years later, Slack returned to England, and the elder Littlejohn died in Prince George's County, Maryland, where he had emigrated with the remainder of his family. Now a ward of Mr. Allison in Norfolk, Virginia, Littlejohn moved across Chesapeake Bay to a fourth apprenticeship with Eldred Fisher, a Norfolk harnessmaker. Fisher also ran a bachelor's house, where the English teen lived "as to my morals w^t. out restraint," making pocket money by selling "the private [pornographic] adventures of Sailors" and supplying the mariners with "Red Birds," or cardinals, popular items for trade in the West Indies. Littlejohn used his portion of the profits to satisfy his "Itch" for gaming, cockfighting, and other laboring-class pleasures, pursuing these, as he was later to express in hyberbolic evangelical style, "till few of my age had done as much in the service of

Satan as I did (drunkeness excepted)." On Saturday nights, Fisher's apprentices and their friends regularly joined one of their master's journeymen for oyster suppers, gambling, and cockfighting by candlelight. "Often the Sabath's Sun, would be hours high before we were dispersed."

Littlejohn spent two years in Norfolk. During this time, while following his usual entertainments, he "could not withstand the ding dong of the 2^d bell for Church." He first heard revival preaching in 1769 when the Irish Methodist preacher Robert Williams, newly arrived from Britain, climbed the steps of the Norfolk courthouse and began to sing, "Come, sinners, to the gospel feast." Looking out from the door of Fisher's shop, Littlejohn called to his shopmates, "[T]here is a Crasy fellow at the C^t house & I will go & see him." Joining the growing crowd, he quickly recognized Williams as a religious man and "paid great attent^n." The mayor of Norfolk, another attentive listener, remarked curtly, "If we permit such fellows as these to come here we shall have an insurrection of the Negars." Williams returned for future visits, as did Joseph Pilmore, Richard Wright, William Watters, and others from among the first preachers, speaking in Portsmouth on Sunday mornings and in the theater in Norfolk at night. "I was a constant hearer," Littlejohn remembers.

Although now attending preaching regularly, Littlejohn regretted that "the word did not reach my heart, altho it did many others." Among these was the household seamstress, Elizabeth Crawley, with whom he shared religious conversations, although these exchanges "had an effect upon my conduct but did not reach the heart." When Eldred Fisher died in 1772 or 1773, Littlejohn, once more between apprenticeships, moved temporarily to Baltimore, where his mother now lived. Here he was "restrained from my former courses of vice for fear of her." Within a few weeks, he was employed by Joseph Selby in Annapolis. Now "finding I had nothing to recommend me to the World but a good char[ac]t^r, I resolved to gain one." Littlejohn left off gambling and determined to become proficient in his trade. He attended church twice on Sunday. At the same time, to his dismay, his master took in tradesmen to board and dispensed with family prayers on Saturday evenings. The fines collected for breaches of household bylaws were used to purchase alcohol for drinking frolics. Littlejohn quarreled with Selby, and in December 1773 he left to become foreman and manager at Thomas Armat's shop in Alexandria, Virginia. Despite the ridicule of an Irish journeyman working in the shop, Littlejohn began to attend Methodist preaching with the Armats. In February 1774, while listening to John King at a private house, he was struck by the analogy King made between the cost of salvation and a tradesman's simple exchange. "I sat under his voice as I had done before, till he s^d 'let us count the cost [of salvation], here is a parodox, we are to come & buy, yet without Money; I will therefore draw up a bill of the cost.' I was all ear wondering what Preachers had to do with bills of cost." King continued, " 'It will cost you y^r Cards, Dice, &c &c.' " It would cost Littlejohn, that is, his laboring-class pleasures.

In the summer of 1774 Littlejohn's religious awakening was fermented by the preaching of John Sigman, a Methodist exhorter from Philadelphia. "He related to us what God had done for his Soul. His words got to my heart as never any did before, tears gushed from my eyes as voluntary as the water from a fountain." Later, sleepless by his bed, Littlejohn prayed, and suddenly: "all my sins were before me, pirticularly the Sins of obstancy & hypoc[risy] & those things I loved turned against me. The pit was moved f^m beneath to meet me; & I ready to be swallowed up of sorrow. . . . I acknowledged my sin & cryed unto the Lord to spare & pluck me as a brand f^m ye burning."[1]

John Littlejohn's conversion from carousing apprentice to sober evangelical took place across the boundaries of the North Atlantic world, from the ancient frontier of northern Britain to the hinterlands of the northern Chesapeake. The changes in his life and consciousness reflect the extensive geographic mobility of Anglo-Americans in this period, the constant changes in livelihood circumscribed by clear social boundaries, the central place of the household. Littlejohn lived and moved within a trading and tradesman's world, where admission to a craft still followed from apprenticeship to the stages of journeyman, foreman, and master. In Britain and in the colonies, church attendance was something of a habit among Anglicans, taken more seriously by women, the chief spiritual guides for children. For teenage males, the main diversions were cardplaying, cockfighting, and other schemes for making petty cash. The differences between America and Britain also appear: the casual mixing of Protestantism and Catholicism in Maryland, the immigrant subculture along the mid-Atlantic coast, and the ubiquitous presence of slavery.

Littlejohn's introduction to Methodism was a gradual, even haphazard, process, with little initial connection to the Methodist organization of chapels, societies, and class meetings. He first heard a Methodist itinerant, one of the British missionaries, on the steps of the Norfolk, Virginia, courthouse. Despite his immersion in the local apprentice culture and the racial anxiety of the local magistrate, fearful of an "insurrection of the Negars," Littlejohn began to participate in revival meetings, sharing spiritual intimacies with a young servant woman at his master's house. Out of work, he briefly lived in his family's home, where his mother's authority reminded him of his religious upbringing. As he became socially self-conscious and anxious to rise in the world, he began to reform his behavior and to "hear" what the itinerants had to say: that the cost of salvation would be his "Cards, Dice, &c, &c." While working as a foreman in Alexandria, he was awakened to his sins under the preaching of an exhorter from Philadelphia: "The pit was moved f^m beneath to meet me; & I ready to be swallowed up of sorrow."

The pattern of Littlejohn's religious experience was replicated among a remarkable variety of Methodists, male and female, across social, racial, and ethnic lines. Like Littlejohn, few of those awakened by revival preaching appear to have formally joined a Methodist society by the time of their conversion. Nor did they acquire their scriptural and theological knowledge through the institutions of churches, schools, or universities. Rather, Methodists' religious education typically occurred over three phases, beginning with the initiating ritual of the revival meeting, climaxing in the "secret" experience of "conversion," and resolving itself in the social experience of the Methodist society. The upheaval of the revival, the solitary trauma of redemption, and the orderly discipline of the Methodist community appear as contradictory as any set of historical phenomena can be; but the three steps to Methodist conviction were essential elements in an experiential process that drew increasing numbers of Revolutionary-era Americans into the Methodist movement and transmuted them into a major cultural force.

THE REVIVAL RITUAL

Revival meetings were the primary ritual events of the new religious enthusiasm. As such, revivals were purposefully designed, their settings selected for uniqueness or accessibility, their forms of worship repeated, their proceedings administered by officers—the itinerants—endowed with special powers, and their immediate outcomes relatively predictable.[2] In the Wesleyan formulation, revivals provided the locus for the missionary recall to Primitive Christianity. They also served as the forum in which the great variety of Methodism's converts first heard Wesleyan preaching and experienced the beginnings of the personal transformation that led to their spiritual rebirth.[3]

Depending on the location, the occasion, and the numbers of participants involved, as well as the duration of the meeting, the outward appearance of Methodist revival meetings varied considerably. Revivals were convened outdoors and indoors, were led by many and few preachers, attracted large and small crowds, and lasted for long and short periods of time. Besides relying on the relatively few though increasing numbers of Methodist chapels built before 1800, itinerants in the Middle Atlantic region and beyond convened revival meetings on town greens, before county courthouses, on racing fields and in potters' fields, aboard ships and ferries, and even in the churches of other denominations.[4] At the 1789 revival in Baltimore, one of the largest before 1800, preaching was held at the town common, in the market-house, and on Howard's Hill, as well as in the church of the German Brethren and the Methodist chapels.[5] As in the cottage revivals of the 1760s and 1770s, meetings continued to be called together at private residences, sometimes the result of a simple conversational exchange between preacher and host,[6] but more often organized in the same way as public revivals, with prior announcement of the gathering's place and time.[7] If the occasion was a quarterly meeting or love feast, more than the usual one or two preachers would be present.[8] If the meeting was at a household, family members, servants, and slaves might constitute the entire gathering; if outdoors, an assemblage of many tens, hundreds, or even thousands of diverse listeners were often in attendance.[9] And while some assemblies lasted satisfactorily for an hour, others were convened and reconvened for several days running.[10]

The basic scheme of the revival meeting, however, varied very little. While containing any of a number of elements, the revival ritual centered on the impact of sound and rhetoric, from hymn singing and preaching to the accompanying Scripture reading and prayer—loosely defined by the Methodist discipline as the ingredients of "public worship"—as well as the testimonies that composed the chief part of love feasts, class meetings, and exhortations to repent.[11] Translated through the medium of oral culture, these elements of public and private worship not only replaced the visual iconography of medieval Christianity, as did most Protestant sectarian forms of worship, but also supplied the dramatization of Christian experience at the center of evangelical Protestantism. The sound-ritual of the Methodist revival in effect transformed the austerity of Puritanism's religion of the Book into a popular musical and rhetorical event, complete with compelling melody and verse, hortatory performance, scriptural recitative, and stirring personal narrative.[12]

Methodist itinerants customarily opened their meetings with vigorous hymn singing. As he was able to recall nearly sixty years later, John Littlejohn was introduced to the Methodist sound-ritual by Robert Williams's rendition of the hymn "Come, Sinners, to the Gospel Feast" on the steps of the Norfolk courthouse, a Wesleyan standard stressing the central missionary credo that "every soul be Jesu's guest" as the "invitation is to all."[13] A practiced singer like Williams committed verses and recommended tunes to memory and knew which were best suited to each of his multivarious audiences and revival circumstances. We find Jesse Lee praising his brother John as "a good singer" who knew "many hymns and spiritual songs by heart, suitable to the condition of any person, or any company."[14] Since there were generally no choirs in Methodist chapels, hymns were initiated by a "setter of tunes," who stood below the pulpit at requisite times in the service.[15]

John Wesley intended the hymns to replicate the "spiritual biography" of "a real Christian."[16] With his brother Charles, he accomplished this in 1780 with the *Collection of Hymns for the use of the People called Methodists*, the contents of which form a summary of the Methodist's progress, from "Beseeching to Return to God" to "Interceding for the World."[17] The collection arrived in America in the form of *A Pocket Hymn-Book*, reprinted in Philadelphia, New York, and Baltimore in the mid-1790s and distributed by the itinerants on their circuits.[18] With use of these various compilations, "fitted for private devotion . . . as well as for family, social, and public worship," the American itinerants, like the British preachers, were able to familiarize their audiences with the chief principles of Methodist theology as well as the sensibility of Wesley's heart-religion.[19]

Verses from the hymns form a poetic continuum through the Methodist journals and correspondence, a scriptural stream of consciousness reflecting the new evangelicals' newfound identity. "I felt such raptures," Maryland convert Joseph Everett exclaimed, ". . . that I could with the poet sing . . .: I rode on the sky / Freely justify'd I / Nor envied *Elijah* his feat: / My soul mounted higher / In a chariot of fire, / And the moon it was under my feet."[20] More than an encapsulation of Scripture, however, or a form of entertainment designed to attract "hearers," the hymns embodied the Wesleyan sensibility and what might be called the religious seeker's proper posture in the presence of the sacred. In the hymns the Wesleys shaped the language of evangelical eroticism to the purposes of the revival, transcribing into written and then spoken or sung form the images through which the singers "saw" themselves wedded to Jesus bloodied and crucified before them, the evangelical Protestant equivalent of the Catholic reverence for painted and sculpted depictions of Christ.[21] In the hymns, singers are beckoned to Christ, transformed into spiritual seekers in quest of the Divine, mourners longing for a return to the heights of sensate grace achieved at first awakening, triumphant victors over sin. So the singer pleads that Christ "Turn, and look upon me" and "break my heart of stone."[22] "Thee will I love, my strength, my tow'r," the seeker chants, "Thee will I love, my joy, my crown, / Thee will I love with all my pow'r, / In all my works, and thee alone." Other hymns limned the stereotype of the Methodist at the revival, heart tendered and soul "swallowed up": "Each moment draw from earth away / My heart, that lowly waits thy call; / Speak to my inmost soul, and say, / 'I am thy Love, thy God, thy All!' / To feel thy power, to hear thy voice, / To taste thy love, be all my choice."[23] Christ appears in these and other guises, as the believer's master or conversely his or her best friend, and always as the embodiment of overpowering love: "Jesu, lover of my soul, / Let me to thy bosom fly, / While the nearer waters roll, / While the tempest still is high. . . ."[24]

Treating Wesleyan hymns as rhetorical artifacts, Edward Thompson argued that the hymns' "sexual and womb-regressive imagery" and their "overpowering sacrificial imagery of blood" underlay Methodism's seductive appeal to the British working class at the turn of the nineteenth century. While recognizing the importance of Wesley's movement to laboring people confronting industrialization and the hostile reaction of the British government to attempts at democratic reform, Thompson characterized the hymns as a "ritualized form of psychic masturbation" that sustained a chiliastic religion of despair, social conformity, and political passivity.[25]

The Methodists did not invent the love poem to Christ, however. The mystical-erotic relationship between believer and Holy Ghost is a constant through much of the history of Christianity. In the eighteenth century, Christian eroticism resurfaced among Puritans praising the "double espousal" of believers to Christ and to the marital relation, and conversely among the Moravians espousing the rejection of marriage. Thompson's critique, then, is one that may be extended to any religious culture that represents the world as an ephemeral phenomenon and the transformation of the heart as the only lasting reality.[26]

In the same way, the central sound-ritual of the revival meeting—evangelical preaching—was designed to persuade listeners of the essential ingredients of Methodist doctrine. Once the hymns were sung, it was the preacher's preaching that best relayed the core of Wesleyan discourse.

Dwelling on the Christian doctrines of original sin, redemption through Christ's sacrifice and resurrection, free will, justification, and final judgment as well as the perfectionist emphasis on the Holy Spirit's transformation of the emancipated heart, Methodist preaching, like that of other evangelical movements, impressed its hearers as inspired oratory. The itinerants, it was understood, preached rather than delivered sermons.[27] Hearing Asbury in Maryland before the Revolutionary War, Freeborn Garrettson "found him to be a workman that need not be ashamed, rightly dividing the word." At the same time, Garrettson felt Asbury "began to wind about me in such a manner that I found my sins in clusters, as it were, around me." He was "ready to cry out, 'How does this stranger know me so well!' "[28] Virginian Jesse Lee's oratory, his biographer emphasized, was "plain and artless." Lee "never either read or memorized his sermons, seldom committing any thing more of them to paper, than merely the leading ideas, or general propositions." Instead, he "entered the pulpit in the name of the Lord, confiding in the aids of the Holy Spirit to assist his powers of invention as well as delivery."[29]

Methodist preaching was far from unpremeditated, however. The itinerants were instructed to appear "at the time appointed," with a "serious, weighty, and solemn" demeanor, and arrived at the predetermined location with the Bible and a parcel of notes on hand. They were urged to pray *ex tempore* for no more than "eight or ten minutes (at most) without intermission." Sermons were considered long if they lasted more than an hour.[30]

Methodist preaching possessed a pronounced didactic content as well. The American itinerants were careful to adopt the three-part form—preamble, points of doctrine, and application—favored by Wesley.[31] In the fall and winter of 1774–1775, James Dempster, a Scottish recruit traveling in the Middle Atlantic, filled a small notebook with fifty-five sermon outlines while on shipboard and twenty-five more while stationed in New York and Philadelphia. Each was fashioned on the three-part Wesleyan model and filled with perfectionist emphases.[32] In one sermon, Dempster took as his text a line from the Seventy-second Psalm, "He shall come down as the rain upon the mown grass," and prepared to explain to his listeners what was necessary for salvation as well as for "our present usefulness and comfort." In question-and-answer form, he set out the main points of doctrine regarding Christ's person in the Trinity, concluding that when Christ comes down like the rain, he appears "in the various graces of His holy Spirit" to the poor soul and to such as are "weary," "Tempted," and "Afflicted."[33] Those who believe in Christ as the fulfillment of the Moral Law, Dempster concluded in the application of another sermon, shall pass from "Death unto Life," "shall never die," "shall have the heavenly Bread," "shall be perfected in love," and "shall walk in the light as God is in the light."[34] Imitating the Wesleyan model, Dempster's sermon preparations, while more elaborate than some, were not markedly different from those of Francis Asbury, Jesse Lee, or others among the early preachers for whom records remain.[35] As a group, the American preachers favored the texts of the New Testament and Book of Revelation, managing always to codify these in straightforward, "practical" terms.[36]

The apparent extemporaneity of preaching derived from aspects other than its Wesleyan inspiration. Among these were the skillful use of metaphor, analogy, and vernacular imagery disdained by their classically educated counterparts in other churches;[37] the application of topics to the circumstances at hand, whether war, epidemics, bad harvests, the temptations of laboring-class culture, or apathy;[38] the itinerants' own personal involvement in the revival, exhibited by repeated efforts to preach "with liberty" and "with power," and exasperation with unresponsive audiences;[39] and impromptu contests with other ministers that provided itinerants the opportunity to test their newly defined manhood.[40] Altogether, as Thomas Lyell recalled, "[t]he affecting themes of the corruption of the human heart—its Sinfulness and utter depravity, the necessity of redemption in the blood of Christ, the forgiveness of Sins and the sufficiency of the grace of God to renew the Soul of penitence, in righteousness and true holiness—were dwel[t] on with fervor and feeling."[41]

The improvised appearance of the revival emerged at other moments of the revival ritual, during prayer and exhortation, when the participants themselves sought to communicate with Christ and the Holy Spirit. It was in this phase of the meeting that the sound-ritual of the revival combined with religious enthusiasm to create the ecstatic event for which the Methodists were notorious. Episodes of religious ecstaticism abounded among the first generation of Methodists, as at the Baltimore revival in 1789 where participants made "such a noise among them, that many of the christian people were measurably frightened, and . . . many of them went out at the windows, hastening to their homes," while others "lost the use of their limbs, and lay helpless on the floor, or in the arms of their friends."[42] In rural Maryland, a participant at a meeting led by Benjamin Abbott "lay for near an hour, as though she had been dead, and then came to, and sang, with such a melodious note, as [the preacher] never had heard before," and more extraordinarily still, "[t]he voice seemed as if four or five were singing together."[43] At a revival at St. George's Chapel in Philadelphia, the seekers fell on the floor and "the cry of mourners, and the joyful acclamations of the christians, were so great" that the preachers could not be heard.[44] And during a household revival in Prince Georges County, Maryland, the "black friends" were "carried away with raptures of joy, while the good woman of the house felt as tho' the angels were hovering round us."[45]

To contemporary observers these apparently uncontrolled, "emotional" responses to revival rituals—fainting, trance states, involuntary cries, shouting, and glossolalia—were something new, an innovative, even intentionally designed, feature of evangelical revivalism and other forms of radical sectarianism that distinguished these popular religious outbursts from the reasonable Christianity of the Anglican and Reformed churches.[46] But the ecstaticism of the Methodist revivals, like the eroticism of the Methodist hymns, tapped deeper roots and uncovered previously buried veins of popular belief that account for the similarity of revival responses among different populations at great distances from each other and among other revival movements as well.[47]

As historians of early modern religion have stressed for some time, one such deep vein was the widespread belief in the palpable manifestation of the supernatural in everyday life. Many inhabitants of the North Atlantic world, well into the Revolutionary era, were heirs to a magical worldview that absorbed features of hermeticism, astrology, freemasonry, divination, and alchemy whenever useful.[48] While magic and its attendant practices declined in repute among Europe and America's educated elite, occult knowledge and efforts to invoke the supernatural to control the material universe had not lost their allure for middling and laboring folk, servants, and slaves and had survived as a fundamental element of British, German, and American popular religious culture.[49] In his chronicle of the segregation of magic from religion in seventeenth-century Britain, British scholar Keith Thomas has also observed that the "practical attraction of enthusiastic religion during [the English Revolution] closely matched those of the magic arts," a correlation which only became more marked over time.[50] Albert Raboteau has correspondingly noted that in addition to belief in a transcendent divinity, all West African religions featured sacrifice, divination, music, dance, and the phenomena of spirit possession and faith healing, cultural forms readily available to American slaves for translation into revivalistic counterparts.[51]

Displays of the miraculous, from omens, visions, theophanies of Christ and God, to angelic visitations, and other signs of Providence, were yearned-for marvels in the often austere world of Protestant persuasions. The coming of the Revolution, furthermore, and the successful break with Britain strengthened the conviction of many Americans that Providence guided the affairs of the new states and, together with an ascendant republicanism, would shape their destiny.[52] Thus while traveling his Greenwich circuit in New Jersey and Delaware in December 1775, Methodist William Duke conversed on the "Deplorable State of the Country" with the local people who reported on the remarkable celestial exhibition they had witnessed in the sky some time previously. Here had appeared "Streams of Blood fearfull to behold and Armies furiously moving to and fro which moved round Northward" until the spectral panorama "stood directly over the City of Philadelphia." This, Duke concluded, was "an evident Token of heavy Judgments coming upon this Land."[53]

For Methodists absorbed with their mission to "reform the continent, and spread scripture-holiness over these lands," millennial or utopian oracles foretelling national decline or triumph were of less concern, however, than the decline or triumph of manifestations of the Holy Spirit. To the "mission of the Holy Spirit" they were "indebted for blessings infinitely more valuable than any which the revolution of states can possibly afford."[54] Revival participants also reported numerous interventions of the supernatural in less sweeping capacity in the midst of, or otherwise in association with, revival meetings. During her father's preaching at St. George's, John Dickins's young daughter reported seeing a deceased fellow believer return to life as an angel with a "Garment hung lose about him of a Shining silver colour."[55] In Albany, a revival participant told the preacher of a premonition during her religious seeking that had spared her from injury from a falling tree.[56] Near Tuckahoe, New Jersey, a Baptist woman testified that she had seen her hearth open wide to reveal hell in front of her eyes just as the house was filled with the "glory of God, brighter than the sun at noonday"—a constellation of visions that her church rejected, insisting that God "did not come to people in such a manner now a-days."[57] In an episode anticipating Joseph Smith's discovery of the Golden Plates that held the Book of Mormon, a revival participant in Kent County, Delaware, informed Benjamin Abbott that he had beheld the spectral form of his mother directing him to where he might dig up a dozen plates she had buried for him when he was a child.[58]

Distinctive to the revival was another feature of the miraculous that shaped its ecstaticism and, in the case of the Methodists, substantiated the movement's perfectionism. In the belief in possession, the incarnation of a supernatural force or forces within the religious seeker's body, many Americans, whether European,

African, or Indian in background, shared a common conviction in the power of the supernatural to transform the individual through direct contact with his or her person. In the seventeenth century, episodes of possession were invariably interpreted as the work of the devil or one or another evil spirit, evidenced by the widespread fear of witchcraft and its punishment in seventeenth-century New England.[59] For those who shared what one historian has called "a vivid sense of the malice of Satan,"[60] possession continued to be perceived as a threat several generations after the provincial governments ceased to prosecute witchcraft as a crime. Hence in the 1770s Joseph Pilmore was confronted with a New York woman who believed herself to be possessed by the devil. In Cambridge, New York, where the Palatine founders of New York City's John Street Chapel had migrated in the 1770s, fears of witchcraft, obliquely associated with the Shakers, disrupted the peace of the Methodist society.[61] The itinerants used various means to address and allay these tensions. Pilmore held a prayer session for the afflicted follower in New York. Benjamin Abbott eased a mourner out of a revival-induced fit by singing what he called "the hymn composed for one possessed of an evil spirit," the words of which—"King of Kings, spread thy wings, / Christ our weakness cover, / Till the storm is over"—were indistinguishable from the many other hymns calling on Christ's protection.[62] In Delaware, William Colbert promised a black servant girl who believed she had been put under a spell that he would "pull out my knife and ask her if I should drive the witch away."[63]

By the late eighteenth century, the Methodist leadership, like the clergy of other churches, associated these episodes of what may be called "negative" possession with soul sickness, or mental illness.[64] In America, an account of the possession of a British woman was reprinted in the *Methodist Magazine*, along with other tales of amazing and providential events, but accompanied by a postscript emphasizing how the story was intended to "magnify the power and goodness of Almighty God in His relieving a reasonable creature from insupportable misery, and in curing a disease which far surpassed the skill of human physicians."[65] It was generally understood among Methodists that the condition resembling demonic possession required healing rather than exorcism, and while all Methodists believed in the literal existence of the devil, the Evil One's role was generally that of the harasser who assaulted, challenged, and haunted, rather than possessed, the seeker at his or her times of spiritual darkness.[66] Scottish preacher William Glendinning was so distraught by "Lucifer's" alarming presence during his conversion that he suffered a nervous breakdown; but throughout his ordeal, the devil was a powerful adversary rather than the insinuating incubus of medieval and Puritan cosmology.[67]

"Positive" possession—the incarnation of the Holy Spirit in the body of the revival participant—was another matter, however. As the seizures, fainting spells, trance states, and shouting multiplied at revivals, revival participants believed the Holy Spirit to be working its transformative effects. In ecstasy the Holy Spirit was made manifest. The experience of positive possession in this way became popular proof that God was at work in the revival ritual.[68]

Filled with the Spirit, the believer fell into a faint, was struck down, exclaimed, sang, or shouted. A cloud might descend before his or her eyes, and then a sudden, glittering light throw him or her to the floor.[69] "While you was speaking of the Cherubims overshadowing the mercy seat," an awakened listener told one preacher, "I felt such a power of Love flow through my Soul that all my distress departed, and my tongue was unloose to praise GoD."[70] Benjamin Abbott recalled his own vivid moment of sanctification at a small household meeting. Here the preacher instructed Abbott to repeat the incantation "Come Lord and sanctify me soul and body!" "That moment," Abbott recalled, "the Spirit of God came upon me in such a manner, that I fell flat to the floor, and lay as one strangling in blood, while my wife and children stood weeping over me. But I had not power to lift hand or foot, nor yet to speak one word; I believe I lay half an hour, and felt the power of God, running through every part of my soul and body, like fire consuming the inward corruptions of fallen depraved nature."[71]

Possession by the Holy Spirit was directly and indirectly encoded into revival rhetoric as well as into the hymns and sermons that formed the ritual's cultural core. Whether Methodists interpreted this language literally or figuratively, they were reminded repeatedly of God's power to seize them. "Come quickly, gracious Lord," one hymn appeals, "and take / Possession of thine own! / My longing heart vouchsafe to make / Thine everlasting throne!" "Conqu'ror of hell, and earth, and sin," another intones, "Still with thy rebel strive; / Enter my soul, and work within, / And kill, and make alive!"[72] "True Religion consists in nothing less," James Dempster preached, "than an Heart tuned to the Love of God, and a Life devoted to his service. . . . An Heart freed from wrong tempers and possessed of pure Love."[73] To be holy was to be fully possessed of God, a state Nelson Reed yearned for in the "second work in the heart" or sanctification: "the prayer of my heart [was] now 'Come and possess me whole, Nor hence again remove, Settle and fix my wavering soul; With all thy weight of Love.' "[74] At the height of ecstatic experience, the revival participant was at a loss for words to describe the power of spirit possession: "How inexpressible are the pleasures of those, who are filled with the raptures of a Saviour's love?" one itinerant recorded of a successful revival: "Ecstatic pause! 'Silence heightens heaven.' "[75]

For Thomas Coke and Francis Asbury, anxious to establish that their new movement was not the antinomian harbinger of moral and social chaos that their Anglican and Presbyterian opponents predicted, the more extreme instances of ecstaticism came as unwelcome side effects to the revival. Coke discouraged the itinerants from falling into "extravagant" preaching, as "[i]t is a ground of lamentation to every liberal and devout mind, that the Christian world has been ever running to extremes; that of *infidelity* on the one hand, and that of *gross superstition* on the other."[76] Visions, Asbury instructed the itinerants, were to be "brought to the standard of the Holy Scriptures," in keeping with St. Paul's admonitions to the Galatians that if an angel from heaven preach any other doctrine, "Let him be accursed." Methodists were warned not to succumb to the "power of sound."[77]

The bishops' condemnation of the preaching of miracles only verifies its wide-spread appeal, however. Freeborn Garrettson was regularly called an enthusiast, on one occasion "because I talked so much about feelings; and impressions to go to particular places," but, he added, "I also know, that both sleeping and waking, things of a divine nature have been revealed to me."[78] After a deadened meeting at the start of which he had been reprimanded for extravagant preaching, Benjamin Abbott reflected, "O! how careful ought the preachers, to be, how they censure or speak against a work, merely because there are some things attending of it, which are not exactly agreeable to their views or wishes."[79] Revival meetings, as the most skilled of the early itinerants knew, were ephemeral events, easily punctured if the carefully constructed relationship between preachers and hearers was disturbed. The Holy Spirit after all might speak to the hearer in any number of ways. William Watters, after a day of hymn singing with sympathetic friends, found "a divine light beamed through my inmost soul, which in a few minutes encircled me around, surpassing the brightness of the noon day sun." When Watters left the meeting "(strange and enthusiastic as it may appear to those who have not experienced any thing of the sort) the Heavens over me, the Earth with all around me spoke in a powerful, though silent language, to my calm mind, while all appeared to stand in quite a new relation to me."[80]

The revival sound-ritual—hymn singing, preaching, prayer, exhorting, and testifying—operated on many revival participants with altogether intoxicating effects. As revival meetings proliferated throughout the Middle Atlantic, the South, and then the West, the ecstatic episodes that characterized these events came to be perceived as the central religious phenomena of the new evangelicalism.

But they represented a small part of the conversion experience. The preachers were aware, in fact, that the revival of religion went beyond the convening of public meetings where many were awakened but few were converted. The greater ambition of the revival preacher was to initiate the ultimately more profound process of the "rebirth" of the awakened seeker. For this change to have a lasting effect, or so the Methodists believed, the recruit had to undergo two further tests: the "reality" of redemption and induction into the larger Methodist system.

RELIGIOUS EXPERIENCE

On the night of his religious awakening, John Littlejohn had a dream that was "forciable fixed in my memory" and "afterwards almost literally fulfill[d]." In his words:

> I dreampt That I was at preech[g] in Norfolk. M[r] W[m]. Watters was Preech[g], when several Men of Wars men came w[t] Swords to persecute the Meth[s] & disturb[d] the people. M[r] W[illia]ms exhort[d] them not to fear, but in vain. I got into y[e] Pulpit, & cry[d] "Blessed are they who are persecut[d]. for R[ighteous]ness sake for theirs is the Kingdom of heaven."
> . . . I went out & was supprised to see no persons in the Street. I was sorry so many were afraid to suffir. Walk[g] home (think[g] I lived in Norfolk) not in the least afraid I saw

the Lieu^t w^t his sword draw[n] in the Street. . . . [I] got home and to my great supprise found two Candles burn^g on the floor, w^t two pillows lying near them. [T]ak^g up the Pillows I blew out the lights & went to see a nieghb^r. Here I saw Betsy Crawley lay^g over a table weeping bitterly. I ask^d w^t are you cry^g for. She ans^d I feared you wl^d be killed. I rebuked her sharply & left the home. . . . I had not got far, before many persued, threw mud, Stones &c but none fell upon me, this enraged 'em the more, see^g their labour lost. I was surrounded on every side, I saw no way to escape, (yet w^{t}out fear) I looked up, saw a piece of Timber project^g f^m a house. I got upon it, when one of the Mob took hold of it. I looked up again, saw a second peice, got upon it, one of the mob took hold. I look^d up a 3^d time, saw anoth^r, but could only sit on it with my legs hanging down. The Man persued but cl^d only touch the soles of my Shoes. Those below still pelt^g me w^t dirt & stones, find^g their lab^r lost, they left me sit^g on the timb^r. I awoke & behold it was a dream.

"This dream," Littlejohn extrapolated, "was a great blessing to me [and] its interpretation to me was easy." Paraphrasing from the thirty-third chapter of Job, he continued, "In a dream, in a vision of the night, when deep sleep fallith upon men, in slumberings upon the bed, then he openth the ears of Men, & sealeth their instruction."[81]

If the purpose of the revival was to induce a transformation of state, then dreams provided the instruction. In Littlejohn's, he saw himself metamorphosed into a preacher and one of a people apart. Escaping the violence of the "Men of Wars men" with swords drawn—whether British or American is unclear and largely irrelevant—he is transformed into the solitary Christian hero, rejecting the light and comfort at home and the conjugal state, and scolding his new friend, Elizabeth Crawley, for doubting his newfound power. Returning to the dangers of the world in the streets of Norfolk, he experiences near martyrdom but is able instead to climb the timbers of a house, three in sequence, like the three stages of conversion, until he rises above his enemies, the last of his pursuers left looking up at the bottoms of his shoes. Which parts of the dream were "afterwards almost literally fulfill^d" is not relayed, but the religious and social elements of Littlejohn's imagination are here intertwined in a vinelike fashion, combining military conflict, exhorting, and missionizing with rejection of the conventional world, near death, and literal transcendence.

For the months before and after this dream, Littlejohn "doubted my convict^n for Sin . . . till the good Lord show^d me that my exircises were the fruit of his Spirit." But as an attentive hearer at Methodist revivals, Littlejohn believed that he "must be Sanctified." At the beginning of October in 1774, he attended evening preaching. On returning to his room he "got into a doze," and was "suddenly startled, at hear^g (as I tho^t) Mr Armat [his employer] calling sharply, John." Littlejohn rose in the bed, and listening he heard "a small still voice w^t in me cry 'Thy Sins be forgiven thee.' "[82] Now overcoming the central obstacle of his religious rite of passage, Littlejohn believed himself to be a doubly redeemed Christian.

Following the revival meeting, the frequently solitary experience of conversion was the central drama of the new evangelical's rebirth. Among Methodists, this event was intensified by the expectation of the paired experiences of justification and sanctification. As in the case of revival ecstaticism, new converts shared remarkably similar experiences despite differences in ethnicity, age, gender, and race. The shaping of the consciousness of four Methodists—Philip Gatch, Benjamin Abbott, Lucy Watson, and Richard Allen—attests to the power of the Methodist conversion prototype.

Philip Gatch, one of Robert Strawbridge's earliest American supporters, was born in Baltimore County, Maryland, in 1751, his father of German descent, his mother Burgundian. Gatch's parents conformed to the dominant Anglican Church, and their son was taught to read at an early age.[83] As a teenager, Gatch was briefly attracted by "vain and wicked associations" and ceased going to church, but the death of a sister followed rapidly by that of an uncle sparked a depression in which Gatch was "alarmed by dreams, by sickness, and by various other means, which were sent by God, in his mercy, for my good." He was attracted to the Society of Friends, but having no opportunity to attend their meetings, he instead paricipated in a revival meeting held in January 1772 by Nathan Perigau. "His prayer alarmed me much," Gatch recalled; "I never had witnessed such energy nor heard such expressions in prayer before." Gatch's father opposed his son's newfound interest. "He said I was going beside myself, and should go to hear the Methodists no more; that his house should not hold two religions," although, Gatch caustically observed, "I thought this was no great objection, fearing there was little religion in the house." Despite being of age, Gatch, a dutiful son, obeyed his father's command for about five weeks until he found himself drawn back into the Methodist orbit, his heart "tendered" in a conversation with a pious follower.[84]

Gatch now believed "there was no mercy for me," and he "continued under these awful apprehensions for some time," until during a prayer meeting he "felt the power of God to affect me body and soul. It went through my whole system. I felt like crying aloud." Gatch "instantly submitted to the operation of the Spirit of God, and my poor soul was set at liberty. I felt as if I had got into a new world." The moment reminded him of the lines from a hymn: "Tongue can not express / The sweet comfort and peace / Of a soul in its earliest love." Now absorbed in the vocal culture of the Methodist revival, Gatch before he knew what was happening was "shouting aloud, and should have shouted louder if I had had more strength. I was the first person known to shout in that part of the country."[85]

Benjamin Abbott, another Methodist of the first generation, was twenty years Gatch's senior and of a strikingly different temperament. Apprenticed to a Philadelphia hatter after the early death of his parents, Abbott spent his leisure hours boxing or picking fights with his fellow laborers, washing his bloodied clothes in the city pumps. Even as an adult, Abbott was a great fighter "in order to shew his manhood and bravery in that line." Abbott went on to work as a laborer and tenant farmer near Elmer in Salem County, New Jersey, where he also married. Before the age of forty, he knew nothing of "experimental religion," and even though his wife was a devout Presbyterian, she "knew nothing about a heart work."[86] Abbott's conversion was foreshadowed by a series of dreams, including one in which a pack of demons threatened to throw him into a fiery lake and another in which his mother-in-law, a woman of great piety, stood before the throne of the "Ancient of Days" and intoned, "Benjamin, this place is not for you yet."[87]

Like Philip Gatch, Abbott first attended a Methodist revival in 1772. The preacher, one of the British missionaries, described witnessing a ball of fire fall through the sky during his voyage to America. A ball of fire exists in everyone, the preacher freely construed, just as hell exists dreadful beyond imagination.[88] Abbott began seeking solace in communal hymn singing and attending Methodist meetings with his wife. Returning to his farm from a local mill, it was "suddenly suggested to my mind, as I was one of the reprobates and there was no mercy for me, I had better hang myself and know the worst of it." But instead he "drove home under the greatest anxiety imaginable," convinced that the devil was behind him "with his hand just over my head, threatening to take me away both soul and body."[89] Looking "like death," Abbott isolated himself, sleeping alone, reading hymns, and furtively feeding his uneaten dinner to the family dog. While mowing grass with a scythe, he feared the earth would open and swallow him up, "while my troubled heart beat so loud that I could hear the strokes," like "two men a boxing or threshing." In a solitary place he prayed aloud for the first time.[90]

Several days later, Abbott awoke at dawn and, like many converts at this stage of their conversion crisis, fell into a dozing state flooded with images. Abbott dreamed that he wrestled with the devil to free an angel-child from drowning in a clear river. In the same test he liberated a sorrel-colored horse chained in the water, the horse springing out of the water "like a cork, or the bouncing of a ball." On waking, he witnessed "by faith" Christ with his arms extended assuring him, "I died for you." And again, "by faith" he saw the "Ancient of Days," who proclaimed, "I freely forgive thee for what Christ has done." The Scriptures, Abbott now observed, "were wonderfully opened to my understanding."[91]

The product of a more resolutely religious background than either Gatch or Abbott, Lucy Watson was born in Groton, Connecticut, in 1755, the tenth and youngest child of John Fanning, a Baptist merchant, and Abigail Minor, a Presbyterian—both Whitefield supporters. Frequently "discontented or changeful," John Fanning was a business failure and was forced by poverty to move his family first to Walpole, New Hampshire, and then to Little Egg Harbor, New Jersey, when Lucy Watson was still a child.[92] In New Jersey, like other young pious girls, Lucy took to reading the Bible and books of divinity and became so persuaded of the ungodliness of the people around her that she covered her head during thunderstorms "that I might not see what was coming upon us." But she was also, as her son John Fanning Watson later recalled, a person of "great animal spirits" who loved to dance and sing. After her marriage to William Watson, a sea captain and shipowner, her religious convictions began to fade. She sought happiness in her husband, her firstborn son, and the diversions of music and clothing.[93]

Lucy Watson's story, however, early takes on the features of a Methodist narrative: that of a personal crisis resolved through a felicitously timed redemption experience. The war brought hard times to the Fannings and Watsons alike. Abigail Minor Fanning died, an event "almost insupportable" to her daughter. In March 1778, in separate incidents, two of Watson's brothers, both naval officers, also died, one killed in action near Barbados. In 1781, Watson's husband and the crew of the privateer *Captain Mifflin* were captured by loyalists off the Jersey shore and confined to a prison ship and then to a hospital ship in New York Harbor. Captain Watson eventually returned home, but impoverished by postwar depreciation of continental currency, the Watson family moved to Gloucester County, New Jersey, and then in 1785 to the Northern Liberties in Philadelphia. Here William Watson was able to reestablish himself in his trade.[94]

Lucy Watson's first exposure to the Methodists occurred in about 1780 or 1781, coincident with her husband's imprisonment. Although she had heard that "they made people crazy," she began to attend evening prayers led by Methodists at a neighboring house where several itinerants were lodging. At one small revival meeting, one of the preachers exhorted Lucy that she "must first *do* what was in [her] power, & that God would bless [her] endeavours." The preacher compared the awakening converts to a field of corn. "If we plant it, God will bless it & give the increase; but *if we never plant*, we cannot expect to reap." He then testified to his own spiritual transformation. Watson thought that this was what she knew from her Bible reading, "a something called conversion or new birth, but [I] never could understand how it was to be wrought or obtained." Praying on her knees for the first time, "being formerly used to pray standing, sitting or lying down," Watson felt that "my heart was very hard, and my affections very cold." She began to avoid her worldly acquaintances and even her two small children lest they hinder her in her new "single object." She kept a dark room as her "place of secret prayer," and it was here that it she "*felt* the change *to take place*."[95] A so-called justified Christian, Watson joined the fledging society at St. George's. At a prayer meeting, her experiences intensified: "while one [of the participants] was praying & mentioned that Christ might appear in the greatness of his strength, with his garments rolled in blood," Watson saw Christ "by the eye of faith, pass by in that appearance, and [He] gave *me* a touch with his hand [and then] *I felt* as if my heart was taken out." She was "so filled & melted with divine love," that she sank to the floor, exclaiming, if diffidently, "I dare not say I was sanctified . . . [But] what can this *be*, but perfect love."[96]

Presenting the greatest contrast in social experience, Richard Allen, the fourth Methodist in this sampling, was born in 1760, a slave on Benjamin Chew's Delaware plantation and grew up on the farm of his second master, Stokeley Sturgis, outside Dover, Delaware.[97] Allen recollected that Sturgis behaved "more like a father to his slaves than anything else," but faced with bankruptcy around the beginning of the Revolutionary War, he sold Richard's mother and three siblings while keeping title to Richard himself, a brother, and a sister.[98] Allen does not associate his family's breakup with his conversion in his much later account of his early life, but it seems hardly possible that separation from their mother even as teenagers did not prompt the simultaneous religious crises of Allen and his two siblings. Allen wrote, "I was awakened and brought to see myself, poor, wretched and undone, and without the mercy of God, [I] must be lost." Despite conversations with "many old, experienced Christians"—Dover was a Methodist strong-hold—his anxieties did not pass. Instead he "cried to the Lord both night and day" and was sure that "hell would be my portion." At last, Allen experienced the second of two convictions of faith, one that he describes in the manner of a hymn verse: "[A]ll of a sudden my dungeon shook, my chains flew off, and, glory to God, I cried. My soul was filled. I cried, enough, for me the Saviour died."[99]

The full conversion of these four Methodists, and dozens of others for which evidence remains, conform to the cross-cultural stages of religious transformation long familiar to scholars of religion: from an awareness of personal sinfulness; to rejection of the corrupt world through self-imposed solitude; to comprehension of what Clifford Geertz has called the "really real" (and what Methodists, by way of Moravian discourse, called sanctification).[100] Proto-Methodists might be prepared for such changes long before coming into contact with Methodist preaching, both through exposure to unorthodox religion and from personal circumstance. Many came from religious families or were often the children of devout mothers from whose example they felt they had strayed. Philip Gatch and Lucy Watson both were religiously serious children and considered themselves as lacking piety through their teenage years. Often the shock of family deaths—or, in the case of slaves, the sale and removal of family members—drove the future convert to seek refuge in the company of religious folk. Religious awakening or reawakening and the impulse to separate from temptations and from tempting acquaintances followed upon the revival experience, conferences with pious Christians, and advice rendered by itinerating missionaries who make fleeting appearances in the Methodist narratives. At first, candidates for conversion are not comforted but rather made more insecure by their new spiritual sensibility: Philip Gatch, already "alarmed by dreams," appeared to his family to be going "beside myself"; Abbott looked "like death"; Watson felt "my heart was very hard, and my affections very cold."

With the unexpectedly tranquil awareness of the "really real," however, those under "the work" move from near spiritual defeat to fearless triumph over sin and evil spirits. Instead of being cast off by God, he or she is loved by Christ. As the clouds obscuring understanding begin to lift, previously opaque passages of Scripture are suddenly rendered clear: "[T]he scriptures," Abbott writes, "were wonderfully opened to my understanding."

Each convert's recounting of the critical moments of religious experience is likewise anticlimactically brief. Of his justification, Gatch writes that he "submitted to the operation of the Spirit of God, and my poor soul was set at liberty. I felt as if I had got into a new world." "By faith," Abbott witnesses Christ and then "the Ancient of Days," who assures him of his forgiveness. On her sanctification, Watson "by the eye of faith" beholds Christ, whose seeming touch upon her hand "so filled & melted" her with divine love that she collapses. Allen cries out: "all of a sudden my dungeon shook, my chains flew off. . . ."

Provocative differences also mark the converts' recollections, passing as they do through individual filters of generational, gender, and racial experience. Philip Gatch, still under his father's control but old enough to marry and run a household, feels as if in a new (independent) world. Abbott, a middle-aged man, witnesses Christ and the "Ancient of Days" together, as if requiring the company of the patriarchal person in the Trinity to adjust to his own embodiment of an elder's authority. Watson, a female convert, is the only initiate to sense the impression of Christ's hand, at the same time that she writes, "I dare not say I was sanctified." It seems hardly a coincidence that the slave convert among these Methodists feels as if freed from prison.

A brief recounting of the spiritual coming-of-age of another female Methodist, Catherine Livingston, supplies further insight especially into the gendered character of Methodist conversion. Introduced to Methodist revivals by preachers who held exhortation and prayer meetings at her mother's estate on the Hudson River, Livingston, unmarried and dependent on her mother's support, was propelled by her religious convictions into dream states and visionary trances over the several years following her awakening. For days at a time, Livingston was "swallowed up in God" while "a Devine sweetness" coursed through her "whole frame." In one afternoon Livingston was "struck down upon my back, lost in solemn awe and wonder. . . . I knew it was impossible to see God and live; I knew that out of Christ he is a consuming fire. With my bodily Eyes I saw nothing, all was presented to my mind." Upon rising, she threw herself on her knees, "cried to my beloved, and my Friend, to come and stand between the Awful Holy God and his poor Catherine." In an altered state that night, she was "espoused to Jesus, and [through] Him united to the Glorious Trinity." In full-bodied Wesleyan language, she exclaimed: "I found myself a drop in the Ocean of love. . . . I contemplated his wounded hands—his side—his feet. God is love—I feel It—I know it."[101]

Earlier, in an extended dream, Livingston had met up with the shade of her maternal grandfather Beekman, who greeted his granddaughter with the warning "Nature, Nature, Nature—Following thee leads not to peace." She then entered "the place of Sanctified Souls" (which she was able to identify on the basis of a similar night-journey traveled by her betrothed, the preacher Freeborn Garrettson) through the entrance of a modest cottage inhabited by three holy women, its linen ceiling studded with crystal stars. "[A]ll four of us joining hands, I kissed them all, and found myself most happy." At the same time, two men, one of whom she recognized as her father, Judge Livingston, now a "Glorified being" dressed in "robes of the purest white," and an unidentified male companion, entered the cottage and took their places on a high seat. "I sank to the flore in speechless ecstacy," Livingston recorded in her journal the next day. "When I came to my speech, I claped my hands, giving Glory to God, for the Wonders of redeeming Love."[102]

Livingston's expositions of religious devotion at first glance appear stereotypically feminine: overflowing with marital imagery, spousal devotion, and expressions of sexual and filial submission and childlike imaginings of life after death. Like many devout women, she found particular solace in the company of likeminded women. She appears especially susceptible to the authority of men—her grandfather, father, and fiancé—and the romanticizing of the Christ figure.

Similarly, there can be little doubt that the language of liberation embedded in evangelical conversion—of freedom from error, the shackles of sin, and the illusory ways of the world—was of vastly greater importance to black converts than to white, separated as they were from white society by chasms of social, legal, and racial difference.[103] The impact of the inequalities of gender and race on the ways in which conversion was interpreted, in other words, was real.

It is testimony to the power of Wesleyan discourse, then, that Methodist converts sound so much alike. While they brought the framework of their quotidian lives and social identities to their religious experiences, they also endowed them with the meaning and significance of Wesleyan language and doctrine imbibed from their new revivalist culture.[104] Thus Methodist men also experienced union with Christ as a form of betrothal undertaken by their figuratively female souls rather than their persistently masculine bodies. "[Wha]t Comfort doth my Soul enjoy, while She sweetly reclines herself on the blessed Jesus," James Dempster confessed. "For my part," William Jessop declared, "my cup ran over, and my soul was full, and I could say with the Spouse in the Canticles—'I am sick of LOVE.' "[105] For slaves and free black people, conversion was the moment of universal connection despite the racial barriers erected by slavery. In their first publicly issued statement, Richard Allen's African Methodists would proclaim (echoing Gal. 3:28) that there is "neither male nor female, barbarian nor Scythian, bond nor free, but all are one in Christ Jesus." Repeatedly, one of the fundamental attractions of Methodism was the escape it provided from constrictive social taxonomies. Methodist ideology, as Donald Mathews writes, represented "an abrupt, oral, radical intrusion into a world of rank, invidious distinctions, and careless convention."[106]

Just as they entered the trauma of religious conversion in the same way, so converts otherwise separated by rigid social boundaries reported on the "ecstatic pause" that left them suspended between the chorus of the revival and the clamor of the outside world. For Methodists the change of consciousness wrought by conversion perfected the process in which "the flame of holy love" consumed "all the remains of a carnal mind" and purified the soul: an experience shared across sexual, racial, and social differences. Likewise all Methodists shared the language of the Wesleyan "heart-work," legitimating a historically feminine rhetoric of affection and surrender while arming themselves in the battle against sin in a historically masculine language of militancy.[107]

Like the popular ingredients of positive possession that typified the ecstaticism of the Methodist revival, so the essential features of the Methodist conversion were not unique to the group. Medieval, Puritan, and Quaker observers would have been familiar with the power of this internal spiritual pilgrimage. The most distinguishing characteristic of Wesleyan conversion, then, was also its most prosaic: the decision to join a Methodist society.

This step was more fundamental than may at first appear. For while Congregationalists, Presbyterians, and many Baptists came to their religious experiences after years of familiarity with Scripture and Reformed theology,[108] and Quakers, while eschewing learned knowledge, still expected their members to be fully familiar with the distinguishing features of their church, if not already born into it,[109] Methodists customarily joined Methodist societies and became fully familiar with Wesleyan doctrine *after* their awakening, in many cases, often after their full conversions.

Those reading further into John Littlejohn's life will find that the young convert became "bett^r acquainted with the principles & economy of the Methodists & desired to be joined w^t them" at the end of his double conversion rather than at its conception.[110] Similarly, in an effort to make sense of his religious tumults, Philip Gatch read Wesley's sermon on salvation by faith following the first part of his two-step conversion, rather than before it. Benjamin Abbott attempted to reconcile the Westminster and Baptist Confessions of Faith with the Bible after the heights of a visionary double conversion; only then did he realize he was destined for another group altogether: "[O]n a sudden I cried aloud, several times, '*I am a methodist! I am a methodist!*' "[111] In her "Experience," Lucy Watson associated her full conversion with the "precious means of Grace" and "such as watched over me in love," rather than with the formal society of Methodists at St. George's with which she had been only briefly associated. Richard Allen joined a Methodist class in the forest near Dover only after his conversion and a preliminary itinerancy "from house to house" to exhort his friends.[112] Catherine Livingston experienced several years of religious turmoil before calling herself a Methodist. Through the entirety of his spiritual transformation John Littlejohn does not mention John Wesley's name.[113]

In the throes of their often solitary religious experience, Methodists-in-the-making rarely if ever mentioned Wesley, appear not to have attended Methodist societies (as opposed to revival meetings) with any regularity, had not read or heard a recital of the *General Rules*, or for that matter the numerous other writings with which Wesley had blanketed Britain and Ireland, and which the MEC reprinted in increasing numbers in North America. They were, that is, part of a diverse, and often mobile and neophyte, population whose religious identity was shaped as much by experience as it was by denominational allegiance or education: as unmoored from past traditions as republican radicals like Thomas Paine and Thomas Jefferson fondly hoped Americans would be.

Yet it was in the Methodist society that converts were able to give retrospective shape to what had happened to them, as they poured out their religious impressions to fellow class members and attended regular sessions of hymn singing, preaching, and exhorting. In brief, for those who became Methodists, it was membership in the religious society rather than participation in the fleeting revival that would direct the course of their lives thereafter and turn them into thoroughgoing Wesleyans.

THE METHODIST SOCIETY

The connection between revivalist religions and the social behavior of their adherents, as Max Weber once wrote, in fact contains "no small inherent difficulties."[114] Revivals were by definition liminal, antistructural, disorderly events that challenged the norms of the dominant culture and provided alternative spaces for religious exercises. Men and women, rich, middling, and poor, black and white, were joined in the all-encompassing ritual of the revival with the common aim of achieving the first stage of conversion's rite of passage. In this process the worldly dross of nature was burned out of the individual and the believer's body and soul made sacred: the flesh made Word.[115]

The greater paradox within Methodism, however, was the degree to which the movement managed to make sectarianism a "catholic" form. Like other Protestant sects, Methodism required the internalizing of strictly defined social norms that resulted not in a daily demeanor of liminal ecstasy but rather in a powerful organizational commitment and a sometimes rigid, even morbid, self-control. In effect, Word was turned into flesh as Methodists, one after another, even before their conversion was complete, adopted the sober, religiously literal demeanor that marked them as members of their sect. Beyond this, however, Methodists believed they could defy the limitations of sectarianism and convert the larger society. The Methodists' goal was to "reform the continent and spread scripture-holiness over these lands," requiring the opposite of brooding self-examination.

These two conflicting impulses—to withdraw from the world and to convert it at the same time—underlay the individual's socialization into the larger Methodist system.

Regarding Methodism's antiworldliness: The Methodist society was the convert's select band or substitute family, where members called each other "brother" and "sister," and the society officials were men who had themselves endured initiation into Methodism's fraternal organization of preachers.[116] Society membership required participation in Sunday services, the Lord's Supper, and especially the weekly class meetings, which provided continued solidarity and consciousness-raising with the new recruits' fellow believers. In their most intense form, classes were small revival meetings, where "mourners" were set "at liberty," with shouting and singing, and participants "fit to fly out of their bodies."[117] But more important, among other goals, they permitted the stationed preacher to know who remained in the society and to "instruct the ignorant in the first principles of religion: if need be, to repeat, explain, or enforce, what has been said in public preaching."[118]

In the class meetings, society members were probably first introduced to Wesley's *General Rules*, the instructions that served as a guide for Methodist social intercourse. Wesley's rules were exhortations to avoid evil, do good, and observe the sacraments. But they may also be understood more broadly as a set of norms that proscribed particular forms of excessive or exploitive behavior and promoted conduct that benefited or sustained the Methodist movement. Methodists were instructed to avoid profanity, drunkenness, quarreling, brawling, gossip, ornate clothing, indebtedness, hoarding, and tax evasion, as well as "giving or taking things on usury" and speaking ill of magistrates and ministers. In keeping with many of the first itinerants' opposition to slaveholding, the "buying or selling of men, women, or children, with an intention to enslave them," was also, at first, strictly forbidden. At the same time, Methodists were urged to do good "as far as is possible, to all men" and "especially to them that are of the household of faith" by "employing them preferably to others, buying one of another, helping each other in business."[119]

Like all proscriptions, the *General Rules* were designed to separate the sacred from the profane where the lines demarcating the two spheres, in everyday experience, were particularly ambiguous.[120] As such, the rules that seemed to matter most to American initiates were those, in Rhys Isaac's observation regarding the Baptists, that "must be considered to have been shaped to a large extent in reaction to the dominant culture."[121] Where Saturday night drinking frolics were the custom, Methodists were sober; where men were prolific gamblers, Methodists were frugal; where boxing and cockfights were common, Methodists rejected physical challenges and blood sports; where extravagant dress was the fashion, Methodists were plain. Reflecting the character of popular secular culture in America, Methodists condemned all forms of exhibitionism, including fighting for public display, sport shooting, and horse racing, as well as the mixed-gender activities of dancing, theatricals, and public festivals—behaviors long associated with gentry and laboring-class pleasures.[122]

Methodists' antiworldliness may also be found in the melancholic strain that runs through the accounts of Methodist meetings and individual Methodists' post-conversion consciousness, serving as a counterweight to the potential eroticism of religious devotions. To join with the Methodists was to assume a preoccupation with death, and it was perhaps this psychic orientation that most distinguished the early Methodists from their Anglican cousins. When Ezekiel Cooper sat at the deathbed of Mary Killen at the height of the 1789 revival, he "took out my pensill and wrote the following sentences as they flowed from her lips," assiduously recording the dying woman's expressions of joy and expectancy of reward.[123] In New Jersey in 1792, Richard Swain shared Dr. Blare's poem "The Grave" with a prayer group, "which seemed to make us all happy."[124] Methodists gathered at scenes where siblings were passing away from childhood illnesses, mothers from puerperal fever, fathers from accidents and war, and grandparents from the infirmities of old age, tableaux that were set forth in spiritual diaries and broadcast in Methodist books and journals, then shared in family readings.[125] Tendencies toward a morbid fascination with the process of dying would only multiply in the nineteenth century when deathbed pieties, especially those expressed by young women and "worn-out" itinerants, accumulated in the *Methodist Magazine*.[126] Affecting melancholic passages recur in Methodists' records of their daily lives as they found that their troubles were not completely banished by membership in Methodist societies or the traveling fraternity. "I once thought that in a few years I should so Mortify the flesh and conform it to the will of god that I would find Little or no trouble, But rather a constant Delight in the Se[r]vice of god," one itinerant wrote. "But I see the path to glory still continnues Narrow and the Longer I walk therein the Narrower it appear to be." "I am like an *Eagle* wounded in the wing," wrote another, "and having fell to the earth, for a season, take up my residence in the Dust; and make frequent efforts to arise, but cannot."[127]

At the same time, the Methodist narratives reveal the new converts' profound desire for personal control and independence from the rigid social restrictions that continued to govern so many facets of the larger culture in the years after the

Revolutionary War. For women and men locked into positions of filial subservience, tenantry, servitude, and slavery, the Methodist society's promise of protection from social behaviors marked by loss of control (excess), display (exhibitionism), or indulgence in force (exploitation) was as tempting as the temporary liberation of the revival meeting. For the wealthy as well, involvement in Methodist societies meant freedom from the responsibilities of social and political dominance so frequently expressed in forms of physical, even violent mastery. "[I]t was a miracle," William Weems, a former Whig, wrote ironically, "that I ever came from among the Rich and Honourable to become a dispised follower of the Lord."[128]

But Methodism's true distinction lay in the second half of its system: its missionary core. For while Methodism shared an emphasis on ritual, prayer, and communion with the Anglicans, on faith and conversion with the Calvinists, and on behavioral proscriptions with the Quakers and Moravians, it was Methodism's extraordinary ability to sustain both the missionary organization and preaching drive that most distinguished it. In its system of circuits and conferences, the Methodist Church possessed an unparalleled structure for continental expansion. And as the instrument that guided the Methodist believer from sin to salvation, missionary preaching was something most Methodists found difficult to resist, both as "hearers" and as practitioners. Asbury and other Methodist leaders' desire to define and control this force was to cause some of the most serious fissures in the early church.

John Littlejohn's final transition from religious seeker to traveling Methodist speaker underscores this point. Following his conversion, on the eve of Independence, John Littlejohn, the new English-born convert, was drawn by the preaching of American itinerant William Duke to a small class of twelve members in Alexandria, Virginia. Littlejohn and two Methodist friends in short time gathered together a regular prayer meeting in a "large thatched pen [in Falls Church], where some hundreds came to hear us pray." And although the "Magisterates & the [Anglican] Minister tried to stop the work," Littlejohn began to exhort in public. Near the end of 1775 or beginning of 1776, William Watters appointed him class leader for the Fairfax County circuit. In the spring of 1776, as the Revolutionary crisis came to a head, Littlejohn was admitted to the Methodist conference as an itinerant in training and began traveling on Virginia's Berkeley County circuit.[129]

Speaking as a fully formed Wesleyan, Littlejohn now outlined a personal economy for himself and daily reminder of his commitment to the Methodist discipline:

Ist Every night to exam[e] myself. 2[d] To rise every Morn[g] before or by the peep of day, & to have family pray[r] where practicable the 1[st] thing that the Blacks may attend; & to engage heads of Familes to do so. 3[d] To avoid talk of World[l]ly things as much as possiable; others may yea must I need not. 4[th] To converce with all I can on the Salvat[n] of their souls, Rich & poor. 5[th] Never to stay at any place longer than necessary. 6[th] To avoid lightness & reprove those who joke & laugh to excess. 7[th] Strictly to enforce the rules on every memb[r]. of society *Rich* or *poor*. 8th Never to triffel or while away time, &

to guard ag^st talk^g too much. 9th to read the bible, & [Wesley's] notes every Morn^g & even^g w^t pray^r to God & to read other books occasionaly.

Dressed in the mourning coat his mother had bequeathed him in memory of his father—although "she feared I wl^d turn a Preacher"—Littlejohn now set off in a wholly new direction, leaving his father's world behind.[130]

For just as the revealing references to the fundamental elements of Revolutionary society, from families and their heads to slavery and to divisions of wealth, appear through Littlejohn's account of his personal economy, so Methodist missionizing did not occur in a social vacuum. In this sense, Methodism, to use Edward Thompson's phrase, had a "transforming power";[131] and John Wesley's distinctive brand of Primitive Christianity was to have both a complex and unexpectedly ascendant future in the new republic.

PART II

Social Change

CHAPTER FOUR

Evangelical Sisters

IN THE SECOND book of *The Pilgrim's Progress*, a devotional tract favored by
American Methodists, John Bunyan recounts the adventures of Christiana, her
four sons, and her friend Mercy as they make their way to the Celestial City, the
destination already attained by her Pilgrim husband Christian. A woman, like a
man, Bunyan demonstrates to his readers, can in her own way survive the ordeals
necessary to attain the prize of salvation. And women, like men, were essential to
the propagation of Christianity. "I will now speak on the behalf of women," Bunyan pauses in his narration to exclaim: "For as death and the curse came into the
world by a woman, so also did life and health: *God sent forth his Son, made of a
woman. . . .* Women therefore are highly favoured, and show by these things that
they are sharers with us in the grace of life." Women succored Christ at his moment
of sacrifice, just as Mary had given him birth. Although daughters of Eve, Bunyan
granted that women, "with us," could escape the taint of original sin.

Relayed "in the similitude of a DREAM," Christiana's trials are no less heroic
than her husband's, if less often marked by physical challenges. Unlike Christian's
solitary pilgrimage, however, Christiana's journey is a decidedly social one, inter-
woven with the responsibilities and securities of family and friendship. Her quest
is not simply her own but that of her children and her confidante and spiritual
sister.[1]

Certain similar generalizations hold true for the American women who joined
Methodist societies one hundred years later. For one thing, the contributions of
women to Methodism were significant but more often assumed than acknowledged. For another, women's participation in the movement emanated from their
households and their world of female association, strengthened by early Methodism's origins as a household-centered or "cottage" religion. As Bunyan would
have predicted, much of the cohesion of American Methodism in the Revolutionary years may be attributed not only to its fraternal corps of preacher itinerants
but also to the often lifelong support of a host of women in and outside the church.

At the same time, the sponsors of "enthusiastic" religion were less inclined to
publicize the degree to which becoming a female evangelical was also a rebellious
act, one, as Christine Heyrman has shown for southern evangelicals, that drove
a wedge between many women and their families, before and after marriage.[2]
Methodism, furthermore, sustained a religious culture of female association that
was explicitly separate from the family and community. And unlike their counterparts in the older, seventeenth-century churches, the women who joined Methodist societies in the main Middle Atlantic cities—New York, Philadelphia, and
Baltimore—following the Revolutionary War were often young, single, and ethnically and racially diverse, arriving at Methodist societies on their own or in the

company of one or another female relation. In short, women's place in the new movement reflected the rapidly changing—often unpredictable—social conditions of the new nation as much as it did the enduring role of women within Christianity.

As such, women's engagement with Methodism provides a suitable point of departure for understanding the complex relationship between the new evangelicalism and the Revolutionary age. And as with most early American social developments—and nearly all relating to women—the story begins in the household.

The Female Methodist Network

The son of a female household exhorter, John Wesley consistently encouraged women to participate privately and publicly in his movement. Wesley appointed deaconesses in Georgia and female as well as male "band," or prayer group, leaders at the first Methodist society at Bristol in 1739. By the early 1740s, forty-seven women and nineteen men led class meetings at London's Foundery Chapel. Numerous women served as unlicensed preachers, and a significant number, including Grace Murray, Sarah Crosby, Elizabeth Ritchie, and Mary Bosanquet, traveled.[3] When in the early nineteenth century the increasingly respectable Wesleyan Methodist Church restricted women's public speaking, the sectarian Primitive Methodists—like the first English Methodists, a household-centered faith—sponsored female proselytizers and preachers through the industrializing Midlands.[4]

American Methodism also originated as a cottage religion with a strong private and public female component. Among the earliest of the new evangelists was Barbara Heck, by tradition the "Mother" of American Methodism. It was Heck, during the Irish Palatines' unsettled years in New York City, who discovered the lapsed Wesleyans playing cards and in a gesture redolent of female domestic authority—and sufficiently memorable to have endured in Methodist oral tradition—swept the cards into her apron and from there into the nearby hearth fire. It was through Heck's insistence that Philip Embury resumed local preaching in 1766, and she, her husband, a man servant, and a woman servant formed the core of New York's first Methodist society.[5]

Heck is only the best known of the first women Methodists, however, one of an expanding network of female members and supporters in the 1760s and 1770s. In New York, the Methodist society constructed a chapel from the proceeds of a subscription in 1768 that included the contributions of thirty-six women.[6] In Philadelphia, the first British itinerants were sustained, emotionally and physically, by Methodists Mary Thorn, Mary Wilmer, and Hannah Baker. Thorn, a recent widow, moved from Charleston, where she had been a favored congregant in Oliver Hart's Particular Baptist Church, back to Philadelphia sometime before the first itinerants' arrival in the colonies. Submitting herself to divine guidance, Thorn discovered Joseph Pilmore preaching at the local Methodist society and joined the group while remaining a member of the Baptist Church, which, as she put it, "it may be Remembered was not inconsistent with Mr Wesley's first intention of methodism."[7] An ecstatic revival participant, Thorn was appointed to head a class meeting, one of ultimately three women leaders in Philadelphia. Her loyalty to the English movement won her little public sympathy during the war with Britain, and she claimed to have been pelted through the streets and her effigy stoned.[8] Another Philadelphian, Mary Wilmer, Lambert's wife, was also appointed class leader by the first preachers. Her lifelong fellow member, Hannah Smith, joined the society as a nineteen-year-old before marrying Jacob Baker, and she hosted Methodist itinerants as a "mother in Israel" until the revival of 1800.[9] In Annapolis in the 1780s, the founding members of the Methodist society were all women.[10]

In addition to these early members and class leaders, the Methodist itinerants, as sponsors of an ecumenical movement, relied on the advocacy of prominent women from other churches. The John Street Chapel in New York was constructed on land supplied by Mary Barclay, widow of the Anglican vicar of Trinity Church and a Methodist sympathizer.[11] In Baltimore, Mary Magdalen Tripolet, a German-speaking congregant of Otterbein's German Reformed Church, hosted Methodist preachers from John King's first appearance in that town.[12] Mary Woodward of Primrose Hill near Annapolis, later wife of the Swedish portrait painter John Hesselius, was also a Methodist advocate.[13] Among Francis Asbury's long-term women friends was Rebecca Grace, widow of one of Pennsylvania's ironfounders.[14] Mary Withey, the proprietor of the Columbia Hotel in Chester, Pennsylvania, supported the Methodist itinerants and antislavery activists—another set of Revolutionary-era reformers. She also raised a small Methodist society in Chester and by 1800 had been "treating" the itinerants for twenty-eight years.[15] And despite a later falling-out with her Methodist daughter Catherine, Margaret Beekman Livingston, an evangelically inclined member of the Dutch Reformed Church, hosted the Methodist preachers at her Clermont estate in the Hudson River Valley until her death in 1800.[16]

Perhaps the densest concentration of early Methodist female members and patrons was to be found in and around Baltimore, among the Ridgely, Gough, and Owings families, significant players in Maryland's gentry. Priscilla Hill Dorsey, wife of Caleb, the "Iron Master," invited Methodist preachers to the Dorsey plantation at Belmont on a regular basis before the war.[17] Two of her daughters, Rebecca and Priscilla, married into the Baltimore branch of the Ridgely family: Rebecca in about 1760 to Captain Charles Ridgely, one of the city's richest merchants and an ambivalent but powerful patriot; and Priscilla in 1782 to Ridgely's nephew Charles R. Carnan, a Maryland legislator and eventually governor of the state, who changed his surname to Ridgely to qualify as his uncle's heir. Both men were Anglicans, but their wives, drawn into the movement before the Revolution, remained lifelong Methodists.[18] Another child of the Dorsey family, Deborah Lynch, converted sometime before her husband, Samuel Owings, Jr., whom she married in 1765. The family estate of Ulm (later Owings Mills) was open to the Methodist preachers before and after the war, and by the early 1770s the Owingses were influential figures at the Light Street Chapel in Baltimore Town.[19]

Figure 5. *Rebecca Dorsey Ridgely*, by John Hesselius, ca. 1770. The first
mistress of Hampton Hall before her conversion. Courtesy of Collection of
Hampton National Historic Site, National Park Service.

The Dorsey-Ridgely links to Methodism were strengthened by intermarriage.
Captain Ridgely's older sister, Achsah Chamier, was a Methodist benefactor. Two
of her nieces, Rachel Goodwin and Pleasance Goodwin, joined the movement.
Closer to home, Chamier's daughter Prudence converted to lifelong Methodism.
She was the young wife of the Baltimore County landholder and Baltimore City
merchant Harry Dorsey Gough, the Dorsey sisters' first cousin. Unlike Charles
Ridgely, his chief commercial and political rival, Gough briefly followed his wife
into the new church.[20] The Goughs' Perry Hall manor, moreover, served as a way
station for itinerants during the Revolutionary War, and was the scene of the
preconference meeting in 1784 at which Thomas Coke and Francis Asbury drew
up their blueprint for the Methodist Episcopal Church.[21]

Figure 6. *Priscilla Dorsey Ridgely*, by Rembrandt Peale, ca. 1800.
Rebecca's sister, a convinced Methodist. Courtesy of Collection of Hampton
National Historic Site, National Park Service.

By this time, the family connections among Methodists were plentiful outside
Baltimore as well, particularly along the Eastern Shore and in Delaware, already
the most pronounced Methodist region in the country. In Dover, the Delaware
branch of the Ridgely family, headed by Dr. Abraham and Ann Ridgely, were
important sustainers of the itinerants.[22] On the basis of his Dover connections,
Asbury established his alliance with Judge Thomas White, whose wife, Mary,
was instrumental in her husband's conversion.[23] Among the wartime converts was
Richard Bassett, later a delegate to the Federal Convention and governor of the
state, who joined the Methodists simultaneously with his wife, Ann Ennalls Bassett. The Bassetts provided Bohemia Manor, the former Labadist colony in Cecil
County, Maryland, as another way station for the itinerants.[24] In another part of

the Eastern Shore, Ann Bassett's sisters, Catherine and Mary Ennalls, converted their brother Henry and another relation, Henry Airey, both prominent local planters in Dorchester County. These and other Methodist ties among powerful Delaware and Eastern Shore families in no small way account for Methodism's phenomenal expansion through these areas.[25]

Women sympathizers and acolytes, old and young, many of them widows, guided young converts along their paths and supplied holy conversation to friends and family. Among families, perhaps the greatest influence was exercised by pious mothers over their impressionable daughters. Thus the original inspiration for Rebecca Ridgely's religious quest in the 1760s was her Quaker mother's urgings that she not be "Like the Rest . . . to pray with our Lips and at the Same time our hearts be far from God."[26] Her sister-in-law, Achsah Chamier, shared her own religious impressions with her daughter, Prudence. The two maintained an evangelically laden correspondence that emphasized the leveling impact of religious conversion on generational differences: "I have often though[t] my Dear Mamma," Prudence Gough wrote to her mother, "that an intercourse between friends is the highest satisfaction that absence can bestow, but I never experienced it in a more sensable degree then when I received your first Letter."[27] One by one, the daughters and granddaughters of the itinerants' first female advocates joined the movement: Mary Killen and Caroline Zolikofer, daughters of Mary Magdalen Tripolet in Baltimore;[28] Rebecca, wife of Philip Rogers of the Light Street Chapel and daughter of Mary Woodward;[29] Elizabeth Lusby, wife of Josiah Lusby, a Philadelphia physician, and daughter of longtime Methodist supporter "mother Steele";[30] Martha Potts, granddaughter of Rebecca Grace and later wife of Thomas Haskins;[31] and Catherine Livingston, Margaret Beekman Livingston's fifth child and eventually wife of itinerant Freeborn Garrettson.[32]

Old and young women shared their spiritual struggles and fantasies with the young itinerants. Mary Thorn in Philadelphia was the recipient of more than one male convert's assurances of support, expressed in the physical language of Wesleyan discourse: "I love you in the bowels of Jesus," Richard Sause wrote to Thorn before the war, "[and] could rejoyce at your Souls prosperity." Those seeking perfection, Richard Boardman confided to Thorn, will feel "inward temptations: dejections: a struggling painful to feel: impossable to be *discribed*."[33] "[B]e not discouraged," Joseph Pilmore wrote in a more martial tone, "but bring these Enimies that would not that Christ should reign over them, and let them be slain before his face—don't spare one."[34] Years after Thorn's move to England, Asbury grieved, "Surely you sometimes think how often we have sat and talked together at your own house and the houses of others, about the precious things of God."[35] Asbury corresponded with fewer female followers than did Wesley, yet references to women friends are multitudinous in his letters and in his journal. His grief at their absences and deaths reveals a strong mutual attachment.[36]

The itinerants were also unembarrassed to rely on women for more material support. "Women are weak," Asbury began a letter to wealthy Philadelphia Methodist Martha Haskins, before continuing in a more ingratiating vein: "but remember Eve, and Sarah, Miriam, Deborah, Hannah, Shebah's Queen, Elizabeth, Anna,

Phebe and such like, bring the gifts to enrich the temple of God."[37] Considering the affluence of many of the itinerants' female supporters in and around Baltimore—Rebecca Ridgely, Priscilla Ridgely, and Prudence Gough were each recipients of substantial estates from their fathers and husbands—and of their women followers in Delaware, Philadelphia, and the Hudson River Valley, it is hardly surprising that Methodist leaders hoped to reap some advantage from the association.[38] Asbury in particular relied on cash support from prominent Methodists to bolster his small stipend after the war. And as he was to write to Rebecca Ridgely, "my Benefactoress," years later, his stipend would not have been sufficient income "[i]f I had not here and there a Friend like Mamma Ridgely."[39]

The wealth of most of these women, however, was tied up in family and dower arrangements, controlled by their male relatives or reserved as bequests for other women in the family. Itinerants seeking cash support from their wealthy patronesses were likely disappointed.[40] More often than not, women's material maintenance came in the form of gifts in kind, some quite generous. Thus Robert Strawbridge and his wife lived rent-free on a farm at Rebecca and Charles Ridgely's Hampton estate before Strawbridge died in 1781.[41] At Perry Hall, the Goughs converted one room of their Georgian manor house into a "Preachers Room" where in spartan quarters itinerants could stay for brief or extended visits, and where they might worship in a chapel built for their and the Goughs' use.[42] But the most important gifts were the great consumers of women's time: the repeated rounds of meals, lodging, and nursing provided to the itinerants by women householders, their daughters, and their, mostly female, servants. The preachers rarely stayed in one place for more than a few days at a time, and since only the city societies provided regular lodging, they spent most of their nights at the house of one or another recruit: taking breakfast, dinner, and supper, and sometimes late afternoon tea. A formidably restless missionary like Asbury relied unspokenly on the hundreds of women who made ready his rooms, prepared his meals, mended his clothes, and washed his laundry for the nearly forty-five years he was on the road.[43]

Altogether, through the first decades of the movement, women played critical spiritual and material roles in the propagation of Methodism, forming close alliances with the itinerants and influencing the conversion of men and other women in their families; so much so that it is unlikely that American households "turned" Methodist without the consent and frequently the fervent advocacy of the women who managed them.

METHODISM AND FAMILY CONFLICT

To say that Methodism relied on the sustenance of women within their families and households, however—just as conversion experiences were conducted like electricity through family connections—is not to say that Methodism was initially compatible with American family life, or for that matter with republican family rhetoric. On the contrary, in Revolutionary America as in Britain, Methodism was widely interpreted as representing an attack on family relations, and a woman by her conversion might be as easily led to reject as to celebrate her family ties, including her responsibilities as a republican wife and mother.

Scholars disagree on the distinguishing features of the American family at the time of the Revolution. But recent studies suggest that the model patriarchal family, in which the male head of household exercised significant control over the legal, economic, and emotional life of the family and laboring dependents, was already in decline by the war's end. High premarital pregnancy rates in parts of the country, the legalization of divorce in many states, and intestate practices favoring widows and daughters as well as sons reveal widespread familial change after the war.[44] The symbolic import of the representation of the worthy infant colonies' rebellion against a tyrannical imperial parent, which accounts for so much of the rhetorical power of Thomas Paine's antimonarchical *Common Sense*, for example, could not have been lost on Americans.[45]

Attempting to come to terms with these changes, republican theorists generated a prescriptive literature on how women and children were to be shaped to fit the new mold of civic responsibility and educated decision making. Gendered definitions of citizenship, as Mary Beth Norton and Linda Kerber each elucidated in their pathbreaking studies of Revolutionary-era women, associated women's patriotic duty with "Republican Motherhood." In a further transfiguring of republican rhetoric, virtue, once an overtly masculine value, was increasingly identified with feminine piety in the home, as Ruth Bloch has explained.[46] Altogether, these ideas strongly proposed that the American political experiment depended on its citizens' imbibing of virtue from their mothers. Under "Maxims for Republics," a new American magazine announced, "[I]t is of the utmost importance, that the women should be well instructed in the principles of liberty in a republic. Some of the first patriots of antient times, were formed by their mothers." In his "Thoughts Upon Female Education," Benjamin Rush urged that young women, as the future mothers of American citizens, should be better trained in many areas, among these history, geography, natural philosophy, and religion. The last was especially important.[47] As Martha Blauvelt writes, "Development of the belief that, as Benjamin Rush put it, 'the female breast is the natural soil of Christianity,' simultaneously calmed patriot nerves and exhorted women to fulfill their natural destiny."[48]

Women's adherence to Methodist piety, however, did not necessarily strengthen their pedagogical proclivities or allegiance to motherhood or their families. Wesley, like his contemporaries, defined the family not as an affective unit but rather as a collectivity coincident with the household, consisting of master, wife, children, and servants (whom he called "secondary children"). With characteristic detail, Wesley defined the appropriate Methodist domestic economy, from the powers of the heads of families to the dangers of overindulgent grandmothers.[49] But most tellingly he identified the true father of the Methodist family as himself or, more specifically, Christ. Methodist fathers were in effect human surrogates for a higher power.[50] Hence when the 1785 American discipline called for "Family-Religion," it did not seek to promote the authority of families per se. Rather, the family provided the conduit by which the Methodists might promote religion. "For what avails *Public Preaching alone*, though we could preach like Angels?" the discipline asked. "We must, yea, every Travelling-Preacher must instruct them *from House to House*. Till this is done, and that in good earnest, the Methodists will be little better than other People."[51] By 1798, the discipline more overtly expressed the pragmatic point about families, which was that "[t]he whole world is composed of families. A travelling preacher may bring as many souls to glory by his fidelity in the families which he visits, as by his public preaching."[52] The Methodists, that is, saw themselves as a "peculiar people" for the fervency of their religious belief and ministry rather than their emphasis on the centrality of family life. The future of the Methodist household, the proper relation of children and servants to their fathers, mothers, masters, and mistresses, along with the always problematic question of what was to become of families torn apart by the urgencies of religious conversion, were issues rarely addressed by the traveling preachers.

Instead, the itinerants pressed their followers—rich, middling, and poor; white and black; men and women—to listen to Christ first, confront parental and spousal authority if necessary, and above all to resist being "unequally yoked" with unbelievers. While the movement was often embraced by the members of one family, it also overturned conventional family discipline and order and led to at times violent family conflict, especially between parents and children, and husbands and wives.

The story of Catherine Livingston's five-year struggle with her mother illuminates the peculiar intensity of the impact of Methodism on one family. Like many of the New York Dutch aristocracy, the Livingstons were Calvinist by sentiment and patriarchal by class, the family's wealth based on ancestor Robert Livingston's successful manipulation of the Indian trade and generous land grants from the provincial assembly. Catherine's father, Judge Robert R. Livingston, was an active opponent of Parliament through the early years of the American resistance but had not come around to supporting independence when he died in 1775. Catherine's mother, Margaret Beekman Livingston, patroness of Methodist itinerants, was the offspring of a wealthy Dutch Reformed family.[53] Hence Catherine, born in 1752, was a product of New York's hierarchical caste system. As a young woman she frequented dancing assemblies in New York City with her family's allies and relations, including Elizabeth Schuyler and Schuyler's fiancé, Alexander Hamilton. She was courted by at least one suitor but by her late twenties had settled into a well-connected spinsterhood, living with her mother at Clermont Farm in the Hudson River Valley with a small army of servants and slaves.[54] Her eight surviving siblings were each in his or her own way destined for renown in Whig and then Democratic-Republican circles.[55]

Livingston's dutiful acceptance of her circumstances underwent a dramatic change at the time of her religious conversion. Spiritually awakened in 1786 while at communion at New York City's St. Paul's Church, she experienced an intensification of her religious crisis two years later on the eve of her thirty-fifth birthday.[56] Livingston scoured the Christian devotional literature, including the letters of St. Paul, her "favorite" apostle St. John, the apocalyptic Book of Revelation, Calvinist tracts, and several works by John Wesley, for answers to her spiritual quandaries. She learned of the Methodist doctrine of sanctification and approved of it. Altogether she was unusually well informed on doctrinal issues.[57]

But like most Methodists, her first exposure to the new evangelism came from religious experience rather than from religious texts, followed by association with fellow travelers of less privileged background. She is said to have heard of Methodism from a female servant who was a member of the New York City society. The small class Catherine joined in Rhinebeck near Clermont included, among others, a Dutch fisherman and, only later, her wealthy neighbors John and Phebe Rutsen and their daughters, Sarah and Catharine. Livingston formed an especially close association with Catharine Rutsen, with whom she shared descriptions of dreams and spiritual experiences.[58] In a short time she also became engaged to marry Freeborn Garrettson, the Maryland-born itinerant and antislavery activist, who first traveled to Rhinebeck in May 1788 at the invitation of Margaret and Thomas Tillotson, Catherine's sister and brother-in-law.[59]

Livingston described her decision to stand by Garrettson through subsequent crises with family and friends as having been "prepared by dreams," and these took on an increasingly sensual character as her marriage was delayed and she found herself "ever engaged for Sanctification."[60] In an illuminating night vision, she dreamed that the betrothed pair discussed their wedding plans while a maidservant washed the room, as if cleaning the slate of Livingston's former life. Catherine told her fiancé that he had "great obsticles to encounter," and she "doubted wether there was one in the Family, that would not oppose his pretentions." In his dream-guise, Freeborn responded, "He that is for us, is greater than all that are against us."[61] Later Catherine wrote to Freeborn in the language of religious intimacy: "I do not think I have a wish, or thought that I would conceal from you. O what exalted Friendships does the love of Jesus form!"[62]

Over the next several years, Livingston's mysticism reached new heights: "God is love," she wrote of one intoxicating encounter with the Divine, "boundless! boundless Love! . . . I gazed at uncreated love, love in its Original Source! Here was nothing solemn—Nothing Awful! It was extacy!"[63] As her religious experiences escalated, Livingston's relationship with her family deteriorated. Francis Asbury continued to be welcome at Clermont.[64] But Margaret Beekman Livingston, like Catherine's siblings, was wary of the emotional turmoil into which Wesley's heart-religion had cast her daughter. And then there was Livingston's engagement: while favoring a plebeian missionary movement in the spirit of religious experimentation or Christian charity was a privilege of noblesse oblige, forming a marital alliance with a Methodist missionary was a social test of the first order. The potentially leveling power of Methodism was fully apparent at this one juncture: the matter of marriage. Jettisoning her mother's protection and authority, Catherine met her lover clandestinely and eventually left her mother's house altogether.[65]

"I have continual sorrow from without, and from within," Livingston wrote to one of her sisters; "I have been cast from my Mothers affections, and house, and have now no other home than such I derive from the bounty of a kind sister, upon whom I have been thrown." But her association with the Methodists had provided her with the thing her family had consistently refused her: an autonomous identity. "I declare to you," she exclaimed to her sister, "I would not be what once I was, If every other thing which the world can bestow or enjoy were at my free choice."[66] When Livingston and Garrettson set their wedding date, various friends were still silent on the engagement, and Margaret Livingston was unreconciled to the marriage.[67]

Episodes of women's filial and spousal disobedience, covert and overt, permeate the Methodist narratives. Rebecca Ridgely, for one instance, during years of religious seeking before and after her marriage and some distress at not having been baptized by her Quaker mother, attempted to conform to her husband's Anglicanism. But during Anglican services she remembered her mother's warning her not to "Lett my toung give my Heart the Lye." She took stock of other church services—Quaker, Baptist, and Presbyterian—before hearing of Captain Thomas Webb's return to Baltimore in 1774. "Doe go," an acquaintance urged her; "it is as good as a play to hear him." Attending with two women friends, she heard Webb preach: "Now is the appointed time, now is the Day of Salvation." Ridgely observed that he "spoke so plain of the spiritual Baptism and how we might through prayer Come to Receive that Blesing and through Neglect must Lose it." She added: "[B]eing of a Gay Desposition [I] Danced a[nd] Claptt my hands and said it was the truth [Webb] had spoke that Night . . . and that I would go to hear him every Night as Capit Ridgely was gone to annapolis." Ridgely later prohibited his wife from frequenting Methodist meetings hosted by a neighbor with whom he had had a disagreement, no doubt prompting further subterfuge on his wife's part.[68]

More trying was Mary Evans Thorn's altercation with her mother around the same time. Both widows, the two women lived together with Thorn's siblings outside Philadelphia before the Revolutionary War. Much to their mother's dismay, Thorn's brothers and two of her sisters one by one converted to Methodism. Widow Evans was heard to exclaim on the subject, "[T]hese birds of passage [the itinerants] have bereaved me of my Children, they will all be in bedlam." She then presented her daughter with the ultimatum that she "[e]ither forsake the methodists" or be cut off from all contact with her family. Thorn's "mind was in an agony and that word of our Lord, thundered in my Soul, He that loveth father or mother more than me is not worthy of me. . . . I gave my final answer to my Dear mother." As a result of her loyalty to the itinerants and subsequent marriage to British Methodist merchant Samuel Parker, Mary Thorn "never saw [her family] more."[69]

Elsewhere, a young woman in Annapolis was ejected from her father's house for joining the Methodists, and a female convert in western Pennsylvania was "turn'd out of doors by her husband" for giving one of the preachers a quarter of a dollar.[70] In Penn's Neck, New Jersey, local rumor had it that the husband of one convert "wanted to heat [the kitchen fire] nine times hotter than it had ever been, and he intended to burn his wife in it as soon as she came from meeting."[71]

Alarmed spouses confronted the itinerants on public thoroughfares, as when Free-born Garrettson was halted on the road near Saratoga, New York, by a stranger "raving like a madman." "Stop, sir," he commanded Garrettson, "and clear up one thing. Is it right for you to part man and wife? My wife joined your church last night. We are parted, we are parted!"[72] Family divisions spilled over into the ritual drama of the revival itself. In Maryland, a husband trailed his wife to a revival meeting, wielding a club and threatening the preacher with physical as-sault.[73] When an awakened Quaker acolyte confided to Benjamin Abbott that she was disobeying her mother by attending his preaching, Abbott prayed that God might pursue the new convert "through the streets, . . . in the parlour, in the kitchen, and in the garden," notwithstanding the consequences to her family life.[74]

Making the wrong marital choice—including one determined by their family rather than their faith—conversely led new converts into trouble with their Meth-odist society or the stationed preacher. "We are well assured that few things have been more pernicious to the work of God, than the marriage of the children of God with the children of this world," Coke and Asbury informed their followers.[75] Converts of both sexes could be expelled for marrying "*unawakened* persons." The question was put as to whether a woman might marry without her parents' consent. The discipline conceded to social convention when it advised that "[i]n general she ought not." But if she was "under the necessity of marrying" (that is, was among the as many as 25 percent of late-eighteenth-century American women who became pregnant before marriage), and her parents "absolutely re-fuse to let her marry any christian: Then she may, nay, ought to marry without their consent."[76] In good conscience, women might go so far as to neglect their maternal duties if religious strenuosity demanded it. Lucy Watson's two small children saw little of their mother when she was in the throes of her conversion. After Mary Thorn had moved to Britain with her future husband and raised a family, Asbury reminded her that her religious convictions had once transcended mere family concerns: "You are become a joyful mother of children. Oh, let not these dear little creatures draw your heart from God."[77]

In fact, as in the early English movement, many American itinerants considered marriage and family life to be bad influences on the movement. While households formed the base of operations for most of the preachers, Asbury preferred that the itinerants themselves remain unattached, and was deeply suspicious of the power of sexual attraction to lead men astray from their missionary vocation. As he warned one young recruit, "Stand at all possible distance from the female sex, that you be not betrayed by them that will damage the young mind and sink the aspiring soul and blast the prospect of the future man."[78] Before republican rheto-ric made femininity and virtue logical equivalents, the image of the "daughter of Eve" died hard, and many Methodists continued to perceive women as weak in body and mind but paradoxically powerful in sex and guile; they believed that a clever woman might easily draw the innocent male convert from his chosen path as a solitary and faithful evangelist.[79] As one of the Wesleyan virtues, furthermore, celibacy for both men and women was applauded in the American discipline and supported by scriptural passages directing the reader to "flee youthful lusts."

Elizabeth Rowe's guide to solitary female devotions, *Devout Exercises of the Heart*, was an American favorite.[80] Catherine Livingston observed of one "un-equally yoked" woman before her own marriage to Garrettson: "O with what regret did she recal those happy days when she had none to protest her in the service of God. . . . Let others do as they please, for my part was I free from every engagement, I would sooner wed my Coffin; than a Man that was not converted."[81]

In Wesley's movement, the celibate ideal had soon waned. It was similarly doomed in the American movement, and the church quickly made efforts to ac-commodate their married preachers. For this purpose the 1780 conference con-ceived an ambitious plan to build residences for the preachers' wives on each circuit, so that the preacher might be free to travel.[82] When the plan failed to gain the support of the local societies, the preachers instead urged that itinerants' wives receive the same support as their husbands when necessary, as had been the case in the English connection. In 1783, this provision was criticized by "leading men" at the local societies who "thought it unreasonable that they should raise money for a woman they never saw; and whose husband had never preached among them." Hence in this year, the allowances for preachers' wives were allotted sepa-rately to northern and southern annual conferences, with the names of individual wives printed in the annual minutes.[83] But at the Christmas Conference, an annual stipend of £24 Pennsylvania currency, equivalent to the preachers' stipend, was reserved for preachers' wives, the amount updated to $64 in 1792. Overall, despite the poverty of the connection, the church continued through 1800 to direct annual conferences and local societies to fully support the preachers' wives, children, widows, and orphans. As Coke and Asbury reminded Methodists in the 1798 discipline: "the wife is to have *the same claim* in respect to salary as the travelling preacher," and any income raised in a circuit traveled by a married preacher and a single preacher "is to be divided into three parts, one part of which belongs to the wife."[84]

The wives of the itinerants no doubt derived satisfaction from being so publicly maintained by their church. But underlying the MEC's sponsorship was the under-standing that itinerants' spouses would be spending time without their husbands, adjusting to long months of separation, and even moving back to parents' house-holds if the circuits' stipends proved inadequate, as was often the case. William Watters's wife, Sarah Adams, whom he married in spring 1778, continued to live with her father until 1779 when she moved into the household of Watters's older brother.[85] Another preacher reported that his wife was boarding nearby since "I found if I did not break up house keeping, I should collect so much of this worlds goods . . . that I should be quite oppressed."[86] While her husband's long absences provided some respite from the physical uncertainties of pregnancy and child-birth, the preacher's wife must also have been aware of how hers was not the typical marital relationship. Like Christiana, Bunyan's Pilgrim's wife, she was frequently as dependent on friends and family as she was on her spouse.[87]

Despite these challenges, women continued to attend revivals, join Methodist classes and societies, and marry the Methodist itinerants. Often talking alike, in Wesleyan "holy conversation" and the plain language of Quakers, and frequently looking alike, their gowns, caps, and bonnets fashioned from muted fabrics, "so that the preachers could not but observe the remarkable uniformity of appearance thus presented,"[88] women also constituted the majority of the Methodist societies about which significant information has survived. The Middle Atlantic city societies in particular reveal the social parameters of women's participation in the movement and the degree to which Methodism depended on women's association with other women in an unprecedentedly diverse community.

WOMEN IN THE CITY SOCIETIES

The records of the postwar Methodist societies in the major Middle Atlantic cities—New York, Philadelphia, and Baltimore—provide the only surviving social profile of early American Methodism. The earliest dating from 1785, these local societies' registers reveal a church membership of remarkable variety and geographical and social mobility. No simple generalizations may be made about the Americans first drawn to Methodism in its urban, or for that matter its rural, context.[89]

Yet one significant point is immediately apparent: women formed a majority, frequently a large majority, of the Methodist city societies in the postwar years. Counted in selected years from 1786 to 1801, women emerge as constituting nearly two-thirds of New York's membership in the 1780s and 1790s, and from nearly 60 to more than 64 percent of Philadelphia's Methodists between 1794 and 1801. In Baltimore City in 1800, women made up 60 percent of the Methodist society, and in 1801, they composed more than 63 percent of Baltimore's smaller Fell's Point congregation.[90]

Women's social experience in the city societies reveals a number of important trends. As was to be the case in northern evangelical churches before the Civil War, women were just as likely as men to join at times of revival, and many enrolled in the company of female relations. Patterns of Methodist membership, that is, were predictors of developments that were to characterize the revivals in New York's "burned over district," the western New York region swept by evangelical fervor in the 1820s and 1830s.[91]

In the 1780s and 1790s, however, these patterns were just taking shape, and female participation in the Methodist city societies, despite an important family component, reflected the changing and changeable world in which these Methodists lived and worshiped. Five trends stand out. First, women dominated church membership in and outside revival years; second, women by all appearances joined in the company of their women relations, many of them probably sisters, many others impossible to identify; third, these new members were most likely young and single; fourth, married women also joined as "single" women, that is, without the company of their husbands; and fifth, social and ethnic diversity was a fact of life for women in the city congregations. Altogether, the record of these women's experience confirms the larger impression that the missionary drive within Methodism redefined both the character of family relationships among Methodists and the nature of the religious society itself.

To look first at the consistently high proportions of women: Through most of the first half of the eighteenth century, revivals were known to attract greater numbers of men than women. In one study covering a 150-year period, women in selected New England churches were found to regularly outnumber men except at times of religious revival, in particular during the Great Awakening of the 1740s. Similarly, with the exception of the 1740s, women in eighteenth- and nineteenth-century Connecticut formed as much as 78 percent of church member-ship.[92] By contrast, the percentage of women at the New York Methodist society was much the same in the low-tide revival year of 1786 (63.2 percent) as it was in the high-tide year of 1791 (65.9 percent). And the proportion of women in the Philadelphia society *rose* substantially, from 59 percent, when revival fervor was ebbing in 1796, to 64.1 percent when it was soaring in 1800.[93]

More telling is the second consistent trend characterizing women's member-ship: Methodist women joined the city societies in the company of other women. This conclusion is drawn from a simple examination of members' last names.

In New York, Philadelphia, and Baltimore alike, Methodist women with the same last names appear in the record with striking repetitiveness. In New York, for example, 242 white women (nearly 38 percent) and 54 black women (more than 32 percent) belonging to the Methodist society in the sample years of 1786, 1791, and 1796 shared last names with at least one and often three or more woman of the same race, In Philadelphia, a similar pattern emerges: In the years 1794, 1796, and 1801 collectively, 291, or close to 45 percent of all white women in the society, shared last names with other women (often three at a time). And in Baltimore City, in 1799, 1800, and 1801 collectively, 265 white women (again, close to 45 percent), possessed the same last name as another white woman in the church, and, likewise, 124 black women (or more than 36 percent) shared last names with other black women.[94]

To relay these findings more generally, more than a third of the white women belonging to the New York society and nearly half in the Philadelphia and Balti-more City societies shared last names with at least one other woman in the congre-gation, and often with two or *more* other women. Likewise, nearly a third of black women Methodists in New York and more than a third in Baltimore held a sur-name in common with another black woman in the local church.

A comparison of the clustering of women's last names with men's, moreover, strongly suggests a gender-specific pattern. At the New York society, the 640 white women appearing in the record for the years 1786, 1791, and 1796 collec-tively were 1.5 times more likely than the society's 374 white men to share a last name with another member of the same sex; they were nearly five times more likely to share last names with *more* than one other member of the same sex. In Philadelphia, for the years 1794, 1796, and 1801 collectively, the 650 white women in the record were again 1.5 times more likely than the society's 377 white men to hold a last name in common, and 3.5 times more likely than men to share a last name with more than one other member of the same sex.[95]

The repetition of last names among Methodist women is so persistent as to leave the impression of great family interconnectedness among city members—but it is a tie that women appear especially to possess. Women, that is, were joining the city societies in the company of their female relations. In light of the frequency with which women from the same natal families—mothers, married daughters, and married sisters—bore differing last names, the incidence of family connections among Methodist women was probably even greater than the duplication of names suggests. But another explanation may account for the sheer numbers of women with common names: a common attraction to Methodism among groups of sisters of the same generation.

Indeed, negative evidence, together with the urban historical context in which these women joined the Methodists, is persuasive of the most tentative but suggestive conclusion regarding women in the city societies: many were young and unmarried. The first generation of Methodist women in New York, for example, were remarkably removed from the familial rites of their local churches. In 1786, just twenty-five of the ninety-six white women Methodists in New York, and two of the nineteen black women, or a little under a quarter of all female members, appear in the marriage and baptism records before or after joining. Women members' lack of engagement with rituals supporting family life only increased with their rising numbers. Between 1786 and 1796, it becomes difficult to trace women in marriage and baptism records; and the proportion of women, black and white, for whom there is no record of marriage within the church—despite strictures against marrying nonbelievers—rose by more than ten points, from an already high 71 percent of female membership to 82 percent in these years.[96] Similarly, in Philadelphia between 1794 and 1801, the proportion of women for whom there is no record of marriage or childbirth rose from 74 percent to 83 percent.[97]

In short, the city societies reveal little in the way of active family formation before 1800. Infant baptism was relatively rarely administered, and marriages were infrequent. The familial status of members, whether as parents, husbands, wives, or widows, was also rarely if ever recorded by the stationed preachers.[98]

While the numbers of spinsters, widows, and divorcées were escalating in New England and the Middle Atlantic after the Revolution, the sheer proliferation of women in the Methodist city societies militates against assuming that female Methodists were part of a rising population of older single women.[99] Rather, another prototype emerges from the record: a teenage girl or young adult, likely between the ages of 16 and 24, still dependent on her natal household or working as a servant, not yet entered into marriage and the responsibilities of motherhood and household management, or bound to her life's employment.[100]

The vestiges of Philadelphia Methodist Elizabeth McKean's short life confirm this third trend. A young, as yet unmarried woman, sober, serious, and "cast down" by the responsibilities of attending her Methodist class—she "dare not stay away"—McKean relied on her female kin, especially her sisters, to carry her through her spiritual travails. "What reason I have to be thankful to God, who has answered prayer in behalf of my dear sisters?" McKean observed when two of her siblings also joined St. George's. "It gives me more joy than I can express!" Other women and men, even relations, outside this magic circle, were not quite trustworthy. "I pray that the Lord may protect me, until I return home, from the dangers of visiting," McKean exclaimed of the prospect of a social call to family members outside of town. So much better to be with her like-minded Methodist sisters, perhaps equally tested by their loyalty to their new religious faith.[101]

McKean's sentiments also open to view Methodism's reshaping of the family, as converted women came to rely upon like-minded female relations regarding the critical choice of religious affiliation. Similarly, married women's influence on their husbands in religious matters, as well as their often single state within the Methodist city societies, the fourth trend here, further illuminates Methodism's transformative impact on American family culture.

On first glance, the city churches appear to have sustained a healthy number of married couples. Both in New York in 1791 and in Philadelphia in 1796, for example, 43 percent of the members known to be married had joined in the company of their spouses. Some women in these congregations were to make the evangelically desirable match with a conference preacher.[102] With minor variations in these years, however, the proportion of husbands of Methodist women who did not join the church—including those already married to women members in 1791 and those who *were to* marry women from this year—was close to half.[103] By contrast, the proportion of men whose *wives* were not, or were not to be, communicants of the New York and Philadelphia societies in the sample years ranged from a low of 15 percent in Philadelphia in 1794 to only a little over a quarter (27 percent) in New York in 1796. In sum, a large majority of men at these urban congregations were married to women in the church, or had followed their wives into membership, whereas close to a majority of women were married to or were to marry men who never joined.[104]

Hence Methodist women were entering a unique social world, one in which female association predominated, separate from patriarchal family structures and community ties alike. The movement further encouraged such association by institutionalizing gendered worship. Like the Moravians and Quakers before them, the Methodist societies partitioned men and women into separate sections of their preaching houses, dispensing with family pews such as were common to Anglican and Congregational churches.[105] The MEC discipline did not require gender segregation in class meetings, but once a congregation reached a critical size, women and men, as well as whites and blacks, usually met separately in groups ranging from ten to more than thirty-five, and the preacher's class was almost always all female.[106] While exceptions to gender segregation did exist, other distinctions— of marriage, wealth, or free or slave status—seemed to matter less than the two basic divides within the church, whether one was black or white, and whether one was female or male. In this way, the Methodists sustained the Moravian experiment in gender segregation and provided their female members with a Protestant version of a Catholic sisterhood, at least while women were within the bounds of their chapels or class meetings.[107]

But Methodist women were also joining a missionary church, one that sought out all manner of converts. Thus they shared with Methodist men a remarkably heterogeneous social profile: the fifth major trend evident among the city societies' women. German, Dutch, French, and Swiss, as well as English, Scottish, Irish, and Welsh, surnames pepper the church registers. From the first preaching of Philip Embury in New York City, African American women especially had participated in revivals and attended worship at the city cottages and chapels, forming an important minority of the Methodist population thereafter.[108] In 1786, 16.5 percent of the female membership in New York was black, and in 1791, 23.5 percent. In Baltimore City, 184 black women members formed 34.8 percent of the women in the church in 1800. At the smaller societies as well, black women constituted substantial proportions of female membership: more than 14 percent in Philadelphia (not including Richard Allen's chapel) in 1794, and 25 percent at Fell's Point in 1801. Again, with the exceptions of Allen's congregation and the Fell's Point society, black women were more likely to be attracted to Methodism than were black men. By the 1790s, they not only helped to form the majorities of women in the New York and Baltimore congregations but accounted for significant proportions of the total membership: 15.5 percent in New York in 1791 and 13.6 percent in 1796; 20.9 percent in Baltimore City in 1800 and 19.9 percent in 1801.[109]

At the same time, women of significantly differing social class joined these congregations, sometimes briefly, sometimes for the rest of their lives. In New York, for example, wealthy members included merchants' wives Elizabeth Arcularius, Ann Disosway, and Mary Staples. Ann Jarvis, a descendant of John and Charles Wesley's sister and mother of the future painter John Wesley Jarvis, with her husband was a worshiper at the John Street Chapel before the couple moved to Philadelphia.[110] In Philadelphia, among prominant Methodist women were Hannah Baker, Catherine Comegys (Hannah's daughter), Margaret Doughty, and Ann Harvey; Martha Potts Haskins, the preacher Thomas Haskins's first wife, and, after Martha's death, Elizabeth Richards Haskins, the preacher's second wife, both products of wealthy ironfounding families; Zibiah Hewson, wife of English immigrant calico designer and manufacturer John Hewson; and Elizabeth Bennis, an Irish correspondent of Wesley's who emigrated to Philadelphia in the 1790s.[111] In Baltimore City, several wealthy women were drawn from the broad circle of female Methodist acolytes who were so critical to the success of the new movement: Prudence Gough, Rachel Hollingsworth, Deborah Owings, and Caroline Zolikofer.[112]

In keeping with Methodism's missionizing goals, just the same, many more of these urban women appear to have come from the ranks of America's middling and laboring classes. Philadelphia Quaker merchant Henry Drinker's wife, Elizabeth Drinker, found little to recommend in Methodism. "We must have but a poor opinion of the Methodists," she noted in her diary after reading the British anti-Methodist James Lackington's *Memoirs*, "if all he says relating to them is true." But Drinker's servant Sally Dawson happily attended a love feast at one of the Methodist chapels, away from her mistress's watchful eye.[113] The few Methodist women in any of the city societies whose occupational status can be identified—widows or single women—were white women laboring as grocers, seamstresses, and mantua-makers.[114] Other middling women, widows and spinsters, took in boarders—Methodist itinerants included—for income.[115] New York Methodist Mary Dando, an English immigrant from Asbury's home county of Gloucestershire, despite being unmarried adopted the honorific title "Mrs." and earned her keep by managing her nephew's household.[116]

In New York, finally, evidence of indigent members survives in a unique tabulation of poor relief distributed by the society to its members in the second half of the 1790s. Women appear throughout its pages. In 1795, fifty-two out of sixty-seven recipients of church aid—mainly allotments of cash or firewood—were women. Altogether, 14 percent of Methodist women in this year received aid at least once. The New York chapels continued to provide assistance to their neediest communicants thereafter.[117] Many of these poor Methodists, like Pallas Jackson, were servants and former slaves, unemployed or disabled by any of the ailments or misfortunes that so often befell laboring women. The church assisted "Blind Bette," probably also a slave, among numerous others in the winter of 1799–1800. Widows appear throughout the record.[118] Most recipients of the society's poor relief, however, were white, and many were of childbearing age. Betsy Dewint's child was baptized in 1801, some six years after her mother had been a resident of the poorhouse. In April 1795, cash was donated to ten children of poor women.[119] And if a member failed to survive a harsh winter, childbirth, accident, the yellow fever that swept through the city every several years, or the debilities of old age, the society paid for her burial.[120]

In sum, the Methodist city societies were complex social organisms, where a great variety of women and men, but especially women, found their place apart from the claims of family loyalty. They were also changeable organisms—a direct product of missionizing revivalism—as the ranks of long-standing married communicants with each new revival were swamped by new young and single recruits. Thus while many more women than men joined these urban chapels, equal proportions of women and men also fell away: to marriage, geographic mobility, and backsliding. For women especially, exclusion would result from their consorting too freely with the opposite sex, drinking too heavily, dressing too gaudily, and gossiping too loudly.[121] In New York in 1786, 41 percent of the women in the society and 39 percent of the men still belonged five years later. Over the longer ten-year period, from 1786 to 1796, just 23 percent of women and 22 percent of men remained.[122] In Philadelphia, in just two years, from 1794 to 1796, the society experienced a 50 percent turnover in white membership.[123]

Methodist adherence, in other words, was a demanding commitment, one that not all members could sustain, nor all members, tied down by marriage, children, and the cares of life, could afford. For women in particular, belonging to a Methodist society required a kind of single-mindedness that became increasingly less acceptable as young women moved into married adulthood. Thus falling short of Wesley's *General Rules*, or worse, Christ's forgiveness, was a risk to be ever vigilant of, and falling into ecstatic states provided a thrilling release from social decorum and entrance into Christian sisterhood: "Betsy Crooks fell down at prayer Meet[g] last Week," a Delaware woman reported of the excitement attending a Methodist class meeting in Dover, "and [she] was carried, at Midnight, from McNatts to her Mothers in an Arm'd Chair, follow'd by all the Class, shout[g] most vehemently all the way."[124] And converts could rely on their classmates for advice at the great turning points in their lives, not least of all the deciding matter of marriage, always a dangerous transition for the faithful. As Catherine Garrettson wrote to her classmate Catharine Rutsen, regarding "a Young Gentleman" proffering her friend "many worldly advantages," "We are enlisted under Christ's [B]anners, and have to war with the pomps and vanities of this life."[125]

The transition that few Methodist women made, however, was that which concluded the spiritual crises of their most devout male counterparts: recruitment to the local or traveling ministry. It may be persuasively argued, in fact, that in moving from households to religious societies, Methodist women simply exchanged one form of patriarchy for another: from obeying their fathers' dictates to those of the MEC preachers. In the absence of significant female participation in church governance, in fact, Methodism first showed signs of the domestic conservatism that was to accompany its future expansion.

GENDER, PUBLIC AUTHORITY, AND THE HOUSEHOLD

Despite the prevalence of female Methodist networks throughout the greater Middle Atlantic and the sheer numbers of women of all kinds in New York, Philadelphia, and Baltimore's Methodist churches, most women appear to have come to the movement in search of something other than explicitly public authority; or, if they did seek such power, they were soon disappointed.

Indeed, American Methodist women's exclusion from or reluctance to accept official capacities in the MEC is another of the movement's distinctive features, setting Methodism apart from the Moravians, who provided so many other models for Methodist experimentation, as well as the Quakers, similarly interested in confessional piety. Women like Barbara Heck, Mary Thorn, Mary Magdalen Tripolet, Prudence Gough, and Deborah Owings were notably active in early Methodism, but few of them spoke in public and none was permitted to join the Methodist preachers' conferences. After the Revolutionary War, Mary Wilmer remained the only female class leader in Philadelphia, and then only briefly.[126] At the larger New York churches, six white women (Mary Anderson, Sarah Day, Elizabeth Burnet, Sarah Riker, Catherine Warner, and Susan Lamplain) and one black woman (Jane Barsary) were class leaders in the 1780s and 1790s.[127] Yet, although Catherine Warner's weekly class was the largest in New York City in any given year between 1786 and 1796, she was the sole female leader by 1791. In 1793, Susan Lamplain was the only other female leader, and by 1795, no women were among the society's thirty-six leaders.[128] In Baltimore City in 1792, Asbury appointed three "sisters" as class leaders: Christina Keener, Rachel Owings, widow of the preacher Richard, and Martha Fonerden, wife of manufacturer

Adam Fonerden. By 1793, however, just one class in Baltimore City was headed by a woman. As of 1800, all thirty classes were run by men.[129]

Women traveling or preaching as exhorters appear occasionally in the Methodist narratives, and their significance should not be underestimated. In the 1770s, an unidentified female Methodist preached from house to house in New Jersey.[130] The first missionary in the area of Sudlersville, Maryland, after Strawbridge introduced Methodism to the Eastern Shore was said to have been one Mrs. Rogers, about whom little else is known except that she may have been blind. In the summer of 1792, Sarah Riker, shortly to be one of the church's regular recipients of poor relief, "Preach[d] with freedom" to the congregation at New York's Wesley Chapel. At another time, "Sister Mills" also preached.[131] Rachel Bruff in Maryland was credited as being a public speaker by Wesley's *Arminian Magazine*. Lorenzo Dow, the charismatic itinerant, was converted in the 1790s by one preacher's unofficial assistant named Abigail Leister.[132]

But American Methodist women's public presence was minimal compared with the numerous publicly active women in Britain, and their lack of authority within the structures of their own church did not go unobserved by interested outsiders. Anne Emlen, a Philadelphia Quaker attending a service at St. George's, criticized the congregation for preventing a young woman from preaching, "seeing Male & Female are declared to be one in Christ!" The stationed preacher countered that women were allowed to talk in private meetings (the classes), but their proper public role was a subject of controversy in the church.[133] Those attempting to defy the congregation probably ran into resistance such as Deborah Owings experienced when John Littlejohn censured her performance at a quarterly meeting near Baltimore. "S[r] Owings is impress[d] w[t] an Ideal that God has called her to preech," Littlejohn wrote. "[S]he did & made an attempt to address the people, and *failed*." He added, without irony, "[T]his cured her enthusiasm."[134] The Methodist itinerants, that is, responded to women's preaching ambitions in much the way the Anglican establishment had reacted to theirs.

Considered as a social problem, American Methodist women's lack of visible public stature in their societies—in fact the apparent diminishing of what little public authority they claimed as the movement matured—was the consequence of a number of related circumstances. Probably most important was the gendered character of the itinerancy. Although Methodist itinerants came from all social backgrounds, and by 1800 black local deacons were among their ranks, women were never considered potential conference members. As Francis Asbury and Thomas Coke wrote in their "Explanatory Notes" to the 1798 discipline, the class leaders "are the sinews of our society, and our revivals will ever, in a great measure, rise or fall with them." More tellingly the bishops continued, "[O]ur classes form the pillars of our work, and, as we have before observed, are in a considerable degree our universities for the ministry."[135] Thus as the class meeting became one route to professional mobility for Methodist men, class leadership became a more restrictively male office.

There is good reason to believe that exclusion from the itinerancy was not by women's choice, especially in light of the close association of conversion and missionizing among the Methodists. Deborah Owings was convinced that God would not bless her unless she preached.[136] During the time she was courted by Freeborn Garrettson, Catherine Livingston mourned her inability to contribute to the Methodist cause in the same way as her preacher fiancé. "What can I do, equal to the Service you are engaged in," she wrote to Garrettson in 1791. "What more noble employment, than bringing souls to Christ. . . . if you knew how painfully I feel my own insignificance you would pity me. No Doubt you have many cares that I know nothing of," she continued, "but have the consciousness that I have never felt, that of being useful."[137] After attending a Quaker meeting in Pennsylvania, preacher William Colbert reflected sympathetically on the "volotility of women" and how if "they were to cultivate the Art of speaking they would make great orators."[138] Few among Colbert's fellow itinerants appeared to agree.

The changing composition and size of many Methodist churches in the 1780s and 1790s was another reason for women's diminishing official authority in the churches. In short, the larger a Methodist society became, the more it emulated the power relations of the larger world and barred women from positions of power. A brief comparison of the evolution of the Baltimore City and the Fell's Point societies will illustrate this point.

The Baltimore Methodist churches, like all the city societies examined here, originated as gatherings in private households before moving to larger rented spaces. Construction on the first chapel, in Strawberry Alley on Fell's Point—Baltimore's maritime district on the eastern side of the Patapsco Basin—was begun in 1774. Another chapel, in Lovely Lane in Baltimore Town on the northwest side of the basin, opened in the same year. Among their wealthy male supporters, both groups initially attracted merchant entrepreneurs as trustees. By the time the Christmas Conference was convened at Lovely Lane in 1784, a larger city chapel was already under construction at the corner of Light Street and Wine Alley in Baltimore Town. Opening in 1786, the church burned ten years later, along with the Methodist (Baltimore) Academy, but the chapel reopened in 1797 with the aid of another group of merchant-trustees. In the meanwhile, another chapel had opened on Green (later Exeter) Street in Old Town in 1789, and a number of black members were meeting on Fish and on Sharp Streets.[139]

By 1799, the character of the two Methodist societies—the congregation on Fell's Point; and the Baltimore City society, encompassing the members of the Light Street and Green Street Chapels along with the two African meetings—was markedly different. The bulk of Baltimore Methodists, including wealthy patrons like the Hollingsworths, Prudence Gough, Caroline Zolikofer, and the Chalmers family of merchants and preachers, worshiped at the Baltimore Town and Old City chapels. The society was sustained by an impressive array of deacons, local preachers, class leaders, and exhorters.[140] A significant black membership—more than a third of the communicants between 1799 and 1801—also belonged to these two chapels and the two black congregations, probably many of them the servants or slaves of the city's middling and wealthy inhabitants.[141]

Over the same years, Fell's Point sustained a significantly smaller Methodist congregation. Here the phrases "from country" and "from Town" or "removed" and "moved away" follow many members' names in the registers, marking the comings and goings of a poorer, geographically mobile population. By 1800, among the trustees, Jesse Hollingsworth and Philip Rogers had resigned, another had moved, and three more had died. Only Job Smith, resident in Shakespeare's Alley, and Isaac Sutton in Philpot Street remained in office.[142] No merchants were members by 1800; instead, most of the society's men were mariners or worked in marine-related crafts. Among the women, as many as six may have been self-employed widows.[143] While a smaller percentage of the Fell's Point congregation were black than was the case at the Baltimore City Society, by 1800 the numbers of black men and women were virtually equal, and many fewer of them appear to have been slaves. Instead they formed part of the population of free black laborers setting up households in the poorer section of the city.[144]

The place of women among the Baltimore Methodists reflected their larger surroundings. In Baltimore City, after 1799, black men were appointed as exhorters, but no women of either race held any of the fifty-five offices by 1801.[145] By contrast, the women at Fell's Point, in a pattern unique among the Methodist societies in any of the cities examined here, took on public roles approximately commensurate with their numbers. Three of the six class leaders in 1800—Elizabeth Shaffer, Margaret Smith, and Martha Timms—were women, as were five of eight leaders the following year: Shaffer, Smith, Timms, Ruth Reese, and Margaret Sampson. The female-led classes were substantially populated. Elizabeth Shaffer's group in 1800 was the largest, with thirty-three names on the rolls, ten more than in the preacher's class. It is likely, furthermore, that four black members—Hannah Montgomery, Jane Waller, William Ellis, and John Hoy—whose names appear at the top of their class lists were also class leaders.[146]

Regrettably little is known about the Fell's Point women. They receive no mention in Asbury's journal beside the numerous wealthier female Methodists who were his patrons. It is likely that they were married to men in the church: Elizabeth Shaffer to Frederick, a brushmaker in Gough Street; Margaret Smith to Job, the trustee, a joiner by trade; and Margaret Sampson to Joseph, a rigger in Alisanna Street.[147] Ruth Reese was perhaps the only single woman or widow holding the office of class leader, indicating the unusual importance of married women to the chapel.

Altogether, the contrasting development of the Baltimore City and Fell's Point societies reveals that the larger and more prestigious a Methodist congregation became, the less likely were women to have a public voice within it. Societies that remained relatively small or poor, on the other hand, similar to the original cottage or household meetings in which Methodism first thrived, continued to feature women prominently.[148]

The movement's unspoken reliance on women in their households also helps to explain Methodist women's relative silence regarding their roles in the church, particularly what collectively may be called their declining public presence. Overtly excluded from preaching, Methodist women turned to the one arena in which they had undisputed moral authority: the household itself. In so doing, they worked within the long-standing framework of the movement. In the "home,"

Methodist women were able to remain engaged, like their male counterparts, in Methodism's missionary zeal while at the same time adhering to the Wesleyan credo that the most important setting for the propagation of "heart-religion" was right where they already were.

Concentration on the domestic sphere, however, and magnification of its relevance to women, also consigned the largest segment of the Methodist population to an increasingly private sphere, removed from the public domain of America's fastest-growing religious movement. It was precisely into this latter arena that the other Methodist outsiders, "African" converts, especially black men, sought to make their way in the years after the Revolutionary War.

CHAPTER FIVE

The African Methodists

OF THE GOALS of the SPG, former employers of the Wesleys and George Whitefield and inspiration for the upsurge of British and colonial missionizing before the Revolution, perhaps none was as potentially visionary as the conversion of the African population of British America. Facing opposition from many slaveholders and hampered by the drawbacks of their own formal catechizing, the SPG failed to bring substantial numbers of Africans into the church in most parts of the colonies. Instead, in the twenty years following the Revolutionary War, Methodist preachers attracted more free blacks and slaves into their religious societies than had the SPG in the previous seventy-five. As early as 1790, 11,682 blacks were tallied as members of the Methodist Episcopal Church, or one-fifth (20.3 percent) of a total membership of 57,600. By 1800, 13,449, or 21 percent of 64,000 members, were black. Many more, perhaps several thousands of slaves, attended churches or preaching without formally joining a Methodist class meeting.[1]

The relationships among the itinerants, black Methodists, and white Methodists were necessarily fraught with difficulty, reflecting race relations within the larger republic. Blacks frequently encountered Methodism within the households of their masters and mistresses. But more often than not they were set apart. Itinerants matter-of-factly formed distinct black classes on their circuits. Even in the city societies, where many fewer black members were likely to have been the bondsmen and -women of fellow white communicants, class meetings were segregated by race.

These social and institutional partitions imply strong cultural divisions between blacks and whites as well. As Donald Mathews writes of evangelicals in the post-Revolutionary South: "Blacks experienced the century before Emancipation much differently [from whites]. . . . For the last one hundred years of legal slavery, all events which whites saw as sequential were experienced by blacks as persistently contemporaneous, as if history were an objective drama of subjective perception and meaning." This drama was realized in an ideological context of Bible narratives and prophecies that slaves applied to their confined existence, frequently as a form of covert opposition to white culture.[2]

The black Methodists of the greater Middle Atlantic, from New York to northern Maryland, however, represented a distinct segment within the slave and free population of the United States. Their religious experience coincided with the beginnings of the halting transition from slavery to freedom. Newly freed slaves moved through the region with unprecedented geographical mobility, flooding into the port towns and developing an inchoate race consciousness. In the MEC, these slaves and former slaves discovered a church that publicly espoused the elimination of slaveholding among its members and a vanguard of preachers determined to carry these measures into effect—a denominational distinction the Methodists shared with just Quakers, Congregationalists, and select groups of Baptists and Presbyterians.

The Methodist Church all too quickly jettisoned its antislavery militancy. But black followers applied the religious message of liberation to their own condition. Like Methodist women, a significant minority of whom were also black, African Americans played instrumental roles in early Methodism. And in the Middle Atlantic city societies, black Methodists pressed for greater public authority—including the raising up of their own body of preachers—than did most Methodist women.

By the end of the century, blacks not only represented a fully engaged portion of the Methodist movement but had initiated a viable African Methodist alternative within the movement, one that would serve as a spiritual wellspring for African Americans for generations to come.

THE FIRST EMANCIPATION AND METHODIST ANTISLAVERY

Methodism boomed among the Middle Atlantic black population, slave and free, at a significant moment of transition in American slavery, one that promised far greater change for Middle Atlantic and many southern slaves than the years leading up to the Revolution. In 1780, antislavery activists brought forth their first legislative success with the passage of Pennsylvania's Act for the Gradual Abolition of Slavery, legislation that would ultimately serve as a model for other northern states. Modest progress was also made in the lower Middle Atlantic and the South. In 1782 the manumission of adult slaves under the age of forty-five was legalized in Virginia, and in 1784 manumission of slaves by individual will as well as by deed (as formerly permitted) was agreed to by the Maryland legislature. In Delaware, the requirement that manumitters post an indemnity bond of £60 per emancipated slave was eliminated for adult blacks in 1787, and the sale of slaves out of state was severely curtailed. By 1805, with the exception of North Carolina, manumission was legal throughout the South, although the greatest numbers of manumissions continued to occur in Virginia, Maryland, and Delaware.[3]

Despite unprecedented state action against slaveholders' property rights, the First Emancipation, as the Revolutionary-era experiment with liberation of slaves has come to be called, had significant drawbacks. The new emancipation laws in the North, including Pennsylvania's, liberated the children of slaves only. Gradualist legislation, furthermore, consistently protected slaveholders against the immediate loss of their bondspeople's labor by replacing slavery with a form of indentured servitude. Under this new system individual blacks were often bound until well into their twenties. Although manumissions continued apace in the other northern states, New York did not pass a gradual emancipation law until 1799, nearly twenty years after Pennsylvania, and the banning of slavery in the state did not occur until 1827. New Jersey's gradual emancipation was finally legislated in 1804, nearly twenty-five years after Pennsylvania's.[4]

In both Maryland and Virginia, furthermore, legal incentives for manumission were offset by legislation holding whites who assisted blacks in freedom suits liable for court costs.[5] In some parts of Maryland, the absolute numbers of slaves actually rose, as in the case of Baltimore City, where, despite an increasing percentage of free people, the numbers of slaves quadrupled in the years 1790–1810.[6] In Monmouth County, New Jersey, hundreds of blacks remained in bondage into the nineteenth century. Shane White has estimated that in New York City, 43.2 percent of the black population was still enslaved in 1800.[7]

The slow progress of the First Emancipation nonetheless reflected profound changes in the culture of racial and social dominance that had perpetuated slavery through the colonial era. The contradiction between the rhetoric of natural rights that infused Revolutionary-era discourse and the practice of holding black men, women, and children in captive bondage was patently obvious to, if not publicly acknowledged by, large numbers of Americans. At the same time, older religious proscriptions against the commerce in bond servants slowly but inexorably drove Quakers, then Congregationalists and individual Baptist and Presbyterian churches out of the business of slave trading and eventually the use of slave labor altogether. By the last quarter of the eighteenth century, an "antislavery international" of Quaker and evangelical Anglican reformers had united to challenge prevailing European perceptions of Africans as an inferior people.[8]

The Methodist position on slavery was forged in this transatlantic drama. In early 1772, when John Wesley discovered Anthony Benezet's work on slavery, he immediately placed it in the context of Christian history, exclaiming that he had read of "nothing like it in the heathen world, whether ancient or modern." In 1774, as the imperial crisis deepened, he published his own antislavery salvo, *Thoughts Upon Slavery*, reprinted in Philadelphia in the same year.[9] Thomas Rankin, Wesley's first superintendent for the American work, arrived in Philadelphia in 1773 just as a wave of antislavery tracts was released by the presses, and he promptly befriended several Philadelphia abolitionists.[10] In 1780, his successor, Francis Asbury—perhaps aware of the debate over gradual emancipation then ongoing in the Pennsylvania legislature—led the preachers at the Baltimore conference to issue their first condemnation of slavery. "[S]lavery," the annual minutes announced to Methodist members, "is contrary to the laws of God, man, and nature, and hurtful to society, contrary to the dictates of conscience and pure religion, and doing that which we would not others do to us and ours." More important, as an example to their followers, the preachers agreed to free their own slaves.[11] Wesley's appointment of Thomas Coke as American superintendent in 1784 furthered the antislavery cause among the preachers. Coke's plans for evangelizing the "heathen" population of the West Indies coincided with his first trip to America. He likely drafted, although the American preachers likely pushed for, the antislavery plank that graced the MEC's first discipline in 1785. The section condemning slavery was resounding. The MEC pronounced the institution as "contrary to the Golden Law of God . . . and the unalienable Rights of Mankind, as well as every Principle of the Revolution to hold in the deepest Debasement, in a more abject Slavery than is perhaps to be found in any Part of the World except America, so many Souls that are capable of the Image of God."[12]

In many respects, the MEC's new rules on slavery correlated significantly with the church's position on women within the unconverted—"heathen"—family. In both cases, the Methodist movement initially undermined conventional family authority. In the greater Middle Atlantic in particular, slavery and servitude had long been features of the household economy, with individual slaves and servants working on white farms and in white workshops and residing in or near white family dwellings, their actions directly controlled by the restraining force of the household master or mistress as well as provincial and, subsequently, state laws. Even on the larger plantations in the Chesapeake (including Maryland) Tidewater—where Allan Kulikoff has estimated that 75 percent of slaves lived in autonomous slave quarters and within networks of slave families on large farms—the livelihood and security of bondsmen, women, and children were dependent on their master's life span and the largesse of his heirs.[13] The Methodists' relatively sudden assault on slaveholding within their ranks, like the so-called Methodist seduction of women, had the potential to alter dramatically the character of family culture and the structure of households, not only in the greater Middle Atlantic but throughout the South and the rising western territories as well.

The truly radical implications of the 1785 discipline's section on slavery, however, and the one that ultimately consigned it to failure, lay in the Methodist preachers' efforts to regulate their members' "property." In no other area did the itinerants attempt to exercise direct control over what many American Whigs, especially southern patriots, considered another natural right. The preachers' often bold tactics to bring an end to slaveholding among their coreligionists were not lost on many southern Methodists, inevitably less susceptible to the claims of the antislavery international than their Middle Atlantic brothers and sisters. While Methodist women were able to mitigate the responses of their fathers, husbands, and brothers to their newfound faith through the exercise of female moral authority, slaves, male or female, only occasionally enjoyed equivalent leverage. And while American households provided the Methodists with the most common setting for recruitment of both women and blacks to the movement, this milieu provided few material advantages for slaves and servants seeking to attract the attention of Methodist preachers.

The church's bold assault on slavery was quickly pushed back. In early 1785, when the two superintendents circulated a lengthy petition in Virginia, calling for the abolition of slavery by the state legislature, slaveholders outside the church circulated counterpetitions reminding their fellow Virginians of the Methodists' dubious war record and claiming that these "Tools of the British Administration" were attempting to deprive slaveholders of one of their jealously guarded rights. Within six months, the discipline's section on slavery had been suspended and the regulation of slaveholding left to the local quarterly meetings and regional annual conferences.[14] But a decade later, in 1796, the general conference revisited the subject of what they called the "crying evil of African slavery." While still leaving the quarterly and annual conferences to judge whether or not slaveholders could remain members, the conference recommended that the MEC's "lay officials"—local preachers and class leaders—be required to emancipate their slaves either immediately or gradually, banned the selling of slaves by members, and specified that manumissions were to be executed for all newly purchased slaves.[15]

In 1800, several members of the general conference took more resolute steps to eliminate slaveholding from among their followers. Nicholas Snethen moved that "this General Conference resolve, that from this time forth no slaveholder shall be admitted into the Methodist Episcopal Church." Two other motions—to emancipate all children born after 4 July 1800 to slaves owned by Methodists, and to require that "every member of the Methodist Episcopal Church, holding slaves . . . within a term of one year . . . give an instrument of emancipation for all his slaves"—were introduced. All three, one after the other, failed to pass.[16] Instead, the conference issued an address, once again exclaiming that slavery was "repugnant to the unalienable rights of mankind, and to the very essence of civil liberty, but more especially to the spirit of the Christian religion." The general conference called for the initiation of an elaborate process by which the preachers' connection might "give a blow at the root to the enormous evil" by sponsoring petitions that favored gradual emancipation for distribution in states where no such laws existed. These were to be drawn up by committees formed "out of the most respectable of our Friends for the conducting of the business" and the process to be carried on yearly " 'till the desired end be fully accomplished."[17]

The church's antislavery address was received unenthusiastically. By 1804, the general conference, headed by a now more pragmatic Asbury and reflecting the increasingly pessimistic mood of abolitionists and antislavery reformers in the wake of Gabriel's Rebellion, an uprising of slaves in Virginia in 1800, withdrew the call to petition state legislatures. While itinerants were still expected to free slaves in conformity with the laws of their states, the MEC discipline permitted slave sales under certain circumstances and admonished slaves to "render due respect and obedience to the commands and interests of their . . . masters." As Donald Mathews writes, "The Conference's most telling decision . . . was to suspend the whole Section on Slavery south of Virginia." For the first time, the MEC published two disciplines, one for Virginia and the northern states that included the section on slavery, and one for the southern states that excluded it.[18]

It would be a mistake, however, to equate the rules passed by the preachers' conferences with the totality of the Methodist experience with antislavery. While Coke and Asbury revealed themselves early on to be ameliorationist—morally opposed to slavery but willing to accommodate proslavery forces for the sake of the missionary goals of the movement—rather than abolitionist, other important American itinerants were ardent emancipationists in the decades following the war, determined, that is, to free as many slaves as possible even if unable to change state laws.

Freeborn Garrettson was among the best known of these activists. Garrettson's decision to free his slaves came at the peak of his conversion experience and was closely tied to his visionary propensities. As he wrote in his manuscript journal—

Figure 7. *Freeborn Garrettson.* Garrettson Family Papers, Drew University Library. Reprinted with permission of the Methodist Collection, Drew University Library, Madison, New Jersey.

his description of the apparition was omitted from the published version—Garrettson was standing before his assembled family, preparing to sing from his psalmbook, when he felt "as if some person stood by me" who said, "[I]t is not the will of the Lord that you should keep your fellow creatures in bondage." Astonished by this apparent manifestation of the Divine, Garrettson "paused about a minute, afraid to go in worship, for the person appeared to be waiting for an answer."[19] The preacher at last responded as if by necessity, "Lord, the oppressed shall go free," and announced to his bondspeople that "they did not belong to me, and that I did not desire their services without making them a compensation." As he proceeded with psalm singing, Garrettson's "dejection and that melancholy gloom, which preyed upon me" vanished, and "a divine sweetness ran through my whole frame."[20]

Garrettson claimed that until this moment he had never had any doubts about slavery. "[T]ill then," he wrote, "I had never suspected that the practice of slave-keeping was wrong; I had not read a book on the subject, nor been told so by any." But news of his decision to abandon mastership of his bondspeople passed quickly through the neighborhood, as did his rising reputation for emancipationist preaching.[21]

The equally unanticipated impact of Wesleyan conversion on other Maryland slaveholders is evident in the changed "hearts" of Philip Gatch, Joseph Everett, and Thomas Haskins, all known to have rejected slaveholding before or during their itinerancy.[22] While stationed in Annapolis over the winter of 1790–1791, Ezekiel Cooper went further by publishing a series of pseudonymous letters in the *Maryland Gazette* and *Maryland Journal and Baltimore Advertiser* condemning all manner of slaveholding as contrary to the lessons of the Revolution. "Is not LIBERTY the grand American shrine?" Cooper demanded of his Maryland audience. Several correspondents retorted that the British had forcibly imported slavery to the continent, freeing the slaves would leave the daughters of southern families without inheritances, and the "mildness of the Christian religion" would prevent the worst abuses. An especially hostile rebuke, in verse form, labeled Cooper "The monarch of the blacks." Cooper retaliated: "I hope to see the repeal of all laws which empower tyrants to treat human creatures like horses or dogs." It was melancholy to see "enlightened citizens" influenced by "*groundless, absurd prejudices*."[23] The year before, James O'Kelly, Virginia Methodist and radical republican, also published an impassioned attack on slavery. "The primitive Christians," O'Kelly argued, referring back to Methodism's original inspiration, "did not support their ministers upon the hire of slaves procured for that purpose." His fellow laborers in other denominations should "no longer support the gracious general gospel by the sweat and blood of the objects of GOD's mercy and subjects of gospel-grace!"[24]

Maryland itinerant William Colbert's running commentary on slavery in his journal reveals how a number of itinerants responded to many of their fellow Methodists' attachment to the institution. On separate occasions in Maryland, Colbert rejected a society member for putting irons on her servants and chastised slaveholders "on the impropriety of holding their fellow creatures in Bondage." When a master near Gunpowder Falls north of Baltimore balked at Colbert's restrictions on the treatment of slaves, claiming that "God Almighty gave them [his slaves] to him, and he intended to keep them," Colbert replied that "God Almighty never gave them to him." Later the same day, Colbert again met with resistance to his emancipationism at a class meeting. Transferred to the Milford circuit in Delaware—crossroads for a thriving illegal trade in kidnapped servants and slaves—Colbert remained undaunted. "I felt it my duty," he wrote, "to bear my testamony against the horrid practice of dealing in human flesh and blood— buying—selling, and stealing the poor negroes."[25]

Over these years, Colbert developed an increasingly radical perspective on race relations, one that stressed the interchangeability of white and black believers and the economic underpinnings of the slave system. "O that I may meet them in glory, both black and white," he exclaimed after participation in a revival meeting in the early 1790s, "for the Lord has many precious in this part of the world that are clothed with black bodies." Criticized by white members near Milford,

Delaware, for addressing black adherents as *"brethren"* and *"sisters,"* Colbert wondered "[w]hat objection can be brought to speaking to them in this manner, seeing that, God has made of one blood all nations of men, for to dwell on all the face of the earth." Traveling in Somerset County, Virginia, he was dismayed by the ostentation of the local women, whose gay apparel "no doubt is at the expense of the labour and sweat of the poor black people." When a trader in Maryland casually offered him a slave for purchase, Colbert shot back "that I look'd upon [slave traders] to be the grandest set of vilians on this side of hell." On meeting another trader not more than a mile further on, Colbert declared that "if he did not repent for what he was doing he would be damned as sure as the devil was damn'd." Shortly thereafter he performed "the painful task" of expelling one of his hosts from a Methodist society for selling a black servant into lifetime servitude.[26]

These preachers and others like them had a significant impact on slaveholding and trading within the movement. The Methodist manumission record in the lower Middle Atlantic—the numbers of members who willingly set limited terms of service for their slaves—is impressive. In a study of Talbot County on the Eastern Shore, Kenneth Carroll attributes as many as 441 manumissions in the years 1783 to 1790, and 306 more from 1791 to 1799, to Methodists acting on a combination of evangelical and Revolutionary fervor. Thomas Airey, the Dorchester County planter, for just one example, freed thirty slaves in 1790, stating that he believed that "freedom and liberty is the unalienable right and privilege of every person," and slaveholding "is repugnant to the pure precepts of the gospel of Jesus Christ. . . ."[27] Prompted by the actions of preachers like Woolman Hickson— whose emancipationist strategy consisted of appealing "by the moste earnest (personal) application" to slaveholders' consciences and then immediately distributing blank manumission forms to the same audience—rank-and-file Methodists in and around Baltimore City were also moving toward free-labor households, with as many as 220 slaves emancipated by Hickson's efforts alone.[28] By 1776, Jesse Hollingsworth's Baltimore City household already included just one slave out of fifteen servants. Hollingsworth's Quaker background may account for this unusual balance, but Anglican planter-merchant Harry Dorsey Gough, "[c]onvinced of the injustice of detaining my fellow Creatures, in Slavery and Bondage," manumitted forty-five of his slaves at Perry Hall outside the city in April 1780. Likewise, at the time of his death in 1786, Richard Moale, a Baltimore Methodist merchant, promised immediate emancipation to six of his black servants and gradual emancipation to one other.[29] After 1796, the Baltimore and Harford Quarterly Meetings actively set the length of the terms of service for members' slaves and excluded or disciplined members who sold or otherwise abused slaves. Other circuits for which records have not survived likely did the same.[30]

Strong evidence of the Methodist commitment to antislavery, finally, was the participation of prominent Wesleyans on the boards of the various abolition societies organized after the war. Among the founding members of the Pennsylvania Abolition Society were three early members of St. George's—Jacob Baker, Lambert Wilmer, and Thomas Armat. Wilmer served on the PAS's militant Acting

Committee. Two more Methodists, Burton Wallace and Duncan Stewart, were elected to the PAS in 1786.[31] In Delaware, state senator Richard Bassett, patron of Francis Asbury, freed his own bondspeople and then successfully introduced bills into the Delaware assembly outlawing the sale of slaves to the Carolinas, Georgia, and the West Indies and eliminating the £60 bond previously required on manumitted slaves between the ages of eighteen and thirty-five. In 1788, he and Quaker Warner Mifflin founded the Delaware Society for Promoting the Abolition of Slavery in Dover. By the late 1790s, Bassett and several other Methodists were part of the large minority of Delaware legislators who supported, ultimately unsuccessfully, a gradual emancipation law in that state.[32]

In 1803, Allen McLane, another Methodist and Revolutionary War hero, was elected president of the Delaware Society for the Gradual Abolition of Slavery in Wilmington. Six years later, the short-lived Sussex County Abolition Society was headed by Methodist supporter Caleb Rodney from Lewes, with Methodists Daniel Hudson and William Russell serving as the group's first secretary and treasurer.[33] The substantial if brief-lived Maryland Abolition Society, established in Baltimore in 1789, also included several Methodists in prominent offices: Philip Rogers, a Baltimore merchant, was its first president; Adam Fonerden and William Hawkins served on the Election Committee; and James McCannon was a member of the Acting Committee. Fonerden and Jesse Hollingsworth were also among the participants at the first Convention of American Anti-Slavery Societies, held in Philadelphia in January 1794.[34]

Reiterating the faith in enlightened progress these evangelicals shared with so many other antislavery activists of their generation, William Watters could look back on the early years of the Methodist experience with slavery and observe that his eldest brother had not freed his slaves when he died in 1774 because this was before there was "talk amongst us about the impropriety of holding our fellow creatures in bondage." Watters added, "I believe it was entirely owing to the prejudice of education and the want of not weighing the matter thoroughly."[35] His brother, that is, had not lived long enough to partake in the battle against slavery, a struggle also left largely untouched by the patriots.

Nonetheless, in the matter of antislavery as in many other areas, the Methodist experience was as varied as the people they tried to convert. Many Baltimore County Methodists continued to purchase black servants in the 1790s and beyond, and the slaves of Methodists frequently worked ten years and more before arriving at the promised date of manumission. Harry Dorsey Gough, so generous in the First Emancipation's wave of religious and natural rights enthusiasm, once again owned fifty-one enslaved laborers when he died in 1808.[36] And more troubling still was the inability of many Methodists to escape the economic laws that kept slavery in place. Hence when Richard Owings, poor cousin of the Owings Mills family and one of the first American-born itinerants, drew up his will in 1786, he directed that his two bondspeople, Will and Esther, were to be "set free" upon his wife's death. But Owings's widow was forced to sell Will to pay off her husband's debts, accrued during his years of traveling for the Methodists. The decision appears to have been purely economic: Will's value represented 38 percent of the estate sale.[37]

Hence for the thousands of black people attending revivals, Methodist class meetings, and chapel services in the last quarter of the eighteenth century, the emancipationist message of the Methodist movement was ambiguous at best. But there is no doubt that the Methodist evangelization of the black population in the greater Middle Atlantic, slave and free, was a stunning success.

BLACK METHODISTS AND SOCIAL EXPERIENCE

African Americans came to the movement that would so significantly shape their destinies in numerous ways. Depending on their status as slaves or free people, whether they lived and labored in rural or urban settings, and the nature of the religious meetings, black Methodists probably had more varied social experiences within Methodism than any other demographic group.

African American slaves and free people formed a substantial part of Methodist gatherings from the start. The first specific estimate of black Methodist membership was made by Thomas Rankin in 1774 when he reported back to England that five hundred blacks belonged to the Methodist societies, or 25 percent of the total tally. Since Rankin's figure did not include slaves, the total proportion of African Americans attracted to Methodism was undoubtedly higher, perhaps close to 30 percent.[38] Black audiences were a regular feature of early Methodist revivals. In the early 1770s, both Pilmore and Asbury met with separate black classes in New York City and in Baltimore. Thomas Rankin and George Shadford were both impressed by the responsiveness of black listeners to love feasts and revival meetings in Maryland.[39] By the 1780s, black classes were meeting throughout the greater Middle Atlantic, from New York to Delaware and Maryland. In the mid-1780s, Robert Ayres met with a black class at night "amongst y^e. poor Slaves" on the Dorchester circuit on the Eastern Shore as well as similar groups in Delaware, including a black society near Lewes comprising nearly fifty participants.[40] William Colbert, traveling on the Calvert, Maryland, circuit in 1790, regularly met with individual blacks, black groups, and mixed black and white assemblies. Around 1800, Henry Boehm ministered to a class of twenty-seven slaves, mainly men, in Cambridge, Maryland. Some circuits were almost exclusively black populated, as in the Annapolis Methodist society in the early 1790s, where African Americans outnumbered whites two to one, and in the Georgetown, Maryland, society, where their numbers predominated by the early nineteenth century.[41]

In 1786 when the Methodist Church began to tally its membership by race, 1,890 blacks, presumably both free and slave, were counted as formal members of the Methodist United Societies, 9.9 percent of the full membership, with the highest concentration of black members—from 100 to 300 each—on the Baltimore, Caroline, Calvert, and Talbot circuits in Maryland and on the Dover circuit in Delaware. The numbers and proportions of black members rose quickly thereafter to a full fifth of the church by 1790. By the end of the century, while the bulk of close to 13,500 black Methodists continued to be concentrated in Delaware, Maryland, and points further south, black members might be found on virtually every one of the MEC's circuits, with the exceptions of New England and upstate New York.[42]

In fact, these figures are too modest, as numerous blacks who attended Methodist revivals before and after the Revolutionary War were prohibited by recalcitrant masters from joining Methodist societies or forming their own classes. At the start of his ministry in New York, Joseph Pilmore received a petition from a slave woman who, despite her mistress's resistance, was determined to attend services at the John Street Chapel, thinking it better to be "beaten for hearing the word of GoD here, than to burn in Hell to all eternity." In 1771, another "poor Negro Slave" sent word to Joseph Pilmore that "I wanted much to come to the church at the Watch-night, but could not get leave."[43] Similarly, on the Calvert circuit in Maryland at the war's end, the itinerant Nelson Reed was approached by a number of black people "desiring I would advise how to serve God & save their souls, telling me that their masters never suffer'd them to go to hear preaching." In the 1790s, in Prince Georges County, Maryland, slaveholders were still attempting, unsuccessfully by this time, to restrict their slaves' attendance at Methodist meetings.[44]

The fast-rising black population among greater Middle Atlantic Methodists may be attributed to a number of causes. But among the most important factors were the household proselytizing of Methodist itinerants, cultural syncretism, and the transitional state of slavery in the region.

The household imperative of Methodism served the region's black population exceedingly well. From the start of the movement, itinerants came into regular contact with servants and slaves in their masters' and mistresses' kitchens, and some of the earliest Methodist classes—in New York and then later throughout the region—were composed of white families and their servants.[45] At the large farms and plantations where the African American population was concentrated, household meetings drew in large numbers of black listeners, and the itinerants probably had their greatest impact on the manumission of slaves. At plantations like the Gough estate at Perry Hall, Methodist preachers had contact with many more black listeners at one time than on almost any other occasion, and it was frequently in this setting that itinerants drew their conclusions regarding the intensity of black spirituality. Here conversions involving both white householders and their servants acquired intercultural significance as the revival ritual leveled barriers between whites and blacks and each group's response to Wesleyan preaching served as a model for the other, adding a potent ingredient to that mainstay of Methodist narratives: the wholesale household conversion.[46]

At the same time, there was a distinct limit to the largesse of the revival. At household meetings and in Methodist classes and chapel meetings alike, the races were quickly segregated as soon as black participation reached what whites perceived to be a critical mass. Henry Boehm recollected that it was a commonplace that "[w]e not only had separate classes for the colored people, but separate lovefeasts; they were generally held in the morning previous to the love-feasts for the whites."[47] Larger crowds of black listeners were relegated to secondary status on the itinerants' visits to farms and plantations, waiting out-of-doors and in out-buildings for the preachers to attend their meetings. At one gathering in Delaware in the 1780s, servants listened from the kitchen while Benjamin Abbott and another itinerant conducted family worship in a different part of the house. At an outdoor meeting on the Calvert circuit in 1790, William Colbert struggled to be heard over a partition separating the two races. The Methodist chapel in Annapolis, from the time it was built in about 1788, required blacks to enter the gallery by a separate stairway.[48]

To a remarkable extent, the affinity of free black people and slaves for evangelicalism in general and Methodism in particular overcame these obstacles. Scholars have long proposed a variety of reasons why. Among the most persuasive is the striking resemblance between features of evangelicalism and African, particularly West African, religious culture. While the nature of the survival and geographical dispersal of African cultural forms in North America continue to be a subject of controversy, there is little doubt that a distinctive African American culture developed rapidly in the colonies, deriving from the enormous variety of West African cultural, social, and religious practices brought to America by slaves and from the conditions of slavery itself.[49] Often just a generation removed from their West African homelands, many North American blacks were familiar with pre-modern magical rituals—divining, healing, casting of spells—and ecstatic behavior. Wherever they had access to Christian teachings and ritual, beginning with the Anglicans, and then through Baptists, Moravians, Quakers, and Methodists, American slaves mixed biblical, African, and European folk elements into distinctly American religious forms.[50]

Black Christians were not all alike, however, with the level of syncretism between Christianity and African religion varying according to the density of the slave population and temporal distance from African origins.[51] Within Methodism as well, black Methodists constituted one part of the religious spectrum and Middle Atlantic black Methodists yet another, based on the changing social circumstances of the population. While slavery remained a fact of life for most black people in many of the Methodists' major areas of evangelization, particularly the South and the new Southwest Territory, in some areas it was being eroded very quickly, in others more slowly, as a result of manumissions and mandated gradual emancipation—a transition that was particularly important where the system of slavery was most pervasive.[52] Thus while large numbers of blacks remained in bondage in Maryland, New Jersey, and New York, in Maryland the free black population also more than doubled in the decade from 1790 to 1800, rising to nearly 20,000 at the end of the century and close to 30,000 in 1810, or approximately 23 percent of the black population in the state. After Pennsylvania, the process was most rapid in Delaware. In 1790, freemen, women, and children formed 30.5 percent of the state's black population; by 1810, the proportion had risen to an extraordinary 75.9 percent.[53]

In the 1780s and 1790s, newly liberated free people crowded into the Middle Atlantic port cities, escaping the confines of rural society and seeking to establish livelihoods. Between 1790 and 1810, while Baltimore's slave population increased substantially, brought in by the city's newly prosperous white inhabitants, the city's free black population also rose from 323 to 5,671.[54] In Philadelphia, nearly 70 percent of the 800 black people living in the city in 1780 were bondspeople; twenty years later, just 55 individuals out of 6,000 (less than 1 percent) were still slaves.[55] Even in New York, where two-thirds of the 3,000 blacks living in the city in 1790 were still enslaved, and nearly half continued in this status in 1800, by 1810 the proportion of slaves in a much greater black population of 8,900 had fallen to 16.2 percent.[56]

The changes in the social profile of African American membership in the New York Methodist society between 1786 and 1796 and in the Baltimore societies between 1799 and 1801 reflect the speed and social complexity of this transition.

In New York, blacks formed a significant minority of the Methodist society in the years after the Revolutionary War. In 1786, the first year for which full records survive, blacks represented 14.8 percent of the New York membership. By 1791, this proportion had risen to 19.8 percent, or close to a fifth of the New York Methodist population. By 1796, despite an incoming wave of new members, blacks still constituted 17.7 percent of the society, that is, continued to be an important presence despite turnover in the society's composition.[57]

In the immediate postwar years, the majority of New York's black Methodists, male and female, were probably slaves. In 1786, for example, 10 of the 19 black women in New York's single chapel and 3 of the 8 men were identified by first names only, while several of those *with* last names—Francis Rapalja and Deidama Sherrard, married at the John Street Chapel in 1790, as well as Elizabeth Courland, married to Glascow in the same year—were also bondspeople.[58] Since slaveholders discouraged their slaves from formally joining the Methodist society, a significant number of slaves overall was probably in attendance.[59]

By the early 1790s, the numbers of free blacks at the New York society had begun to rise. In 1791, just 3 of 27 men—or 11.1 percent of the black male membership—can be identified with certainty as slaves, and 16 of 97 women, or 16.5 percent of the black female membership. By 1796, 2 men out of 30, and 7 women out of 102, or less than 7 percent of both men and women, were probably slaves. Since two-thirds of New York City's black population were still held in bondage in 1790, and close to one half in 1800, the Methodist society may be said to have attracted a disproportionate number of free blacks.[60]

Black women constituted an important segment within this group. Through the late 1780s and 1790s, the great majority of black members—70.4 percent in 1786 and 78.2 and 76.7 percent in 1791 and 1796 respectively—were female. Black women in fact represented more than 15 percent of the New York Methodist society as a whole in 1791. Of the twenty-five all-female Methodist classes in New York in 1796, six were for black women exclusively.[61]

Many of these women had probably reached a stage of life similar to that of their white counterparts: young, unmarried, attempting to establish an independent identity. Their relative autonomy is evident in the fact that many had acquired their freedom (or had at the least adopted the free-style identity afforded by a last name) by the time they joined the Methodist society.[62] Like their white peers, these women appear to have joined their congregations with other female relations.[63] And like the white women in the church, they found themselves worshiping with men of their race who were more likely to be married than they were, and more likely to be married to other members.[64]

Black Methodists, however, whether female or male, single or married, almost certainly traveled in spheres limited by race as much as by gender. As Shane White has shown, in 1790 as many as one-third of New York's free blacks lived in white households—that is, households other than their own or their parents'— working as domestic servants.[65] Others made their livelihoods at the low-wage work available to free people: men as mariners, day laborers, and chimney sweeps; women as nurses, cooks, and launderers; men and women alike, as small vendors and dealers.

More of New York's black Methodists than can be documented undoubtedly were small proprietors and artisans, struggling for a competency in the port towns' fluid economies. Joseph Munro was probably the proprietor of the beer, mead, and oysterhouse in William Street listed in the city's directory. Similarly, Anthony Reed was likely a fruiterer in Frankfort Street and John Southerland a "teawaterman," or small vendor, in Bowery Lane.[66]

Peter Williams, sexton at the John Street Chapel and later a significant actor in African Methodist affairs, is the best known of these New Yorkers. Born in 1749, the son of an African couple bound to the Boorite family in Beekman Street, Williams joined the New York society after hearing Philip Embury and Thomas Webb preach in the late 1760s. He was subsequently purchased by a tobacconist named Aymar. During the Revolutionary War, Williams was relocated to work for the Durham family in New Brunswick, New Jersey, where he met his future wife, Mary (Molly) Durham, a native West Indian and family servant. A loyalist, Aymar sold his slave to the trustees of the now ten-year-old Wesley (John Street) Chapel before leaving for Canada at the end of the war. Still called "Negro Peter," Williams paid back the trustees in installments, including the barter of his watch. By December 1783, he had taken his surname; by November 1795, his freedom payments were complete.[67]

Williams made his way swiftly through the tradesmen's ranks. Trained by his former master as a tobacconist, he opened his own tobacco shop in Liberty Street and eventually turned this business into a full-fledged manufactory.[68] But despite their upward mobility, Peter and Mary Williams were still denizens of a black social world, separate from whites. They attended the funerals and weddings of their fellow black Methodists, turning these occasions into communal celebrations. In the early 1790s, John Street Chapel boasted a black chorus that the Williamses and their cohort may well have organized.[69] And they belonged to all-black classes, held at the chapels and at private residences throughout the city. These usually convened on Sundays, when most slaves were not on call to their masters and free black laborers were not bound to their daily work. While the stationed preachers, instructed by the MEC discipline, continued to appoint white leaders to head black classes, black spirituality was undoubtedly most profoundly shaped by the groups of fifteen and more class members, the Williamses among them, testifying together to the power of their religious experiences.[70] The Methodist society, in other words, supplied the setting for blacks' solidarity as it did for women's.

The relevance of a critical mass of black members to the development of a black community is more evident still in the Baltimore Methodist societies. The racial profile of the Baltimore Methodists was not significantly different from that of the New York contingent in the late 1780s. In 1786, just 14.5 percent of the Baltimore total membership (including city and county together) was black, as compared to 15 percent in New York in the same year, likely reflecting the large numbers of slaves, as opposed to free blacks, attending revivals. By 1795, however, the proportion of black members at Baltimore City and Fell's Point combined had risen to 29.5 percent. And by 1801, 361 African Americans belonged to the Baltimore City society—now comprising the Light Street and Green Street chapels and the all-black Fish Street and Sharp Street congregations—and 72 belonged to the Fell's Point chapel. Altogether an extraordinary one-third of Baltimore's Methodists were black.[71]

The successful recruitment of African Americans to the Baltimore societies was one result of the Methodists' missionary focus in that city, for more than fifteen years after the Revolutionary War the movement's most important urban center. But the attraction of slaves and free people to Methodism also reflected what one historian has called the "black drive for autonomy," which took the form of freedom petitions and other demands for independence by Baltimore's African American population after the Revolution.[72] By 1800, in keeping with their numbers and diversity, black Methodists in Baltimore formed three distinct populations. One continued to be slaves. In 1800, at least 12 percent and probably more of Baltimore's black members were still bondspeople—including Levin Wales, a black Methodist in the Fell's Point society, who, despite his surname, was a still slave. The great majority of these men and women belonged to the Baltimore City society and probably worshiped at the Light Street and Green Street chapels. Many more undoubtedly had been bound to or lived with white Methodists. A significant proportion of the black women in the Baltimore City society were also slaves.[73]

At the same time, an unusually substantial proportion of Baltimore City's black members were men: just above and under 40 percent in the years from 1799 to 1801. In 1795, a cohort of these men had already petitioned Asbury for the formation of "a distinct African, yet Methodist Church," one that "in temporals, shall be altogether under their own direction." The petitioners undoubtedly included local preacher "Father" Thomas Dublin and others from among the eleven black preachers, exhorters, and prayer leaders listed in the Baltimore City register.[74]

The black members at Fell's Point, nearly half of whom were also men, represented a third segment of Baltimore's African American population: relatively independent, laboring-class folk. Many more of the black congregants at the Point's Strawberry Alley Chapel than at the other chapels in the city bore the symbol of free status, a last name, and were undoubtedly employed in much the same way as other free blacks: as household servants, but especially as artisans' assistants, mariners, stevedores, carters, nurses, and launderers.[75]

Overall, this survey of black involvement in postwar New York and Baltimore Methodism demonstrates the movement's strong African American base. But it also suggests that black Methodists were drawn from a geographically mobile, socially self-conscious, and economically ascending population. It was only a matter of time before black Methodists sought to shape the Methodist movement in return.

The precedents for the formation of discrete black Methodist congregations existed as early as the 1780s. In rural parts of the Middle Atlantic, freestanding black or multiracial religious meetings, some predating Methodist affiliation and some large enough to be called "societies" by the traveling preachers, were surely more common than their scant appearance in the historical record implies. In one instance, Benjamin Abbott was invited by an "African" to attend a religious meeting of blacks and Indians on Long Island "who professed themselves to be congregationers" though not members of any church. "The man, who had given me the invitation," Abbott wrote, "told me that they knew nothing of our hymns, and requested me to tell them to sing their own. When we arrived at the place, we found them gathered; accordingly, I told them to sing their own hymns; they did so." Regrettably, Abbott does not report on the content and sound of the music—whether deriving from African sources, sea chanteys, or some other inspiration. But he expressed his own response to the group in what were increasingly common refrains among antislavery evangelicals: "I was as happy among these Indians and Africans, as I could live in the body. God is no respecter of persons; but all them, who fear him and work righteousness, of every nation are accepted of him." The following day, he invited the congregation to form a Methodist class, to which they readily agreed.[76]

Similarly, in 1794 William Colbert discovered "a congregation of Black people," free and slave, who had built their own Methodist meetinghouse in Oxenhill, Maryland, near Alexandria, Virginia. In the only extended description of the organization of a rural black society in the Middle Atlantic before 1800, Colbert elaborated:

> [T]heir society is very numerous, and very orderly, and to their great credit with pleasure I assert, that I never found a white class so regular in giving in their Quarterage, as these poor people are, and the greater part of them are slaves, of whom never request anything. But they will enquire when the Quarterly Meetings are from time to time, and by the last time the preacher comes round before the Quarterly Meeting they will have five Dollars in silver tied up for him: as they are so numerous the circuit preacher cannot meet them all, there are 2 leading characters among them, that fill their station with dignity. They not only have their Class meetings, but their days of examination in order to find out anything that may be amiss among them and if they can settle it among themselves they will, if not, as the Elders of Israel brought of matters which they concieved were of too great importance for them to decide on before Moses, so would these people bring matters of the greatest moment before the preacher.[77]

Like the several thousands of black Methodists in the rural Middle Atlantic and in the city societies after the Revolutionary War, the black Methodists of Oxenhill were a part of the MEC but also apart from it, members of a new evangelical subculture whose numbers were growing yearly with the manumission and emancipation of the region's slave population. It was testimony to Richard Allen's perspicacity, and to some extent his wishful thinking, that this former slave was able to conceive of the Methodist movement as a context in which blacks might thrive and a distinctly African American identity might be forged.

RICHARD ALLEN, BLACK PREACHERS, AND THE RISE OF
AFRICAN METHODISM

Richard Allen is renowned as one of the first black ministers in American history. But as a young man he was just one among unknown numbers of African American evangelicals who fit W.E.B. Du Bois's familiar description of "the most unique personality developed by the Negro on American soil"—the black preacher.[78]

Other more or less freelance black exhorters and self-appointed preachers were working among the Methodists in the years after the end of the Revolutionary War, including one runaway slave, among others, described by his new master as having lived with a Methodist family "ON TERMS OF PERFECT EQUALITY" and being accustomed to "INSTRUCTING AND EXHORTING HIS FELLOW CREATURES OF ALL COLORS IN MATTERS OF RELIGIOUS DUTY."[79] During Allen's young adulthood, the best known among early black Methodist travelers was freeman Harry Hosier. "[V]ery black, an African of the Africans," Hosier was the traveling companion and backup exhorter for several of the leading preachers.[80] The kind of preacher-genius that the Methodists were known to produce, he was an especially efficacious exhorter with white audiences in Virginia, where he accompanied Asbury, and in northern venues. In New Rochelle, New York, Freeborn Garrettson found that "the people of this circuit are amazingly fond of hearing Harry," and in Hudson, New York, the "different denominations heard him with much admiration, and the Quakers thought that as he was unlearned he must preach by immediate inspiration."[81] In the 1780s, the New York Methodists advertised Hosier's arrival in the city in the *New York Packet*, describing him as "a very singular black man, who . . . is quite ignorant of letters, yet he has preached in the Methodist church several times to the acceptance of several well-disposed, judicious people." He speaks "with great zeal and pathos," the notice continued, "and his language and connection is by no means contemptible," so much so that he might "rouse the dormant zeal of numbers of our slothful white people."[82] One of Methodism's original celebrities, Hosier suffered a painful decline in the years to follow, succumbing to alcoholism before he died in Philadelphia in 1806, once again a redeemed man.[83]

Hosier's fame in his young manhood did little to alter one of the key obstacles African American men confronted in the Methodist movement, however: while the new church welcomed black exhorters and unlicensed itinerants among the ranks of the preachers, it was cautious about, if not downright hostile to, the advancement of black itinerants. Indeed, the assumption that the class meeting served as the "university" for preachers seeking to rise in the church was as exclusionary for black men as it was for women of whatever race. As the 1785 discipline specified, white leaders were to be appointed to head black classes at local societies.[84]

The MEC leadership's ambivalence regarding the role of black preachers in the church—first embracing the talents of black preachers and then denying them promotion through the church hierarchy—goes a long way toward explaining Richard Allen's behavior as his prominence rose within the movement: for while he was loyal to the faith that had freed him from slavery as well as from sin, he was simultaneously eager to escape the official dictates of the church that bound him to second-class citizenship.

Allen's conversion to Methodism and subsequent emancipation took place in the heart of postwar Methodist territory, in Kent County, Delaware.[85] In the various stages of his early life—birth in 1760 and infancy as part of Benjamin Chew's labor force on the Whitehall plantation near Dover; sale with his mother and a number of siblings to Stokeley Sturgis, a lesser planter in the same neighborhood; and then loss of his mother in a subsequent sale to pay off Sturgis's debts—Allen experienced the varying conditions of rural slave life, from the "big house" to the small farm, and from the security of his mother's protection to forced teenage labor.[86] The appearance on the local scene of Francis Asbury and emancipationist preacher Freeborn Garrettson, among other itinerants, proselytizing among blacks as well as whites before and through the long years of the Revolutionary War, would not have escaped Allen's attention, nor would he have failed to be aware that several of Delaware's most prominent planters—Richard Bassett among them—had joined the new movement.[87] Perhaps nowhere else in the new states outside Baltimore was it quite so evident as it was in and around Dover that the Methodists possessed an extraordinary ability to bring rich and poor, black and white, under one cultural roof.

Stokeley Sturgis's slaves—Richard, his brother John, and a sister—discovered Methodist preaching sometime in the 1770s, on the eve of American Independence.[88] But Independence did not bring liberation for Allen; association with the Methodists did. In this new context, Allen's life narrative takes on the characteristics of a providential story, one in which the protagonist watches painstakingly for every sign of a change in the terms of his present confinement. With his brother Allen joined a Methodist class led by white leader John Gray near Sturgis's farm and began to make contact with the leading preachers in the movement. Like other slaves in the area, the two brothers, Richard and John, spent what little free time they had growing produce to sell on the local market, delivering part of the profits to the Methodist itinerants, while laboring conspicuously on their assigned tasks "so that it should not be said that religion made us worse servants." At the same time, they attended their Methodist class meeting once a week and public preaching every other week. "At length," Allen continued, "our master said he was convinced that religion made slaves better and not worse, and often boasted of his slaves for their honesty and industry." Allen reflected: "I had it often impressed upon my mind that I should one day enjoy my freedom," for slavery was a "bitter pill." While the price was high, the cost of the brothers' enslavement was far higher: their "day's work" was never done, and the likelihood of sale on their master's death was a chillingly constant threat.[89]

Allen describes Sturgis as "an unconverted man," but the Kent County planter and his wife quickly succumbed to the pressures of the new movement. Attending their servants' prayer meetings, the couple eventually permitted religious assemblies in their parlor, first under the aegis of the local class leader, then under the itinerants.[90] Sometime in September 1778 or July 1779, Freeborn Garrettson, at the beginning of his antislavery crusade, joined the Sturgises and their servants for religious worship at the Sturgis farmhouse. Reading from the Book of Daniel, Garrettson exhorted Sturgis, "Thou art weighed in the balance and art found wanting," a text, he later recalled, he had chosen purposefully to underscore the "necessity of religion" and the "propriety of loosing the bands of wickedness, and letting the oppressed go free."[91] In a crisis of conscience, and perhaps recognizing his bondsman's compelling abilities, Stokeley Sturgis offered to sell Richard his time for £60 in gold and silver, or about $2,000 in continental money, to be paid off in five yearly installments. The agreement was sealed on 25 January 1780, on the eve of Richard's twentieth birthday. A similar manumission appears to have been drawn up for Richard's brother John. The two youths now adopted their last name, and Richard Allen set out on an extended itinerancy to pay the price of his emancipation.[92]

Freed from forced toil, Allen hired himself out as an itinerant day laborer, cutting cordwood and earning a monthly income of $50 working in a brickyard. In the waning years of the war, he was able to transform a teamstering job into a salt dealership, the first outlet for what would turn out to be his considerable entrepreneurial talents. On 27 August 1783, just three and a half years after the original agreement, he paid Sturgis the price of his manumission, at the same time presenting his former master with a gift of eighteen bushels of salt. With this transaction—emblematic of the freeman's hard-won independence and his new contract-worthy equality—Allen moved on to his life's work.[93]

For a number of years, Richard Allen's life followed the course of many other Methodist itinerants-in-the-making, with the added empowerment that such freedom of movement signified to a former slave. Leaving Delaware, he first traveled north to New Jersey, where he met the charismatic preacher Benjamin Abbott, a "friend and father to me." He then traveled in wider circuits through the Middle Atlantic and South, including two months as a missionary among an unidentified Indian tribe, probably in the Carolina backcountry. Like the other itinerants, he relied on the hospitality of Methodist followers, white and black, such as Caesar Waters and his wife, both slaves in Radnor Township outside Philadelphia. Here he preached on a Sunday to "a large congregation of different persuasions," and one of the numerous whites in attendance gave him a horse, symbol of itinerant independence. In Lancaster he was a success among the town's German population. By 1785 he was a member of the Baltimore society, probably at the Fell's

Figure 8. *Richard Allen*, ca. 1785. Probably
sketched in Baltimore. Courtesy of the Moorland-
Spingarn Research Center, Howard University.

Point chapel, home to so many freemen and women. Sometime during his itinerancy he also learned to read and write.[94]

Yet all the while that Allen's reputation among the white preachers was rising
and his sense of belonging to a Methodist people was likewise increasing, his
awareness of the racial divide separating him from the other preachers remained
acute. Invited to accompany Bishop Asbury on a circuit of the South, Allen,
unlike Harry Hosier, balked at the conditions: restrictions on his intermixing with
slaves and the requirement that he sleep in the bishop's carriage rather than in the
residences of the Methodists' hosts. Referring to the insecurities of a freeman's
life, Allen responded to the bishop's offer by noting that "people ought to lay up
something while they were able, to support themselves in time of sickness or old
age." While Asbury "would be taken care of, let his afflictions be as they were,"
Allen "doubted whether it would be the case with myself." Absorbed with issues
of economic as well as personal autonomy, Allen now returned to Pennsylvania,
where he alternatively preached and worked. In early 1786—possibly under pressure from Francis Asbury, who sought to raise up black speakers but not itinerating preachers—Allen accepted one of several entreaties by the stationed itinerant
that he become a local preacher in Philadelphia.[95]

For many reasons, Philadelphia was an attractive destination for a young black
man keen to make his own way. Most important was the growing free population

of the city. By 1790, more than 2,000 blacks, nearly 1,850 of them free people, were living within the limits of greater Philadelphia (the city, Southwark, and Northern Liberties combined), a small but growing portion of the greater city's population of 44,000. By 1800, fueled by in-migration, Philadelphia's black population had nearly tripled, but its slave population had dwindled to insignificance. Blacks composed close to a tenth of the city's inhabitants. The majority, almost all free people, lived in the Northern Liberties and in the New Market, Cedar, and Locust Wards skirting the mariners' district of Southwark.[96] Most worked in the unskilled occupations of food vending, chimney sweeping, laundering, and domestic work. But the early success of James Forten, an African American war veteran and artisan who had taken over his former employer's sail-making business, suggested the possibilities at hand. By 1795, 381 families of "free People of Colour" lived in the city; and blacks owned ninety-nine single-family dwellings, worth an average of $200 each.[97]

In addition to providing a haven for ex-slaves in search of work and the company of fellow free people, the city was the capital of the nation's first antislavery movement. While its status as the seat of the federal government through the 1790s brought few benefits for African Americans—on the contrary, the Federal Congress refused to legislate restrictions on either slavery or the slave trade, and congressmen and senators brought their bondspeople into the city with impunity—Philadelphia's abolitionist activism set it apart. The Pennsylvania Abolition Society (PAS), founded in 1775 and reorganized in 1787, in its first years attracted the attention of the city's elite, including Benjamin Franklin as well as numerous less well known Quakers, Baptists, and Episcopalians. The society has been credited with the successful passage of Pennsylvania's two gradual emancipation laws in 1780 and 1788 and was among the nation's most important advocates for freemen and women. Hundreds of former slaves, like Allen himself, deposited their manumission certificates with the PAS for safekeeping and were to rely in future years on its defense against the claims of slaveholders and slave kidnappers.[98]

Philadelphia's black population was consequently a mixture of slave and free, aspiring and laboring class. As early as 1781, the efficacy of black activism in the city was evident when a group of African Americans successfully petitioned the state legislature to oppose measures designed to delay the enforcement of gradual emancipation in the state. At the same time, many black folk in the city were only recently removed from their African pasts. Many were known to gather at the Potter's Field on holidays for dancing and singing "after the manner of their several nations in Africa, and speaking and singing in their native dialects." Altogether, that is, they were one part of the diverse slave population that Methodism had so successfully attracted in the past.[99]

Arriving in Philadelphia in February 1786, Richard Allen took the full measure of this urban panorama. He observed, "I soon saw a large field open in seeking and instructing my African brethren, who had been a long forgotten people and few of them attended public worship." Moving away from his earlier mission as a black itinerant crossing racial lines, Allen's focus now centered exclusively on recruiting blacks into the Philadelphia Methodist society. Over the next several years, he preached in common areas in the city, in Southwark, and in the Northern Liberties. He organized black prayer meetings and quickly succeeded in gathering together an informal black Methodist meeting of forty-two members. He also befriended several other African Americans at St. George's, among them Absalom Jones, a fellow former slave from Delaware and twenty-five-year resident of the city. Together Allen and Jones devised a plan to tap into the potential resources and meet the needs of Philadelphia's growing numbers of black inhabitants. The two men decided that nothing would better suit these goals than the formation of a black religious society.[100]

The pursuit of the idea of an exclusively black church was to consume the energies of Allen, Jones, and their allies for the next seven years. Its evolution into two black churches quite different from the one originally planned has been recounted by numerous historians, beginning with Allen's biographer, Charles Wesley, and more recently by Gary Nash.[101] The narrative bears retelling nonetheless for the insights it provides into the emergence of African Methodism within the Methodist movement, and, not least of all, for just how important a black ministry was to this first generation of free people.

The officials at St. George's, the Methodist society, opposed the idea of a separate society from the start.[102] Anxious to stay within the MEC, Allen and Jones were initially forced back upon a less controversial project: the organizing of the Free African Society (FAS), a self-help association for Philadelphia's freemen, women, and their children. As announced in the group's opening minutes, Jones and Allen proclaimed "a love to the people of their complexion whom they beheld with sorrow, because of their irreligious and uncivilized state." While the "creation of some kind of religious society" had been put aside for the time being, the two men had determined that "a society should be formed, without regard to religious tenets" so long as the members "lived an orderly and sober life," supported each other in sickness, and cared for members' widows and children.[103] William White and Dorus Jennings, two other black Methodists associated with Jones and Allen, quickly joined the group, and others followed: Quaker Cyrus Bustill; William Wilshire, a free black manumitted through the efforts of Methodist Lambert Wilmer the year before and probably from St. George's; Moses Johnson, also recently freed; William Gray, the proprietor of a West Indian fruit and confectionery shop; and Caesar Cranchell, Cato Freeman, William Gardiner, Caesar Worthington, and Henry Stewart—men whose names appear repeatedly in the FAS records, and several of whom may have been members of the Anglican, now Protestant Episcopal, Church.[104]

The FAS was unaffiliated with any church, but the FAS minutes are replete with Wesleyan values. As the society wrote to the Union Society of Africans, a similar group in Boston:

> Here is encouragement for us of the African race. The scriptures declare, that God, is no respecter of persons. We beseech you, therefore, in much brotherly love, to lay aside all superfluity of naughtiness, especially gaming and feasting; a shameful practice, that we as a people are particularly guilty of. While we are feasting and dancing, many of

our complexion are starving under cruel bondage; and it is this practice of ours that enables our enemies to declare that we are not fit for freedom,—and at the same time, this imprudent conduct stops the mouths of our real friends, who would ardently plead our cause.[105]

The folk culture of slavery would be left behind as free Africans accepted the egalitarian message of the Scriptures and the call to religious sobriety.

Shared goals did not necessarily translate into consensus on how to reach them, however, and in the spring of 1791, Allen, likely favoring Methodism over the increasing Quaker influence on the group, was expelled "for attempting to sow division among us." Nevertheless, the FAS temporarily resolved their disagreements by returning to a more sharply defined version of Allen and Jones's original proposal: the creation of a Christian but nondenominational "union" church, one that would serve black members from all the various congregations in the city.[106] They now contracted Benjamin Rush, Philadelphia's best-known antislavery spokesman, and Robert Ralston, one of the city's new merchants, for assistance in sponsoring the church. In July 1791, Rush presented "sundry articles of faith and a plan of church government" to about a dozen Free Africans meeting at William Wilshire's house. The group agreed to Rush's draft, as did the FAS in a formal session on 28 July.[107]

In an address published at the end of August, the "Representatives of the African Church," Absalom Jones and seven other society members, set out the purpose of their association and sought further fiscal support. The church, the address asserted, aimed to gather otherwise scattered black religious folk under one roof. Why convene separately from whites? Because, the address continued, the degree to which men are more often influenced in their morals by their equals than by those placed over them by "accidental circumstances," as well as the ties of color and condition that held blacks together, "all evince the necessity and propriety of their enjoying separate, and exclusive means, and opportunities of worshipping God, of instructing their youth and taking care of their poor." These statements were probably drafted by Rush, himself an evangelical who increasingly conceived of the Revolution as a moral as much as a political victory. At the same time, as is evident from later events, Rush's outline must have included another vital provision: the appointment of church elders. The plan, that is, contained within it the germ of black religious independence: a black ministry.[108]

Like the original Wesleyan "old plan," the scheme for the union church would not require members to abandon their current denominational affiliation, proposing instead a form of dual membership. Presiding elders Caleb Boyer and Richard Whatcoat, the officials at St. George's, were unsympathetic nonetheless, despite, or perhaps because of, Allen's renewed cooperation with the plan. Whatcoat in particular used "degrading language" in responding to the FAS's actions, suggesting not only deep tensions between this British preacher and the black Methodists now requiring his affirmation but Whatcoat's rising awareness that the new society might very well draw off black members from the MEC.[109]

The efforts to form an African union church moved apace over the winter and spring of 1791–1792, nonetheless. In February, the Free Africans purchased for £450 two lots on Fifth Street below the Statehouse for the African chapel. In March they began to circulate subscription papers to help defray the cost of construction.[110] The racial stresses generated by these efforts boiled over at St. George's during Sunday service in early June 1792. On this day, Allen, Jones, and several of the other Methodist Free Africans arrived for worship at the chapel and were directed to sit in the new galleries running down either side of the church hall—a sign of trouble to come. Shortly into the service, as singing ended and prayer began, the Free African representatives were suddenly and forcibly interrupted by Henry Manley and another trustee demanding that they move, presumably to the back of the galleries where they would be less visible. Allen recalled: "I raised my head up and saw one of the trustees, H[enry] M[anley], having hold of . . . Absalom Jones, pulling him up off of his knees, and saying, 'You must get up—you must not kneel here.' " Jones insisted that they wait out the remainder of the prayer. Profoundly disturbed by this sudden display of white dominance, Allen and his fellow FAS members walked out of the chapel. Allen, still angry about the incident years later, recollected that "[b]y this time prayer was over, and we all went out of the church in a body, and they were no more plagued with us in the church. This raised a great excitement, and inquiry among the citizens, in so much that I believe [the trustees] were ashamed of their conduct."[111]

The MEC's segregating tendencies, both accepted and resented by its black followers, came to a head with the incident at St. George's. The crisis was exacerbated when the new presiding elder, John McClaskey, threatened to expel the black members associated with the union church. In a heated argument, Allen and the remaining Methodist Free Africans challenged McClaskey to show "where we have violated any law of discipline of the Methodist Church," and declared that if McClaskey turned them out illegally, they would "seek further redress." In a pointed reference to their spiritual equality with white Christians, they reminded the elder that "we were dragged off of our knees in St. George's church, and treated worse than heathens." McClaskey pronounced the group "not Methodists." In a second meeting, the Free Africans insisted that they would not return to St. George's. It was, Allen said, "a trial that I never had to pass through before."[112] In November 1792, further fueling McClaskey's wrath, the union church chose its first elders: now former Methodists Absalom Jones, William White, and Dorus Jennings. In April of the following year, the society initiated construction on the building.[113]

Allen's struggles—internal as well as external—over his continuing connection with the Methodists were profoundly significant for the early Methodist movement. The temptations for Allen to leave the Methodists behind were many. A remarkable gathering of white workingmen and Free Africans in Southwark in August 1793, celebrating the building of the African church, held out the promise of greater unity between blacks and white workingmen in the city away from the influence of white church hierarchies. The ongoing battles with the Methodist elders suggested that most avenues of advancement for black members, especially advancement into the preachers' ranks, would be closed well into the future.[114]

Allen was also one of Philadelphia's rising black entrepreneurs and as such no doubt expected greater esteem from his own religious society. Through a chimney-sweeping business, a brief venture in nail manufacturing, and a shoe dealership, Allen had risen swiftly through the black trades, employing sweeps, indentured servants, and apprentices, and purchasing a property at 150 Spruce Street near Dock to house his growing family.[115] By the late 1790s, Allen, along with Absalom Jones, Cato Freeman, and William White from the FAS, owned substantial housing stock in the expanding black district of the New Market Ward and had accumulated a considerable fortune in rents.[116] While he and Absalom Jones stressed their support for poor blacks in their defense of black nurses and gravediggers accused of profiting from the 1793 yellow fever epidemic, the temptations of the comforts of prosperity might well have been enough to draw Allen from the Methodists as it did so many of his white counterparts.[117]

A significant change in the plans for the union church, furthermore, provided Allen with an extraordinary opportunity for professional as well as social advancement, the deferral of which reveals much about Allen's inner struggles through this time. Late in 1793, the proposers of the black church abandoned what Will Gravely has called the "elusive dream of black communal unity" in exchange for the denominational security of affiliation with the Protestant Episcopal Church, one of the few instances in which the Anglicans one-upped their Methodist competitors. Exempted from the Greek and Latin tests usually required of Anglican clergy, Allen was offered ordination as the first African Episcopal minister in the nation.[118] Allen turned the offer down. In his place, Absalom Jones was ordained as deacon of the first African Protestant Episcopal Church, soon to be called St. Thomas's. The Methodist Free Africans, including Dorus Jennings and William White, now formally left the Methodists to join the new Episcopal congregation.[119]

Allen's reasons for staying with the Methodists were, in the long run, straightforward, and recognizable to any convinced Methodist. Recollecting this critical decision, Allen speaks in the repetitive, vocalizing manner of a transformed convert: "I told them [the FAS] I could not accept of their offer, as I was a Methodist. . . . I informed them that I could not be anything else but a Methodist, as I was born and awakened under them, and I could go no further with them [the FAS], for I was a Methodist. . . ." Methodism, furthermore, was the religion of Allen's people. "I was confident that there was no religious sect or denomination would suit the capacity of the colored people as well as the Methodist," he still insisted years after the event. The "plain and simple gospel" was best for all people, but especially for the poor and uneducated, "for the unlearned can understand, and the learned are sure to understand." "The Methodists," moreover, "were the first people that brought glad tidings to the colored people," an approach based on "spiritual and extempore preaching" that had benefited "thousands and ten times thousands." The Methodists, Allen emphasized, were a missionary movement, one that, intentionally or not, had transformed former slaves and oppressed free blacks into religiously empowered, racially conscious, independent agents.[120]

Methodism, furthermore, provided potentially limitless chances for advancement for black preachers if the white leadership would only permit it. Not even Allen at this point pressed for a black traveling fraternity. But the advancement of black officers within the church was a central feature of Allen's movement within the movement.

Hence Allen was not willing to return to the church in exactly the same capacity as in the past. In May 1794, as St. Thomas's prepared to open, Allen met with ten other black Methodists, who agreed to furbish "a house to meet in for religious worship . . . separate from our white brethren." For this purpose, the group transported the frame of a blacksmith's shop to a lot on Sixth Street above Lombard that had been in Allen's possession for several years.[121] The "African Methodist Episcopal Church," or Bethel, as the spin-off society was doubly christened from the start, was supported by the new presiding elder, Allen's old mentor, Freeborn Garrettson. Francis Asbury preached the inaugural sermon on 29 June.[122]

The approval of Bethel's congregation may not have seemed particularly risky to the bishop at first. Asbury noted that "[o]ur coloured brethren are to be governed by the doctrine and discipline of the Methodists."[123] Bethel's trustees likewise downplayed the radical implications of their actions in a public statement published in November. Since "many inconveniences have arisen from white people and people of color mixing together in public assemblies, more particularly places of worship," the trustees declared, they had found it "necessary to provide for ourselves a convenient house to assemble in separate from our white brethren." The arrangement, the trustees explained, would prevent offense on both sides, though the African Methodists believed with St. Paul that there was "neither male nor female, barbarian or Scythian, bond nor free, but all are one in Christ Jesus." The society would remain "in union with" the MEC forever and "did not mean or intend willfully anything bordering upon schism." Rather, they "would rejoice in the prospect of mutual fellowship subsisting between our white brethren and us." In keeping with this agreement, Bethel also accepted white class leaders.[124]

The mission of the church's organizers continued clear when stationed preacher Ezekiel Cooper was called on to draw up Bethel's articles of association in October 1796, two years later. The articles emphasized the racial distinctiveness of the congregation. The society would be run by a board of black trustees, and membership restricted to "Africans and descendants of the African race." All complaints against Bethel's congregants were to be judged by the elder, with the trustees acting as his "advisers and counsellors" and with the possibility of appeal to the trustees and other church officers thereafter, "*[p]rovided always*" that these officers "shall be of the African race." While the elder was to nominate preachers for Bethel, expected to be from among the white itinerants, he was also obliged to license any Bethelites to exhort or preach who "shall appear . . . to be adequate to the task, and to have grace and gifts proper to appear in public." Bethel, that is, would be a fostering ground for black preachers.[125]

A number of these provisions were exceptions to the Methodist discipline, which reserved authority over most chapel affairs to quarterly meetings and the preachers' conferences. Allen later discovered that the second article in particular, in which Bethel was said to be held in "perpetuity" for use of the ministers of the MEC, might be interpreted to vest legal control over the Bethel property in the MEC's general conference. Conflicts with the elders at St. George's over this and other issues would continue to occupy Allen's attention over the next two decades.[126]

But these points were initially overshadowed by the not at all predictable success of the new chapel. Bethel's first congregation comprised just thirty-two individuals, sixteen men and fourteen women, or approximately half of St. George's black membership, a small gathering indeed compared to the several hundred worshipers meeting at St. Thomas's.[127]

The congregation appears to have been composed exclusively of free people, but still mostly poor folk and servants, the majority probably resident outside the city's central wards. Those for whom identifying information survives were current or future members of Allen's family, including John Allen, Richard's brother, a tenant of the Methodist William White in the New Market Ward; Flora Allen, Richard's first wife; and Sarah Bass, "a poor black widow" who served as a nurse in the 1793 yellow fever epidemic and was later to become Allen's second wife.[128] Bethel's trustees have left only slightly firmer traces. William Hogen, a rag-gatherer, lived near the Allens on Spruce Street; Thomas Martin, a sawyer, resided on Cherry Street; John Morris, a master chimney sweeper by trade, also owned property in the South Mulberry Ward; and Jonathan Trusty was probably a coachman resident on Penn Street. The only former member of the FAS appears to have been Robert Green, later a contender with Allen for control of the Bethel Church.[129]

In the next few years, however, the new chapel grew rapidly. By 1795, membership had risen to 121 individuals; by 1797, to 163. St. George's opened a second black Methodist chapel called Zoar in the Northern Liberties in 1796 and another called Beulah was in operation by 1802. Among Zoar's class leaders was William Sturgis, a probable relation of Richard Allen's old master in Delaware. But Zoar's adherents accounted for a small proportion of Philadelphia's black Methodists, most of whom were to be found at Bethel.[130] Black and white audiences alike flocked to the church. In 1798 Allen and Jupiter Gibson wrote to Ezekiel Cooper regarding a revival then ongoing: "Our evening meetings mostly Continue untill 10 or 12 o'Clock, & from 4 to 8 Convinc^d & Converted of a night, Whites & Blacks. Our Churches ar[e] Crouded, particularly Bethel." The chapel building in fact was already too small. "[W]e are now making more s[e]ates & think shortly we must Enlarge the House. [I]t is at Bethel the work is in General. [F]or at Prayer meetings the House is Crouded & persons under Conviction for Weeks Come there to get Converted."[131] By the spring of 1801, while more than 250 new white members joined Philadelphia's Methodist society, raising the total number of adherents at St. George's and Ebenezer Chapel in Southwark to 669, the numbers of black Methodists, chiefly the African Methodists at Bethel, rose to 448. African Methodists now constituted an extraordinary 40 percent of the Philadelphia membership and outpaced even the numbers of African Americans at the Baltimore City and Fell's Point congregations. By 1813, Bethel's 1,272-strong congregation was more than twice the size of St. Thomas's.[132] Most important, the Bethelites and the other African Methodists constituted an increasingly race-conscious segment of the city's black population. When in 1799 Allen and Jones spearheaded a petition to Congress calling for an end to slavery and the slave trade, close to 20 percent of the seventy-one black signers, and probably more, were African Methodists—nearly twice as many as among the original members of St. Thomas's.[133]

Allen made a significant sacrifice by staying with Wesley's movement. Despite the tremendous potential for an African American fraternity of itinerants and the Protestant Episcopal Church's innovative adoption of black ordination, the Methodist conferences consistently declined to bring black preachers through the ranks. It was not until June 1799, when Asbury recognized Allen's special gifts by ordaining him as a local deacon, that Bethel's founder achieved a status approximating those of white preachers on the bottom rung of advancement.[134] A year later, the MEC's general conference gave the bishops authority to ordain local deacons from among black men where a separate house or houses of worship had been established, but the measure was so strongly resisted among the southern white Methodists that it went unprinted in the church's discipline.[135] Overall, the movement's reluctance to sponsor a black ministry was one of its earliest and greatest failures.

Restrictions on the rise of black men in the movement and on contact between the races at revival meetings did not discourage slaves and free blacks from becoming Methodists, however. In fact, barriers within the movement, as well as Methodism's ongoing informality, inspired black leaders in the other Middle Atlantic towns to take the same route to separation as had the Philadelphians.

Separation and African Methodist Identity

In the 1790s and early 1800s, separate African Methodist chapels were swiftly established in three other cities—Baltimore, New York, and Wilmington—all within the greater Middle Atlantic.

In Baltimore, as early as 1787, black Methodists led by Jacob Fortie and Caleb Hyland were meeting for worship in Hyland's boot-blacking cellar near the Belair Market. The activities of Baltimore's black Methodists cannot be followed as closely as developments in Philadelphia, but it is evident that their desire for autonomy within the movement was equally strong. In 1793, black Methodists leased the African School run by the Abolition Society in Sharp Street, west of Baltimore Town center, for use for their meetings.[136] In May 1795, Francis Asbury met with an unidentified delegation of Baltimore's black members likely headed by Fortie to discuss "building a house and forming a distinct African, yet Methodist Church." Several months later he complained that "[t]he Africans of this town desire a church, which, in temporals, shall be altogether under their own direction, and ask greater privileges than the white stewards and trustees ever had a right to claim." Asbury initially rejected the idea, but separate meetings continued nonetheless. In 1797, Hyland, Stephen Hill—a freeman known for his persuasive volubility—and other black men from the Baltimore society leased a lot and building on Fish (later Saratoga) Street for religious meetings. This chapel soon disbanded, though many of the same men were to purchase property in 1812 for a separate black society.[137]

The Sharp Street group, led by black artisans Jacob Gilliard and Richard Russell and supported by the MEC, now more responsive to demands for black autonomy, met with greater success. In 1802, the congregation bought the school building and its lot outright, after profiting from investments in land sales in the city. By 1805, the building had been replaced by a new structure for continued use as a combined school and African Methodist chapel. Although the chapel was unincorporated, the trustees controlled its property and it provided an outlet for the talents of the extraordinary number of black exhorters and local preachers living in the city, led by the gifted mixed-race local deacon Daniel Coker.[138] Through the first decade of the nineteenth century, the Sharp Street Chapel continued to serve as the social center of African Methodist life in Baltimore, with prayer meetings held regularly at the residences of wealthier black members and spiritual uplift supplied by bands of young men renowned for their passionate exhorting and hymn singing.[139]

In New York, the move toward separation was likewise headed by a mix of local preachers and prominent laymen. Peter Williams, the freeman, was as "African"-conscious as the Bethelites.[140] In 1796, he and several others from the New York society—notably James Varick (later an officer among the New York African Methodists); Francis Jacobs; licensed preachers Abraham Thompson, June Scott, and Thomas Miller; and exhorter William Miller—petitioned Bishop Asbury for permission to meet in quarters separate from the white congregation. Asbury, already faced with petitions for separate meetings in Philadelphia and Baltimore, agreed so long as the black members' meetings were not held at the same time as the main services at the larger chapels. The group, calling themselves the Zion Society, began gathering in Cross Street at Thomas Miller's cabinetmaker's shop, refitted as a chapel.[141] Black membership continued to be significant in New York but not to the same degree as in the cities further south. The fear of being outnumbered by whites—and hence gradually pressed out of the larger churches altogether—rather than an overwhelming drive for separation prompted the group to move toward erecting their own chapel. In July 1800, two lots were leased at Church and Leonard Streets, and by means of a successful public subscription, the Zion society was able to construct a frame building for worship in the fall of 1800.[142]

In February 1801, the Zion society was incorporated as the African Methodist Episcopal Church (with the name Zion Church designated in parentheses), and in April the trustees signed on to articles of agreement with the MEC, drawn up by none other than John McClaskey, Richard Allen's adversary in Philadelphia. Control of the African society by a presiding elder, the bishops, and the general conference was encoded into several articles. But the requirement stood that "none but Africans or their descendants" were to be chosen as trustees or as members of the AMEZ. In addition, the elder was to raise up competent preachers from among the congregation, provided they were recommended by a majority of the African officers.[143] Like Bethel in Philadelphia, the Zion Society was a relatively poor group, with little in the way of material resources. Unlike Bethel, the Zion congregation maintained a pacific relationship with the larger New York church, which may account for its initial lack of success at attracting a substantial black membership. At the same time, in 1806, three of Zion's founders—June Scott, Abraham Thompson, and James Varick—were, like Richard Allen before them, ordained as local deacons.[144]

The African Methodists of each of these cities shared a passion for institution building, one at least in part derived from the larger movement, with its bottom-up creation of local societies and provision of legal incorporation. The pattern can be seen once again in Wilmington. Never a large group—Delaware's sizable Methodist population was concentrated in the state's rural districts—Asbury Chapel at Third and Walnut Streets was nonetheless more than half black through the 1790s, with itinerants reporting of a 1799 revival that "the best work seems to be among the blacks."[145] Several years thereafter, in February 1805, Asbury's African members agreed to build their own chapel, advertising the plan in a local paper. As at St. George's in Philadelphia, the Asbury Chapel's trustees responded by segregating black members into the galleries, complaining of broken benches and debris left behind by the class members in the church's lower seats. The trustees announced that "[i]f they [black members] refuse to meet in the gallery, the sexton shall inform them that the door will not be opened for their reception."[146] Forty or more black members, led by class leaders Peter Spencer (like Richard Allen, born a slave in Kent County and now a twenty-three-year-old freeman) and William Anderson, left the chapel. Spencer and six other free black men purchased a lot at Ninth and Walnut Streets, where they constructed the Ezion African Methodist Episcopal Church. Similar to provisions in Bethel's act of incorporation, Ezion's deed stipulated that "none but persons of colour [and members of the church] shall be chosen as trustees of the said African Methodist Episcopal Church."[147]

Neither Spencer nor Anderson was a licensed preacher, and the group continued to rely on Asbury Chapel's white stationed preacher until 1813. In this year, conflicts with the Methodist elder ended in a court case, compelling Wilmington's two black Methodist leaders to found the Union Church of African Members. It was a small society but one with the distinction of being the first independent African Protestant denomination in the United States.[148]

Driving these changes were the aspirations of individual black women and men, many free but others still enslaved, who became African Methodists in the first two decades after the Revolutionary War. Some were solitary figures, like the Eastern Shore slave woman who impressed Freeborn Garrettson with her extraordinary piety, self-denial, and efforts to keep afloat in the shifting currents of slavery's slow demise in northern Maryland. Living alone in a rented room, she labored as a hired servant for her master's profit and attended all available Methodist preaching, sometimes with her "work" at hand, rising "several times in the night to pray." Others gathered together in increasing number in the larger societies, as did the black women who constituted such significant proportions of city society membership by the 1780s and 1790s.[149]

And among black men, and later black women, there were aspiring preachers. Such was George White, born a slave in Accomack, Virginia, before the Revolution and living as a manumitted freeman in New York City when he was transfixed during a revival at the Bowery Church and joined the Methodist ranks. Licensed as an exhorter, White struggled through four unsuccessful trials at the New York Methodist society in his efforts to be accepted as a licensed preacher. Anxious to preach "[a]mong my African brethren," and convinced that his application to the itinerancy had been denied because of his "illiterature," White persuaded his sixteen-year-old daughter to teach him to read the Bible "since she could learn me nothing from the common spelling book," which held comparatively little meaning for him. She then taught her father to write "so far as to be able to keep my own accounts; and, though in a broken imperfect manner, to correspond with absent friends, and minute the travels of my own soul."[150]

Finally licensed through the popular acclaim of the New York quarterly meeting in 1807, White joined the fraternity of traveling preachers. Inspired by dreams and spiritual shouting, he worked especially among Middle Atlantic blacks, who, "being my own blood, lay near my heart." By the early nineteenth century, this was a less difficult task than ever before. Traveling south, White preached to one African Methodist congregation after another: in New Brunswick, Shrewsbury, Middletown, Woodbridge, and Trenton in New Jersey; and in Philadelphia, Wilmington, and Baltimore. In the last city he found more of his old Virginia associates than he did in the Virginia neighborhood of his childhood. Throughout the region he found many former slaves, geographically mobile men and women whose main tie was a religious like-mindedness and shared commitment to their new African Methodist churches.[151]

The metamorphosis of black Methodists into African Methodists, like the rise of African Methodist preachers, had enormous consequences for black Americans and American culture. Like so many aspects of early Methodism, this transformation was not without its paradoxes. For in the process of shaping a racial identity, African Methodists drew upon Wesley's movement for organizational inspiration and, more intimately, the language—scriptural and Wesleyan—of heart-religion. African Methodist men were to find some of their greatest opportunities in an institution in which a not-so-invisible ceiling was held firmly in place by a phalanx of southern slaveholders. At the same time, the first African Methodist organizers were to exhibit some of the same ambivalence regarding *female* preaching as did their white brethren.

Yet as some of the most fervent participants in Wesley's American movement, the first generation of African Methodists engendered a singular form of "Africanized Christianity,"[152] in which the ritual of the revival served as the medium for a wholly new mode of cultural expression, and former slaves, now African

Primitive Christians, were seized with religious confidence and racial boldness. Largely excluded from the benefits of Revolutionary republicanism, the African Methodists exercised an influence well beyond their chapel walls, providing blacks with a route to liberation that would continue meaningful thereafter. In the following examination of the social experience of Methodist men all together, the extraordinary heterogeneity of the Methodist movement comes even more manifestly into view.

CHAPTER SIX

Laboring Men, Artisans, and Entrepreneurs

AMERICAN METHODISTS, like their British counterparts, were ambivalent about wealth. "[I]t is rare—a mere miracle, for a Methodist to increase in wealth and not decrease in grace," Asbury told his American audience, paraphrasing Wesley.[1] Yet acquisition of wealth was also a sign of the creditworthiness, household stability, and sobriety that verified the believer's true conversion to the Wesleyan way of life. The Methodists' fear of the effects of too much or too little wealth—the arrogance and abuse of power by the rich and the dependence of the poor—was one of the unspoken fundamentals of the movement.

For this reason, Methodists were consistently under attack from both ends of the social spectrum and frequently from a combination of the two. Victims rather than beneficiaries of the "gentry-crowd reciprocity" that was both an outlet for unaddressed grievances and an endemic feature of Britian and its colonies,[2] most Methodists had broken from this cycle. As one English itinerant put it, Methodists lived "more in a state of independence and less subject to the influence of superiors" than other folk in British society, in part because of their often middling social background, in part because of the transformative effects of conversion itself. As John Walsh writes regarding the impact of Methodism on social relations in Britain: "In a variety of ways Methodism was an active solvent of patriarchal deference. There was a wide gap between its conservative political theory and the situational reality of continual collision with the representatives of the established order."[3]

Historians of English Methodism have focused on its plebeian origins and the movement's blunting of a potentially revolutionary climate at the end of the 1730s and again in the first decades of the nineteenth century in Britain.[4] But one of the surprises of American Methodism was its social as well as racial heterogeneity. Middle Atlantic Methodists came from a wide array of social ranks: not only women of all classes and blacks—in itself an unusual diversity—but also poor men, middling farmers, greater merchants, and planters. In the Middle Atlantic city societies in particular, the movement attracted laboring men, artisans, *and* the "new men" of late-eighteenth-century capitalist expansion: commercial, industrial, and professional entrepreneurs. While the great proponderance of laboring men and tradesmen, along with servants and slaves, in the city societies warrants calling them plebeian institutions, they were that and more.

When men joined Methodist societies, they brought with them, in Max Weber's words, an "elective affinity" for the features of Wesleyan ideology and organization that best matched their understanding of the purposes of their new community.[5] In this proclivity they were not significantly different from other Methodists or, for that matter, members of any church. But as the individuals possessing authority within the local societies—as class leaders, exhorters, local preachers, trustees, and potential future itinerants—the men in these Methodist congregations, most specifically the white men, operated within a different set of social roles from those of white women and black men and women and shaped the movement in distinctive ways. And depending upon the commitment and ambitions of their male leaders, Middle Atlantic Methodist societies were models of community cohesion or cauldrons of community conflict.

WESLEYANISM, WEALTH, AND SOCIAL CLASS

John Wesley had something to say about wealth, as he did about most subjects. Early on, Wesley favored for his followers what one author has described as a kind of "primitive communism," similar to that of the later utopian socialists. Unlike John Locke, Wesley held that his followers did not possess a natural right to their property but were called to share whatever goods they accumulated. As he saw it, wealth was the "mammon of unrighteousness," held in trust for the service of God. Methodists, he stressed, should gain as much wealth as possible, save as much as possible, and then give away as much as possible.[6]

Wesley's attempts to control the property of his followers fared no better than his attempts to control their sexuality or the American Methodists' efforts to end slaveholding among their ranks. But to the end of his life, he came down hard on the accumulation of overgreat assets. To be rich was to have "above the plain necessaries or (at most) conveniences of life." God entrusted wealth to his people, but not its ownership. Money in excess of what was needed for plain living should be given to charity. Excessive riches led to atheism, idolatry, pride, self-will, contempt, resentment, revenge, anger, and fretfulness.[7] The last of Wesley's sermons, "The Danger of Increasing Riches," was, in the words of one of its editors, a "résumé of a long series of denunciations of greed and surplus accumulation, especially among professing Christians."[8] In many respects Wesley supported what Edward Thompson has called a "moral economy," but one that promoted the voluntary distribution of wealth from the rich to the poor, rather than the forced seizure of property by the poor.[9]

The first American Methodist preachers had more to say on many subjects than they did either on the dangers of riches that the great majority of their followers did not possess or, conversely, on working-class consciousness.[10] But it is evident that the Methodist itinerants and their followers were well aware of differences in social rank among Americans and attempted especially to evangelize among the poor, as called for by Wesley and the MEC discipline. In addition to preaching to slaves and free blacks—the largest segment of the American laboring classes—Methodist preachers regularly sought out locations where other workers and day laborers were congregated. Iron forges, the first industrial sites in Pennsylvania, New Jersey, and northern Maryland, manned by blacks and poor immigrants, were favored stops. Despite rumors that the colliers planned to shoot him, Benjamin Abbott preached at Pott's Furnace in Pennsylvania during the war; he reported that "several of the colliers' faces were all in streaks where the tears ran down their cheeks." Near the Batsto Iron Works in New Jersey, Asbury urged that a chapel be built "for the benefit of those men . . . employed . . . in the manufacture of iron—rude and rough, and strangely ignorant of God."[11]

Many preachers were not far removed in background from the men among whom they proselytized. Abbott, it will be recalled, was himself a tenant farmer and former street-fighter. While any number of the itinerants—Freeborn Garrettson, Ezekiel Cooper, and Philip Gatch stand out—were the scions of long-established families of Maryland's lesser gentry, many others were farmers, artisans, and laboring men before they joined the itinerant ranks. Still others, whatever their backgrounds, subscribed to the value of daily labor and what Ronald Schultz has called the "small-producer tradition" of artisans and other men of middling wealth.[12] "My parents were neither rich nor poor," Joseph Everett wrote, "but laboured and taught me to labour for my living." With his conversion, he likewise "set out to labour and keep under the wicked flesh. . . . I now earned my bread by the labour of my hands: and believe no man can live long in the favour of GOD, without using proper care to provide for himself and his houshold." In this way, Everett continued, "I lived, and studied divinity at the plow, axe, or hoe, instead of the college." Another American itinerant preacher wrote in the margins of an official tally of the terms of service remaining for slaves manumitted by Baltimore Methodists: "And when ought a poor Methodist Travelling Preacher to be free? Ans. When he can do no more work, and his Master says to him, 'Rest from thy labours.' "[13] Echoing a conviction held in common by English and American Methodists, Thomas Webb's wife, Grace, exhorted her son, living in America, "[I]f Jesus is but with you the morsel earned by the sweat of your brow, will be far sweeter than if you had come to an independant fortune, without the enjoyment of his presence."[14]

Whether they came to Methodism from above, within, or below the middling ranks of Revolutionary society, however, the itinerants were a serious threat to a social order in which distinctions in wealth were widely touted and exhibitionist displays were regular features of male culture. Not surprisingly, the first Methodists' commentary on the social dependency of the poor and the arbitrary power of the rich emerged in connection with episodes of physical confrontation between them and their opponents that continued after the Revolutionary War.

Benjamin Abbott, the laboring preacher, appeared to attract special hostility, as well as to take some pleasure in recording his peaceable triumphs over violent assailants. Hence, on Long Island in the early 1790s, while Abbott led a meeting, with the disabled daughter of a local gentleman in attendance, several local "grandees" appeared on the scene, blaming the Methodists—well-known critics of gambling and other sports of excess—for a horse-racing accident that had occurred the same day. A crowd of unidentified social composition then attacked the building where the Methodist meeting had been held, although, as Abbott remarked, "we were in a free country." In the following year, in Upper Penn's Neck, New Jersey, local people reportedly planned to disrupt one of Abbott's meetings by running a horse past the house where he was appointed to preach.

When Abbott was holding forth in a meetinghouse in nearby Salem, a group of "club-gentry" invaded the premises, one positioning himself in the middle of the house, another stationed three feet from the door, a two-foot truncheon in hand, and several more standing sentry outside, similarly armed. Abbott pronounced Salem famous for vice. One of his adversaries retorted that it was as good a place as ever. Abbott replied that his assailants were breaking the law and would be fined £20 or sent to jail. When he then proceeded to delineate the various points of law relevant to the case, followed by an accounting of the rigors of God's judgment, his assailant fled from the room exclaiming, "Do not judge, do not judge!" A Quaker standing watch by the door called out as he rushed past, "Thou hast met with thy match."[15]

The Methodists were confronted with this mixture of "club-gentry" and laboring-class opposition in other parts of the Middle Atlantic. In rural Crosswicks, New Jersey, the locals subverted a Methodist meeting by converting the revival into a town event. The officiating itinerant reported that the "people seemed as if they would over run us for awhile. For they broke the door open once or more, and a number of them a selling watermellons and cake, and beer, and rum etc. through the whole Meeting." "This is not a market house," one preacher exclaimed in exasperation at those mocking a Methodist revival in Gunpowder Neck, Maryland.[16]

In the cities, Methodists faced other kinds of challenges. Here the temptations of material wealth were perhaps the greatest, as were the twin lures of socializing and Sabbath-breaking. Although Asbury regularly condemned the mass of urban inhabitants of even relatively small towns like Dover in Delaware, Philadelphia, the nation's largest city, was especially a cause for his lamentation. "O Philadelphia!" he wrote in distress in the late 1790s, "I have had very little faith for that city. I have often remarked the general contempt of the Sabbath; the constant noise of carriages; there is a perpetual disturbance of worshipping assemblies."[17] The regular visitations of yellow fever seemed only to confirm a number of Methodists' impressions that divine punishment awaited the city's inhabitants at some suitable future time.[18]

Here too the Methodists experienced the threat of mob violence. In 1792, the stationed preacher at St. George's reported that the previous winter "the civil rights" and "religious privileges" of worshiping Methodists had been invaded when "ill-behaved people" forced open the doors and windows of the church, throwing in brickbats that injured one member of the congregation. During the week,

> [t]he rabble collected at the door, among whom were some young men armed with musquets, & who spoke as if they intended to shoot the minister in the pulpit. Soon after the mob rushed in at the door, perhaps to the amount of 100 or 150 persons; they then crowded up the ile towards the pulpit & there mocked & insulted the minister, laughing & swearing as loud as common to be heard in the streets; & then with their hands & stamping their feet on the floor with the utmost violence, so that the minister's voice was quite lost in the noise.[19]

Southwark's Ebenezer Chapel was also subject to a crowd assault. In 1792 Asbury reported that "the *mobility* came in like the roaring of the sea; boys were around the doors, and the streets were in an uproar." The next day, as the crowds came to service and the preacher was barely able to control their "fighting, swearing, threatening," Asbury waxed uncharacteristically apocalyptic: "This is a wicked, horribly wicked city. God will send pestilence amongst them, and slay them by hundreds and thousands. . . . [F]or their unfaithfulness they will be smitten in anger. . . . [T]he Lord will visit their streets with the *silence of desolation*."[20]

Without evidence from the assailants themselves, it is difficult to know what provoked specific anti-Methodist attacks. But, as with slaveholders' responses to the Methodists' antislavery activism, it is evident that great social unease and fear of social devolution shadowed the itinerants wherever they traveled. In a sermon delivered in Maryland in 1791 on the Methodists' overrighteousness—a common theme in Anglican antievangelical discourse—the Reverend J.G.J. Bend insisted that "[i]t is impolitic in those in inferior stations, to set themselves up, as teachers of those above them. 'Who made thee a prince & judge over us?' will be the natural question." The Methodists, another Anglican report complained, empowered their black and women followers and ensnared gullible folk with their enthusiastic preaching.[21] They were, in short, social levelers, threatening the good order of society just as they undermined traditional family relations. "Away with you. I want no more of you here," one woman shouted at Benjamin Abbott when he claimed her son was converted. "Whitefield was here like you, turning the world upside down: I want no more of your being born again."[22]

The Methodists' efforts to keep their movement free of control by the elites is reflected in Bishop Asbury's advice to Freeborn Garrettson regarding the hazards of chapel building. The building of preaching houses, Asbury noted, was a complicated process, for "[y]ou will make rich men necessary and they will rule you and impede your discipline if you are not well aware." Referring to the city societies themselves, he added, "We groan under heavy debt in [New] York, Philadelphia, and Baltimore and it weakens the hands of the poor among us and strengthens the hands of the few Rich, to oppose our strictness of discipline." Methodism, in short, was a movement designed for the lower and middling ranks in society, to be controlled by a missionary fraternity rather than vestrylike trustees. "I am for no trade but truth," Asbury wrote to a friend in England.[23]

From the start, however, Asbury and his preachers relied on the support of wealthy patrons of the movement, whose gifts they accepted (in the form of land grants for chapels and donations of money), whose servants they converted, and whose wives and daughters formed a bulwark sustaining Methodist itinerants' daily rounds.[24] The itinerants were able to convert many of these patrons themselves. Historian William Williams has identified numerous such adherents among the Eastern Shore and Delaware gentry: Benton Harris of Worcester County; Henry Airey and Henry Ennalls of Dorchester County; General James Benson, Thomas Harrison, William Hindman, and Henry Banning of Talbot County; Capt. William Frazier, Phillip Harrington, and Henry Downes of Caroline County; Col. William Hopper, William Bruff, Robert Emory, and James Bordley

Figure 9. Dudley's Chapel, 1783, Sudlersville, Queen
Annes County, Maryland. The oldest surviving chapel
built for Methodist worship, typical of the Methodists'
steepleless preaching houses. Photograph by author.

of Queen Annes County; Thomas White, Philip Barratt, and Allen McLane of
Kent County, Delaware; and David Nutter, Rhoads Shankland, John Wiltbank,
Ezekiel Williams, and Lemuel Davis of Sussex County, Delaware. Methodist law-
yers and physicians in the same areas included Richard Bassett and Dr. Abraham
Ridgely of Dover, and Dr. James Anderson of Chestertown. Dr. Sluyter Bouchell
of Cecil County was a strong sympathizer.[25]

Another wealthy convert, Henry Foxall, was the son of the forge-operator in
West Bromwich near Birmingham under whom Asbury had served as an apprentice. In the late 1790s Foxall emigrated to Philadelphia, where he formed a partnership with Robert Morris to establish the Eagle Iron Foundry and was subsequently awarded one of the first defense contracts from the new federal
government. When the government moved to the District of Columbia in 1800,
Foxall followed, erecting the Columbia Foundry above Georgetown for the con-

tinued production of armaments. He quickly adopted a southern lifestyle, purchasing slaves and fashioning himself into a great host to federal luminaries, including Thomas Jefferson, at his house on Frederick (now Thirty-fourth) Street. At the same time, Foxall was the main contributor to the construction of a church for the Georgetown Methodists in 1803, nearly a third of whom were black. Epitomizing the multiple characteristics of some of Methodism's rich men—geographical and social mobility, engagement in the new trades and professions, easy movement between the greater political world and the often lesser Methodist one—Foxall also represented some of the potential hazards of rich men's involvement with the new religious societies: not least of all the power of slaveholders among their ranks.[26]

Almost invariably the expectation was that these wealthy members would indeed become trustees or, at the least, major subscribers to the building of preaching houses. As Eleanor Dorsey wrote to her cousin Harry Dorsey Gough in 1802 from Lyons Town, Ontario County, New York, praising Gough's return to the faith, "the Man who was first made usefull to my Soul at Perry Hall is once more engaged in God['s] service." Now the "poor Breathren in this wilderness" required the help of the Baltimore gentry to build a preaching house for the thirty members on their circuit. Dorsey hoped that Gough, along with "Mr. [Jesse] Hollingsworth, Mr. [James] McCannon, Mr. R[obert] Carnan" and "many more of our Ritch Breathren" would help out.[27]

The coexistence of the Methodists' missionary goals with their frequent reliance on the wealthy "new men" of the early republic produced significant stresses in the early years of the movement. For while Wesley's *General Rules* called for restraint in business practices and adherence to a moral political economy, Methodist men's attitudes toward the acquisition of wealth continued to represent as wide a spectrum as the social backgrounds from which they came. For the itinerants there was always the danger that the wealthy men in the movement would, as Asbury put it, "decrease in grace" and move on to other associations, leaving the Methodists with a strong workingmen's contingent but without the material resources that kept churches afloat.

At the same time, individual accounts of the Middle Atlantic city societies—once more in New York, Philadelphia, and Baltimore—suggest that in addition to perceiving their churches as centers of male sociability, much as they were for women and blacks, Methodist men also expected to run their local societies, sometimes in defiance of the traveling ministry, sometimes in defiance of their own fellow Methodists.

NEW YORK CITY: WORKINGMAN'S CHURCH

While not the fastest-growing urban center in the nation after the Revolutionary War—Baltimore held that distinction—postwar New York City was nevertheless a study in urban expansion. With a fire destroying much of the lower city in 1776, and the dislocations brought on by British occupation ending only in 1782, New

York's population dwindled to fewer inhabitants than before the war. But in 1790, census takers reported 31,225 residents in the city; by 1800, this total had grown nearly twofold to 57,663; and by 1810, the city was to grow by more than a third to 91,659 residents.[28]

Growth did not automatically produce grandeur. In the mid-1780s, New York was still "a neglected place, built chiefly of wood, and in a state of prostration and decay." Noah Webster described parts of lower Manhattan around the Stock Exchange on Broad Street as "recovering from its ruins."[29] But the city's extension seemed unstoppable. In the mid-1790s, its rural hinterlands were retreating with each new ward surveyed, and the city's boundaries had reached Fresh Water Pond below Bayard Street on the north, Rutgers Street on the east, and the vicinity of Greenwich Street on the west. The city's central thoroughfare, Broadway, extended west of and parallel to Bowery Lane, from the old South Ward to as-yet-unbuilt districts above Hester Street. Along this avenue the commercial elite erected their new mansions, far removed from the commotion and noise of the wharves by the East River. Housing for the city's middling and poor classes expanded into the Fourth, Fifth, and Sixth Wards as immigrants from northern Europe and migrants from rural areas (including blacks from Delaware and Maryland) poured in looking for work.[30] Through these years the city's infrastructure was barely able to keep up, creating a notoriously tight housing market. Recent construction in the fields beyond Broadway, as one Methodist itinerant observed, appeared "like a New City built upon them."[31]

In addition to the barracks and battery at the base of the island, now used for promenading, New York's chief public building was its city hall, renamed Federal Hall, the scene of Washington's first inaugural. A conjoined jail, bridewell, and almshouse stood near Broadway in the Sixth Ward. The bulk of the remaining "public" buildings were all religious structures, which multiplied from a total of eighteen before the war to twenty-one by the mid-1790s. Three old Dutch Reformed, Anglican, and Presbyterian churches formed part of New York's urban fabric, as well as "Old" and "New" Quaker meetinghouses, the "Jews Synagogue," German and French Reformed churches, and Baptist and Seceder churches—all of them preceding the Methodists.[32]

The city's growth and economic development, prompting the expansion in the mass-market trades of shoemaking, tailoring, tanning, paper manufacturing, and cabinetmaking, among others,[33] were inevitably accompanied by social restructuring. Sizable fortunes now divided New York's merchant elite from lesser artisans and laboring folk. By the early 1800s, New York's master craftsmen, many of them rising entrepreneurs, were to come into increasing conflict with the poorly paid journeymen and immigrants in their employ.[34] Journeymen, lesser artisans, and small shopkeepers were part of a middling population whose economic status, in the words of one historian, was "not much above that of the poor, and well below that of the rich. These men resided and worked in three-room cottages and two-story houses lining the streets and alleys of the new wards. Many were young, unmarried, and foreign-born journeymen and laboring men without households.[35] The city was known as well for its tradition of "artisan republicanism," first promulgated by the radical anti-British Committee of Mechanics before the war. Artisan republicanism was a distinctly procommercial Federalist faith in the years immediately following the war; but by the mid-1790s, many of the five-hundred-member General Society of Mechanics and Tradesmen had begun the rapid transition from Federalist to Democratic-Republican.[36]

To a remarkable extent, the men in New York's Methodist society mirrored the social character of the city in the postwar years. With the end of the war, the society was an inchoate remnant of the original congregation. Just sixty whites and blacks were in attendance at the solitary chapel on John Street. To attract members, the preachers took liberties with Methodist ritual, such as baptizing a number of adults in the late 1780s.[37] In 1789 stationed preacher Thomas Morrell nevertheless initiated the building of a new chapel in Second Street northeast of the city center. The following year he led a revival in the city's two churches. "Persecution Rages," he wrote of the public reaction to the turbulent revival meetings. "The people say we are going mad—and threaten to complain to the magistrate for our breaking the peace." But the society had "3 Powerful Times on the Sabbath evenings at which Meetings as near as we can Judge about 40 were converted. . . . 76 Joined in Jany., 62 in Feby."[38]

The following year, the society grew dramatically. By 1791, 627 members were attending the two Methodist chapels, in John Street and Second Street near Forsythe, a more than threefold increase from five years before. In 1796, the stationed preacher reported a total Methodist population of 751. At the end of the decade in 1800, approximately 776 New Yorkers, white and black, belonged to five Methodist chapels: John Street, Second Street, North River (also known as the Hudson or Duane Street Chapel), Two Mile Stone Chapel in the Bowery, and the African Zion society.[39]

Large and unwieldy, the New York circuit was a challenging one for the Methodist preachers. The stationed itinerants struggled to keep the various congregations within the MEC discipline. Some of the sixteen hundred people to whom Asbury preached in 1796 were "wicked and wild." It was necessary "to preach conviction and conversion among our own," he continued, "as among other congregations."[40] Turnover was alarming. Just twenty-five, or 38.5 percent, of the men, white and black, who belonged to the society in 1786 were still members in 1791. The balance of more than 60 percent had moved on to other churches, to employment in other towns and regions, or had died. In 1796, eighty-one men, white and black, or once again just 38.2 percent, remained from five years earlier.[41] A significant proportion of the men—young, laboring-class, or geographically mobile individuals drawn in by the revivals of the 1790s—do not appear in the city directories.[42] They included Joseph McCord, excluded in 1787 for "Imoderate Drinking [of] Spirit⁵ Liquors"; William Lasston, excluded "for the habitual neglect of family prayer [and because] he had also treated the preachers with great contempt"; and Cornelius Cupton, "a Poor youth—Ruin'd by bad Example."[43]

Like their female counterparts, New York's Methodist men were ethnically varied, placing yet other demands on the preachers' ingenuity. In addition to black members, men of English, Scottish, Irish, Welsh, Dutch, German, and French backgrounds belonged to the society, itself at the geographical center of similarly diverse Methodist chapels in the greater New York area: in Brooklyn, on Staten Island, and in the village of Tuckahoe in Westchester County.[44] To meet the linguistic demands of the New York congregations, the conference supplied the city's chapels with preaching in German and French whenever possible.[45]

Despite the changeability and heterogeneity of New York's Methodists through these years, however, two other social distinctions characterized the city's Methodist men. One was the enduring core of founding members, composed chiefly of prewar immigrants. The other was the substantial and rising proportion of the city's leading Methodists who were recruits from another sector of the city's economy: skilled tradesman.

Turning first to the "great" men: Among those who had belonged since before the war were English-born William Lupton and Henry Newton;[46] James Harper, another Englishman, who had organized the Newtown society, the first Methodist congregation on Long Island;[47] German-born Philip Jacob Arcularius, who came to the Methodists in 1787 from the German Lutheran Church;[48] Prussian-born John Staples;[49] and Paul Hick, Irish-Palatine relation of Methodist "Mother" Barbara Heck.[50] Israel Disosway, of Huguenot descent, organized the first Methodist society on Staten Island before moving to Manhattan to send his sons to Columbia College.[51] Another member in the 1780s, John Jarvis, the son of original trustee James Jarvis (now dead), had returned from England in about 1783 with his new wife, one of John and Charles Wesley's grandnieces.[52]

Several of these men fit the description of those often expected to play leading roles in religious societies and urban associations. Lupton, Newton, Staples, and Disosway were merchants. James Harper moved, after the war, to Manhattan, where he opened a flourishing grocery business in Maiden Lane.[53] John Jarvis shortly removed with his family to Philadelphia, where he was variously employed as a money-collector, a scrivener, an accountant, and an innkeeper, while his wife took up midwifery: not a wealthy family but one holding professional status, albeit of a lesser kind.[54] Others belonged to a new urban class, artisan-entrepreneurs, interconnected with fellow Methodists. Philip Arcularius was a master baker who also ran a tanning business in the city's industrial "Swamp" district; two of his daughters married into the Harper family.[55] John Staples, a sugar-baker, was also merchant-proprietor of the "Sugar House" in Liberty Street, one of the first American sugar refineries, with the dubious distinction of having been used as a British prison during the war. In 1787, Staples purchased a substantial farm on Greenwich Street in the "Outward" of the city, the first of a number of land purchases that were to elevate him into the ranks of New York's lesser gentry by the end of the 1790s.[56] Paul Hick ran a plaster-of-paris manufactory and was married to Hannah Dean, another Irish-born Methodist from the first congregation in the city.[57]

Most of these men, then, were representative of the "rich" Methodists whose influence both Wesley and Asbury lamented, but whose wealth was often the result of assiduous attachment to the Wesleyan rules of frugality and industry combined with being in the right place at the right time. They supported their chapels in the manner of a patron group, although not without compensation: the creditors of the New York Methodist society, for example, including William Lupton, Henry Newton, Philip Arcularius, and William Chave, annually received as much as £70 interest on church debts. They probably also helped to support the poor members, mainly women, who appeared on the society's relief lists after 1795.[58]

New York's Methodist businessmen also profited from networks of financial and legal support within their religious circles. Among John Staples's many customers in the 1790s were Methodist itinerants and fellow New York artisans Cornelius Warner and Peter McLean, and Staples's brother-in-law Thomas Brinkley. Staples had substantial dealings with George Suckley, a partner in the Newbould & Holy firm of Sheffield, England, and husband of Catharine Rutsen, Catherine Livingston Garrettson's Methodist classmate.[59]

Too much may be made of the affluence of New York's leading Methodists. Few of these men could compete for influence with the heads of the big families in the city: the Livingstons, De Lanceys, Schuylers, Jays, and Clintons. In contrast to the Philadelphia and Baltimore Methodists, as will be evident shortly, the richer New York Methodists filled virtually none of the offices of the numerous civic, ethnic, and voluntary organizations listed in the 1796 city register—including the Society for Promoting the Manumission of Slaves and the General Society of Mechanics and Tradesmen. Instead, Methodist men appear in substantial numbers in another part of the register: the list of more than three hundred carters—teamsters—that formed the bedrock of the city's service economy.[60]

The New York Methodist society, in short, was a workingman's church, and artisans in particular formed its most significant social constituency. The predominance of tradesmen among the New York Methodists is apparent from the start, but even more so with the intensifying political climate of the 1790s.

In 1786, artisans already constituted half of those society members whose livelihoods can be identified with any certainty. By 1791, more than 100 Methodist men, white and black, may be found in the city directories. Of these, 58, or 54.7 percent, were engaged in tradesmen's crafts. By 1796, the numbers of these men had risen to 84, or 60.9 percent of those whose occupations can be identified.[61]

Artisans also greatly outnumbered the Methodists from the ranks of merchants and shopkeepers. In 1791, for example, 4.8 artisans belonged to the New York society for every merchant and retailer; in 1796, the ratio had risen to 5.25.[62] By contrast, in Philadelphia in 1796, just 2.1 artisans belonged to the Methodist society for every merchant and retailer; and in Baltimore City in 1801, the ratio was 1.9.[63] In New York, there were also proportionately many more tradesmen among the Methodists than in the city as a whole: 60.9 percent for the Methodists in 1796 compared to an estimated 40.7 percent for the city around the same time. The Methodist society, that is, can be understood to have held a *particular* attraction to the city's tradesmen.[64]

Filling the ranks of New York's Methodist artisans were men such as house carpenters Stephen Rudd, Cornelius Warner, and Abraham Russell, the last a longtime Methodist who superintended construction of the city's Methodist chapels; hatter Abraham Brower and shoemaker Elias Vanderlip (later recruited to the itinerancy);[65] wheelwright William Cooper, ship carpenter William Valleau, and baker Jonas Humbert;[66] as well as Andrew Mercein, a baker of Swiss descent; and John Sprosen, a Windsor-chair maker, who together with Samuel Stilwell, a grocer, was one of the original trustees of the Second Street Church.[67]

As is evident from these men's occupations, certain kinds of tradesmen, notably from the city's low-capital crafts—house carpentry, woodworking, shoemaking, and tailoring—were especially prevalent among the Methodists. In 1791, for example, eleven house carpenters and three other men in the building trades accounted for 14.1 percent of all the white Methodist men whose names appear in the city directories. Fourteen shoemakers and five tailors constituted another 19.2 percent. Altogether, men in these four occupations made up a third (33.3 percent) of all white men in the Methodist society whose occupations are known and 57.9 percent of all white artisans.[68] Over the next five years, the society witnessed a steady increase in small merchants and specialty tradesmen like cabinetmakers. But the numbers of middling craftsmen remained much the same. By 1796, nineteen carpenters and eleven men in other building trades now made up 24 percent of the white men with identifiable occupations. The other two largest categories—nine shoemakers and nine tailors—still accounted for 14.4 percent of these men. Taken together, the four occupational categories—carpentry, woodworking, shoemaking, and tailoring—comprised 38.4 percent of the white Methodist men and 60 percent of all white artisans in this year.[69]

The social class of these Methodist men, of course, says little about their cultural mentalité. Insofar as they were men of middling rank, it can be assumed with some legitimacy that they subscribed to the "small-producer tradition" favored by so many artisans; insofar as they were Methodists, it can be taken for granted that they adhered to Wesley's *General Rules* prescribing self-control and upright business practices. The significant presence of shoemakers may perhaps be seen as a remnant of a proclivity for religious radicalism that inspired Jakob Boehme, the German Reformation mystic, and George Fox, ecstatic founder of the Quakers, both cordwainers. Others still may have been attracted to the artisan republicanism whose evolution into trade-union activism Sean Wilentz has traced back to New York's immediate postwar years.[70]

A handful of New York Methodists, particularly artisan-entrepreneurs, were headed for careers in democratic politics in the next century. Thus in 1801, Philip Arcularius, master baker and tanner, ran for the state assembly on the Democratic-Republican ticket, although several years earlier he had opposed the wage demands of New York's journeyman shoemakers.[71] Another of the society's master bakers, Jonas Humbert, rose through the ranks of the General Society of Mechanics to run for city alderman and was associated briefly with the radical "workingmen's" movement of the late 1820s.[72] Grocer Gilbert Coutant, originally from a New Rochelle Huguenot family, was a "Tammany fixer" by the 1820s.[73] A Methodist lower down the social scale, teamster Uzziah Coddington, defying any direct links among religion, social class, and political affiliation, had been an operative for the Federalists in ward elections in the 1790s.[74]

But the main source of authority for artisan Methodists, especially men from the poorer trades, lay closer to home. Tradesmen ran the New York chapels and appeared to do so with bravado. In 1786, just one merchant, William Lupton, and one artisan-entrepreneur, John Staples, may be found among New York's Methodist class leaders; the others were hatter Abraham Brower, chair-maker William Tillow, and baker Jonas Humbert, along with English immigrant Cornelius Cook and two women, Mary Anderson and Jane Barsary.[75] By 1791, John Staples was the solitary trustee from among the society's elite; and all but two of the class leaders were tradesmen, among them comb-maker Daniel Carpenter and housepainter Thomas Hutchinson, coheads of the Methodist class at the poorhouse.[76] In 1796, twenty-one artisans along with one sea captain and one carter filled the vast majority (88.5 percent) of positions as class leaders in New York, making the city's lay leadership the most plebeian among the Middle Atlantic city societies.[77]

An assertive group, New York's class leaders ran into trouble with the Methodist hierarchy—with some frequency. As early as 1787, Philip Ebert was expelled "for charging the Preachers with misconduct & refusing either to be silent among the people or to prove it from the bible or form of discipline."[78] Another controversy, its content unknown, centered on house carpenter Stephen Rudd. Rudd was removed as a class leader in 1791, along with a host of other artisans and members of unknown social identity. Two years later he was expelled from the society altogether.[79]

In the mid- to late 1790s, other events suggest that the middling men in the New York society, mainly tradesmen, were trying to maintain control and were willing to abandon the Methodists for churches more sympathetic to the claims of their rank. In 1795, one group attempted unsuccessfully to vote out the old trustees, again for reasons not specified.[80] By the following year, seven of the eleven members who had left with Rudd had returned. But they may have been the same group who departed the Methodist society shortly thereafter, identified as "Universalists," i.e., members of another religious society with much more explicit ties to artisan-radicals.[81] A year later, a vocal minority objected to the building of church pews, which, it was feared, would lead to pew rents, always a hardship for the poor. Suggesting the resolute, perhaps even reckless, independence of the New Yorkers, Asbury complained that the chapel class leaders were ignorant of sections of the Methodist discipline and indifferent to the bishop's labors in other parts of the republic.[82]

New York's Methodist artisans were thus products of two often conflicting worlds: the Wesleyan culture of sobriety, work, and "heart-religion" and the New York tradesmen's culture of increasingly radical political consciousness. Not for the first time, religion and politics were potentially in serious conflict for Methodists. The ramifications of the politicized 1790s were even more evident for Philadelphia's richer—and much more divided—Methodist community.

PHILADELPHIA: ANATOMY OF A METHODIST SCHISM

According to one member's recollection, at the end of the Revolutionary War St. George's Chapel in Philadelphia was a "dreary, cold-looking place," heated in winter by a leaky stovepipe from which "smoke would frequently issue, and fill all the house." Women brought portable woodstoves to warm their feet during services. Incongruously, in an effort to improve the appearance of worship at the chapel, the stationed preachers adhered to Wesley's Sunday Service, and itinerant Henry Willis led services wearing a black silk gown, an Anglican-style pretension that "gave offence to many" and was soon given up. At the start of worship, Johnny Hood, the "setter of tunes," stood below the pulpit to lead the congregation in hymn singing. The society also installed a floor and erected a box pulpit, "a square thing not unlike a Watch box, with the top sawed off," for the use of stationed preachers until more elegant renovations might be carried out.[83]

Despite the condition of their chapel, membership at the Philadelphia society rose substantially in the 1780s. When it began to decline again at the end of the decade, Asbury, despite his reservations about empowering wealthy members, persuaded a small group to accept appointment as trustees for incorporation. In August 1790, construction was completed on a second chapel, called Ebenezer, on Second Street in Southwark, south of the central wards, on land supplied by shipbuilder John Petherbridge. In this neighborhood, a class had been meeting at Robert Fitzgerald's block-and-pump shop in Penn Street since the late 1760s.[84]

Asbury typically expressed frustration at the Philadelphia society's slow rate of growth: "My soul longs for more religion in this city. . . . [T]wenty years have we been labouring in Pennsylvania, and there are not one thousand in society: how many of these are truly converted God knows:"[85] Part of the society's difficulties rested with its need to compete with the numerous denominations in the city: the well-established Anglicans, as well as New Side and Old Side Presbyterians, Baptists, Moravians, Lutherans, German Reformed, Roman Catholics, Jews, and, of course, the city's founding denomination, the Religious Society of Friends, or Quakers. The Methodists recruited members from Philadelphia's laboring folk and hence were, in Asbury's words, "generally poor," although, he added, "perhaps it is well; when men become rich, they sometimes forget that they are Methodists."[86]

In the 1790s, in Philadelphia as in New York, Asbury's efforts began to pay off. At the start of the decade, after a steep decline, several hundred Methodists were meeting in nine white and two black classes. The tally of members rose steadily thereafter, from 532 in 1795, to 543 in 1797, to 622 in 1799. By the last date, Philadelphia Methodists were meeting in the four chapels now operating in the city: St. George's, Ebenezer, and the specifically black chapels of Bethel and Zoar.[87]

Over the same period, St. George's trustees initiated a series of renovations at the city's main building, paid for by subscriptions and loans, chiefly from the trustees themselves. Much of the work appears to have been contracted out to the numerous non-Methodist artisans working in the city.[88]

Philadelphia also regained some of the prominence among Methodists that it had lost to Baltimore during the war. John Dickins moved the MEC book business to Philadelphia in 1789, taking over the book stewardship from James Kinnear, an Irish auctioneer. In 1790, Dickins was also appointed treasurer of the MEC and its circuit collections. Another located preacher, Thomas Haskins, was at work editing Asbury's journals. By 1796, the general conference of the church recognized the creditworthiness of the Philadelphia members by appointing Haskins and eight other trustees as managers of the Chartered Fund, a pension plan for indigent itinerants and their families. Preaching was held regularly for large crowds in the statehouse yard.[89]

For other reasons, the Philadelphia society was a different entity from its pre-war predecessor. Much changed from the relatively homogeneous gathering of the early 1770s, the Philadelphia Methodists like their New York brethren were now racially and socially polyglot. As in New York, the greatest variety was ethnic. The majority of Philadelphia Methodists were Anglo-Americans, but Scottish, Welsh, Irish, and German names appear with frequency. About an eighth of the members were black, bearing the surnames of liberated slaves: Barbary, Boss, Gibbs, Green, Lux, and Solomon.[90] As in New York, an unknown number of Methodists may have been immigrants. At least two members of Ebenezer Church, Cuthbert and David Landreth, were English-born Wesleyans who ran a nursery above Twelfth Street.[91]

As in New York, many of the Philadelphia Methodists were tradesmen and laboring men. In 1794, the earliest year for which membership records survive, 354 men and women, white and black, belonged to the society as a whole. Of the 141 white men in this year, 33, or 50.8 percent of those with known occupations, were artisans. Eleven more, or 16.9 percent, were mariners, transport and service workers, or laborers, although a substantial proportion of the 76 men too poor or low in status to appear in the city directories probably also fit these categories. In 1796, with a relatively static membership, the majority of Methodist members, old and new, were still workingmen.[92]

Unlike their counterparts in New York, however, the aggregate of Philadelphia's Methodist artisans in particular more closely mirrored the proportion of artisans in the city as a whole, estimated to have been approximately 42 percent in 1798. And while the representation of the mercantile classes in the Methodist churches was distinctly lower than in the city—the latter an estimated 40 percent of the working population in 1798—the Philadelphia Methodist society contained within it a much greater constituency of merchants and retailers than did New York's Methodist congregations. In 1794, 14 men, or 21.5 percent of white men with known occupations, and in 1796, 15 men, or 26.8 percent, were merchants or shopkeepers. As mentioned above, in 1796, just 2.1 artisans belonged to the Philadelphia society for every merchant and/or retailer: a significant contrast to the strong tradesmen's presence (5.25 artisans for every merchant and/or artisan) at the New York congregations in the same year.[93]

Accentuating the social divides among the Philadelphia members, Philadelphia's leading Methodists, mainly merchants, were forming themselves into a modest but prosperous mercantile elite in the two decades after the war. In 1784, Jacob Baker, one of the society's founders, joined in a partnership in the dry goods business with Cornelius Comegys, a Revolutionary War veteran who had worked under Robert Morris in the Confederation Congress's Department of Finance and as a partner in Morris's mercantile house, Willing & Morris. Comegys joined the Methodists after marrying Baker's daughter Catharine.[94] The two partners engaged in some land speculation in the 1790s and appear to have lived in increasing comfort and leisure, on one occasion taking a holiday with preacher Ezekiel Cooper at the New Jersey shore.[95] In the late 1790s, Baker exhibited his upward mobility by making a number of improvements to his new house at the corner of Arch and Sixth Streets, assessed at a high $3,500 at the end of the decade.[96] Another merchant, Samuel Harvey, joined the Methodist society after his marriage to member Caleb North's sister Ann in 1794. By 1797, Harvey had established an importing and hardware partnership, Harvey & Worth, at 62 North Front Street, a neighbor of the Baker & Comegys firm, and an ironmongering business. His work as St. George's treasurer reveals an orderly mind, strict with accounts.[97] Along with founding member Lambert Wilmer (a flour merchant) and the other trustees, these men thrived on the profits of Philadelphia's regional and, in some cases, international trade.[98]

Even at Ebenezer Chapel in Southwark, the mariners' district, a "wooden town" with "a large proportion of the [city's] working people and but few of the wealthy,"[99] the two leading Methodists were doing well. Founding member Robert Fitzgerald was a man of "ample means." Another Ebenezer trustee, James Doughty, a shipwright, owned a brick house, stable, lot, and assorted personalty worth £253 in 1791. Eight years later, now a lumber merchant, Doughty had expanded his residence to two stories, with the addition of a countinghouse and a piazza. The Doughtys' taxable property was now valued at $2,100.[100]

Other important actors in the Methodist society were former itinerants engaged in commerce. John Dickins entered the publishing trade to support his work as the MEC book agent. Daniel Ruff ran a shoe warehouse on North Second Street.[101] The most successful of the located preachers, Thomas Haskins, was a former Maryland slaveholder and law student, and reluctant participant in the Christmas Conference in 1784. In 1785, he married Martha Potts, a descendant of one of the founders of Coalbrookdale in Britain and daughter of the Coventry, Pennsylvania, ironworks family.[102] He subsequently opened a grocery business in the city. In 1796, he formed the merchanting firm North & Haskins at 38 North Water Street with Caleb North, also a Methodist, who had seen active service with the Ninth Pennsylvania Regiment under General Anthony Wayne in the Revolutionary War.[103] Still other members were men in the rising professions: Josiah Lusby, who divided his time between practicing medicine and running a store, and William Penn Chandler, who was studying dentistry with Benjamin Rush when he received the call to preach.[104]

The men at the Philadelphia church benefited from the prosperity of, and their interconnectedness with, their fellow Methodists, including members of the Free African Society. One Methodist retailer, Thomas Armat, proprietor of a hardware and yard-goods store, for example, carried on business with a Methodist network that extended throughout the surrounding region. Over the fourteen years between 1781 and 1794, Armat's customers ranged from preachers Asbury, Robert Cloud, John Dickins, John Littlejohn, William Glendinning, Richard Allen, and Absalom Jones; to Philadelphia members Jacob Baker, Lambert Wilmer, Richard Mosely, Burton Wallace, Duncan Stewart, William Bell, Josiah Lusby, John Petherbridge, James Armstrong, John Hewson, William Wood, Robert Fitzgerald, Henry Manley, Richard Tolliff, John Dennis, and the firm North & Haskins; to Delaware Methodists Richard Bassett and Allan McLane; and Maryland Methodists Adam Fonerden, Richard Dallam, Henry Dorsey Gough, and Emanuel Kent. In the 1780s, Armat's business accounts contained several for the Methodist society itself, recording numerous cash advances for improvements for St. George's, as well as supplies of hardware and payment of the society's debts and ground rent.[105] In contrast to the relatively uninvolved (or uninvited) merchant members in New York, a number of Philadelphia's leading men participated in civic affairs as members of the Pennsylvania Abolition Society.[106]

Altogether, the Philadelphia Methodists were markedly divided between a merchant and retailing elite and an artisanal and laboring rank and file, more specifically between merchant trustees and artisan class leaders. In the 1790s, part of the latter group were shoemakers John Dennis, William Blair, William Pigeon, and Manley Smallwood; tailors Reiner Gilbert and Joseph Elton; cabinetmaker Pennel Beale; and carpenter Hugh Smith. The founding member Lambert Wilmer and shoe-dealer Henry Manley were among the few leaders who were not artisans. Trustees Hood and Doughty also served as class leaders; leaders Smith and Manley also served as trustees. For the most part, however, multiple officeholding was the exception rather than the rule, and the Philadelphia artisans played a significantly lesser role in their church than did their counterparts in New York.[107]

The bifurcation of the Philadelphia Methodists into leading founders and located preachers versus middling mechanics and lower-class laborers would accelerate with the increasing popularity and fervor of their religious meetings in the late 1790s. One outsider's account of a New Year's watch night at St. George's reveals the Philadelphians to have been gaining rather than declining in enthusiastic vigor, as well as acquiring an increasingly younger clientele. "I have just returned from a Methodist meeting," the young Connecticut observer wrote in 1797,

> where I have witnessed the most extraordinary scene that I ever viewed. . . . [W]e found them work'd up to a very extravagant pitch of zeal . . . the spirit progressed as the night advanced & before the old year had expired the house exhibited a scene of the utmost distress and confusion—groans issued from every quarter—one half the congregation were on their knees praying audibly at the same time. God—Jesus—and holy Ghost issued constantly in wild language from fifty tongues—young lads were bellowing, and

girls wringing their hands calling on the Lord and nearly fainting in a state of delirium—
the groans of the damned cou'd not be more terrible, nor the confusion of Babel more
compleat.[108]

The artisan members of the Methodists' two chapels, moreover, could not have
been entirely immune to the radical republican ideology that characterized labor
relations in Philadelphia and issued from its presses in the late 1790s and early
nineteenth century. Elhanan Winchester's Universalist Society in Lombard Street,
with close ties to the Democratic-Republican Society in the 1790s, was a strong
competitor with the Ebenezer Chapel Methodists for workingmen's allegiance.[109]
Tom Paine's egalitarianism was now familiar in *The Rights of Man*, and the
"small-producer" values of workingmen found expression in Benjamin Bache and
William Duane's newspaper, *The Aurora*. The city, location of both federal and
state governments, was the scene of some of the most vociferous party conflict
in the decade. Proto-socialist opinion was soon to make its way into the Philadelphia press with the reprinting of Irish radical James Reynold's *Equality* in the
deist magazine *The Temple of Reason* in 1802.[110]

At least one Philadelphia Methodist, English immigrant John Hewson, was a
product of this political world. In the late 1760s, Hewson had actively participated
in London's radical political clubs while baptizing his children in one of London's
dissenting chapels. Like Paine, Hewson read broadly in history and the Scriptures
to determine the origins of monarchical rule, coming to the conclusion, much as
Paine would in *Common Sense*, that monarchy was a usurpation of the sovereignty
of the people. Like Paine, in the early 1770s Hewson sought out Benjamin Franklin in London to inquire about the possibilities of succeeding as a tradesman in
the colonies, in his case as a calico-printer. The Hewson family left England in
1773, complete with textile-printing machinery and Franklin's letter of recommendation. In Philadelphia, Hewson set up shop in Kensington, north of the city
center.[111]

Unlike the English Methodist preachers, Hewson was an ardent patriot from the
start. He and his second wife, Zibiah Smallwood, named their first child Catherine
Washington Hewson, born in 1777 "while the brittish was [in] Possession of the
City." In 1775 Hewson joined the first republican grenadier company in Philadelphia and then the Philadelphia county militia as a commissioned officer.[112] He
is credited with marketing one of the first iconographic depictions of General
Washington, a portrait at the center of a calico handkerchief, based on a miniature
supplied by Martha Washington. In the spring of 1778, the Hewson family fled
to New Jersey with several hundred pounds' weight of printing works and tools.
Here Hewson formed a body of volunteers to seize goods headed to the British
army from New Jersey Tories. Hewson was soon captured by the British and
taken to Long Island, but made a dramatic escape by canoe back to the New
Jersey shoreline.[113]

After the war, however, Hewson's path diverged from that of his fellow radicals. Rather than going on to participate in the democratic and deistic causes of
the Revolutionary age, Hewson followed his wife into the Methodist society and

became an artisan-entrepreneur. With William Lang, an English immigrant designer and engraver, he produced some of the finest textiles available from an American manufactory. A firm Federalist, Hewson advertised his wares during Philadelphia's 4 July 1788 celebration of the ratification of the Federal Constitution. For this occasion, Hewson's muslin-printing machine formed the centerpiece of the float for the Pennsylvania Society for the Encouragement of Manufactures and Useful Arts, which also featured Hewson's partner cutting patterns for shawls, and Zibiah Hewson and four of the Hewson daughters stenciling designs on Hewson chintz under a Hewson Stars and Stripes while dressed in Hewson cottons. When he died in 1821, the manufacturer left a much-prized collection of Washington memorabilia to his children.[114]

No longer an immigrant artisan but an American entrepreneur, Hewson succeeded in the Middle Atlantic's burgeoning protoindustrial economy.[115] Some Philadelphia Methodists were doing so well that the hazards that Wesley and Asbury both associated with wealth were beginning to appear, as Methodists attempted to keep up with their conspicuously consuming neighbors. John Wrenshall, another English immigrant, commented on the apparently widespread indebtedness of the city's inhabitants and of his coreligionists in the 1790s: "Our neighbours on all sides of us were coming allmost daily to borrow money for the purpose of paying their notes in the bank, which surprised me much, on account of some of those who most frequently applyed in this way, keeping one or two Carriages with a pair of prancing horses, glittering trapping, and servants in proportion to attend them." One Methodist "expres'd to me his regret in being under the necessity of being at so much expence."[116]

By contrast, many laborers and journeymen and some artisans prospered less well. In the two decades following the Revolutionary War, Philadelphia journeymen—printers in 1786, carpenters in 1791, cabinet- and chair-makers in 1796, and shoemakers in 1799—for the first time resorted to strikes against their artisan-entrepreneur employers to resist falling wages, rising prices, and long hours. From their outreach at the city poorhouse, the Methodists would have been familiar with the fate of the city's inhabitants who fell victim to poverty and ill health in this otherwise affluent time, folk whom one itinerant called "the *poor*, the *mamed*, the *halt*, and the *Blind*."[117]

In conformity with Wesleyan principles, many Methodists would not have expected to increase in wealth or to obtain more than a competency, whatever the conditions of the economy. Bookseller John Dickins had no desire "to make an estate" but sought to live simply on an "abundance of labour, from year to year" (although he later observed that he found this difficult to do in the city "where *everything* must be bought"). Dickins was still a tenant at his death, as were a number of class leaders, renting houses from the richer members of the church.[118] Hugh Smith may well have been the prototypical small-producing Methodist in the congregation. Raised in Salem, New Jersey, Smith first joined the Philadelphia society in the mid-1770s and was a class leader as early as 1787. A carpenter, Smith made one of his many contributions to St. George's Chapel when he and another member constructed its new galleries in the early 1790s—scene of Richard Allen's and the other Free Africans' confrontation with the chapel trustees, but symbol as well of the society members' affection for their now thirty-year-old sanctuary.[119]

Smith's hero was Benjamin Abbott, his New Jersey mentor and the Methodists' shining example of the proud street-fighter converted to lover of Christ. Abbott also supported devout workingmen. As Smith recalled, "I have known him in the time of harvest, to take his men from the field to go with him to meeting, and yet pay them for the full day's work." Describing Abbott's transformation from rough youth to Christian traveler, Smith, still moved by the story years later, exclaimed: "Surely his conversion was a remarkable instance of sovereign grace and divine mercy! The lion, became the lamb! The hero in the service of the devil, became a bold veteran in the service of God."[120]

The Methodist movement was able to contain any number of Hewsons and Smiths so long as its members' commitment to its missionary goals remained paramount. But the Philadelphia society was also affected by the city's own growing divisions among rich, middling, and poor, and the radical consciousness that was a by-product of the city's place at the center of the 1790s' political maelstrom. Thus as the Philadelphia Methodist society's population boomed at the end of the decade, tensions between its prospering artisan and merchant entrepreneurs, like Hewson, and its middling workingmen, like Smith, suddenly came to a head, leading to a full-fledged crisis by 1800.

The conflict was provoked by stationed preacher Lawrence McCombs's dismissal of several of the society's class leaders. Hugh Smith along with David Lake and new member William Sturgis, all artisans, apparently disagreed with McCombs over a disciplinary matter, one that may have related to Henry Manley, whose tendency toward high-handedness was already evident in his treatment of Free Africans in the chapel's gallery. McCombs replaced the leaders with five new appointees, none of whom had held the office before. In keeping with the MEC discipline, the dismissed leaders appealed to the judgment of the presiding elder, Joseph Everett. In Everett's opinion, the three petitioners had been unjustly removed, and in accordance with the MEC discipline, he reappointed them to office. When McCombs refused to comply with the decision, Everett promptly replaced him with a new stationed preacher, Richard Sneath. The society rapidly disintegrated into two contending factions, the one supporting McCombs's action and the other Everett's decision.[121]

Asbury attributed the crisis in Philadelphia to the peculiarly disputatious character of Philadelphians of all religious persuasions. He might have added, of all political persuasions, as the contentious presidential election of 1800 had only just been resolved.[122] But as McCombs's supporters began to boycott attendance at the church, Ezekiel Cooper, the new book agent, recruited to mediate the conflict, reluctantly but assuredly characterized the two factions as distinct social interests, the "wealthy and respectable minority" on the one side and the "poor majority" on the other.[123]

Cooper's observations were apposite. Preacher McCombs's "wealthy" party consisted of Thomas Haskins, newly located preacher Charles Cavender, long-

standing members Lambert Wilmer, John Hood, and Jacob Baker, as well as John
Hewson and Samuel Harvey, all from St. George's, and James Doughty from
Ebenezer. The "poor" were led by Hugh Smith and David Lake and the class
leaders appointed to office by preacher Sneath, among them Manley Smallwood,
William Pigeon, and John Petherbridge. The dispute, the original cause of which
had by this time been forgotten, became, in Cooper's words, a matter of which
had more authority in the church, "wealth and worldly respectability on the one
side, or the majority on the other." Cooper initially attempted to moderate between
the two sets, repeatedly referring to their social differences. "The wealthy and
respectable were surprised at me to take part with what they called the poor and
ignorant part of the society," he wrote, ". . . and the others lamented . . . that I did
not give them a more desided support in opposition to what they considered the
overbearing measures of . . . 'the great men.' " "In the midst of this business,"
Cooper continued, "a work of religion broke out and amongst us which the others
[the wealthy party] opposed with much severity, and endeavoured to make it be
believed that it was a delusion."[124]

The 1800–1801 revival significantly altered the social composition of the Philadelphia Methodists. By the spring of 1801, of the 669 members meeting at St.
George's and Ebenezer, just 14 can be identified as merchants or retailers, a low
13.5 percent of men with known occupations, and a 50 percent drop from five
years before. Merchants, professional men, and government workers together accounted for just 24 percent of the male membership fitting this category. The
proportion of artisans, on the other hand, had climbed to 60.6 percent of those
with known occupations, and altogether, artisans and other laboring men formed
close to three-quarters (73.1 percent) of the communicants whose livelihoods can
be identified. The proportion of women had also risen from 59 to 64.1 percent.
The black societies at Bethel and Zoar, chiefly Bethel, sustained a healthy membership of 448, forming a substantial proportion of the city's Methodists. At least
953 of the 1,117 members meeting at the four chapels in Philadelphia (more than
85 percent) were women, blacks, and laboring men.[125] At the same time, even with
preacher Sneath's reinstatement of the ejected artisan class leaders, 40 percent of
class leaderships were held by merchants, professionals, and government workers—a socially skewed representation in a set of congregations with such a significant tradesmen's presence.[126]

The crisis in Philadelphia tested the limits of the Methodist missionary model.
Francis Asbury was torn between his friendship with Thomas Haskins, still editing his journals, and the MEC's structure of authority. Although he was accused
of imperious methods in his dealings with the itinerants, when it came to the
affairs of the local congregations, Asbury and the other church leaders generally
left the solutions in local hands. Thus when in June 1801 the "malcontents," as
Asbury called McCombs's supporters, petitioned the Philadelphia annual conference for redress, he and Richard Whatcoat, his cobishop, issued a broadside emphasizing the problems the dispute was causing the larger preachers' connection:
"How can you expect your preachers to live and labour among you in the fire of
contention, and always to be wading through the waters of strife?" The preachers

added that the yearly conference was not authorized to do more than hear complaints, with "each society as standing in its own accountability" and quarterly meetings given full authority over their own affairs. Asbury then wrote to Haskins, urging that the located preacher and his associates lobby the quarterly meeting to have their case heard, considering "how improper, if not impossible, it might be for you to obtain [your property] if [you are] withdrawn."[127]

When their appeal to the annual conference of preachers in Philadelphia fell on deaf ears, the group prepared hastily but resolutely to leave the MEC. On the same day that Asbury and Whatcoat addressed the Philadelphia society, Haskins, resorting to the language of social reputation, wrote to the stationed preachers to decline reappointment as a local preacher: "For me to *exercise* any Official functions in the Methodist Churches in *Philadelphia in the present Situation of its affairs*," he emphasized, "would be repugnant to those feelings, as well as a violation of that sense of propriety & duty which ought to activate every upright honest Man, *Sacrifices* which your enlightened & feeling hearts cannot expect me to make." A few days afterwards he and his aggrieved associates resigned their memberships.[128]

To make up for the loss of the chapel they had been renovating for so many years, the seceding group secured for their use the north end of the Philadelphia Academy building—formerly the preaching hall constructed for George Whitefield.[129] Joining the seceders were the Philadelphia society's oldest members: Lambert Wilmer, John Hood, and Jacob and Hannah Baker, Methodists for more than thirty years. With them came new merchants and entrepreneurs John Hewson, James Doughty, and Caleb North, and their wives Zibiah, Margaret, and Lydia. Thomas Haskins also joined with his second wife, Elizabeth Richards Haskins (like his first, the daughter of a Middle Atlantic iron-founding family).[130] In August, the group held their own small conference to found what they called the "Academy" society, which they optimistically projected would be part of a new connection called "The United Societies of the People called Methodists (late in connection with the Methodist Episcopal Church)." Now associating their grievances against the middling and poor members of St. George's with the excesses of the missionary system, they determined that the main authority in the church was to reside in the "Private Members" rather than itinerant preachers. The church's trustees and members, following a congregational model, were to make all the major decisions, including those concerning admission of new members and appointment of preachers.[131]

Altogether, thirty-eight men and forty-four women formed the new "Academy" church. The new society was by no means a strictly mercantile organization. A total of 28.9 percent of the men in the church were without identifiable occupations, probably journeymen or unskilled laborers. Fourteen of the men whose occupations are certain, furthermore, or 51.9 percent, were artisans and service workers. Nevertheless, eight of the men at the Academy—a high 29.6 percent of those with known occupations—were merchants or retailers. Twelve, or 44.4 percent, of the same category hailed from the ranks of merchants, shopkeepers, professionals, and government and clerical workers combined. A number of the tradesmen, like John Hewson, are also better identified as entrepreneurs. These last, and undoubtedly their wives, considered themselves part of a new class in American society, similar in status to the located preachers and other businessmen who had supported St. George's with their financial largesse through the previous two decades.[132]

By contrast, the remaining Philadelphia Methodist society, comprising the congregations at St. George's, Ebenezer, Bethel, and Zoar, was ever more a religious community for workingmen, women, and blacks. Led by stationed preacher Ezekiel Cooper and trustees Hugh Smith, David Lake, John Dennis, and Alexander Cook, the Philadelphia Methodists countered the impression, widely held among the Academy group and many preachers, that their "poverty, . . . want of skill in management, . . . [and] small influence among those who were able to contribute to [their] relief" would lead to the mortgaging of the chapel building. By November 1801, through a matching subscription among leaders and members, as well as public and class collections and an anonymous gift, the society had accumulated more than four thousand dollars and begun to pay off their substantial debts. In addition, the new leaders made back payments on the ground rent, insured the church against fire, and finished the interior of Ebenezer Chapel.[133]

St. George's continued to have a reputation for enthusiasm into the early 1800s. "I found the people in St. George's in a great flame with Brother McClaskey for reproving them publickly for some of their wild working in meetings," Asbury wrote in 1802.[134] The Episcopalians attributed the schism to the "noisy, enthusiastic, and apparently trifling and irreverend Behavior, of the Congregation assembled professedly for the Worship of God."[135] But a more compelling explanation was the peculiar conjunction of class consciousness, political awareness, and evangelical fervor that the city's Methodists brought to their denominational experience. For artisan and laboring-class Methodists, this confluence of events resembled, if not precisely duplicated, that of their African Methodist counterparts in the same city.

Indeed, it is only in turning to the Baltimore Methodists that one finds a Methodist society in which all the parts of the urban fabric fit smoothly together, typical of the rising city that Methodism had made its American capital by the mid-1780s.

BALTIMORE: NEW MEN

In the two decades following the Revolutionary War, the Baltimore Methodist churches presented a marked contrast to New York and Philadelphia. In brief, the Baltimore Methodists were by far the most cohesive of the city societies. At the center of a thriving Methodist population that extended from Dover, Delaware, to northern Virginia, Baltimore was the capital of the first American Methodist heartland. But Baltimore Methodists' ability to get along with each other was by no means a sure thing: they were also the most socially and racially heterogeneous of the Methodists' urban congregations. To some extent the calm at the Baltimore societies was a credit to Methodism's inclusiveness, but it was also a reflection

Figure 10. *Perry Hall, Baltimore County, Maryland.* The Gough family seat outside Baltimore
City. Courtesy of the Henry Francis Du Pont Winterthur Museum, Delaware.

of the degree to which Baltimore was able to absorb increasing varieties of inhabitants into its ever-expanding economy.

   The inhabitants of the lower Middle Atlantic and the Chesapeake responded
with extraordinary alacrity to Wesley's movement. Numerous families within a
fifty-mile radius of Baltimore had adhered to the movement since the 1760s,
among them Robert Strawbridge's converts and Francis Asbury's earliest allies.
"[W]hat is somewhat remarkable, and out of the usual course of things," one
itinerant wrote, was that the Methodists could number among their friends "The
Ridgeleys—The Dorseys—The Goughs—The Hallidays—The Rogers—The
Bucchanans—The Hollingsworths—the Carnans, & others of great respectability
and influence in society."[136]

   Baltimore's Methodist churches accounted for a healthy proportion of these
Methodists. In 1789, the city experienced one of the largest American Methodist
revivals up to that time. The following year, membership for the city and county
together skyrocketed to 2,196, the largest concentration of Methodists in the new
states. Approximately half of these members lived in Baltimore City itself.[137] After
a decline, the numbers rose again. By 1798, 926 Baltimoreans belonged to the
city's various Methodist chapels and societies and another 615 members belonged

to the Baltimore County Methodist societies. The tallies for the city continued to rise thereafter. By 1801, 400 more had joined the city's Methodist churches, for a grand total of 1,320.[138] The Methodists now also had the largest number of church buildings in the city and a rapidly increasing proportion of the city's churchgoers. Its closest competitors were the Roman Catholic and Protestant Episcopal Churches, both with a more than 150-year advantage over the Methodists.[139]

The Methodists' success may in part be attributed to its missionary zeal that drew in a great variety of "hearers" who might otherwise have sought out the German and other English churches in the city. Thus in Baltimore as in New York and Philadelphia, Methodist men ran the gamut of northern European ethnic diversity, with Irish, Scottish, and Welsh, German, Dutch, and French as well as English surnames.[140]

But diversity of race and class, rather than ethnicity, was the Baltimore Methodist societies' hallmark, exemplary of the historical development and complicated social fabric of the city itself.

In the fifteen years following the Revolutionary War, Baltimore expanded at an unprecedented rate. With its merchants reaping the benefits of the international wheat trade, the city's population doubled every ten years, growing from just 7,000 inhabitants in 1776 to 13,500 in 1790, 26,500 in 1800, and 46,600 in 1810. Baltimore's new inhabitants were a mix of European immigrants, Irish and English indentured servants, farm folk, slaves, and free people. French refugees from St. Domingue flooded the city after 1792—fifty-three ships unloading 1,000 white and 500 mulatto and black islanders at Fell's Point in July 1793 alone.[141] The Revolutionary War, moreover, accelerated rather than hindered Baltimore's commercial success and fostered the beginnings of industrial development.[142]

The city was hardly free of social differences. By the time the three neighborhoods of Baltimore Town, Old Town, and Fell's Point were incorporated as Baltimore City in 1796, merchants and artisan-entrepreneurs had begun to turn upper Calvert, Charles, and Lexington Streets into a wealthy enclave, and a cluster of new civic buildings would soon be erected along the rim of the Basin. By this date, Fell's Point had become an exclusively working-class and mariners' district, with two-story frame buildings and back-lot cottages lining alleys off the larger thoroughfares. As one historian writes, "Despite a few imposing brick homes belonging to captains and shipbuilders along the waterfront, Fell's Point had the reputation for being the poorest section of town and the bawdiest." After 1800, some 40 percent of Baltimore's free black population lived on the Point.[143]

But Baltimore was a distinctive town with a great deal of municipal esprit. A new mercantile center at the northern tip of an aging rural region, set in the midst of a slavery-based economy, Baltimore's various classes were tied together by the city's urban distinction and a long struggle with the planter-dominated provincial assembly over the city's chartering. In 1763 during the Revolutionary agitation, Baltimore's new merchants cooperated with the city's artisans in the radical Baltimore Mechanical Company to train militia and promote self-government, as well as in the Baltimore Whig Club, organized in 1777. The two groups—merchants

and artisans—were similarly allied as Democratic Republicans in the 1790s: artisans in the Baltimore Mechanical Society, which provided benefits to the city's
journeyman and master mechanics alike, and merchants and lawyers in the Baltimore Republican Society.[144] Its merchants and entrepreneurial artisans, as evidenced by the Methodists' participation in various civic organizations, were unusually progressive, although Baltimore's black population was often left
dangling between the coercion of slavery and promises of manumission.[145] In
1799, nevertheless, more than a third of the three central Baltimore City chapels'
collective membership—287 of 825—was black. The proportion remained much
the same in the following two years. At Fell's Point, the 72 black men and women
at the chapel represented more than 30 percent of the members in 1801.[146]

Racial and other internal politics at the Baltimore societies were far less anguished than in Philadelphia, however. The proposers of the African church in
1795—probably Jacob Fortie along with several other black Methodists—faced
responses to their proposal for a separate black society very different from those
that confronted Richard Allen. This relative peace may have been partly a result
of racism: Baltimore Methodists may have more readily accepted or, conversely,
encouraged the segregating of congregations. Nor did revivals bring on significant
changes in what was already a diverse Methodist population, as they would in
the more northern city.[147]

By the mid-1790s, the Baltimore City Methodist society was meeting in a new
house on Light Street near Wine Alley—the successor to the original Lovely Lane
Chapel where the Christmas Conference had convened in 1784—in the Green
Street Chapel in Old Town and the African Methodist meetings on Fish Street and
on Sharp Street. The Fell's Point congregation continued to convene in Strawberry
Alley Chapel.[148] In December 1796 a fire destroyed the Light Street building and
the adjoining Methodist Academy. A new church was built on the opposite side
of Light Street and dedicated in October 1797.[149] Altogether the society supported
an unusually large roster of officers. In 1799–1800, these included two elders and
four deacons (located itinerants), five white and three black local preachers, six
white and six black exhorters, thirty-seven white class leaders, and two black
prayer leaders.[150]

To some extent, the cohesiveness of the society may be attributed to the
involvement of many men from the city's ascending classes. Among these were
a substantial proportion of merchants and shopkeepers. In 1801, these men made
up 26.3 percent of the white members in the Baltimore City society whose names
appear in the city directories. Collectively, merchants, shopkeepers, professionals,
and government workers formed more than a third—37.6 percent—of white
men with identifiable occupations; many points higher than the comparable
groups in New York and Philadelphia. The mercantile members at the Baltimore
City congregations also more closely approximated the proportion of merchants
and retailers in the city as a whole than was the case for either New York or
Philadelphia.[151]

Merchants, retailers, and artisan-entrepreneurs played an important role in the
Baltimore societies, most notably in Baltimore City. The Chalmers family—John

Sr. and sons John Jr., James, and Daniel—is a case in point. Originally from Annapolis, John Sr., a silversmith and sometime traveling preacher, had donated the lot for the Annapolis Methodist society. Sometime after 1789 he followed his customers to Baltimore and by 1800 had opened a merchanting house in Cheapside. John Jr. was an ordained Methodist elder.[152] Another located preacher among the City society's officers in 1799 was Joseph Toy, originally a founder of the Trenton Methodist society and for a time an instructor at Cokesbury College.[153] Local preachers included William Hawkins, a merchant-tailor; Jacob King, an industrial comb-maker; and Abner Neale, a stationer.[154] Among the society's class leaders in the same year were James McCannon, a merchant-tailor; George Baxley and Paul Ruckle, both grocers; and Caleb Hewitt, a wealthy tobacco merchant.[155]

Compared to the New York and Philadelphia groups, the society drew a disproportionate number of its class leaders from the merchant ranks. These men included Emanuel Kent, a tea merchant, formerly from Queen Annes County; William H. Wood, a hardware merchant;[156] and Samuel Owings, Jr., wealthy cousin of preacher Richard Owings and husband of the influential female Methodist Deborah Lynch Owings. A former patriot militia colonel and provincial assemblyman, Owings was the proprietor of the Ulm estate and gristmills in Baltimore County and was known as the nation's leading hydraulic expert. Among the first Baltimore Methodists, Samuel and Deborah Owings were also among the richest, with a townhouse on Hanover Street in addition to their county properties.[157]

Other prominent men at the Baltimore City society did not hold office but undoubtedly influenced its proceedings. Among these were Philip Rogers, Owings's business partner in the firm Rogers & Owings, one of the trustees at Lovely Lane Chapel before the Revolutionary War, and still an active Methodist twenty years later;[158] Jesse Hollingsworth, patriot and a long-standing trustee at Fell's Point in the process of moving to a new residence on elite Hanover Street in 1800;[159] and Adam Fonerden, one of the founders of the Green Street Chapel in Old Town, and proprietor of a wool and cotton card manufactory on Baltimore Street.[160]

These leading members and officeholders thus represented a cross section of the city's new merchants and rising craftsmen. Providing yet another contrast to Philadelphia and New York, they were also important actors in Baltimore's civic culture. Members of the Maryland Abolition Society, the board of the African Academy, and the Mechanical Society, Baltimore Methodists also shaped Baltimore's local politics in ways unheard-of in New York and Philadelphia.[161] Emanuel Kent—known to practice cures by "animal magnetism," or hypnosis—in a less intriguing manifestation was superintendent of the City's pumps. Jesse Hollingsworth and Samuel Owings both served terms as state assemblymen between 1786 and 1787. Fonerden, Hollingsworth, McCannon, Owings, and Rogers were elected into various municipal offices in 1797.[162] By the time of his death in 1803, Samuel Owings, in his country guise, had served terms as deputy sheriff of Baltimore County, justice of the peace, county commissioner, and county delegate to the Maryland legislature.[163]

The prominence of the leading figures at the Baltimore City society, in fact, can draw attention away from the strong tradesmen's presence among the Baltimore Methodists. In 1801, artisans constituted more than half—50.4 percent—of the City members listed in the town's directories; artisans, mariners, and transport and other service workers combined accounted for 60.9 percent of these adherents.[164] Middling artisans also filled the ranks of class leaders. Among these, for example, William Tilyard was an English sign-painter who had emigrated to America in 1773 and named three of his sons—Philip Thomas Coke, John Wesley, and Henry Willis—after Methodist preachers;[165] John Armstrong (a shoemaker), John Parker (a bricklayer), and Jacob Rogers (a hatter) all led black classes in the City society; and Job Smith—one of two men by this name, the other a trustee at Fell's Point— was a wheelwright and class leader in Old Town. Fifteen (40 percent) of the city's white officers do not appear in the city directories, suggesting their relatively low social status.[166]

An impression of the wide social range of the Baltimore Methodists may be gained from the wills and inventories of those who died before the turn of the century. Men of modest means had formed the bulwark of the city's Methodist churches for many years. Emanuel Stansbury, Nicholas Jones, and Joseph Perigo are illustrative cases. A class leader at Fell's Point, Stansbury died in 1791, leaving a personal estate of a little over £112. He owned real estate in the city, but his personal effects amounted to little more than furniture.[167] Nicholas Jones, whom Asbury called "a happy, simple soul," had been a participant in the agitation against the Tea Act in 1773/74, and a class leader in Baltimore City, and a trustee at Cokesbury College, along with a number of other Baltimoreans. At his death in 1797, his main wealth was in silver plate, and his total estate was valued at just slightly more than £105.[168] Joseph Perigo, a class leader at Baltimore City and a bricklayer, owned miscellaneous properties, but at his death in 1800, he left household goods worth just $249.15. His wife died three years thereafter, with an equally sparse legacy. None of these men owned slaves or servants, partly a sign of their Methodist convictions, partly indicative of their middling status.[169]

But in some respects, Baltimore Methodists were tied together by the degree to which many, whatever their specific status, were "new men." They were, that is, men moving between two worlds: the colonial past and the new republican future. The Baltimore City society's new men included, for example, Dr. Henry Wilkins, a physician and a local preacher (as well as Samuel Owings, Jr.'s son-in-law), who made an effort to evangelize the American public on good health practices in *The Family Adviser*, first published in 1795 with Wesley's *Primitive Physic*.[170] A more numerous group at the society were portrait and landscape painters in great demand among Baltimore's gentry and ascending merchant elite as well as more middling folk. A mobile lot, artists' attraction to the Methodist movement may have resulted at least in part from the marginal but increasingly visible status that they shared with the traveling ministry. Philip Thomas Coke Tilyard, son of William, the sign-painter, was an aspiring painter at the City society. By 1807, his business partner was Moses Hand, another Methodist artist.[171] Thomas Ruckle, a historical and landscape painter, was a business partner with another Methodist, John Coffie, and father of Thomas Coke Ruckle, who would become a prominent portrait artist in the next century.[172]

During the same period, Baltimore's Methodists encompassed an important constituency of workingmen, white and black, the future working class of the city and "new men" in their own right. A solid cohort of these men made up the majority of male membership at the Fell's Point congregation: artisans alone constituting 55.6 percent of the white men with known occupations; workingmen as a group (artisans, together with mariners, transport and service workers, and laborers), fully three-quarters (77.8 percent) of the white men in the congregation whose livelihood can be identified.[173]

By 1800, these Methodists were increasingly concentrated in distinct working-class enclaves, especially at Fell's Point. At the turn of the century, most of the original Strawberry Alley merchant-trustees had, like Richard Moale, either died or, like Philip Rogers and Jesse Hollingsworth, moved to the City. Only Job Smith and Isaac Sutton, artisans, remained in office.[174] None of the twenty-seven men members listed in the city directory were merchants, and only two were retailers and three grocers. Fell's Point, as explored earlier, was unusual in other ways. Five out of the eight classes were run by women; and most of the black members were likely freemen and freewomen. Altogether, it is not surprising that it was at the Point's working-class Methodist chapel that Frederick Douglass, although still a slave, first took his place at the center of a free black community.[175]

Overall, Methodist men's experience in Baltimore demonstrates the degree to which Wesleyanism had the cultural power to unify a strikingly diverse community of believers. The Baltimore Methodists, in this respect, foreshadowed the successful Americanized future of the movement and epitomized Methodism's capacity for evangelical ascendancy in all manner of settings.

But the collective experience of men in these three major American cities also reveals the underlying political as well as social tumult of the 1790s that even the nonpartisan Methodists could not or would not entirely ignore. Except, that is, when engaged in their primary religious calling: as missionary preachers of the gospel.

PART III

Politics

CHAPTER SEVEN

Methodism Politicized

IN 1789, as a revival swept through Baltimore, riveting worshipers to meetings that lasted until two and three o'clock in the morning, enemies of the Methodists charged that the devil was in the revivalists and Methodism should be suppressed before the danger spread further. The meetings, Ezekiel Cooper reported, "were very noisy." But fortunately the Methodists' enemies' "hands were bound by our civil and religious rights and privileges. Lord grant that these rights may extend to, and be maintained in every nation." Religious hierarchy "supported by a civil establishment," Cooper continued, "scarse ever fails, to create a species of tyranny over the simple gospel truth, as it would otherwise operate in the consciences of men." Americans should praise the helpful effects "of a free unshackled toleration" and give thanks to providence "for knocking off, every human compulsion over the consciences of men in our government."[1]

Perhaps alone among the American churches, the Methodist Church, freed from attachment to the colonial religious establishments and heirs to Wesley's doctrine of separating political and religious spheres, could speak so confidently of the future of religious toleration in the new states. As John Murrin has written, with the Revolution "the [American] churches were no longer the official spokesmen for public values." Instead, the "civic humanism" of the founding generation—apparent in the deist language of the state constitutions, the "gentle" anticlericalism of men like Franklin, Jefferson, and Madison, and the absence of any reference to God in the U.S. Constitution—guaranteed a constitutional settlement in which churches, clergy, and theology played a distinctly secondary role.[2] Perhaps at no time in the eighteenth century had circumstances so favored an upstart group like the Methodists.

Maintaining the separation of churches and government proved more difficult than enlightened thinkers or their Methodist allies had hoped, however. Initially, the pressures came from outside the churches themselves: from the radicalization of the French Revolution, the rise of the Democratic Republicans, and the American publication of Thomas Paine's *Age of Reason* in 1794. As party conflict—anathema to the constitution-builders of the previous decade—deepened in the 1790s, the Methodist preachers were only partly able to maintain the high road in political affairs or to prevent their followers from taking sides.

Nor was the MEC free from internal dispute. Still ambivalent about their British origins, Methodists continued to struggle with issues that had divided the preachers at the time of the church's formation: the connection with Wesley, Francis Asbury's authority, Thomas Coke's ambition. More important, the language of political conflict—antifederalism versus federalism, democracy versus monarchy, the people versus tyranny—suffused preachers' contests with Francis Asbury over the future of the movement and the place of rank-and-file Methodists, mainly the preachers themselves, within it.

In short, the collective destiny of American churches and religious sects, as evident in the writings of Methodists and their contemporaries, was far from clear in the first years of the republic, and the MEC's relationship with the new American states was less comfortable than it at first seemed. For most denominations, the 1780s and 1790s were decades of retrenchment. The Methodists themselves witnessed discord at local societies, battles within the church hierarchy, and the secession of renegade preachers. Struggling with chronic bad health, Francis Asbury in 1797 despaired of the future of his itinerant connection and "that order which I have been seeking these many years to establish."[3]

These events appeared in no way, however, to undermine the resolve of Asbury's missionaries to push on into the American continent. With each passing year, the itinerants—underpaid, unprotected, pouring their thoughts into their journals, traveling to their far-flung circuits alone or with a single companion—worked in ever-expanding networks, farther south and farther west. Although few American pundits would have predicted a great future for Wesley's Methodists in the new republic's prodigious cultural marketplace after 1800, the Methodist movement had become more American than either its adherents or its enemies realized, and the makings of the Methodist triumph in the next century were already in place.

POLITICS WITHOUT: CHURCH, STATE, AND PARTISANSHIP

"RELIGION is no less important to states than to individuals," William Duke began his *Observations on the Present State of Religion in Maryland* in 1795. "Whatever difference there may be between private and public weal, and consequently between the influence of religion as it effects the salvation of an individual, and as it maintains the vigour of the body politic, it is equally necessary to both."[4] Separation of church and state—the new creed of the new republic—suggested just the opposite, and the role of religion and of ministers remained ambiguous under both the Confederation and the new federal government of 1787. Both Federalists and Anti-Federalists were aware of the potentially central role of religion in the new nation but at varying levels of comfort. Suspicious of political conflict and popular unrest, Federalist writers were fearful of the effects of religious dispute, particularly religio-political dispute. Thus James Madison, defending the concept of an expansive republic, predicted that "a religious sect may degenerate into a political faction in a part of the Confederacy," but in a large republic "the variety of sects dispersed over the entire face of it must secure the national councils against any danger from that source." The best republic was one in which strife—political and religious—was neutralized by large numbers of competing factions.[5]

For their part, Anti-Federalists esteemed the moral authority provided by churches and clergy, but like many religious dissenters—chief among them Isaac Backus's Baptists—were wary of religious establishments. To varying degrees, the separation of religious and political realms at the state level had been guaranteed by clauses in state bills of rights or other legislation supporting religious freedom. Jefferson's Bill for Establishing Religious Freedom, passed by the Virginia legislature in 1786, as described earlier, was the strongest statement among these.[6] The succinct clauses of the First Amendment, prohibiting "an establishment of religion" by Congress and protecting "the free exercise" of religion, incorporated the Anti-Federalist position into the U.S. Constitution, further removing churches from their traditional place at the right hand of government upholding morality among the folk.[7]

Adding to the ambiguous position of churches in the new republic was the ascending popularity of Deism among American leaders and many men of the nascent working class. At the same time, many devout Protestants, as Ruth Bloch has shown, were persuaded that the century's approaching end would bring with it the millennium and Christ's judgment on the nation. At its most extreme, millennialist opinion solved the church-and-state conundrum simply by willing both church and state out of existence; as when a Delaware legislator attempted, unsuccessfully, to convince preacher Ezekiel Cooper that at the end of the century an armed conflagration would annihilate the U.S. Constitution and state governments alike.[8]

Surveying the American religious landscape for his *Observations*, William Duke, the former Methodist preacher, now an ordained Protestant Episcopal minister, was concerned for the future of his, the least millennially inclined of the American churches. Duke understood that "the people of this country is a mixture of various nations, and consequently distinguished into various religious denominations," but nevertheless believed that a "national religion" could be achieved if certain ideal standards were shared by all Christians: especially belief in the divine origin of the Bible, a confession of basic Christian beliefs, maintenance of public worship, acceptance of Jesus Christ as savior, and observance of the Sabbath. "A habitual sense of the divine presence is the essence of religion," Duke wrote, "and such a sense renders our life a continued act of worship, varied according to the vicissitude of human affairs." In Maryland, this had not always been the case, partly because of distracting religious dispute in a religiously diverse province and partly because "the most numerous and wealthy church in Maryland [the Anglicans] was also the most supine and careless of its interests." The Methodists took advantage of this moral torpor and the Anglican laity's disdain for their own clergy, and, seeking a kind of popular martyrdom, "calculated upon being ducked, mobbed, or ludicrously set at nought" whenever they entered an Anglican stronghold. Critical of the degree to which the Methodists were known to "estimate their success in proportion to the disorder and tumult of their audience," Duke nonetheless stressed that the Anglicans' evangelical offspring had succeeded in winning away the church's membership for two reasons: churchpeople lacked knowledge of their own system; and, until the formation of the MEC, many Methodists had remained loyal members of the church.

While Duke recognized that the return to a church establishment was impossible, the absence of a consensus regarding a "national religion" was troubling.

"We do not enjoy uniformity, and almost every denomination is either rising or falling." The problem, Duke asserted, was not religion versus no religion but whether or not churches would degenerate as a result of their own "collision of parties, and the intemperate stir of religious animosity."[9]

Other members of the Anglican establishment, as in the past, were less sanguine about the Methodists' impact on Anglican uniformity. Wesley's assumption of ordination and extraecclesiastical power was profoundly unpalatable to many churchmen, clerical and lay alike. One Anglican parish in the late 1780s described Wesley as a "Contumner of Authority, Ambitious and revengeful," whose follow-ers "to divert you from noticing *their deficiency of Authority*" claimed "their Con-versions and their Extacies as proofs of divine Mission." The Methodists assumed a social authority that undermined the church's influence among the middling and poorer folk. As already noted, the Reverend J.G.J. Bend complained of the Methodists as lesser folk who "set themselves up, as teachers of those above them." Such social assumptions clearly made the Methodists, in Bend's view, disrespecters of *all* authority. By the late 1790s, Bend was resorting to more overtly political language to describe the Methodists' usurpation of Anglican power. "I have been fully convinced, for some time, of the Jacobinic principles of the Methodists," he charged, "nor is this fact wonderful. They, are for the most part, persons of the lower classes in life, & distinguished by that ignorance upon which the Jacobin chiefs work so successfully."[10]

In 1797, the vestry of St. Peter's Parish in Talbot County elaborated on these themes by issuing a virtual catalog of the Quakers' and Methodists' social sins: the promotion of ecstatic experience, support for antislavery, and the empow-erment of women. The Methodists were susceptible to "extravagant Stories" and "relished the manumitting Subject as highly as the Quaker preachers." The report concluded, "[T]he religion of not a few seems to be guided by their Wives & Sweet-hearts apron Strings, too many of whom inherit the Curiosity of Lot's wife, and the Confidence of their old Mother Eve."[11] Other Maryland vestrymen were equally hostile to what they perceived as Methodist pretentions, as William Col-bert was to discover on receiving a letter from "an officer in the Church of England . . . informing me, that he looks upon my appearance among them as a preacher, both an insult upon their reason and relegion."[12]

The Methodists themselves were at least in part to blame for the Anglican antipathy directed toward them after the Revolutionary War. Not only had the itinerants rapidly, even precipitously, formed their own church independent of the Episcopalians, but they had also publicly accused the Protestant Episcopal Church of hegemonic ambitions. The Episcopal Church, the 1789 discipline charged, sought to set up "a national establishment, which we cordially abhor as the great bane of truth and holiness, and . . . a great impediment to the progress of vital Christianity." The Methodists, by contrast, depicted themselves as the true lega-tees of the Revolution. In an address to President Washington published in the New York press, Methodists called for "the preservation of those civil and reli-gious liberties which have been transmitted to us by the providence of GOD, and the glorious revolution."[13] While the Anglicans and Calvinists aspired to national domination and political power—the old temptations—the Methodists eschewed such ends. At one of the annual conferences in 1795, the preachers instead gave public thanks for

> the goodness and wisdom of God displayed towards America, by making it an asylum for those who are distressed in Europe with war and want, and oppressed with ecclesiastic and civil tyranny; the merciful termination of our various wars; the pacifications of the savage tribes; and the rapid settlement and wonderful population of the continent. . . . For the general union and government, that this may be kept pure and permanent—For the admirable revolution, obtained and establish[ed] at so small a price of blood and treasure—That religious establishments by law, are condemned and exploded, in almost every spot of this extensive empire. And for African liberty; we feel gratitude, that many thousands of these poor people are free and pious.[14]

A more comprehensively liberationist program—personifying the new republic as the "asylum" of oppressed European peoples where peace and Indian pacification, national expansion and political union, disestablishment and "African liberty" would thrive—could not have been written by Thomas Paine himself.

The intensification of political and religious dispute in the 1790s, however, made it more difficult for individual Methodists to remain indifferent to governmental affairs, or for the MEC to sound like Tom Paine. Once in the political arena, Methodists demonstrated as great a degree of political partisanship as any other Americans, religious or otherwise.

The Methodists' reactions to the political developments of the 1790s, like those of most Americans, were shaped by events in France. The outbreak of the French Revolution in 1789 had been greeted with enthusiasm by many Americans, including itinerant John Kobler, who copied the liberal Abbé Fauchet's memorial to Benjamin Franklin, a celebration of international republicanism, into his commonplace book. The "foundations of a new city are created in the two worlds," Kobler copied down the Abbé's words; "brother nations hasten to inhabit it; it is the city of mankind."[15] But as the Revolution moved from liberal imitation of the American constitutional model to execution of the king and radical imposition of one-man rule under Robespierre, support for its political innovations collapsed among the Federalists while becoming a badge of honor among Democratic Republicans. The new French regime's rigorous enforcement of dechristianization of the French state, despite its focus on what for many Protestant Americans was the despised Catholic Church, sent alarms through American religious circles. The escalating events in France provoked American churches as different as the Congregationalists and the Methodists to close ranks against Deism and Unitarianism. With the exception of religious dissenters in New England, where resentment of the Congregational establishment ran high, many American clergy were more willing to publicly support the Federalists against the Democratic Republicans than would otherwise have been the case.[16]

Thomas Paine once again came forward as the leading shaper of discourse. In 1794, the first American edition of part one of Paine's *The Age of Reason* was published, part two to follow two years later.[17] In many respects a conventional deist critique of organized religion as an affront to God's rational plan for humankind, *The Age of Reason* also delivered a blistering attack on the validity of Scripture, made all the more devastating by Paine's apparent knowledge of the Bible and what he characterized as its superstitious tales about primitive Israelites and accommodationist Christians. In a kind of anticatechism, Paine exclaimed, "I totally disbelieve that the Almighty ever did communicate anything to man, by any mode of speech, in any language, or by any kind of vision or appearance . . . otherwise than by the universal display of Himself in the works of creation. . . . The most horrid cruelties," Paine continued, "and the greatest miseries that have afflicted the human race have had their origins in this thing called revelation, or revealed religion."[18] The accumulated grievances of the Revolutionary Age against not only tax-supported state churches but the whole deadweight of tradition found their way into Paine's tract, written in his customary blistering, blunt prose. Tom Paine now proclaimed the plain man's Deism as John Wesley proclaimed the plain man's gospel, and the two had almost nothing in common.[19]

For the Methodists, such an uncompromising rejection of the twin bases of their religious worldview—the Bible and the experience of revelation—raised the specter of a republic in which religion had no place at all. The MEC formally rejected Paine's work in the *Methodist Magazine*, reprinting Thomas Erskine's defense of Christianity at the trial of Paine's British publisher. Stith Mead, one of Asbury's preacher-spokesmen, ritualized the church's position against Paine by rendering it into the doggerel of a spiritual song: "The world, the devil and Tom Paine / Have done their best, but all in vain / They can't prevail, the reason is / The Lord defends the Methodis."[20] Itinerant William Colbert feared that "the deciples of Paine will triumph" as long as Christians, by whom he meant American Calvinists, "hold up the idea of God the father being so angry with the world of mankind" that he "punished his son in their stead." Despite accusations of Jacobinism leveled by Anglicans unhappy with the invasion of Wesley's preachers into formerly secure Anglican domains, many Methodists harbored the suspicion that republicanism, while protecting churches from political persecution, would replace religion altogether. In 1795, John Mann wrote in New York, "Republican principals & politics eats [religion] out of many hearts."[21]

At the same time as the Democratic-Republican challenge to the Federalists gathered speed in the mid-1790s, a distinct tendency toward tyranny of the majority in the Methodist stronghold of Delaware belied the Methodists' claims to disinterest in public affairs. The ranks of the state's officeholders boasted three Methodist Federalists: Governor Richard Bassett, Secretary of State Dr. Abraham Ridgely, and Court of Common Pleas Justice Andrew Barratt. Impressionistic evidence suggests that the bulk of Delaware's rank-and-file Methodists also supported the Federalists, as William Williams writes, since the "the specter of Jacobin atheism, cleverly associated by Federalist propagandists with the Democratic Republican party, was much on Methodist minds."[22] With the XYZ affair— in which the French foreign minister attempted to bribe agents of the American government in Paris—in the news and French invasion rumored, Willamina Ridgely, Abraham's daughter in Dover, wrote glowingly to her brother of the universal accolades President Adams was reportedly receiving in Philadelphia, including a patriotic procession of a thousand young men in his honor. A Dover local preacher had delivered a sermon to the Methodist meeting that was "very well suited to the occasion and as much in the political way as you may imagine. . . . [E]ven the hymns were patriotic. . . . You'll think I'm turnd politician," Ridgely continued. But with the threat of foreign invasion, "even the Women and children might be allowed to become patriots."[23]

Philadelphia was at ground zero for Federalist and Democratic-Republican strife in the 1790s. As in the years before the Revolution when Thomas Paine spearheaded the movement toward independence, the city continued to be a magnet for immigrant radicals. The majority of these men, like printers Mathew Carey and his brother James and radical deist James Reynolds, were Irish political refugees from the Irish anti-imperial rebellion of 1798, but immigrants included as well English and Scottish constitutional reformers and religious radicals like Joseph Priestley, Jr., and William Cobbett (the latter soon to abandon the cause of democratic reform), many of them activists with the London Corresponding Society, which sought to introduce democratic reforms to the British electoral system. Altogether these were men in their mid- to late twenties, from small-producing and professional and lesser-professional backgrounds, Roman Catholic or most often with a strong proclivity for dissenting religion or Deism: a mirror profile of many American Methodist men.[24]

Once in America, the immigrant radicals joined forces with Jefferson's Democratic Republicans, also called Republicans or Democrats, in outright ideological warfare against Hamilton's and Washington's pro-British, hierarchical policies. As Michael Durey writes, the "political careers" of the radical exiles from Britain and Ireland are best comprehended within the "framework of what they perceived to be a militant Painite-Jeffersonian radicalism, premised on the doctrines of participatory democracy." A series of events, many of them taking place in Philadelphia, where the federal government was convened until the eve of Jefferson's presidential election, alternatively braced first the Republicans' and then the Federalists' views of their opponents' machinations. From President Washington's Proclamation of Neutrality in 1793, to the Federalist suppression of the Whiskey Rebellion in 1794, and the Jay Treaty in 1795, in which the Federalists appeared to cave in to the British on the Mississippi frontier, the Republicans saw monarchical tyranny afoot. Conversely, from the Federalist perspective, the Republicans had formed dangerously close ties to the French, evident in their enthusiasm for egalitarian rhetoric and susceptibility to French manipulations in the Citizen Genêt and XYZ affairs in 1793 and 1797. When President Adams, convinced that Republican opposition to his administration was fueled by foreign radicals living in the United States, persuaded the Congress to pass the Alien and Sedition Acts in 1798, the Republicans responded with the Kentucky and Virginia Resolutions, anonymously composed by Jefferson and James Madison, which renewed antifederalist jibes against consolidated power in the federal government. Altogether, these episodes served to inflame a fierce party conflict that just a decade before had been proclaimed the worst of all possible outcomes for the new American republic.[25]

Among the most persistent of democratic polemicists was William Duane, an Irish patriot who had been born in America but spent most of his young adulthood in Ireland, London, and India where he had honed his journalist skills. In 1795, he arrived in New York, sporting an unconventional beard and uncut hair, and then moved to Philadelphia, where he went into partnership with Benjamin Bache, Benjamin Franklin's grandson, in the publication of the Democratic-Republican *American Aurora.*[26] By the spring of 1800, the *Aurora* was in a full-fledged battle with the Federalist *Gazette of the United States* over the future of religion under a President Jefferson whom the *Gazette* dubbed a "howling Atheist" and the *Aurora* defended as the champion of religious liberty against those "who laugh at religion in private, who cant about it in public, and accuse of Atheism all those who are content to take as their motto, 'By their fruits shall ye know them.' "[27]

In April 1800, the *Aurora* also turned its attention to the Methodists in Delaware, claiming that Methodist itinerants readily preached from the pulpit against the Republicans. Like the Illuminati in Connecticut, the paper charged, Methodist itinerants sought to supersede the operations of constitutional suffrage and to prey on the gullibility of their followers. "It is to be regretted, while it cannot be denied, that the society of methodists, are more liable to imposition from ignorant imposters than other sects," the paper asserted. "[S]everal methodist preachers have already commenced political preaching in Delaware, and among other things, that no salvation is to be expected by those who support the election of *Thomas Jefferson*, to be President of the United States."[28] Governor Bassett, it was further claimed, had lent the Methodists £800 for the erection of a meetinghouse, an advance for which the Methodists would be beholden in the elections. Another influential Methodist had informed the Duck Creek society that those who did not support the Federalist ticket would have their names publicly struck from the membership rolls. At a quarterly meeting in Dover, the *Aurora* charged that "it was preached that no methodist could be a *democrat* [i.e., Democratic Republican], for the principles of the latter were to destroy all government, and their church to support it."[29]

In retaliation, Federalist Thomas Rodney, speaking to Methodists at a political rally in Kent County, Delaware, later in the same month, depicted the publisher of the *Aurora* as "an alien to our government and a stranger among our Citizens," who had printed "what every jacobin in private thinks, but is too wise to avow publickly, 'that Methodism is made to answer the purposes of political intrigue.' " The Methodists were subject to Duane's attack because they voted for the Federalists, and "because in a word ye think not as the democrats think, nor act as they advise." "Do ye think my fellow Citizens," Rodney closed with gusto, "that those men who are averse to toleration when out of office, would become proselites to religious liberty by being put in office?"[30]

Throughout the tense year of 1800, overt partisanship was once again hard for Methodists to resist, just as it had been during the Revolutionary War. Washington, now dead, was portrayed by Methodists as a virtuous and even a pious man, a foreshadowing of the canonization of the former president as the epitome of homely rectitude in Mason Locke Weems's popular biography.[31] The former general was perceived as the true protector of religious liberty against a new threat of Democratic-Republican irreligion. On Washington's birthday in 1800, Ezekiel Cooper urged upon his listeners "that our civil and religious rights and liberties, invaluable privileges, obtained and improved under the military and civil administration of Washington may forever be held sacred, and maintained against every secret machination or public attack of domestic or foreign foes."[32] Thomas Coke wrote to England with unfeigned partiality: "Political dispute runs very high indeed in this country; and I have considerable fears that the Democratic party gains strength. . . . I trust the Almighty God will grant such success to the armies of the Allied Powers, that the French interest in these States will receive a mortal blow. . . ." The Pennsylvania preacher Henry Boehm recollected the "great political excitement" that heralded the election. "Federalism and Democracy ran high, and Jefferson and Adams were talked about everywhere."[33]

As in the case for the MEC's waning support for antislavery after 1785, however, it is important to distinguish between the movement's English-born leaders, with their often wealthy Federalist patrons, and the church's rank and file, both clerical and lay. Not all of the Methodist itinerants nor their followers were the Anglophilic advocates of Washington's and Hamilton's party. Thomas Ware, attending the annual conference in Philadelphia in 1800, objected to the politicization of the proceedings when he refused to vote in favor of a partisan address to President Adams, in keeping with standard conference practice. Ware recalled, "I made some remarks on the changes which would be likely to take place in the administration of our government, upon which those who were influenced by a political frenzy put such construction as suited them."[34] Also in Philadelphia, William Colbert attended the debates in Congress in March 1800 and praised a speech by Democratic Republican Albert Gallatin as "much to the purpose." When fellow preacher Daniel Fidler expressed preference for the British government, Colbert was "disgusted with him" and "did not let him go without asking him why he could prefer a Monarchical Government to a *free* one?" Fidler replied that "he was *born* under it," hardly a satisfactory response in Colbert's mind. John Ffirth, a New Jersey Methodist and compiler of Benjamin Abbott's journal, was an ardent Jeffersonian and after the presidential election claimed that as many as eight out of ten preachers of his acquaintance also backed the Republicans. There is good reason to believe that the social-conflict-laden schism at the Philadelphia Methodist society, taking place just after Jefferson's victory in fall 1800, was a further example of the impact of the rancorous politics of the election. And in New England, where opposition to the standing order of the Congregational Church ran high among other denominations, many Methodists were strong proponents of Jefferson and his well-known repugnance for religious establishments.[35]

Within the church as well, opposition to the MEC's leaders and their perceived high-handedness accelerated in the 1790s, and the MEC was unable to bar the influence of contemporary politics from among their ranks. Methodists, like many Americans in a decade riven with class, ethnic, and ideological enmities, now read their differences in the language of the people versus the aristocrats and democracy versus federalism. For the Methodist itinerants, this meant a return to the struggles that had divided the movement from the start: Irish iconoclasts versus English disciplinarians, grass roots versus the Methodist hierarchy, American versus British control. These dualities were no more apparent than in the contest between Francis Asbury and James O'Kelly over the future of the movement—a contest that spanned much of the decade.

POLITICS WITHIN: FRANCIS ASBURY, JAMES O'KELLY, AND THE MEC

Asbury and O'Kelly's struggle over the future of the Methodist Episcopal Church is best understood in the context of internal Methodist affairs combined with external political ones. The Methodists, for one matter, continued to have important and potentially controversial ties to Britain before and after 1800. For another, the church's leadership, embodied in Francis Asbury, exhibited a distinct preference for Federalist-style governance. In the view of many preachers—and undoubtedly in the view of many followers with strong attachments to popular sovereignty—the bishops and their supporters appeared to be monarchical conspirators determined to hold on to their places in the face of democratic challenges to concentrated power.

To look at these problems separately: Although its American leaders labored to legitimize the MEC as an American institution, there was little doubt of the church's debt to their English father-in-Christ, John Wesley. Wesley dominated the intellectual and doctrinal affairs of American Methodists. As Frank Baker has shown, the MEC's first official publication, *Minutes of Several Conversations Between The Rev. Thomas Coke, LL.D., The Rev. Francis Asbury and Others*, later converted into the church's discipline, duplicated the format and reproduced three-quarters of the contents of the English minutes, with the names of Coke and Asbury simply replacing those of the Wesley brothers as leaders of the preachers. The Americans temporarily adopted the *Sunday Service*, Wesley's abridgment of the Anglican Thirty-Nine Articles of Religion into the twenty-five Methodist ones with the formation of the church in 1784. Wesley's teachings, encoded in the *Notes on the New Testament*, which he had forwarded to the American itinerants as early as the 1775 conference, as well as in the *Forty-four Sermons* and selected doctrinal tracts, formed the doctrinal bedrock of the movement.[36]

Works written or abridged by Wesley, furthermore, appeared in the American issues of the *Arminian Magazine* (its title taken from Wesley's London magazine) in 1789 and 1790, as well as in the renamed *Methodist Magazine*, first published in Philadelphia in 1797.[37] American preachers sent letters and copies of their life accounts to Wesley, receiving letters of paternal encouragement in return. Thus in the late 1780s Freeborn Garrettson corresponded with Wesley regarding that all-important itinerant avocation of journal writing, as did Ezekiel Cooper. In 1790, Cooper wrote to the English leader with sentiments shared by many of his traveling brethren: "It is my happy lot to be numbered with your sons in the gospel, who in my feble way, am striving to win my fellow mortals to the embraces of a loving Saviour."[38]

The Americans also cooperated with the English connection when necessary. Hence American itinerants continued to be appointed to British circuits in Canada and the West Indies into the 1790s, and tallies of the American preachers and American membership were recorded in the English minutes through 1790 and 1800 respectively.[39] Thomas Coke, Asbury's British co-"bishop" and Wesley's chief counselor on American affairs, made nine trips to the United States between 1784 and 1804, his name always imprinted ahead of Asbury's in broadsides and Methodist publications issued by the two men. And in a move important for ecclesiastical legitimacy, the American bishops claimed apostolic succession through John Wesley, adopting the term *bishop* as a sign of this link (and, less overtly acknowledged, as a useful way to compete with the Anglicans). While it may be argued that the adoption of the term was a distinct sign of American independence from Wesley, the conference nevertheless deferred to the founder's feelings when they continued to describe Coke and Asbury as having been elected to "superintend"—Wesley's word—the American work.[40] When in 1800 the British connection requested that Coke be allowed to turn his focus to missions in the West Indies and Ireland, the American general conference, in light of Asbury's frail health, agreed to "lend" Coke back but only so long as was necessary. To replace Coke, the American preachers chose Richard Whatcoat, nine years Asbury's senior and from the same iron-founding district of Gloucestershire, over Virginian itinerant Jesse Lee. Remarkably, the church did not have an American-born bishop until the election of William McKendree in 1808.[41]

The American preachers had learned some important lessons from the Revolution, nonetheless—not least of these, the need to adapt to American mores whenever possible. As early as 1787, the preachers had dispensed with the liturgical details of Wesley's Anglican-style *Sunday Service*, especially what many rank-and-file Methodists considered the socially pretentious formality of their bishops' wearing gowns, cassocks, and bands. In the same year, the MEC minutes were revised by John Dickins and christened with an original American title, *A Form of Discipline*, changed again to *The Doctrines and Discipline* in 1792.[42] When Wesley attempted to appoint Richard Whatcoat and Freeborn Garrettson as new bishops for the American church in 1787, with intimations of removing Asbury, the American conference of preachers voted overwhelmingly to excise their promise of obedience to Wesley as well as to strike the founder's name from the head of the discipline's list of preachers (it was restored two years later, but only through respect for the aging English founder). Coke, at the same time, was made to sign an "Instrument of Abdication" declaring he would neither expand his authority when in the country nor exercise authority over the Americans when out of the country. In 1796, the general conference erupted in controversy when Coke suggested that he might serve as bishop without an election. The American preachers' leverage over their leaders contrasted sharply with the British preachers' position in England, where Wesley controlled nearly all features of their work and voting was forbidden.[43]

From Wesley's perspective, Francis Asbury and Thomas Coke, his former trusted deputies, had stepped out of line in their pursuit of American fame. In 1788, the English leader wrote bitterly to Asbury regarding the founding of Cokesbury College, the Methodist academy for preachers' sons, and Asbury's and Coke's mutual adoption of the title "bishop" over "superintendent." Invoking the old paternal metaphor, Wesley dubbed Asbury the "elder brother" of the American connection, but "I am under God the father of the whole family. . . . I study to be little, you study to be great. I creep: you strut along. I found a school: you a college! nay, and call it after your own names!" And although Wesley had himself ordained his "primitive presbytery" in 1784 for apostolic work in America, he was particularly aggrieved by what he believed to be Asbury's attempt to claim a place in the apostolic succession. "How can you, how dare you suffer yourself to be called Bishop?" he wrote his former helper. "I shudder, I start at the very thought! Men may call me a knave or a fool, a rascal, a scoundrel, and I am content; but they shall never by my consent call me a Bishop!"[44]

The American leaders indeed were indulging in a Federalist-style taste for elevated names and titles—one that would cause significant problems in the church over the next number of years. But, as in the case of the Federalists, such titles portended far less in the United States than they did in Britain. As American preacher Thomas Morrell observed of Wesley, the English leader "claimed, possessed, and exercised greater power than any ecclesiastic ever had done before him in England since the Reformation." The "whole Bench of Bishops" headed by the king himself "could not station, change, or suspend which preachers they pleased, in every part of England, Scotland and Ireland, as Mr. W. did, for a number of years." The MEC bishops, Morrell continued, "neither claim, possess, nor exercise the powers Mr. W. had."[45]

Since claims to what had once been the mighty moral force of apostolic power united to the arm of the English state, furthermore, were incongruous with the intentionally humble, apolitical features of the Methodist movement, these American "bishops" were likewise less lofty. This disjuncture was nowhere more evident than in Francis Asbury's own circumstances. No longer a young man in the 1790s, Asbury had honed his preaching and administrative skills throughout his long residence in America, carefully setting up the round of itinerants' appointments before each conference, reviewing the itinerants' performances, and keeping a paternal eye on their welfare, successes, and failings. Over this time, what little wealth he had accumulated he as often as not passed on to these men and their widows.[46] Although inured to pain from years of outdoor travel, Asbury nevertheless suffered from constant bouts of asthma, rheumatism, and pleurisy, a combination of ailments which became so severe that he was not expected to live long past the 1800 conference. As he himself thought, his frequent physical incapacities may have accounted for his relative lack of sexual drive and resistance to the temptations of location and marriage, altogether an advantage for a religious leader who insisted on the same sacrifices from his much younger disciples.[47]

Figure 11. *Francis Asbury*, portrait by Charles Peale Polk, 1794.
Painted in Baltimore. Courtesy of the United Methodist Historical
Society, Lovely Lane Museum, Baltimore.

Asbury was nonetheless described as making a striking physical impression,
and in numerous respects exerted authority in a manner suitable to a Primitive
presbyter, the kind of "bishop" he aimed to be. Coke observed that while Asbury
exhibited a Christian demeanor of meekness and love, he also possessed "though
hardly to be perceived, so much command and authority." Henry Boehm recalled
that Asbury's eyes were "so keen that it seemed as if he could look right through
a person." He was, like all successful leaders, "born to sway others." The few
surviving portraits depict him as a man of acute, pugnacious dignity, his face
strained by illness but with the healthy patina of a workingman, his clothes dark
and plain. Long accustomed to running the American movement, Asbury was no
longer emotionally susceptible to Wesley's frequent disapproval. As he wrote to
an English confidant in 1789 of one such moment, "I am sorry our dear old Daddy
is so offended with me. . . . Indeed I am not the same man in the main as I always
was."[48] Never a great writer or polemicist, he dedicated himself to a lifework of
a decidedly pragmatic kind. In the face of numerous obstacles—John Wesley's

assumption of social and ecclesiastical superiority, Thomas Coke's expectations of continuing cosuperintendence, and the proliferation of attacks on his governance by the American preachers—Asbury unwaveringly, assiduously forwarded the Methodist cause as he saw it: as a missionary church, separate from the crises and conflicts of the American republic but virtually designed for the nation's evangelization. He was in fact an American evangelist like none other before or since: self-punishing, determined, psychologically solitary, and consumed by the task at hand; and one who traveled to the prodigiously far reaches of the American republic—by his own count, sixty times across the Appalachians, twenty-nine times to the states south of Virginia; in all nearly forty-five years on the road.[49]

From Asbury's perspective, his greatest challenge—one that Federalist politicians would have appreciated—was to maintain order in the potentially amorphous American Methodist connection, a task logically following from English precedent but made more difficult by the movement's English ties. Writing to one of the British preachers in 1788, Asbury elaborated on the problems presented by affiliation with the English wing. Referring to Wesley's reputation during the Revolutionary War, Asbury noted, "There is not a man in the world so obnoxious to the American politicians as our dear old Daddy." But the larger problem was the practical one of government. No man or group of men, Asbury wrote, "unless he or should they possess divine powers, be omnipotent, omniscient and omnipresent," could run the Methodist system from so great a distance. Nor did attempts to do so go over well with the itinerants and local preachers and thirty thousand members who currently made up the MEC. "For our old, old Daddy to appoint conferences when and where he was pleased, to appoint a joint superintendent with me," Asbury observed, overturning the father-son metaphor, "were strokes of power we did not understand."[50]

One change was distinctly to the American Methodists' advantage. Americans *outside* the movement had long forgiven or forgotten Wesley's "strokes of power," not least of all because he appeared no longer to be meddling in affairs of state on either side of the Atlantic. When word of Wesley's death on 2 March 1791, at age eighty-seven years, reached Americans, he was posthumously saluted in the American press.[51] In New York, the papers reprinted obituary notices from London and praised Wesley's support for "our excellent constitution in church & state." The *Maryland Journal* reprinted verbatim the London *Argus*'s glowing tribute: "His Loss will long be deplored by Thousands of the Poor, who subsisted through his Influence!" Methodism had succeeded "from his unremitted Vigilance, his unexampled Labours, and unceasing Attention to his original Plan."[52] Once a radical Christian accused of disloyalty to both church and state and excoriated by the American patriots for attacks on their resistance to Parliamentary oppression, Wesley had once more metamorphosed, emerging at the end of his life as the tolerant leader of a particularly useful "missionary" plan for poor folk: testimony to Wesley's claim that his movement was uninterested in political disputes.[53]

With Wesley's death, Asbury's main English contact continued to be Thomas Coke. For Asbury, Coke presented difficulties somewhat different from those

Wesley had embodied. While Coke appreciated Asbury's ability to hold sway over his young itinerants, he several times mismeasured Asbury's commitment to a fully American movement. Such misjudgment was especially evident in April 1791, when Coke, predicting John Wesley's death and newly persuaded of the importance of the English Methodists' Anglican ties, attempted to backpedal the American Methodists' break with the church as well. Writing uninvited and confidentially to the American bishop William White, and without Asbury's knowledge, Coke proposed an unorthodox union between the Protestant Episcopal and Methodist Episcopal Churches. According to Coke's scheme, if the Episcopal bishops were to agree to waive the article on ancient languages, the Methodist preachers would agree to receive ordination from the Protestant Episcopal bishops. The Methodists would maintain their separate organization but the Anglicans would benefit from the recruitment of the now many thousands of Methodist members.[54]

Coke provided White with the statistical profile of a burgeoning movement:

We have now above 60,000 Adults in our Society in these States, & about 250 Travelling Ministers & Preachers; besides a great number of Local Preachers, very far exceeding the number of Travelling Preachers; & some of those Local Preachers are men of very considerable abilities. But if we number the Methodists as most people number the members of their Church, viz. by the Families which constantly attend the Divine Ordinances in their places of worship, they will make a larger Body than You probably conceive. The Society, I believe, may be safely multiplied by five on an average to give us our stated Congregations; which will then amount to 300,000. And if the calculation which, I think, some eminent writers have made, be just, that three fifths of mankind are un-adult (if I may use the expression) at any given period, it will follow that all the families, the Adults of which form our Congregations in these States, amount to 750,000. About one fifth of these are Blacks.[55]

Exhibiting the Methodist proclivity for enlightened calculation, Coke painted a picture of the Methodists that he believed could hardly be ignored by their former Anglican comrades. "[S]omething must be done before the death of M[r]. Wesley," Coke urged. He warned that "M[r]. Asbury, whose influence is very capital, will not easily comply: nay, I know he will be exceedingly averse to it." In subsequent conversations with White, Coke added that Asbury would have to be ordained for the plan to succeed, as would Coke himself, since, as White reported of the exchange, "it would not be fit, considering he was Mr. Asbury's senior, that he should appear in a lower character than this gentleman."[56]

Bishop White was taken by surprise at Coke's sudden renewal of contact, just a few years after the Methodist discipline had accused the former Anglicans of a willful inability to distinguish between the proper spheres of state and church governance. Consequently, despite Coke's impressive enumeration of Methodist potential, when White raised the Methodist offer to his fellow Anglican bishops at the Protestant Episcopal Convention of 1792, the subject was quickly dropped. "It was evident," White wrote, "from some circumstances which passed in conversation with Dr. Coke, that there was a degree of jealousy, if not of misunderstanding, between him and Mr. Asbury." White's observation was prescient: Coke's proposal was quickly jettisoned when Asbury learned of it.[57]

Far more challenging through the 1790s was the centerpiece of Methodist political dispute: the conflict between Asbury and James O'Kelly. An Irish-born veteran of the Revolutionary War, celebrated itinerant in the Virginia Southside, anti-British radical, and published opponent to slavery, O'Kelly first expressed his opposition to the American Methodist leadership in 1787 when Wesley's plan to appoint Richard Whatcoat and Freeborn Garrettson as cobishops, in place of Coke and Asbury, was disclosed to the American itinerants. At this time, and in his numerous anti-Asbury forays thereafter, O'Kelly couched his grievances in terms of the Revolutionary struggle, including the struggle against slavery of all kinds.[58] Already in 1787 he had staked out his ground on the pitfalls of episcopal power: "The question is, Shall we give all the power incorporated in us and agree that if the Doctor [Coke] and Brother Asbury [agree] it is enough, putting nothing to vote if possible . . . and, for our consolation, they may say by us as the oppressors do by the slaves, 'They have nothing to do but work eat and sleep.' " On the contrary, O'Kelly demanded, "let our dear preachers have this liberty, to choose their master."[59]

O'Kelly and his supporters were equally vocal regarding Asbury's introduction of a short-lived executive council in 1789. Fashioned after Wesley's council of senior preachers, the group was to be composed of the bishops and presiding elders, including O'Kelly himself. For Asbury, concerned with smooth governance, the council's purpose was to streamline and consolidate the actions of the preachers' conferences, now meeting in a variety of different locations each year. Objecting to Asbury's veto power over the new consulting body, O'Kelly was expelled from the American connection of preachers in 1790 until his supporters were able to gain his reinstatement.[60]

Unpacified, O'Kelly again challenged Asbury at the first quadrennial general conference in 1792, placing a motion on the floor that called for the preachers' right to appeal the bishop's appointments to circuits. The motion was debated for several days, Asbury having absented himself from the proceedings. At the end of the fourth day, it failed by "a large majority." But Asbury's opponents did not take their arguments or defeat lightly, "some of the brethren," according to one preacher, being "rather too warm" and "giving way to a false zeal." O'Kelly made his own statement by submitting a letter of resignation, charging that the "superintendents," as he pointedly called the bishops, "was on a stretch for power." He and his followers then went on to form the Republican Methodist Church, centered in the southern counties of Virginia and in North Carolina, prompting a schism that Nathan Hatch has estimated cost the MEC approximately thirty preachers and ultimately as many as twenty thousand members.[61]

One of O'Kelly's young followers, Virginia preacher William Spencer, later returned to the MEC and criticized his former mentor for his high-pitched political rhetoric, so removed from the missionary credo: "Instead of 'Glory to Jesus, Glory to God, I am happy I am bound for Heaven, O Brother! I love you, O! Sister, I am bound to meet you in Heaven, &c.' " Spencer wrote, "I say, instead of this blessed, heavenly talk, it was 'Government, Government, Government, we shall all be ruined, we shall be oppressed to death, we and our children are lorded over! Popery, popery! Despotism! Despotic power, and whatnot!' "[62] O'Kelly's language was a unique blend of Old Testament and antifederalist rhetoric, reflecting a mental landscape peopled by modern patriarchs and warrior democrats on a collision course with pro-monarchy men. "What have I done?" he wrote to a fellow Virginian: "Overturned government? What? the Council—not Methodism. I only say no man among us ought to get into the Apostle's chair with the Keys, and stretch a lordly power over the ministers and Kingdom of Christ. 'Tis a human invention, a quicksand. . . ." More to the point, O'Kelly argued, along antifederalist lines, "A consolidated government is always bad." He then painted an unsavory picture of Asbury's mastership over his young preaching ranks and their contrast to the true workingmen of the church: "Boys with their Keys, under the absolute sway of one who declares his authority and succession from the Apostles," "these striplings" would dare "rule and govern Christ's Church" as if they were "master workmen" who "could finish such a temple."[63]

O'Kelly's break with the Methodist connection was just one of a number of divisions among the preachers that threatened Asbury's control of the MEC in the 1790s. In 1791, William Hammett, an Irish preacher newly arrived from evangelizing the West Indies, accused Asbury of episcopal tyranny and disloyalty to Wesley. Hammett organized the short-lived Primitive Methodist Church in Charleston, South Carolina—the first breakaway denomination from the American Methodists. His congregation, a mix of whites and their slaves, dissolved upon his death in 1803.[64] In 1792, an anonymous New York Methodist published an address to the members of the Methodist Church calling for enfranchisement of Methodist members in the conferences and instatement of their rights to refuse appointments of stationed preachers and to choose their own class leaders and other officers. The present Methodist government, he wrote, "*may be called an aristocracy rather bordering on monarchy.*" Submission to the authority of the conferences "is only giving us a sleeping potion, by means of which the chains of aristocracy may be rivetted on us with more ease." "[E]very man," the same disputant exclaimed, "ought to be at liberty to think and speak freely about religion [without fear of expulsion], and this, perhaps, would contribute more to the propagation of truth than any other means."[65]

By the mid-1790s, Jesse Lee observed increasing dissension among southern Methodists, who called for enfranchisement of local preachers in the conferences and inclusion of a delegation of lay members. The church leadership responded with what would be their main retort to O'Kelly's opposition: representation was warranted in a government that supported itself for purposes of taxation; whereas the MEC governed only those who volunteered for the itinerants' connection. The arguments over these issues became so rancorous that the Reverend Devereux Jarratt, the Methodists' former friend in Virginia, wrote, "I have seen and heard so much of the party zeal, party interest and party spirit of the people called Methodists, and the nefarious methods made use of to put down one and set up another, that I really doubt whether there would be any propriety in giving them the epithet of a religious society." The people, William Watters reported from Virginia, were frustrated by their lack of influence over the preachers' conferences.[66]

The conflicts among the preachers, not least of all many American preachers' awareness of their lack of clout in the church and how this contrasted with the American rhetoric of equality, came to a head at the 1796 general conference. Here Thomas Coke, as noted earlier, offered to continue in the office of bishop without an election. From the floor, one of the remaining Irish preachers shouted at the English superintendent, "Popery, Popery, Popery!" Coke tore up his proposal, striking back in a revealing spate of anger, "Do you think yourself equal to me?" Nelson Reed quickly took up the challenge: "Dr. Coke has asked whether we think ourselves equal to him—I answer, yes, we *do* think ourselves equal to him, notwithstanding he was educated at Oxford and has been honored with the degree of Doctor of Laws—and more than that, we think ourselves equal to Dr. Coke's king." "He is hard upon me," Coke remarked, whereupon Asbury bluntly retorted, "I told you our preachers were not blockheads."[67]

Now head of the Republican Methodist—later Christian—Church, James O'Kelly continued to verbally assail Asbury and the Methodist hierarchy. In 1798, when Federalist and Democratic-Republican contention was at an all-time high, O'Kelly initiated a rare Methodist print controversy by pseudonymously publishing *The Author's Apology for Protesting Against the Methodist Episcopal Government*, in which he used a chronicle-style narrative and the discourse of Revolutionary polemic to allegorize the grievances of the American Methodist rank and file against their bishops." [T]he people of America groaned, by reason of oppression," he began, "[and] they prayed the king of Britain to ease their burden. But the king consulted the young men, and refused to remove any of their burdens, but sent his army and shot the people of Columbia." With the American revolt and the assistance of "the resolute Franks," the Americans were able to prevail. Analogously, "Francis," as O'Kelly referred to the Methodist leader, in his "absolute manner," along with his young henchmen, had imposed episcopacy, a form of "Ecclesiastical Monarchy" on the Methodists.[68]

In a second foray, O'Kelly made the contemporary political comparisons more overt. With the creation of the council in 1789, he argued, Asbury had effected a change in Methodist government "from a confederacy of the districts, to an Ecclesiastical Monarchy." Drawing further on the Federalist critique of consolidated government, O'Kelly claimed that the council was designed to "remove the foundation, and utterly destroy the suffrage of the districts." By contrast, O'Kelly was "a true friend to liberty, and considered *sovereignty* to be an inherent right of the people." Reaching the conclusion of his argument, O'Kelly at last landed an ad hominem attack on Asbury's nationality: "Ah, Sir, we are too sensible of the *sweets* of liberty, to be content any longer under British chains!" A "son of America" and a "Christian," O'Kelly vowed opposition to Asbury's "political measures" and dedicated himself to "Bible government, Christian equality, and the Christian name."[69] In short, O'Kelly's theology, as Russell Richey writes, "laid claim to a republican language that would increasingly become the Protestant idiom and eventually also the Methodist idiom"—but largely under pressure from schismatic groups.[70]

More specifically, O'Kelly's attacks on Asbury suggested a fear of the consolidating tendencies of the movement. Indeed, the very bases for the organizational expansion of Methodism rested on addressing some of the same problems tackled by the Federal Convention of 1787: how to create an overall structure in which the constituent units—from the local societies and quarterly meetings up through the annual conferences—had a say in church affairs while assuring that the central unit of the church—the general conferences—would govern decisively over increasingly massive extents of territory.

Asbury was hard-pressed to reply to O'Kelly's very American critiques of his leadership. In fact, he did not reply directly himself but worked behind the scenes to control the future direction of American Methodism. His first action was to direct Nicholas Snethen, his right-hand assistant, to respond to O'Kelly's assaults in suitably polemical form.[71]

At the start of the first of two published replies to O'Kelly, Nicholas Snethen satirized the older preacher's biblical style and claims to prophetic authority, resorting to a gendered metaphor to belittle the older preacher. Since O'Kelly had depicted the episcopacy as the monster out of the Book of Revelation, Snethen claimed, perhaps he "had an eye to the dragon, and the woman that brought forth the man child, in the Revelations. What a grand thought! this great dragon, episcopacy, pouring out of his mouth a furious flood, after the helpless, the innocent woman, republican Methodism, and her man child, Mr. O'Kelly and his friends."

Snethen swiftly moved on to the political heart of the matter. Providing a strict constructionist interpretation of the Revolution, he asserted that the conflict between the Americans and Britain had been about taxation: "The dispute between Great Britain and America, did not originate in any objection to the British government, but solely in the question of the right of taxation. . . . It never was the wish of the American people to dethrone the king of Great Britain, or to destroy the English constitution; they only asked for equal rights as British subjects." Independence "was an afterthought, forced upon the Colonies by the coercive measures of the British ministry." O'Kelly already had equal rights in the Methodist connection; he now refused to accept the will of the majority. Besides, Snethen continued, with a pointed reference to the Methodist mission, "[t]he business of a Methodist preacher is not to take care of this or that society only, but to save as many souls as he can; he is not to show how fallen the church is, but how fallen the people themselves are!"[72] Referring to Asbury's indisputably relentless labors on behalf of the movement, Snethen depicted the bishop as the benefactor of the MEC's young preachers, struggling with O'Kelly, the willful man-child: "In him [Asbury] we see an example of daily labour, suffering, and self-denial, worthy the imitation of the young preacher. In a word, we have every reason to esteem him as a father, and not one reason to suspect or discard him as a '*tyrant or despot*.' "[73]

Asbury and Coke dispensed with the paternal metaphor in favor of more overtly American symbols when they undertook a more elaborate if indirect refutation of

O'Kelly's charges. This counterattack took the form of a series of dense annotations in the church's discipline regarding the meaning of its numerous provisions, a project that the bishops buttressed with innumerable scriptural allusions and various analogies to American politics.

"It cannot be needful in this country," the bishops observed in their commentary, "to vindicate the right of every christian society, to possess, within itself, all the privileges necessary or expedient for the comfort, instruction, or good government of the members thereof." It followed that the MEC had a "right," like any other church in America, to choose the episcopal plan with the purpose of supporting the missionary goals of the church. Hence those who opposed the MEC government would "utterly destroy our *itinerant plan*." These opponents "would be concerned chiefly, if not only, for the interests of their own constituents. They could not be expected, from *the nature of things*, to make the necessary sacrifices, and to enter impartially into *the good of the whole*." Conflicts would then emerge, since "such is the *nature* of man, and perhaps such is the *duty* of man, that he will always prefer the people for whom he acts, and to whom he is responsible, before all others." By contrast, the traveling ministry "who know not, when they meet [in conference], what may be their next sphere of action, and are willing to run any where on the errands of their Lord, are not nearly as much exposed to the temptations mentioned above."[74]

The bishops went on to codify the governing structure of the church, observing that "Mr. Wesley was the patron of all the Methodist pulpits in Great Britain and Ireland *for life*, the sole right of nomination being invested in him by all the deeds of settlement, which gave him exceeding great power." This was not so for the Americans; nevertheless, the question remained, "How could an itinerant ministry be preserved through this extensive continent, if the yearly conferences were to station the preachers?" The conferences, rather, would be solely concerned with "the spiritual and temporal interests of *that part* of the connection, the direction of which was intrusted to them." In the final analysis, "*that grand spring, the union of the body at large* . . . would be gradually weakened, till at last it might be entirely destroyed." Addressing O'Kelly directly, although the preacher remained unnamed, Asbury and Coke asserted that those who called such church government tyrannical indulged in "the common cry of restless spirits even against the best governments, in order that they may throw every thing into confusion, and then ride in the whirlwind and direct the storm."[75]

Inclined toward a top-down Federalist-style exercise of authority, Asbury and Coke were nonetheless unable to fully disregard the issues of democratic governance within the MEC. Pertinent questions were obvious to both the bishops and the rank and file: In what way was it suitable for clerics in the United States to exert control over their fellow preachers? Was the Methodist Church a remnant of British constitutionalism in the midst of the American republic? Were Asbury and Coke assuming a form of governance that most Americans found inimical? Was O'Kelly basically correct?

Asbury's and Coke's answer came in the new but conservative American language of opportunity. The church was a "people's" institution, they claimed, not because the preachers ran the church—although they had a significant say in its policies and direction—but especially because of the process by which Methodists *became* preachers. They invented, that is, the simile of the itinerancy as a university for the upwardly mobile: "[O]ur societies form our grand nurseries or universities for ministers of the gospel," the bishops wrote. Ideally any man might initiate a career in the itinerancy by attending class meetings, joining a Methodist society, and seeking appointment as a class leader, and then proceed to the critical steps: as exhorter, local preacher, and probationary itinerant; and finally as an ordained itinerant and even presiding elder. "From all that has been observed," the bishops concluded, referring to the continual process of recommendations, appointments, and elections that accompanied this upward trajectory, "it must be clear to every candid reader, that it is not the yearly conference *only*, or the bishops or presiding elders *only*, in the intervals of the conferences, who choose the local or travelling preachers. On the contrary, *they* have no authority to choose at all, till the people, through their leaders, stewards, &c. recommend."[76]

As observed earlier, the bishops' resorting to the trope of a university of preachers effectively excluded women and blacks from the itinerant ranks. The language of social mobility too exclusively assumed the gender and race of those who were rising to apply satisfactorily to the extraordinarily broad base of Methodist membership. But in the long run, it was decidedly the "experience" and "labors" of Asbury's "boys," as O'Kelly depicted them—often far removed from rancorous disputes over central power, absorbed in the problems of their daily ministry, and driven on to ever greater distances by their evangelical calling—that guaranteed Methodism's place as the *American* phenomenon it was to become in the new century.

THE CIRCUIT RIDERS

The Methodist preachers maintained their network of societies and circuits through the discouraging trends of the 1790s—downward spirals in membership and attendance, resistance to antislavery, the unsettled conditions of churches in general, Hammett's and O'Kelly's schisms—by spending relentless hours on the road. Heirs of Wesley's missionary vision, subject to the discipline of the new American church and Francis Asbury's paternal oversight, the circuit riders piloted Methodism through the rough waters of religious and political strife in the early republic, sharing Wesleyan doctrine and "remarkable" dreams and experiences with thousands of household, class, and society members and "hearers," and turning themselves into a formidable evangelical vanguard that, year by year, increasing numbers of Americans found hard to resist.

The ranks of Methodist itinerants also grew. Jesse Lee, the MEC's first official historian, calculated their numbers, dividing the pioneering generation of preachers—those who had entered the itinerancy between 1769 and 1806—into four chronological "classes." The first class, a total of 125 men, was made up of itinerants licensed to preach between 1769 and 1784, from the arrival of Wesley's first

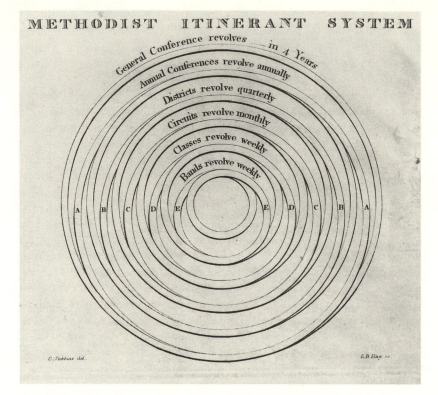

Figure 12. *Methodist Itinerant System*, ca. 1818. A chart of the American Methodist missionary structure: as natural as the solar system, or the perpetual motion of the new industrial age. Courtesy of Methodist Episcopal Church Records, 1791–1945, Manuscripts and Archives Division, The New York Public Library, Astor, Lenox, and Tilden Foundations.

assistants to the Christmas Conference; the second class, 289 men, were licensed between 1785 and 1792, the date of the first general conference; the third class, 259 men, joined between 1793 and the critical year of 1800; and the fourth class, comprising 317 men, joined between 1801 and 1806, several years before the publication of Lee's history. In addition to the regular itinerants, 251 probationers had traveled between 1773 and 1806.[77] Altogether, a total of 1,241 individuals in one capacity or another served as traveling preachers in the first generation of the movement, 832 of whom had been admitted to the connection or as probationers before 1800.[78]

The Methodist itinerants—retaining the title "preacher" despite their new ministerial status—were recognizable to most Americans by a number of external features. Chief among these were their distinctive "social age," demeanor, and dress.

Regarding the preachers' age: A minority manifested the patriarchal manner of charismatic preachers like James O'Kelly and Benjamin Abbott, the latter an old man "with large shaggy eyebrows, and eyes of flame, of powerful frame, and great extent of voice, which he exerted to the utmost . . . which, with an occasional stamp of his foot, made the church ring."[79] But impressionistic evidence suggests that most itinerants were young by the standards of their times. That is, while the average age of itinerants received on trial at the New York conference in 1801 was twenty-four, they were not yet heads of households. In this respect, O'Kelly's repeated references to Francis Asbury's "boys" needs to be understood with some qualification: the preachers were young by virtue of their removal from household responsibilities. And like many boys, they spent much of their time associating with same-sex bands—set apart from a society in which most adult men, including ministers, were married.[80]

The Methodist itinerants had also internalized the responsiblities of their mission and exhibited the serious demeanor of their sect, or what John Fanning Watson, before his own conversion, called "a continual selfish sulleness, a continual railing against the world in which it has pleased kind heaven to place us." Their sobriety was thus another means by which they were readily identified in a crowd. Traveling to Europe in 1799, Lorenzo Dow, a twenty-two-year-old charismatic preacher, was quickly deemed a Methodist by one of his fellow passengers because he did not "drink and be jovial and cheerly, as what the rest of us are; but are gloomy and cast down; like that people, always melancholy."[81] Past the turmoil of their religious conversions, Methodist preachers imbibed the disciplinary demands of their sect to the point of morbidness.

But Methodists were probably most easily identified by their traveling gear, what was rapidly becoming the uniform of a distinct traveling ministry. The preachers did not always dress like poor men. When he died, itinerant Jacob Brush left a silk-hair suit to a fellow itinerant.[82] More common was the preacher's dress of black, gray, or blue-gray breeches and leggings, topped by a vest, an overcoat, and a low-crowned white hat: the standard livery until about 1810 when, much to Asbury's disapproval, the itinerants began to adopt the new style of long pants.[83] One preacher recollected the details of Richard Whatcoat's appearance: "His dress was very plain, in Methodist minister style: the shad-belly coat, and vest buttoned snug up to his neck." Like many of his cohort, Whatcoat wore his hair long, unpowdered, and combed "straight over his forehead," considered the "Methodist fashion in those days." Reflecting on the Methodists' antiexhibitionist conception of virility, the preacher noted, "It would have been considered out of order to have worn [one's hair] so as to exhibit a noble forehead." Like Asbury, Whatcoat's skin was tanned like a workman's, the result of years of riding out-of-doors. Others, as if entering a monastic order, cut their hair.[84] Most of all, the preachers prized their saddlebags, symbols of their traveling life, into which they packed journal notebooks, pocketbook hymnals, extra clothing, medicines for themselves and their followers, and, among the antislavery preachers, preprinted manumission forms. "It used to be said," an itinerant recollected, "that 'Methodist ministers kept house in their saddle-bags.' " They kept their appointments, punctuality being an important Methodist value, through one more critical component of the itinerant wardrobe—a pocket watch.[85]

Americans, however, were usually more intrigued by the reputation that preceded the preachers wherever they made their rounds than by their external characteristics. Marginal figures in most of the neighborhoods and territories through which they traveled, the Methodists occupied a place in the American imagination somewhere between medicine men and deviant vagrants. From the start, rumors abounded regarding Methodist itinerants' ability to wield shamanistic powers. Preachers were said to use magic powder that made people fall down at revivals, and to carry knives to ward off the devil.[86] Some practiced a form of folk medicine, as when Philip Gatch applied a prescription from the New Testament to heal a man injured in a fall from the top story of a tobacco house. Others resorted to outright faith healing, Freeborn Garrettson observing that after a Methodist itinerant effected a cure for a New Jersey woman who had been dumb for two years, "some thought the Methodists could work miracles."[87] Among unsympathetic obervers, the preachers were perceived as troublemaking outsiders and seducers of women. One of the Methodists' ploys, it was reported, was to lock themselves in corn houses with young women. Little elaborating was necessary for their rivals and opponents to describe the itinerants—leading uninhibited revival meetings filled with female acolytes—as sexual predators.[88]

Consequently, the first Methodist preachers in Flanders, New Jersey, a town populated by Presbyterians, Baptists, Quakers, and Moravians, appeared "only as a few Stragling Vagrants Scarcely worth notice" but for their heretical teachings. "Some Said they were antechrist or the fals prophess that Should come in the last time to Deceive, if it were possible, Even the Verry Elect. [O]thers Said they preached fals Doctrine teaching Sinners to pray and that they were to be Saved by their works." For their Flanders followers, however, Methodists were "a little Spartan Band" who, in keeping with Revolutionary salvos, "Supported the Gosple flag of Equel Rights to full and free Salvation."[89]

Indeed, it was in the prosaic rounds of their work and association, not just with their followers but with each other, that the itinerants laid the groundwork for Methodist expansion. The preachers' daily lives revolved around four essential elements: traveling, compliance with Methodist discipline, income, and sociability.

Foremost was the itinerancy. William Colbert's commentary on his circuit riding through western Pennsylvania, when the area still had few roads and fewer public hostelries, illuminates the kinds of conditions the preachers faced in the outermost circuits of the Middle Atlantic. On the Tioga circuit, Colbert wrote that he

> [p]aid one and sixpence for my accomodations (the man was moderate in his charge) and being impatient to see Dayly Town I set off without my breakfast: but O perplexing! missed my way again. . . . This morning breakfasted on a frozen turnip. After which I call'd at a house—wanting something for me and my horse, but the uncomfortable reply, "*no bread*," again was heard. . . .[A]greeable to directions I crosst a towering mountain to Dayly Town that long desired place, but how am I mistaken. [I]nstead of finding a tavern here where man and horse should be refresh'd with that, which repairs the wastes of decaying nature, the Ideal Dayly Town vanishes away, when the real one heaves a smokey Cabin or two in view.[90]

On the eve of the Whiskey Rebellion, Colbert complained that the Susquehanna River Valley abounded "with whore[s], whoremongers and drunkards, and for all I know murderers." His listeners were relatively indifferent, those who could discern his words over the cries of discontented children: "I would wish such people to know that I do no[t] preach for the sake of hearing myself," Colbert wrote caustically; "if I did, I could have as much satisfaction in preaching to the trees, as to them that cannot hear me."[91]

The traveling plan for preachers was entirely under Asbury's control, but the preachers set their own pace. Partway through his years on the road, Freeborn Garrettson determined "not to travel less than an hundred miles a week, and Preach twice a day." Most itinerants appear to have covered ground daily, with occasional breaks owing to illness or other obligations. In addition to the duties associated with the Methodist societies, the itinerants regularly preached in public venues, ministered to populations in local poorhouses, and attended executions, where they attempted to provide solace to, and of course to save the souls of, the condemned.[92] Along their routes they lodged at the houses of the increasingly dense network of supporters, where they received their room and board gratis, or rented rooms at inns. The potential tedium of circuit riding is evident in Richard Whatcoat's account of several days of traveling in August 1790:

> [August 12] I Rode To John Evans & preach[d] To About 30 people [August 13] Rode with Bro[r] Green To Elis Jones. I preach[d] in the Evning &c. [August 14] Rode to Baltimore. [P]reach[d] in the Evening at Fels point. Bro[r] willis Exhorted &c. [August 15] I preach[d] Morning. Bro[r] willis & Hagerty Gave the Sacrament, Also I prech[d] in the Afternoon To I Supose as many more as the House Could hold . . . [August 16] Rode to Abingdon. [P]reach[d] in the Evning. [W]e were comforted Together. I Slep at Jos Toys [August 17] Rode To Josiah Delams &c. [August 18] Dined at W[m] Mackintears. Slep[t] at Sol[m] Hercys [August 19] Rode To Wilminton. Dined with W[m] Daugherdy [and] Bro[r] Thelwels D.T. [Dinner and Tea] at Sister Matsons; preach[d] To a Smal Congregation in the Evning [with] Liberty.[93]

Incessantly on the road as they were, it is no wonder that the preachers treated their horses like favored consorts, for there was "scarcely anything of all that he possesses of this worlds goods that a Methodist preacher prefers to his horse, and in general they have very fine ones." Itinerants labored to keep their horses fit and were particularly panicked or pained by lost, injured, or ill animals. "My poor horse I have rode for four years over many mountains, and thousands of miles, has never failed me, until now," William Colbert wrote dispiritedly in 1795. "Had I been by myself, this had not happened. If I am allways in the mind, I am now in, I will never punish my horse to please any man."[94] In December 1782, Thomas Haskins's horse took ill and was frequently too lame to travel until it died the following April, after a grueling twelve-mile journey. Haskins recorded: "about 7 O'Clk my Beast espired, tho' the loss to me was great, yet I felt no repining or murmuring in my breast ag[t] the providence, but was sorry I forced her to travel when she was so sick." Over the next two months, Haskins borrowed various mounts until he purchased his own, partially on credit, for £25. Asbury compared his mare, "supple joynted Jane," in value to one of Harry Dorsey Gough's thoroughbred racehorses.[95]

These travels, while usually pursued alone or with just one other itinerant, were carried out under the terms of the MEC's discipline: the second important element in the itinerating life. The itinerants' performances were regularly assessed by fellow preachers and elders at quarterly meetings and annual and general conferences. Although their schedules kept them away from the oversight of their superiors on most days of the year, the preachers took these disciplinary judgments seriously, even when they reflected more a want of skills than virtue on the itinerants' parts. In trials made by the New York conference in and after 1800, for example, the church hierarchy's chief concerns were many of the preachers' lack of experience and alienating personality quirks rather than the more deleterious infractions of drunkenness, profanity, and fornication. Phrases such as "apt to be sick perhaps more apt to complain," "weak in Preaching[,] excellent in Conversation & class," "holy, useful, Objection Management of Voice" were common refrains. Ebenezer Washburn was "not admitted on account of debts & further likely debts."[96] Lorenzo Dow—soon to be known as "Crazy Dow" for his intentionally slovenly appearance and cabalistic-style oratory—was dropped by the New York conference for having "gone to Ireland, nothing immoral against him," rather than his lack of conformity to social mores. Another itinerant, Mitchell Bull, was not accepted: "Urged against him his forwardness of Spirit. Obstinancy. Want of Knowledge of the Scriptures."[97] Likewise, when examined at the annual and general conferences for full admission into the preachers' connection, "which at that period of Methodism was a trying and somewhat perilous process, even where nothing worthy of death or of bonds, had been committed by the individual," the new itinerants were as often as not rebuked for their character and works rather than for more repellent sins. Thomas Lyell recalled running into trouble when his innate high spirits prompted him to whip a fellow itinerant's horse, although he knew that the discipline catechized the preachers: "Do you deny yourself every useless Pleasure of Sense? Imagination? Honour? Are you temperate in all things?"[98] For most of the itinerants, these daily elements of self-denial, rather than the rejection of more exotic temptations of drink, gambling, and sex, formed the core of their missionary identity.

In a brief memoir of his friend Francis Spry, Ezekiel Cooper summarized the qualities of the ministerial prototype that the Methodists were attempting to sponsor. In Cooper's words, Spry was "a man of exemplary piety, great meekness, full of patience, unfeignedly humble even to a great diffidence, always less in his own esteem, than in the esteem of his friends: he was an ingenious preacher of sound judgment, and good method." The two had engaged in frequent religious conversations, and Cooper's record of an exchange between them when both were ill and fatigued from traveling exudes the sometimes maudlin sensibility that Wesleyan discourse shared with the sentimental novel:

> "My dear brother C[ooper]," Spry began, "I have lately been thinking that you and I shall never have the happiness of travelling another circuit together; or indeed at all.

Our complaints seem foreboding of a dismission from our laborious fatigue and toil, travelling too and fro preaching to poor sinners striving to win them unto Jesus."

"O brother Spry!" Cooper replied, "I hope we shall travel another circuit before we die, our complaints tho' thretning I don't expect will take us off so soon as you have been thinking."

"It may be so," Spry returned, continuing after some reflection, "they are only thoughts, which have passed my mind in prayer and meditation."

"Well!" Cooper answered, "if the Lord takes us from the vineyard, no doubt he will raise up others to supply our place; so we will be resigned. Let us stand in a state of readiness."

Cooper concluded with the common Wesleyan refrain: "A melting time we had of it, and I trust a profitable time."[99]

In fact, "idle talk," or gossip, a common source of power in small, homogeneous communities like the Methodist fraternity, was a weakness for which the preachers might be disciplined. "No people on earth *mean* better," Joseph Pilmore wrote after he had left the Methodists, "but many of them are very unfit for *Familiar Friendship*. . . . Through a kind of *puerile simplicity*, they are often drawn into a sort of loquacity, which proves very hurtful to the Characters of Individuals, and the [Methodist] Society in general."[100] Thus while the itinerants engaged in intimate conversations on all manner of religious topics, they were hard-pressed not to spread the word on those members of the fraternity who were less forthcoming, not to complain in a moment of indiscretion about fellow itinerants who were failing to make the grade, and not to compete with one another for the attentions of their elders and bishops.

The itinerants' stipendiary compensation for these trials—the third essential ingredient of their daily experience—was minimal. Initially, the local societies paid the preachers' quarterage as well as compensating the itinerants for the costs of clothing, housekeeping, laundering, haircuts, and traveling to the next appointment.[101] By the late 1770s, the preachers' income was set by the annual conference to be paid by the quarterly meetings. In 1778, the itinerants were allotted a quarterage of £8 Virginia currency, amounting to an annual stipend of £32, one that took wartime inflation into account. With the conclusion of the Revolutionary War, the preachers at the 1783 annual conference determined that all of the preachers' income, "either in money or cloathing," was to be valued by the stewards at the quarterly meetings and the balance due reported to the annual conferences for distribution to the itinerants. The first discipline, published in 1785, set this annual stipend at £24 Pennsylvania currency plus expenses (translated into $64 at the 1792 general conference), for the support of the preachers, along with their wives, children, and widows, and men who had left the field owing to fatigue or age. These allotments were not raised again until 1800, when the annual stipend for all eligible preachers and their wives and widows was set at $80.[102]

The same bodies that determined the preachers' salaries, however, frequently did not have enough to pay the preachers' "deficiencies," that is, were indebted to the preachers for back pay. In 1785, the annual collection to help defray this expense was only £300 and fell to £182 6s. 6d. in 1786. In 1788, little more—£185 8s. 5d.—was contributed toward paying the connection's backlog of debts to its itinerants, "many of whom after all, did not receive more than eighteen or twenty pounds, and several not more than fifteen pounds per annum."[103] Many preachers, another itinerant recalled, attended annual meetings "often but *poorly clad* and evincing by their appearance, that they had the year preceding, not only laboured hard in the word and doctrine, but encountered many hardships and Endured no small portion of afflictions."[104] By 1790, the connection owed its itinerants more than £1,000. In the same year, William Jessop wrote disconsolately that he was broke: "All I had, was a fipeny Bit, and a few old Coppers." Asbury was fully aware of and often uneasy about his young disciples' poverty. "I am a bishop and a beggar," he wrote in 1788, "our connection is very poor, and our preachers on the frontiers labour the whole year for 6 to 8 pounds."[105] While collections might rise in one area—in 1796, for example, the Philadelphia annual conference was able for the first time to pay salaries in full to from forty to fifty preachers—in others, they might not. In 1802, the New York annual conference reported a deficit of more than $1,000 owed to forty-three preachers.[106] It may have galled some probationers that the chief failing for which they were tested at the New York annual conferences after 1800 was whether or not they were free of debt.[107]

The greatest burden for collection of monies to pay the itinerants continued to rest with the local societies and quarterly meetings. A majority of the business of the Baltimore quarterly meeting, for example, was taken up with collection of donations from classes and love feasts and distribution to the preachers and their families.[108] Quarterly meeting balances might be completely cleared out by the preachers' salaries. In 1795, the Long Island circuit, for example, collected $41.41 from eighteen classes and public collections; $41.41 was then disbursed to the three stationed preachers.[109] The quarterly meetings might sponsor special drives, such as the collection in the Baltimore circuit that raised £17 to buy one itinerant a horse. Preacher Lawrence McCombs attempted to extract the same generosity from the Philadelphia quarterly meeting when he complained of the expense of keeping a horse "in Town" and requested that the society "pay for the keeping of my Creature."[110] Asbury's own horses and, when he was ill, carriages were provided or paid for by local Methodist societies from Maryland to New York. In 1800, several of the local societies from New York to Alexandria submitted petitions to the 1800 general conference requesting that appropriate measures be taken to improve the finances of the connection. An elaborate plan for culling money from all possible sources—from preachers' contributions to public collections at the annual and general conferences, to surpluses from the chartered fund for superannuated preachers—was proposed, with unrecorded results.[111]

By comparison, despite the loss of tax support and the disruptions of the Revolutionary War, Anglican clergymen could expect to receive a comfortable income from salaries and glebes as well as from teaching and practicing medicine. A large parish like St. Paul's in Baltimore paid as much as £500 per annum to its incumbent clergyman. Ministers appointed to the rural parish of St. Petersburg,

Virginia, received between £100 and £134 in annual stipends in the 1790s, in addition to the earnings from schoolteaching and a glebe of forty acres.[112]

Even the Methodists' own local preachers might profit more than the itinerants, as Asbury noted whenever these men demanded a voice in the annual or general conferences. Local preachers, Asbury pointed out, "go where and when they please; can preach anywhere and nowhere; they can keep plantations and slaves, and have them bought or given by their parents. The local preachers can receive fifty or a hundred dollars per year, for marriages." By contrast, "we travellers, if we receive a few dollars for marriages, must return them to the conference, or be called refractory or disobedient." Of the preachers' paltry income and its uncertain supply, Thomas Haskins observed that "[t]he prejudiced suppose we under take to preach for a livelihood, or that we are Lazy & so take this easy way to Get our living. . . . But can money, can a design of living easy [be] our aim," Haskins asked rhetorically; "if so th[e]n methodist preachers are the most Stupid men in the world."[113]

To make up for what was lacking in their livelihood, the itinerants relied heavily on sociability among their fellow travelers and their "hearers"—the last but not least important aspect of their daily experience. It is safe to say that preachers' conferences, revival meetings, and visiting among the households of the faithful were the mainstays of many itinerants' lives whatever their background. Those traveling through familiar territory after the Revolutionary War were now received with open arms by fellow Methodist relations and neighbors. In the early 1780s, Maryland-born Thomas Haskins, journeying on his Maryland circuit to a total of twenty-eight different households over one month, pursued a cheerful round of visiting, beginning with a stay at Perry Hall, and including stops at the residences of various relatives.[114] The MEC forestalled what might otherwise have been a daunting solitude on the itinerant trail by assigning itinerants to travel in pairs. Consequently the "Preachers Room" at Perry Hall was equipped with furnishings for two men: one high-post and one low-post bedstead, two chests of drawers, two tables, two washstands with two pitchers and two basins, two carpets, and, for the occasions when the members of the household came to join them in prayer, five walnut chairs.[115]

But those who traveled on less-populated circuits expressed an at times painful loneliness as they forged into unknown terrain, often just barely removed from Indian territories. Even if assigned in pairs, the itinerants frequently traveled separately in order to attend to as many as twenty or more classes and societies in each circuit.[116] Haskins's formerly happy tone changed to gloom when he was appointed to a frontier circuit in Maryland at the end of 1782, where he endured "poor lodging & eating" and "*Bethlehem fare*," far from the friendly climate of the eastern counties of the state. The preachers' greatest challenge was that itinerancy was indeed designed to *prevent* them from forming attachments to their followers: the social separation of minister and congregation was a given, one that was in keeping with the missionary ethos of Methodism and the formation of Methodist societies as distinct from traditional communities of any sort—social, political, or religious.[117]

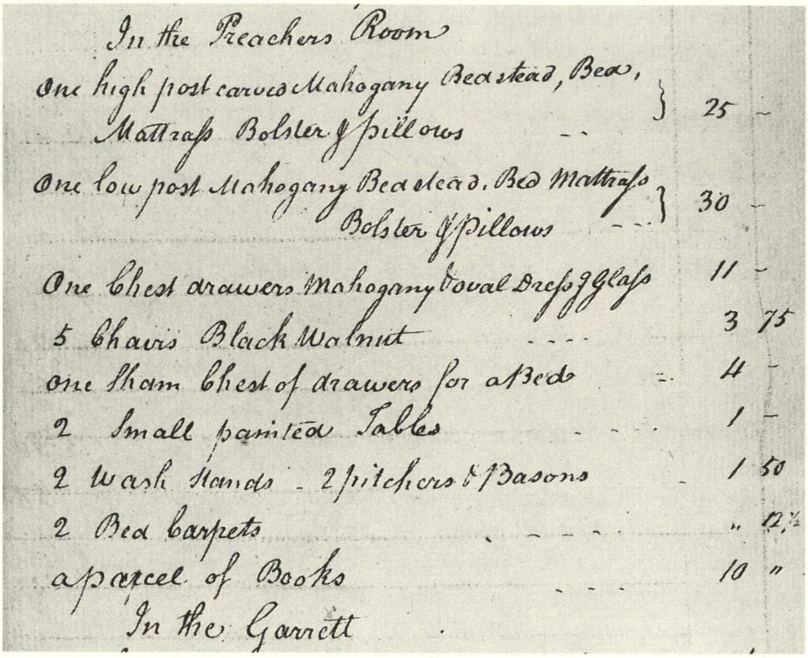

In the Preachers Room

One high post carved Mahogany Bedstead, Bed, Mattrass Bolster & pillows	25 –
One low post Mahogany Bedstead. Bed Mattrass Bolster & Pillows	30 –
One Chest drawers Mahogany & oval Dress g Glass	11 –
5 Chairs Black Walnut	3 75
one Sham Chest of drawers for a Bed	4 –
2 Small painted Tables	1 –
2 Wash stands - 2 pitchers & Basons	1 50
2 Bed Carpets	" 12½
a parcel of Books	10 "

In the Garrett

Figure 13. The Preachers Room at Perry Hall. One segment of the 1808 inventory, listing the furnishings of a room set aside for Methodist preachers. Courtesy of Maryland State Archives/Baltimore County Register of Wills (Inventories) 25 [MSA C 340, MdHR 11678], Annapolis.

For consolation and motivation, preachers poured their thoughts into letters and journals, setting out rules for themselves and their correspondents and chastising fellow itinerants for tardy replies. As one itinerant wrote angrily to another in 1791: "This comes to inform you that I did not Receive a Letter from you Since conference. I heard of your being on my Circuit and going off again without droping one line. [V]ery well, very well, Mabe I Shall come into your Circuit Some time & I will not Serve you so."[118] It is perhaps not surprising that the preachers occasionally fell in love with each other. "I love God, I love his people, I love all the dear Preachers," Stith Mead wrote to John Kobler in 1795, in an exchange not unlike that among many Methodists. In response to Kobler's passionate address, however, he continues with a mixture of metaphor and unalloyed emotion: "Yet none seems so much like my own flesh as yourself. I love you with a pure love fervently, I think of you with tears, I dream of you, I dream of embracing you, in the fond arms of Nuptial love I dream of kissing you with the kisses of my mouth. I am Married to you."[119]

By the end of the 1790s, several of the Methodist itinerants had been traveling for twenty years and were spiritual father figures for followers of all ages. As he lay dying, William Watters's brother-in-law saluted him, calling the itinerant "his spiritual father—his father in Christ—his God Father—and the good old Veteran that had been long in the field."[120] But it is further testimony to the difficulties of the preaching trade that few itinerants in the first generation held out for long. Jesse Lee's census of the first preachers traveling between 1769 and 1806 again provides critical information.

A small segment (fifteen) of these men were expelled or otherwise turned out by their annual conferences or the general conference. Among these were Abraham Whitworth and James Dempster, ejected before the Revolution, the former for intemperance, the latter likely for returning to his native Presbyterianism. Adam Cloud was forced to leave in 1783 for improper conduct. Beverly Allen was expelled in 1792 for an unspecified crime.[121]

Another small number (twenty-eight men) withdrew voluntarily from the Methodist connection. Several, including Thomas Vasey—one of Wesley's three-man presbytery sent to America in 1784—Robert Ayres, William Duke, John Coleman, Samuel Spraggs, John Wade, and Thomas Lyell, returned to the Anglican Church and a more comfortable living as Protestant Episcopal ministers.[122] Others, like James O'Kelly and his numerous followers, among them Scottish-born William Glendinning, left the connection over the political disputes that rocked the church in the 1790s.[123]

More significant, seventy-nine of the first generation died while on appointment to a circuit. Among these losses were Methodist book agent John Dickins, who succumbed to yellow fever in Philadelphia in 1798; Benjamin Abbott, who died weakened by old age in 1796; and Bishop Richard Whatcoat in 1806. The preachers' record of longevity was not encouraging. Sixty-six of the 850 full and probationary preachers had died by the end of 1800, that is, as the phrase went, were "worn out" in their labors. Thirty-four, or more than half of these men, died after just five years or less in the field.[124] As Nathan Hatch has found, an astonishing 63.1 percent of the Methodist preachers who died in the field between 1780 and 1818 were under forty years of age. The great majority of this cohort served less than ten years. One preacher remarked curtly on the deleterious effects of his calling, "From the Labours of this Year I am convinced that traveling and preaching is far more impairing to helth then my former employment has been."[125]

Overall, the largest proportion of itinerants—two-thirds of those who entered the traveling ministry between 1769 and 1800—simply "located," that is, stopped traveling.[126] While preachers were known to quit viable trades and the professions of medicine and the law to join the itinerancy, the opposite was more generally the case. "[O]ur preachers [are] getting into the trade," Asbury lamented of backsliding among the Methodists in the 1790s, "now here and there marrying fortunes, and some going into trade and cheating their dear brethren out of hundreds."[127] Others were likely attracted to the more settled life of local preachers, combining business with service at their local society where, as William Watters pointed out, the local preachers often got to know their congregations far better than itinerants were able to.[128]

But most of the men probably quit the itinerancy for a more predictable reason: to engage in what Asbury called a "ceremony awful as death"; that is, to marry.

"Well may it be so," Asbury continued, noting the cost of this worldly temptation, "when I calculate we have lost the travelling labours of two hundred of the best men in America, or the world, by marriage and consequent location." Bemoaning the loss of preachers to women and wedlock, Asbury made it clear that he would have preferred to serve at the head of a celibate brotherhood.[129] Yet, as the MEC's efforts to accommodate preachers' wives indicates, not all the itinerants were single to begin with: many, that is, had already moved beyond "boyhood" socially defined. In 1801, for example, the New York Annual Conference paid the salaries of fifteen married and twelve single men. Other features of the movement—the payment of allowances to the wives and children of married preachers[130] and the opening of Cokesbury College for the accommodation of preachers' sons[131]— suggest the important presence of men who had temporarily abandoned their hearthsides to join the itinerancy.

Despite the gratifications of Methodist sociability among the Methodist fraternity, furthermore, many single itinerants found it difficult to resist their sexual needs or the call to fulfill the common expectation of mature men: in the parlance of the time, to set up housekeeping.[132] Certainly, the common assumption among the traveling preachers was that marriage—or exhaustion—was the only legitimate reason for retiring from traveling. "O my brother!" John Dickins wrote to Ezekiel Cooper in 1794, "if you are under no necessity to marry, stick by the work till nature is worn out, & then you can return to your property & abide till you die."[133] Preachers who chose not to settle down after marriage left lonely if sympathetic wives at home and sometimes pathetic legacies to their children. At his death in 1789, widower Cornelius Cook left his son in the care of his executors—John Bleeker, the New York Methodist merchant, and preacher Thomas Morrell—who were instructed to send the boy to Cokesbury College, away from the influence of his (non-Methodist) grandmother, the Widow Van Vlack. Bleeker and Morrell were to sell Cook's modest effects to pay for his son's clothing and to meet unforeseen emergencies.[134]

The prospect of marriage provoked deep spiritual conflicts for individual preachers. The progress of Thomas Haskins's relationship with Martha Potts, heiress to the Potts family iron fortune, is illustrative. Haskins, twenty-three years old, met his future wife in July 1783 while lodging at her grandmother Rebecca Grace's residence near Coventry Forge, Pennsylvania. Martha Potts, Haskins wrote in his journal, "has retrenched and taken a serious turn." Almost immediately, Haskins expressed dismay at his own changing emotions and lack of loyalty to his Methodist mission: "Oh What would I have given to have got away from Preaching today—The Cause is evident, I have not kept my heart—Oh my unfaithfulness, my unfaithfulness." Over the next year, while continuing on his circuit appointments, he made frequent stops at Widow Grace's, where he still "found my Affection strong toward M[iss] P[otts]" and "my mind variously & deeply agitated." He spent his time "between hope & fear; Oh, What a cruel thing is it to Get so much in L[ov]e as I am." But he was sure that were he "to live to Methuselah's age," he would "to the last warmly regard M[iss] P[o]tts."

Despite her wealth and good connections, Martha Potts was the ideal Methodist wife: "[H]er piety, her sweetness of temper, her sensibility and her amazing artlessness of disposition," Haskins wrote, "must recommend her to *all* her Acquaintances." But his greatest fear was that mere sexual attraction was luring him away from the traveling ministry. "Lord I am in danger," Haskins concluded, and lapsing from his scriptural training, he quoted Homer's *Iliad* on the dangers of female entanglement: "Unhappy Paris / But to woman brave." By this time, Haskins had engaged himself to Potts for a June marriage. Still, on the eve of his wedding, he hesitated leaving the ministry. "All things are now ready,—But we will procrastinate it a few months longer." He at last concluded his journal on a foreboding note: "Spent the morning in writing & preparing for my intended Journey to Pensylvania—Not Knowing what shall befal me."[135]

Several years earlier, John Littlejohn expressed something of the same ambivalence, as well as inability to resist the inevitable, on the eve of his engagement to Monica Talbott of Fairfax County, Virginia.

> [I] was much dissatisfied w^t my intentions & desired every thing [the engagement] might be forgotten. I told her she might do just as she pleased. [T]hese things deprived me of my sleep for the night. In the morn^g I got my Horse & was just biding he[r] farewell, some conversation passed, it began to rain, I staied & what the result will be I know not.[136]

Implored by admiring women—many young and marriageable, eager to break from parental control and shape their own destinies—the preachers faced the daily temptations of sexual desire. Their religious imaginations fired by the erotic imagery of the Wesleyan sound-ritual—infused with the language of Christ's passion and love—Asbury's "boys" were unlikely to remain separate from the demands of the most fundamental social relationship, that of sexual connection, or to remain suspended forever in filial obedience to the emerging church hierarchy.

Nor did the itinerants develop an immunity to democratic politics. The general conference of 1800, like its 1796 predecessor, continued much affected by the political concerns of the preachers. Held in Baltimore for two weeks in May, the meeting opened with a vote on an elaborate set of rules designed to quell disorder. Motions, nonetheless, were made, passed, and rejected in rapid-fire succession. The resolution that the conferences be represented by delegation rather than by direct participation of the preachers was promptly negatived. While the preachers elected Englishman Richard Whatcoat as Asbury's cobishop rather than the Virginian Jesse Lee, a longtime opponent of Asbury, the first ballot was a tie and the second just four votes over a majority. A number of the participants, furthermore, attempted to rein in the power of this new bishop, proposing that the annual conferences appoint a committee to "aid the bishop in stationing the preachers"— an appeal to the preachers' deep-seated grievance that Bishop Asbury exercised too much control over this essential feature of their vocation.[137]

In a poignant moment, Asbury, visibly failing in health and responding to a request from the floor for information on his future plans, "intimated that he did not know whether this General Conference were satisfied with his former services." One of the preachers suggested that the conference vote on this matter, like all others. Asbury "then rose, he said, to speak on his own behalf." His "affliction had been such," he reported, that he was unable to travel alone or by any other means except by carriage, and had had to locate several times in the past year. "[H]e did not know," he repeated, "whether this General Conference, as a body were satisfied with such parts of his conduct." Yes, the participants agreed, they did "earnestly entreat a continuation of Mr. Asbury's services as one of the general superintendents of the Methodist Episcopal Church, as far as his strength will permit."[138] Nothing more, nothing less.

So rough-hearted might the new democracy be, subjecting all things to majority rule and renouncing the deferential courtesies of the past. But was Methodism to become a democratic faith? In becoming American, did Methodism also join revivalism with the expansive expectations of popular sovereignty? Did being a movement with a passion for the plain gospel and spiritual equality also make Methodism a movement with a passion for the new principles of Jeffersonian republicanism?

In its years of greatest triumph, those coinciding, indeed often interchangeable, with the Second Great Awakening, Methodism reflected many of the attributes of the world in which the circuit riders and ever-rising numbers of followers found themselves. But the Americanization of Methodism was as much about the survival of Methodism's eighteenth-century roots—its household origins, missionary call, experiential appeal to the heart, and the ability to outcompete all and sundry denominations in a diverse, even chaotic, religious economy—as it was about an expansive, democratic republic. Throughout all the changes the MEC and its adherents would experience in the sixty years up to the Civil War, and the tremendous benefits the church accrued from the dynamic forces shaping American life, Methodism remained at its core a Wesleyan movement: a part of, but as often as not in conflict with, the main currents in American history.

CHAPTER EIGHT

The Great Revival and Beyond

In 1800, the American Methodists had reason to boast of an impressive record of survival and growth. From a minor religious reforming movement, overshadowed by the greater fame of George Whitefield and struggling for legitimacy during and after the Revolutionary War, the Wesleyan Methodists had survived the vicissitudes of patriot suspicion, Anglican disdain, proslavery attack, local schism, political partisanship, and itinerant secession to emerge at the end of the century with preaching houses in full tilt in every part of the new republic, an infinitely expandable conference structure, a discipline that privileged the critical role of the traveling preacher, a major African component working within the larger church, ever-increasing popularity among women, young and old, and the cooperation of white men of all ranks.

The MEC annual minutes for 1800 paint a profile of healthy increase. A total of 317 preachers now traveled for the church, including influential elders—among them Freeborn Garrettson, Joseph Everett, Thomas Morrell, Jesse Lee, Thomas Lyell, and Thomas Ware—from the years of the Revolutionary conflict, and three "superintending" bishops: Francis Asbury and Thomas Coke having held office for sixteen years, and Richard Whatcoat newly elected. Just three preachers had been lost to location. Four, all under the age of forty, appeared by way of their obituaries, including Benton Riggin, possessed of "a very close and delicate connexion between his soul and body," who succumbed to the yellow fever. But the strenuous labors of these often physically fragile yet spiritually powerful men had borne fruit. A grand total of 63,958 Methodists were joined to local societies: nearly 6,000 in New England, a new sphere of influence; another 22,500 in the greater Middle Atlantic; 33,000 in the South below the Potomac; and 2,800 in the West beyond the Appalachians. Fifty-six percent of Methodists lived in the South and West, regions previously known for their religious indifference. While the West witnessed a largely white movement, 5,000 blacks, concentrated in Delaware and northern Maryland, were formal members in the greater Middle Atlantic, close to one-quarter of the region's adherents. Another 6,500, mostly slaves, formed 18 percent of the South and West's membership. Altogether, eighteen presiding elders kept watch over seventy-six circuits in seven annual conferences from Maine to Georgia and from the Northwest Territory to Natchez.[1]

But even the most ardent of boosters could not have predicted the exponential growth of American Methodism in the years after 1800. In the first third of the nineteenth century, in political parlance the Democratic-Republican era, beginning with the Great Revival in 1800, Methodist itinerants and their followers, loyal and fleeting, were to make their movement the largest in the nation, surpassing Anglicans, Congregationalists, Presbyterians, and Regular and Freewill

Baptists alike. In 1810, the MEC comprised 636 preachers and close to 175,000 members. By 1830, despite several secessions, 1,900 preachers traveled for the church, and more than 475,000 adherents belonged to its societies.[2] The Methodist circuit riders, already a generic American type, perforce prompted other denominations, seeking to exercise equivalent popular effectiveness, to co-opt their revivalist style and methods. The Wesleyan gospel of spiritual rebirth year by year became the rallying call of Calvinist innovators. Religious opinion-makers witnessing the igniting of this Wesleyan explosion would soon dub the middle years of the new century as the Methodist Age.[3]

How did this spectacular increase in size and influence occur? Was there something distinctive about the connection between religion, especially evangelical religion, and the nation itself that accounted for the Methodist juggernaut?

Nathan Hatch, in his richly observed study of the democratization of Protestant churches in the new republic, has argued that "American Methodism veered sharply away from the course of British Methodism" in the years between 1780 and 1830. Unlike English Methodism, Hatch stresses, the American movement "experienced a rare incubation period [during the Revolution] that permitted it to establish its own agenda without sharp class antagonism blunting the force of the movement." Francis Asbury and his itinerants were to triumph as the stern and strenuous supporters of the people, self-educated proponents of a system of "primitive simplicity" with "accordionlike power of expansion into every corner of the country." The American Methodists, in other words, epitomized the democratic fervor of American religion in the burgeoning American republic.[4]

As evidenced by the early history of their city societies, however, the American Methodists could no more escape the impact of class divisions than could any other Americans. As a "catholic" evangelizing force attracting a vast array of followers, Methodists were inevitably drawn into the social and political antagonisms of their times, before and after 1800. With the preachers, including Asbury, advocating greater Christian militancy in the first years of the nineteenth century, the Methodist itinerancy was masculinized as much as democratized, with strong ideological efforts to elevate the preachers above their striving followers, and aspirations to gentility that supplied Methodism with a middle-class patina scarcely imagined in the past, and greater distance between public and private Methodist forums. The church also faced schisms on a national scale, most important the withdrawal of the African Methodists in 1816 and 1822, the Protestant Methodist schism in 1830, and the long-feared breakup of the church over slavery in 1844—more than fifteen years before the nation itself was to suffer such a divide.

The Methodists, without question, benefited from what Gordon Wood has called the "explosion of energy" that drove American development in the decades after 1790.[5] But the more American the Methodists became, the more they suffered from the often splintering forces at work in early national and antebellum America as much as they benefited from the nation's booming democratic culture. Several questions then remain regarding the course of Methodist history. Did the Americanization of Methodism entail only schismatic breakup and reflexive responses to American historical development? Wherein lay the fundamental unity of Methodism, and what, if any, was its connection to the greater American context of which it was so much more a part with every passing year?

1800 AND THE COMING OF THE GREAT REVIVAL

As the Revolutionary era drew to what at first seemed an unsettled end in 1800, revival upon revival swept through Methodist meetings. "The high and low, rich and poor flock out," George Roberts reported from Annapolis. "As Whitefield said we have Tag rag and bobtail."[6] The numbers were impressive. Rather than the small clusters of converts reported in previous years, in the winter and spring of 1800 the preachers began to tally up tens and hundreds of adherents. On New Year's Day 1800, about 70 were said to be converted in Baltimore, in meetings that continued into spring, interrupted only by the yellow fever at Fell's Point. In Smyrna, Delaware, "people would not leave the house day or night; in short, such a time hath been seldom known: the probability is, that above one hundred souls were converted to God."[7] The May 1800 general conference in Baltimore was attended by an exuberant revival meeting. In Philadelphia, an observer exclaimed, "there had never been so great a revival [among the city's Methodists]," despite the Philadelphia Methodist Society's preoccupation with its own internal crisis. In New York, religion was "coming very fast into Fashion."[8] By the fall of 1800, after several yellow fever epidemics in a row, congregation among all denominations surrounding Baltimore surged ahead, with 1,000 especially attending a Methodist love feast in Baltimore City. "[S]uch a general shout I hardly ever heard," Roberts wrote to another itnerant, "& when I tell you that near a thousand were present you may form some Idea how great was the noys."[9] By the spring of 1801, Asbury claimed that nearly 3,000 had converted in the previous year on the Eastern Shore alone.[10]

For Americans concerned with the passing of an era there did seem a providential quality about the coming of the nineteenth century. The events marking its arrival came one after another: the Democratic-Republican victories in the elections of 1800, what Jefferson somewhat immodestly called the Second American Revolution; the dramatic magnification of American territory with the Louisiana Purchase in 1803; the ongoing explosion in national population growth—from approximately 5,300,000 in 1800 to over 7,200,000 in 1810, a 36.4 percent increase and a record repeated for decades thereafter—and unrestricted demographic movement south and west; the nation's economic expansion, slowed just temporarily by the 1807 Embargo, propelled forward by merchants and artisan-entrepreneurs as well as market-minded wheat-farmers and cotton-planters.[11] The full force of early industrial development would not be felt until the years after the War of 1812, and then only in the North and Midwest in what remained an overwhelmingly rural country. But as early as the 1810s, whole sections of upstate New York and the old Northwest were being surveyed for towns that would turn the region into one of the fastest growing in the new republic, filled with new families and young potential converts to evangelicalism, as in the South.[12]

For churches and sects, the most astonishing changes were those among themselves. Through the early nineteenth century and beyond, multiple denominations and their schismatic offspring jockeyed for place in a competitive religious marketplace, confirming recent historians' judgments that the real revolution in American religion followed rather than preceded the Revolutionary War. In the half century after the Revolution, Jon Butler writes, Christian churches especially "would begin to master the new American environment by initiating a religious creativity that renewed spiritual reflection and perfected institutional power, all to serve Christian ends."[13] Some confessions, like the Shakers, were small communities holding no pretense to universal membership. Instead, the high admission bar to most religious sects all but guaranteed their future as small utopian experiments. Other "experts," like the alchemist writers who informed the teachings of Mesmerists, Swedenborgians, and later Mormons and spiritualists, exerted an influence from outside that of churches and sectarian communities. Still other groups, like the Universalists popular among workingmen, sought to free the religious seekers' consciences from the remnants of church coercion.[14]

Then there were the "mass movements," among them the Christians (together with the Disciples of Christ), Mormons, Methodists, Baptists, and African Methodists and Baptists, espousing new forms of popular Christianity and depending on directly inspired, loosely educated, peripatetic preachers to broadcast their "good news."[15] These movements—the Methodists rapidly advancing to the head—without question derived power and credibility from the rising hegemony of Jeffersonian democracy itself.

Despite Thomas Jefferson's reputation for both political and religious radicalism, some evangelicals claimed a direct connection between the political victory of his party and the hoped-for triumph of their mode of Christianity. Renegade Methodist John Ffirth defended Jefferson against Federalist attack by comparing the relatively small size of the Methodist Church in 1791 to its rapid growth in the first three years of the new administration. Ffirth concluded that Jefferson's presidency had been good for religion in general, and the Methodists in particular. This proposition was derided by one Federalist, who pronounced that had Ffirth "attributed the declension of religion, *for ten years previous to the year 1801*, to the prevalence of the *abominable principles* of jacobinism and deism, introduced by his beloved French brethren, and his democratic brother Tom Paine, whose writings and detestable operations spent their *full force* during that period, he would have been more correct. . . ."[16] Ffirth retorted that numerous "democratical" Methodists might be found in Gloucester and Salem Counties, New Jersey, including preachers running on Democratic tickets. It was "a known fact" that at least two of the stationed preachers were "zealous advocates and firm friends" to Jefferson's administration; eight out of ten of the approximately one hundred Methodist itinerants known to him, Ffirth claimed, were "decided democrats."[17]

As in the past, however, the political identity of most Methodists appeared to follow from their religious identity, depending on what was good for the Methodists: the majority party (the Federalists in Delaware) where they were strong; the opposition party (the Democratic Republicans in New England and New Jersey) where they were weaker.[18]

More easily correlated with Methodist growth were the benefits of Jefferson's hands-on territorial policies and hands-off economic policies. The expected defeat and assimilation of the Northwest and Southwest Indian nations provided Americans limitless prospects for westward movement and personal improvement and, for Methodists, horizonless possibilities for missionizing. Thus located preacher Philip Gatch, Robert Strawbridge's early convert, reluctant "to die [in Virginia] and leave my offspring in a land of Slavery," moved from Virginia to Ohio with his extended family in 1798, happy to cross the Ohio River, "which separates between slavery and freedom."[19] The West produced new leaders for the church: William McKendree made his name as a western apostle, spending so much time in the region that his eastern brethren barely knew who he was when he arrived at the general conference of 1808. But his oratorical skills, born of years of preaching to tough frontier audiences, won Asbury and the other itinerants over to him, and led to his election at the same meeting as the MEC's first American-born bishop.[20]

Wesleyanism might have even come full circle, returning to its origins as a reform society born of the cultural imperative to convert the "heathen," i.e., American Indians. Up to this time resistant to the appeal of evangelical preaching, Native Americans facing the decimation of their tribes were more susceptible to the sway of revival preaching, which they freely translated into a visionary call for tribal rebirth. In about 1814, the first Methodist mission to the Indians opened among the Ohio Wyandot, initiated by John Stewart, a mixed-race (part black and part Indian) convert. In the 1830s, the first white migrants to Oregon were Methodist missionaries drawn west by what would turn out to be a fabricated report of the Pacific coast tribes' plea for preaching. As in the past, the Methodists faced the limits of their appeal when confronted with a population resistant to Christianization, and Native Americans resented the Methodists' marked tendency to favor white settlers in Indian-white disputes. By 1844, only 2,992 Indians belonged to the church's Indian Mission Conference.[21]

Better prospects were augured by American capitalist growth. Methodists might now evangelize among bourgeois women as they had among their gentry counterparts; among the newly displaced artisans and their wives; among girl millworkers and immigrants; as well as among frontierspeople, cotton-planters, yeomen and women, and slaves.[22] At the same time, Methodism continued to be the religion of choice for aspiring urban blacks. It comes as no surprise that Frederick Douglass, preparing for his escape from slavery, worshiped at the Fell's Point Chapel in early industrial Baltimore, although his experience growing up in Maryland left him with bitter recollections of the hypocrisy of Christian (mainly Methodist) slaveholders.[23]

By the 1820s and 1830s, the expansionists among Congregationalist and Presbyterian ministers were claiming that God might be brought to earth by the tactical methods of revivalism and acknowledging the power of the less-than-classically-educated Methodists. Presbyterian renegade Charles Finney praised the work of the Methodists' "plain, pointed and simple, but warm and animated mode of preaching" in his *Lectures on Revivals of Religion*, published in 1835. The revivals that had swept through New York's "burned over district" under his sway, and that now formed so significant a part of popular religion, were neither miraculous nor uncontrolled by human input but the natural philosophical result of appeals to God. "*Religion*," he wrote more brazenly than Wesley ever would have or would have wanted to, "*is the work of man.*"[24]

MUSCULARITY, DOMESTICITY, AND DISUNION

The Methodists did not become America's reigning religious movement without significant sacrifices to unity, however, or—the problem considered from a different perspective—to the egalitarian universalism of their original message. The church, for one matter, ran the risk of not only popularizing but lionizing their circuit riders, ever more visible at ever more sizable revivals. Its relationship with its "minority" populations of women and blacks, for another, was more strained after 1800 than before. The continuation of a largely autocratic church organization that excluded rank-and-file preachers from important decision making and lay representation of any kind troubled even some more conservative Methodists. The small but vocal abolitionist contingent in the church was unable to change the minds of most Methodists, even nonslaveholding northerners, to favor the immediate emancipation of slaves. All in all, Methodism exhibited a notable propensity for resisting reform and tolerating fissure in the years following Francis Asbury's death in 1816.

The elevation of circuit riders to a caste apart—and above—their coreligionists began with the camp meeting. Initially designed as interdenominational gatherings to embrace the scattered population of the frontier, camp meetings quickly became associated with Methodist evangelization and were held in every part of Methodist territory.[25] At the helm of the meetings were new preachers raised up in the 1790s and early 1800s, eager to put the business of the Methodist revival at the forefront of American attention. One such promoter, William Penn Chandler, a former dentistry student under Benjamin Rush at the University of Pennsylvania's new medical school, entered the itinerancy in 1797 and by 1804 had risen to presiding elder. At his first revival meetings, held on his Eastern Shore circuit in the late 1790s, he employed the ritual technique of the "altar call," in which revival participants possessed by the Holy Spirit might approach the chapel altar to set themselves apart for special ministerial attention. The mourners' bench, a similar tactic, was adopted for the outdoor camp meetings.[26]

In the summer of 1805, Chandler masterminded a camp meeting near Smyrna, Delaware, that demonstrated the ways in which the new revivals were departures from past practice. Lasting from 25 to 29 July, the Smyrna meeting was closely orchestrated, with no detail left unattended. At the center of the camp were the worshipers' benches, enough to accommodate some four thousand participants.

Figure 14. *Camp Meeting of the Methodists in N. America*, engraving by M. Dubourg, ca. 1817. A camp meeting under construction in the North American forest.
Reprinted with permission of the Methodist Collection, Drew University Library, Madison, New Jersey.

These were set out in rows and divided into front and back courts by aisles labeled "Philadelphia" and "New York" after the two participating annual conferences. Mourners' benches, covered with bowers of tree branches and separated at some distance, were set up for men and for women. Facing the audience was the preachers' stand, elevated about four feet above the ground. The largest space was reserved for two hundred "tents"—sails or pieces of tow-linen nailed to surrounding trees or to the ground—and about eighty carts and wagons taken off their axles to serve as overnight lodging for the campers. Black attenders were restricted to the back of the preachers' stand. The entire encampment was enclosed by makeshift fences and barriers.[27]

The Smyrna meeting lasted all four days and four nights with little or no intermission, an all-consuming round that added to the drama of the event. The hours of the days were carefully ordered. According to a sympathetic British observer, on 25 July the proceedings commenced at five o'clock in the morning with the blast of two trumpets sounding the time for prayers. Preaching was held at eight and three o'clock each day, "with the intervening time taken up with singing and praying." The camp was then illuminated through the night by lamps and candles. "From time to time scores were struck to the ground," some "appearing lifeless," while "others in agonies" called out to God for mercy.[28] By Chandler's estimate—probably accurate as to the numbers of "officials" involved—32 itinerants, 37 local preachers, 15 exhorters, and 24 leaders performed in one capacity or another at the meeting. Less reliably as it later turned out, he also claimed upwards of 9,000 to 10,000 people in attendance; it is probable, though, that the 4,000 seats at least were filled. When the meeting concluded at seven in the morning on the 29th, with the further blowing of horns, "the preachers collected at the stand before all the assembly, and fell on each others necks and wept."[29]

The new camp meetings differed from the Methodists' earlier revivals in several ways. The Revolutionary-era revivals, unorthodox ritual events held in all manner of venues, were rarely as closely controlled. Much briefer and smaller, they usually attracted from ten to twenty listeners, occasionally one hundred or more, on rare occasions one thousand or more. The bulk of these audiences were outsiders, passing by or drawn in by the theatricality of a given preacher's performance. Regarding assertions as to the sum of those "converted" at the camp meetings, realistic comparisons with past revivals break down. Chandler, and no doubt many other preachers, inflated the numbers converted at the encampments, a telling example of the way in which camp meetings altered the understanding of the revival ritual itself, as preachers were pressured by the sheer singularity of the event to produce results. The careful distinctions among the experiences of spiritual awakening, justification, and sanctification fell away in the new revivals, legitimizing the gibes of Methodist critics that camp-meeting conversions were trumped up at best, a snare and a delusion at worst.[30]

Despite their critics, camp meetings were popular among Americans, white and black alike, and smaller, more intimate encampments proliferated along with mass meetings throughout the republic. These gatherings might be more freewheeling than Chandler's, especially if men like Lorenzo Dow, traveling without church sponsorship, led the preaching.[31] But for ambitious evangelists, the prospect of harvesting so many souls at the largest of the events, and the raising up of the lowly preacher's status, were hard temptations to resist, and many camp meetings, as their name in part implied, also became militant gatherings where preachers were determined to exhibit their persuasive talents and prepared to administer rough justice to miscreant insiders and outsiders alike. At Chandler's encampments, local preachers, exhorters, and class leaders, called managers, or, more colorfully, "dog whippers," were formed into separate guards, each led by a captain and wearing identifying badges, to patrol the periphery of the campsite. Smoking and drinking were strictly forbidden—Chandler was an early temperance advocate—and violators might be incarcerated in the camp-meeting jailhouse.[32] One of the participating guards observed, reflecting the Methodists' new attraction to military metaphor, "I have no doubt many [of the guards] thought themselves as highly honoured as General Washington and his officers did, when they took command of the armies of the united colonies at the revolution." Chandler wrote glowingly to Asbury, "[E]very thing was as orderly . . . as in a Court of Justice."[33]

These efforts were to lead Chandler into his own legal trouble in 1806 when, at two encampments, one again near Smyrna and the other in Pungoteague, Virginia, revival participants "jailed" several young outsiders who were attempting, in the tradition of mobbing, to intrude on the faithful. In Virginia, the wrong man was detained, and Chandler, several of the preachers, and local supporters were arrested by the local sheriff's posse. Chandler and six preachers were charged with trespassing, assault and battery, and false imprisonment. Two of the preachers were found guilty and fined $2,000. In Delaware, where Methodist dominance in the region was resented, the camp meeting "proceedings looked to[o] much like fire and Sword to compell men to Submit to *Methodis' dictation*."[34]

The tide had certainly turned when the Methodists were now found guilty of assault. But the "arming" of Chandler's meetings was a sign of a new muscular Methodist itinerancy, one in keeping with masculine metaphors of military preparedness. "Camp Meetings," Bishop Asbury wrote in 1805, "are like the great plough that tears up all by the roots. These meetings are our forts and fortifications, our warships and gondoliers, these holy meetings are our soldiers, these temporally and spiritually will keep far our foes, of all kinds and keep peace and liberty at home."[35] This rhetoric was accompanied by a tendency to treat the preachers as not only a caste apart from everyday Methodists but a cut above them as well. At one of Chandler's encampments, for example, the planners arranged for another innovation: the erection of a separate "marquee," or large tent, next to the preachers' stand for the feeding and housing of the participating ministers. Campers could enter by invitation only. Such exclusive treatment of the preachers' circle would have been unheard-of at the earlier public revivals.[36]

In fact, contrary to Christine Heyrman's thesis that the Methodists were compelled to masculinize their clergy, often accurately perceived as effeminate, in order to lure in male supporters otherwise resistant to a movement run by weaklings, Methodist militancy appears to have increased alongside Methodist popularity rather than before it and especially in response to the rising competitive climate among the nation's clergy. The Methodists, especially on the frontier, now produced more explicitly pugnacious, even worldly, preacher-heroes. Among these were homegrown geniuses like Peter Cartwright who spent their youths indulging in boyish pleasures until conversion turned them into manly advocates of the gospel. Preacher Cartwright was famed for his aggressive recruitment of sinners for Methodist reformation. In the early years of his ministry, Cartwright observed that the itinerancy was in danger of losing its appeal to young men with plans to rise in the world, especially in the rough but economically developing environment of the early-nineteenth-century Southwest Territory: "no members hardly to support a preacher, the discipline only allowing a single man eighty dollars, and in nine cases out of ten he could not get half that amount." But the challenge of bringing souls to Christ, while casting out devils, expelling young toughs intent on disrupting the faithful at public worship, opposing those who called the itinerants "illiterate, ignorant babblers," combined with countering Baptists, Presbyterians, and what Cartwright labeled the "blasphemous organization called the Mormons," was just too great for a young evangelical to resist, and Cartwright confidently moved ahead into a lifetime career of itinerant ministry. In 1828, he demonstrated his ability to survive robustly in the masculine world of political competition by winning a seat in the Illinois General Assembly and then going on to defeat Abraham Lincoln in a second race in 1832.[37]

In short time, as Heyrman has well shown, Methodists began to absorb elements of the Revolution's political legacy, turning to their own uses what had previously been a Revolutionary discourse out of bounds for all but the most rebellious of Asbury's "boys." Hence the preachers glorified their (unconverted) fathers' patriot pedigrees while calling attention to their own privations for their cause. Stressing the continuing indigence of the itinerants during his early ministry, Cartwright could unblinkingly adopt the rhetoric of Tom Paine as suitable to the conditions of evangelical campaigning as well, pronouncing firmly, "These were the times that tried men's souls and bodies too."[38] By the 1840s many more Methodist preachers than in the past were willing to participate in party politics, drawn in by "the tide of American popular culture," and gradually persuaded of what had heretofore been the Calvinist view of the need to "promote righteousness and eliminate national sins." Among these last were hard liquor, Roman Catholicism, and slavery, opposition to which turned increasing numbers of Methodist men into Whigs by the time of the Mexican War.[39]

The masculinizing of the Methodist itinerancy was mirrored by other efforts to make the church more respectable, and to more sharply delineate the divide between public and private Methodist cultures so often blurred in the household meetings of the past. These changes inevitably affected who would or would not be welcome as public actors in the church.

The leading proponent for adapting Methodism more conspicuously to the bourgeois ethos of the nation's cities was the presiding elder and book agent Nathan Bangs. Altogether Bangs sought to reshape the church in dramatic ways. His most ambitious plan was to transform the Methodist Book Concern into a viable business, one that would keep up with the explosion of American religious print media in the first part of the century. He succeeded even more extravagantly than Methodists were accustomed to succeeding, building up the largest publishing house in the world by 1860, and issuing periodical publications, among them the weekly paper *Christian Advocate and Journal* and the more academic—itself a telling development—*Methodist Magazine and Quarterly Review*, that collectively achieved an annual circulation of over one million.[40] In 1820, Bangs headed an MEC committee directed to explore the "expediency of digesting and recommending the outline of a plan for the institution of schools and seminaries of learning," a mandate quickly adopted by a number of annual conferences. Augusta College, the first Methodist institution of higher learning since Cokesbury School had been abandoned, was organized in Kentucky in 1821. Randolph-Macon, Wesleyan, Dickinson, Allegheny, Emory, Indiana Asbury (now DePauw), and Ohio Wesleyan followed in rapid succession. At the same time, in 1828 the Methodist Sunday School Union, organized just a year earlier with Bangs at the helm, was superintending more than 1,000 schools enrolling 63,000 children. In 1833, the union was combined with the Methodist Bible and Tract Society, thereby creating a formidable organ for Methodist propagation of the gospel in and outside the family.[41]

The quest for gentility also underlay efforts to replace the unadorned, steepleless meetinghouses of the movement's first generation with the imposing Greek Revival, and later the neo-Gothic, structures favored by the urban bourgeoisie. In 1820, Bangs led the drive to replace the 1768 John Street Chapel with a new classical edifice, forcing a secession of members, no doubt many artisans among them, who objected to this "departure from the primitive simplicity of Methodism."[42] The new Methodist churches were clearly designed to impress upon their viewers Methodism's rising public presence in Jacksonian America.

By contrast, the household—formerly indistinguishable from the public sphere for purposes of Methodist evangelization—was rapidly subsumed into the obverse of public life, the private, domestic sphere. Home and family, once sources of conflict for the converted woman, were now often glorified as her exclusive objects of attention. "When each family member was converted," Gregory Schneider writes, "they together became an internal unit bound together by their sanctified affections." The key word here is "internal," as the home, abiding by the teachings of Wesley's heart-religion, became more and more separate from a heartless world.[43]

Women were not invisible in the nineteenth-century church. They continued to be vital advocates for their local societies, to attend love feasts and class meetings, and, not least important, to marry preachers and sustain the social life surrounding their husbands' vocation. The *Methodist Magazine* was replete with renderings of women's religious experiences, most especially poignant accounts of the deaths of pious young women. The *Ladies' Repository and Gatherings of the West*, published in Cincinnati, was directed toward the massive market of serious Methodist women readers, many of whom expressed themselves in public for the first time in letters to the *Repository*'s editors.[44] Most significant, the MEC, true to its support of preachers' wives in the past, was a pioneer in women's education, especially in the South and West, where schools for girls were few and far between. Wesleyan Female College in Georgia opened as a freshly chartered Methodist institution in 1839. Greensboro College in North Carolina, the Cincinnati College for Young Women, and MacMurray College in Illinois followed within ten years.[45]

The drive for gentility nonetheless meant that women seeking masculine roles (most particularly preaching) were unwelcome in the MEC and left for its various splinter groups described below. Likewise, men emulating feminine piety, unlike in the past, were suspect. Thus Lorenzo Dow, the Connecticut-born charismatic, suffering from epilepsy and asthma, affecting the long hair and wan, feminized aspect of the first preachers, while otherwise exhibiting a cultivated indifference to his physical appearance, was described by one itinerant as "clownish in the extreme; his habit and appearance more filthy than a *Savage Indian*." Dow was accordingly forced to devise his own irregular career on the camp-meeting circuit, just barely tolerated by the regular preachers but popular with those Methodist audiences in America, Ireland, and Britain for whom a "masculinized" clergy was not necessarily a priority.[46]

In a flood of autobiographical, "historical," and prophesying tracts, published wherever he happened to be, "Crazy" Dow served himself up as the anti-Calvinist biblical watchman of convinced Christians.[47] His influence among British Methodists prompted the exiling of the Primitive Methodists from the main church in Britain in 1811, and later in the United States, where a group of Primitives formed their own Methodist Church in Philadelphia in 1829. Among the Primitive Methodists' chief offenses, according to English Methodist hierarchy, was their celebration of female preaching and traveling.[48] Dow himself readily included his wife's memoir in one of his many volumes of collected works. For Disciple of Christ preacher Nancy Towle, he composed a testimonial that formed the preface to her spiritual autobiography, stating matter-of-factly: "[W]hy a *female*, should not be as accountable, to God for her talents and ministration,—as the opposite gender,—I know not."[49]

The multiple, often conflicting, impact of social change on the Methodists was especially evident among black Methodists. Still marginalized in local deaconships in the church and prohibited from traveling or pursuing other forms of clerical advancement, the African Methodists now also faced rising resentment against black independence on the part of MEC church leaders and growing restrictions on their use of church property. In 1805, when Philadelphia's presiding elder, a white southerner, threatened to seize control of the Bethel Church property, Allen and his trustee allies responded with a court-approved supplement to Bethel's original articles of association. This legal instrument significantly modified the power of the presiding elder in the chapel's property transactions, gave the trustees and official members greater disciplinary control, and amplified their power to raise up exhorters and local preachers from among Bethel's male members.[50] After several challenges to the court's ruling in 1814, the congregation, now numbering more than twelve hundred, en masse refused another MEC presiding elder access to Bethel's pulpit. The state supreme court ruled in favor of the "African Supplement," and Bethel's long detente with the MEC was over.[51]

At the same time, the African Methodists in Baltimore, led by deacon Daniel Coker, were struggling with the limitations placed on Baltimore's many talented black preachers.[52] In April 1816, just one month after Asbury's death, and perhaps dismayed at the prospect of the loss of the bishop's mediating influence with southern slaveholders, delegates from the African churches in Philadelphia, Baltimore, and Wilmington, as well as Attleborough, Pennsylvania, and Salem, New Jersey, met in Philadelphia to form a "General Society" of African Methodists, soon renamed the African Methodist Episcopal (AME) Church.[53] In keeping with Richard Allen's enduring loyalty to Methodist teaching and organization, the AME Church adopted the discipline of their parent organization while eliminating the office of presiding elder and proscribing slaveholding. But the new church provided the most important of disciplinary advantages: there were now effectively no bars to the advancement of black men into the ranks of fully ordained preachers, affording, in the words of one of its young recruits, a "sweeping field

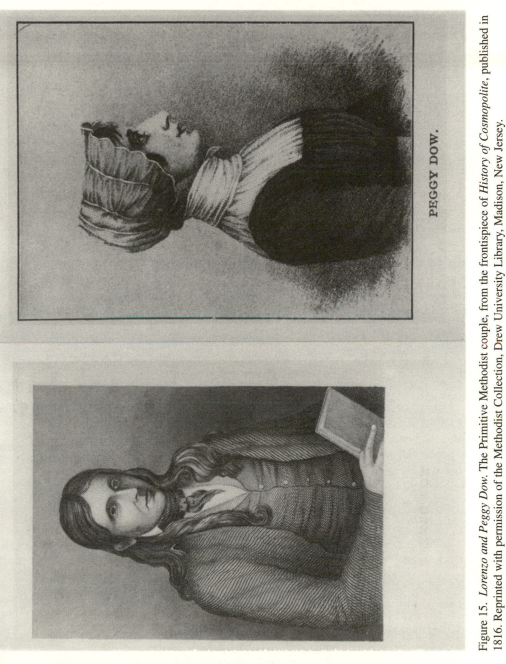

PEGGY DOW.

Figure 15. *Lorenzo and Peggy Dow.* The Primitive Methodist couple, from the frontispiece of *History of Cosmopolite*, published in 1816. Reprinted with permission of the Methodist Collection, Drew University Library, Madison, New Jersey.

. . . for the development of Christian manhood." With Coker stepping aside, Allen was elected bishop of the new denomination. He was subsequently ordained by Anglican bishop William White, assisted by Absalom Jones, a fitting conclusion to Philadelphia's leading Methodist's long crusade to achieve ministerial parity with his white counterparts.[54]

The central place that preaching already held in African American culture was evident in other developments. New York City's African Methodist Zion congregation, for example, remaining a part of the MEC into the 1820s, was literally suffering from a surfeit of preachers with no professional outlet. After several schisms and an unsuccessful effort to get the MEC to recognize an "African Conference," the New Yorkers formed their own conference in 1821. A year later, in June 1822, three of Zion's deacons, Abraham Thompson, James Varick, and Leven Smith, ordained by several sympathetic presiding elders from the MEC, organized another African Methodist Episcopal Church, later called AME Zion, one that would compete with Allen's church for members and influence among free blacks.[55]

Free agents, black-identified, and hostile to slavery, the AME and AMEZ preachers and their followers were constant reminders to Methodist slaveholders of the emboldening possibilities of Methodist conversion among their bondsmen and women. The two churches' influence among southern slaves was thus restricted and then further blunted after 1822 when Denmark Vesey's slave conspiracy was rumored to have started among communicants at the African Methodist Church in Charleston.[56] Southern slaves were subsequently subject to the MEC's special Mission to the Slaves. Black adherence to the churches of the Baptists, the Methodists' rivals, rose accordingly.[57]

African Methodist women, in the meanwhile, were no less spiritually empowered than their brethren. Through sheer persistence, Philadelphia African Methodist Jarena Lee was able to persuade Deacon, then Bishop, Allen to license her as a traveling exhorter. Her published remarks on the matter of preaching, focusing on gender rather than race, underscore the extent to which being an African Methodist was no longer out of the ordinary for northern blacks; but being a female preacher still was. "If a man may preach, because the Saviour died for him," Lee exclaimed in the emerging feminist refrain of the 1830s, "why not the woman? seeing he died for her also. Is he not a whole Saviour, instead of a half one?"[58] Another independent black woman Methodist, Zilpha Elaw, although careful to espouse only the most conservative views regarding women's "place" in her published autobiography, was still prompted to wonder how St. Paul could deny women's voice in the church and yet sponsor the work of Phoebe, the Primitive deaconness. "[I]t was strange indeed," Elaw mused, "if she [Phoebe] was required to receive the commissions of the [Primitive] Church in mute silence, and not allowed to utter a syllable before them."[59] Well may the many Methodist women sustaining the preachers on their circuits have asked.

The MEC was also unable to escape the other major divides that followed from their close ties to the larger society. In 1820, disputes once more broke out over the political rights of the MEC preachers (by this time represented by delegates in the general conferences) and the less often championed rights of the laity. The conflict escalated when the reformers, led by Nicholas Snethen—formerly Asbury's ally on the opposite side of this struggle but now a located preacher, settled on a farm in Frederick County, Maryland—published a new monthly periodical, the *Mutual Rights of Ministers and Members of the Methodist Episcopal Church*, and organized corresponding societies to spread word of their activities. Reforming preachers were subsequently expelled, one by one, from the church.[60] The MEC, the bishops argued, much as Asbury had in the past, refrained from "all interference" in the rights of Methodists as citizens; "but that it should be inferred from these, what are your rights as Methodists, seems to us no less surprising, than if your Methodism should be made the criterion of your rights as citizens."[61]

At a remarkable gathering in late 1827 in Baltimore, the wives of the expelled preachers convened to mount a defense of their husbands, and the resulting "Associated Methodist Reformers," organized among their menfolk, was to serve as the founding core of the Methodist Protestant Church in 1830, attracting five thousand members with annual conferences from Vermont to Alabama. The reformers, propelled by the primordial Methodist urge to be a "catholic," all-embracing church that rose above social controversy, declined to enfranchise their assertive women, and, like the parent church, left the issue of slaveholding to the local conferences. But they more closely resembled a true republican church than did the MEC in their adoption of equal clerical and lay representation at conferences and the adoption of presidents in preference to the "papal" offices of bishop and presiding elder.[62]

And in the next several years, even the moderates and conservatives remaining with the still dominant MEC found it increasingly difficult to ignore the issue of slavery. The Methodist call for the immediate emancipation of slaves was first made by Vermont preacher Orange Scott in Boston's Methodist paper, the *Zion's Herald*, in 1835. Up to this time, the MEC had supported the American Colonization Society to further the voluntary removal of slaves to Liberia: a solution to slavery satisfying to "genteel" slaveholders, Democratic politicians, and state legislatures. Scott was opposed by Nathan Bangs, who argued that slaves were not helped by "inflammatory harangues, but by deeds of charity." Bangs then blocked all discussion of abolition in the *Christian Advocate and Journal*.[63]

In 1840, Scott formed the American Wesleyan Anti-Slavery Society, initiating attacks on the "Slave Power." The society sponsored a small number of auxiliaries. In November 1842, Scott and his fellow Methodist abolitionists, further inspired by a renewal of the Wesleyan doctrine of perfection, split off to form the separate Wesleyan Methodist Church, comprising six thousand members and eighty ministers. "It is holiness of heart and life," the new church announced, combining eighteenth-century Wesleyan discourse with nineteenth-century Methodist militancy, "that will arm you against every assault, that will give you moral power to oppose the evils and corruptions in the world, against which we have lifted up a standard."[64]

The fate of the section on slavery in the MEC discipline, still calling for the "extirpation of slavery," was now in the hands of moderate preachers from the North and West—some of them antislavery Whigs, but the majority opposed to both abolitionism and slaveholding—and increasingly rigid proslavery preachers from the South. At the 1844 general conference, these two contingents came into irresolvable conflict as the southern delegates attempted to eliminate the MEC's condemnation of slavery and to permit the church to pass regulations on the domestic slave trade, separation of enslaved families, and other treatment of slaves. The proposed changes were voted down. "For the first time in the history of the Methodist Episcopal Church," Donald Mathews writes, "Southerners had lost an important vote."[65]

The southern preachers, that is, found themselves in a position within the MEC analogous to that the South held within the nation: slowly but inexorably losing a majority voice. Much like the northerners and westerners who would come to form the bulk of the Republican Party, the northern preachers were far from being abolitionist but resented the prospect of a church held hostage to southern interests. With the conference's rejection of the ordination of one slaveholding preacher, and suspension from episcopal office of Bishop James Osgood Andrew, recently the recipient of two slaves by bequest, the southerners declared themselves no longer in the church and by consensus were permitted by the conference to form the Methodist Episcopal Church, South. A later ballot among all Methodist preachers had less conciliatory results. The measure failed the three-quarters' vote necessary for constitutional separation; by this vote the preachers rejected the conference agreement, forcing the new southern church to sue to secure church properties throughout the region.[66]

For the Methodists, then, the years of democratic triumph in the new republic were marked by often deep discord. The universal American church was beset with universal American dualisms: popularity versus respectability; public versus private roles for women; unresolved racial tensions between black and white; and the enduring dichotomies of freedom versus slavery, and democracy versus authority. At the head of a religious organization rather than a nation-state, the MEC's movers and shakers resolved these problems straightforwardly: those in the minority were either forced out or left on their own initiative. Before the Civil War, the last of these secessions was that of the Free Methodists in 1859, devoted to the proposition that Methodism was first and foremost about the "second blessing" of sanctification. From its seeds were to spring another dualism: the inward-dwelling Pentecostalism of the rural South versus the outward-marching social gospel of the urbanizing North and West.[67]

But there is little doubt that Methodism in all its many guises remained the preferred faith of vast numbers of Americans, more so than any other individual denomination. The ranks of Wesley's collective heirs continued to multiply with phenomenonal speed: in round numbers, from more than 475,000 in 1830 to more than 800,000 in 1840. By 1855, more than 1,500,000 Methodists belonged to the various branches of the church: 780,000 to the MEC, 580,000 to the MEC, South; 70,000 to the Methodist Protestant Church; 23,000 to the Wesleyan Methodists;

21,200 to the AME; 6,200 to the AME Zion; and 1,100 to the Primitives. Despite the devestation of the Civil War, the approximately 1,900,000 Methodists of all stripes in 1865 still numbered more than the approximately 1,400,000 Baptists, who continued to be their closest contestants. The MEC, South, alone was larger than all Presbyterian churches combined. Methodist dominance continued well after the war had ended, virtually to the end of the nineteenth century, despite, by this time, the extraordinary array of religious choices—ever more complex and sensitive to distinctions in doctrine and discipline—available to Americans.[68]

THE MEANING OF METHODISM AMERICANIZED

Within ten years of 1800, the Methodists knew they were making astonishing progress in the American republic and, they more than ever believed, were destined for great things. "Among the many surprizing occurrences that have transpired since the commencement of the last century," one Methodist, James Sowden, wrote in 1809 in his *Inquiry into the Cause of the Prosperity of the Methodist Episcopal Church in the United States*, "perhaps none have attracted the attention of a certain part of the community more than the singular rise and rapid progress of that branch of the church of Christ called *Methodist*." Sowden continued, "That a people almost every where misrepresented, and frequently severely persecuted, without funds, without the immediate aid of the civil power, should still, against all opposition, so prosper as in less than half a century to be able to number upwards of *one hundred and fifty thousand* communicants, is very surprising [indeed]."

Sowden went on to defend "methodism" against its detractors, asserting that the real reason for the movement's flourishing was "*the power of God.*" But God might be persuaded by various "*means*" to hearken unto the seeker's quest for salvation. Among the Methodists' means was their straightforward doctrine, encompassing the basic Christian teachings (as seen through the prism of Wesleyan interpretation) of original sin, justification by faith, the free agency of the believer, the free grace of God, and the second conversion of holiness. "By thus addressing the human race as rational beings," Sowden continued, disparaging Edwardsean doctrine that was making a comeback among the New Divinity men, "composed of *spirit* as well as *matter* and not comparing them to machines as inanimate as a pair of lifeless scales," the Methodists deprived sinners of their Calvinist escape: that all was predetermined do what they might. Under Methodist persuasion, the sinner "feels that he has sinned *voluntarily* and not *necessarily*."

In Sowden's view, a brief history of the Methodists in America confirmed the superiority of the Methodist discipline. Underscoring the Methodists' geographical mobility and informal organization in their first years, Sowden emphasized that the new group was at a great advantage against the sacramental rigidity of the Baptists and the formality of the "government church," as he called the Anglicans. The Methodists, consequently, were *everywhere*: "They have called to the north beyond the [Great] [L]akes to give up; and to the southern extremities of the union to keep not back.—In the humble dwelling of the indigent, and the magnificent seat of the wealthy," their voices had been heard, and their success "is well known." Among these new Christians were the "sons and daughters of Ethiopia who bound in iron chains of slavery are lorded over by tyrannical despots." All these disparate believers were then joined by a "REGULAR" system of circuits, districts, and conferences, run by a regular order of preachers, presiding elders, and superintendents, "or, (as some prefer calling them) Bishops."

But how American were the Methodists? Here Sowden had something further to say. Methodism, he wrote, "in a remarkable manner contributes to the cementing of the union. . . . If we search the continent at large where shall we find a people so widely extended whose laws, whose regulations are so universally the same, and which bear so equally upon all." Much of this unity could be attributed to the itinerant plan, which, among other things, guaranteed access to the Methodists despite social class distinctions among their followers: without it the "largest and most respectable societies would have the . . . greatest *orators*—The poor would no longer have the gospel preached unto them." The missionizing drive of the movement continued to be one of its most original and dynamic features, and, as Sowden stressed, one of its claims to extraregional American-wide influence.[69]

In a weak moment, Asbury took the analogy between Methodism and the American union one step further. "All men of sense," he wrote, in 1809, "know that our church government was founded before the Federal Government and state rights in that they copied our government as far as humans could follow or ought to follow a divine government, all offices being elected except offices of special trust and confidence as presiding elders and bishops."[70] More appositely, several years later, reflecting on the health of his movement while still rankling from the common charge that the Methodists were upstarts with little historical legitimacy, Asbury contrasted the Methodists' mobility and Primitive Christianity with the sedentary conventions of other denominations: "Instead of *going* to preach, they *stay* to preach," he wrote. "Hence it is that schools, colleges, and universities undertake to make men ministers that the Lord Jesus Christ never commanded to be made."[71] The Anglican and Reformed churches were now corrupt remnants of the once pure Primitive Church. By contrast, the "traveling apostolic order and ministry" was at the heart of the Methodist "constitution," and "the generations to come may read our Church records and Conference journals, where they shall see what vast tracts of country we traveled."[72]

Together, Sowden and Asbury, concerned chiefly with ecclesiastical structure, convey a picture of a movement with three major advantages for evangelizing the vast, diverse, and changing United States. The first of these was its bold claim to offer salvation to all, and not just salvation, but holiness within this life. Quite removed from any familial, community, or regional context, Wesley's heart-religion promised personal transformation on a grand scale, not limited to sectarian commitment or ethnic or prior religious identity. Second, through the agency of the itinerancy and religious revivals, Methodism thrived on action and innovation. The "expectation of being entertained with something new, together with the novelty of the scene of [the revival meeting]," Sowden wrote candidly of these particular Methodist "means," "has drawn forth the multitude."[73]

And, third, there was the matter of the Methodist organization, indeed not unlike the design of federal and state governments, though clearly unconnected to these. Under this "regularity," Methodist societies formed in far reaches of the continent would be much the same however great the distances between them. Methodists in Vermont, then, could expect to share a common religious culture and style of life with Methodists in Ohio, and points further west and south.

As much as the Methodists loved their universal doctrine and orderly discipline, however, and possessed the fundamental proof in their rising numbers of the remarkable appeal of this system to Americans, there was no organic link between Methodism, even in its many guises, and the United States. Except, paradoxically, for an important similitude: both Methodism and the new emerging American democratic republic were eighteenth-century products of *disassociation* from organic community, familial hierarchy, classical tradition, and the church and state connection. Various aspects of Methodist culture and development were indeed closely tied to those of early republican culture and development: a democratic ethos that foreswore allegiance to social or religious elites and was dedicated to the popular voice; a potent revivalism that in its most effective form equalized, even dissolved, if temporarily, the racial, gender, and social differences that republican rhetoric, in its most visionary form, lent credence to; and a sometimes blunt indifference to intellectual and academic tradition.

The Jeffersonian proponents of republican change, however, devoted their energies to reenvisioning the relationship of the individual to the state, the dismantling of the public prerogatives of social elites, and the reshaping of passive subjecthood into active citizenry. Republicanism, that is, was about natural rights, representative government, and democratic progress. The Methodists, by contrast, were about fundamental personal change—the triumph of holiness over adversity and sin, and the planting of spiritual roots in the shifting sands of the American social landscape. The possibilities held out by such a metamorphosis would transfix millions of Americans in the course of the nineteenth century, and it was the bread and butter of evangelicalism. For all the differences among them, and their wrestlings with the greatest issues of their day, it was loyalty to John Wesley's understanding of the "circumcision of the heart" that made a Methodist a Methodist.

To the extent that Methodism became the American church in the Revolutionary years and the decades that were to follow, and as often as not the church of those left out of the Republican prescription for democratic progress—women, blacks, and the rural and urban poor—it was increasingly what Americans were about as well.

A Plain Gospel for a Plain People

IN 1795, the witness to a Methodist service in Norwich, Connecticut, published an exposé of the "manner and stile of those class of Preachers denominated *Methodists . . .* who in large numbers, are itinerating these states." Reporting the contents of the preacher's sermon verbatim and ridiculing its homely discourse, the writer unintentionally left historical traces of Methodism's popular appeal. However much couched in the syntax of biblical English and translated through the arch probity of the New England mind, the preacher's message resonates for the reader today, so familiar with the intimate entreaties of evangelical exhortation and the ubiquitous appeals for personal reformation. "WITNESS, O woman!" the preacher urges his listeners, many probably young women and men, ambivalent about familial obligations but anxious to move to the next stage of their lives, ". . . when in thy house, pursuing thy domestic concerns; has thou not been arrested, and stopped in thy career: brought to reflect on thy own state and condition." You may wonder, the preacher continues, " 'How does he know I am cross, peevish, fretful, and the like!' I'll tell thee woman, if the Preacher don't know this, the Lord knows thy heart, and how thou art conducting." And men! no longer should you follow the ways of your fathers and grandfathers: "for if thou worship the religion of thy forefathers, instead of thy forefathers God . . . thou might as well expect to ride to heaven, on thy Grandfather's old grey mare, who has been dead above forty years ago." No! "[T]hou must have, and live, the power and life of religion, if thou mean to be a Methodist christian, and gain heaven in the end."

"[I]n this way," the outsider lamented, expressing his dismay at the new faith, "many converts . . . are said to be converted to God . . . when they know no more about God, Christ, or Heaven in reality, than the untutored savage. . . ." Methodism, in this view, was hardly a form of Christianity at all but a natural religion like that of the Indian who "pays homage to the sun, or moon, and borrows all his ideas, and expectations of Heaven, in a place for hunting deer. . . ."[1] Thus, for their severest critics, the Methodists were not only deluded but unscriptural, radically divorced from recognizable Christian theology and civilized society, themselves no different from the American heathen that formed the cultural "other" of so many eighteenth-century Anglo-American imaginations.

The Methodists, of course, saw things differently. But one can detect in the observer's words the frustration of Anglican and Calvinist intellectuals with Americans' susceptibility to the new movement's blandishments and their bafflement at the power of Wesley's Primitive Christianity. Here it was, the Methodist message, pared down to its popular essentials, with a simplicity verging on childishness and a curt indifference to standards of historical legitimacy and learned discourse. In matching this message to the most basic of human concerns and the deepest of human yearnings, the Methodists found their most enduring mission. But theirs was a church that had to overcome numerous barriers to find its way into the pantheon of American religious movements, as well as one that was not without its own divided social vision.

At the time of its first expansion, Methodism was a maverick faith, a cultural import attempting to lay claim to American allegiance just as Americans were shaping their first ideas of nationality; an apolitical evangelical force coming to maturity in tandem, often awkwardly, with the political maturation of the nation. Espoused by British as well as American preachers and aimed at everyone from the gentry to their slaves, Methodism was widely perceived as an outsider faith, sponsored by Tory sympathizers, as a few Methodists indeed were, and seducing common folk into religious delusion. As late as the 1790s, James O'Kelly could launch a persuasive assault on Francis Asbury's credibility by attacking the bishop's English origins.

Upon the formation of the MEC, the Methodists leaders—in contrast, they claimed, to their Anglican forebears—labored to present their movement as respectful of the values of the Revolutionary struggle: independence, popular sovereignty, and the separation of church and state, Many of the preachers had been deeply influenced by the libertarian and egalitarian rhetoric of the Revolution and the boundless prospects of American nationhood. Responding to a Maryland vestryman's complaint in the 1790s that "[o]ne sermon in a day, if religiously attended to, is certainly enough for any ordanary memeory to digest," William Colbert exclaimed to his audience, "I concidered myself in a free Country, where the roads were forty feet wide, [thus] I should preach where I pleased. . . ."[2] Many preachers, and many more followers, were swept up into the political fray that ended the Revolutionary era, relishing the freedom of speech and participation in popular expression that independence brought.

But Methodism was neither a classless nor a democratic movement. On the contrary, gender, racial, and social distinctions were conspicuously part of its every development. Women formed the great core of eighteenth-century Methodist adherents and Methodist societies. Young and single women, often with their like-minded sisters, flocked into the city congregations; older women, many widows, hosted preachers on their daily rounds, supplying essential material and spiritual sustenance; still others were married to itinerants, often drawing them away from their all-consuming vocations, other times willingly sacrificing their own security, even a household itself, as long as their husbands were on the road. Blacks, slave and free, were likewise drawn in by the Methodist revivals. From attendance at small class gatherings concentrated in rural Maryland and Delaware, to active engagement in the city societies, black men and women initiated unprecedented cultural change among fellow slaves and free people. By the end of the century, a new, explicitly black form of Methodism, African Methodism, advanced in Philadelphia and the other Middle Atlantic ports, was fast becoming the faith of choice for northern blacks. So much so that self-appointed black itinerants were able to travel throughout the region depending exclusively on the support of African Methodist congregations, and no doubt their black women members.

At the same time, the movement's white men—far more socially diverse than historians have thought—came to Methodism with expectations of shaping their local societies to suitable evangelical ends. To them the movement held out the convention-breaking temptation of a career as a traveling preacher: for many Methodist men the logical, if not necessarily long-lived, culmination of their religious experience. In the cities, and especially in New York City, Methodism was strong among artisans, men who, like the itinerants, labored at their calling from day to day. But it was by no means exclusively a workingman's movement, here or elsewhere. Many poorer Methodist men—immigrants, servants, day laborers, mariners—appear only once in the historical record: on a Methodist class list. At the other end of the scale, in Baltimore in particular, the movement expanded among rising numbers of "new men"—merchants and artisan-entrepreneurs who had learned to flourish in the capitalist economy of the new republic. The two Baltimore Methodist societies together represented a social microcosm of the larger movement, including the expected majority of female members as well as slaves, free blacks, mariners, carters, ship-caulkers, shoemakers, bricklayers, carpenters, portrait painters, clerks, shopkeepers, international merchants, local gentry, and the superintendent of the city pumps.

Methodism was, in other words, an extraordinarily inclusive movement. Yet, a product of its time, it inevitably placed limits on the kinds of social, as opposed to spiritual, change permissible among these various constituencies. Women, white and black, were discouraged from not only preaching but also class leading, and were urged toward the increasingly segregated arena of domestic evangelizing. The African Methodists were ultimately forced ever closer to full separation from the MEC by the unresolved issues of access to clerical advancement and, closer to home, control over their local societies, the home ground for the raising up of preachers. And white men in the church were as torn as ever between the imperatives of their religious calling and the imperatives of wealth—by no means exclusively their dilemma but one that especially applied to them, the bearers of family wealth. Nineteenth-century Methodism's momentum toward gentility may in many respects be seen as an effort not to draw rich men into the church but to keep them there.

The preachers' connection, furthermore, was among the least democratic of American churches. Francis Asbury and Thomas Coke, adopting the socially superior title "bishop" over the more popularly acceptable "superintendent," ran a purposely top-down organization designed to maximize the impact of missionary outreach. Whatever the bishops' claims to having created a church that embodied the will of the Methodist "people," particularly through the "university" of the class meeting and avenues of advancement for aspiring preachers, local societies had no formal voice in the church's annual or general conferences. The bishops continued to control the church as best they could through the appointment of powerful presiding elders and the unappealable assignment of itinerants to their circuits. The numerous efforts by traveling preachers, local preachers, and laymen to modify this system ultimately ran into the same explanation: the rights of Methodist ministers, voluntarily joined to the cause of holiness, were not the same as the rights of Americans. It was a defense of episcopal power oddly reminiscent of John Wesley's support for imperial rule in *A Calm Address to Our American Colonies.*

The more "American" many Methodists became after 1800, finally, the more they clung to the conservative prerogatives of American life: the power of men within the ministry, the privatization of the household, the respectability of the rising middle class, and the protected position of slaveholders within the church. Herein lay the greatest of Methodist challenges: how to remain true to the radical vision of John Wesley's Primitive Christianity while wielding the influence suitable to an institution of its size and public authority.

The Methodists, however, continued to be different from the other American churches with which they vied so well. Unlike the Anglicans, Calvinists, and Quakers, the Methodist movement was a product of eighteenth- rather than sixteenth- and seventeenth-century religious experimentation. Hence its innovations, so often copied by other denominations, derived from eighteenth-century precedents: missionizing, revivalism, the privileging of religious convictions rising out of experience rather than doctrine, as well as "social" worship in local societies independent of customary communities and standing authority. The Methodists, that is, were "a people," but an intentionally inclusive rather than exclusive people.

Coming of age in an era of relative religious toleration and denominational proliferation, the Methodists—again in contrast to the Anglicans and Calvinists, who continued to make no secret of their ambitions to speak for the "nation," whether British or American—represented a wholly different cultural prospect. For while they declared their fealty to the American Constitution, were quick to acknowledge the authority of the republic's newly elected leaders, and were as susceptible to political dispute and the allure of millennial prophecy as any group of Americans, they considered these to be relatively superficial pursuits. The fundamental goal of Asbury's movement and its many offspring lay elsewhere: in a supranational, all-embracing, missionizing evangelism that stood outside the claims of political allegiance and national destiny.

Methodism, finally, had one more distinct eighteenth-century attribute: it was as much a reform movement as it was a church—hence the ease with which the two terms may be interchanged in the narration of its rise. Appropriately, Methodism thrived on movement and change in both geographical and social senses, mirroring first the socially unsettled years of the Federalist Republic and then the explosive expansion of Jeffersonian America after 1800. In this respect, the missionary origins of Methodism remained critical. For many non-Methodists, increasingly sympathetic to the church's claims, the itinerancy was the great homogenizing force of evangelical Christianity. Hence in 1850, David Campbell, former Virginia governor, would describe Methodism as "completely a missionary system," designed, in his words, "to carry the Gospel to the very fire sides of the most ignorant and benighted of our countrymen."[3] But the real power of

Methodism for Americans lay in the spiritual egalitarianism of the revival: in its capacity to transcend conventional social distinctions and create new men and women.

For better or for worse, the Methodists revolutionized American culture by popularizing the confessional religious life, making religious regeneration the great American equalizer and source of social happiness. In this way, Wesleyan discourse—plain preaching for plain folk, by birth or aspiration—furnished a powerful alternative to republican civic culture and harnessed the energies of a restless American people.

APPENDIXES

Tables

TABLE 1

The New York Methodist Society by Gender, Selected Years, 1786–1796

	1786		1791		1796	
	No.	%	No.	%	No.	%
Men	65	35.7	212	33.8	256	34.1
Women	115	63.2	413	65.9	486	64.7
Gender unidentified	2	1.1	2	0.3	9	1.2
Total	*182*		*627*		*751*	

Sources: John Street MEC, "Members of the Church" (1786), "The Names and number of those persons in Society" (1791), and "The Names and Number of Persons" (1796), in Methodist Records, no. 233 and no. 241, NYPL.

TABLE 2

The Philadelphia Methodist Society by Gender, Selected Years, 1794–1801

	1794		1796[a]		1801[a]	
	No.	%	No.	%	No.	%
Men	141	39.8	143	40.7	240	35.9
Women	212	59.9	207	59.0	429	64.1
Gender unidentified	1	0.3	1	0.3	0	0.0
Total	*354*		*351*		*669*	

Sources: St. George's MEC, "The Names of the Officers, and Members" (ca. 1794), "The Names of the Officers, and Members" (1796), and "A List of the Classes" (1801), in Register Book, 1785–1817, OSHS.

[a] White members only.

TABLE 3
The Baltimore Methodist Societies (Baltimore City and Fell's Point) by Gender, 1799–1801

	1799		1800				1801			
	Baltimore City		Baltimore City		Fell's Point		Baltimore City		Fell's Point	
	No.	%	No.	%	No.	%	No.	%	No.	%
Men	319	38.7	346	39.4	72	35.0	414	38.1	86	36.8
Women	496	60.1	528	60.0	134	65.0	657	60.5	148	63.2
Gender unidentified	10	1.2	5	0.6	0	0.0	15	1.4	0	0.0
Total	*825*		*879*		*206*		*1,086*		*234*	

Sources: Baltimore City Station MEC, "A List of the Names" (1799), [A] list of the Society" (1800), and "A List of the members" (1801), in Class Records, M408, MDSA; East Baltimore Station (Fell's Point) MEC, "A list of the members" (1800) and "Register for Whites ... [and] Blacks" (1801), in Annual Register, 1800–1818, M411, MDSA.

TABLE 4
Women in the New York Methodist Society,
Selected Years, 1786–1796

	1786		1791		1796	
	No.	%	No.	%	No.	%
Whites	96	83.5	316	76.5	384	79.0
Blacks	19	16.5	97	23.5	102	21.0
Total	*115*		*413*		*486*	

Sources: See table 1.

TABLE 5

Women in the Baltimore Methodist Societies (Baltimore City and
Fell's Point), 1799–1801

| | *1799* | | *1800* | | | | *1801* | | | |
| | Baltimore City | | Baltimore City | | Fell's Point | | Baltimore City | | Fell's Point | |
	No.	%	No.	%	No.	%	No.	%	No.	%
Whites	333	67.1	344	65.2	104	77.6	441	67.1	111	75.0
Blacks	163	32.9	184	34.8	30	22.4	216	32.9	37	25.0
Total	*496*		*528*		*134*		*657*		*148*	

Sources: See table 3.

TABLE 6

The New York Methodist Society by Race,
Selected Years, 1786–1796

| | *1786* | | *1791* | | *1796* | |
	No.	%	No.	%	No.	%
Blacks	27	14.8	124	19.8	133	17.7
Whites	155	85.2	503	80.2	618	82.3
Total	*182*		*627*		*751*	

Sources: See table 1.

TABLE 7

Blacks in the New York Methodist Society,
Selected Years, 1786–1796

	1786		1791		1796	
	No.	%	No.	%	No.	%
Men	8	29.6	27	21.8	30	22.6
Women	19	70.4	97	78.2	102	76.7
Gender unidentified	0	0.0	0	0.0	1	0.7
Total	*27*		*124*		*133*	

Sources: See table 1.

TABLE 8

The Baltimore Methodist Societies (Baltimore City and
Fell's Point) by Race, 1799–1801

	1799		1800				1801			
	Baltimore City		Baltimore City		Fell's Point		Baltimore City		Fell's Point	
	No.	%	No.	%	No.	%	No.	%	No.	%
Blacks	287	34.8	309	35.2	54	26.2	361	33.2	72	30.8
Whites	538	65.2	570	64.8	152	73.8	725	66.8	162	69.2
Total	*825*		*879*		*206*		*1,086*		*234*	

Sources: See table 3.

TABLE 9

Blacks in the Baltimore Methodist Societies (Baltimore City and Fell's Point), 1799–1801

| | 1799 | | 1800 | | | | 1801 | | | |
| | Baltimore City | | Baltimore City | | Fell's Point | | Baltimore City | | Fell's Point | |
	No.	*%*	*No.*	*%*	*No.*	*%*	*No.*	*%*	*No.*	*%*
Men	115	40.1	124	40.1	24	44.4	141	39.1	35	48.6
Women	163	56.8	184	59.6	30	55.6	216	59.8	37	51.4
Gender unidentified	9	3.1	1	0.3	0	0.0	4	1.1	0	0.0
Total	*287*		*309*		*54*		*361*		*72*	

Sources: See table 3.

TABLE 10

The AME Congregation, 1794

	No.	*%*
Men	16	50.0
Women	14	43.8
Gender unidentified	2	6.2
Total	*32*	

Source: St. George's MEC, "List of the members of the African Methodist Episcopal Church," ca. 1794, Register Book, 1785–1817, OSHS.

TABLE 11
Occupations of Men in the New York Methodist Society,
Selected Years, 1786–1796

	1786 No.	1786 %	1791[a] No.	1791[a] %	1796[b] No.	1796[b] %
Merchants and retailers	4	40.0	12	11.3	16	11.6
Professionals	0	0.0	5	4.7	4	2.9
Government employees and clerical workers	0	0.0	3	2.8	2	1.4
Artisans	5	50.0	58	54.7	84	60.9
Marine, transport, and service workers	1	1.0	19	18.0	27	19.6
Unskilled laborers	0	0.0	9	8.5	5	3.6
Total	*10*		*106*		*138*	

Sources: See table 1. Occupations identified in *The New York Directory for 1786*, reprint ed. (1786; New York, [1905]), *The New-York Directory, Register, for 1790* (New York, 1790), *The New-York Directory, and Register, for the Year 1791* (New York, 1791), *The New-York Directory, and Register, for the Year 1792* (New York, 1792), *The American Almanack, New-York, Register, and City Directory* (New York, 1796), *Longworth's American Almanack, New-York Registery, and City Directory* (New York, 1797).

[a]In 1791, 1 artisan, 5 marine, transport, and service workers, and 1 unskilled laborer were black.

[b]In 1796, 4 artisans, 6 marine, transport, and service workers, and 3 unskilled laborers were black.

TABLE 12

Occupations of Class Leaders in the City Societies, Selected Years, 1796–1801 (in percent)

	New York, 1796	Philadelphia, 1796	Philadelphia, 1801	Baltimore, 1801
Merchants, professional, government, and clerical	11.5	25.0	40.0	56.5
Artisans, marine, transport, and service	88.5	75.0	60.0	43.5
Unskilled	0.0	0.0	0.0	0.0

Sources: See tables 1–3. Occupations identified in city directories, 1795–1802, cited in tables 11, 13, and 14.

TABLE 13

Occupations of Men in the Philadelphia Methodist Society, Selected Years, 1794–1801

	1794[a]		1796[b]		1801	
	No.	%	No.	%	No.	%
Merchants and retailers	14	21.5	15	26.8	14	13.5
Professionals	3	4.6	3	5.3	4	3.8
Government employees and clerical workers	2	3.1	1	1.8	7	6.7
Artisans	33	50.8	31	55.4	63	60.6
Marine, transport, and service workers	6	9.2	4	7.1	6	5.8
Unskilled laborers	5	7.7	1	1.8	7	6.7
Other	2	3.1	1	1.8	3	2.9
Total	*65*		*56*		*104*	

Sources: See table 2. Occupations identified in *The Philadelphia Directory and Register,* 2d ed. (Philadelphia, 1794), *The Prospect of Philadelphia and Check on the Next Directory* (Philadelphia, 1795), *Philadelphia Directory For 1796* (Philadelphia, 1796), *The Prospect of Philadelphia and Check on the Next Directory,* pt. 1, 2d ed. (Philadelphia, 1796), *Philadelphia Directory For 1797* (Philadelphia, 1797), *The Philadelphia Directory For 1801 ... Also Register* (Philadelphia, 1801), and *The Philadelphia Directory, City and County Register, For 1802* (Philadelphia, 1802).

[a]In 1794, 1 artisan, 3 marine, transport, and service workers, and 1 unskilled laborer were black.

[b]Includes white men only.

TABLE 14

Occupations of White Men in the Baltimore Methodist Societies
(Baltimore City and Fell's Point), 1801

	Baltimore City		Fell's Point	
	No.	%	No.	%
Merchants and retailers	35	26.3	5	18.5
Professionals	5	3.8	0	0.0
Government employees and clerical workers	10	7.5	1	3.7
Artisans	67	50.4	15	55.6
Marine, transport, and service workers	14	10.5	5	18.5
Unskilled laborers	0	0.0	1	3.7
Other	2	1.5	0	0.0
Total	*133*		*27*	

Sources: See table 3. Occupations identified in *The New Baltimore Directory and Annual Register; For 1800 and 1801* (Baltimore, [1801]) and *The Baltimore Directory for 1802* (Baltimore, [1802]).

Occupational Categories for
Tables 11–14

GROUP I: MERCHANTS AND RETAILERS

merchant / dealer
grocer
shoe-dealer
storekeeper
bookseller
broker

GROUP II: PROFESSIONALS

minister
lawyer / attorney at law
physician / apothecary / dentist
teacher / professor
schoolmaster
musician
other professional

GROUP III: GOVERNMENT EMPLOYEES

tax collector
constable
inspector
other government

GROUP IV: CLERICAL WORKERS (NONGOVERNMENTAL)

clerk / scrivener
accomptant
other clerical

GROUP V: ARTISANS

building trades
food / tobacco / distillery trades
leather crafts
marine crafts
metal crafts

textile trades
woodworker / box-maker / stay-maker
cabinetmaker / chair-maker / turner /
    coach-maker
house carpenter
ship carpenter / shipbuilder
comb-maker / card-maker
foundryman
hairdresser / barber / surgeon
instrument-maker / clock-maker / jeweler
printer / engraver / bookbinder
shoemaker / cordwainer
soap- and candle-maker / tallow chandler
tailor
painter / glazier
other artisan

GROUP VI: MARINE / TRANS-PORTATION / SERVICE WORKERS

captain
pilot / boatman / ferryman
coachman / liveryman
carman / carter / drayman
tavernkeeper / innkeeper
small dealer
chimney sweep / wood-sawyer
gardener
mariner
other transportation
other service

GROUP VII: UNSKILLED LABORERS, SERVANTS, SLAVES

laborer
servant
slave
other unskilled

GROUP VIII: OTHER

gentleman
farmer
fisherman
nurseryman
other miscellaneous

Methodological Note

THE MEMBERSHIP data in Part II are taken from a sampling of the records for the New York, Philadelphia, and Baltimore Methodist societies between 1786 and 1801. The records are a combination of admission registers, class lists, and marriage, baptism, and occasional burial records. The stationed preachers inscribed these in large register books without distinguishing among the different chapels in a given city, with the exception of Richard Allen's AME congregation in Philadelphia and the Fell's Point Methodist Society in Baltimore (also called East Baltimore Station). These records provide the only substantial quantifiable evidence to have survived for American Methodism prior to 1800.

For this study, I compiled four separate data sets based on the class lists for each city. The choice of years depended on the availability of records combined with the desirability of comparing like years in the different cities at consistent intervals. In each case the first year of the data set is the first for which records are extant. The Baltimore records before 1799 were likely destroyed in a 1796 fire, and the 1801 class lists for New York City likewise have not survived. The results are a New York City data set of 1,247 cases for 1786, 1791, and 1796 (including the John Street or Wesley Chapel, the Second Street Chapel by 1791, and the Two Mile Stone Chapel by 1796), a Philadelphia data set of 1,105 cases for 1794, 1796, and 1801 (including St. George's Chapel and Ebenezer Chapel); a Baltimore City data set of 1,490 cases for 1799, 1800, and 1801 (including the new Light Street Chapel—successor to the original Lovely Lane Chapel—the Green Street Chapel, and the two African Methodist meetings on Fish and on Sharp Streets); and a Fell's Point, Baltimore, data set of 329 cases for 1800 and 1801 (for the Strawberry Alley Chapel). The total number of cases came to 4,171 individuals.

I asked the same questions of each set: in which of the chosen years did a member appear and what was his or her race and gender, as well as office-rank and, if known, occupation for each year in the sample? For New York and Philadelphia, I also asked what each members' marital status was for the sampled years and whether his or her spouse joined before or after the marriage, or at all. Marital status was identified from marriage and baptism records in New York and Philadelphia through 1810, and first appearance in the marriage records was assumed to be a first marriage unless otherwise known.

Since the class lists are divided by race, this was the easiest variable to identify. If a first name was missing or gender was unclear, gender was considered to be a missing variable. Office-rank was taken from the list of officers in each sample year's record, and multiple officeholding was included as a variable. Occupations for the men in the societies were identified from city directories cited in the tables.

As with any historical document, imperfection is the norm rather than the exception with the Methodist society records, and the effort to locate identifying information on these Revolutionary-era Methodists was sometimes futile. The records, furthermore, rarely indicate family relationships, making family reconstitution a matter of deduction. Nevertheless, the Methodist city society records provide indispensable insights into the gender, race, and class of the first generation of American Methodists, information that may be drawn from no other source.

Methodist Statistics

As PROPONENTS of a missionary church, the Methodists were perhaps unusually absorbed in the collection of numerical data. As the MEC discipline instructed, it was "necessary that the yearly conference should have an exact account of the numbers in society, and of every thing material relating to each circuit under its controul, otherwise it could not possibly judge of the progress of the work. . . ."[1] Membership tallies, listed circuit by circuit, were published each year in the church's annual minutes. In 1786, the preachers began to divide circuit tallies into totals for white and black members, thereby providing the only numerical "series" on eighteenth-century African American evangelical adherence.

How accurate were these tallies? Christine Heyrman suggests that the numbers were "padded by clergymen eager to claim success for their ministries and churches."[2] A comparison of membership numbers as reported in the MEC minutes, however, and those listed in the city society registers for selected years between 1791 and 1801 indicates that the annual tallies of the Methodist conferences were remarkably precise, and in the case of Fell's Point in 1801, under- rather than overrepresented the size of one local congregation. The comparison is as follows:

New York City, 1791
    From MEC *Minutes*: 636
    From New York City Society class records: 627

New York City, 1796
    From MEC *Minutes*: 786
    From New York City Society class records: 751

Philadelphia, 1794
    From MEC *Minutes*: 367
    From Philadelphia Society class records: 354

Philadelphia, 1801 (white members only)
    From MEC *Minutes*: 707
    From Philadelphia Society class records: 669

Baltimore City, 1800
    From MEC *Minutes*: 880
    From Baltimore City Society class records: 879

Fell's Point, 1801
    From MEC *Minutes*: 208
    From Fell's Point Society class records: 234

The discrepancy in Philadelphia's 1801 count, furthermore, may be attributed to the loss of members to the Academy Church in that year, one example perhaps of a stationed preacher's attempt to mask divisions within a local congregation.

Of course no historian can determine precisely how carefully preachers working with an often changeable population of believers and backsliders tallied up their numbers. The membership lists in the minutes need to be used with care for other reasons as well, since Methodist circuits were often more geographically comprehensive than their names suggest. Before 1790, for example, the Baltimore circuit included the city and county. None of the Methodist annual conferences was interchangeable with the state, region, or, obviously, city for which it was named: in 1796, the Philadelphia annual conference included part of New York, all of New Jersey, Pennsylvania east of the Susquehanna River, all of Delaware, and the remainder of the Eastern Shore. The timing of the collection of the data might also vary from year to year. Most numbers were reported to the annual conferences in the spring, but in his *Short History,* Jesse Lee cites occasional irregularities, as in 1790 when local society totals were collected in October rather than the previous May, thereby inflating the increase in members for that year (and deflating those for the following year). Yearly totals for the entire church also often included circuits in Antigua and Canada.[3] Distinctions should be made, finally, between the numbers of members of Methodist societies and numbers of individuals actually converted at often publicly accessible revival meetings: claims as to the latter, especially at camp meetings, were without question exaggerated by nineteenth-century preachers.

The argument may be made, however, that the MEC annual minutes seriously *undercounted* Americans within the Methodist orbit. The figures in the minutes did not include the significant numbers of followers who regularly attended Methodist revival meetings without joining the local society; nor, but for rare exceptions, did the preachers include the children of members in their tallies. As quoted in chapter 7 above, in the early 1790s Bishop Thomas Coke attempted a statistical revision of the total numbers of Americans belonging to Methodist societies to include the families of members, noting that "if we number the Methodists as most people number the members of their Church, viz. by the Families which constantly attend the Divine Ordinances in their places of worship, they will make a larger Body than You probably conceive."[4] Slave members were undoubtedly also undercounted.

The Methodists' affinity for enumeration, furthermore, suggests the degree to which they valued "scientific" accuracy, however often individual itinerants might fall short of this test. The annual minutes were often little more than lists of information, data that reappear in Jesse Lee's plain and pioneering but often rote-like first history of the church.[5] Itinerants also itemized information in their personal journals that they considered important to their vocation: hence one finds lists of the biblical texts from which a given journal-writer preached and the topics of his sermons, among other enumerated information. Richard Whatcoat recorded the location of each of his meals while he traveled. Henry Boehm counted the number of times he had heard Francis Asbury preach. Perhaps the most startling example of the Methodist passion for counting is Peter Cartwright's conclusion to his *Autobiography*. In this, the life of a so-called backwoods preacher, the author is as vigorous a numbers man as his eastern counterparts. The autobiography concludes with tallies of the years Cartwright had traveled (as a single preacher and then as a married one); the number of his children, grandchildren, and great-grandchildren; the years he served as a presiding elder; the number of annual conferences he had attended; his cumulative salary minus losses from incapacitated horses, robbery, and other causes; the cumulative value of the books he had sold ($10,000); his net income in marriage fees (unspecified) along with presents received in money, clothing, and horses ($500), and donations for other church purposes ($2,300); as well as numbers of circuits and districts he had traveled, the numbers of members he had received into local societies, a tally of the children and adults he had baptized and funerals at which he had officiated, and sermons he had preached. Regarding the last: Cartwright claimed that at approximately 400 sermons per year for the first twenty years of his ministry, and 200 sermons per year for the last thirty-three years of his ministry, he had preached a grand total of 14,600 sermons. A greater love of itemization—and the record keeping it entailed—can hardly be imagined.[6]

One final word may likewise be useful regarding the magnitude of revival crowds reported in the Methodist preachers' journals. Frank Lambert has suggested that George Whitefield inflated his reports on the size of crowds that greeted him on his 1740 tour of the colonies.[7] The first Wesleyan Methodists, working later in the century before the rise of the camp meeting, describe gatherings of significantly smaller scale. Judging by the extent to which the itinerants prided themselves on data gathering, it can be assumed that their eyewitness assessment of the numbers in their audiences is as close to a correct count as any historian's retrospective reconstruction is likely to be.

AHR	*American Historical Review*
AME	African Methodist Episcopal
AQ	*American Quarterly*
BA	Baltimore
BC	Barratt's Chapel, Frederica, DE
BDML	*Biographical Dictionary of the Maryland Legislature*, ed. Papenfuse et al.
BM	British Museum, Manuscripts Division, London
CH	*Church History*
CLG	Catherine Livingston Garrettson
DAB	*Dictionary of American Biography*
D&D	MEC, *Doctrines and Discipline*, various years
DNB	*Dictionary of National Biography*
DSA	Delaware State Archives, Bureau of Archives and Records Management, Dover, DE
DU	William R. Perkins Library, Duke University, Durham, NC
DUL	United Methodist Church General Commission on Archives and History at Drew University Library, Madison, NJ
EC	Ezekiel Cooper
FA	Francis Asbury
FAS	Free African Society
FG	Freeborn Garrettson
FP	Fell's Point
GTS	The United Library, Garrett-Evangelical Theological Seminary / Seabury-Western Theological Seminary, Evanston, IL
HSD	Historical Society of Delaware, Wilmington, DE
HSP	Historical Society of Pennsylvania, Philadelphia, PA
HSWP	Historical Society of Western Pennsylvania, Pittsburgh, PA
JAH	*Journal of American History*
J&L	Francis Asbury, *Journal and Letters*, ed. Clark, Potts, and Payton
Journal	JW, *Journal*, ed. Curnock
JW	John Wesley
KWC	Kentucky Wesleyan College, Owensboro, KY
LCMD	Library of Congress, Manuscripts Division, Washington, DC
LCP/HSP	Library Company of Philadelphia, on deposit at HSP
Letters	JW, *Letters*, ed. Telford
LHP	Files of the Legislative History Project, MDSA
MAM	Methodist Archives, John Rylands Library, Manchester, England
MDA/PEC	Maryland Diocesan Archives, Protestant Episcopal Church, Baltimore, MD

MDHM	*Maryland Historical Magazine*
MDHS	Maryland Historical Society, Baltimore, MD
MDSA	Maryland State Archives, Annapolis, MD
MEC	Methodist Episcopal Church
MH	*Methodist History*
Minutes	MEC, *Minutes*, various years
MTSO	John W. Dickhaut Library, Methodist Theological School in Ohio, Delaware, OH
NJHS	New Jersey Historical Society, Newark, NJ
NJSL	New Jersey State Library, Trenton, NJ
NRB	The New Room, Bristol, England
NY	New York City
NYHS	New-York Historical Society, New York City, NY
NYPL	New York Public Library, Rare Books and Manuscripts Division, New York City, NY
OSHS	Old St. George's Historical Society, Philadelphia, PA
PAS	Pennsylvania Abolition Society
PCA	Philadelphia City Archives, Philadelphia, PA
PH	Philadelphia
PMHB	*Pennsylvania Magazine of History and Biography*
PP	*Past and Present*
PSL	Pennington School Library, Southern New Jersey Methodist Historical Society, Pennington, NJ
PWHS	*Proceedings of the Wesley Historical Society*
RA	Richard Allen
SHC/UNC	Southern Historical Collection, University of North Carolina, Chapel Hill, NC
SPG	Society for the Propagation of the Gospel in Foreign Parts
TC	Thomas Coke
UMHS	United Methodist Historical Society, Lovely Lane Museum, Baltimore, MD
WL	Joseph Downs Collection of Manuscripts and Printed Ephemera, Winterthur Museum, Winterthur, DE
WMQ	*William and Mary Quarterly*, 3d ser.
Works	John Wesley, *Works* (Oxford/Abingdon ed.)

INTRODUCTION: HOW AMERICAN WAS EARLY AMERICAN METHODISM?

1. MEC, *Minutes of the Methodist Conferences, Annually Held in America; From 1773 to 1813, Inclusive* (New York, 1813), 243.

2. Roger Finke and Rodney Starke, *The Churching of America, 1776–1990: Winners and Losers in Our Religious Economy* (New Brunswick, NJ, 1992), fig. 3.1, p. 55; Edwin Scott Gaustad, *Historical Atlas of Religion in America* (New York, 1962), 43.

3. Nathan O. Hatch, "The Puzzle of American Methodism," *CH* 63 (1994): 177–78. See also idem, "The Christian Movement and the Demand for a Theology of the People," *JAH* 67 (1980): 545–67, and *The Democratization of American Christianity* (New Haven, 1989), including "Redefining the Second Great Awakening: A Note on the Study of Christianity in the Early Republic," 220–26, for fuller expositions of Hatch's thesis regarding the democratic onslaught of religious "mass movements" in the new republic.

American Methodist historians have not been idle over the last three decades: see especially the church anthology, Emory Stevens Bucke et al., ed., *The History of American Methodism*, 3 vols. (New York and Nashville, 1964); the set of essays by Frank Baker in *From Wesley to Asbury: Studies in Early American Methodism* (Durham, NC, 1976); William Henry Williams's *The Garden of American Methodism: The Delmarva Peninsula, 1769–1820* (Dover, DE, 1984); Donald G. Mathews's felicitious essay, "Evangelical America: The Methodist Ideology" and the other useful articles in *Rethinking Methodist History: A Bicentennial Historical Consultation*, ed. Russell E. Richey and Kenneth E. Rowe (Nashville, 1985), a number, including Mathews's, reprinted in *Perspectives on American Methodism: Interpretive Essays*, ed. Russell E. Richey, Kenneth E. Rowe, and Jean Miller Schmidt (Nashville, 1993); as well as recent work in *MH*. The dearth of social studies has also been corrected in new work, especially on the American South: see Russell E. Richey, *Early American Methodism* (Bloomington, IN, 1991), Christine Leigh Heyrman, *Southern Cross: The Beginnings of the Bible Belt* (New York, 1997), and Cynthia Lynn Lyerly, *Methodism and the Southern Mind, 1779–1810* (New York, 1998); as well as the discussion of women and Methodist domesticity in A. Gregory Schneider, *The Way of the Cross Leads Home: The Domestication of American Methodism* (Bloomington, IN, 1993), the Baltimore African Methodists in Christopher Phillips, *Freedom's Port: The African American Community of Baltimore, 1790–1860* (Urbana, IL, 1997), chap. 5, the lively Hatch-inspired study by John H. Wigger, *Taking Heaven by Storm: Methodism and the Rise of Popular Christianity in America* (New York, 1998), which focuses on the "enthusiastic" features of the movement, and the discussion of women preachers in Catherine A. Brekus, *Strangers and Pilgrims: Female Preaching in America, 1740–1845* (Chapel Hill, NC, 1993). Of these, Heyrman's is the most sweeping in interpretation, arguing that the southern evangelical churches, the MEC prominently among them, succeeded in the region only after accepting and imitating the "mastery" of white men. See also discussion of Methodism's early-nineteenth-century triumph and relative twentieth-century decline in religious "market share" in Finke and Stark, *Churching of America*, 54–108 and 145–98.

But Hatch's observations regarding the neglect of the movement by non-Methodist historians remain apposite, especially in comparison to the central place held by the Methodist narrative in English historiography. This prominence may be traced to Elie Halévy's influential essay, "La naissance du Méthodisme en Angleterre," first published in the *Revue de Paris* in August 1906 (reprinted in *The Birth of Methodism in England*, trans. and ed. Bernard Semmel [Chicago, 1971]). In part derived from the treatment of Methodism in W.E.H. Lecky's *A History of England in the Eighteenth Century*, 8 vols. (New York, 1891), 2:598–695, and chiefly known for Halévy's largely unproven assertion that Methodism prevented a social revolution in mid-eighteenth-century Britain, Halévy's discussion was nonetheless of great sociological sophistication and offered a series of bold insights into the basically liberal nature of Wesley's movement, reiterated for the early nineteenth century in Halévy's *A History of the English People in the Nineteenth Century*, vol. 1, *England in 1815*, trans. E. I. Watkin and D. A. Barker, 2d ed., rev. (1913; London, 1949), 389–485.

The main social studies of English Methodism have in one way or another followed from Halévy, including V. Kiernan, "Evangelicalism and the French Revolution," in the first issue of *PP*, no. 1 (February 1952): 44–56; E. J. Hobsbawm's counter-Halévy thesis in "Methodism and the Threat of Revolution in Britain," *History Today* 7 (1957): 115–24, revised in a postscript to a reprint of the essay in *Labouring Men: Studies in the History of Labour* (New York, 1964), 33; E. P. Thompson's masterful reworking of the Halévy thesis as it applied to the suppression of working-class politics in early industrial Britain in *The Making of the English Working Class*, reprint ed. (1963; London, 1980); the sympathetic use of the thesis in Bernard Semmel, *The Methodist Revolution* (New York, 1973); and three assessments: J. D. Walsh, "Elie Halévy and the Birth of Methodism," *Royal Historical Society*, 5th ser., 25 (1975): 1–20, Elissa S. Itzkin, "The Halévy Thesis—A Working Hypothesis? English Revivalism: Antidote for Revolution and Radicalism, 1789–1815," *CH* 44 (1975): 47–56, and Michael Hill, "The Halévy Thesis," in idem, *A Sociology of Religion* (London, 1973).

Social and cultural studies of English Methodism are also numerous: important overviews and monographs include Anthony Armstrong, *The Church of England, the Methodists and Society, 1700–1850* (Totowa, NJ, 1973), Robert Moore, *Pit-Men, Preachers and Politics: The Effects of Methodism in a Durham Mining Community* (London, 1974), James Obelkevich, *Religion and Rural Society: South Lindsey, 1825–1875* (Oxford, 1976), Hugh McLeod, *Religion and the People of Western Europe, 1789–1970* (Oxford, 1981), idem, *Religion and the Working Class in Nineteenth-Century Britain* (London, 1984), Frederick Dreyer, "Faith and Experience in the Thought of John Wesley," *AHR* 88 (1983): 12–30, Deborah M. Valenze, *Prophetic Sons and Daughters: Female Preaching and Popular Religion in Industrial England* (Princeton, 1985), Julia Stewart Werner, *The Primitive Methodist Connexion: Its Background and Early History* (Madison, WI, 1984), and Richard Carwardine, *Trans-Atlantic Revivalism: Popular Evangelicalism in Britain and America, 1795–1865* (Westport, CT, 1978), which uniquely discusses American influences on Britain. Seminal work on eighteenth-century Methodism has also been produced by John Walsh in a series of important essays: "Methodism at the End of the Eighteenth Century," in *A History of the Methodist Church in Great Britain*, ed. Rupert Davies and Gordon Rupp (London, 1965), 1:277–315, "Methodism and the Mob in the Eighteenth Century," in *Popular Belief and Practice*, ed. G. J. Cuming and Derek Baker (Cambridge, 1972), 213–27, and "Origins of the Evangelical Revival," in *Essays in Modern English Church History in Memory of Norman Sykes*, ed. G. V. Bennet and J. D. Walsh (London, 1976). See also Henry Abelove's innovative biography, *The Evangelist of Desire: John Wesley and the Methodists* (Stanford, 1990), and David Hempton's three historiographically rich volumes: *Methodism and Politics in British Society, 1750–1850* (Stanford, 1984), *The Religion of the People: Methodism and Popular Religion, c. 1750–1900* (London, 1996), and *Religion and Popular Culture in Britain and Ire-*

land from the Glorious Revolution to the Decline of Empire (Cambridge, 1996). My own ideas have been shaped especially by W. A. Speck's discussion of eighteenth-century Methodism in *Stability and Strife: England, 1714–1760* (Cambridge, MA, 1979), Michael R. Watts, *The Dissenters: From the Reformation to the French Revolution* (Oxford, 1978), and idem, *The Dissenters: The Expansion of Evangelical Nonconformity* (Oxford, 1995).

4. Hatch, "Puzzle of American Methodism," 183–86.

5. John Locke, *Epistola de Tolerantia [A Letter on Toleration]*, ed. Raymond Klibanksy and J. W. Gough (Oxford, 1968), 71, 85.

6. Rupert E. Davies, introduction to *Works*, vol. 9, *The Methodist Societies: History, Nature, and Design* (Nashville, 1989).

7. Parish Report, 5 June 1797, St. Peter's Parish, Talbot County, MD, MDA/PEC.

8. Paul S. Boyer and Stephen Nissenbaum remarked on the contemporaneous coincidence of the decline of witchcraft beliefs with the rise of revivalism in *Salem Possessed: The Social Origins of Witchcraft* (Cambridge, MA, 1974), 25–26.

9. See informative discussions in Valenze, *Prophetic Sons and Daughters*, and Frederick Dreyer, "A 'Religious Society under Heaven': John Wesley and the Identity of Methodism," *Journal of British Studies* 25 (1986): 62–83.

10. John Mann to Daniel Fidler, 19 July 1795, DUL.

Connections between the Great Awakening and the American Revolution are a mainstay in recent American historical interpretation. Two influential social treatments are: Rhys Isaac, "Evangelical Revolt: The Nature of the Baptists' Challenge to the Traditional Order in Virginia, 1765 to 1775," *WMQ* 31 (1974): 345–68, and Harry S. Stout, "Religion, Communications, and the Ideological Origins of the American Revolution," *WMQ* 34 (1977): 519–41. For critiques, see Jon Butler, "Enthusiasm Described and Decried: The Great Awakening as Interpretative Fiction," *JAH* 69 (1982): 305–25, and John Murrin, "No Awakening, No Revolution? More Counterfactual Speculations," *Reviews in American History* 11 (1983): 161–71. Among the few studies that take the connection through the Revolution are Rhys Isaac, *The Transformation of Virginia, 1740–1790* (Chapel Hill, NC, 1982), Stephen A. Marini, *Radical Sects in Revolutionary New England* (Cambridge, MA, 1982), and John Brooke, *The Heart of the Commonwealth: Society and Political Culture in Worcester, Massachusetts, 1713–1861* (Cambridge, 1989).

Ironically, studies of religion and the Revolution have been comparatively rare. For contrasting overviews of religion's relationship to the coming and course of the conflict, see Patricia U. Bonomi, *Under the Cope of Heaven: Religion, Society, and Politics in Colonial America* (New York, 1986), and Jon Butler, *Awash in a Sea of Faith: Christianizing the American People* (Cambridge, MA, 1990). Other works, such as Nathan O. Hatch's *The Sacred Cause of Liberty: Republican Thought and the Millennium in Revolutionary New England* (New Haven, 1977), and Ruth H. Bloch's *Visionary Republic: Millennial Themes in American Thought, 1756–1800* (Cambridge, 1985), have tended to concentrate on New England. See also J. William Frost, *A Perfect Freedom: Religious Liberty in Pennsylvania* (Cambridge, 1990), and essays in Mark A. Noll, *Religion and American Politics: From the Colonial Period to the 1980s* (New York, 1990). Gordon S. Wood devotes all of six pages in his new study, *The Radicalism of the American Revolution* (New York, 1992), to a discussion of the impact of the Revolution on religion (329–34). Stanley Elkins and Eric McKitrick, *The Age of Federalism: The Early American Republic, 1788–1800* (New York, 1993), likewise make little or no mention of religious developments for the period, and no reference to the Methodists.

Social historical studies of revivalism with reference to Methodism pick up dramatically for the years of the Second Great Awakening after 1800. Among the pioneering assessments are those by Methodist scholar William Warren Sweet, who attributed the impact of Methodist and other revival movements to the individual's assertion of power in a democracy. Sweet's works include *Methodism in American History*, rev. ed. (1933; New York, 1954), *Revivalism in America: Its Origin, Growth and Decline*, reprint ed. (1944; Gloucester, MA, 1965), and *Religion in the Development of American Culture, 1765–1840* (New York, 1952), the last covering the fuller Revolutionary period. Other major work includes Whitney R. Cross, *The Burned-Over District: The Social and Intellectual History of Enthusiastic Religion in Western New York, 1800–1850* (Ithaca, NY, 1950), Timothy L. Smith, *Revivalism and Social Reform: American Protestantism on the Eve of the Civil War* (1957; New York, 1965), C. C. Goen, "The 'Methodist Age' in American Church History," in *Religion in Life* 44 (1965): 562–72, Winthrop Hudson, "The Methodist Age in America," *MH* 12 (1974): 3–15, Donald G. Mathews, "The Second Great Awakening as an Organizing Process," *AQ* 21 (1969): 23–43, John B. Boles, *The Great Revival, 1787–1805: The Origins of the Southern Evangelical Mind* (Lexington, KY, 1972), Nancy Cott, "Young Women in the Second Great Awakening," *Feminist Studies* 3 (1975): 15–29, Paul E. Johnson, *A Shopkeeper's Millennium: Society and Revivals in Rochester, New York, 1815–1837* (New York, 1978), Mary P. Ryan, *Cradle of the Middle Class: The Family in Oneida County, New York, 1790–1865* (Cambridge, 1981), Nancy Hewitt, *Women's Activism and Social Change: Rochester, NY, 1822–1872* (Ithaca, NY, 1984), and Carroll Smith-Rosenberg, "The Cross and the Pedestal," in *Disorderly Conduct: Visions of Gender in Victorian America* (New York, 1985), 129–64. Probably the most pronounced thesis for the influence of awakenings on American culture is put forth by William G. McLoughlin in *Revivals, Awakenings, and Reform: An Essay on Religion and Social Change in America, 1607–1977* (Chicago, 1978), in which McLoughlin argues that revival cycles underlie the most significant changes in American history. See also suggestive discussion in Daniel Walker Howe, "The Decline of Calvinism: An Approach to Its Study," *Comparative Studies in Society and History* 14 (1972): 306–27.

11. Important discussions of the region may be found in Douglas Greenberg, "The Middle Colonies in Recent American Historiography," *WMQ* 36 (1979): 396–427, Michael Zuckerman, "Introduction: Puritans, Cavaliers, and the Motley Middle," in *Friends and Neighbors: Group Life in America's First Plural Society*, ed. idem (Philadelphia, 1982), Robert J. Gough, "The Myth of the Middle Colonies: An Analysis of Regionalization in Early America," *PMHB* 107 (1983): 393–419, Jack P. Greene, *Pursuits of Happiness: The Social Development of Early Modern British Colonies and the Formation of American Culture* (Chapel Hill, NC, 1988), and Wayne Bodle, "The 'Myth of the Middle Colonies' Reconsidered: The Process of Regionalization in Early America," *PMHB* 113 (1989): 527–48. My broader usage is based on sociogeographic measures rather than political boundaries and is in keeping with contemporaries' observations, which describe the Middle Atlantic in even more expansive terms: see, for example, frontispiece of this book and discussion of various editions of Lewis Evans's map of the Middle Atlantic in Henry N. Stevens, *Lewis Evans: His Map of the Middle British Colonies in America* (New York, 1971). Geographer D. W. Meinig divides the Middle Atlantic coastal region into four large subregions: the Hudson River Valley, the Delaware River Valley, Pennsylvania, and Greater Virginia, in *The Shaping of America: A Geographical Perspective on Five Hundred Years of History*, vol. 1, *Atlantic America, 1492–1800* (New Haven, 1986), 86–160.

12. FA, *J&L*, ed. Elmer T. Clark, J. Manning Potts, and Jacob S. Payton, 3 vols. (London and Nashville, 1958), 3:133.

CHAPTER ONE
RAISING RELIGIOUS AFFECTIONS

1. For select work on the state of British religion in the long eighteenth century, see W. A. Speck, *Stability and Strife: England, 1714–1760* (Cambridge, MA, 1979), chap. 4, Michael R. Watts, *The Dissenters: From the Reformation to the French Revolution* (Oxford, 1978), G. E. Aylmer, "Unbelief in Seventeenth-Century England," in *Puritans and Revolutionaries: Essays in Seventeenth-Century History Presented to Christopher Hill*, ed. Donald Pennington and Keith Thomas (Oxford, 1978), 22–46, Robert Currie, Alan Gilbert, and Lee Horsley, *Churches and Churchgoers: Patterns of Church Growth in the British Isles since 1700* (Oxford, 1977), Hillel Schwartz, *The French Prophets: The History of a Millenarian Group in Eighteenth-Century England* (Berkeley, 1980), and J. L. McCracken, "The Ecclesiastical Structure, 1714–60," in *A New History of Ireland*, vol. 4, *Eighteenth-Century Ireland, 1691–1800*, ed. T. W. Moody and W. E. Vaughan (Oxford, 1986), 88–89. On the numbers of Dissenters in England and tentative estimates in Wales compared to the general population, Anglican and non-Anglican combined, see Watts, *Dissenters*, tables 2 and 3, p. 270, and tables 12 and 13, pp. 509–10. Watts estimates that Dissenters formed 6.21 percent of the English population and 5.74 percent of the Welsh population in the early eighteenth century.

2. For overviews, see James Axtell, *The Invasion Within: The Contest of Cultures in Colonial North America* (New York, 1985), Patricia U. Bonomi, *Under the Cope of Heaven: Religion, Society, and Politics in Colonial America* (New York, 1986), and Jon Butler, *Awash in a Sea of Faith: Christianizing the American People* (Cambridge, MA, 1990), 182–87. For an in-depth study of the dissenting churches in the Delaware Valley, see also Jon Butler, "Power, Authority, and the Origins of American Denominational Order: The English Churches in the Delaware Valley, 1680–1730," *Transactions of the American Philosophical Society* 68, pt. 2 (February 1978).

3. John Locke, *Epistola de Tolerantia* [*A Letter on Toleration*], ed. Raymond Klibansky and J. W. Gough (Oxford, 1968), 71, 85.

4. Speck, *Stability*, 91–93. The Toleration Act also maintained Anglican control at the national level by confining dissenting religious activities to individual chapels and congregations, thereby limiting the national ambitions of Presbyterians and Independents: see Russell E. Richey, "Effects of Toleration on Eighteenth-Century Dissent," *Journal of Religious History* 8 (1975): 350–63. Also see *Oxford English Dictionary*, rev. ed., s.v. "denomination," and Sidney Mead, "Denominationalism: The Shape of Protestantism in America," *CH* 23 (1954): 291. Nevertheless, the Quakers were already expansive missionizers, the only dissenting church with meetings in every English county (Watts, *Dissenters*, 280–85).

5. Thomas Bray wrote, with unintentional humor, "Whilst the Papists, the Dissenters, and the very Quakers have such Societies for the carrying on their Superstituous Blasphemies, Heresies and Fooleries[,] we have had nothing of this nature yet set up": quoted in Butler, "Power," 26. Another late-seventeenth-century group were the Philadelphians, whose formal name—The Religious Society for the Reformation of Manners, for the Advancement of an Heroical Christian Piety, and Universal Love towards All—reveals the multiple inspirations for the new religious societies (Schwartz, *French Prophets*, 45). For representative work on the Anglican societies, see R. A. Knox, *Enthusiasm: A Chapter in the History of Religion, with Special Reference to the Seventeenth and Eighteenth Centuries* (Oxford, 1950), 427, William A. and Phyllis W. Bultmann, "The Roots of Anglican Humanitarianism: A Study of the Membership of the S.P.C.K. and the S.P.G., 1688–1720,"

Historical Magazine of the Protestant Episcopal Church 33 (1964): 3–48, and John Frederick Woolverton, *Colonial Anglicanism in North America* (Detroit, 1984), 81–106.

6. Schwartz, *French Prophets*, 64. The Anglican, John Lacy, was later approvingly read by JW: see Schwartz, 85–97, 207.

7. *DNB*, s.v. "Wesley, Samuel [1662–1735]." See also background of the Wesley family's political and religious allegiances in Frank Baker, *John Wesley and the Church of England* (Nashville, 1970), 7–8, and Samuel Wesley's missionary plan in Adam Clarke, *Memoirs of the Wesley Family, from Original Documents*, 2d ed., rev. and enl. (New York, 1848).

8. Susanna Wesley to JW, 24 July 1732, reprinted in Clarke, *Memoirs*, 325–26, and partially quoted in JW, *Works*, vol. 3, *Sermons III*, ed. Albert C. Outler (Nashville, 1984), 367–68. See also Clarke, *Memoirs*, 318–24, and Frank Baker, "Salute to Susanna," *MH* 7 (April 1969): 3–8.

9. Quoted in Richard P. Heitzenrater, *Mirror and Memory: Reflections on Early Methodism* (Nashville, 1989), 44.

10. For more critical views of Susanna Wesley, see Majorie Bowen, *Wrestling Jacob* (London, 1938), quoted in Robert F. Wearmouth, *Methodism and the Common People of the Eighteenth Century* (London, 1945), 207, and Philip Greven, *The Protestant Temperament: Patterns of Child-Rearing, Religious Experience, and the Self in Early America* (New York, 1977), 36–38.

11. [Susanna Wesley], "Mrs. Wesley's Conference with Her Daughter," Wesley Historical Society, *Publications*, no. 3 (London, 1898), 34, 37, 40. See also Samuel Wesley to [Susanna] Wesley, 13 January 1709/10 in Clarke, *Memoirs*, 347–73.

12. Clarke, *Memoirs*, 386–87.

13. An original copy survives in the rare book collection at Van Pelt Library, University of Pennsylvania: [Bartholomew Ziegenbalgh], *Propagation of the Gospel in the East: Being an Account of the Success of Two Danish Missionaries Lately Sent to the East-Indies for the Conversion of the Heathen in Malabar*, 2 pts. (London, 1709–1710). See esp. 1:37, 68, 72. JW refers to the Malabar missionaries in *A Plain Account of the People Called Methodists*, in *Works*, vol. 9, *The Methodist Societies: History, Nature, and Design*, ed. Rupert E. Davies, 258, comments that were reprinted in *The Arminian Magazine* (London) 12 (1789) and 13 (1790). The missionaries were Germans in the employ of the Danish king: see *Propagation*, xxvii–xxviii, and *Works*, 9:258–59n.

14. Clarke, *Memoirs* 388–89.

15. JW reprinted his mother's letter in his sermon "On Obedience to Parents": *Works*, 3:367–68, 368n.

16. Baker, *John Wesley*, 10–19, and Heitzenrater, *Mirror*, 69–76.

17. See extended discussion in Baker, *John Wesley*, 10–28. Baker notes that it was a number of years before JW's attempts to rise regularly at 4:00 A.M. were successful (19–20).

18. Quoted in Richard P. Heitzenrater, ed., *Diary of an Oxford Methodist: Benjamin Ingham, 1733–34* (Durham, NC, 1985), 120n. Other derivations of the name point to a group of ancient physicians, a term used to describe students who adhered to a particular "method of study," and the seventeenth-century "new methodists," a theological school favoring good works: see *Works*, 9:32–33, and Heitzenrater, *Mirror*, 18. See also Charles Wesley to Dr. Chandler, 28 April 1785, in *Charles Wesley: A Reader*, ed. John R. Tyson (New York, 1989), 59, *DAB*, s.v. "Whitefield, George [1714–1770]," and Baker, *John Wesley*, 19.

19. The insight is Elie Halévy's in *The Birth of Methodism in England*, trans. and ed. Bernard Semmel (Chicago, 1971), 44. An extended discussion on the later movement's identity appears in Frederick Dreyer, "A 'Religious Society under Heaven': John Wesley and the Identity of Methodism," *Journal of British Studies* 25 (1986): 62–83.

20. *DNB*, s.v. JW [1703–1791].

21. Baker, *John Wesley*, 39–57, and idem, *From Wesley to Asbury: Studies in Early American Methodism* (Durham, NC, 1976), 3–27, 29–30. See also Richard S. Dunn, "The Trustees of Georgia and the House of Commons, 1732–1752," *WMQ* 11 (1954): 555–57; Phinizy Spalding, *Oglethorpe in America* (Chicago, 1977), 83–84, and G. E. Milburn, "Early Methodism and the Huguenots," *PWHS* 45 (1985): 72.

22. James Edward Oglethorpe, *Some Account of the Design of the Trustees for establishing Colonys in America*, ed. Rodney M. Baine and Phinizy Spalding (Athens, GA, 1990), 13. See also Spalding, *Oglethorpe*, 18–32.

23. JW to the Reverend John Burton, 10 October 1735, in *Works*, vol. 25, *Letters I (1721–1739)*, ed. Frank Baker (Oxford, 1980), 439. On JW's spiritual crisis, see Albert C. Outler, ed., *John Wesley* (New York, 1964), 7, and preconversion narrative in *Works*, vol. 18, *Journal and Diaries I (1735–1738)*, ed. W. Reginald Ward and Richard P. Heitzenrater (Nashville, 1988), 242–49. Charles later noted that JW was in Georgia "waiting for an opportunity of preaching to the Indians" (CW to Dr. Chandler, 28 April 1785), 59.

24. Baker, *From Wesley*, 8–11.

25. CW, "Journal Selections: 9 March—4 December 1736," in Tyson, *Charles Wesley*, 66–81. On Ingham, see *Works*, 18:175.

26. Alexander Garden, Anglican commissary, quoted in Garden to Bishop Gibson, 22 December 1737, partially reproduced in John A. Vickers, "Lambeth Palace Library: Some Items of Methodist Interest from the Fulham Papers," *MH* 9 (1971): 24–25. See also Baker, *John Wesley*, 47–52, and Harvey H. Jackson, "Parson and Squire: James Oglethorpe and the Role of the Anglican Church in Georgia, 1733–1736," in *Oglethorpe in Perspective: Georgia's Founder after Two Hundred Years*, ed. Phinizy Spalding and Harvey H. Jackson (Tuscaloosa, AL, 1989), 62–65.

27. JW to the Reverend John Burton, 10 October 1735, in *Works*, 25:439.

28. Reprinted in *Works*, 25:464–66.

29. *Works*, 18:193; Baker, *From Wesley*, 12–13, 30–31.

30. Baker, *From Wesley*, 13, 21, idem, *John Wesley*, 47–52, and Milburn, "Early Methodism," 71.

31. Luke Tyerman, *The Life and Times of the Rev. John Wesley, M.A., Founder of the Methodists* (New York, 1872), 1:155–56.

32. For overviews, see Gillian Lindt Gollin, *Moravians in Two Worlds: A Study of Changing Communities* (New York, 1967), and Beverly Prior Smaby, *The Transformation of the Moravian Brethren: From Communal Mission to Family Economy* (Philadelphia, 1988).

33. Gollin, *Moravians*, 9–24, 67–130. On Ingham and Delamotte, see Heitzenrater, *Diary*, 46–47, and *Works*, 18:136n.

34. On the Moravian "diaspora," see W. Thomas Smith, "Attempts at Moravian and Methodist Union, 1785–1786," *MH* 8 (1970): 36–48, Watts, *Dissenters*, 395–96, and Knox, *Enthusiasm*, 400–404. For further details, see Susan O'Brien, "A Transatlantic Community of Saints: The Great Awakening and the First Evangelical Network, 1735–55," *AHR* 91 (1986): 825, and Knox, *Enthusiasm*, 398–99.

35. Schwartz, *French Prophets*, chap. 6; David S. Lovejoy, *Religious Enthusiasm in the New World: Heresy to Revolution* (Cambridge, MA, 1985), 168–70; Milburn, "Early Methodism," 75–77.

36. Schwartz, *French Prophets*, 198. For further pioneering discussion, see Halévy, *Birth of Methodism*, 52–62.

37. Heitzenrater, *Mirror*, 121–26.

38. Quoted in Tyerman, *John Wesley*, 1:182.

39. Davies, introduction to *Works*, 9:6. See also *Works*, 25:509n and 18:236–37, 236n.

40. For JW's spiritual state, see *Works*, 18:242–51, culminating in these last sentences, 249–50. The full title of Luther's work was, perhaps not surprisingly, *A Methodicall Preface prefixed before the Epistle of S. Paule to the Romanes. . .* (London, [1594]). See Outler, *John Wesley*, on the relative importance of this episode (14–16).

41. *Works*, 18:252n.

42. Heitzenrater, *Mirror*, 124–26; Bernard Semmel, *The Methodist Revolution* (New York, 1973), 32–33.

43. Semmel, *Methodist Revolution*, 33; *Works*, 18:252n. The "Rules of the Band Societies" are reprinted in *Works*, 9:77–78.

44. See descriptions in Watts, *Dissenters*, 277–80, and Speck, *Stability*, 112.

45. Watts, *Dissenters*, 346–66, and Speck, *Stability*, 101–3.

46. *Works*, 18:221.

47. Whitefield's conversion experience in spring 1735 also preceded that of the Wesleys. Whitefield was ordained as an Anglican priest in January 1739, and his first outdoor sermon was to the Kingswood miners on 17 February 1739 (*DAB*, s.v. "Whitefield, George"). Other preachers were also speaking in the fields: see Halévy, *Birth of Methodism*, 59–62, R. B. Knox, "The Wesleys and Howell Harris," in *Studies in Church History*, ed. G. J. Cuming, vol. 3, *Papers Read at the Third Winter and Summer Meetings of the Ecclesiastical Historical Society* (Leiden, 1966), 267–76, and Schwartz, *French Prophets*, 70n.

48. *Works*, vol. 19, *Journal and Diaries II (1738–1743)*, ed. W. Reginald Wald and Richard P. Heitzenrater (Nashville, 1990), 67.

49. *DNB*, s.v. JW, and Outler, *John Wesley*, 28–29.

50. *Works*, 19:33–34; Schwartz, *French Prophets*, 206. David Hume summarized the basic Enlightenment view of religious enthusiasm: "Human reason, and even morality are rejected as fallacious guides; And the fanatic madman delivers himself over, blindly, and without reserve, to the supposed illapses of the spirit, and to inspiration from above" (quoted in Semmel, *Methodist Revolution*, 15).

51. *Works*, 18:252. See also the case of a gentlewoman in a chapel near Chester in *Works*, 18:231, and ibid., vols. 18 and 19, passim.

52. Ibid., 19:16, 16n. See also Charles A. Rogers, "John Wesley and Jonathan Edwards, *Duke Divinity School Review* 31 (1966): 20–38. JW objected to Edwards's Calvinism, writing in his preface to the abridgment of *Religious Affections*: "He heaps together so many curious, subtle, metaphysical distinctions, as are sufficient to puzzle the brain and confound the intellects, of all the plain men and women in the universe . . ." (quoted, 29–30). Edwards for his part mentions JW just once in his writing, criticizing JW's support for the doctrine of perfection.

53. *Works*, 19:70. On response to JW's preaching in Bristol and surrounding areas, see ibid., 49–62, and on a case of possession, see ibid., 109–112.

54. Ibid., 59.

55. "The Nature of Enthusiasm," in *Works*, vol. 2, *Sermons II*, ed. Albert C. Outler (Nashville, 1985), 46–60. See also Frederick Dreyer, "Faith and Experience in the Thought of John Wesley," *AHR* 88 (1983): 12–30, and Heitzenrater, *Mirror*, chap. 6, esp. 139–41.

56. *Works*, vol. 1, *Sermons I*, ed. Albert C. Outler (Nashville, 1984), 103–4. See also Semmel, *Methodist Revolution*, 23–55.

57. Jonathan Edwards, *Religious Affections*, in *The Works of Jonathan Edwards*, vol. 1, ed. John E. Smith (New Haven, 1959).

58. Harry S. Stout, *The Divine Dramatist: George Whitefield and the Rise of Modern Evangelicalism* (Grand Rapids, MI, 1991), 4, 22.

59. Ibid., 41–45.

60. "Free Grace," in *Works*, 3:544–63. Fletcher quoted in Semmel, *Methodist Revolution*, 53.

61. JW, "The Late Work of God in North America," in *Works*, 3:598.

62. On the theological basis for the split with the Moravians, see Semmel, *Methodist Revolution*, 36. JW was also suspicious of the Moravians' relaxed view of sexuality: see Henry Abelove, *The Evangelist of Desire: John Wesley and the Methodists* (Stanford, 1990), 54.

63. Davies, introduction to *Works*, 9:10. On the preaching houses in Bristol, London, Newcastle, and Cardiff, established between 1739 and 1743, see Leslie F. Church, *The Early Methodist People* (New York, 1949), 57–62.

64. JW, *A Plain Account of the People called Methodists*, in *Works*, 9:257, 256.

65. Dreyer, "Religious Society," 72, 80.

66. Davies, introduction to *Works*, 9:1–15; Church, *Early Methodist People*, 59.

67. Davies, introduction to *Works*, 9:11–12, 69–70. See also Church, *Early Methodist People*, 153–82, Thomas William Madron, "Some Economic Aspects of John Wesley's Thought Revisited," *MH* 6 (1965): 37–38, and Abelove, *Evangelist*, 58–60.

68. See, e.g., Mary Bosanquet, *Jesus, Altogether Lovely: or a Letter to some of the single women in the Methodist Society*, 2d ed. (Bristol, 1766), 4, and Elizabeth Rowe, *Devout Exercises of the Heart in Meditation and Soliloquy, Prayer and Praise* (Philadelphia, 1798). For the Moravian influences on Rowe, see Margaret Maison, " 'Thine, Only Thine!' Women Hymn Writers in Britain, 1760–1835," in *Religion in the Lives of English Women, 1760–1930*, ed. Gail Malmgreen (Bloomington, IN, 1986), 11–40. See also Abelove, *Evangelist*, chap. 5.

69. Davies, introduction to *Works*, 9:15–23. In about 1753 Wesley codified the evolving Methodist discipline in the so-called Large Minutes of the preachers' conference. Beginning in 1765, the *Minutes* of the conferences were published annually for the information of preachers and members alike (21).

70. Earl Kent Brown, *Women of Mr. Wesley's Methodism* (New York, 1983), 239–46; on Crosby, see 166–76.

71. Davies, introduction to *Works*, 9:17.

72. Phrases quoted in Speck, *Stability*, 113; see also E. J. Hobsbawm, "Methodism and the Threat of Revolution in Britain," *History Today* 7 (1957): 28.

73. John Walsh, "Methodism and the Mob in the Eighteenth Century," in *Popular Belief and Practice: Papers Read at the Ninth Summer Meeting and Tenth Winter Meeting of the Ecclesiastical History Society*, ed. G. J. Cuming and Derek Baker (Cambridge, 1972), 218–19; on "insolent boys," see idem [J. D. Walsh], "Elie Halévy and the Birth of Methodism in England," *Transactions of the Royal Historical Society*, 5th ser., 25 (1975): 19.

74. Abel Stevens, *The History of the Religious Movement of the Eighteenth Century Called Methodism*, 4 vols. (New York, 1858), 1:318–19.

75. R. B. McDowell, "Ireland in 1800," in Moody, *New History of Ireland*, 4:688.

76. JW, *Primitive Physic*, reprint ed. (1747; London, 1960), 26–28.

77. Reprinted in *Works*, 9:67–75.

78. Introduction to *Works*, vol. 7, *A Collection of Hymns for the use of the People called Methodists*, ed. Franz Hildebrandt and Oliver Beckerlegge (Oxford, 1983), 1–69. The Wesley brothers emphasized the social purposes of the hymns in a preface to one of their early hymnbooks, available to Americans: "The Gospel of CHRIST, knows of no Religion but Social; no Holiness but Social Holiness" (*Hymns and Sacred Poems* [Philadelphia, 1740], vi). Charles Wesley is estimated to have written some 7,300 hymns, over 400 of which are part of contemporary hymnals of various churches: Tyson, introduction to *Charles Wesley*, 20–21.

79. See Knox, *Enthusiasm*, 448.

80. On Whitefield and the Tennents, see Ned C. Landsman, "Revivalism and Nativism in the Middle Colonies: The Great Awakening and the Scots Community in East New Jersey," *AQ* 34 (1982): 156–58, idem, *Scotland and Its First American Colony, 1683–1765* (Princeton, 1985), chap. 8, Butler, *Awash in a Sea of Faith*, 182–87, Stout, *Divine Dramatist*, chap. 6, and Frank Lambert, *"Pedlar in Divinity": George Whitefield and the Transatlantic Revivals, 1737–1770* (Princeton, 1994), chap. 3. By contrast, the Quakers were largely resistant to Whitefield's appeal: see Frederick V. Tolles, *Quakers and the Atlantic Culture* (New York, 1960), 104–9.

81. Sanford H. Cobb, *The Rise of Religious Liberty in America: A History* (1902; New York, 1968), 362–453. For recent studies of Middle Atlantic pluralism, see Butler, "Power," idem, *Awash in a Sea of Faith*, 174–77, Martin E. Lodge, "The Crisis of the Churches in the Middle Colonies, 1720–1750," *PMHB* 95 (1971): 195–220, Landsman, *Scotland*, Bonomi, *Under the Cope of Heaven*, 72–85, Sally Schwartz, *"A Mixed Multitude": The Struggle for Toleration in Colonial Pennsylvania* (New York, 1987), Richard W. Pointer, *Protestant Pluralism and the New York Experience: A Study of Eighteenth-Century Religious Diversity* (Bloomington, IN, 1988), and Randall Balmer, *A Perfect Babel of Confusion: Dutch Religion and English Culture in the Middle Colonies* (New York, 1989).

82. On the Anglican renaissance, see Butler, *Awash in a Sea of Faith*, 99–116. See also Robert W. Shoemaker, "Christ Church, St. Peter's, and St. Paul's," in *Transactions of the American Philosophical Society* 43, pt. 1, *Historic Philadelphia, from the Founding until the Early Nineteenth Century* (1980): 187–98, and Dell Upton, *Holy Things and Profane: Anglican Parish Churches in Colonial Virginia* (Cambridge, MA, 1986), esp. 194. In nonrevival periods, church attendance appears to have been highest in communities settled by one religio-ethnic group, or among groups, like the Quakers and German sectarians, moving toward a cultural tribalism that defined membership by birthright rather than by religious experience: see examples in Bonomi, *Under the Cope of Heaven*, 72–160. For an analysis of the 1724 queries and the argument that church adherence was relatively high in the colonies, see Patricia U. Bonomi and Peter R. Eisenstadt, "Church Adherence in the Eighteenth-Century British American Colonies," *WMQ* 39 (1982): 245–86, esp. appendix, 277–86.

83. William Stevens Perry, ed., *Historical Collections Relating to the American Colonial Church*, vol. 4, *Maryland*, reprint ed. (1878; New York, 1969), 190–231. See also Bonomi, *Under the Cope of Heaven*, 41–61.

84. Perry, *Historical Collections*, 4:212.

85. "Proceedings on the Comissarie's Visitat^{n}," Oxford, Md., 16 June 1731, in Perry, *Historical Collections*, 4:304. See also [George] Ross, "History of his Church at New

Castle," 1 March 1727, in Perry, *Historical Collections*, vol. 5, *Delaware*, reprint ed. (1878; New York, 1969), 48.

86. Stout, *Divine Dramatist*, and Lambert, *Pedlar in Divinity*, chap. 2. See also rendition by Whitefield's traveling companion and publicist: William Seward, *Journal of a Voyage from Savannah to Philadelphia and from Philadelphia to England, 1740* (London, 1740).

87. See O'Brien, "A Transatlantic Community," Landsman, *Scotland*, 232–55, William Becket to SPG, 4 March 1740/41, in Nelson Waite Rightmyer, *The Anglican Church in Delaware* (Philadelphia, 1947), 113.

88. Benjamin Franklin, *The Autobiography*, ed. Leonard W. Labaree, et al. (New Haven, 1964), 176. On Whitefield and Franklin's friendship, see Stout, *Divine Dramatist*, chap. 12.

89. Quoted in Gerald J. Goodwin, "The Anglican Reaction to the Great Awakening," *Historical Magazine of the Protestant Episcopal Church* 35 (1966): 370.

90. For Anglican references to Methodists in the 1740s, see [Archibald] Cummings to the Secretary, 29 August 1740, in Perry, *Historical Collections*, vol. 2, *Pennsylvania*, reprint ed. (1871; New York, 1969), 203; [H. A.] Brockwell to the Secretary, 15 June 1741, in Perry, *Historical Collections*, vol. 3, *Massachusetts*, reprint ed. (1873; New York, 1969), 356–57; [Robert] Jenney to the Secretary, 26 January 1744 [extract], in Perry, 2:236; [Philip] Reading to the Secretary, 14 November 1746 [extract], in Perry, 5:89. On the expectation that the Wesleys would come to New England in 1741, see Charles Brockwell to Bishop of London, excerpted in Vickers, "Lambeth Palace Library," 25. See also discussions in Nelson R. Burr, *The Anglican Church in New Jersey* (Philadelphia, 1954), chap. 6, Goodwin, "Anglican Reaction," and William Howland Kenney, 3d, "George Whitefield, Dissenter Priest of the Great Awakening, 1739–1741," *WMQ* 26 (1969): 75–93.

91. Stout, *Divine Dramatist*, chap. 14, and Lambert, *Pedlar in Divinity*, 214–25.

92. *Early American Imprints*, 1st ser., nos. 5310, 4207, 4624, 4838, 5511, 5881, 7814, 9867. In *Methodism Anatomized: Alarm to Pennsylvania, by a Lover of True Piety, In Opposition to Enthusiasm* ([Philadelphia], 1763), the anonymous author, an English Anglican traveling in America, warned Philadelphians about the numbers of itinerant preachers that would follow in Whitefield's wake, and the salaciousness of love feasts, both more commmon attributes of Wesleyan than of Whitefieldian Methodism: 3, 11.

93. Bernard Bailyn, *Voyagers to the West: A Passage in the Peopling of America on the Eve of the Revolution* (New York, 1986), 26, 205, and extended discussions in chaps. 4 and 6.

94. Robert V. Wells, *The Population of the British Colonies in America before 1776: A Survey of Census Data* (Princeton, 1975), 112, 147, 284; Gary B. Nash, *The Urban Crucible: Social Change, Political Consciousness, and the Origins of the American Revolution* (Cambridge, MA, 1979), chaps. 9 and 10, and Bernard Bailyn, *The Peopling of British North America* (New York, 1986), 111–31.

95. The best treatment of the Irish Palatine Methodists is William Crook, *Ireland and the Centenary of American Methodism* (London, 1866), esp. 40–55, 73–84. On Embury's preaching house, see ibid., 80, and JW, *Works*, vol. 21, *Journal and Diaries IV (1755–1765)*, ed. W. Reginald Wald and Richard P. Heitzenrater (Nashville, 1992), 156, 156n. Embury's conversion statement is reprinted in J. B. Wakeley, *Lost Chapters Recovered from the Early History of American Methodism* (New York, 1858), 33.

96. For overviews, see Ruthella Mory Bibbins, *How Methodism Came: The Beginnings of Methodism in America* (Baltimore, 1945), 85–109, and Baker, *From Wesley*, chaps. 3 and 4. For various details, see John Embury et al., "Petitions" (1763–1765), nos. 1–7, Embury Papers, DUL; J. L. McCracken, "The Social Structure and Social Life, 1714–60," in Moody and Vaughan, *A New History of Ireland*, 4:42; Crook, *Ireland*, 74, 89; Frank

Baker, "Early American Methodism: A Key Document," *MH* 8 (1965): 3–15; and Baker, *From Wesley*, 41. Embury advertised his ability to teach "Reading, Writing, and Arithmetick; in English" in the New School-House in Queen-Street, and the availability of his brother, John Embury, "who teaches several Branches belonging to Trade and Business": *New York Gazette* (Weyman), 16 March 1761.

97. Frank Baker writes, "A small book could be written about the complex historiography of this event, of which there are scores of accounts varying considerably in detail": *From Wesley*, 42. For rendition of the event by descendants of the participants, see William M. Chipp to Rev. Joseph B. Wakeley, 8 April 1858, in Embury Papers, and George Heck to Henry B. Dawson, 17 January 1885, in Heck Family Papers, DUL. See also lively discussion in Crook, *Ireland*, 89–95, and partially inaccurate but myth-making accounts in Wakeley, *Lost Chapters*, 34–41, and Abel Stevens, *The Women of Methodism: Its Three Foundresses, Susanna Wesley, The Countess of Huntingdon, and Barbara Heck; with Sketches of their Female Associates and Successors in the Early History of the Denomination* (New York, 1866), 175–212.

98. Crook, *Ireland*, 90, Bibbins, *How Methodism Came*, 102, and Baker, "Early American Methodism," 9.

99. Crook, *Ireland*, 96–97. For earliest members, see "Peter Parks true Statement of the first rise of the Methodist in america, in the year, 1766," EC Collection, GTS; and for more information on the early society, see Thomas Taylor to JW, 11 April 1768, in Baker, "Early American Methodism," 9–11 (where Embury is described as a Wesleyan "Helper"), and idem, *From Wesley*, 73–78. On the likely location of the "upper room," see Bibbins, *How Methodism Came*, 107, and Baker, "Early American Methodism," 10.

100. The best treatment of Robert Strawbridge and his place in American Methodism is Bibbins, *How Methodism Came*, 25–74, which corrects Crook on the dates for the Strawbridge family's migration to Maryland: esp. 30–31. See also Crook, *Ireland*, 149–69, Edwin Schell, "Beginnings in Maryland and America," in *Those Incredible Methodists: A History of the Baltimore Conference of the United Methodist Church*, ed. Gordon Pratt Baker (Baltimore, 1972), 2–19, and Frederick E. Maser, *Robert Strawbridge: First American Methodist Circuit Rider* (Rutland, VT, 1983). On Lawrence Coughlan, see also *Works*, 21:175n, and George H. Cornish, *Cyclopaedia of Methodism in Canada: Containing Historical, Educational, and Statistical Information* (Toronto, 1881), 14.

101. Bibbins, *How Methodism Came*, 27–28, and Schell, "Beginnings," 2–5.

102. For overviews of Strawbridge's travels, see Bibbins, *How Methodism Came*, 25–54, Schell, "Beginnings," 8–9, Baker, *From Wesley*, chap. 3, and Maser, *Robert Strawbridge*, 27–28. Strawbridge eventually traveled to PH in 1770, to Trenton, New Jersey, in 1774, and to Lancaster, Pennsylvania, in 1781, where he met with Martin Boehm, founder of the United Brethren; he may also have initiated a society in Fairfax, Virginia, in 1766, although evidence is scanty: Schell, 10–11, and Maser, 33–38.

103. Crook, *Ireland*, 158–59; Bibbins, *How Methodism Came*, 51–52.

104. Bibbins dates the earliest baptism to 1762 based on the recollection of a participant: *How Methodism Came*, 31. See also Baker's comments in *From Wesley*, 32n, and Maser, *Robert Strawbridge*, 47.

105. Crook, *Ireland*, 156. Bibbins provides a list of the male members of Strawbridge's society in *How Methodism Came*, 35. See also [Edwin Schell], "New Light on Robert Strawbridge," *MH* 9 (April 1971): 62–63, Baker, *From Wesley*, 34–37, Bibbins, *How Methodism Came*, 59, and Schell, "Beginnings," 2–14.

106. Burr, *Anglican Church*, 82–83, and Deborah Mathias Gough, "Pluralism, Politics, and Power Struggles: The Church of England in Colonial Philadelphia, 1695–1789" (Ph.D. diss., University of Pennsylvania, 1978), 309–12.

107. Hugh Neill to the Secretary, 18 October 1764, extract in Perry, *Historical Collections*, 2:365–66. Barclay was a former catechist to the Mohawk Indians: Wakeley, *Lost Chapters*, 54.

108. Edward Evans to JW, 4 December 1770, reprinted in Frank Baker, "Edward Evans, Founding Philadelphia Methodist," *MH* 14 (1975): 57–59. Baker has modernized the spelling and punctuation. Evans's name appears on the 1740 list of trustees for George Whitefield's preaching house (John Fanning Watson, *Annals of Philadelphia and Pennsylvania in the Olden Time; Being a Collection of Memoirs, Anecdotes, and Incidents of the City, Its Inhabitants, and of the Earliest Settlements of the Inland Part of Pennsylvania* rev. ed. [Philadelphia, 1881], 3:274), and on the deed for the Moravian Church, PH, dated 20 August 1743 (Abraham Ritter, *History of the Moravian Church in Philadelphia from its Foundation in 1742 to the Present Time* [Philadelphia, 1857], 42, 70–71).

109. John Lednum, *A History of the Rise of Methodism in America, Containing Sketches of Methodist Itinerant Preachers, From 1736 to 1785* (Philadelphia, 1859), 39–42, and Baker, *From Wesley*, 32.

110. John L. Brooke, *The Refiner's Fire: The Making of Mormon Cosmology, 1644–1844* (Cambridge, 1994), pt. 1.

111. Burr, *Anglican Church*, 559. Evans died in 1771: see reference to funeral sermon in St. George's MEC, "A Book of Collections," 14 October 1771, OSHS. Another early Irish immigrant who converted to Methodism in New Jersey was John Early, for many years a class leader in Gloucester County (Burr, *Anglican Church*, 313).

112. For in-depth treatments, see Marvin Ellis Harvey, "The Wesleyan Movement and the American Revolution" (Ph.D. diss., University of Washington, 1962), 183–226, and Baker, *From Wesley*, 51–69.

113. The treatise is advertised in *Pennsylvania Journal; and Weekly Advertiser* (PH), 24 May 1759. See also John Pritchard, *Sermon Occasioned by the Death of the Late Capt. Webb; And Preached at Portland-Chapel, Bristol, December 24, 1796, At the Time of his Interment* (Bristol, 1797), 12–14.

114. Quoted in Baker, *From Wesley*, 60–61. See also JW to Thomas Rankin, 4 December 1773, in *Letters*, ed. John Telford, 8 vols. (London, [1931]), vol. 6 (1772–1780), 56–57, on Webb's tendency to exaggerate.

115. Baker, "Early American Methodism," 10, and Arthur Bruce Moss, *Thomas Webb: A Founder of American Methodism* ([Lake Junaluska, NC], 1975), 9.

116. Baker, "Early American Methodism," 12; Harvey, "Wesleyan Movement," 183, 183n.

117. Baker, *From Wesley*, 58–59. On the new members, see Wakeley, *Lost Chapters*, 80–86, 533–40, and Arthur Bruce Moss, ed., "Two Thomas Webb Letters at Drew University," *MH* 13 (1974): 55n. Webb probably also founded a Methodist class in Schenectady when he was stationed in Albany: Gabriel P. Disosway, *The Earliest Churches of New York and Its Vicinity* (New York, 1865), 415.

118. Thomas Taylor to JW in Baker, "Early American Methodism," 10.

119. Lednum, *History*, 9–4. On Wrangel, see JW, *Works*, 22:161, 161n.

120. Baker, *From Wesley*, 58–59; FA, *J&L*, ed. Elmer T. Clark, J. Manning Potts, and Jacob S. Payton, 3 vols. (London and Nashville, 1958), 1:540n.

121. Thomas Taylor to JW, 11 April 1768, reprinted with slight revisions in Baker, "Early American Methodism," 9–15. In *From Wesley*, Baker updates his discussion of the

Taylor letter on the basis of his discovery of a published version, probably printed by William Pine in Bristol in 1768 (72–79).

122. Thomas Taylor to JW, 11–12. On the conveyance of the NY property, see Frank Baker's extended discussion in "Early American Methodism," 12–13n. On the model deed, see Davies, introduction to *Works*, 9:18–19, and E. Benson Perkins, *Methodist Preaching Houses and the Law: The Story of the Model Deed* (London, 1952), chaps. 1–3. In Britain, the distinction was made between a "meetinghouse," usually referring to a dissenting chapel requiring licensing under the Toleration Act, and a "preaching house," the legal term for Methodist buildings (Davies, introduction to *Works*, 9:18n). These distinctions were not observed in the colonies, however.

123. Thomas Taylor to JW, 12–14. Taylor adds "excepting Mr. Whitefield's Orphan House in Georgia" to his description of the "first preaching-house," but the John Street Chapel was in fact the first American chapel specifically tied to JW's connection.

124. The subscription paper is reprinted in Wakeley, *Lost Chapters*, 69–72.

125. For profiles, see ibid., 74–93, Harvey, "Wesleyan Movement," 75–76, and Harold E. Dickson, *John Wesley Jarvis: American Painter, 1780–1840* (New York, 1949), 2–3.

126. *DAB*, s.v. "Livingston, Philip [1716–1778]," "De Lancey, James [1732–1800]," and "De Lancey, Oliver [1718–1785]"; and Wakeley, *Lost Chapters*, 94–103.

127. Crook, *Ireland*, 115.

128. JW, *Works*, 22:161, 161n.

129. William Bell to George Cussons, 1 May 1769, *Methodist Magazine* (London) 30 (1807): 45–46; Joseph Pilmore, *The Journal of Joseph Pilmore, Methodist Itinerant, for the Years August 1, 1769 to January 2, 1774*, ed. Frederick E. Maser and Howard T. Maag (Philadelphia, 1969), 15.

130. Crook, *Ireland*, 135–46, Baker, *From Wesley*, 44–49, and *Works* 22:161–62.

131. See discussion of JW and personal control in Abelove, *Evangelist*, 48.

132. Lester J. Cappon, ed., *Atlas of Early American History: The Revolutionary Era* (Princeton, 1976), 38.

CHAPTER TWO
THE WESLEYAN CONNECTION

1. Frank Baker, *From Wesley to Asbury: Studies in Early American Methodism* (Durham, NC, 1976), 44–52, William Crook, *Ireland and the Centenary of American Methodism* (London, 1866), 120–21, 135–46, and Arthur Bruce Moss, "Philip Embury's Preaching Mission at Chesterfield, New Hampshire," *MH* 16 (1978): 101–9.

2. John Street MEC, "Cash Book," in Treasurer Accounts (1768–1796), Methodist Records, no. 249, NYPL. Williams appears to have reprinted at least ten of JW's publications before 1773: Baker, *From Wesley*, 48–49. See also James Penn Pilkington, *The Methodist Publishing House: A History*, vol. 1 (Nashville, 1968), 26–29.

3. Baker, *From Wesley*, 86; Joseph Pilmore, *The Journal of Joseph Pilmore, Methodist Itinerant, for the Years August 1, 1769 to January 2, 1774*, ed. Frederick E. Maser and Howard T. Maag (Philadelphia, 1969), 15–21. On Pilmore, see Frank Bateman Stanger, "The Rev. Joseph Pilmore, D.D.: A Biographical Sketch," in Pilmore, *Journal*, 235–49.

4. Joseph Pilmore to JW, 31 October 1769, reprinted in *Methodist Magazine* (NY) 6 (1823): 462; Richard Boardman to JW, 4 November 1769, reprinted in *Arminian Magazine* (London) 7 (1784): 163–64. See also Joseph Pilmoor to JW, 5 March 1770, reprinted in ibid., 222–24.

5. Pilmore, *Journal*, 40, 70, 72. See Frank Baker, "Early American Methodism: A Key Document," *MH* 8 (1965): 12–13, for the somewhat convoluted transactions for the new deed for John Street. The indenture and deed are at DUL; see also J. B. Wakeley, *Lost Chapters Recovered from the Early History of American Methodism* (New York, 1858), 58–63.

6. Pilmore, *Journal*, 27–28. See *Pennsylvania Archives*, 8th ser., 7:6302–3, 6307, 6340, for a brief history of the Reformed congregation and its financial problems. Photostats of the deeds for St. George's, dated 14 June 1770 and 11 September 1770, are located at OSHS. James Kinnear, an Irish member of the NY society, became the first American Methodist book agent: see Pilkington, *Methodist Publishing House*, 1:38–39.

7. Pilmore, *Journal*, 29.

8. Baker, *From Wesley*, 48–59; Pilmore, *Journal*, 58; Ruthella Mory Bibbins, *How Methodism Came: The Beginnings of Methodism in England and America* (Baltimore, 1945), 60.

9. Pilmore, *Journal*, 103.

10. Ibid., 38–123.

11. Joseph Pilmore to unidentified [ca. 1770–1771], NRB; reprinted in Frederick Maser, ed., "A Revealing Letter from Joseph Pilmore," *MH* 10 (1972): 54–58.

12. *DNB*, s.v. "Whitefield, George"; Pilmore, *Journal*, 61.

13. Baker, *From Wesley*, 31–33. See chap. 3 below.

14. J[ohn] Fletcher to Joseph Benson, 12 February 1773, DU, and Baker, *From Wesley*, 60–61; and *DNB*, s.v. "Benson, Joseph." JW acknowledged Whitefield's influence in "On the Death of George Whitefield," in *Works*, vol. 2, *Sermons II*, ed. Albert C. Outler (Nashville, 1985), 330–47.

15. Baker, *From Wesley*, 90–95.

16. *J&L*, ed. Elmer T. Clark, J. Manning Potts, and Jacob S. Payton, 3 vols. (London and Nashville, 1958), 1:3–4n, 123–25, 720–22. See also Elmer T. Clark, introduction to *J&L*, 1:xi–xiv.

17. *J&L*, 1:123–25, 720–22. On FA's circuit traveling in England, see John A. Vickers, "Francis Asbury in the Wiltshire Circuit," *MH* 16 (1978): 185–89.

18. *J&L*, 3:9–10; 1:4–5.

19. On FA's journal, see *J&L*, 1:xv–xviii. The journal's first number was published in *Arminian Magazine* (PH) 1 (1789). The only other publication issued under FA's name alone (as opposed FA's and TC's names together) was *The Causes, Evils and Cures of Heart and Church Divisions* (1792), a collection of extracts from the works of Richard Baxter and Jeremiah Burroughs. See Pilkington, *Methodist Publishing House*, 1:52–53, 53n, and FA's brief introduction to the book, reprinted in *J&L*, 3:45–46. See also FA to EC, 31 December 1801, in *J&L*, 3:231–33. On updates of FA's journal since the publication of *J&L*, see Frederick Maser, "Francis Asbury's Journal," pts. 1 and 2, in *MH* 9 (1970): 53–57, and 9 (1971): 34–43.

20. See reference to "Methodist Plan," *J&L*, 1:10, and to "Old Plan," William Duke, "Minutes" (1774–1778), 1777, MDA/PEC.

21. *J&L*, 1:6–61; Bibbins, *How Methodism Came*, 119–20; "The Death of the Rev. Joseph Toy," *Methodist Magazine* (New York) 9 (1826): 438–39.

22. Pilmore, *Journal*, 138–42.

23. Ibid., 141; Bibbins, *How Methodism Came*, 47–49; Edwin Schell, "Beginnings in Maryland and America," in *Those Incredible Methodists: A History of the Baltimore Conference of the United Methodist Church*, ed. Gordon Pratt Baker (Baltimore, 1972), 1–31.

24. William Watters, *A Short Account of the Christian Experience and Ministereal Labours of William Watters Drawn Up By Himself* (Alexandria, VA, 1806), 20; Frederick E. Maser, *Robert Strawbridge: The First American Methodist Circuit Rider* (Rutland, VT, 1983), 25.

25. *J&L*, 1:46–73. The new United [German] Brethren were an evangelical association among Lutherans, Mennonites, and Dunkers organized at a meeting in Lancaster County, Pennsylvania, in 1767: see J. Steven O'Malley, *Pilgrimage of Faith: The Legacy of the Otterbeins* (Metuchen, NJ, 1973), 167–84.

26. *J&L*, 1:53–54, 59–60.

27. Among the Irish members in BA County were William Hawkins and James McCannon (class leaders appointed by FA); John Kelso and his two brothers; Robert and Thomas Armstrong; the Ruckle brothers; James Morrison; and Alexander Russell (Crook, *Ireland*, 168–69). The house of Captain Patton (or Paten) on Fell's Point was used as a Methodist meeting place in the early 1770s (*J&L*, 1:65n). William Moore, another Irish supporter in BA, was English preacher John King's host (*J&L*, 1:98n).

28. See Trenton MEC, "Minute Book" (1772–1838), DUL: entries between 19 April 1772 and 15 November 1773 reveal consistent support, paid chiefly out of class collections, for the licensed itinerants working in the colonies, including FA, Wright, Abraham Whitworth, Boardman, King, and Shadford. A subscription circulated for the purchase of a lot at Broad and Academy Streets attracted contributions from 122 individuals (18 women, 103 men, 1 gender unidentified), including Methodists in NY and PH: Trenton MEC, "A List of the Subscribers, for building a Methodist Preaching House, in Trenton, Nov.ʳ 25. 1772," DUL.

29. For example, see FA's itinerary from PH to Burlington, Trenton, Greenwich, and Gloucester and their vicinities in May 1772 (*J&L*, 1:29–32). In his five months in Maryland beginning in October 1772, FA preached 150 times in forty-three different locations: Schell, "Beginnings," 29.

30. *J&L*, 1:19, 26, 29, 32; Bibbins, *How Methodism Came*, 67–68.

31. FA first preached at the Goughs' in March 1776: *J&L*, 1:180. In 1774, Gough purchased the BA County property and unfinished house that he renamed Perry Hall, presumably after the Gough estate in England: Edith Rossiter Bevan, "Perry Hall: Country Seat of the Gough and Carroll Families," *MDHM* 45 (1950): 34–36.

32. *J&L*, 1:98n, 201n. See Strawberry Alley (Model) Deed, 22 October 1776, MS copy, MDHS. On Lovely Lane, see *J&L*, 1:150n; Bibbins, *How Methodism Came*, 62. Lovely Lane Chapel opened in October 1774, and the property remained in the merchant Philip Rogers's name until 1792 (Schell, "Beginnings," 27). On location of Lovely Lane, see J. Thomas Scharf, *The Chronicles of Baltimore; Being a Complete History of "Baltimore Town" and "Baltimore City" from the Earliest Period to the Present Time* (Baltimore, 1874), 76–78.

33. Schell, "Beginnings," 26–29, Bibbins, *How Methodism Came*, 67–69, and *J&L*, 1:66–80.

34. *J&L*, 1:28, 45–46; "The Life of Mr. Thomas Rankin," in *The Lives of Early Methodist Preachers, Chiefly Written by Themselves*, ed. Thomas Jackson, 6 vols. (London, 1866), 5:184; [George Shadford], "Memoir of George Shadford," *Methodist Magazine* (NY) 1 (1818): 137.

35. Rankin, "Life," 136–52, 143, 153–56, 159; Thomas Rankin to Stewards, Leaders, and Society in York, 24 June 1773, PLP86.17.11, MAM.

36. Rankin, "Life," 183–84.

37. MEC, *Minutes of the Methodist Conferences, Annually Held in America from 1773 to 1794, inclusive* (Philadelphia, 1795), 5–7.

38. Rankin, Journal (1773–1778), typescript, GTS, 1 September 1774–23 February 1776, 24 March 1776.

39. Ibid., 23 September and 23 October 1775.

40. Ibid., 20 July 1775.

41. Ibid., 25 May 1774; *Minutes* (1795), 10–18.

42. See Philip Gatch, Certificate of Conference Membership, 24 May 1776, Gatch Microfilm, Group I, MTSO.

43. *Minutes* (1795), 7–18. In 1774 Rankin reported to Lord Dartmouth that five hundred—or approximately 25 percent—of the American members were black (Thomas Rankin to Lord Dartmouth, 29 December 1774), reprinted in [Frederick V. Mills, Sr.], "Thomas Rankin to Lord Dartmouth on the State of Religion and Political Affairs in America," *MH* 23 (1985): 118. Rankin notes in his Journal that the conference statistics did not include slaves; hence the published totals do include free blacks (Journal, 165).

44. JW to Thomas Rankin, 21 July 1774, in *The Letters of the Rev. John Wesley*, ed. John Telford, 8 vols. (London, [1931]), vol. 6 (1772–1780), 102–3; *J&L*, 1:146–47.

45. John Lednum, *A History of the Rise of Methodism in America, Containing Sketches of Methodist Itinerant Preachers, From 1736 to 1785* (Philadelphia, 1859), 142. Dempster had preached to the Palatines in Ireland (Crook, *Ireland*, 60n).

46. Quoted in John A. Vickers, "Lambeth Palace Library: Some Items of Methodist Interest from the Fulham Papers," *MH* 9 (1971): 27. See also Deborah Mathias Gough, "Pluralism, Politics, and Power Struggles: The Church of England in Colonial Philadelphia, 1695–1789" (Ph.D. diss., University of Pennsylvania, 1978), 312–13.

47. R. C. Simmons, *The American Colonies: From Settlement to Independence* (New York, 1976), 337–39.

48. Ibid., 333–49.

49. Thomas Jefferson, *A Summary View of the Rights of British America*, in idem, *The Papers of Thomas Jefferson*, vol. 1 (1760–1776), ed. Julian P. Boyd et al. (Princeton, 1950), 121–37.

50. Rankin, Journal, 2 October 1774. On virtue and the formation of American republicanism, see discussions in Bernard Bailyn, *The Ideological Origins of the American Revolution* (Cambridge, MA, 1967), Linda Kerber, *Women of the Republic: Intellect and Ideology in Revolutionary America* (Chapel Hill, NC, 1980), and Gordon S. Wood, *The Radicalism of the American Revolution* (New York, 1991).

51. *The Character of a Methodist*, in *Works*, vol. 9, *The Methodist Societies: History, Nature, and Design*, ed. Rupert E. Davies (Nashville, 1989), 33, 41; and *Reasons against a Separation from the Church of England*, in ibid., 337.

52. JW to "My Dear Brethren," 1 March 1775, in *Letters*, 6:142–43.

53. In 1768, for example, JW wrote: "Which do you think is the safest guide—a cursing, swearing, drinking clergyman . . . or a tradesman who has in fact 'from his childhood known the Holy Scriptures', and . . . who has given attendance to reading, has meditated on these things and given himself wholly to them? Can any reasonable man doubt one moment which of these is the safest guide?" (quoted in Frank Baker, *John Wesley and the Church of England* [Nashville, 1970], 258).

54. On Whig bishops, see W. A. Speck, *Stability and Strife: England, 1714–1760* (Cambridge, MA, 1979), 96–98, and D. R. Hirschberg, "The Government and Church Patronage in England, 1660–1760," *Journal of British Studies* 20 (1981): 125–39.

55. Bernard Semmel, *The Methodist Revolution* (New York, 1973), 56–80.

56. JW to Earl of Dartmouth, 14 June 1775, quoted in [Frederick V. Mills, Jr.], "New Light on the Methodists and the Revolutionary War," *MH* 28 (1989): 57–65. A slightly different copy appears in *Letters*, 6:155–60. See also stronger statement in JW to Earl of Dartmouth, 23 August 1775, *Letters*, 6:175–76, and JW to Lord North, 15 June 1775, *Letters*, 6:160–64. Dartmouth was also a land investor in Nova Scotia, another destination for Methodist migration: see Bernard Bailyn, *Voyagers to the West: A Passage in the Peopling of America on the Eve of the Revolution* (New York, 1986), 367–77.

57. See commentary on the radical John Wilkes's attacks on the king's ministry in JW to "a Friend" [December 1768], in *Letters*, vol. 5 (1766–1772), 370–88: here JW defends the king and his family, and declares London tradesmen unqualified to judge affairs of state.

58. *A Calm Address to Our American Colonies* (London, [1775]), 9, 13; Frank Baker, "The Shaping of Wesley's 'Calm Address,' " *MH* 14 (1975): 3–12. JW discussed the first edition in a letter to Thomas Rankin: see *Letters*, 6:181–82. On the king's proclamation, see Mills, "New Light," 60. On the probability that Johnson encouraged Wesley to publish a popular edition of the address, see Allan Raymond, " 'I fear God and honour the King': John Wesley and the American Revolution," *CH* 45 (1976): 321.

59. Baker, "Shaping," 8; Raymond, "I fear God," 324–28; and Donald H. Kirkham, "John Wesley's 'Calm Address': The Response of the Critics," *MH* 14 (1975): 22–23. On similar writings by JW's associates, see Donald S. Baker, "Charles Wesley and the American War of Independence," *PWHS* 34 (1964): 159–64, and 40 (1965): 125–34, 165–82; idem, "Charles Wesley and the American Loyalists," ibid., 35 (1965): 5–9; John Fletcher, *A Vindication of the Rev. Mr. Wesley's "Calm Address to Our American Colonies": In some Letters to Mr. Caleb Evans* (London, n.d.); and idem, *American Patriotism Farther Confronted with Reason, Scripture, and the Constitution: Being Observations on the Dangerous Politicks Taught by the Rev. Mr. Evans, M.A. and the Rev. Dr. Price, With a Scriptural Plea for the Revolted Colonies* (Shrewsbury, 1776).

60. Philip Gatch, "Minutes," 1775, in Gatch Microfilm, "Minutes" (1774–1779), Group II, MTSO. The wording in the published version leaves out the phrase "and great brittain": *Minutes* (1795), 15.

61. Simmons, *American Colonies*, 350; Thomas Rankin to Lord Dartmouth, 20 December 1775 and 15 January 1776, quoted in Marvin Ellis Harvey, "The Wesleyan Movement and the American Revolution" (Ph.D. diss., University of Washington, 1962), 156–57, 158n.

62. *J&L*, 1:181.

63. See, for example, Eric Foner, *Tom Paine and Revolutionary America* (London, 1976), 19–69, and Steven Rosswurm, *Arms, Country, and Class: The Philadelphia Militia and "Lower Sort" during the American Revolution, 1775–1783* (New Brunswick, NJ, 1987), 76–108. There were sixteen different sects and denominations in Pennsylvania in 1775, many pacifist: see Lester J. Cappon, *Atlas of Early American History: The Revolutionary Era, 1760–1790* (Princeton, 1976), 38.

64. Thomas Paine, *Common Sense*, ed. Isaac Kramnick (1776; London, 1988).

65. Foner, *Tom Paine*, 107–82.

66. Sanford H. Cobb, *The Rise of Religious Liberty in America: A History*, reprint ed. (1902; New York, 1968), 501, 503–4. Benjamin Franklin failed to keep a religious test for officeholding out of the Pennsylvania Constitution but succeeded in eliminating a test against Roman Catholics in particular; a test excluding Roman Catholics from public office was instituted in New Jersey, and one excluding Unitarians was in effect in Delaware (ibid., 501–4).

67. Ibid., 501.

68. Cobb, *Rise*, 497–98; and Jon Butler, *Awash in a Sea of Faith: Christianizing the American People* (Cambridge, MA, 1990), 258–67.

69. "Methodist Petition," 28 October 1776, reprinted in *Virginia Magazine of History and Biography* 18 (1910): 143–44.

70. *J&L*, 1:458. As Shadford writes, he was glad to return to England where subjects were free to "worship God according to our conscience" (Jackson, *Lives*, 6:175).

71. John Adams, *Diary and Autobiography*, 4 vols., *Diary, 1771–1781*, 2:156; Thomas Webb to Lord Dartmouth, 21 March 1775, extracted in [Mills], "New Light on the Methodists," *MH* 28 (1989): 58–60. For discussion of the correspondence with Lord Dartmouth, see Harvey, "Wesleyan Movement," 189–92. On Grace Gilbert and Nathaniel Gilbert, see Baker, *From Wesley*, 62, and John A. Vickers, "One-Man Band: Thomas Coke and the Origins of Methodist Missions," *MH* 34 (1996): 138.

72. Thomas Webb's Memorial to the Loyalist Commissioners, cited in Harvey, "Wesleyan Movement," 202. Rankin and another British preacher, Martin Rodda, probably also provided intelligence: ibid., 202–8.

73. Quoted in E. B. D[awson], "The Early Methodists and the American Revolution," *Historical Magazine, and Notes and Queries, Concerning the Antiquities, History, and Biography of America* 10 (1866): 366; Harvey, "Wesleyan Movement," 209–11.

74. Douglas R. Chandler, "Prelude to a Church," in Baker, *Those Incredible Methodists*, 52. On Judge White, see below. See also discussion of the loyalist Deveaus of New Rochelle in [Daniel De Vinne], "History of Methodism in New Rochelle," [n.d.], microfilm, R-7, vol. 64, NYPL.

75. *BDML*, s.v. "Owings, Samuel, Jr. [1733–1803]."

76. Walter W. Preston, ed., *History of Harford County, Maryland, from 1608 . . . To the Close of the War of 1812*, reprint ed. (1901; Baltimore, 1972), 93–102, 124; Littlejohn, Journal, vol. 3 (1777), 30 August 1777; *Maryland Archives*, 18:343–44.

77. J. Thomas Scharf, *Chronicles of Baltimore; Being a Complete History of "Baltimore Town" and "Baltimore City" from the Earliest Period to the Present Time* (Baltimore, 1874), 57 and passim; Bernard C. Steiner, "Maryland Privateers in the American Revolution," *MDHM* 3 (1908): 99–103; *Maryland Archives*, 11:489, 522; and 16:160–161, 165, 171, 272, 335, 349, 353, 404.

78. Harvey, "Wesleyan Movement," 332–33. Fitch, however, complains of lack of support from the NY Methodists during this trial: John Fitch, *The Autobiography of John Fitch*, ed. Frank D. Prager, in *Memoirs of the American Philosophical Society*, vol. 113 (Philadelphia, 1976), 100.

79. Harvey, "Wesleyan Movement," 214–15; *Journals of the Continental Congress, 1774–1789* (Washington, DC, 1909), 7 (1777): 367.

80. Webb struggled for many years thereafter to restore his military pension. He died in Bristol in 1796: Harvey, "Wesleyan Movement," 218–26, and Baker, *From Wesley*, 64–67. See also Thomas and Grace Webb Correspondence, 1777–1785, in Edward Wanton Smith Collection, HSP; two letters, Thomas Webb to Elias Boudinot, 7 April 1778, and Grace Webb to Elias Boudinot, [30 April 1778], in the Elias Boudinot Papers, HSP; and John Pritchard, *Sermon Occasioned by the Death of the Late Capt. Webb; And Preached at Portland-Chapel, Bristol, December 24, 1796, At the Time of his Interment* (Bristol, 1797).

81. JW to Thomas Rankin, 28 July 1775, in *Letters*, 6:168.

82. Gatch, "Minutes," 1777, in Gatch Microfilm, "Minutes" (1774–1779), Group II, MTSO. See also *J&L*, 1:238–39, and Baker, *From Wesley*, 99–100.

83. Thomas Rankin to Stewards and Leaders at Society at Mantua Creek, attached to Rankin to William Duke, 14 February 1776, MDA/PEC.

84. Littlejohn, Journal, vol. 3 (1777–1778), 7 September 1777; Thomas Rankin to Matthew Mayer, 7 July 1778, Lamplough Collection, 657:159–60, MAM.

85. James W. May, "Francis Asbury and Thomas White: A Refugee Preacher and His Tory Patron," *MH* 14 (1976): 146, and Harvey, "Wesleyan Movement," 293–95. See description of Rodda's escape in Littlejohn, Journal, vol. 3, 11 October 1777.

86. Jackson, *Lives*, 6:173; Harvey, "Wesleyan Movement," 298–99; and Wakeley, *Lost Chapters*, 253–66.

87. *J&L*, 3:21–22. See also JW to Thomas Rankin, 1 March 1775, 21 April 1775, and 19 May 1775 in *Letters*, 6:142, 148, 150.

88. *J&L*, 1:267.

89. Rankin to Matthew Mayer, 7 July 1778. See also Harvey, "Wesleyan Movement," 178.

90. Baker, *From Wesley*, 97. James Dempster, the other British itinerant, went behind British lines in NY: Wakeley, *Lost Chapters*, 250–54. Rankin's returning entourage was relatively small since a number of the British preachers had left the connection for reasons other than the war: of the preachers in attendance at the 1773 conference, Richard Boardman and Joseph Pilmore returned to Britain in January 1774 (Pilmore, *Journal*, 233); Richard Wright and Joseph Yerbury returned in 1774 (Rankin, Journal, 81); Abraham Whitworth was expelled for intemperance in 1774 or 1775 (*J&L*, 1:76n; Rankin, Journal, 85); Robert Williams left traveling to marry and died in Virginia in 1775 (Baker, *From Wesley*, 47–49); and John King married in 1776 and quit the itinerancy to practice medicine in North Carolina, where he died in 1795 (Schell, "Beginnings," 19–20).

91. Jesse Lee, *A Short History of the Methodists, in the United States of America: beginning in 1766, and continued till 1809* (Baltimore, 1810), 316–20.

92. Ibid., 316–20, and Maser, *Robert Strawbridge*, 38.

93. Chandler, "Prelude," 44; *J&L*, 1:196, 406.

94. Educated preachers included English-born John Dickins, who may have come to the colonies as an indentured servant tutor (Pilkington, *Methodist Publishing House*, 1:66–68); William Duke, a former tutor at Captain Charles Ridgley's estate (Chandler, "Prelude," 35); Thomas Haskins, a former law student (*J&L*, 1:375); and FG, who studied mathematics and accounting until he was seventeen (Robert Drew Simpson, comp., *American Methodist Pioneer: The Life and Journals of the Rev. Freeborn Garrettson, 1752–1827* [Rutland, VT, 1984], 39).

95. Joseph Everett, "An Account of the most remarkable Occurrences," *Arminian Magazine* (PH), 2 (1790): 558–59, 560–61, 601–4.

96. Littlejohn, Journal, vol. 1 (n.d.–1776), June 1775; see also Jackson, *Lives*, 6:172.

97. Chandler, "Prelude," 48. On the Abbotts, see Roll of Captain Jacob DuBois's Company, Salem County, New Jersey Militia, 1 February 1777, Revolutionary War Records, NJSL. Brothers Freeborn and Richard Garrettson appear on "A List of Non Associators," in Preston, *History of Harford County*, 344–51.

98. Harvey, "Wesleyan Movement," 286–88.

99. Littlejohn, Journal, vol. 3, 11 October 1777.

100. Chandler, "Prelude," 46–47; Richard A. Overfield, "A Patriot Dilemma: The Treatment of Passive Loyalists and Neutrals in Revolutionary Maryland," *MDHM* 68 (1973): 147.

101. Chandler, "Prelude," 46–47. On Pennsylvania, see Sally Schwartz, *"A Mixed Multitude": The Struggle for Toleration in Colonial Pennsylvania* (New York, 1987), 282–86.

102. Harvey, "Wesleyan Movement," 307, and Chandler, "Prelude," 49. Hartley was discharged from jail after a grand jury returned a bill of ignoramus in February 1780 (*J&L*,

1:335). On Anglicans, see St. Peter's Parish Report, 5 June 1797, Talbot County, Maryland, photostat, MDA/PEC.

103. Harvey, "Wesleyan Movement," 307–10.

104. Simpson, *Pioneer*, appendix 1, 391, 404–5.

105. Quoted in May, "Francis Asbury," 145.

106. Harvey, "Wesleyan Movement," 293–95.

107. May, "Francis Asbury," 157–58, 158n. Clow was later convicted and hanged for the murder: ibid., 158n.

108. Lee, *Short History*, 74–75.

109. Watters, *Short Account*, 49–52.

110. Littlejohn, Journal, vol. 2 (1776–1777), 22 May 1777 and 4 July 1777; vol. 3, 20 August 1777.

111. Ibid., vol. 4, 19 January 1778, 15 March 1778, and 30 May 1778; Nelson Reed quoted in Chandler, "Prelude," 48. Col. Thomas Dorsey was commander of the Elk Ridge Battalion: *J&L*, 1:386n.

112. Minton Thrift, comp., *Memoir of the Rev. Jesse Lee With Extracts from his Journals* (New York, 1823), 26–34.

113. Simpson, *American Methodist Pioneer*, 64, 149.

114. Ibid., 69–71. On Brown's identity, see William H. Williams, *The Garden of American Methodism: The Delmarva Peninsula, 1769–1820* (Wilmington, DE, 1984), 33.

115. Gatch, "Autobiography," Gatch Microfilm Group I, MTSO, pp. 25–27, recapitulated in slightly altered form in John McLean, comp., *Sketch of Rev. Philip Gatch* (Cincinnati, 1854), 44–49.

116. Benjamin Abbott, *The Experience and Gospel Labours of the Rev. Benjamin Abbott: To Which is Annexed a Narrative of His Life and Death by John Ffirth* (Philadelphia, 1801), 30–32.

117. Littlejohn, Journal, vol. 4, 15 March 1778.

118. Wakeley, *Lost Chapters*, 454–55, and Lednum, *History*, 194.

119. For Methodist preaching scheduled to coincide with militia exercises with open invitation to women, see EC, Journal (1784–1800), 13 vols., GTS, 1:2.

120. Simpson, *American Methodist Pioneer*, 189. On masculine values, see Christine Leigh Heyrman, *Southern Cross: The Beginnings of the Bible Belt* (New York, 1997), 206–52.

121. *J&L*, 1:267; May, "Francis Asbury." See also Williams, *Garden*, 44–49, Lednum, *History*, 203–72, and *J&L*, 1:262–345, 253n.

122. May, "Francis Asbury," 150–59; Lednum, *History*, 206–11; *J&L*, 1:346. On letter from FA to Rankin, see Thomas Ware, *Sketches of the Life and Travels of Rev. Thomas Ware, Who Has Been an Itinerant Methodist Preacher for More than Fifty Years*, rev. ed. (New York, 1839), 251–52; on White's arrest, see also Caesar Rodney to General [William] Smallwood, 5 April 1778, and [General] W[illiam] Smallwood to Caesar Rodney, 6 April 1778, National Archives, Washington, DC (photostats, HSD).

123. *J&L*, 1:262–80.

124. Williams, *Garden*, 49.

125. *J&L*, 3:298. Anglican supporters included Sydenham Thorne of Milford; Hugh Neill, the former Methodist opponent, now a nonjuror, of St. Paul's parish, Queen Annes County; and Samuel Magaw of Dover (Williams, *Garden*, 51–53).

126. *J&L*, 1:313, 325n; May, "Francis Asbury," 159–64; Littlejohn, Journal, vol. 4, 12 June 1778.

127. *Minutes* (1795), 25, 33, 53.

128. Ibid., 18; Jarratt, *A Brief Narrative of Religion in Virginia*, extracted in *J&L*, 1:207–24.

129. *Minutes* (1795), 21.

130. Ibid., 21, 40, 53; John Fanning Watson, *Annals of Philadelphia, and Pennsylvania, in the Olden Time; being a Collection of Memoirs, Anecdotes, and Incidents of the City and Its Inhabitants, and of the Earliest Settlements of the Inland Part of Pennsylvania*, 3 vols. (Philadelphia, 1881), 1:456; Lednum, *History*, 194. On the business of the NY society, see John Street MEC, "Cash Book." The society was damaged at the end of the war by the loyalist exodus to Nova Scotia, already a destination for Methodists from Yorkshire: see John Dickins to Edward Dromgoole, 4 July 1783, Edward Dromgoole Papers, microfilm edition, SHC/UNC; and Bailyn, *Voyagers to the West*, 420–26.

131. Simpson, *American Methodist Pioneer*, 91; *J&L*, 1:308.

132. R[ichar]d Smith to Pres. Reed, 24 February 1781, *Pennsylvania Archives*, vol. 8 (1779–1781), 740–41.

133. Harvey, "Wesleyan Movement," 312–15; Overfield, "Patriot Dilemma," 159.

134. Williams, *Garden*, 64, and Bibbins, *How Methodism Came*, 73–74.

135. *Minutes* (1795), 91–93.

136. Gatch, "Autobiography," 37.

137. *Reasons against a Separation from the Church of England*, in *Works*, 9:334.

138. Carol Van Voorst, *The Anglican Clergy in Maryland, 1692–1776* (New York, 1989), 122, 206–16, and Sandra Ryan Dresbeck, "The Episcopalian Clergy in Maryland and Virginia, 1765–1805" (Ph.D. diss. University of California, Los Angeles, 1976), 232–34. On the traditional view of Anglican failure, see William Warren Sweet, *Religion in the Development of American Culture, 1765–1840* (New York, 1952), 67 ff.; on the Anglicans' ambivalent acceptance of religious pluralism in PH, see Gough, "Pluralism," 361–431.

139. John Frederick Woolverton, *Colonial Anglicanism in North America* (Detroit, 1984), 233, and David L. Holmes, "The Episcopal Church and the American Revolution," *Historical Magazine of the Protestant Episcopal Church* 48 (1978): 270–71.

140. Wallace N. Jamison, *Religion in New Jersey: A Brief History* (Princeton, 1964), 63–67, Holmes, "Episcopal Church and the American Revolution," 261–91, Butler, *Awash in a Sea of Faith*, 206–12, and Richard W. Pointer, "Religious Life in New York during the Revolutionary War," *New York History* 66 (1985): 357–73.

141. Paul S. Sanders, "The Sacraments in Early American Methodism," in *Perspectives on American Methodism: Interpretive Essays*, ed. Russell E. Richey, Kenneth E. Rowe, and Jean Miller Schmidt (Nashville, 1993), 81–92.

142. Lee, *Short History*, 90.

143. Quoted in Gatch, "Minutes," 1779, in Gatch Microfilm, "Minutes" (1774–1779), Group II, MTSO. See also Lee, *Short History*, 67–70; *J&L*, 1:238–39; and account of the conference from Gatch's minutes in McLean, *Sketch of Rev. Philip Gatch*, 67–73.

144. Baker, *From Wesley*, 39. See also Chandler, "Prelude," 54–55, 541n. For subsequent conferences dealing with the same issues, see *J&L*, 1:346–50, 346n; *Minutes* (1795), 35–41; Watters, *Short Account*, 30–32; and Simpson, *American Methodist Pioneer*, 104, 174–76.

145. *J&L*, 1:411; Maser, *Robert Strawbridge*, 55–57. Robert Strawbridge's inventory after his death lists the basic possessions of a small farmer, and no slaves: Inv., 1782, BA Invs., Box 25, fold. 39, MDSA. Strawbridge's sons Robert and Theophilus were apprenticed as orphans: Orphans Court Proceedings, BA County, 1783, MDSA.

146. Lee, *Short History*, 84–85; *J&L*, 1:462, 462n.

147. Among these were William Duke, Thomas Haskins, and John Littlejohn: see chap. 7 below. See also Robert T. Handy, *A History of the Churches in the United States and Canada* (New York, 1977), 146–47, William White, *Memorials of the Protestant Episcopal Church in the United States of America* (New York, 1880), 13–27, and Butler, *Awash in a Sea of Faith*, 212–24.

148. "Minutes of Conference held April 16. 1781. at Choptank. Deleware state & adjourn'd to Baltimore," Cole Collection of the Bond Family Papers, Special Collections, 1571, MDSA.

149. Ware, *Sketches*, 104.

150. *J&L*, 3:29–31.

151. JW to the Preachers in America, 3 October 1783, *Letters*, vol. 7 (1780–1787), 190–91; *J&L*, 1:450. JW also appears to have been prejudiced against FA's leadership by Thomas Rankin, who had reportedly announced at one of the English conferences that "[i]f he . . . had the power and authority of Mr. Wesley, he would call Frank Asbury home directly": *J&L*, 3:547.

152. Frank Baker, *John Wesley and the Church of England* (Nashville, 1970), 209–12.

153. Ibid., 222–28, 265–78. For further details on the Deed of Declaration, see E. Benson Perkins, *Methodist Preaching Houses and the Law: The Story of the Model Deed* (London, 1952), 43–45. JW wrote to the bishop of London regarding his frustration with the church's refusal to ordain Methodist preachers because of their lack of Greek or Latin: 10 August 1780, *Letters*, 7:29–31.

154. *DNB*, s.v. TC; John Vickers, *Thomas Coke: Apostle of Methodism* (Nashville, 1969), chap. 4, "Right-Hand Man"; TC and Thomas Parker, *A Plan of the Society for the Establishment of Missions among the Heathens* ([London], [1784]).

155. Letters quoted in Vickers, *Thomas Coke*, 76–78.

156. After the formation of the American church, Charles Wesley wrote: "But what are your poor Methodists now? Only a new sect of Presbyterians!" Charles Wesley to Dr. Chandler, 28 April 1785, in *Charles Wesley: A Reader*, ed. John R. Tyson (New York, 1989), 61. Wesley wrote several poems on the subject of TC and FA's later adoption of the title "bishop," including one attacking Asbury's low status:

> A Roman emperor, 'tis said;
> His favorite horse a counsul made;
> But Coke brings greater things to pass,
> He makes a bishop of an ass.

Quoted in W. Thomas Smith, "Attempts at Methodist and Moravian Union," *MH* 8 (1970): 40.

157. For overviews, see Baker, *From Wesley*, 137–59, and Vickers, *Thomas Coke*, 68–99. Among the other English Methodists, the Calvinists in Lady Huntingdon's connection ordained new preachers beginning in 1783; Howel Harris's movement, the North and South Wales Associations, introduced ordained preachers in 1810–1811 (Michael Watts, *The Dissenters from the Reformation to the French Revolution* [Oxford, 1978], 448–50). See profiles of TC, Whatcoat, and Vasey in *Works*, vol. 23, *Journal and Diaries VI (1776–1786)*, ed. W. Reginald Ward and Richard P. Heitzenrater (Nashville, 1995), 372n, 329–30n.

158. *Works*, 23:330n; [JW], "Certificate of appointment for T. Coke as superintendent," 2 September 1784, photostat, Coke MSS, Methodist Missionary Society, London; [JW], "Certificate of Ordination as elders, to R. Whatcoat and T. Vasey" [2 September 1784], MS draft, Department of Manuscripts, Additional 41295, f. 20, BM.

159. JW to "Our Brethren in America," 10 September 1784, reprinted in *Letters*, 7:237–39.

160. JW to FA, 31 October 1784, Manuscript Letters of John Wesley, Archives, Center for Methodist Studies at Bridwell Library, Perkins School of Theology, Southern Methodist University. The founding Christmas Conference had probably already occurred by the time FA received this communication.

161. For the commonly accepted view that Wesley intended to found a new church, see Frank Baker, "The Status of Methodist Preachers in America, 1769–1791," in *Rethinking Methodist History: A Bicentennial Consultation*, ed. Russell E. Richey and Kenneth E. Rowe (Nashville, 1985), 29–36, and Vickers's defense of TC's actions in *Thomas Coke*, 69–70. The strongest statement to the contrary was made many years ago by church historian John A. Faulkner, who attributed the formation of the MEC to a combination of Wesley's expedience, TC's ambition, and Asbury's experience: "Did Wesley Intend to Found the Methodist Episcopal Church?" in idem, *Burning Questions in Historical Christianity* (New York, 1930), 207–32. Closer to the events, Charles Wesley thought likewise: Vickers, *Thomas Coke*, 101–4.

Further evidence of TC's hand in the creation of the church comes from his correspondence and meetings with Bishop William White in 1791, when TC attempted a union of the Protestant Episcopal and Methodist Episcopal Churches. As TC wrote at the time: "I am not sure but I went farther in the seperation of our Church in America, than M^r. Wesley, from whom I had received my commission, did intend. He did indeed solemnly invest me, as far as he has a right so to do, with Episcopal Authority, but did not intend, I think, that an entire seperation should take place": TC to Bishop William White, 24 April 1791, microfilm, NYHS.

162. Baker, "Status of Methodist Preachers," 33; TC, *Extracts of the Journals of the Late Rev. Thomas Coke, L.L.D.; Comprising Several Visits to North-America and the West-Indies; His Tour Through Part of Ireland, and His Nearly Finished Voyage to Bombay in the East Indies* (Dublin, 1816), 40.

163. Warren Thomas Smith, "The Christmas Conference," *MH* 6 (1968): 6; quotation from Vickers, *Thomas Coke*, 80–81.

164. Simpson, *American Methodist Pioneer*, 243. When FG published his journal in 1791, he wrote, "Mr. Wesley had gratified the desires of thousands of his friends in America, in sending a power of ordination, and giving his consent to our becoming a separate church" (ibid., 122). But William Williams has discovered that FG crossed out the phrase "and giving his consent" in his personal copy of *Experiences and Travels*: see Williams, *Garden*, 68.

165. TC, *Extracts of the Journals*, 45. See also Williams, *Garden*, 64.

166. *J&L*, 1:471–72; and TC, *Extracts of the Journals*, 45–46.

167. Simpson, introduction to *American Methodist Pioneer*, 7; Adam Fonerden to unidentified, 28 November 1784, UMHS; Edward Dromgoole to FA, 29 December 1805, MS copy, Bruce Cotten Collection, in Edward Dromgoole Papers Microfilm edition, SHC/UNC.

168. Journal, no. 6 (1784–1785), 22 December 1784, microfilm, LCMD. Jesse Lee also complained of the haste with which the meeting was called, and that FG had failed to reach a number of the preachers "who were in the extremities of the work" (*Short History*, 93–94).

169. Rev. John Andrews to Dr. Smith, 31 December 1784, in William Smith, *Life and Correspondence of the Rev. William Smith*, ed. Horace Wemyss Smith, 2 vols. (Philadelphia, 1880), 2:243–46; Devereux Jarratt to Edward Dromgoole, 31 May 1785, in Edward

Dromgoole Papers. Jarratt, up to this time a Methodist ally, may have been excluded from the conference because he was an advocate of southern slaveholders: see TC, *Extracts of the Journals*, 68.

170. *Minutes* (1795), 75–82. The attendance is reconstructed in Smith, "Christmas Conference," 20–21.

171. Journal, no. 6, 24–31 December 1784.

172. *J&L*, 1:474. FA's ordination certificate, dated 27 December 1784, is housed at UMHS and reprinted in *J&L*, 1:474.

173. Edward Dromgoole to Nicholas Snethen, 24 February 1802, MS copy, Bruce Cotten Collection, in Edward Dromgoole Papers.

174. *Minutes of Several Conversations Between The Rev. Thomas Coke, LL.D., The Rev. Francis Asbury and Others, at a Conference, Begun in Baltimore, in the State of Maryland, on Monday, the 27th of December, in the Year 1784. Composing a Form of Discipline for the Ministers, Preachers and Other Members of the Methodist Episcopal Church in America* (Philadelphia, 1785), 3.

175. Among the twenty elders ordained in 1784–1785, only James O'Kelly and Henry Willis had been among the earlier Gatch supporters; LeRoy Cole, Reuben Ellis, and Nelson Reed had all moved to Asbury's side by the 1781 meeting at Choptank, Delaware: Lee, *Short History*, 94–95; Smith, "Christmas Conference," 20–21.

176. Ware, *Sketches*, 106. For the minute on slavery, see chap. 5 below.

177. TC, *The Substance of a Sermon, Preached at Baltimore, in the State of Maryland, Before the General Conference of the Methodist Episcopal Church, on the 27th of December, 1784, at the Ordination of Francis Asbury to the Office of Superintendent* (Baltimore, 1785), 6–7. In this sermon, TC overtly attributes to Wesley the decision to form a separate church in America: "After long deliberation, he saw it his duty to form his Society in *America* into an independent Church . . ." (8). The Anglicans believed Wesley was angling to raid their churches: see Abraham Beach to SPG, 8 February 1785, quoted in Nelson R. Burr, *The Anglican Church in New Jersey* (Philadelphia, 1954), 312.

178. For the varying goals of American churches at the end of the war, see William G. McLoughlin, "The Role of Religion in the Revolution: Liberty of Conscience and Cultural Cohesion in the New Nation," in *Essays on the American Revolution*, ed. Stephen G. Kurtz and James H. Hutson (Chapel Hill, NC 1973), Stephen Botein, "Religious Dimensions of the Early American State," in *Beyond Confederation: Origins of the Constitution and American National Identity*, ed. Richard Beeman, Stephen Botein, and Edward C. Carter II (Chapel Hill, NC, 1987), 315–30, and Ruth H. Bloch, *Visionary Republic: Millennial Themes in American Thought, 1756–1800* (New York, 1985), chap. 5. Bloch observes elsewhere that by the 1780s a number of the American churches that had favored close ties between politics and religion before the Revolution now saw greater possibilities of influence outside the political sphere: "Religion and Ideological Change in the American Revolution," in *Religion and American Politics: From the Colonial Period to the 1980s*, ed. Mark A. Noll (New York, 1990), 56–57.

179. Ware, *Sketches*, 245–46.

C H A P T E R T H R E E
T H E M A K I N G O F A M E T H O D I S T

1. John Littlejohn, Journal, 10 vols. (1776–1832), vol. 1 (n.d.–1776), opening pages, microfilm, KWC.

2. See overviews in Anthony F. C. Wallace, *Religion: An Anthropological View* (New York, 1966), and Clifford Geertz, "Religion as a Cultural System," in *Anthropological Approaches to Religion*, ed. Michael Banton (New York, 1966), 1–46.

3. Wallace, *Religion*, 106, 130–32. For recent historical treatments of ritual, see Leigh Eric Schmidt, *Holy Fairs: Scottish Communions and American Revivals in the Early Modern Period* (Princeton, 1989), 69–114, and David D. Hall, *Worlds of Wonder, Days of Judgment: Popular Religious Belief in Early New England* (New York, 1989), 166–212.

4. Examples appear throughout Methodist correspondence and journals. Methodists' efforts to speak at other denominations' chapels were not always successful: In Shrewsbury, New Jersey, "a town in which the quakers, baptists, presbyterans and episcopalians each had a house of worship," Benjamin Abbott found that "they all, as with one accord, refused me the liberty of their houses": *The Experience and Gospel Labours of the Rev. Benjamin Abbott: To Which is Annexed a Narrative of His Life and Death by John Ffirth* (Philadelphia, 1801), 184.

5. Jesse Lee, *A Short History of the Methodists, in the United States of America: beginning in 1766, and continued till 1809* (Baltimore, 1810), 139.

6. See e.g., Thomas Ware, *Sketches of the Life and Travels of Rev. Thomas Ware, Who Has Been an Itinerant Methodist Preacher For More than Fifty Years*, rev. ed. (New York, 1839), 63.

7. For examples of advance publicity, see Joseph Pilmore, *The Journal of Joseph Pilmore, Methodist Itinerant, for the Years August 1, 1769 to January 2, 1774*, ed. Frederick E. Maser and Howard T. Maag (Philadelphia, 1969), 108, and *J&L*, ed. Elmer T. Clark, J. Manning Potts, and Jacob S. Payton, 3 vols. (London and Nashville, 1958), 2:279.

8. Richard O. Johnson, "The Development of the Love Feast in Early American Methodism," *MH* 19 (1981): 74–78, and Russell E. Richey, *Early American Methodism* (Bloomington, IN, 1991), 21–32. See also examples in Ware, *Sketches*, 62–69, and *J&L*, 1:382.

9. William Duke estimated a crowd of 1,500 listeners at preaching in PH before the war (William Duke, Journal, 26 vols. [1774–1825], vol. 1 [1774], 17 April 1774, MDA/PEC); FG spoke to crowds of 300 to 2,000 listeners on the Eastern Shore at the end of the war ("Notes and Manuscript Material," in *American Methodist Pioneer: The Life and Journals of the Rev. Freeborn Garrettson*, ed. Robert Drew Simpson [Rutland, VT, 1984], 220–21). In 1787 FA attracted a crowd estimated at 700 near Newburgh, NY, and another 1,000 in the woods near Flanders, NJ (*J&L*, 1:543, 544).

10. Extended descriptions survive for two Methodist revivals: see Devereux Jarratt's account of the 1775–1776 revival in Sussex and Brunswick Counties, Virginia, in *A Brief Narrative of the Revival of Religion in Virginia, In a Letter to a Friend*, reprinted in *J&L*, 1:207–24; and EC, on the 1789 BA revival, in *A Brief Account of the Work in Baltimore*, reprinted in George A. Phoebus, *Beams of Light on Early Methodism in America. Chiefly Drawn from the Diary, Letters, Manuscripts, Documents, and Original Tracts of the Rev. Ezekiel Cooper* (New York, 1887). Both accounts refer to all-night meetings. In BA, a particularly lively meeting at the Brethren Church lasted for two and one-half hours after the sermon ended: Lee, *Short History*, 139–40. During the same revival, about 1,000 attended a watch night where the "shout" lasted until 2:00 A.M. (EC, Journal, 13 vols. [1784–1802], vol. 5 [1788–1790)] p. 69, GTS).

11. *The Doctrines and Discipline of the Methodist Episcopal Church in America* (1798; reprint ed., Rutland, VT, 1979), 120–21.

12. Methodist ideology, Donald Mathews writes, was a "collage of sound, symbol, and act. It was a style and mood evinced in oral communication": "Evangelical America: The

Methodist Ideology," in *Perspectives on American Methodism: Interpretive Essays*, ed. Russell E. Richey, Kenneth E. Rowe, and Jean Miller Schmidt (Nashville, 1993), 19. See also Hall, *Worlds of Wonder*, 22–31, Harold Bloom on the Bible as talisman in *The American Religion: The Emergence of the Post-Christian Nation* (New York, 1992), 220–21, and Harry S. Stout on the spoken word as event in the Great Awakening in "Religion, Communications, and the Ideological Origins of the American Revolution," *WMQ* 34 (1977): 519–41.

13. Hymn no. 2 in *Works*, vol. 7, *A Collection of Hymns for the use of the People called Methodists*, ed. Franz Hildebrandt and Oliver A. Beckerlegge (Oxford, 1983), 81–82.

14. Jesse Lee, *A Short Account of the Life and Death of the Rev. John Lee, A Methodist Minister in the United States of America* (Baltimore, 1805), 26.

15. John Fanning Watson, *Annals of Philadelphia and Pennsylvania in the Olden Time*, 2 vols. (Philadelphia, 1856), 1:457–58. Singing at revivals was often managed by line reading, in which a preacher spoke the verse of a hymn, which the participants sang in response. An account of line reading and alternative verse singing by men and women at the African Methodist Bethel Church in PH, ca. 1811–1813, appears in Robert Stevenson, *Protestant Church Music in America: A Short Survey of Men and Movements from 1564 to the Present* (1966; NY, 1970), 95–96. See also "Of the Spirit and Truth of Singing," in *D&D* (1798), 122–25. Later, at the camp meetings, "[v]erses were shortened, refrains added, and expressions and ejaculations interpolated. Familiar tunes were put to use. A common practice was to reduce each stanza of text to four lines and follow this by a chorus, which was to be repeated at the end of each stanza": Robert Emerson Coleman, "Factors in the Expansion of the Methodist Episcopal Church from 1784 to 1812" (Ph.D. diss., State University of Iowa, 1954), 357.

16. An examination of the hymnbooks suggests the extent to which the Wesleyans focused as much on holiness as on damnation, the latter overemphasized in Christine Leigh Heyrman, *Southern Cross: The Beginnings of the Bible Belt* (New York, 1997).

17. Bernard Manning, quoted in introduction to *Works*, 7:26. Preface in *Works*, 7:79, 606.

18. On Methodist hymnbooks available in America before 1800, see Leland D. Case, "Origins of Methodist Publishing in America," Bibliographical Society of America, *Papers* 59 (1965): 12–23. See also James Penn Pilkington, *The Methodist Publishing House: A History*, vol. 1 (Nashville, 1968), 26–29, 79–115: John Dickins, the first American Methodist book steward, issued a number of hymnbooks beginning in 1787, by far the most popular being *A Pocket Hymn-Book, Designed as a Constant Companion for the Pious*, based on Robert Spence's pirated edition of JW's *Collection of Hymns for the Use of the People Called Methodists* (1780), and not to be confused with JW's volume of same name. Pilkington, *Methodist Publishing House*; editions of the *Pocket Hymn-Book* were first published by other printers in PH, NY, and BA between 1791 and 1795. Between 1799 and 1804, EC, the second book steward, printed 50,300 copies of the hymnbook, which accounted for nearly one-third of all volumes printed: EC, "Account of Books, pamphlets etc. published for the Methodist Connection by E Cooper since the 10th of June 1799," EC Papers, DUL.

19. On the English tune books, *Sacred Melody* and *Sacred Harmony*, see introduction to *Works*, 7:25; *A Pocket Hymn-Book, Designed as a Constant Companion for the Pious. Collected from Various Authors*, 20th ed. (Philadelphia, 1795), i.

20. See "An Account of the most remarkable Occurrences in the Life of Joseph Everett, In a Letter to Bishop Asbury. (Written by himself) [1788]," *Arminian Magazine* (PH) 2 (1790): 510. Hymn singing or reading was also a form of private devotion. Henry Boehm

writes of FA: "The bishop sang as he walked the floor, and this he often did when in deep meditation": *Reminiscences Historical and Biographical of Sixty-Four Years in the Ministry* (New York, 1866), 443.

21. See Methodists' reaction to Roman Catholic iconography and worship in Abbott, *Experience*, 94, and William Jessop, Journal (1790–1791), 41–42, OSHS.

22. *Pocket Hymn-Book*, Hymn no. 20, p. 24. The gist of the contents of the pocket edition did not differ significantly from the other Wesleyan collections. See, for example, an early volume available to Americans: John Wesley, *Hymns and Spiritual Songs, Intended for the Use of Real Christians of all Denominations*, 14th ed. (reprint ed., Philadelphia, 1770). In the preface, Wesley stresses, typically, the "truly catholic spirit" and the "spirit of love" now arising among men of different opinions and denominations (iii–iv).

23. *Pocket Hymn-Book*, Hymn no. 55, p. 59; Hymn no. 71, p. 74. See also Hymn no. 56, p. 60 ("Infinite, unexhausted Love! Jesus and love are one . . ."), for another of numerous examples throughout the hymnal.

24. Ibid., Hymn no. 55, p. 59; and Hymn no. 71, p. 74. See also no. 45, p. 49.

25. E. P. Thompson, *The Making of the English Working Class* (1963; London, 1980), 405, 408–9, 411–30. For Thompson's full statements on religion and the working class, see ibid., 28–58, 385–440. See also Thompson's defense of his anti-Methodist argument in ibid., 917–23, and Barbara Taylor's sympathetic but critical assessment of Thompson in "Religion, Radicalism, and Fantasy," *History Workshop*, no. 39 (1995): 102–12. The definitive treatment of Methodist hymns is introduction to *Works*, 7:1–69.

26. Richard Godbeer, " 'Love Raptures': Marital, Romantic, and Erotic Images of Jesus Christ in Puritan New England, 1670–1730," *New England Quarterly* 68 (1995): 373. See also Caroline Walker Bynum, *Jesus as Mother: Studies in the Spirituality of the High Middle Ages* (Berkeley, 1982), Gillian Lindt Gollin, *Moravians in Two Worlds: A Study of Changing Communities* (New York, 1967), 9–22, 90, and introduction to *Works*, 7:1–22, 31–38.

27. Stout, "Religion," 527–30, Sandra Rennie, "The Role of the Preacher: Index to the Consolidation of the Baptist Movement in Virginia from 1760 to 1790," *Virginia Magazine of History and Biography* 88 (1980): 430–41, and Rhys Isaac, "Preachers and Patriots: Popular Culture and the Revolution in Virginia," in *The American Revolution: Explorations in the History of American Radicalism*, ed. Alfred F. Young (De Kalb, IL, 1976), 125–56. The Methodist Articles of Faith were printed in the MEC discipline: see *D&D* (1798), 9–30, and "Of Christian Perfection" and "Against Antinomianism," in ibid., 184–87. The main source of doctrine was JW's *Notes Upon the New Testament* and his four volumes of *Sermons*: Frank Baker, *From Wesley to Asbury: Studies in Early American Methodism* (Durham, NC, 1976), 168–72.

28. Simpson, *American Methodist Pioneer*, 41.

29. Minton Thrift, comp., *Memoir of the Rev. Jesse Lee With Extracts from His Journals* (New York, 1823), 355–56. See also FA in Boehm, *Reminiscences* (441). The texts of Methodist sermons were often copied down after they were preached: R. A. Knox, *Enthusiasm: A Chapter in the History of Religion, with Special Reference to the Seventeenth and Eighteenth Centuries* (Oxford, 1950), 514, and EC, Journal, vol. 13 (1798–1802), 6 January 1799.

30. "Of the Matter and Manner of Preaching, and of other public Exercises," in *D&D* (1798), 84–85. In their notes, TC and FA also urge the preachers to be especially punctual at the city societies "where they have clocks and watches to direct them" (88). On the length of sermons, see John Lee, who spoke "loud, fast, and long" for an hour and a quarter at a Long Island meeting and then complained of a New Light minister who "prayed

till I was quite weary, and then he spoke near two hours": Lee, *Short Account of John Lee*, 47, 60.

31. On JW's sermon formats, see preface to *Works*, vol. 1, *Sermons I*, ed. Albert C. Outler (Nashville, 1984), 97.

32. James Dempster, "A few remarks on Some Select Texts for my own use," in Preaching Notes I (1774–1776, 1779–1783), 1774–1775, microfilm, DUL.

33. Ibid., 7.

34. Ibid., 172–76.

35. Outlines of FA's sermons appear in *J&L*, passim. See, for example, 1:44, 323, 771. See also Thrift, *Memoir*, appendix, 355–60.

36. In a five-month period in BA, Richard Whatcoat preached from sixty-two Old Testament texts, seventy New Testament texts, and five texts from the Book of Revelation: Richard Whatcoat, "List of texts," in Journal, vol. 2 (1792–1793), LCMD. Robert Ayres favored the New Testament and Book of Revelation: see "memorandum of Texts preach'd" (1785), in Journal, 5 vols. (1785–1845), vol. 2 (1785–1786), microfilm, DUL. Dempster wrote in one sermon outline: "Many lay aside the greater part of the Old Testament, as a nonintelligable book. . . . [N]evertheless, by Divine assistance, we may all understand as much as is necessary for our present and future Comfort": see "A few remarks," 188–89.

37. Stout, "Religion," 530–40. Perhaps the best source for laboring men's language turned to religious uses is Abbott, *Experience*. Abbott's biographer, John Ffirth, refers to the preacher as "a truly primitive methodist preacher" ("A Narrative of the Life and Death of the Rev. Benjamin Abbott," in ibid., 222).

38. During the Revolutionary War, FA's sermons were frequently on the subject of Christian divisions: see *J&L*, 1: passim. See also Boehm, *Reminiscences*: "The bishop [FA] was peculiar in adapting his subject to times and circumstances": 441–42.

39. James Dempster, Preaching Texts (1770–1774), microfilm, DUL: typical abbreviations are "c. Pot." (with power), "c. Lib." (with liberty), and "c. Dul." (with sweetness). William Jessop wrote of an unsuccessful meeting filled with such "hard-hearted hearers" that "I found it almost as hard work as splitting a black Gum": Journal (1790–1791), 1 September 1790.

40. See, for example, William Watters and Abraham Whitworth's confrontation with an Anglican minister in *A Short Account of the Christian Experience and Ministereal Labours of William Watters Drawn Up By Himself* (Alexandria, VA, 1806), 38–39.

41. Thomas Lyell, "Autobiography" (ca. 1837), 7 vols., vol. 2 (1790/91–ca. 1795), n.p., SHC/UNC.

42. Lee, *Short History*, 139–40.

43. Abbott, *Experience*, 190.

44. Ibid., 165–66.

45. Colbert, Journal, 10 vols. (1790–1833), vol. 2 (1794–1798), p. 3, microfilm, GTS.

46. The description of evangelical religion as "emotional" has been a commonplace since the eighteenth century. For a critique, see Frederick Dreyer, "Faith and Experience in the Thought of John Wesley," *AHR* 88 (1983): 12–30.

47. John L. Brooke, *The Refiner's Fire: The Making of Mormon Cosmology, 1644–1844* (Cambridge, 1994), 30–58, and Jon Butler, *Awash in a Sea of Faith: Christianizing the American People* (Cambridge, MA, 1990), 164–93.

48. Butler, *Awash in a Sea of Faith*, esp. 67–97, and Brooke, *Refiner's Fire*. See also Hall, *Worlds of Wonder*, on seventeenth-century New England, and Alan Taylor, "The Early Republic's Supernatural Economy: Treasure Seeking in the American Northeast,

1780–1830," *AQ* 38 (1986): 6–34. James Obelkevich, *Religion and Rural Society in South Lindsey, 1825–1875* (Oxford, 1976), provides examples of long-lived magical beliefs in Britain. On the ritual bases of African survivals, see Sidney W. Mintz and Richard Price, *The Birth of African-American Culture: An Anthropological Study* (1976; Boston, 1992), 45–47, and Albert J. Raboteau, *Slave Religion: The "Invisible Institution" in the Antebellum South* (New York, 1978), 24–36.

49. See recent work on the Mormons: D. Michael Quinn, *Early Mormonism and the Magic World View* (Salt Lake City, 1987), Bloom, *American Religion*, 77–128, and Brooke, *Refiner's Fire*.

50. Keith Thomas, *Religion and the Decline of Magic* (New York, 1971), 638, 641–68; see also Butler, *Awash in a Sea of Faith*, 92–93.

51. Raboteau, *Slave Religion*, 11–15, 24–36.

52. See especially Ruth H. Bloch, *Visionary Republic: Millennial Themes in American Thought, 1756–1800* (Cambridge, 1985), 188, and idem, "The Social and Political Base of Millennial Literature in Late Eighteenth-Century America," *AQ* 40 (1988): 378–96.

53. Duke, Journal, vol. 5 (1775–1776), 14 December 1775.

54. *D&D* (1798), iii, 89.

55. CLG to [Catharine Rutsen], 17 December 1793, Garrettson Papers, DUL.

56. Nathan Bangs, ed., *The Life of the Rev. Freeborn Garrettson; compiled from his printed and manuscript journals, and other authentic documents* (New York, 1829), 224–25. Likewise, a Quaker woman believed she had been led to Benjamin Abbott's preaching by a premonitory dream: Abbott, *Experience*, 51–52.

57. Abbott, *Experience*, 61.

58. Ibid., 100.

59. Representative work is John Putnam Demos, *Entertaining Satan: Witchcraft and the Culture of Early New England* (New York, 1982), Carol F. Karlsen, *The Devil in the Shape of a Woman: Witchcraft in Colonial New England* (New York, 1987), and Richard Godbeer, *The Devil's Dominion: Magic and Religion in Early New England* (Cambridge, 1992). Regarding African and Indian varieties of possession, see Melville J. Herskovits, *Myth of the Negro Past* (1941; Boston, 1990), 215–35, and Raboteau, *Slave Religion*, 59–65.

60. Obelkevich, *Religion and Rural Society*, 231.

61. Pilmore, *Journal*, 73, and FG, "The Garrettson Journals," in Simpson, *American Methodist Pioneer*, 299. Other examples abound: see references to the Greenwich circuit in New Jersey (Duke, Journal, vol. 5, 24 January 1776), and to Sussex County, Delaware (Ayres, Journal, vol. 1 [1785–1786], 25 April 1786). As late as 1810 in Camden, New Jersey, a woman was thought "crazy, or bewitched" when she converted to Methodism: G. A. Raybold, *Annals of Methodism or Sketches of the Origin and Progress of Methodism in Various Portions of West Jersey: derived from the most Authentic Sources* (Philadelphia, 1847), 19–21.

62. Pilmore, *Journal*, 73; Abbott, *Experience*, 39–40.

63. Colbert, Journal, vol. 4 (1801–1804), p. 45.

64. The transition in diagnosis from possession to mental illness occurred among the Anglican intelligentsia at the end of the seventeenth century: Michael MacDonald, *Mystical Bedlam: Madness, Anxiety, and Healing in Seventeenth-Century England* (Cambridge, 1981), 121, 207.

65. *Methodist Magazine* (PH) 1 (1797): 167.

66. For examples of Methodists' belief in the devil, see William Jessop, Journal (1788), MSS, AM08611, HSP, 42; *J&L*, 1:319–20; and John Atkinson, *Memorials of Methodism*

in New Jersey, from the foundation of the first society in the State in 1770, to the Completion of the first twenty years of its history, 2d ed. (Philadelphia, 1860), 130 ff. Devil-fearing Benjamin Abbott nevertheless told a backsliding schoolmaster that his vision of two devils was in his imagination: Abbott, *Experience*, 42–43.

67. William Glendinning, *The Life of William Glendinning, Preacher of the Gospel, Written by Himself* (Philadelphia, 1795), 19–35. Glendinning forms the centerpiece of chap. 1, "Raising the Devil," in Heyrman's *Southern Cross*. Compared to that of other Methodists, however, Glendinning's experience more closely resembled a psychotic break-down than an altered religious state, or so Benjamin Rush, himself an evangelical advocate, believed: see description of Glendinning's ordeal in *The Autobiography of Benjamin Rush: His "Travels Through Life" Together with his Commonplace Book for 1789–1813*, ed. George W. Corner (Princeton, 1948), 220–21.

68. The ecstatic features of early Methodism were similar to what I. M. Lewis has called the "main morality" or "central possession religions": *Ecstatic Religion: An Anthropological Study of Spirit Possession and Shamanism* (1971; Harmondsworth, England, 1978), esp. 34. Both Herskovits (*Myth*) and Raboteau (*Slave Religion*) distinguish between American revival ecstaticism and African possession, but Lewis (*Ecstatic Religion*, 37–44) suggests a greater affinity between Christian and non-Christian forms of possession.

69. EC, Journal, vol. 12 (1795–1798), 13 June 1796.

70. John Kobler, Diary, vol. 1 (1789–1792), UMHS, p. 178. References to shouting appear throughout Methodist journals. See, e.g., reference to Zech. 9:9 on scriptural shouting in Abbott, *Experience*, 192. In this instance it is useful to distinguish between the revival shout, a response to external or internal stimuli, and the African ring-dance shout, a course of ritual action to induce a trance state: see Raboteau, *Slave Religion*, 35–36.

71. Abbott, *Experience*, 32–33.

72. *Pocket Hymn-Book*, Hymn no. 56, p. 61; Hymn no. 74, p. 77. See also Hymn no. 68, p. 71, on sanctification; and Hymn no. 104, p. 104, "Refining fire, go through my heart . . . ," as well as hymns throughout the section "Petitioning."

73. Dempster, "A few remarks," 1.

74. Nelson Reed, Diary (1778–1782), vol. 2 (1779), pp. 131–32, typescript, UMHS.

75. Abbott, *Experience*, 193.

76. TC, *The Substance of a Sermon on the Godhead of Christ Preached at Baltimore, in the State of Maryland, on the 26th Day of December, 1784 Before the General Conference of the Methodist Episcopal Church* (London, 1785), 5–6; *J&L*, 1:278. See also *D&D* (1798), 80, for directive to preachers to watch that followers not fall into extremes of behavior.

77. *J&L*, 1:278, quoting from Gal. 1:8–9; and Hymn no. 196, in *Works*, 7:327. JW stressed that the purpose of music was to stir the sensations and common sense together, so that the seeker or believer might thus be better turned to God: JW, "Thoughts on the Power of Music, 1779," appendix I, in ibid., 766–69.

78. Simpson, *American Methodist Pioneer*, 77.

79. Abbott, *Experience*, 151.

80. Watters, *Short Account*, 14–17.

81. Littlejohn, Journal, vol. 1, opening pages. The scriptural reference is to Job 33:15–16.

82. Ibid.

83. John McLean, *Sketch of Rev. Philip Gatch* (Cincinnati, 1854), 6–7.

84. Ibid., 7–11.

85. Ibid., 12–13.

86. Abbott, *Experience*, 5–6; John Ffirth, "A Narrative," in ibid., 218–19; Hugh Smith to EC, 7 October 1801, in ibid., 236–40. On the location of Abbott's farm, see Richard Swain, *Journal of Rev. Richard Swain*, ed. Robert Bevis Steelman (Rutland, VT, 1977), 5n.

87. Abbott, *Experience*, 8.

88. Ibid., 9.

89. Ibid., 11–12.

90. Ibid., 12–14.

91. Ibid., 14–17.

92. [Lucy Fanning Watson], "Wesley M. Watson Family History By His Mother," (1803), WL; idem, "memory and account of New Settlers in the American Woods in 1762 chiefly at Walpole, N.H." (1825), MS copy, WL; idem, "Experience & Incidents in the life of Mrs Lucy Watson, who died at Germantown P^a 5th June 1834, aged 79 Years," MS copy, 4–10, WL; John Fanning Watson, preface to "Experience."

93. Watson, "Experience," 10–13, John Fanning Watson, preface to ibid., and Deborah L. Dependahl, "John Fanning Watson, Historian, 1779–1860" (M.A. thesis, University of Delaware, 1971), 5.

94. Dependahl, "John Fanning Watson," 5, [Watson], "Family History," and idem, "Experience," 14–15.

95. Watson, "Experience," 15–18.

96. Ibid., 20; John Fanning Watson, preface, ibid., n.p.

97. Gary B. Nash, "New Light on Richard Allen: The Early Years of Freedom," *WMQ* 46 (1989): 334–35. On Allen's conversion, see RA, *The Life Experience and Gospel Labours of the Rt. Rev. Richard Allen*, ed. George A. Singleton, reprint ed. (Nashville, 1960).

98. RA, *Life Experience*, 16.

99. Ibid., 15–16. Minor changes in punctuation have been made to clarify the rhyme.

100. On the cross-cultural character of religious seclusion, see Raboteau on African religion, *Slave Religion*, 73, Wallace on Plains Indians' vision quests in *Religion*, 129, and on the Iroquois in *The Death and Rebirth of the Seneca* (1969; New York, 1972), 59–75.

101. CLG, Diary, 15 vols. (1787–1817), vol. 5 (1788–1792), 3 June 1792, Garrettson Papers, DUL; and vol. 6 (1793), 7–12 March 1793. For overview, see [Diane Lobody Zaragoza], "Lost in the Ocean of Love: The Spiritual Writings of Catherine Livingston Garrettson," in *Rethinking Methodist History: A Bicentennial Historical Consultation*, ed. Russell E. Richey and Kenneth E. Rowe (Nashville, 1985), 175–84, and idem [Diane H. Lobody], " 'That Language Might Be Given Me': Women's Experience in Early Methodism," in Richey, Rowe, and Schmidt, *Perspectives*, 127–44.

102. CLG, Diary, vol. 5, 31 August 1791.

103. Caroline Walker Bynum, "Introduction: The Complexity of Symbols," in *Gender and Religion: On the Complexity of Symbols*, ed. idem, Stevan Harrell, and Paula Richman (Boston, 1986), 2–3, and idem, "Women's Stories, Women's Symbols: A Critique of Victor Turner's Theory of Liminality," in *Anthropology and the Study of Religion*, ed. Robert L. Moore and Frank E. Reynolds (Chicago, 1984), 105–25. See also Susan Juster, " 'In a Different Voice': Male and Female Narratives of Religious Conversion in Post-Revolutionary America," *AQ* 41 (March 1989): 34–62, and idem, *Disorderly Women: Sexual Politics and Evangelicalism in Revolutionary New England* (Ithaca, NY, 1994).

104. Methodist men more often divided their life accounts into pre- and postconversion stages. The call to preach was an essential part of the second stage: hence William Jessop writes: "I am now 25 Years of Age, Which time has been spent as follows—viz. First 10 Years in childhood, before I arrived to the Years of understanding, to know good from evil,

in every point. 2ly. 5 Years in Sin. 3ly. 10 Years in the service of GoD . . ." (Jessop, Journal [1790–1791], 56); while FG summarizes his conversion: "It was three years from my conviction, before I was brought through the pangs of the new birth. Eight months elapsed after I was called to preach, before I was willing to leave my all and go out" (Garrettson to JW, 20 April 1785, reprinted in Simpson, *American Methodist Pioneer*, 245). See also Richard T. Vann, *The Social Development of English Quakerism, 1655–1755* (Cambridge, MA, 1969), on Quaker testimony that emphasized the length of conversion rather than a single date, though the Quakers also distinguished between convincement and complete conversion (28–39).

105. James Dempster, Journal (1768–1769), microfilm, 85, DUL; Jessop, Journal (1788), 59. Cf. sec. 2, "For Believers Fighting," in *Works*, 7:398–436. In a typical passage, Kobler writes of contemplating Jesus "in a retired room": "I sit with silent wonder Gazing upon him that is alpha and omega, the beginning and the end, O the boundless perfection of Omnipotence" (Kobler, Diary, vol. 1 [1789–1792], p. 15).

106. B. T. Tanner, *An Outline of Our History and Government For African Methodist Churchmen[,] Ministerial and Lay, In Catechetical Form* (n.p., 1884), 145; Mathews, "Evangelical America," 30.

107. Edward Dromgoole to Henry Waters, 12 September 1776, DUL.

108. See, for example, Schmidt, *Holy Fairs*, 115–68.

109. Barry Levy, *Quakers and the American Family: British Settlement in the Delaware Valley* (New York, 1988), 53–85.

110. Littlejohn, Journal, vol. 1, opening pages.

111. McLean, *Sketch*, 17; Abbott, *Experience*, 21–23.

112. Lucy Fanning Watson, "Experience," 19; RA, *Life Experience*, 16.

113. CLG, Diary, vol. 5, 29 June 1791; Littlejohn, Journal, vol. 1, opening pages.

114. Max Weber, *The Protestant Ethic and the Spirit of Capitalism*, trans. Talcott Parsons (1930; New York, 1958), 140.

115. Victor Turner, *The Ritual Process: Structure and Anti-Structure* (1969; Ithaca, NY, 1977), 94–130; Mathews, "Evangelical America," 23–24.

116. Mircea Eliade, *Rites and Symbols of Initiation: The Mysteries of Birth and Rebirth* (1958; New York, 1975), introduction, 61–103, 127–30. Further affinity between conversions and rites of passage may be found in the numbers of converts in their teenage or young adult years and the itinerants' select membership in the fraternity of the Methodist conference.

117. Swain, *Journal*, 23–24; Colbert, Journal, 3 (1797–1801), p. 35.

118. " 'On the right METHOD of meeting CLASSES and BANDS, in the Methodist Societies' [By the late Mr. Charles Perronet]," *Methodist Magazine* (PH) 1 (1797): 413–15. The directions for the bands were longer, more stringent, and more monastic (see *D&D* [1798], 146–53).

119. *D&D* (1798), 133–34. In *Primitive Physic*, JW further extolled moderation: "Abstain from all mixed, all high-seasoned food. Use plain diet, easy of digestion; and this as sparingly as you can, consistent with ease and strength. Drink only water, if it agrees with your stomach; if not, good clear, small beer" (reprint ed. [1747; London, 1960], 29).

120. Mary Douglas, *Purity and Danger: An Analysis of the Concepts of Pollution and Taboo* (New York, 1966). Douglas writes: "[I]deas about separating, purifying, demarcating and punishing transgressions have as their main function to impose system on an inherently untidy experience" (4).

121. Rhys Isaac, *The Transformation of Virginia, 1740–1790* (Chapel Hill, NC, 1982), 163–64. See also idem, "Evangelical Revolt: The Nature of the Baptists' Challenge to the Traditional Order in Virginia, 1765 to 1775," *WMQ* 31 (1974): 345–68.

122. Examples appear throughout Methodist journals and histories: on fighting, see Atkinson, *Memorials of Methodism*, 353–55, G. A. Raybold, *Reminiscences of Methodism in West Jersey* (New York, 1849), 130–31, and Duke (Journal, vol. 3 [1774–1775], 30 January 1775), who reported on fistfighting in Leesburg: "[O]ne of them who I saw at a distance appeared to be as bloody as if the skin was plead [*sic*] off"; on dancing, see Watters, *Short Account*, 3–17, John Hagerty to Edward Dromgoole, 19 January 1778, in *Religion on the American Frontier, 1783–1840*, ed. William Warren Sweet, vol. 4, *The Methodists: A Collection of Source Materials* (Chicago, 1946), 125–28, and Reed, Diary, vol. 3 (1779–1781), p. 105; on sport shooting, see Colbert, Journal, 1:63, for Colbert's efforts to discourage an elderly man from a turkey shoot on St. Patrick's Day; on theatricals, see Atkinson, *Memorials of Methodism*, 240–41. Regarding sectarian Protestant attitudes toward pagan practices, see James Axtell, "The Indian Impact on English Colonial Culture," in idem, *The European and the Indian: Essays in the Ethnohistory of Colonial North America* (Oxford, 1981), 272–315, and EC, Journal, 5:123–24; EC also criticized a St. Tammany's Day parade in New York in which participants were painted like Indians: ibid., 158.

123. EC, Journal, 5:67–68.

124. Swain, *Journal*, 18. See also Littlejohn, Journal, vol. 2 (1776–1777), 2 August 1777: Littlejohn "was much pleased with" verses on the thoughts of a dying Christian: "I come I come, & joyfully obey / The fatal Voice y^t summons me away / With pleasure [I] resign this mortal breath / And fall a will^g sacrifice to death."

125. For examples, see George Shadford, "A short account of the death of Mrs. Moore, of Baltimore, in Maryland . . . in a letter to a friend," *Arminian Magazine* (PH) 2 (1790): 147; William Glendinning, *A Short Account of the Exemplary Life and Triumphant Death of Theodosia Maxey, A Young Woman of Virginia, Whose Death happened on the 3d day of March, 1793* (Philadelphia, 1794); and Edward Dromgoole, "On the Death of my Son Edward" (1784), Edward Dromgoole Papers, microfilm edition, reel no. 1, SHC/UNC. For a typical reference to a dying man's weeping interpreted as spiritual joy, see Simpson, *American Methodist Pioneer*, 209.

126. See biographical obituaries throughout *Methodist Magazine* (NY) 1–11 (1818–1828).

127. Elijah Ellis to Henry Waters, 3 December 1785, Miscellaneous MSS, DUL; and Jessop, Journal (1790–1791), 18 July 1790.

128. William Weems to FA, 15 March 1791, EC Collection, GTS. For a less sympathetic interpretation of Methodism's impact on the poor and middling classes and the effects of "work-discipline," see Thompson, *Making*, 402, 416–17, and idem, "Time, Work-Discipline, and Industrial Capitalism," *PP*, no. 50 (1971): 56–59.

129. Littlejohn, Journal, vol. 1, opening pages.

130. Ibid., vol. 2, 25 November 1776.

131. Thompson, *Making*, 385–440. Thompson uses the phrase ironically, quoting from Andrew Ure's 1835 *Philosophy of Manufactures* (398).

CHAPTER FOUR
EVANGELICAL SISTERS

1. John Bunyan, *The Pilgrim's Progress* (Harmondsworth, England, 1985), 215, 315–16.

2. Christine Leigh Heyrman, *Southern Cross: The Beginnings of the Bible Belt* (New York, 1997), 117–60.

3. Frank Baker, *From Wesley to Asbury: Studies in Early American Methodism* (Durham, NC, 1976), 13; Robert F. Wearmouth, *Methodism and the Common People of the Eighteenth Century* (London, 1945), 223–24; Leslie F. Church, *More About the Early Methodist People* (London, 1949), 136–76; and Earl Kent Brown, *Women of Mr. Wesley's Methodism* (New York, 1983), 15–37, 90–99, and appendix, 239–46.

4. Barbara Taylor, *Eve and the New Jerusalem: Socialism and Feminism in the Nineteenth Century* (New York, 1983), 118–82, Julia Stewart Warner, *The Primitive Methodist Connexion: Its Background and Early History* (Madison, WI, 1984), 140–45, and Deborah M. Valenze, *Prophetic Sons and Daughters: Female Preaching and Popular Religion in Industrial England* (Princeton, 1985).

5. Abel Stevens, "Barbara Heck and American Methodism," in idem, *Women of Methodism* (New York, 1866), 175–212; Baker, *From Wesley*, 42–43.

6. J. B. Wakeley, *Lost Chapters Recovered from the Early History of American Methodism* (New York, 1858), 69–72.

7. Mary [Evans Thorn] Parker to TC and Adam Clarke, 29 July 1813, OSHS.

8. Ibid. Thorn's former Baptist pastor in Charleston, South Carolina, warned that "[t]hese rapturous Thoughts have, I doubt not, raised you to the invisible World of Spirits; . . . you will soon find that you are yet in the Body": Oliver Hart to [Mary Thorn], 1 April 1772, OSHS.

9. John Lednum, *A History of the Rise of Methodism in America, Containing Sketches of Methodist Itinerant Preachers, From 1736 to 1785* (Philadelphia, 1859), 42–44. Mary Wilmer's maiden name was Baker; she was likely Jacob Baker's sister: see chap. 6 below.

10. Ruthella Mory Bibbins, *How Methodism Came: The Beginnings of Methodism in America* (Baltimore, 1945), 80–82.

11. Baker, *From Wesley*, 77–78.

12. Lednum, *History*, 90; EC, Journal, 13 vols. (1784–1802), vol. 8 (1791–1792), 4 December 1791, GTS; *J&L*, ed. Elmer T. Clark, J. Manning Potts, and Jacob S. Payton, 3 vols. (London and Nashville, 1958), 1:89n. See also references to sixteen German books in Mary Magdalen Tripolet, Inv., 22 March 1792, BA Invs., bk. 16, fol. 413, MDSA.

13. *J&L*, 2:446n.

14. Ibid., 1:187n.

15. Ibid., 26n; 2:235; see also Henry Boehm, *Reminiscences, Historical and Biographical, of Sixty-Four years in the Ministry* (New York, 1866), 283–84.

16. *J&L*, 2:242.

17. Harry Wright Newman, *Anne Arundel Gentry* (Baltimore, 1933), 115; Caleb Dorsey, Will, 14 March 1772, Anne Arundel Wills, 1772, bk. 38, fol. 819, MDSA.

18. *BDML*, s.v. "Ridgely, Charles [1733–1790]," and "Ridgeley, Charles Carnan [born Charles R. Carnan; 1760–1829]." Also *Biographical Directory of the Governors of the United States, 1789–1978*, ed. Robert Sobel and John Raimo (Westport, CT, 1978), s.v. "Ridgely, Charles Carnan [1816–1819]."

19. Lynch was the daughter of Caleb Dorsey's sister Eleanor: *BDML*, s.v. "Owings, Samuel, Jr. [1733–1803]." See also Owings Family Chart in LHP; Dawn F. Thomas, *The Green Spring Valley: Its History and Heritage* (Baltimore, 1978), 164; and *J&L*, 1:122n.

20. *J&L*, 1:386n; *BDML*, s.v. "Ridgely, Charles [1733–1790]"; Ridgely Family Chart in LHP; *BDML*, s.v. "Gough, Harry Dorsey [ca. 1745–1808]." Prudence Gough was the daughter of Achsah Chamier by her second marriage, to John Carnan; Chamier's third husband, Daniel Chamier, was a Tory who died in exile in NY City: Ridgely Family Chart in LHP, and *J&L*, 1:386n. On the Gough-Ridgely rivalry, see correspondence between

Harry Dorsey Gough and Charles Ridgely, 1785–1792, in Ridgely Family Papers, micro-film reels 2, 3, and 5, and Charles Ridgely to Harry Dorsey Gough, 8 August 1787, Broad-sides, MDHS.

21. Lednum, *History*, 153–57, Stevens, *Women*, 235–46, Edith Rossiter Bevan, "Perry Hall: Country Seat of the Gough and Carroll Families," *MDHM* 45 (1950): 38–40.

22. *J&L*, 1:304n, and Leon de Valinger and Virginia E. Shaw, eds. and comps., *A Calendar of the Ridgely Family Letters, 1742–1899, in the Delaware State Archives*, 2 vols. (Dover, 1948, 1951), vol. 1.

23. Lednum, *History*, 269–72, and Stevens, *Women*, 220–27.

24. Lednum, *History*, 272–77, Stevens, *Women*, 227–30, and William H. Williams, *The Garden of American Methodism: The Delmarva Peninsula, 1769–1820* (Wilmington, DE, 1984): 99–100. Also *DAB*, s.v. "Bassett, Richard [1745–1815]." On Bohemia Manor, see Lednum, *History*, 277–78, and *J&L*, 1:26n, 57n, 337n, and 414.

25. Richard Bassett's second wife, Rachel Bruff, was also a Methodist and Catherine Ennalls's future sister-in-law: Stevens, *Women*, 230–35, Williams, *Garden*, 99–100, and *BDML*, s.v. "Bruff, William."

26. Rebecca Ridgely, "Experience" (1786–1798), Ridgely Family Papers, MS 693, Box 2, 2 February 1786, MDHS.

27. Prudence Carnan Gough to Achsah Chamier, 29 January 1777, Gough-Carroll Papers, MDHS.

28. *J&L*, 1:89n, and EC, Journal, vol. 5 (1788–90), 67–68. In another possible instance of evangelical mother-daughter bonding, Mary Magdalen Tripolet restricted her son-in-law's access to her daughter's inheritance on the latter's death: Mary Magdalen Tripolet, Will, [2?] May 1791, BA Wills, 1791, bk. 5, fols. 24 and 29, MDSA.

29. *J&L*, 1:99n, 2:446n.

30. Ibid., 2:93.

31. Ibid., 1:401n, 2:477n, 3:140n.

32. See discussion in the next section of this chapter.

33. Richard Sause to Mary Thorn, 13 January 1774, and Richard Boardman to Mary Thorn, 19 March 1774, OSHS. See additional correspondence at OSHS.

34. Joseph Pilmore to Mary Thorn, 4 November 1772, and additional correspondence, OSHS.

35. *J&L*, 3:156.

36. Ibid., 3: passim. See also FA's letters to Rebecca Ridgely: 24 May 1804, 16 August 1804, 10 March 1807, and 7 May 1810, Ridgely Family Papers, MS 693, Box 2, MDHS; and William Colbert, Journal (1790–1833), GTS, vol. 1 (1790–1794), 15–16, where Colbert records speaking to groups at at least seven different widows' houses on the Calvert circuit, Maryland, in a two-week period in July 1790.

37. *J&L*, 3:141.

38. For the Dorsey sisters' inheritance of £1,000 each, see Caleb Dorsey, Will, 14 March 1772. Captain Charles Ridgely left his wife Rebecca the choice of a house and eight acres or Hampton itself, as well as furniture, silver plate, slaves, £3,000 current money, and another £500 current money to be paid as an annuity to Rebecca by Ridgely's nephew and brother-in-law, Charles Carnan Ridgely (Charles Ridgely, Will, 7 April 1786, BA Wills, 1790, lib. 4, fols. 450–82, MDSA). For Prudence Gough's inheritance, see Harry Dorsey Gough, Will, 17 April 1808, BA Wills, 1808, lib. 8, fol. 315, MDSA. For Deborah Owings, see Samuel Owings, Jr., Will, 7 May 1803, BA Wills, 1803, bk. 7, fol. 197, MDSA.

39. FA to Rebecca Ridgely, 10 March 1807, and idem to Rebecca Ridgely, 7 May 1810, MDHS. See also Catherine Ennalls Bruff's legacy of £300 to FA in William Bruff, Will, 21 July 1802, BA Wills, 1802, bk. 7, fol. 108, MDSA.

40. Tripolet left a bequest of just £100 to the Methodist preachers (Mary Magdalen Tripolet, Will, [2?] May 1791); Achsah Chamier bequeathed £30 to "my Friend Francis Asbury" and suits of mourning to FA and several BA Methodist preachers (Achsah Chamier, Will, 18 June 1785, BA Wills, 1785, bk. 4, fol. 96, MDSA). See also Rebecca Ridgely's conflict with her nephew over the terms of Captain Ridgely's will: [Charles Carnan Ridgely], Estate Agreement with Rebecca Ridgely in Rebecca Ridgely Legal Papers, 29 July 1790; and idem, Inv. 1798, in Bills and Receipts, 1794–1799, Ridgely Family Papers, MS 693, Box 2, MDHS.

The small women's collection at the NY City society in 1802—just $57 out of a total collection of $608—suggests the limited financial resources available to many women Methodists (NYC MEC Collection, NY Annual Conference, Journals, 1800–1820, 5 June 1802, microfilm reel 3, vol. 12, Methodist Records, NYPL).

41. J. Thomas Scharf, *History of Maryland From the Earliest Period to the Present Day*, 3 vols., reprint ed. (1879; Hatboro, PA, 1967), 2:554; Robert Strawbridge, Inv., 19 June 1782, BA Invs., Box 25, fold. 39, MDSA.

42. Harry Dorsey Gough [Perry Hall] Inv., 24 August 1808 and 17 December 1808, BA Invs., 1808, bk. 25, fols. 447–63, MDSA.

43. Philip Barratt's new widow, for example, hosted the eleven preachers who constituted the first Methodist Council before the Christmas Conference (TC, *Extracts of the Journals of the Late Rev. Thomas Coke, L.L.D.; Comprising Several Visits to North-America and the West-Indies; His Tour Through Part of Ireland, and His Nearly Finished Voyage to Bombay in the East-Indies* [Dublin, 1816], 45–46); "Mrs. Crossfields" served dinner to seven preachers in NY City in 1791 (William Jessop, Journal [1790–1791], 45–46, OSHS); widow Ann Miller, previously host to General Washington in White Plains, opened her house to the preachers ("Short Account of Mrs. Ann Miller, of White-Plains, N. York," *Methodist Magazine* [NY] 2 [1819]: 459–61); and widow Abigail Sherwood hosted the itinerants in New Rochelle, NY (*J&L*, 2:131). See also daily references to meals at private residences in Richard Whatcoat, Journal, vols. 1 (1789–1790) and 3 (1794–1796), typescript, GTS, and vol. 2 (1792–1793), typescript, LCMD.

44. Representative works are Daniel Scott Smith, "Parental Power and Marriage Patterns: An Analysis of Historical Trends in Hingham, Massachusetts," in *The American Family in Social Historical Perspective*, ed. Michael Gordon (New York, 1978), 87–100, Allan Kulikoff, *Tobacco and Slaves: The Development of Southern Cultures in the Chesapeake, 1680–1800* (Chapel Hill, NC, 1986), Barry Levy, *Quakers and the American Family: British Settlement in the Delaware Valley* (New York, 1988), Jan Lewis, *The Pursuit of Happiness: Family and Values in Jefferson's Virginia* (Cambridge, 1983), Joan M. Jensen, *Loosening the Bonds: Mid-Atlantic Farm Women, 1750–1850* (New Haven, 1986), Jacqueline S. Reinier, "Rearing the Republican Child: Attitudes and Practices in Post-Revolutionary Philadelphia," *WMQ* 39 (1982): 150–63, and idem, *From Virtue to Character: American Childhood, 1775–1850* (New York, 1996). Also cf. Mary Beth Norton, "The Evolution of White Women's Experience in Early America," *AHR* 89 (1984): 601–19, Glenna Matthews, *The Rise of Public Woman: Woman's Power and Woman's Place in the United States, 1630–1970* (New York, 1992), 32–51, and Carole Shammas, "Anglo-American Household Government in Comparative Perspective," *WMQ* 52 (1995): 104–44.

45. Thomas Paine, *Common Sense*, reprint ed. (Harmondsworth, England, 1984).

46. Mary Beth Norton, *Liberty's Daughters: The Revolutionary Experience of American Women, 1750–1800* (Boston, 1980), 242–50, and Linda K. Kerber, *Women of the Republic: Intellect and Ideology in Revolutionary America* (Chapel Hill, NC, 1980), 265–88. Ruth H. Bloch pioneered work on gendered definitions of virtue in "American Feminine Ideals in Transition: The Rise of the Moral Mother, 1785–1815," *Feminist Studies* 4 (1978): 101–26. See also the implications for female preaching of the "republican language of female virtue" in Catherine A. Brekus, *Strangers and Pilgrims: Female Preaching in America, 1740–1845* (Chapel Hill, NC, 1998), 146–54.

47. *United States Magazine* 1 (January 1779), quoted in Norton, *Liberty's Daughters*, 247. On Benjamin Rush, see ibid., 267–68, and Reinier, "Rearing the Republican Child," 156–60.

48. Martha Tomhave Blauvelt, "Women and Revivalism," in *Women and Religion in America*, ed. Rosemary Radford Ruether and Rosemary Skinner Keller, vol. 1, *The Nineteenth Century* (San Francisco, 1981), 3. For the argument that women gained little from the Revolution, see Joan Hoff Wilson, "The Illusion of Change," in *The American Revolution: Explorations in the History of American Radicalism*, ed. Alfred F. Young (De Kalb, IL, 1976), 384–445, and Linda K. Kerber, " 'History Can Do It No Justice': Women and the Reinterpretation of the American Revolution," in *Women in the Age of the American Revolution*, ed. Ronald Hoffman and Peter J. Albert (Charlottesville, VA, 1989). See also Edith B. Gelles's comments on the limitations of the concept of the "Republican Mother," and the corresponding importance of the concept of sisterhood, in *Portia: The World of Abigail Adams* (Bloomington, IN, 1992), 129–35.

49. "On Family Religion" (1783) in *Works*, vol. 3, *Sermons III*, ed. Albert C. Outler (Nashville, 1986), 338. See also "On the Education of Children," in ibid., 347–60.

50. JW, "On Obedience to Parents" in ibid., 361–72.

51. MEC, *Minutes of Several Conversations Between The Rev. Thomas Coke, LL.D., The Rev. Francis Asbury and Others, at a Conference Begun in Baltimore . . . Composing a Form of Discipline for the Ministers, Preachers and Other Members of the Methodist Episcopal Church in America* (Philadelphia, 1785), 6.

52. Ibid. (1798), 93; see also "An Exhortation to family Godliness: extracted from a late Author," *Methodist Magazine* (PH) 2 (1798): 332–34.

53. *DAB*, s.v. "Livingston, Robert [1654–1728]."

54. CL[G] to [unidentified], 18 August 1781, and idem to Edward Livingston, 20 October 1785, DUL; Margaret Livingston Tillotson to Robert R. Livingston, 15 December [1783], Livingston Family Papers, microfilm reel 3, NYHS. By this time, Margaret Beekman Livingston had released her dower rights to the Lower Manor: Margaret Beekman Livingston, Release of Dower, 17 August 1783, in ibid. Robert R. Livingston, CLG's brother, took no fewer than six slaves and one manservant with him to PH when he was secretary of the United States for foreign affairs: see facsimile opposite title page in copy of Charles Haven Hunt, *Life of Edward Livingston* (1864; New York, 1875), NYHS.

55. CLG's brother Robert was one of the signers of the Declaration of Independence as well as a minister of foreign affairs in the Confederation government; as minister to France in 1803, he was an architect of the Louisiana Purchase. CLG's younger brother Edward was elected to the U.S. Senate and appointed secretary of state by Andrew Jackson: *DAB*, s.v. "Livingston, Robert [1718–1775]," "Livingston, Robert R. [1746–1813]," and "Livingston, Edward [1764–1836]." The Livingston daughters Janet, Gertrude, and Alida married, respectively, Continental Army generals Richard Montgomery, Morgan Lewis, and John Armstrong, and daughter Margaret was the wife of Thomas Tillotson, the Continental

Army surgeon general; another brother, Henry, was a Continental Army colonel: Hunt, *Life of Edward Livingston*, 15–16.

56. CLG, Diary, 15 vols., (1787–1817), vol. 1 (1787–1788), pp. 14–15, DUL. CLG's conversion can be dated in idem to Janet Montgomery, 25 January 1791, DUL. See also Stevens, *Women*, 256–72.

57. CLG, Diary (1787–1817), 1:23, 53, 59, vol. 2 (1788), pp. 18, 36–37, vol. 3 (1788), p. 6, vol. 5 (1788–1792), p. 13.

58. Stevens, *Women*, 260–61, 272–75; and [CLG], "A Short Account of the Late Sarah Schuyler," and [idem], "Memoir of Mrs. Catharine Suckley," *Methodist Magazine* (NY) 9 (1826): 248–54, 330–35. See also CL[G] to FG, 6 August [1790?], DUL.

59. FG went to Rhinebeck after converting Tillotson's half-brother in Maryland: Nathan Bangs, *The Life of the Rev. Freeborn Garrettson, compiled from his printed and manuscript journals, and other authentic documents* (New York, 1829), 193.

60. CL[G] to FG, 6 September 1790; idem, Diary, 5:13, DUL. See also Diane H. Lobody, " 'That Language Might Be Given Me': Women's Experience in Early Methodism," in *Perspectives on American Methodism: Interpretive Essays*, ed. Russell E. Richey, Kenneth E. Rowe, and Jean Miller Schmidt (Nashville, 1993), 127–44.

61. CLG, Diary, vol. 5 [15 May 1789].

62. CL[G] to FG, 6 August [1790?], DUL.

63. CLG, Diary, vol. 6, 11 March 1793.

64. CLG caustically observed regarding her mother and FA, bishop of the MEC: "You know titles go a great way with many people": CL[G] to FG, 25 September 1790, DUL. See also EC, Journal, vol. 9 (1792–1793), 14 January 1793.

65. See correspondence between CLG and FG, 1790–1793, esp. 10 January 1791, DUL.

66. CL[G] to Janet Montgomery, 25 January 1791, DUL.

67. CL[G] to Catharine Rutsen, 30 March 1793, DUL; idem, Diary, vol. 6a (1793–1795), 30 June 1793.

68. On the captain's return, Rebecca continued to attend preaching as he permitted: Ridgely, "Experience," 2 February 1786, and later entries dated 1788–1798.

69. Mary [Evans Thorn] Parker to TC and Adam Clarke, 29 July 1813; see also Lednum, *History*, 42–44. Thorn consequently moved in with a married couple and was able to rent or purchase a house where she hosted the preachers (ibid., 43, and Thomas Rankin to Br. & Sister Dower and Sister Thorn, 30 March 1774, OSHS). She also took on odd jobs, such as making shirts for the itinerants (St. George's MEC, "A Book For the Collections etc. to Defray the Expences of the Methodist Meeting House," 11 February 1772, OSHS). She eventually married an English preacher, Samuel Parker, and left for England before the end of the war (Lednum, *History*, 43–44).

70. EC, Journal, vol. 7 (1790–1791), 18 December 1790; Colbert, Journal, vol. 1, 25 April 1793.

71. G. A. Raybold, *Reminiscences of Methodism in West Jersey* (New York, 1849), 44–45: the woman offered to get into the oven herself. Such counterobedience was recommended in Methodist publications: see "A Pattern for Christian Wives," *Arminian Magazine* (PH) 2 (1790): 464.

72. Bangs, *Life of the Rev. Freeborn Garrettson*, 225.

73. Colbert, Journal, 1:14–15.

74. Benjamin Abbott, *The Experience and Gospel Labours of the Rev. Benjamin Abbott: To Which is Annexed a Narrative of His Life and Death by John Ffirth* (Philadelphia, 1801), 216–17. Methodist men, esp. in the 1770s, also faced opposition from their families, particularly parents, to their new lives. John Cooper's father threw a shovelful of burning

embers at him when he found him preaching: Philip Gatch, "Autobiography," Gatch Microfilm Group I, p. 22, MTSO.

75. MEC, *The Doctrines and Discipline of the Methodist Episcopal Church in America* (1798; reprint ed., Rutland, VT, 1979), 157.

76. "Of unlawful Marriages," in ibid., 156–59. This rule was changed from expulsion to six-month trial in 1804: Jesse Lee, *A Short History of the Methodists, in the United States of America: beginning in 1766, and continued till 1809* (Baltimore, 1810), 299. Evidence of the rejection of members for exogamous marriage is scanty, but Thomas Haskins records one such action: Journal, no. 6 (1784–1785, 1816), 26 January 1785, LCMD. Robert Ayres also records a case of formal separation near Milford, Delaware, in 1785: "Here an Unhappy man and his Wife Sign'd the Bonds of final Separation": Robert Ayres, Journal (1785–1845), vol. 1 (1785–1786), 7 October 1785, microfilm, DUL. On premarital pregnancy, see Daniel Scott Smith and Michael S. Hindus, "Premarital Pregnancy in America, 1640–1971: An Overview and Interpretation," *Journal of Interdisciplinary History* 5 (Spring 1975): fig. 1 and appendix 1.

77. Lucy Fanning Watson, "Experience & Incidents in the Life of Mrs Lucy Watson, who died at Germantown P^a 5th June 1834, aged 79 Years," 18, MS copy, WL; *J&L*, 3:156.

78. *J&L*, 3:19.

79. Thomas Rankin refers to a "Jezubel" who drew James Dempster astray, apparently before the latter's emigration to America (Journal [1773–1778], 98, typescript, GTS). See also ibid., 119; and R[obert] Lindsay to Edward Dromgoole, 22 March 1788, in *Religion on the American Frontier, 1783–1840*, ed. William Warren Sweet, vol. 4, *The Methodists* (Chicago, 1946), 136, where Lindsay expresses his dismay at the loss of preachers in the American work: "*They are Married*, So there is an end of them."

80. *D&D* (1798), 62; Elizabeth Rowe, *Devout Exercises of the Heart, in Meditation and Soliloquy, Prayer and Praise*, abridged (Philadelphia, 1798); EC, "Account of Books, pamphlets etc. published for the Methodist Connection by E Cooper since the 10th of June 1799," EC Collection, DUL, in which EC orders three thousand copies printed.

81. CL[G] to Catharine Rutsen, 4 April 1791, DUL.

82. *J&L*, 1:356; MEC, *Minutes of the Methodist Conferences, Annually Held in America from 1773 to 1794, inclusive* (Philadelphia, 1795), 38. On the English connection, see Lindsay to Edward Dromgoole, 22 March 1788, in Sweet, *Religion on the American Frontier*, 136.

83. *Minutes* (1795), 38; Lee, *Short History*, 83; *Minutes* (1795), 63–64.

84. *Minutes of Several Conversations* (1785), 13, 27; abstract of Journal of the General Conference, 1792, in [MEC], *The General Conferences of the Methodist Episcopal Church from 1792 to 1896*, ed. Lewis Curts (Cincinnati and New York, 1900), 15, 29–30; *D&D* (1798), 69; [MEC], *Minutes of the General Conference of the Methodist-Episcopal Church, Begun in Baltimore on the Sixth, and Commenced Till the Twentieth of May, One Thousand Eight Hundred* (Philadelphia, 1800), in *Early American Imprints*, 1st ser., no. 37958, p. 8. The 1785 provisions for childrens' stipends—£6 Pennsylvania currency for children under age 6, and £8 for children aged 6 to 10—was suspended in 1787, to be restored in 1800 at $14 for children under age 7, and $24 for children aged 7 to 14, unless supported by other means: Lee, *Short History*, 100–101; [MEC], *Minutes of the General Conference* (1800), 8. The support for widows was set at £20 at the Christmas Conference in 1784, $53⅓ at the 1792 general conference, and at $80, that is, raised to the same amount as the preachers' and wives' stipends, at the 1800 general conference. For example of the local payment of these at times burdensome expenses, see Old Union MEC, Blackbird, Delaware, Quar-

terly Conference Minutes, 12 and 13 October 1805, 26 February 1808, 23 April 1808, 14 January, 1809, HSD.

85. William Watters, *A Short Account of the Christian Experience and Ministereal Labours of William Watters Drawn Up By Himself* (Alexandria, VA, 1806), 69–77.

86. William McLenahan to William Colbert, 23 June 1806, William Colbert Collection, GTS.

87. Henry Abelove, *The Evangelist of Desire: John Wesley and the Methodists* (Stanford, 1990), 64–66, 70–73. For summary, see idem, "The Sexual Politics of Early Wesleyan Methodism," in *Disciplines of Faith: Studies in Religion, Politics, and Patriarchy*, ed. Jim Obelkevich, Lyndal Roper, and Raphael Samuel (London, 1987), 86–99.

88. Describing a women's class in Camden, New Jersey, no date: G. A. Raybold, *Annals of Methodism; or Sketches of the Origins and Progress of Methodism in Various Portions of West Jersey; derived from the most authentic of sources. First series. Camden and Vicinity* (Philadelphia, 1847), 23–24.

89. Discussion based on the records of the NY, PH, BA, and FP Methodist societies. See individual citations below.

90. See tables 1–3 and "Methodological Note" in appendixes below.

91. See esp. Mary P. Ryan, "A Women's Awakening: Evangelical Religion and the Families of Utica, New York, 1800–1840," in *Women in American Religion*, ed. Janet Wilson James (Philadelphia, 1980), 90, and idem, *Cradle of the Middle Class: The Family in Oneida County, New York, 1790–1865* (Cambridge, 1981), 79–80; and Martha Tomhave Blauvelt, "Society, Religion, and Revivalism: The Second Great Awakening in New Jersey, 1780–1830" (Ph.D. diss., Princeton University, 1975), 61, 179–87. Terry D. Bilhartz has estimated that 7 in 10 women in BA compared to 3 in 10 men were churchgoers, and the proportion of women to men was higher in nonrevivalist denominations: *Urban Religion and the Second Great Awakening: Church and Society in Early National Baltimore* (Rutherford, NJ, 1986), 21–22.

92. Gerald Francis Moran, "The Puritan Saint: Religious Experience, Church Membership, and Piety in Connecticut, 1636–1776" (Ph.D. diss., Rutgers University, 1973), and Stephen R. Grossbart, "Seeking the Divine Favor: Conversion and Church Admission in Eastern Connecticut, 1711–1832," *WMQ* 54 (1989): 696–740. For other important overviews, see Mary Maples Dunn, "Saints and Sisters: Congregational and Quaker Women in the Early Colonial Period," *AQ* 30 (1978): 582–601, and Susan Juster, *Disorderly Women: Sexual Politics and Evangelicalism in Revolutionary New England* (Ithaca, NY, 1994).

93. See tables 1 and 2 in appendix below.

94. Mary Ryan makes use of a similar deductive method in her study of three Presbyterian congregations and a Baptist one during the Second Great Awakening in Oneida County, NY: "Women's Awakening," 91, and *Cradle of the Middle Class*, 81. See also "Methodological Note" in appendix below. In NY, 48 names were held in common by at least two white women, and 38, by three or more; in PH, the analogous numbers are 62 and 46; in BA City, 64 and 36 for white women, and 19 and 18 for black women. Records are: John Street MEC, "List of Baptisms, Marriages, Burials & Members of the Methodist Episcopal Church" (1784–1798), Methodist Records, microfilm, vol. 23, NYPL (hereafter cited as NY "List of Baptisms"), and idem, "The Names and number of those persons in Society in the City of New York" (1791–1796), Methodist Records, microfilm, vol. 241, NYPL; St. George's MEC, "The Names of the Officers, and Members of the Methodist Church in Philadelphia" (1785–1816), in Register Book, Church Records, OSHS (hereafter

cited as PH "Names of the Officers"); and BA City Station MEC, Class Records (1799–1803), microfilm 408, MDSA (hereafter cited as BA Class Records).

95. Class Lists, 1799, 1800, and 1801 in BA Class Records.

96. For the society as a whole, the percentage rose from 72 to 79 percent: Marriages, 1791–1794, and Baptisms, 1784–1795, in NY "List of Baptisms"; Marriages, 1799–1801, in idem, "Methodist Marriage Register for the City of New York" (1799–1820), Methodist Records, microfilm, vol. 72, NYPL; and Baptisms, 1796–1801, in idem, "Register of Baptisms For The Methodist Episcopal Church in N York" (1796–1820), Methodist Records, microfilm, vol. 234, NYPL.

97. For the society as a whole, the percentage rose from 73 to 81 percent: Marriages, 1789–1799, and Baptisms, 1785–1798, in PH "Names of the Officers."

98. The city societies appear to have included as high a proportion of widowers as widows in their ranks, or higher. In the sample years for PH, e.g., 2 widows appear in 1794, 3 widowers and 1 widow in 1796, and 2 widowers and 1 widow in 1801.

99. See, for example, Robert V. Wells, "Quaker Marriage Patterns in a Colonial Perspective," *WMQ* 29 (1972): table 7, p. 426, and pp. 423–28: 23.5 percent of selected Middle Atlantic Quaker women born after 1786 never married, compared with 9.8 percent of those born before 1786. In PH, 15 percent of the city's households were headed by women in 1791, and this proportion was to increase in the early nineteenth century: Claudia Goldin, "The Economic Status of Women in the Early Republic: Quantitative Evidence," *Journal of Interdisciplinary History* 16 (1986): table 2, p. 388.

On widows, see Goldin, "The Economic Status of Women," 384, and Lisa Wilson, *Life after Death: Widows in Pennsylvania, 1750–1850* (Philadelphia, 1992). See also Carole Shammas, "The Female Social Structure of Philadelphia in 1775," *PMHB* 107 (1983): 72–77; Nancy F. Cott, "Divorce and the Changing Status of Women in Eighteenth-Century Massachusetts," in Gordon, *American Family*, 115–39, and Marylynn Salmon, *Women and the Law of Property in Early America* (Chapel Hill, NC, 1986), 58–71.

100. See similar conclusions regarding unmarried Methodists in England in Gail Malmgreen, "Domestic Discords: Women and the Family in East Cheshire Methodism, 1750–1830," in Obelkevich, Roper, and Samuel, *Disciplines of Faith*, 60; and for Oneida County, NY, women in Ryan, "Women's Awakening," 91n, 94.

On age at marriage, see Smith, "Parental Power and Marriage Patterns," table 4, p. 96, and Wells, "Quaker Marriage Patterns," table 3, p. 420; cf. with figures from other studies provided in table 8, p. 429. See also summary statistics in table 2 in James M. Gallman, "Determinants of Age at Marriage in Colonial Perquimans County, North Carolina," *WMQ* 39 (1982): 181.

101. "An Extract from the Diary of Elizabeth McKean," *Methodist Magazine* (PH) 1 (1797): 227–29.

102. The matches with itinerants included Margery Smith to David Abbott, Ann Abraham to Lemuel Green, Mary Davis to William Penn Chandler, Mary Long to Hugh McCurdy, and Elizabeth Richards to Thomas Haskins after the death of his first wife, Martha Potts Haskins.

103. The full range of percentages for husbands for NY are 49 percent in 1786, 47 percent in 1791, and 45 percent in 1796. The full range of percentages for PH are 36 percent in 1794, 31 percent of husbands in 1796, and 41 percent of husbands in 1801. These figures are derived from matchings between individual members and marriage and baptism records through 1810 for both societies.

104. The full range of percentages for wives for NY are 25 percent in 1786, 26 percent in 1791, and 27 percent in 1796. The full range of percentages for PH are 15 percent in

1794, 16 percent in 1796, and 20 percent in 1801. These gender differences continued into the nineteenth-century revivals in New York's "burned over district": see Ryan, "Women's Awakening," 91, and 91n.

105. *Minutes of Several Conversations* (1785), 28. For a local example, see Asbury MEC Church in Wilmington, Delaware, where men and women entered the chapel by different entrances and were separated inside by a four-foot-high partition kept in place until 1845; in rural Camden, south of Dover, gender separation remained in force until the 1860s (Williams, *Garden*, 107–8).

106. For examples, see Class List, 1796, in NY "List of Baptisms"; Class List, 1799, in BA Class Records; East BA Station (Fell's Point) MEC, Class Lists, 1800 and 1801, in FP "Annual Register For the Methodist Episcopal Church on Fells Point" (1800–1818), microfilm 411, MDSA (hereafter cited as FP "Annual Register"). See also list of nine bands, including one black band, in "Band Society," ca. 1793, Methodist Records, no. 241, NYPL; bands of "Young Men" and "Young Women" in "United in Band," 1799, and 8 bands in "A List of Band Societies in Philadelphia," 1800, in PH "Names of the Officers." See also St. George's MEC, "List of the members of the African Methodist Episcopal Church in the City of Philadelphia," ca. 1794, reprinted in Dee Andrews, "The African Methodists of Philadelphia, 1794–1802," *PMHB* 108 (1984): 471–86.

107. By contrast, classes in rural areas, like the earliest city societies, may have been made up of 50 percent or more married couples: see MEC, Sussex County, New Jersey, Class List, 1800, NJHS, and [Bond Family], Class List, 1790–1791, Cole Collection of Bond Family Papers, SC 1571, MDSA.

108. A slave or servant woman named Betty was one of the original members of Barbara Heck's class in NY in 1766 (Stevens, "Barbara Heck and American Methodism," 187) and several black women and men contributed to the subscription list for the John Street Chapel in 1768 (Wakeley, *Lost Chapters*, 69–72).

109. See tables 4 and 5 in appendix below.

110. On husbands, see chap. 6 below.

111. Ibid. On Bennis, see William Crook, *Ireland and the Centenary of American Methodism* (London, 1866), 222n.

112. "Caroline Zolicoffer" is identified as a "gentlewoman" in *The New Baltimore Directory and Annual Register; For 1800 and 1801* (Baltimore, [1801]). Mary Gray, a NY Methodist who died in 1794, left a significant proportion of her personal property to women Methodists and the itinerants: Mary Gray, Will, 18 December 1794, in Abstracts of Wills, NYHS *Collections* 14 [1786–1796] [New York, 1905], 287–88.

113. Elizabeth Drinker, *The Diary of Elizabeth Drinker*, ed. Elaine Forman Crane, 3 vols. (Boston, 1991), 1:656, 3:1748.

114. Examples in BA include Mrs. Ann Caldwell, grocer; Mary Davis, storekeeper; Martha Hay, seamstress; Anne Matthews, huckster; Elizabeth Mitchel, mantua-maker; Polly Oram, tailoress; Mary Smith, grocer; Sophia Squires, mantua-maker: *New Baltimore Directory* (1800–1801), and *The Baltimore Directory for 1802* (Baltimore, [1802]).

115. 1 July 1799, 15 April 1800, and 9 February 1801 in St. George's Receipt Book (1795–1800), OSHS.

116. "Memoir of Mrs. Mary Dando," *Methodist Magazine* (NY) 8 (1825): 327–38.

117. John Street MEC, "Poor Disbursements," in Poor Fund Treasurer Accounts (1790–1820), Methodist Records, microfilm, vol. 94, NYPL. See also "Poor Collections," 1795–1801, in ibid. In the winter of 1797–1798, 32 of the 43 members too poor to spare the twelve shillings for heating fuel were women.

118. NY "Poor Disbursements," passim.

119. Baptisms, 1801, in John Street MEC, "Register of Baptisms For The Methodist Episcopal Church In N York" (1796–1820), Methodist Records, microfilm, vol. 234, NYPL; NY "Poor Disbursements," 1795. All but one of the members of the "Poorhouse" class were women: "List of the Trustees, Stewards, Leaders, Local Preachers and members of the Methodist Church and Society in the City of New York," 1795, in Methodist Records, no. 241, NYPL. On women in the NY City poorhouse, see Christine Stansell, *City of Women: Sex and Class in New York, 1789–1860* (New York, 1986), 235–36n.

120. Women also borrowed large and small sums of money from the church: see references in St. George's MEC, Receipt Book, 1795–1806, March 1798, 4 April 1798, 30 August 1799, and 14 May 1802, OSHS. The society hired a laborer "for Nursing the poore 2 weeks" and paid Peter Parks, the sexton, for burying the dead (ibid., 1797–1798).

121. In 1791–1795, seventeen women were read out of or suspended from the NY society, usually for "immoral conduct": John Street MEC, List of Exclusions, 1791–1793, in Methodist Records, microfilm, no. 241, NYPL.

122. White and black members have been counted. Those who did stay were disproportionately the married members. Married couples account for 39 percent of all members who remained at the NY society between 1786 and 1791, 33 percent of those remaining between 1791 and 1796, and 35 percent of those remaining between 1786 and 1796. See "Methodological Note" in appendix below.

123. The proportion of married members staying at the PH society for the shorter 1794–1801 period is much the same as that for NY.

124. Ann Ridgely to Henry Ridgely, 30 July 1795, passage dated 2 August, Ridgely Collection, fold. no. 228, DSA.

125. CLG to [Catharine Rutsen], 17 December 1793, DUL. Rutsen's husband later won her friend's grudging approval (idem to Catharine Rutsen, 7 March 1794, DUL). On female bonding among British women evangelicals, see Valenze, *Prophetic Sons and Daughters*, 67, 67n.

126. For lists of officers only, see St. George's MEC, Blotter, 25 April 1787–17 April 1795, Church Records, OSHS; and Class List, 1794, in PH "Names of the Officers."

127. Class Lists, 1786, 1787, and 1791, in NY "List of Baptisms." Jane Barsary's name appears at the head of the single "Negroe Class" in 1786; she can be assumed to have been class leader.

128. Warner's class had 37 members in 1791; only the preacher's class, with 35, came close. See Class Lists, 1791, 1793, and 1795, in NY "List of Baptisms."

129. *J&L*, 1:735; list of 1793 BA class leaders, in Whatcoat, Journal, vol. 2, 14–31 July 1793; Class List, 1800, in BA Class Records.

130. Abbott, *Experience*, 67–68.

131. Arthur A. Walls, *History of Dudley's Chapel, 1782–1917* (n.d., n.p.), microfilm, M2091, 5, MDSA; Williams, *Garden*, 108; Whatcoat, Journal, vol. 2, 8 June 1792 and 7 August 1792.

132. Brown, *Women of Mr. Wesley's Methodism*, 242; Lorenzo Dow, *The Life and Travels of Lorenzo Dow, Written By Himself: In Which Are Contained Some Singular Providences of God* (Hartford, CT, 1804), 17–22.

133. Quoted in Norton, *Liberty's Daughters*, 128. See also Jensen, *Loosening the Bonds*, 145–66, and Jean R. Soderlund, "Women's Authority in Pennsylvania and New Jersey Quaker Meetings, 1680–1760," *WMQ* 44 (1987): 722–49, for the strength of women's voice in eighteenth-century Quakerism.

134. John Littlejohn, Journal, 10 vols. (1776–1832), vol. 2 (1776–1777), 3 August 1777, microfilm, KWC.

135. *D&D* (1798), 147–48.

136. Littlejohn, Journal, vol. 3 (1777–1778), 21 September 1777.

137. CL[G] to FG, 10 January 1791, DUL. Livingston's public role appears to have been limited to the gentlewoman's art of making shirts: idem to FG, 27 January 1790.

138. Colbert, Journal, vol. 2 (1794–1798), 133. Robert Ayres reported on a rare instance where members of a class near York County, Pennsylvania, objected to submitting to the authority of a woman leader: Journal, vol. 1 (1785–1786), 10 January 1786.

139. Scharf, *History of Maryland*, 2:77–79, 2:556; idem, *History of Baltimore City and County*, 2 vols., reprint ed. (1881; Baltimore, 1971), 2:573–75. See also *J&L*, 1:98n, 150n, 201n, 608n; 2:90, 90n.

140. Class Lists, 1799, 1800, and 1801, in BA Class Records; Douglas R. Chandler, "Growth and Consolidation, 1800–1820," in *Those Incredible Methodists: A History of the Baltimore Conference of the United Methodist Church*, ed. Gordon Pratt Baker (Baltimore, 1972), 89. On the Fish Street and Sharp Street congregations, see chap. 5 below.

141. See table 5 in appendix below.

142. Class List, 1800, in FP "Annual Register." See Scharf, *History of Maryland*, 2:243; on Smith and Sutton, see *New Baltimore Directory* [1800–1801]. Another Job Smith, resident in Old Town, was probably the class leader at the BA City society (Class List, 1799, in BA Class Records).

143. Class List, 1801, in FP "Annual Register." On occupations, see chap. 6 below. The women whose names appear in the directory are Isabella Foster, Kitty Hall, Mary Hall, Eliza Inloes, Sarah Johnson, and Mary Norris (*New Baltimore Directory* [1800–1801]).

144. The ratio of black men to black women at the FP society was 4:5 in 1800, and nearly 1:1 in 1801. Just 9 of the 108 black members in the sample years had one last name; just 3 of these were women.

145. Class List, 1801, in BA Class Records.

146. Class Lists, 1800 and 1801, in FP "Annual Register."

147. *The Baltimore Directory for 1802* (Baltimore, [1802]).

148. See, for example, [Bond Family], Class Paper, MDSA.

CHAPTER FIVE
THE AFRICAN METHODISTS

1. C. E. Pierre, "The Work of the Society for the Propagation of the Gospel in Foreign Parts among the Negroes in the Colonies," *Journal of Negro History* 1 (1916): 349–60. On the black Methodist population in 1790 and 1801, see MEC, *Minutes of the Methodist Conferences, Annually Held in America from 1773 to 1794, inclusive* (Philadelphia, 1795), 146, and MEC, *Minutes of the Methodist Conferences, Annually Held in America; from 1773 to 1813, inclusive* (New York, 1813), 243. About 25 percent of Baptists were blacks in 1793, or between 18,000 and 19,000 members: Albert Raboteau, *Slave Religion: The "Invisible Institution" in the Antebellum South* (1978; Oxford, 1980), 131.

2. Donald G. Mathews, *Religion in the Old South* (Chicago, 1977), 208.

3. Arthur Zilversmit, *The First Emancipation: The Abolition of Slavery in the North* (Chicago, 1967), 113–200; Ira Berlin, *Slaves without Masters: The Free Negro in the Antebellum South* (1974; Oxford, 1981), 29; William H. Williams, *Slavery and Freedom in Delaware, 1639–1865* (Wilmington, DE, 1996), 143–44.

4. On Pennsylvania, see Gary B. Nash and Jean R. Soderlund, *Freedom by Degrees: Emancipation in Pennsylvania and Its Aftermath* (New York, 1991), 101–13; Paul Finkel-

man, *The Law of Freedom and Bondage: A Casebook* (New York, 1986), 42–49. On NY and New Jersey, see Zilversmit, *First Emancipation*, 147–62, 177–99, 208–22, Shane White, *Somewhat More Independent: The End of Slavery in New York City, 1770–1810* (Athens, GA, 1991), and Graham Russell Hodges, *Slavery and Freedom in the Rural North* (Madison, WI, 1997), 135–36.

5. Berlin, *Slaves without Masters*, 81–94.

6. Richard S. Dunn, "Black Society in the Chesapeake, 1776–1810," in *Slavery and Freedom in the Age of the American Revolution*, ed. Ira Berlin and Ronald Hoffman (Urbana, IL, 1983), 63, 63n, 75n, 78; T. Stephen Whitman, *The Price of Freedom: Slavery and Manumission in Baltimore and Early National Maryland* (Lexington, KY, 1997), 9–10; Nash and Soderlund, *Freedom by Degrees*, table 1-2.

7. Hodges, *Slavery and Freedom*, 147–70, and White, *Somewhat More Independent*, table 4.

8. David Brion Davis, *The Problem of Slavery in the Age of Revolution, 1770–1823* (Ithaca, NY, 1975), 213. See also Jean R. Soderlund, *Quakers and Slavery: A Divided Spirit* (Princeton, 1985), and Michael Durey, *Transatlantic Radicals and the Early American Republic* (Lawrence, KS, 1997), 288.

9. Quoted in *Works*, vol. 22, *Journal and Diaries V (1765–1775)*, ed. W. Reginald Ward and Richard P. Heitzenrater (Nashville, 1993), 307. See also Frank Baker, "The Origins, Character, and Influence of John Wesley's Thoughts upon Slavery," *MH* 22 (1984): 80–82: in America, *Thoughts* was first reprinted with Benezet's *The Mighty Destroyer Displayed* under the collective title *The Potent Enemies of America Laid Open* (Philadelphia, 1774); JW's observations reappeared anonymously in Benezet's further tract, *Serious Consideration of Several Important Subjects* (Philadelphia, 1778).

10. Including Israel Pemberton and Anthony Benezet: Thomas Rankin, Journal (1773–1778), typescript, 24 March 1776, GTS.

11. Frederick E. Maser, ed., "Francis Asbury's Journal, Pts. 1 and 2," *MH* 9 (1970–1971): 34–43, 53–57, for excerpts relating to slavery removed from the journal by later editors; see also David H. Bradley, "Francis Asbury and the Development of African Churches in America," *MH* 10 (1971): 3–29. For full discussions of the MEC and antislavery, see Donald G. Mathews, *Slavery and Methodism: A Chapter in American Morality, 1780–1845* (Princeton, 1965), 3–29.

12. MEC, *Minutes of Several Conversations Between The Rev. Thomas Coke, LL.D., The Rev. Francis Asbury and Others, at a Conference Begun in Baltimore . . . Composing a Form of Discipline for the Ministers, Preachers and Other Members of the Methodist Episcopal Church in America* (Philadelphia, 1785), 14. See also TC and Thomas Parker, "A Plan of the Society for Establishment of Missions among the Heathens" [ca. 1784], photostat of printed broadside, DUL. For background, see Frank Baker, *From Wesley to Asbury: Studies in Early American Methodism* (Durham, NC, 1976), 142–61, and Michael R. Watts, *The Dissenters:, The Expansion of Evangelical Nonconformity* (Oxford, 1995), 2, 10–11.

13. Allan Kulikoff, *Tobacco and Slaves: The Development of Southern Cultures in the Chesapeake, 1680–1800* (Chapel Hill, NC, 1986), 343. See also ibid., 317–51, Ira Berlin, "Time, Space, and the Evolution of Afro-American Society on British Mainland North America," *AHR* 85 (1980): 44–78, White, *Somewhat More Independent*, 88–92, and Williams, *Slavery and Freedom*, 99–133.

14. Quoted in Richard K. MacMaster, "Liberty or Property? The Methodist Petition for Emancipation in Virginia, 1785," *MH* 11 (1971): 52. The Methodist petitions were ultimately rejected by the Virginia legislature: 53. See also W. Harrison Daniel, "The Method-

ist Episcopal Church and the Negro in the Early National Period," *MH* 11 (1973): 43, and TC's reference to a similar petition for the North Carolina assembly in TC, *Extracts of the Journals of the Late Rev. Thomas Coke, L.L.D.; Comprising Several Visits to North-America and the West-Indies; His Tour Through Part of Ireland, and His Nearly Finished Voyage to Bombay in the East-Indies* (Dublin, 1816), 66.

15. MEC, *Journals of the General Conference of the Methodist Episcopal Church. Volume I. 1796–1836* (New York, 1855), 22–23.

16. Ibid., 40–41.

17. MEC, *The ADDRESS of the General Conference of the Methodist Episcopal Church, to all their Brethren and Friends in the United States*, dated 20 May 1800, microcard facsimile copy in *Early American Imprints*, 1st ser., no. 37957.

18. Mathews, *Slavery and Methodism*, 26. FA relayed his views on slaveholding to his traveling companion, John Wesley Bond, late in his life. In brief, he believed legislators should favor the right of slaves to purchase their freedom in order to spur improvement among blacks and serve as a model for slaves who might attain their freedom through similar behavior; FA nevertheless continued to believe that slaveholding was a sin based on avarice, and the often poor condition of free blacks was used as a pretext for slaveholders' continuing to hold blacks in bondage: Robert J. Bull, "John Wesley Bond's Reminiscences of Francis Asbury," *MH* 4 (1965): 22.

19. Quoted in FG's MS journal in *American Methodist Pioneer: The Life and Journals of the Rev. Freeborn Garrettson, 1752–1827*, ed. Robert Drew Simpson (Rutland, VT, 1984), 146–47.

20. Ibid., 48.

21. Ibid., 49, 189, 241–42. See also Kenneth L. Carroll, "Religious Influences on Manumission of Slaves in Caroline, Dorchester, and Talbot Counties," *MDHM* 56 (1961): 192.

22. John McLean, *Sketch of Rev. Philip Gatch* (Cincinnati, 1854), 91–94; Henry Boehm, *Reminiscences, Historical and Biographical, of Sixty-Four Years in the Ministry* (New York, 1866), 26–27.

23. *Maryland Gazette* (Annapolis), 11 November 1790, 25 November 1790, 2 December 1790, 13 January 1791, and draft of letter, ca. January 1791 in EC Collection, GTS. The full sequence of columns ran until 3 February 1791. On background, see Mathews, *Slavery and Methodism*, 15–16.

24. James O'Kelly, *Essay on Negro-Slavery* (Philadelphia, 1789), 18.

25. William Colbert, Journal (1790–1833), 10 vols., microfilm, vol. 1 (1790–1794), pp. 9, 44, 45, vol. 2 (1794–1798), p. 104, GTS.

26. Ibid., 1:36, 2:84, vol. 3 (1797–1801), pp. 125–26, vol. 4 (1801–1804), pp. 7–8, 12.

27. Quoted with other examples in Carroll, "Religious Influences," 191–92.

28. T——A——to Thomas Harrison, 21 May 1787, Pennsylvania Abolition Society Collection, microfilm edition, 1976 (hereafter cited as PAS), Loose Correspondence, Incoming, reel 11, HSP.

29. Maryland Council of Safety, Census of 1776, BA County, Deptford Hundred, SSU961; Harry Dorsey Gough, Deed of Manumission, 25 April 1780, BA County Land Records, bk. WG, no. 3, pp. 239–41; Richard Moale, Will, 22 February 1786, BA Wills, 1786, bk. 21, fol. 5, MDSA. Twenty-two of Gough's slaves were to receive their freedom on the following Christmas, 22 more, probably children, to serve terms from 4 to 21 years from the same date, and the remaining mentally disabled slave maintained for life.

30. BA City Station, "An Account of Negroes bought by our Members in Baltimore Town," Methodist Records, microfilm, no. 408, MDSA. See also Harford Circuit Steward's Book [Quarterly Conference Minutes], 1799–1830, UMHS, for similar entries.

31. General Meeting Minute Book, 10/2M, 23/2M, and 8/3M/1784, microfilm, reel 9, PAS. On the Acting Committee, Acting Committee Minute Book, vol. 1 (1784–1788), 6/4M/1784.

32. William H. Williams, *The Garden of American Methodism: The Delmarva Peninsula, 1769–1820* (Wilmington, DE, 1984), 164–65; and idem, *Slavery and Freedom*, 150–55.

33. Williams, *Slavery and Freedom*, 150–55.

34. J. Thomas Scharf, *The Chronicles of Baltimore: Being a Complete History of "Baltimore Town" and "Baltimore City" from the Earliest Period to the Present Time* (Baltimore, 1874), 255–56. See occupational analysis of 167 members of the Abolition Society in 1797 in Berlin, *Slaves without Masters*, 28n.

35. William Watters, *A Short Account of the Christian Experience and Ministereal Labours of William Watters Drawn Up By Himself* (Alexandria, VA, 1806), 40.

36. See BA City Station, "An Account of Negroes," and BA Circuit Steward's Book, 1794–1816. For examples of piecemeal manumissions by a number of prominent Methodists, including Rebecca Ridgely, see BA County Court, Certificates of Freedom, 1806–1851, BA 0290, MDSA. On Gough, see Harry Dorsey Gough, Inv., 24 August 1808, BA Invs., 1808, bk. 25, fols. 447–63, MDSA.

37. Bondspeople as a whole constituted 45 percent of Owings's estate, not including Kentucky landholdings (Richard Owings, Will, 5 October 1786, BA Wills, 1786, bk. 4, p. 180, and Inv., 26 November 1786, BA Invs., 1787, Box 33, fold. 6, MDSA). For dispensation of the estate, see: Rachel Owings, Renunciation of [Richard Owings's] Will, 9 November 1786, Frederick Wills, 1786, Box 11, fold. 17; Richard Owings, Accounts of [Estate] Sales, 5 January 1787, BA County Accounts of Sales, 1787, Box 1, fold. 32; Administration Account, 14 February 1788 and Additional Account, 4 April 1788, BA Administration Accounts, 1788, Box 25, fold. 84, MDSA.

38. Thomas Rankin to Lord Dartmouth, 29 December 1774, reprinted in [Frederick V. Mills, Sr.], "Thomas Rankin to Lord Dartmouth on the State of Religion and Political Affairs in America," *MH* 23 (1985): 118. On omission of slaves from the minutes, see Rankin, Journal, 165.

39. Joseph Pilmore, *The Journal of Joseph Pilmore, Methodist Itinerant, for the Years August 1, 1769 to January 2, 1774*, ed. Frederick E. Maser and Howard T. Maag (Philadelphia, 1969), 74, and Joseph Pilmoor to JW, 5 May 1770, *Arminian Magazine* (London) 7 (1784): 224; *J&L*, ed. Elmer T. Clark, J. Manning Potts, and Jacob S. Payton, 3 vols. (London and Nashville, 1958), 1:190, 200; George Shadford, "The Life," in *The Lives of Early Methodist Preachers, Chiefly Written by Themselves*, ed. Thomas Jackson, 6 vols. (London, 1866), 6:168.

40. Robert Ayres, Journal (1785–1789), 5 vols., vol. 1 (1785–1786), entries dated 12 July 1785, 5 December 1785, and 12 March 1786, microfilm, DUL.

41. Colbert, Journal, 1:1, 5, 6, 15; Boehm, *Reminiscences*, 63; Thomas Morrell, Journal (1789–1809), 6 December 1791, Morrell File, NJSL; Watters, *Short Account*, 135–37.

42. *Minutes* (1795), 93, 146; *Minutes* (1813), 240–43. The one thousand black members listed for Antigua in 1786 are not included in these totals.

43. Pilmore to [unidentified], ca. 1770–1771, MAM; Pilmore, *Journal*, 107.

44. Reed, Diary, typescript, UMHS, 125; Colbert, Journal, vol. 2 (1794–1798), 6 June 1794.

45. For NY, see "Peter Parks true Statement of the first rise of the Methodist in america, in the year 1766," EC Collection, GTS. For class of 20 white women and 1 black man on Kent circuit in Maryland in 1781, see Benjamin Abbott, *The Experience and Gospel La-*

bours of the Rev. Benjamin Abbott: To Which is Annexed a Narrative of His Life and Death by John Ffirth (Philadelphia, 1801), 98; a solitary woman named Violet was among the 34 members of the Bond family class in Harford County: [Bond Family], Class Paper, 1790–1791, Special Collections 1571, MDSA.

46. *J&L*, 2:302. For other examples, see Abbott, *Experience*, 118, 188; Emory Pryor to EC, 23 March 1790, EC Collection, GTS.

47. Boehm, *Reminiscences*, 63. E.g.: FA officiated for the "coloured brethren at sunrise; and at nine o'clock for the whites" in Delaware in 1791 (*J&L*, 1:696); at a love feast at the Calvert Circuit Quarterly Meeting in Maryland black people assembled in a barn and white people in the preaching house (EC, Journal, 13 vols. [1784–1802], vol. 8 [1791–1792], 28 August 1791, EC Collection, GTS); separate love feasts were often held on the Eastern Shore in 1794 (Richard Whatcoat, Journal [1789–1800], vol. 3 [1794–1796], 20 July, 3 August, and 10 August 1794, GTS).

48. Abbott, *Experience*, 102–3; Colbert, Journal, 1:6; Morris L. Radoff, *Buildings of the State of Maryland at Annapolis* (Annapolis, 1954), 111–12.

49. Sidney W. Mintz and Richard Price, *The Birth of African American Culture: An Anthropological Perspective* (1976; Boston, 1992). See also chap. 5, "Slavery and the African Spiritual Holocaust," in Jon Butler, *Awash in a Sea of Faith: Christianizing the American People* (Cambridge, MA, 1990), 129–63.

50. See discussion in Raboteau, *Slave Religion*, especially subtle distinctions among different kinds of possession and ecstatic behavior: 59–75. Like Raboteau, Melville J. Herskovits distinguishes between American revival ecstaticism and African forms (*The Myth of the Negro Past*, reprint ed. [1941; Boston, 1990], 215–21). I. M. Lewis, conversely, suggests a greater affinity between Christian and non-Christian forms: *Ecstatic Religion: An Anthropological Study of Spirit Possession and Shamanism* (1971; Harmondsworth, England, 1978), 37–44.

51. On geographical dispersal of forms of early black culture, see Berlin, "Time, Space."

52. See statistics for NY, New Jersey, and Pennsylvania, 1800–1810, in Peter D. McClelland and Richard J. Zeckhauser, *Demographic Dimensions of the New Republic: American Interregional Migration, Vital Statistics, and Manumissions, 1800–1860* (Cambridge, 1982), tables B-2 and B-3.

53. Berlin, *Slaves without Masters*, 46–47; see revised figures for Virginia and Maryland in 1810 in Dunn, "Black Society," 50n; Williams, *Slavery and Freedom*, 141–42.

54. Berlin, *Slaves without Masters*, 55; Christopher Phillips, *Freedom's Port: The African American Community of Baltimore, 1790–1860* (Urbana, IL, 1997), 14–29, and table 1, p. 15.

55. Nash and Soderlund, *Freedom by Degrees*, table 1-4.

56. White, *Somewhat More Independent*, table 4.

57. See "Methodological Note" and table 6 in appendixes below.

58. Class List, 1786, and Marriages, 1790, in John Street MEC, "A List of Baptisms, Marriages, Burials & Members of the Methodist Episcopal Church" (1784–1798), Methodist Records, microfilm, vol. 233, NYPL (hereafter cited as NY "List of Baptisms"). On the significance of naming among free people, see Berlin, *Slaves without Masters*, 51–52, and extended discussion in Gary B. Nash, *Forging Freedom: The Formation of Philadelphia's Black Community, 1720–1840* (Cambridge, MA, 1988), 20–27.

59. Joseph Pilmore to [unidentified] [ca. 1770], PLP 83.60.3, MAM; Baptisms, 1785–1786, in NY "List of Baptisms."

60. Table 7 in appendix below; Class List, 1786, in NY "List of Baptisms," and Class Lists, 1791 and 1796, in John Street MEC, "The Names and number of those persons in Society in the City of New York" (1791–1796), Methodist Records, microfilm, vol. 241, NYPL (hereafter cited as NY "Names and number"). See also White, *Somewhat More Independent*, table 4.

61. Table 7 in appendix below; Class Lists, 1791 and 1796, in NY "Names and number."

62. Marriages, 1792–1795, in NY "List of Baptisms." Nine of fourteen black women married in the NY society between 1792 and 1795 possessed forenames and surnames both.

63. Class List, 1786, in NY "List of Baptisms," and Class Lists, 1791 and 1796, in NY "Names and number." Collectively in these years, there are 10 clusters of 2 women sharing the same last name, and 9 clusters of 3 or more black women sharing the same last name.

64. In 1791, 1 black man can be identified as single and 4 were married. Five black women were single and 3 were married, and for these members there is no record of a husband's joining within one year. In 1796, all those whose marital status is known were married (4 men and 9 women, just 10 percent of the black membership), but there is no record of the husband's joining for 6 of the women, and just one couple was married prior to membership: Marriages, 1791–1798, and Baptisms, 1784–1795, in NY "List of Baptisms"; Marriages, 1799–1801, in John Street MEC, "Methodist Marriage Register for the City of New York" (1799–1820), Methodist Records, microfilm, vol. 72, NYPL; and Baptisms, 1796–1801, in John Street MEC, "Register of Baptisms For The Methodist Episcopal Church in N York" (1796–1820), in Methodist Records, microfilm, vol. 234, NYPL.

65. White, *Somewhat More Independent*, 156–58, and table 22.

66. These links must be made with caution since race is rarely if ever specified in the city directories. In 1791, the probable occupational tally of black members' occupations is: 1 artisan, 1 gardener, 3 mariners, 1 service worker, and 1 laborer. In 1796, the probable tally is: 4 artisans, 4 small dealers, 1 gardener, 1 service worker, and 3 laborers. See *The New York Directory, and Register, for the Year 1795* (New York, 1795), *The American Almanack, New-York Register, and City Directory* (New York, 1796), and *Longworth's American Almanack, New-York Registery, and City Directory* (New York, 1797). No women's occupations were identified. For background, see also White, *Somewhat More Independent*, 159–66, and Paul A. Gilje and Howard B. Rock, " 'Sweep O! Sweep O!': African-American Chimney Sweeps and Citizenship in the New Nation," *WMQ* 51 (1994): 507–38.

67. J. B. Wakeley, *Lost Chapters Recovered from the Early History of American Methodism* (New York, 1858), 438–79; entries dated 10 June, 12 July, and 7 December 1783 in John Street MEC, Treasurer Account Book (1768–1796), Methodist Records, microfilm, vol. 249, NYPL.

68. William C. Nell, *The Colored Patriots of the American Revolution*, reprint ed. (New York, 1968), 320.

69. "List of Classes February 1793," in NY "Names and number," and Marriages, 1785–1798, in NY "List of Baptisms." On black chorus, see Whatcoat, Journal, vol. 2 (1792–1793), 19 February 1792, LCMD.

70. *Minutes of Several Conversations* (1785), 13–14. In 1787, Jane Barsary, whose name appears at the head of one black class list, appears to have been a black leader: Class Lists, 1786–1787, in NY "List of Baptisms," and Class Lists, 1791–1796, in NY "Names and number."

71. *Minutes* (1813), 154, and table 8 in appendix below. For sources, see Class Lists, 1800–1801, BA City Station MEC, "Class Records" (1799–1803), microfilm no. 408,

MDSA (hereafter cited as BA Class Records); and Class List, 1800, in East BA Station (FP) MEC, "Annual Register For the Methodist Episcopal Church on Fells Point" (1800–1818), microfilm no. 411, MDSA (hereafter cited as FP "Annual Register"). The percentage for NY City is from the church records cited above.

72. Whitman, *Price of Freedom*, 61–92.

73. Class List, 1800, in BA Class Records. See "Levin Wails" in Certificates of Freedom, 1802, p. 3, BA, 0290, MDSA. In 1799–1800 collectively, 48 of the 341 black women in the BA City society bore a single name, and 17 out of 194 black men.

74. See table 9 in appendix below. See also *J&L*, 2:51, 65; "List of black Speakers," 1800, in BA Class Records. On Dublin, see David Smith, *Biography of David Smith of the A.M.E. Church*, facsimile ed. (1881; Freeport, NY, 1971), 17–18.

75. See table 9 in appendix below; Class Lists, 1800–1801, in FP "Annual Register." In 1800–1801 collectively, 3 black women out of 55 bear a single name, and 6 men out of 49. On economic status, see James M. Wright, *The Free Negro in Maryland, 1634–1860*, reprint ed. (1921; New York, 1971), 152–54. Five men at BA City Station and 2 at FP were possibly artisans, not a significant sample: *The New Baltimore Directory and Annual Register; For 1800 and 1801* (Baltimore, 1801). The black members of the Brooklyn Methodist society formed a similar profile: of the 26 black members in 1798, 14 were men and 12 were women, and just 5 may be identified as slaves: Edwin Warriner, *Old Sands Street Methodist Episcopal Church, of Brooklyn, New York* (New York, 1885), 13.

76. Abbott, *Experience*, 159–60. John Lee also appears to have spoken to this group: Jesse Lee, *A Short Account of the Life and Death of the Rev. John Lee, A Methodist Minister in the United States of America* (Baltimore, 1805), 61. On Watts, see C. Eric Lincoln and Lawrence H. Mamiya, *The Black Church in the African American Experience* (Durham, NC, 1990), 354–55.

77. Colbert, Journal, vol. 1, 23 January 1794.

78. W. E. Burghardt Du Bois, *The Souls of Black Folk, Essays and Sketches*, reprint ed. (1903; Greenwich, CT, 1961), 141.

79. Quoted in Raboteau, *Slave Religion*, 146; on black preachers, see 133–49. See also Sidney Kaplan and Emma Nogrady Kaplan, *The Black Presence in the Era of the American Revolution*, rev. ed. (Amherst, MA, 1989), 90–130. The Methodists recruited several black preachers before the Revolution. See reference to a black preacher who returned to England with Rankin in Thomas Rankin to Matthew Mayer, 7 July 1778, Lamplough Collection, 657:160, MAM. On Jacob Toogood, raised up by Robert Strawbridge, see Edwin Schell, "Beginnings in Maryland and America," in *Those Incredible Methodists: A History of the Baltimore Conference of the United Methodist Church*, ed. Gordon Pratt Baker (Baltimore, 1972), 13–14, and Whatcoat, Journal, vol. 2, 18 June 1793. Another early black preacher, Thomas Miller, was emancipated by Catherine Livingston's brother-in-law, Thomas Tillotson: see *Ladies Repository* (June 1864), 324, DUL.

80. Boehm, *Reminiscences*, 91–92; *J&L*, 1:362; Abel Stevens, *History of the Methodist Episcopal Church in the United States of America*, vol. 2 (New York, 1866), 171–74; and John Street MEC, Treasurer Account Book, 21 September 1786 and 11 June 1787.

81. *J&L*, 1:403 ff.; Simpson, *American Methodist Pioneer*, 266–70.

82. *New York Packet*, 11 September 1786: quoted in Samuel Seaman, *Annals of New York Methodism* (New York, 1892), 92–93.

83. Stevens, *History of the Methodist Episcopal Church*, 2:175; see also John Lednum, *A History of the Rise of Methodism in America, Containing Sketches of Methodist Itinerant Preachers, From 1736 to 1785* (Philadelphia, 1859), 282. William Colbert cites the date of Hosier's funeral as May 1806: see Warren S. Napier, "Formed for Friendship: Revi-

sioning Early American Circuit Riders through the Journal of William Colbert, 1790–1833" (Ph.D. diss., Iliff School of Theology and the University of Denver, 1996), 305.

84. *Minutes of Several Conversations* (1785), 13–14.

85. Gary B. Nash, "New Light on Richard Allen: The Early Years of Freedom," *WMQ* 46 (1989): 332.

For the fullest accounts of RA's life, see his memoir, *The Life Experience and Gospel Labours of the Rt. Rev. Richard Allen*, ed. George A. Singleton, reprint ed. (Nashville, 1960), dictated to his son, probably in 1816 at the time of the organization of the AME denomination; Charles H. Wesley, *Richard Allen: Apostle of Freedom*, reprint ed. (1935; Washington, DC, 1969), Carol George, *Segregated Sabbaths: Richard Allen and the Emergence of Independent Black Churches, 1760–1840* (New York, 1973), Barbara Clark Smith, "The Limits of Liberty: Richard Allen, Freedman of Philadelphia," in idem, *After the Revolution: The Smithsonian History of Everyday Life in the Eighteenth Century* (New York, 1985), 139–86, and Nash, *Forging Freedom*, 95–132.

86. RA, *Life Experience*, 15–16. RA could not have spent his earliest years at Benjamin Chew's Cliveden estate in Germantown, PH, as some historians have assumed, since the mansion was not occupied until late 1767 or early 1768: Nancy E. Richards to author, 18 March 1994. RA also refers to leaving his "native place" of Delaware in *Life Experience*, 19. For further details, see Wesley, *Richard Allen*, 162, and Nash, "New Light." Sturgis's will, probated in 1787, lists the assets of a small farmer, including one Negro woman and three children, valued at just £15; since these servants were left to neither of Sturgis's children, it may be assumed they were already manumitted: Stokely [*sic*] Sturgis, Will, 26 April 1787, Kent Co. Wills, pp. 109–10, and Inv., 17 May 1787, A49:112–13, DSA.

87. Black membership on the Dover circuit rose from 158 in 1786 to 350 in 1790; blacks constituted 28 percent of Dover's Methodist population by 1790: *Minutes*, (1795), 92, 146. On Dover's abolition society, see Williams, *Slavery and Freedom*, 154.

88. RA's mother, now living on another farm, was also converted: *Life Experience*, 15–16.

89. Ibid., 29–30, 16–19.

90. RA, *Life Experience*, 16–18. FA refers to preaching at "Sturgis's" near Dover on 13 August 1779: *J&L*, 1:310.

91. RA, *Life Experience*, 17; Freeborn Garretson [*sic*], *A Dialogue Between Do-Justice and Professing-Christian* (Wilmington, DE, n.d.), 35–36. FG continues: "Richard Allen, a colored man, told me some time ago, it [FG's sermon] was a means of his spiritual, and bodily freedom. He is now a man of note and fortune, and a minister in the African church, in Philadelphia."

92. RA, *Life Experience*, 17. Manumission paper is reproduced as Document A in Nash, "New Light," 338. Allen refers to Sturgis's requiring payment of £60 for both his and his brother's time, but his manumission certificate refers only to himself.

93. RA, *Life Experience*, 18–19. See also Document B in Nash, "New Light," 339.

94. RA, *Life Experience*, 18–22. RA worshiped at "a small meeting-house called Methodist Alley" (22); the building at FP was called the Strawberry Alley Chapel and was likely the same place. On details, see Nash, "New Light," 339, and Kathrine Hewit Cumin, "The Blacks in Radnor before 1850," *Bulletin of the Radnor Historical Society* 3 (1973): 14–15.

95. RA, *Life Experience*, 22–24. On FA's possible jealousy of RA, see Lorenzo Dow, *History of Cosmopolite; or the Four Volumes of Lorenzo's Journal, Concentrated in One*, 3d ed., corr. and enl. (Philadelphia, 1816), 558–59.

96. Nash and Soderlund, *Freedom by Degrees*, table 1-4. On residential patterns, see Nash, *Forging Freedom*, 58, 144–69, Emma Jones Lapsansky, *Before the Model City: An Historical Exploration of North Philadelphia* (Philadelphia, [1968]), 10, and idem, "South Street Philadelphia, 1762–1854: 'A Haven for Those Low in the World' " (Ph.D. diss., University of Pennsylvania, 1975), 83–120.

97. Kaplan and Kaplan, *Black Presence*, 50–52, and Nash and Soderlund, *Freedom by Degrees*, 172; General Minutes, Reports, 1788–1795 [Report on the Black Population], 1 December 1795, microfilm, reel 9, PAS. On conditions of black life, see Nash, *Forging Freedom*, 76–77, Billy G. Smith, "Black Family Life in Philadelphia from Slavery to Freedom," in *Shaping a National Culture: The Philadelphia Experience, 1750–1800*, ed. Catherine E. Hutchins (Winterthur, DE, 1994), 87–89, and Susan E. Klepp, "Seasoning and Society: Racial Differences in Mortality in Eighteenth-Century Philadelphia," *WMQ* 51 (1994): 495–502.

98. Nash and Soderlund, *Freedom by Degrees*, 41–73.

99. Quoted in John F. Watson, *Annals of Philadelphia, and Pennsylvania in the Olden Time . . .* , enl. and rev. ed., 3 vols. (Philadelphia, 1881), 1:406.

100. RA, *Life Experience*, 23–24. Jones had been brought to PH in 1762; he purchased his wife's freedom and then received his own in 1784 after a long negotiation with his master: see biographical sketch in William Douglass, *Annals of the First African Church, in the United States of America, now styled the African Episcopal Church of St. Thomas, Philadelphia* (Philadelphia, 1862), 119–22, Nash, *Forging Freedom*, 67–70, and Williams, *Slavery and Freedom*, 127. On earlier Baptist congregations in the South, see Lincoln and Mamiya, *Black Church*, 23–24.

101. See Wesley, *Richard Allen*, George, *Segregated Sabbaths*, Will B. Gravely, "The Rise of African Churches in America (1786–1822): Re-Examining the Contexts," *Journal of Religious Thought* 41 (1984), idem, "African Methodisms and the Rise of Black Denominationalism," in *Perspectives on American Methodism*, ed. Russell E. Richey, Kenneth E. Rowe, and Jean Miller Schmidt (Nashville, 1993), 108–26, Gary B. Nash, "To Arise out of the Dust," in idem, *Race, Class, and Politics: Essays on American Colonial and Revolutionary Society* (Urbana, IL, 1986), idem, *Forging Freedom*, 100–133, and Julie Winch, *Philadelphia's Black Elite: Activism, Accommodation, and the Struggle for Autonomy, 1787–1848* (Philadelphia, 1988).

102. RA, *Life Experience*, 24–25.

103. Douglass, *Annals*, 15.

104. On original FAS members, see: Douglass, *Annals*, 17, Nash, *Forging Freedom*, 98–99, and, more specifically, the profile of Moses Johnson in ibid., 66–67; Bustill in Kaplan and Kaplan, *Black Presence*, 100; William Wilshire in Acting Committee Minute Book, vol. 1 (1784–1788), microfilm, reel 4, p. 74, PAS; endorsement identifying Gray's occupation on back of William Gray to Benjamin Rush, 24 October 1792, Afro-American Collection, no. 1980, LCP/HSP; and reference to Cranchell in A[bsalom] J[ones] and R[ichard] A[llen], *A Narrative of the Proceedings of the Black People During the Late Awful Calamity in Philadelphia, in the Year 1793: And A Refutation of some Censures, Thrown upon them in some late Publications*, reprint ed. (1794; Philadelphia, n.d.), 56–57.

105. Douglass, *Annals*, 31–32.

106. Ibid., 21–42.

107. Ibid., 45–46; Benjamin Rush, "Commonplace Book," in *The Autobiography of Benjamin Rush: His "Travels Through Life" Together with his Commonplace Book for*

1789–1813, ed. George W. Corner (Princeton, 1948), 202. On Ralston, see Nash, *Forging Freedom*, 116.

108. "The Address of the Representatives of the African Church . . . ," *Dunlap's American Daily Advertiser* (PH), 30 August 1791; reprinted in *Extract of a Letter from Dr. Benjamin Rush of Philadelphia to Granville Sharp* (London, 1792). For Rush's comments on the church, see *Autobiography*, 202–3.

109. RA, *Life Experience*, 25–26.

110. Douglass, *Annals*; 43–46, Winch, *Philadelphia's Black Elite*, 9–11, and Nash, *Forging Freedom*, 112–18. Charles Wesley notes RA does not appear to have returned to the FAS despite his later participation in the African Church: *Richard Allen*, 70.

111. RA, *Life Experience*, 25–26. The event at St. George's was traditionally dated to 1787, around the time of the founding of the FAS. Milton C. Sernett has observed, however, that St. George's galleries were not built until 1792: *Black Religion and American Evangelicalism: White Protestants, Plantation Missions, and the Flowering of Negro Christianity, 1787–1865* (Metuchen, NJ, 1975), 117. For other versions of this episode, cf.: Wesley, *Richard Allen*, 52, George, *Segregated Sabbaths*, 54–55, Winch, *Philadelphia's Black Elite*, 9–15, Nash, "To Arise out of the Dust," 323–55, and idem, *Forging Freedom*, 118.

112. RA, *Life Experience*, 27. For McClaskey's background, see John Atkinson, *Memorials of Methodism in New Jersey, from the Foundation of the First Society in the State in 1770, to the Completion of the First Twenty Years of Its History*, 2d ed. (Philadelphia, 1860), 235, 352–56.

113. RA, *Life Experience*, 26–28. Nicholson promised a loan of $2,000, the first half of which the FAS received in February, the second in May: Douglass, *Annals*, 47–57. *Dunlap's American Daily Advertiser* (PH), 5 April 1793, refers to the laying of the cornerstone of the African church. See also discussion in Nash, *Forging Freedom*, 119–21.

114. Nash, *Forging Freedom*, 1, 121; Rush, *Autobiography*, 228–29. Nicholson agreed to lend $1,000 more for the church in August: John Nicholson to Absalom Jones and William Gray, 8 August 179[3], Afro-American Collection, no. 3100, LCP/HSP.

115. On general background, see Wesley, *Richard Allen*, 256, and Nash, *Forging Freedom*, 153–54; on occupations, see *The Philadelphia Directory* (Philadelphia, 1791), *Prospect of Philadelphia* (Philadelphia, 1795), and *The Philadelphia Directory for 1800* (Philadelphia, 1800). In 1793 RA had put up his house on Spruce Street as collateral for a loan from the PAS to "Absalom Jones & Co.," a partnership between the two men for a nail factory: Committee for Improving the Condition of Free Blacks, Minute Book, 1790–1803, 10/7M/1793, pp. 68–69, and 30/7M/1793, p. 69, microfilm, reel 6, PAS.

116. PH Tax Assessments, New Market Ward, 1791–1800, PCA, and PH Tax Assessment, Cedar Ward, 1805. For other wealthy blacks in 1790s PH, see Nash and Soderlund, *Freedom by Degrees*, 172. See also RA's will, dated 9 December 1830, in Wesley, *Richard Allen*, 255, 271–74: RA's inventory lists $3,983.17 worth of property and tenements bequeathed to RA's children and grandchildren; his assets at the time of his death totaled $40,000.

117. Jones and Allen, *Narrative of the Proceedings of the Black People*.

118. Gravely, "Rise of African Churches," 65; Winch, *Philadelphia's Black Elite*, 11; Nash, *Forging Freedom*, 127–28; and RA, *Life Experience*, 30. The FAS reappeared in the form of the St. Thomas's Friendly Society: see *Constitution and Rules to be Observed and Kept By the Friendly Society of St. Thomas's African Church of Philadelphia*, reprint ed. (1797; New York, 1969).

119. Jones was admitted to full priestly orders in 1804, but St. Thomas's was not admitted to the Episcopal Convention until 1862: Gravely, "Rise of African Churches," 61.

120. RA, *Life Experience*, 29–31.

121. B. T. Tanner, *An Outline of Our History and Government For African Methodist Churchmen, Ministerial and Lay, In Catechetical Form* ([Philadelphia], 1884), 144–45, and Wesley, *Richard Allen*, 77.

122. *J&L*, 2:18. RA attributes the naming of Bethel to preacher John Dickins: *Life Experience*, 31. On FG, see *Minutes* (1813) 129; FG's journal ends in May 1794, so his version of the founding of Bethel has not survived.

On 30 October 1794, RA and his wife Flora deeded the land for Bethel to trustees John Morris, William Hoggins, John Allen, Jonathan Trusty, Robert Green, and Phillip Johnston. The Allens retained strict control over the property's ground rents and the right to sell goods on the premises or expel the trustees if payment was not forthcoming: Richard Allen to Trustees of the African Methodist Episcopal Church, Deed, 30 October 1794, Letter of Attorney 2, PCA.

123. *J&L*, 2:18.

124. "Public Statement," reprinted in Tanner, *Outline of Our History*, 144–49. Regarding the white class leaders: see John Clinton in *Prospect of Philadelphia* (1795), not identified as black; Blades Wildgoose was likely from Delaware, where the name was common: see, e.g., Thomas Wildgoose, Will, 28 December 1781, Sussex Co. Wills, A107:112, DSA, in which Wildgoose's son Blades inherits a farm.

125. EC refers to transcribing the Articles of Association "for the incorporation of our African Church" in his Journal, vol. 12 (1795–1798), [7] October 1796. For contents, see African Methodist Episcopal Church, *Articles of Association of the African Methodist Episcopal Church*, reprint ed. (1799; Philadelphia, 1969), 3–10.

126. See chap. 8 below.

127. Table 10 in appendix below. The names of Bethel's first members appear in "List of the members of the African Methodist Episcopal Church in the City of Philadelphia," ca. 1794, in St. George's MEC, "Names of the Officers," reprinted in Dee Andrews, "The African Methodists of Philadelphia, 1794–1802," *PMHB* 108 (1984): 484. Forty-nine blacks belonged to three black classes at St. George's just before the founding of Bethel: see Class Lists, ca. 1794, in St. George's MEC, "Names of the Officers," reprinted in Andrews, "African Methodists," 483. Sixty-six blacks were tallied as members at St. George's for the annual minutes in 1794, probably including both the classes at St. George's and Allen's new church: *Minutes* (1813), 146.

128. Occupations of members and trustees have been identified in *The Philadelphia Directory and Register*, 2d ed. (Philadelphia, 1794), *Prospect of Philadelphia* (1795), and PH Tax Assessments, New Market Ward, 1796 and 1798, PCA. On Bass, see Wesley, *Richard Allen*, 159, and Jones and Allen, *Narrative of the Proceedings of the Black People*, 11.

Little is known of the 42 black Methodists remaining at St. George's. Jonathan York, the solitary black class leader in PH, was a laborer from Southwark: see *Philadelphia Directory* (1794), and PH Tax Assessment, Southwark, West, 1799, PCA, where York is identified as "Negroe." The only members to appear in the *Prospect of Philadelphia* (1795), in which blacks were identified by the abbreviation "Af." for "African," were Jane Gray, a washerwoman, William Hooper, a carter, John Morris, master chimney sweep, David Solomon, a carpenter, and Hester Vandergrief, a cook. Another member, Jacob Gibbs, had petitioned the PAS for freedom from his Delaware master in 1786 (Acting Committee, Minute Book, vol. 1, 1784–1788, pp. 76, 78, 79, microfilm, reel 4, PAS). Cf. St. Thomas's "Register of Members Up to 1794," in Douglass, *Annals*, 107–9. St. Thomas's 239 members, more men than women, were representative of the rising lower classes in the city, among them former Methodists William Gray, William White, and Dorus Jennings. Twenty-eight, or about 17 percent, of the men in the church and 2 women appear in the 1795 PH directory, signifying their relatively high status in the black community: *Prospect of Philadelphia* (1795). Twenty were former Free Africans, and many were to join the African Free Mason Lodge of Pennsylvania: Charles H. Wesley, *Prince Hall: Life and Legacy* (Washington, DC, 1977), 219, William H. Grimshaw, *Official History of Freemasonry among the Colored People in North America*, reprint ed. (1903; New York, 1969), 112, and Harry E. Davis, *A History of Freemasonry among Negroes in America* ([Boston], 1946), 290–91.

129. *Philadelphia Directory* (1794), *Prospect of Philadelphia* (1795), PH Tax Assessment, South Mulberry Ward, 1798, PCA. On Green, see Douglass, *Annals*, 15, 24, 47, and Nash, *Forging Freedom*, 228–29.

130. *Minutes* (1813), 154–56, 190–93. The class lists for Zoar have not survived, but a register of those admitted on trial includes forty-seven probationary members between June 1800 and December 1801: see St. George's MEC, "A List of the Officers," reprinted in Andrews, "African Methodists," 485–86. Several Sturgises, further Delaware connections, belonged to St. George's: Stockley Sturgis is identified as a laborer in *The Philadelphia Directory, City and County Register, for 1802* (Philadelphia, 1802) and hence is unlikely to be Stokeley Sturgis's son who inherited his father's Delaware farm (see reference above), but is probably a relation; Jonathan Sturgis is identified as "from Wilmington" and his marriage is recorded 22 November 1791, in Asbury MEC, Wilmington, Marriages, 1788–1954, DSA. For references to Beulah, see St. George's MEC, "An Account of Appointments and Sacrement days," 1802, in Church Records, OSHS, and Thomas Sargente to Thomas Morrell, 12 June 1803, GTS.

131. RA and Jupiter Gibson to EC, 22 February 1798, EC Collection, GTS. On the significance of singing in black Christianity, see Lincoln and Mamiya, *Black Church*, 348. A famous, unsympathetic description of singing at Bethel in 1811 appears in Avrahm Yarmolinsky, *Picturesque United States of America, 1811, 1812, 1813, Being a Memoir of Paul Svinin . . .* (New York, 1930).

132. Members, 1801, in St. George's MEC, "Names of the Officers"; *Minutes* (1813), 256–57. In June 1803, RA reported that the congregation now included 457 "Communicants," nearly 100 more members than had attended all of St. George's when the FAS Methodists first walked out: "Some Letters of Dorothy Ripley," *Journal of Negro History* 1 (1916): 441. On size in 1813, see Nash, *Forging Freedom*, 193.

133. Thirteen out of 71 signators can be identified as Methodists. Since membership lists for Bethel have not survived past 1794, it is likely a greater proportion of the signators were in fact members of Bethel or St. George's; just 7 appear on St. Thomas's original membership list: Petition to U.S. Congress, 30 December 1799, reprinted in Kaplan and Kaplan, *Black Presence*, 273–76.

134. As Will Gravely writes, through "[t]he unprecedented local nature of the office" of local deacon, RA was permitted to perform marriages and baptisms at Bethel, but not communion, nor marriage and baptism outside Bethel: Gravely, "African Methodisms," 113.

135. MEC, *Journal of the General Conference*, 43; Jesse Lee, *A Short History of the Methodists, in the United States of America: beginning in 1766, and continued till 1809* (Baltimore, 1810), 270. Probably about twelve black local deacons were ordained between 1800 and FA's death in 1816; others were itinerants: see Reginald F. Hildebrand, "Methodist Episcopal Policy on the Ordination of Black Ministers, 1784–1864," *MH* 20 (1982):

126–27, 126n-27n. Full authority for black ministers was finally provided in the "mission conferences" equivalent to annual conferences in 1864 (141–42).

136. James A. Handy, *Scraps of African Methodist Episcopal History* (Philadelphia, [1901]), 23–24, and Wright, *Free Negro in Maryland*, 202–18. Gravely notes that Daniel Coker refers to the existence of two black churches in the city in 1810: "African Methodisms," 118. See also EC, "The Plan of appointments for the stationed preachers in Baltimore from June 1812 to April 1813," EC Collection, GTS, which refers to Eutaw, Old Town, Light Street, and the African churches. On Hill and prayer groups, see *Biography of David Smith*, 18–20.

137. *J&L*, 2:51 and 65; Handy, *Scraps of African Methodist Episcopal History*, 23–24. For further discussion, see Phillips, *Freedom's Port*, 128–30.

138. Gravely, "African Methodisms," 117–18. On the first of several land transactions for the purpose of applying the profits from the sales to the "purchase of some proper and convenient house for the accommodation of the members of the African Methodist Episcopal Church in the City of Baltimore," see Indenture, 4 April 1801, BA County Court Records, bk. WG, no. 142, pp. 243–44; as well as Indenture, 16 December 1801, BA County Court Land Records, bk. WG no. 71, pp. 124–27, and two indentures dated 25 October 1803, BA County Court Land Records, bk. WG, no. 78, pp. 538–40, 643–45. On the Sharp Street lot and deed, see Wright, *Free Negro in Maryland*, 202–3, 213.

139. See further discussion in Phillips, *Freedom's Port*, 129–35.

140. Charles W. Gaddess to James M. Buckley, 14 February 1888, DUL: Gaddess purchased a copy of the 1791 edition of *The Life of Olaudah Equiano* that was inscribed: "Peter Williams his book, Nov 29. 1796." on the front page, and "Peter Williams, Tobacconist, Nov. 29. 1796." on the back.

141. Christopher Rush, *A Short Account of the Rise and Progress of the African Methodist Episcopal Church in America* (New York, 1843), 9–11.

142. Rush, *Short Account*, 10; and David Henry Bradley, Sr., *A History of the A.M.E. Zion Church*, pt. 1 (1796–1872) (Nashville, 1956), 46–47. Black membership fell 1 percentage point from 1796 to 1800 (18 percent to 17 percent) but also remained low compared with the other city societies: Class List, 1796, in NY "Names and number," and *Minutes* (1813), 242. On Zion's lease, dated 21 July 1800, see Bradley, *History of the A.M.E. Zion Church*, 60: all three men had been members at John Street since at least 1796 (Class List, 1796, in NY "Names and number").

143. Rush, *Short Account*, 12–13: the Articles of Association are reprinted, 14–24. See also Gravely, "African Methodisms," 122–24.

144. In 1802, out of 11 black classes, 4 male and 7 female, just 3 were meeting at Zion Church and 1 at Peter Williams's house (John Street MEC, Members and Probationers, 1802–1811, in Methodist Records, microfilm, vol. 237, NYPL). In the same year, Zion contributed just $25.70 to the collection in NY, out of a total of $608.88 donations (NY Annual Conference Journal, 1800–1820, in Methodist Records, microfilm, vol. 12, NYPL).

145. Philip Bruce to Daniel Fidler, 27 December 1799, DUL. The Wilmington membership totaled 30 blacks and 40 whites in 1796, and 87 whites and 47 blacks in 1800: *Minutes* (1813), 175, 241.

146. Asbury MEC, Wilmington, Minutes of the Trustees, 1803–1872, Church Records, 19 June 1805, BC. See excerpt from *The Mirror of the Times and General Advertiser*, 6 February 1805, quoted in Lewis V. Baldwin, *"Invisible" Strands in African Methodism: A History of the African Union Methodist Protestant and Union American Methodist Episcopal Churches, 1805–1980* (Metuchen, NJ, 1983), 41–42; and idem, *The Mark of a Man:*

Peter Spencer and the African Union Methodist Tradition. The Man, the Movement, the Message, and the Legacy (Lanham, MD, 1987), 2, 7n.

147. Quoted in Baldwin, *Invisible Strands*, 43. See also Gravely, "African Methodisms," 120–21, Williams, *Garden*, 116, and idem, *Slavery and Freedom*, 224–30.

148. Baldwin, *Invisible Strands*, 43–51.

149. Simpson, *American Methodist Pioneer*, 227.

150. George White, *A Brief Account of the Life, Experience, Travels, and Gospel Labours of George White, An African* (New York, 1810), 2–16. For further information on White, see Graham Russell Hodges, ed., *Black Itinerants of the Gospel: The Narratives of John Jea and George White* (Madison, WI, 1993), introduction.

151. White, *Brief Account*, 16–29, 34–38.

152. Lincoln and Mamiya, *Black Church*, 348.

Chapter Six
Laboring Men, Artisans, and Entrepreneurs

1. *J&L*, ed. Elmer T. Clark, J. Manning Potts, and Jacob S. Payton, 3 vols. (London and Nashville, 1958), 1:748.

2. E. P. Thompson, "Eighteenth-Century English Society: Class Struggle without Class?" *Social History* 3 (1978): 150. For discussions of American crowds, see Gary B. Nash, *Urban Crucible: Social Change, Political Consciousness, and the Origins of the American Revolution* (Cambridge, MA, 1979), chap. 11, and Rhys Isaac, *The Transformation of Virginia, 1740–1790* (Chapel Hill, NC, 1982), 161–77, 243–69.

3. John D. Walsh, "Elie Halévy and the Birth of Methodism," *Transactions of the Royal Historical Society*, 5th ser., 25 (1975): 13, 19.

4. "La naissance du Méthodisme en Angleterre," *Revue de Paris*, 1906, 519–39, 841–67, reprinted in *The Birth of Methodism in England*, trans. and ed. Bernard Semmel (Chicago, 1971). Halévy later applied his thesis to changes occurring in English society at the start of the nineteenth century: see idem, *A History of the English People in the Nineteenth Century*, vol. 1, *England in 1815*, rev. ed. (1913; London 1949), 387–485.

5. Quoted in Michael Hill, *A Sociology of Religion* (New York, 1973), 108.

6. Thomas William Madron, "Some Economic Aspects of John Wesley's Thought Revisited," *MH* 6 (1965): 37, and John Walsh's reference to JW's "scheme of voluntary Christian communism," in "Elie Halévy," 16. See also JW, "The Use of Money," in *Works*, vol. 2, *Sermons II*, ed. Albert C. Outler (Nashville, 1985), 267, 266–80.

7. "The Danger of Riches" and "On Riches" in *Works*, vol. 3, *Sermons III*, ed. Albert C. Outler (Nashville, 1986), 236–39, 523–27.

8. "The Danger of Increasing Riches," in *Works*, vol. 4, *Sermons IV*, ed. Albert C. Outler (Nashville, 1987), 177–86; see also Madron, "Some Economic Aspects," 33–38.

9. E. P. Thompson, "The Moral Economy of the English Crowd in the Eighteenth Century," *PP*, no. 50 (1971): 76–136.

10. On the concept of class in eighteenth-century England and America, see Thompson, "Eighteenth-Century English Society," Sean Wilentz, *Chants Democratic: New York City and the Rise of the American Working Class, 1788–1850* (New York, 1984), 11–19, and Nash, *Urban Crucible*, x–xiii. See also Stuart M. Blumin's nuanced treatment in "The Hypothesis of Middle-Class Formation in Nineteenth-Century America: A Critique and Some Proposals," *AHR* 90 (1985): 299–338, and idem, *The Emergence of the Middle Class: Social Experience in the American City, 1760–1900* (Cambridge, 1989), chap. 1.

11. Benjamin Abbott, *The Experience and Gospel Labours of the Rev. Benjamin Abbott: To which is Annexed a Narrative of His Life and Death by John Ffirth* (Philadelphia, 1801), 94–95; *J&L*, 1:694. EC remarks of the workers at Speedwell Furnace that the people "generally in such places are very wicked": Journal, 13 vols. (1784–1802), vol. 3 (1787–1788), 27 June 1787, EC Collection, GTS. On Maryland ironworkers, see Richard J. Cox, "Servants at Northampton Forge," *National Genealogical Society Quarterly* 63 (1975): 110–17.

12. Ronald Schultz, "The Small-Producer Tradition and the Moral Origins of Artisan Radicalism," *PP*, no. 127 (1990): 84–116, and idem, *The Republic of Labor: Philadelphia Artisans and the Politics of Class, 1720–1830* (New York, 1993).

13. *Arminian Magazine* (PH) 2 (1790): 505, 604.

14. BA City Station MEC, "An Account of Negroes bought by our Members in Baltimore Town," Methodist Records, microfilm no. 408, MDSA; Grace Webb to Charles Webb, Miscellaneous Manuscripts, 4 August 1797, HSP.

15. Abbott, *Experience*, 157–58, 177–80. Likewise in Newburgh, NY, Abbott describes the town's "sinners" as having "roved round the house like wolves": 139.

16. Richard Swain, *Journal of Rev. Richard Swain*, transc. and ed. Robert Bevis Steelman (Rutland, VT, 1977), 35; William Colbert, Journal, 10 vols. (1790–1822), vol. 1 (1790–1794), 15 May 1791, GTS. In New England, incidents occurred over theology, for example, a dispute with Baptists in Connecticut concerning the Methodist doctrine of grace: "Such a tumult I never saw before. A baptist minister was present, and stood up and spoke to pacify the people; but they said as much against him, as they had said against me": Jesse Lee, *A Short Account of the Life and Death of the Rev. John Lee, A Methodist Minister in the United States of America* (Baltimore, 1805), 102; see also 105–6, 113.

17. *J&L*, 2:132.

18. Ibid., 2:171, and CLG to M[argaret] Tillotson, 2[8] December 1793, DUL; see also EC's more scientific discussion in "Account of the Yellow Fever or American Pestilence," *Methodist Magazine* 2 (1798): 514–20.

19. John Dickins to Thomas Mifflin, 14 September 1792, Record Group 26, Department of State, Secretary of Commonwealth, Executive Correspondence, 2 September–6 October 1792, Pennsylvania State Archives, Harrisburg, Pennsylvania.

20. *J&L*, 1:729–30.

21. J.G.J. Bend, Sermon, 29 August 1791, and St. Peter's Parish Report, Talbot County, Maryland, 5 June 1797, MDA/PEC.

22. Abbott, *Experience*, 90–91.

23. Robert Drew Simpson, "Lost Letters of Bishop Asbury," *MH* 32 (1994): 101; FA to Jasper Winscom, 23 January 1796, typescript, UMHS. See also E. Benson Perkins, *Methodist Preaching Houses and the Law: The Story of the Model Deed* (London, 1952), chap. 1, for examples of English Methodist boards of trustees who attempted to set up appointment of preachers for themselves.

24. John Paca to Trustees of Preaching House, Abingdon, [Maryland], 3 July 1784, [Harford County Court], Chattel Records, 1774–1784, MDSA. BA merchant Richard Moale left £200 in specie to FA "for the express purpose of supplying Preachers sent to new places to publish the Gospel," and £150 to Harry Dorsey Gough "for the benefit of the new Chapple in Baltimore belonging to the people called Methodists": Richard Moale, Will, 22 February 1786, BA Wills, 1786, bk. 21, fol. 5, MDSA.

25. William Henry Williams, *The Garden of American Methodism: The Delmarva Peninsula, 1769–1820* (Dover, DE, 1984), 74.

26. "Memoir of the Late Rev. Henry Foxall," *Methodist Magazine* (NY) 7 (1824): 367–71; Homer L. Calkin, "Henry Foxall, Foundryman and Friend of Asbury," *MH* 6 (1967): 36–49.

27. Eleanor Dorsey to H. D. Gough, 17 September 1802, Gough-Carroll Papers, MS 2560, MDHS. Eleanor was probably the wife of Daniel Dorsey who moved to Genesee, NY, from Anne Arundel County: Abel Stevens, *The Women of Methodism: Its Three Foundresses, Susanna Wesley, The Countess of Huntingdon, and Barbara Heck; with Sketches of their Female Associates and Successors in the Early History of the Denomination* (New York, 1866), 248.

28. Jacob M. Price, "Economic Function and the Growth of American Port Towns in the Eighteenth Century," *Perspectives in American History* 7 (1974): appendix B, p. 176; and Shane White, *Somewhat More Independent: The End of Slavery in New York City, 1770–1810* (Athens, GA, 1991), table 4, p. 26, and "A Note to the Reader," xxv–xxix.

29. Merchant Samuel Breck, quoted in Wilentz, *Chants Democratic*, 24; Noah Webster, "Description of New York," in *The New York Directory for 1786*, reprint ed. (1786; New York, [1905]), 6.

30. See "Plan of the City of New York," in *New York Directory (1786)*, frontispiece; for old wards, see White, *Somewhat More Independent*, 44. See also Howard B. Rock, *Artisans of the New Republic: The Tradesmen of New York City in the Age of Jefferson* (New York, 1979), 1–16.

31. EC, Journal, vol. 12 (1795–1798), 1 May 1795.

32. Richard W. Pointer, *Protestant Pluralism and the New York Experience: A Study of Eighteenth-Century Religious Diversity* (Bloomington, IN, 1988), 45–46; Webster, "Description of New York," 10; "Plan of the City of New York."

33. Price, "Economic Function," 159–60, and appendix E, p. 184; on the postwar and republican city as a whole, see Wilentz, *Chants Democratic*, 23–60, 107–42; on the Swamp, see Alfred F. Young, *The Democratic Republicans of New York: The Origins, 1763–1797* (Chapel Hill, NC, 1967), 475.

34. See the evocative description of 1790s NY in Young, *Democratic Republicans*, 468–76.

35. Blumin, *Emergence*, 35, and discussion, 17–65. On boardinghouses, see Wilentz, *Chants Democratic*, 51–52. For the ages of city-dwellers, see data in ibid., table 7, p. 402, indicating that 47 percent of journeymen in NY in 1816 were between the ages of 20 and 29; while the largest cluster of master artisans, 40 percent, were between the ages of 30 and 39. On immigrants, see Young, *Democratic Republicans*, 401–3, 472–73.

36. Wilentz, *Chants Democratic*, 63–77; see also Young, *Democratic Republicans*, 10–12, 201–2, 201n.

37. Baptism Records, 1786–1788, in John Street MEC, "A List of Baptisms, Marriages, Burials & Members of the Methodist Episcopal Church" (1784–1798), Methodist Records, microfilm, vol. 233, NYPL (hereafter cited as NY "List of Baptisms").

38. Morrell's comments, dated [2] January 1790–4 March [1790], in NY "List of Baptisms."

39. Table 1 in appendix below; *Minutes* (1813), 242; J. B. Wakeley, *Lost Chapters Recovered from the Early History of American Methodism* (New York, 1858), 493–95, 523–25.

40. *J&L*, 2:95–96. Another reason for the New Yorkers' independence was that the chapels on this circuit were incorporated under the authority of their trustees rather than the MEC itself: Frederick Maser and George Singleton, "Further Branches of Methodism

Are Founded," in *The History of American Methodism*, ed. Emory Stevens Bucke et al., 3 vols. (New York and Nashville, 1964), 1:626.

41. Class List, 1786, NY "List of Baptisms"; and Class Lists, 1791 and 1796, in John Street MEC "The Names and number of those persons in Society in the City of New York" (1791–1796), Methodist Records, microfilm, vol. 241, NYPL (hereafter cited as NY "Names and number").

42. Eighty-six white men and 20 black in 1791, and 101 white men and 17 black in 1796, do not appear in the directories for those years.

43. List of Exclusions, 1787, in NY "List of Baptisms."

44. In 1787, Staten Island subscribers built Woodrow Chapel on the west end of the island where "numbers, more especially of the poorer and middling ranks of people, who have not carriages, etc, are necessarily precluded from attending the worship of God": A. Y. Hubbell, *History of Methodism and the Methodist Churches of Staten Island* (New York, 1898), 28–31. See lists of trustees in ibid.; and in Edwin Warriner, *Old Sands Street Methodist Episcopal Church, of Brooklyn, New York* (New York, 1885), 9–10; and for the society founded in Tuckahoe, NY, in 1771 in J. Thomas Scharf, *History of Westchester County, New York, Including Morrisania, Kings Bridge, and West Farms, Which Have Been Annexed to New York City*, 2 vols. (Philadelphia, 1886), 1:60–61.

45. Richard Whatcoat, Journal, 3 vols. (1789–1800), vol. 2 (1792–1793), 4–11 March 1792, LCMD.

46. Wakeley, *Lost Chapters*, 534–40.

47. J. Henry Harper, *The House of Harper: A Century of Publishing on Franklin Square* (New York, 1912), 1–2.

48. "Death of Mr. Philip I. Arcularius," *Methodist Magazine* (NY) 6 (1925): 205–6; Harper, Arcularios, Perigo Genealogy, Arcularius Family, in Harper, Lathrop, Colgate Papers, Box 1, NYHS; Wakeley, *Lost Chapters*, 544–46.

49. Wakeley, *Lost Chapters*, 88–89.

50. "[Death of Mr. Paul Hick]," *Methodist Magazine* (NY) 8 (1825): 247–48; Wakeley, *Lost Chapters*, 542 ff. Paul Ruckle, Barbara Heck's brother, sometimes confused with Paul Hick, died in 1787: see burial record, 16 March 1787, in NY "List of Baptisms."

51. Wakeley, *Lost Chapters*, 554; *J&L*, 1:20n; and Hubbell, *History of Methodism*, 28–30.

52. Harold E. Dickson, *John Wesley Jarvis: American Painter, 1780–1840* (New York, 1949), 3–4. Dickson identifies Ann Lambert Jarvis as the granddaughter of the Wesleys' sister Ann.

53. Harper, *House of Harper*, 2; Eugene Exman, *The Brothers Harper: A Unique Publishing Partnership and Its Impact upon the Cultural Life of America from 1817–1853* (New York, 1965), 11.

54. See background and 1784 letter by John Jarvis in Dickson, *John Wesley Jarvis*, 10–20.

55. Harper, Arcularios, Perigo Genealogy; Exman, *Brothers Harper*, 11.

56. Wakeley, *Lost Chapters*, 88–89. On land purchases, see NY Deeds dated 9 January 1787, 25 August 1791, 20 April 1793, and 14 June 1793 in Staples and Sherman Family Papers, fold. 1, NYPL.

57. *The American Almanack, New-York Register, and City Directory* (New York, 1796).

58. Wakeley, *Lost Chapters*, 440–72; John Street MEC, Treasurer Account Book, 12 September 1791, 17 May 1793, and 1 September 1795 in Methodist Records, microfilm, vol. 249, NYPL. See passim for other contributions to the society by its members.

59. John J. Staples and Son, Account Book, 1792–1794, WL; Rutzen Suckley to Rev. Joseph B. Wakeley, 7 May 1866, DUL.

60. The exception was Philip Arcularius, an officer in the German Society: *American Almanack* [1796], 122–23. See also the names of 18 Methodist men out of 813 in "A List of Cartmen belonging to the City of New York, with the Number of their Carts": ibid., 96–106.

61. See table 11 in appendix below.

62. Ibid.; white and black men counted.

63. See discussion below; white men only counted.

64. Price, "Economic Function," appendix E, 184–85. I have adapted Price's occupational categories into an artisan sector by combining trades listed separately in his "Service Sector" and "Industrial Sector."

65. See table 11 in appendix below. On Russell, see Wakeley, *Lost Chapters*, 551–53.

66. See table 11 in appendix below.

67. Ibid. On Mercein, see Wakeley, *Lost Chapters*, 558–61.

68. Table 11 in appendix below. Black men not included.

69. Ibid. Black men not included.

70. Wilentz, *Chants Democratic*; on shoemakers, see E. J. Hobsbawm and Joan Wallach Scott, "Political Shoemakers," *PP*, no. 89 (1980): 86–114.

71. Rock, *Artisans*, 65.

72. Humbert was charged with having been a Tory, but he claimed that his allegiance to the British was forced (ibid., 144n).

73. Quoted by Wilentz, *Chants Democratic*, 226.

74. On Coddington, see Graham Russell Hodges, *New York City Cartmen, 1667–1850* (New York, 1986), 103.

75. List of officers, 1786, in NY "List of Baptisms"; Wakeley, *Lost Chapters*, 318. See table 11 in appendix below, for city directories.

76. List of officers, 1791, in NY "Names and number." By 1791, 22 of the 23 class leaders were white men. Of the 17 men with identifiable occupations, 13 were artisans, 3 were merchants, and 1 was a schoolmaster. See table 11 in appendix below, for city directories.

77. See table 12 in appendix below, and list of officers, 1796, in NY "Names and number." In 1796, of the 26 class leaders, 21 were artisans, 3 were merchants and retailers, 2 were marine or transport service workers. Among the trustees in 1796, 4 were artisans and 2 were merchants.

78. List of Exclusions, 1787.

79. List of Exclusions, 1791, in John Street MEC, "List of Exclusions" (1791–1793), Methodist Records, microfilm, no. 241, NYPL. The others were Ware Branson, cabinetmaker, Henry Darby, laborer, John McGee, house carpenter, David Renny, taylor, Robert Snow, grocer; and Henry Kelsor, Jacob Mott, John Rikeman, Benjamin Smith, and John Whiteman, occupations unknown. For city directories, see table 11 in appendix below. Rudd later became an artisan activist: see Rock, *Artisans*, 61.

80. See also EC on contested election of trustees at John Street and reference to great amount of work at the NY society: Journal vol. 12, 16 March 1795, 1 May 1795.

81. *J&L*, 2:96. Those returning were Rudd, Branson, Darby, McGee, Mott, Renny, and Smith. It may not have been coincidental that the occupations of three out of four men not returning—Kelsor, Rikeman, and Whiteman—are not identifiable, i.e., were those of geographically mobile laboring men. On the popularity of Universalism among workingmen, see Ronald Schultz, "God and Workingmen: Popular Religion and the Formation

of Philadelphia's Working Class, 1790–1830," in *Religion in a Revolutionary Age*, ed. Ronald Hoffman and Peter J. Albert (Charlottesville, VA, 1994), 137–39.

82. EC, Journal, vol. 12, 17 July 1796; *J&L*, 2:95–96.

83. John F. Watson, *Annals of Philadelphia and Pennsylvania in the Olden Time*, 2 vols. (Philadelphia, 1856), 1:456–57.

84. See account for St. George's in Thomas Armat, Ledger, 12 April 1781, Armat Section, Loudoun Papers, HSP; the new altar and pulpit are described in Fred Pierce Corson, "St. George's Church: The Cradle of American Methodism," in *Transactions of the American Philosophical Society* 43, pt. 1, *Historic Philadelphia: From the Founding until the Early Nineteenth Century*, reprint ed. (1953; Philadelphia, 1980), 232. On members, see MEC, *Minutes of the Methodist Conferences, Annually Held in America from 1773 to 1794, inclusive* (Philadelphia, 1795), 61–146; St. George's MEC, Appointment of Trustees, 7 November 1789, OSHS; idem, *An Act of Incorporating the Methodist Episcopal Church, Known by the Name of Saint George's Church, In the City of Philadelphia, in the Commonwealth of Pennsylvania* (Philadelphia, 1789); and *History of Ebenezer Methodist Episcopal Church of Southwark, Philadelphia* (Philadelphia, 1890), 24–40.

85. *J&L*, 1:603.

86. Watson, *Annals* [1856], 1:447–55; *J&L*, 1:651.

87. MEC, *Minutes of the Methodist Conferences, Annually Held in America; From 1773 to 1813, Inclusive* (New York, 1813), 156, 191, 224.

88. St. George's MEC, Subscription, 25 December 1787, and Henry Willis's bond, 23 April 1794, in Blotter (1787–1795), St. George's MEC, Receipt Book (1795–1806), 1795–1803 passim, and Subscription for roof, 20 January 1797 and 15 May 1798, OSHS.

89. James Penn Pilkington, *The Methodist Publishing House: A History*, 2 vols. (Nashville, 1968), 1:85, 95; *J&L*, 3:212–17; MEC, *Articles of Association of the Trustees of the Fund for the Relief and Support of the Itinerant, Superannuated, and Worn-Out Ministers and Preachers of the Methodist Episcopal Church, in the United States of America, Their Wives and Children, Widows and Orphans* (Philadelphia, 1797), 4. On the statehouse, see EC, Journal, vol. 13 (1798–1800), 11 August 1799 and January 1800.

90. Class records, ca. 1794–1801, in St. George's MEC, "The Names of the Officers, and Members of the Methodist Church in Philadelphia" (1785–1816), in Register Book, Church Records, OSHS.

91. *The Philadelphia Directory for 1800: . . . also a Register* (Philadelphia, 1800). Cuthbert, a local preacher, appears to have been in PH as early as 1767 (see his name on William Smith, Receipt [for books bought at auction], 7 April 1767, WL). David immigrated first to Canada in 1781, and to PH in 1783: *PMHB* 12 (1888): 488–89. See also *History of Ebenezer*, 51–53.

92. Tables 2 and 13 in appendix below. Black classes not included.

93. Ibid. Billy G. Smith, *The "Lower Sort": Philadelphia's Laboring People, 1750–1800* (Ithaca, NY, 1990), appendix C, 214.

94. William Wirt Comegys, "The Comegys Family in America," [ca. 1908], and Comegys-Baker Family Notes [n.d.], B. Hoff Knight Collection, HSP. See also Baker's accounts in Samuel Wetherill, Ledger, 1777–1788, WL; and [Port of PH, Collector], Goods imported on Ship Richmond, 12 June 1795, and Affirmation of goods [ca. 1795] in Baker and Comegys Papers, HSP.

95. Jacob Baker, North Mulberry Ward, 1796–1797, PH Tax Assessments, PCA; Jacob Baker et al., Patent for a tract called "Jupiter" in Upper Bald Eagle Township, Pennsylvania, 20 January 1795; and Jacob Baker and Cornelius Comegys, Deed to Ralph Peacock and John Wrenshall, for land in Mifflin County, 8 April 1800, Edward Carey Gardiner

Collection, HSP. This land originally belonged to James Kinnear, an Irish-born PH Methodist, and John Wrenshall, an English Methodist, briefly a PH member before moving to Pittsburgh: see John Wrenshall, Memoir [ca. 1816], 5 vols., HSWP. On the holiday at the shore, see EC, Journal, vol. 11 (1794), 4 July 1796.

96. Jacob Baker, Bill for carpenter work at new house, 31 7M [July] 1798, and Bill for house carpentry, 2 May 1798, Baker Section, Smyth Collection, HSP. Baker also owned two horses: see North Mulberry Ward, 1799, PH Tax Assessments, PCA.

97. Marriage record, 1794, in St. George's MEC, Marriages, 1789–1799, Register Book, Church Records, OSHS. Harvey and Worth, Invoices for hardware from William and Joseph Wallis in Birmingham, England, 10 February 1797 and 24 February 1798, and Accounts with William and Joseph Wallis, 1796–1809, Samuel Harvey Papers, Business Papers, 1797–1829, HSP. In 1798 Comegys purchased a Dutch servant girl from Harvey for $65: entry dated 17 May 1798 in Samuel Harvey, Receipt Book, 1797–1824, in Samuel Harvey Papers, Receipt Books, 1797–1824, HSP. The ironmongery is listed in *The Philadelphia Directory, City and County Register, For 1802* (Philadelphia, 1802). For Harvey's accounting style, see Note to unidentified [trustees], St. George's MEC, Repairing Fund [1800], OSHS.

98. *Prospect of Philadelphia and Check on the Next Directory* (Philadelphia, 1796). Wilmer's longtime friend, John Hood, was a more modest artisan, a silk and stuff shoemaker who rented his residence from another long-standing member, Jacob Baker: *Philadelphia Directory* [1800]; North Mulberry Ward, 1797, PH Tax Assessments, PCA.

99. John Fanning Watson quoted in *History of Ebenezer*, 35.

100. On Fitzgerald, see *History of Ebenezer*, 24–27; on Doughty, see Southwark East, 1791 and 1799, PH Tax Assessments, PCA.

101. *Prospect of Philadelphia* [1795], and *The Philadelphia Directory and Register* (Philadelphia, 1794). The occupation of the fourth located itinerant, Richard Tolliff, is unidentified.

102. On Haskins, see Kenneth L. Carroll, "Religious Influences on Manumission of Slaves in Caroline, Dorchester, and Talbot Counties," *MDHM* 56 (1961): 191, Douglas R. Chandler, "A New Church in a New Nation, 1784–1800," in *Those Incredible Methodists: A History of the Baltimore Conference of the United Methodist Church*, ed. Gordon Pratt Baker (Baltimore, 1972), 63, 67, *J&L*, 3:140n, and *The Philadelphia Directory and Register* (Philadelphia, 1793). On Martha Potts, see *J&L*, 1:401n, and *Hopewell Furnace: A Guide to Hopewell Village National Historic Site, Pennsylvania* (Washington, DC, 1983), 21.

103. *Prospect of Philadelphia* [1796]. See also Caleb North to the Committee of Safety for the Province of Pennsylvania, 2 January 1775; [Lieut. Col. North], Muster Roll of Co. . . . 9th Pa. Reg^t, April 1780; [Caleb North], Presiding at Brigadier General Court Martial, 12 September 1780; Caleb North, Election Speech, 1819, HSP.

104. *Prospect of Philadelphia* [1796]; Thomas Ware, *Sketches of The Life and Travels of Rev. Thomas Ware, Who Has Been an Itinerant Methodist Preacher For More than Fifty Years*, rev. ed. (New York, 1839), 226 ff.

105. Thomas Armat, Ledgers, 1781–1794; and Journal, 1784–1789, Armat Section, Loudoun Papers, HSP. Armat later left the Methodists for St. Luke's Episcopal Church in Germantown: see Guide to Loudoun Papers, HSP.

106. See references to Jacob Baker, Lambert Wilmer, Thomas Armat, Burton Wallace, and Duncan Stewart in Pennsylvania Abolition Society, General Meeting Minute Book (1784–1786), reel 1, Pennsylvania Abolition Society Collection, microfilm edition (hereafter cited as PAS), HSP. Baker left the PAS to become one of the overseers of the poor:

General Minute Meeting Book, 29 5M 1786. Wilmer was active in the manumission of William Wilshire, one of the officers of the FAS: Acting Committee Minute Book (1784–1788), p. 74, reel 4, PAS.

107. Lists of officers, 1791 and 1796, NY "Names and number." For city directories, see table 12 in appendix below.

108. Roger Griswold to Fanny Griswold, 31 December 1797, typescript, in William Griswold Lane Memorial Collection, Manuscripts and Archives, Yale University Library.

109. Schultz, "God and Workingmen," 148–51.

110. Eric Foner, *Tom Paine and Revolutionary America* (London, 1976), 214–20, Schultz, *Republic of Labor*, 150–52, 201–3, and idem, "Small-Producer Tradition," 111–16.

111. [Sarah Hewson Alcock], *A Brief History of the Revolution with a Sketch of the Life of Captain John Hewson* (Philadelphia, 1843), 5–8; Benjamin Franklin to Richard Bache, 25 July 1773, in idem, *The Papers of Benjamin Franklin*, vol. 20 (1773), ed. William B. Wilcox (New Haven, 1976), 320–21.

112. [John Hewson], Family Record, WL; Alcock, *Brief History*, 9.

113. Alcock, *Brief History*, 9, 22–31; John Hewson, Diary [Memoir] Excerpt, [20 September 1778], Society Collection, HSP.

114. Robert Bishop and Patricia Coblentz, *New Discoveries in American Quilts* (New York, 1975), 24; Helen Comstock, *The Concise Encyclopedia of American Antiques*, 2 vols. (New York, [1958]), 1:192–93; Florence Montgomery, *Printed Textiles: English and American Cottons and Linens, 1700–1850* (New York, 1970), 86–98; John Hewson, Will, photostat, 2 May 1820, WL.

115. On nascent industrial growth in leather, wood, iron, shipbuilding, and rope-making trades, see J. Thomas Scharf and Thompson Westcott, *History of Philadelphia, 1609–1884*, 3 vols. (Philadelphia, 1844), 3:2231. By 1811, PH's industrial infrastructure included 273 looms, 3,648 spinning wheels, 28 soap-and-candle manufactories, 44 copper-brass and tin factories, among others (3:2232).

116. Wrenshall, Memoir, 3:14, 19–22, 25–26.

117. Quoted in William Jessop, Journal, 1790–1791, p. 61, OSHS. On conditions in postwar PH, see Sharon V. Salinger, *"To serve well and faithfully": Labor and Indentured Servants in Pennsylvania, 1682–1800* (Cambridge, 1987), 166–71.

118. John Dickens to Edward Dromgoole, November 1791 and 12 July 1798, in *Religion on the American Frontier, 1783–1840*, ed. William Warren Sweet, vol. 4, *The Methodists* (Chicago, 1946), 144, 149. For rentals, see, for example, Caleb North, North Mulberry Ward, 1797, Manly Smallwood, South Mulberry Ward, 1795, and Reiner Gilbert, Upper Delaware Ward, 1794, PH Tax Assessments, PCA.

119. Hugh Smith, like RA, also accumulated income from investment in real estate in one of the city's poorer wards: see Hugh Smith in South Mulberry Ward, 1809, PH Tax Assessments, PCA. By 1805, Pennel Beale, the cabinetmaker, had also invested in real estate in the Cedar Ward, which he rented to "Coloured People": Pennel Beale, Cedar Ward, 1805, PH Tax Assessments, PCA.

120. Hugh Smith to EC, 7 October 1801, in Abbott, *Experience*, 236–40. See also John Lednum, *A History of the Rise of Methodism in America, Containing Sketches of Methodist Itinerant Preachers, From 1736 to 1785* (Philadelphia, 1859), 55. Remnants of Smith's business records survive: see three items under Hugh Smith, in Society Collection, HSP. See also references to "Hugh Smith & Son," St. George's MEC, Receipt Book, 13 April 1803 and thereafter.

121. See EC, Journal, vol. 13, 1 July 1800, for extended discussion of the crisis; excerpts reprinted in George A. Phoebus, *Beams of Light on Early Methodism in America. Chiefly Drawn from the Diary, Letters, Manuscripts, Documents, and Original Tracts of the Rev. Ezekiel Cooper* (New York, 1887), 271–91. See also EC's correspondence with Lawrence McCombs, 21 February–5 March 1801, GTS.

122. *J&L*, 2:272.

123. EC, Journal, vol. 13, 1 July 1800.

124. Ibid.

125. Tables 2 and 13 in appendix below. See also chap. 5 above. In addition the Germantown Methodists had built their own stone chapel in 1800: Lednum, *History*, 428–29.

126. See table 12 in appendix below.

127. *J&L*, 3:206, 209, 212. See also 3:215, 218.

128. Haskins to Messers. Swain and Coate, 8 June 1801, Conference Records, OSHS; [Lambert Wilmer et al.] under "Hugh Smith," to the Methodist Connection in the City of Philadelphia, 12 June 1801, GTS. The Academy group may have left in conjunction with groups of separatists in Charleston, BA, and NY State whom FA refers to as signing a "declaration of withdrawing" in July 1801: *J&L*, 3:214.

129. John F. Watson, *Annals of Philadelphia, and Pennsylvania, in the Olden Times*, 3 vols. (Philadelphia, 1881), 3:274–77.

130. Academy Church, Membership Register, 1801, in "Register of the Names of Official and Private Members of the Methodist Society Meeting at the College," 1801–1811, OSHS. On Elizabeth Richards Haskins, see EC, Journal, vol. 13, 3–4 April 1799; and Bertram Lippincott, *An Historical Sketch of Batsto, New Jersey*, reprint ed. (1933; Vineland, NJ, 1986). Jacob Baker and Cornelius Comegys ended their partnership by 1803, and Comegys moved to BA: see George Roberts's Estate, Bill from Baker and Comegys, 1801, in Samuel Harvey Papers, Business Papers, 1797–1829, HSP, in particular inscription dated 26 April 1803 in which Baker refers to "the late house of Baker & Comegys"; and John Baker to Mrs. Catharine Comegys, 5 July 1804, Smyth Collection, Comegys Section, Correspondence, 1791–1886, HSP. Cornelius Comegys then joined Christ Church and was buried there in 1844: William Wirt Comegys, comp., "The Comegys Family in America," typescript, [1908], Genealogical Collection, HSP.

131. Academy Church, "[Constitution for the] United Societies 1801," OSHS. See also J. Thomas Scharf and Thompson Westcott, *History of Philadelphia, 1609–1884*, 3 vols. (Philadelphia, 1844), 2:1397, and Watson, *Annals* [1881], 3:276.

132. Academy Church, Membership Register, 1801. For city directories used, see table 13 in appendix below.

133. EC, Journal, vol. 13, 1 July 1800; St. George's MEC, "Monies Received for the Church by E. Cooper and Paid over to the Committee for the Dividend to Creditors," 3 November 1801, in Receipt Book, 1795–1806, OSHS; and "General Statement of the Case and Situation of the [M.] E. Church called St. George's," 14 November 1801, EC Papers, DUL. See also *J&L*, 3:232.

134. *J&L*, 3:244.

135. Joshua M. Wallace to [James Kemp], 16 July 1808, MDA/PEC. The Academy Society returned to the MEC but did not reunite with St. George's. By 1802 the Academy congregation had accepted George Roberts as a stationed preacher: *J&L*, 3:239, 248.

136. Thomas Lyell, Autobiographical Manuscript, 1790–1811, Aldert Smedes Papers, no. 3893, Box 4, folds. 1 and 2, SHC/UNC.

137. *J&L*, 3:74; *Minutes* (1795), 146.

138. *Minutes* (1813), 209; table 3 in appendix below.

139. The full tally of congregations is: 3 Methodist, 1 African Methodist, 3 Roman Catholic, 2 Protestant Episcopal, 1 German Lutheran, 1 German Calvinist, 1 German Reformed Evangelical, 1 Seceders, 1 Presbyterian, 1 Quaker, 1 Regular Baptist, 1 Independent Baptist, 1 Dunker, and 1 New Jerusalem (*The New Baltimore Directory and Annual Register; For 1800 and 1801* [Baltimore, (1801)], 21). In 1790, 4 in 9 Baltimoreans was a nominal churchgoer; in 1810, the Roman Catholic Church had the highest membership in the city, but the Methodists were the fastest-growing denomination: Terry D. Bilhartz, *Urban Religion and the Second Great Awakening: Church and Society in Early National Baltimore* (Rutherford, NJ, 1986), 190–92.

140. BA City Station MEC, Class Lists, 1799–1801, in "Class Records" (1799–1803), microfilm no. 408, MDSA (hereafter cited as BA Class Records); East BA Station (FP) MEC, Class Lists, 1800–1801, in "Annual Register For the Methodist Episcopal Church on Fells Point" (1800–1818), microfilm no. 411, MDSA (hereafter cited as FP "Annual Register"). At BA City, names ran the gamut from Irish, Scottish, and Welsh to German, Dutch, French, and English.

141. Mary Ellen Hayward, "Introduction: Baltimore, 1791–1825," in Carolyn J. Weekley et al., *Joshua Johnson: Freeman and Early American Portrait Painter* (Baltimore, 1987), 21–27; Charles G. Steffen, *The Mechanics of Baltimore: Workers and Politics in the Age of Revolution, 1763–1812* (Urbana, IL, 1984), 4; Tina H. Sheller, "Freemen, Servants, and Slaves: Artisans and the Craft Structure of Revolutionary Baltimore Town," in *American Artisans: Crafting Social Identity, 1750–1850*, ed. Howard B. Rock, Paul A. Gilje, and Robert Asher (Baltimore, 1995), 17–32.

142. Gary Lawson Browne, *Baltimore in the Nation, 1789–1861* (Chapel Hill, NC, 1980), 3–13, 19–50.

143. Quoted in Hayward, "Introduction," 22, 27. See also "Warner and Hanna's Plan" in ibid., 22–24, and "A List of the Streets, Lanes, and Alleys in the City of Baltimore, Alphabetically Arranged," in *New Baltimore Directory* [1800–1801].

144. Steffen, *Mechanics of Baltimore*, 11, 54–55, 102.

145. See T. Stephen Whitman, *The Price of Freedom: Slavery and Manumission in Baltimore and Early National Maryland* (Lexington, KY, 1997).

146. See table 8 in appendix below.

147. See chap. 5 above.

148. J. Thomas Scharf, *History of Baltimore City and County*, 2 vols., reprint ed. (1881; Baltimore, 1971), 2:573–75.

149. Ibid.

150. "A List of the Local Elders, Deacons & preachers in Baltimore Town, April 14th, 1799" and "List of black Speakers [1800]," in BA Class Records.

151. See table 14 in appendix below. The same combined categories yield 15.9 percent in NY in 1796 and 24 percent in PH in 1801: tables 11 and 13 in appendix below. On merchants and retailers in BA in 1796, see Steffen, *Mechanics of Baltimore*, table 1, p. 13: I have combined the percentages for "Merchant" (16 percent) and "Trader" (8 percent) to arrive at a total of 24 percent merchants and retailers in 1801.

152. Edward C. Papenfuse, *In Pursuit of Profit: The Annapolis Merchants in the Era of the American Revolution, 1763–1805* (Baltimore, 1975), 164; Chandler, "New Church," 78; and *The Baltimore Directory for 1802* (Baltimore, [1802]).

153. Chandler, "New Church," 68, and illustration of a silver teapot made by Toy in Lynne Dakin Hastings, *A Guidebook to Hampton National Historic Site* (Towson, MD, 1986), 54.

154. *New Baltimore Directory* [1800–1801] and *Baltimore Directory* [1802].

155. Ibid. Hewitt left an estate worth $5,650.87½ when he died in 1805, including $3,000 worth of BA real estate, valuable personal possessions, household furnishings, and two black servants with time left to serve: Caleb Hewitt, Will, 28 December 1805, BA Wills, 1805, bk. 7, fol. 356, MDSA.

156. See table 12 in appendix below; *New Baltimore Directory* [1800–1801]; *J&L*, 2:357n.

157. On Owings: *BDML*, s.v. "Owings, Samuel, Jr. [1733–1803]." When he died in 1803, Owings's estate was worth $16,149.99, including 24 slave men and women, extensive furnishings, 248 ounces of silver plate, a phaeton and a chariot, land, bank stock, and cash: Will, 7 May 1803, BA Wills, 1803, bk. 7, fol. 197, and idem, Inv., 10 April 1804, BA Invs., 1804, bk. 23, fol. 199, MDSA. Owings's value to the movement was such that, in the style of the Methodist "old plan," he was allowed to remain a member of St. Thomas's vestry in BA County: *BDML*, s.v. "Owings, Samuel, Jr."

158. *New Baltimore Directory* [1800–1801]; Edwin Schell, "Beginnings in Maryland and America," in Baker, *Those Incredible Methodists*, 27; Douglas R. Chandler, "Growth and Consolidation, 1800–1820," in ibid., 100–101; *J&L*, 1:108n.

159. *New Baltimore Directory* [1800–1801] and *Baltimore Directory* [1802]; *BDML*, s.v. "Hollingsworth, Jesse [1732/33–1810]." When Hollingsworth died in 1810, he possessed $3,023 worth of personal property, including two servant girls and one Negro man with time left to serve and $2,170 worth of bank stock, as well as two houses and a wharf and assorted other real estate that he left to his wife and children: Will, 2 September 1808, BA Wills, 1810, Lib. 9, fol. 42, and idem, Inv., 28 November 1810, BA Invs., 1810, bk. 26, fol. 500, MDSA.

160. *New Baltimore Directory* [1800–1801]; *J&L*, 2:137n.

161. Philip Rogers was the first president of the Maryland Abolition Society; Adam Fonerden, William Hawkins, Emanuel Kent, Job Smith (probably of BA), and Walter Simpson were also members. James McCannon, Adam Fonerden, and Quaker William Wilson were the three board members of the African Academy: Weekley et al., *Joshua Johnson*, 38–40; J. Thomas Scharf, *The Chronicles of Baltimore; Being a Complete History of "Baltimore Town" and "Baltimore City" from the Earliest Period to the Present Time* (Baltimore, 1874), 255. Fonerden had also been the first president of the patriot Mechanical Society in 1773–1775 when it held its meetings at the Lovely Lane Chapel, and was still a member when it became the BA Mechanical Society after the Revolution: Steffen, *Mechanics of Baltimore*, 60, 102, 111–13.

162. Scharf, *Chronicles of Baltimore*, 281; on Kent, see *New Baltimore Directory* [1800–1801]; on Hollingsworth, see *BDML*, s.v. "Hollingsworth, Jesse"; on Samuel Owings, *BDML*, s.v. "Owings, Samuel, Jr." Reference to Kent in Whatcoat, Journal, vol. 2, 12 December 1792.

163. Dawn F. Thomas, *Green Spring Valley: Its History and Heritage* (Baltimore, 1978), 362–63, and *BDML*, s.v. "Owings, Samuel, Jr."

164. See table 14 in appendix below.

165. Weekley, introduction to idem et al., *Joshua Johnson*, 73–74, 84; for names, see Thomas Fair William Tilyard, alias William Tilyard, Will, May 1806, BA Wills, 1806, bk. 8, fol. 80, MDSA.

166. *New Baltimore Directory* [1800–1801], and *Baltimore Directory* [1802].

167. Emanuel Stansbury, Will, 2 June 1790, BA Wills, 1791, bk. 4, fol. 513, and idem, Inv. [1791], BA Invs., 1791, bk. 16, fol. 239, MDSA.

168. *J&L*, 1:150n; Nicholas Jones, Inv., 15 July 1797, BA Invs., 1797, bk. 19, fols. 48–50, MDSA.

169. Joseph Perrigo, Will, 12 August 1800, BA Wills, 1800, bk. 6, fol. 319; idem [Joseph Perigo], Inv., 17 November 1800, BA Invs., 1801, bk. 21, fol. 160; and Jemima J. Perrigo, Inv., 16 February 1803, BA Invs., 1803, bk. 22, fol. 499, MDSA. Other examples are John Baxley, a local preacher and class leader at the BA City society, who left a personal etate of just over $360 when he died in 1800 (Inv., 14 February 1800, BA Invs., 1800, bk. 20, fol. 310, MDSA); and John Parker, a bricklayer and class leader, who owned a house and lot in Eutaw Street valued at $800 and another house and lot in Wagon Alley valued at $300 when he died in 1807 (Inv., 8 October 1807, bk. 24, fol. 500; and idem, [Revised] Inv., 1 December 1808, BA Invs., 1808, bk. 25, fol. 441, MDSA).

170. Henry Wilkins, *The Family Adviser, or a Plain and Modern Practice of Physick calculated for the Use of Families Who Have Not the Advantages of a Physician, and Accomodated to the Diseases of America*, 2d ed. (Philadelphia, 1795). For a similar definition of "new men," see Sheller, "Freemen, Servants, and Slaves," 23.

171. On Hand and Tilyard, see Weekley et al., *Joshua Johnson*, 73–74, 84, and *New Baltimore Directory* [1800–1801]. See also *The New-York Historical Society's Dictionary of Artists in America, 1564–1860* (New Haven, CT, 1957), 631.

172. *New-York Historical Society's Dictionary of Artists*, 550. Other Methodists also had connections with painters: John Hesselius, the Swedish portrait artist and mentor of Charles Willson Peale, the Revolutionary era's greatest artist-entrepreneur, was married to Methodist patron Mary Woodward, whose daughter Rebecca was the wife of Philip Rogers (*J&L*, 1:99n, and Edgar P. Richardson, Brooke Hindle, and Lillian B. Miller, *Charles Willson Peale and His World* (New York, 1982), 26–27; Thomas Doughty, the renowned landscape painter, was the son of James and Margaret Doughty of the Ebenezer Church in PH (*New-York Historical Society's Dictionary of Artists*, 185–86); and John Wesley Jarvis, the genre artist, was the son of John Jarvis and Ann Lambert of the Wesley family (Dickson, *John Wesley Jarvis*).

173. See table 14 in appendix below.

174. See "Names of the original trustees for the old Meeting house," 1800, in FP "Annual Register." On Richard Moale, see Scharf, *Chronicles of Baltimore*, 76.

175. Class Lists, 1800–1801, in FP "Annual Register; *New Baltimore Directory* [1800–1801]; *Baltimore Directory* [1802].

CHAPTER SEVEN
METHODISM POLITICIZED

1. EC, "A brief account of the work of God in Baltimore: written by E.C. in an Epistle to Bishop Asbury," 5, 11–13, BC; reprinted in *Beams of Lights on Early Methodism in America. Chiefly Drawn from the Diary, Letters, Manuscripts, Documents, and Original Tracts of the Rev. Ezekiel Cooper*, ed. George A. Phoebus (New York, 1887).

2. John M. Murrin, "Religion and Politics in America from the First Settlements to the Civil War," in *Religion and American Politics from the Colonial Period to the 1980s*, ed. Mark A. Noll (New York, 1990), 26–36.

3. *J&L*, ed. Elmer T. Clark, J. Manning Potts, and Jacob S. Payton, 3 vols. (London and Nashville, 1958), 2:132.

4. [William Duke], *Observations on the Present State of Religion in Maryland* (Baltimore, [1795]), 5.

5. *Federalist 10*, in *The Federalist Papers*, ed. Isaac Kramnick (Harmondsworth, England, 1987), 128.

6. "A Bill for Establishing Religious Freedom," in Thomas Jefferson, *Public and Private Papers* (New York, 1984), 20–22. On the Anti-Federalists, see Herbert J. Storing, *What the Anti-Federalists Were For: The Political Thought of the Opponents of the Constitution* (Chicago, 1981), 22–23.

7. Michael Kammen, ed., *The Origins of the American Constitution: A Documentary History* (Harmondsworth, England, 1986), 383.

8. Ruth H. Bloch, *Visionary Republic: Millennial Themes in American Thought, 1756–1800* (Cambridge, 1985), 119–231; EC, Journal, 13 vols. (1784–1802), vol. 12 (1795–1798), 10 January 1796, EC Collection, GTS.

9. Duke, *Observations on the Present State of Religion*, 5–15, 29, 42–45, 47–48.

10. St. Peter's Parish, Talbot Co. [Maryland], Vestry Report, May 1788, MDA/PEC; J.G.J. Bend, Sermon, 29 August 1791, and idem to [William Duke?], 3 November 1798, MDA/PEC.

11. St. Peter's Parish, Talbot County [Maryland], Vestry Report, May 1788, and Parish Report, 5 June 1797, MDA/PEC.

12. William Colbert, Journal (1790–1833), 10 vols., vol. 2 (1794–1798), 21 September 1794, p. 21, GTS.

13. *The Doctrines and Discipline of the Methodist Episcopal Church in America* (1798; reprint ed., Rutland VT, 1979)), 3; Address to President Washington reprinted in *Arminian Magazine* (PH) 1 (1789): 284–86, and *New York Daily Advertiser*, 3 June 1789. For a description of the bishops' carefully planned meeting with Washington, attended also by Thomas Morrell and John Dickins, see Morrell to EC, 26 August 1827, BC. The potential affront, in light of his Toryism, of TC's participation in this endeavor did not escape one patriot, who wrote to the *Daily Advertiser*: "[I]s it not the extreme of *hypocrisy* for such a man to take the lead of the *Episcopalians* in an address to the *President* of our republican Government?": quoted in John Vickers, *Thomas Coke: Apostle of Methodism* (Nashville, 1969), 127–28.

14. MEC, *Minutes of the Methodist Conferences, Annually Held in America; From 1773 to 1813, Inclusive* (New York, 1813), 164.

15. John Kobler, "Commonplace Book," n.d., UMHS.

16. Bloch, *Visionary Republic*, 150–231; Harry S. Stout, "Rhetoric and Reality in the Early Republic: The Case of the Federalist Clergy," in Noll, *Religion and American Politics*, 62–76.

17. Bloch, *Visionary Republic*, 202–31; for publication history, see Philip S. Foner, introduction to Thomas Paine, *The Age of Reason* (1794, 1795; Secaucus, NJ, 1997), and Eric Foner, *Tom Paine and Revolutionary America* (New York, 1976), 245–49.

18. Paine, *Age of Reason*, 182.

19. See Eric Foner's commentary on Paine's "strangely limited" view of Christianity: *Tom Paine*, 247–49.

20. *Methodist Magazine* (PH), 2 (1798): 19–24, 62–69, 113–21; Stith Mead, *Hymns and Spiritual Songs*, no. 107, quoted with change in punctuation from William Warren Sweet, *Religion in the Development of American Culture, 1765–1840* (New York, 1952), 158.

21. Colbert, Journal, vol. 2, 18 April 1796; John Mann to Daniel Fidler, 19 July 1795, DUL.

22. William Henry Williams, *The Garden of American Methodism: The Delmarva Peninsula, 1769–1820* (Wilmington, DE, 1984), 174–75. See also Jacob Simpson Payton, "Preachers in Politics," *MH* 1 (1963): 15–16.

23. Willamina Ridgely and A[braham] Ridgely to Henry Moore Ridgely, 10 May 1798, Ridgely Collection, fold. no. 231, DSA; for context, see Williams, *Garden*, 176.

24. Michael Durey, *Transatlantic Radicals and the Early American Republic* (Lawrence, KS, 1997), tables 1–3, pp. 5–8. On the London Corresponding Society, see also E. P. Thompson, *The Making of the English Working Class*, reprint ed. (1963; London, 1980), chap. 5.

25. Durey, *Transatlantic Radicals*, 228. For a recent in-depth treatment of these events, from the Federalist perspective, see Stanley Elkins and Eric McKitrick, *The Age of Federalism: The Early American Republic, 1788–1800* (New York, 1993), esp. 330–488, 590–618.

26. Durey, *Transatlantic Radicals*, 181–82.

27. The *Gazette of the United States*, 3 May 1800, and the *American Aurora*, 28 May 1800, cited in Richard N. Rosenfeld, *American Aurora: A Democratic-Republican Returns* (New York, 1997), 782, 801; on religious controversy, see ibid., 829–47.

28. *Aurora General Advertiser* (PH), 8 April 1800.

29. Ibid., 9 April 1800.

30. Thomas Rodney, MS of speech in reply to article in the *Aurora*, April 1800, HSD.

31. Weems, the famous Episcopalian, had strong sympathies with Methodism: see *Mason Locke Weems, His Work and Ways: Letters, 1784–1825*, ed. Emily Ellsworth Ford Skeel, 3 vols. (New York, 1929), 3:432–33. FA conferred with him on episcopal government less than a month before the Christmas Conference of 1784: *J&L*, 2:473.

32. EC, "Brethren, Friends, & Fellow Citizens," [1800], first pages, GTS. See also Thomas Morrell, *A Sermon on the Death of General George Washington* (Baltimore, [1800]).

33. TC to [Alexander Knox], 21 April 1800, Dr. Williams's Library, London; Henry Boehm, *Reminiscences, Historical and Biographical, of Sixty-Four Years in the Ministry* (New York, 1866), 65.

34. Thomas Ware, *Sketches of the Life and Travels of Rev. Thomas Ware, Who Has Been an Itinerant Methodist Preacher For More than Fifty Years*, rev. ed. (New York, 1839), 236.

35. Colbert, Journal, vol. 3 (1797–1801), 6 March and 26 May 1800; John Ffirth, *A Friendly Reply to "A Few Remarks" on the Subject of the Present and Past State of Religion in the United States* (Burlington, NJ, 1803), 5–6; George C. Baker, *An Introduction to the History of Early New England Methodism, 1789–1839* (Durham, NC, 1941), 45.

36. Frank Baker, *From Wesley to Asbury: Studies in Early American Methodism* (Durham, NC, 1976), 163, 162–82; JW, *The Sunday Service of the Methodists in North America. With Other Occasional Services* (London, 1784). Baker emphasizes that JW's *Notes on the New Testament* and four volumes of *Sermons* have remained the doctrinal basis of American Methodism to this day.

37. See reprints of Wesley's writings and articles from English sources in *Arminian Magazine* (PH) 1 and 2 (1789–1790) and *Methodist Magazine* (PH) 1 and 2 (1797–1798), passim. See also TC and FA's letter at beginning of *D&D* (1798), referring to JW as the "most respectable divine since the primitive ages" (7).

38. EC to JW, [1790], EC Collection, GTS; FG to JW, 15 July 1786, and JW to FG, 30 November 1786 and 16 July 1787, DUL; and various letters to William Watters, FG, John Dickins, and EC, in *The Letters of the Rev. John Wesley*, ed. John Telford, 8 vols. (London, [1931]), vol. 7 (1780–1787), passim. JW's last letter to America was to EC, dated 1 February 1791, in which JW urges, "See that you never give place to one thought of separating from your brethren in Europe" (*Letters*, 7:259–60). See also William Jessop's journal for

letter received from JW dated 1 February 1791 copied after JW's death (Journal [1790–1791], 5 April 1791, OSHS).

39. Jesse Lee, *A Short History of the Methodists, in the United States of America: beginning in 1766 and continued till 1809* (Baltimore, 1810), 119, 168; FG to JW, 25 September 1786, DUL; [Wesleyan Connexion], "The Minutes or Journal of the Conference of the People Called Methodists," vol. 1 (1784–1813), MAM, 77–85. See also American preachers and membership tallies in "The Stations of the PREACHERS, and Numbers in Society, in the United States of AMERICA," *Arminian Magazine* (London) 17 (1794): 200–204; and letters from the English connection to the 1796 and 1800 general conferences in MEC, *Journals of the General Conference of the Methodist Episcopal Church. Volume I. 1796–1836* (New York, 1855), 9–10, and MEC, *Minutes of the General Conference of the Methodist-Episcopal Church, Begun in Baltimore on the Sixth, and Commenced Till the Twentieth of May, One Thousand Eight Hundred. At Which Thomas Coke and Francis Asbury Presided* (Philadelphia, 1800), in *Early American Imprints*, 1st ser., no. 37958.

40. Baker, *From Wesley*, 129–30. On the importance of the Methodist apostolic succession through JW, see James William May, "From Revival Movement to Denomination: A Re-Examination of the Beginnings of American Methodism" (Ph.D. diss., Columbia University, 1962), 319, 334–35.

41. [MEC], *Minutes of the General Conference* (1800), 4–7; Thomas Jackson, ed., *The Lives of Early Methodist Preachers, Chiefly Written by Themselves*, 3d ed., 6 vols. (London, 1866), 5:312–20; and Lee, *Short History*, 351. The British preachers, for their part, "know but little . . . of the trials of two-thirds of the Preachers on this Continent": TC, *Extracts of the Journals of the Late Rev. Thomas Coke, L.L.D.; Comprising Several Visits to North-America and the West-Indies; His Tour Through Part of Ireland, and His Nearly Finished Voyage to Bombay in the East-Indies* (Dublin, 1816), 128.

42. Baker, *From Wesley*, 163–64; James Penn Pilkington, *The Methodist Publishing House: A History*, vol. 1, *Beginnings to 1870* (Nashville, 1968), 75–77.

43. Lee, *Short History*, 126–27, 247–48. TC's Instrument of Abdication is reprinted in *J&L*, 3:54, part of a letter by James O'Kelly. See also *J&L*, 3:49–54, 1:538n; and Frank Baker, *John Wesley and the Church of England* (Nashville, 1970), 202–3, 220–28, 233.

44. *J&L*, 3:64–65. FA referred to this letter as "*a bitter pill*" (*J&L*, 1:594). The title "Bishop" first appeared in MEC, *A Form of Discipline for the Ministers, Preachers, and Members of the Methodist Episcopal Church in America* (New York, 1787), 6. The Minutes, however, continued until 1800 to refer to TC and FA as those who were elected to "superintend" the work (cf. *Minutes* [1813], 220 and 236).

45. Thomas Morrell, *A Vindication of Truth Discovered; Designed as an Answer to the Rev. William Hammet's Rejoinder* (Philadelphia, 1792), 25–26.

46. At the time of his death in 1816, FA's property consisted of his clothing, horses, carriages (the number unspecified), and $2,000 deposited with the Methodist Book Concern from legacies left to the bishop "chiefly by persons of the first Generation of Methodists": FA, Will, 7 June 1813, BA Wills (1816), bk. 10, fol. 172, MDSA.

47. John W. Bond to Bishop McKendree, 1 April 1816, reprinted in Robert J. Bull, "John Wesley Bond's Reminiscences of Francis Asbury," in *MH* 4 (October 1965): 11–14, 24.

48. TC, *Extract of the Journals*, 46; Boehm, *Reminiscences*, 438–49; FA to Jasper Winscom, 27 May 1789, typescript, UMHS. TC wrote to England in 1800 that FA "seems to be on the brink of the grave": TC to [Alexander Knox], 21 April 1800, MS24.180, Dr. Williams's Library, London. See also portrait by Charles Peale Polk, 1794, in this volume, and later portrait by John Paradise, 1812, reproduced in *J&L*, 3: frontispiece. John F. Wat-

son noted that Asbury favored a suit of blue-gray cloth and a large white hat, probably for summer preaching: *Annals of Philadelphia and Pennsylvania in the Olden Time*, 2 vols. (Philadelphia, 1856, 1857), 1:459.

49. Bull, "John Wesley Bond's Reminiscences," 26.

50. *J&L*, 3:60–64, letter dated 15 August 1788. In 1789, FA defended TC from association with one of JW's antipatriot publications, which FA refers to as *History of the American Revolution*: "The Bishop would not bel[i]eve [it] had ever been written till I convinced him by directing him to a sight of it—in Georgetown South Carolina last april which Book he ordered to be, I know not—to be burnt may be": FA to Thomas Morrell, 9 September 1789, GTS.

51. See references in Jessop, Journal, 14 April 1791; CLG, Diary, 15 vols., vol. 5 (1788–1792), 15 April 1791, DUL; EC, Journal, vol. 7 (1790–1791), 26 April and 25 May 1791; and TC to Thomas Morrell, 6 May 1791, GTS.

52. Quoted in Jessop, Journal, 15 April 1791; *Maryland Journal and Baltimore Advertiser* (BA), 22 April 1791.

53. On hearing of JW's death at the end of April 1791, FA emphasized the English founder's writing abilities more than his organizational genius, from which he was now trying to distance himself. FA preached a funeral sermon on JW in NY on 26 May 1791 at the request of the congregation: its substance is unknown (*J&L*, 1:673–75).

54. TC to William White, 24 April 1791, microfilm, Miscellaneous MSS, NYHS; reprinted in William White, *Memoirs of the Protestant Episcopal Church in the United States of America*, ed. B. F. De Costa (New York, 1880), 408–12, and *J&L*, 3:94–98. See discussion in Vickers, *Thomas Coke*, 176–91.

55. TC to William White, 24 April 1791.

56. Ibid.; White, *Memoirs*, 198.

57. White, *Memoirs*, 196–200, and reprint of White's reply to TC, 412–13. See also William White to Rev. Simon Wilmer, 30 July 1804, MDA/PEC. TC also wrote to Bishop Seabury, stressing the same themes, including the importance of winning over FA, whom he refers to as "our Resident Superintendent," with the added proviso that he and FA be appointed "Bishops of the Methodist Society in the Protestant Episcopal Church": TC to Samuel Seabury, 14 May 1791, facsimile, NYHS. Discussion in Vickers, *Thomas Coke*, 184–86.

58. For overviews of O'Kelly, see May, "From Revival Movement," 244–47, Nathan O. Hatch, "The Christian Movement and the Demand for a Theology of the People," *JAH* 67 (1980): 545–67, idem, *The Democratization of American Christianity* (New Haven, 1989), 68–81, and Russell E. Richey, *Early American Methodism* (Bloomington, IN, 1991), 88–91.

59. "A Letter of James O'Kelly to an Unnamed Person," April 1787, reprinted in *J&L*, 3:51–53.

60. On the council, see Baker, *From Wesley*, 132, Lee, *Short History*, 151–55, and *J&L*, 1:733–34, 3:81–83, 87–88. The published minutes of the council refrain from any reference to O'Kelly's dismissal: MEC, *Minutes Taken at a Council of the Bishop and Delegated Elders of the Methodist-Episcopal Church: Held in Baltimore, in the State of Maryland, December 1, 1790* (Baltimore, 1791).

61. *J&L*, 3:560. On the 1792 general conference and subsequent schism, see abstract of the 1792 general conference journal in [MEC], *The General Conferences of the Methodist Episcopal Church from 1792–1896*, ed. Lewis Curts (Cincinnati, 1900), 2–4, Lee, *Short History*, 177–80, 203–6, and Hatch,"Christian Movement," 549. See also *J&L*, 3:113, for FA's suggestion that O'Kelly had episcopal ambitions, and *J&L*, 1:734, for FA's letter to

the departing preachers. In 1796, six annual conferences were established for the six greater regions of New England, PH, BA, Virginia, South Carolina, and the West: Lee, *Short History*, 233–34.

62. William Spencer to [John Robinson], 14 November 1809, in *J&L*, 3:419–22.

63. James O'Kelly to [Jesse Nicholson], [December 1792], in *J&L*, 3:114.

64. On background, see D. A. Reily, "William Hammett: Missionary and Founder of the Primitive Methodist Connection," *MH* 10 (1971): 30–43; TC, *Extracts of the Journals*, 217; and Lee, *Short History*, 206–9. Thomas Morrell, stationed in Charleston, reported that Hammett had persuaded "about 24 whites & 35 blacks to Join him, has hired & fitted up a place for preaching, and holds worship at the same hours we do": Morrell to EC, 20 February 1792, EC Papers, GTS. A small pamphlet controversy ensued: see Thomas Morrell, *Truth Discovered or an Answer to the Reverend William Hammet's Appeal to Truth and Circumstance* (Charleston, 1792) and idem, *Vindication*, passim.

65. [Anon.], *A Serious Address to the Candid and Impartial Members of the Methodist Communion* (New York, 1792), 4–5, 8, 11–13; Lorenzo Dow, *History of Cosmopolite; or the Four Volumes of Lorenzo's Journal, Concentrated in One*, 3d ed., corr. and enl. (Philadelphia, 1816), 556–57. One preacher went so far as to insist on his "equal natural right" to attend the 1800 conference with other preachers when he was visibly recovering from the effects of a smallpox inoculation recommended by the conference: Jeremiah Norman, Journal (1793–1801), vol. 17 (1800), 20 May 1800, Stephen Beauregard Weeks Papers, no. 762, SHC/UNC.

66. Jarratt quoted in *J&L*, 3:138–39n; William Watters to Edward Dromgoole, 15 May 1795, in *Religion on the American Frontier, 1783–1840*, ed. William Warren Sweet, vol. 4, *The Methodists* (Chicago, 1946), 147–48. See also Lee, *Short History*, 213.

67. Quoted in Sweet, *Religion on the American Frontier*, 28–29; for elaboration, see Lee, *Short History*, 247–48.

68. James O'Kelly, *The Author's Apology for Protesting Against the Methodist Episcopal Government* (Richmond, VA, 1798), 4, 14–19.

69. Idem, *A Vindication of the author's Apology, with reflections on the Reply, and a few remarks on Bishop Asbury's annotations on his Book of Discipline* (Raleigh, NC, 1801), 3–4, 18, 28, 60–62.

70. Richey, *Early American Methodism*, 90–91.

71. FA refers to dictating nearly three hundred pages in reply to O'Kelly: *J&L*, 3:175–76.

72. Nicholas Snethen, *A Reply to an Apology for Protesting Against the Methodist Episcopal Government* (Philadelphia, 1800), 47–48, 57. On FA's personal responses to O'Kelly, see *J&L*, 2:106, 164, 204.

73. Snethen, *Reply*, 49–51. See also Snethen's further commentary in idem, *An Answer to James O'Kelly's Vindication His Apology, Etc. and an Explanation of the Reply* (Philadelphia, 1802), 15–16, 23.

74. *D&D* (1798), 6–7, 34–35; FA to [George Roberts], 11 February 1797, in *J&L*, 3:159. TC writes of uniting his and FA's ideas for annotations on the "Methodist Economy": TC, *Extracts of the Journals*, 219.

75. *D&D* (1798), 40–42, 51.

76. Ibid., 66–68. FA continued to contend with O'Kelly and the Republican Methodists, later called the Christians, until his death in 1816: see 3:175–76, 411–17, and 531–43. On the creation of the Christian Church, see Hatch, "Christian Movement," 545–67, and idem, *Democratization*, 68–81.

77. Lee, *Short History*, 316–59. For an extended list including those admitted on trial only, see Edwin Schell, "Methodist Traveling Preachers in America, 1773–1799," *MH* 2 (1964): 51–67. For a lucid discussion of the spiritual significance of the Methodist discipline of quarterly meetings and conferences, see Richey, *Early American Methodism*.

78. The separate totals are 673 preachers and 159 probationers: Lee, *Short History*, 316–38. For the different ranks among the traveling itinerancy, see *D&D* (1798), 46–58: The ordained ministry comprised the bishops, presiding elders, deacons, and black local deacons; unordained white preachers were recommended by their quarterly meeting and licensed by the yearly conferences for a two-year probation.

79. Frank Baker, "The Status of the Methodist Preachers in America, 1765–1791," in *Rethinking Methodist History: A Bicentennial Historical Consultation*, ed. Russell E. Richey and Kenneth E. Rowe (Nashville, 1985), 35; Watson, *Annals of Philadelphia* (1856), 456.

80. This average does not include statistically "outlying" itinerants aged 16, 36, 37, and 40: NY Annual Conference Journal, 1800–1802, microfilm, no. R-3, vol. 12, entries for 16–17 June 1801, NYPL.

81. John Fanning Watson to Lucy Watson, 18 October 1800, WL; Lorenzo Dow, *The Life and Travels of Lorenzo Dow, Written By Himself: In Which Are Contained Some Singular Providences of God* (Hartford, CT, 1804), 132–33.

82. Jacob Brush, Abstract of Will, 25 September 1795, NYHS *Collections*, vol. 14 (1905), 328.

83. John Fanning Watson, *Annals of Philadelphia, and Pennsylvania, in the Olden Time; being a Collection of Memoirs, Anecdotes, and Incidents of the City and Its Inhabitants, and of the Earliest Settlement of the Inland Part of Pennsylvania*, 3 vols., enl. ed. (Philadelphia, 1881), 1:459. David Campbell, former governor of Virginia, recalled seeing Mr. Seawell, a preacher from BA and later instructor at Cokesbury College, dressed in the more elaborate style of the late eighteenth century: "Although evidently very zealous and much engaged in the cause of religion, he had not changed his manners nor the fashion of his coat or hair, as was then common;—nor could he have been distinguished in the crowd from any other genteel man": David Campbell to [Rev. James P. Carrell], 30 June 1849, DU.

84. Henry Boehm, *Reminiscences, Historical and Biographical, of Sixty-Four Years in the Ministry* (New York, 1866), 142–43; Benjamin Abbott, *The Experience and Gospel Labours of the Rev. Benjamin Abbott: To Which is Annexed a Narrative of His Life and Death by John Ffirth* (Philadelphia, 1801), 215–16.

85. Quoted in Boehm, *Reminiscences*, 445–46. See also William Black to Daniel Fidler, 3 September 1794, DUL, on ordering saddlebags "made of good leather."

86. Robert Strawbridge was probably the first American Methodist preacher described as a sorcerer: see Nathan Bangs, *The Life of the Rev. Freeborn Garrettson; compiled from his printed and manuscript journals, and other authentic documents* (New York, 1829), 21. For other references, see Simon Miller, "The Experience," *Methodist Magazine* (PH) 2 (1798): 459; and Colbert, Journal, vol. 1 (1790–1794), 7 August 1792. Jon Butler stresses that Methodism's syncretism centered on the "ministers who manifested divine attributes in their being, bearing, dreams, and rituals": *Awash in a Sea of Faith: Christianizing the American People* (Cambridge, MA, 1990), 237.

87. Philip Gatch, Autobiography, Gatch microfilm, Group I, 38–39, MTSO; Robert Drew Simpson, *American Methodist Pioneer: The Life and Journals of the Rev. Freeborn Garrettson, 1752–1827* (Rutland, VT, 1984), 92. Preachers similarly sought miracles from among their dead predecessors: Jesse Lee was among the preachers who viewed

Whitefield's remains at a ceremonial disinterment from its vault at the Presbyterian meet-inghouse in Newburyport, Massachusetts, in the 1790s: *Short History*, 37–38. His description of Whitefield's much decayed corpse in his private journal is less upbeat; nevertheless he took part of the evangelist's gown as a relic: Minton Thrift, *Memoir of the Rev. Jesse Lee With Extracts from his Journals* (New York, 1823), 155–56.

88. Colbert, Journal, vol. 1, 24 January 1794.

89. Nicholas Albertson, "A Sketch of the Rise and Progress of Methodism in Some parts of the State of New Jersey" (ca. 1835), Albertson Family Papers, MG no. 691 (1815–1866), NJHS.

90. Colbert, Journal, vol. 1, 4 December 1792.

91. Ibid., 15 January 1793, 3 March 1793.

92. For examples, see FG to John Coe, [March 1785?], DUL; John Atkinson, *Memorials of Methodism in New Jersey, from the foundation of the first society in the state in 1770, to the Completion of the first twenty years of its history* (Philadelphia, 1860), 205; and Colbert, Journal, vol. 2 (1794–1798), 6 January 1798, where Colbert describes "a dreadful spectakle" of "a living man dressed in his Grave clothes, his Coffin in his room, and a rope about his neck" in jail on the Strasburg circuit, Pennsylvania.

93. Richard Whatcoat, Journal, vol. 1 (1789–1791), microfilm, 11–19 August 1790, GTS. Itinerants were instructed to travel from house to house based on a "Catalogue" of those in each society: MEC, *Minutes of Several Conversations Between The Rev. Thomas Coke, LL.D., The Rev. Francis Asbury and Others, at a Conference Begun in Baltimore . . . Composing a Form of Discipline for the Ministers, Preachers and Other Members of the Methodist Episcopal Church in America* (Philadelphia, 1785), 8.

94. Thomas Lyell, Autobiographical Manuscript, 7 vols., SHC/UNC, vol. 3 (1792–1793), n.p.; Colbert, Journal, vol. 2, 4 October 1795.

95. Thomas Haskins, Journal, vol. 2 (1782–1783), 7 November 1782–7 April 1783, pp. 6–20, LCMD; and *J&L*, 3:221. See also *Minutes of Several Conversations* (1785), in which itinerants are instructed to "Be merciful to your Beast. Not only ride moderately, but see with your own Eyes that your Horse be rubbed and fed" (19).

96. NY Annual Conference Journal, entries for 16–17 June 1801. After 1789, all itinerants were on trial for six months: Lee, *Short History*, 145.

97. NY Annual Conference Journal, entries for 19 and 20 June 1801, and 4 June 1802; Dow, *Life and travels*, 86n.

98. Lyell, Autobiographical Manuscript, vol. 3, n.p.; *Minutes of Several Conversations* (1785), 23.

99. Passages quoted and paraphrased from EC to John Dickins, 25 May 1789, EC Collection, GTS.

100. Joseph Pilmore to Thomas Tatham, 21 March 1784, PLP 83.60.4, MAM.

101. John Street MEC, Account Book, 1768–1796, microfilm, vol. 249, 1769–1772 passim, NYPL.

102. MEC, *Minutes of the Methodist Conferences, Annually Held in America, from 1773 to 1794, inclusive* (Philadelphia, 1795), 25; *Minutes of Several Conversations* (1785), 13, 27; [MEC], *General Conference* (1792), 15, 30; and [MEC], *Minutes of the General Conference* (1800), 8. See also Edwin A. Schell, "Support of the Bishops in Early American Methodism," *MH* 4 (1966): 42–50.

103. *Minutes* (1795), 83, 93, 117.

104. Lyell, Autobiographical Manuscript, vol. 2 (ca. 1790–1792), n.p.

105. *Minutes* (1795), 147–48; Jessop, Journal, 25 June 1790, 61–62; *J&L*, 3:62.

106. *J&L*, 2:102. Most of the preachers in the NY annual conference were paid something depending on what was owed them, with each preacher still holding a $21 "Share" at the end of the conference, a euphemism for back pay: MEC, NY Annual Conference Journal, 5 June 1802. At the same time, the connection made efforts to make payments to support "superannuated" preachers, their widows, and children; money was also collected from the printing business for this fund (Lee, *Short History*, 192).

107. NY Annual Conference Journal, entries for 16–17 June 1801. See also PH Annual Conference, Salem Circuit, Recommendation for Aaron [P]arvin to Yearly Conference, 29 December 1799: "he is a single man clare of dept Some gifts to speak—a good man."

The bequests of two preachers who died in the work suggest their resources. Richard Owings's wealth was concentrated in two thousand acres' worth of landholdings in Kentucky, half of which was a gift from his brother, along with forty-one acres of cultivated land in Maryland, four slaves, animal stock, farm utensils, and modest household goods, all but the Kentucky land valued at £434 11s. 3d., £190 of which was the value of the four slaves: Richard Owings, Will, 5 October 1786, BA Wills, bk. 4, p. 180, and Inv., 26 November 1786, BA Invs., 1787, Box 33, fold. 6, MDSA. Jacob Brush forgave his brother a £5 debt and left his nephew £50 "to be put out at interest by my executors" until his nephew reached the age of 21: Jacob Brush, Abstract of Will, 25 September 1795, 328.

108. BA Circuit Quarterly Conference Minutes, 1794–1816, M1587, MDSA.

109. Long Island Circuit Stewards Accounts, 1795–1830, microfilm, no. R-7, vol. 60, NYPL.

110. Disbursements, 1790–1791, in Salem Circuit Quarterly Conference Minutes (1789–1816), PSL; BA Circuit Quarterly Conference Minutes, 10 and 11 September 1796; Lawrence McCombs to EC, 2 March 1795, EC Collection, GTS. On Asbury's income, see FA to John Dickins, 18 June 1798, in *Methodist Magazine* (PH) 2 (1798): 379–81.

111. [MEC], *Minutes of the General Conference* (1800), 7–10. Love feasts were also seen as opportunities for raising money: Proceedings of the Quarterly Meeting, 1789, in Salem Circuit Quarterly Conference Minutes.

112. Sandra Ryan Dresbeck, "The Episcopalian Clergy in Maryland and Virginia, 1765–1805" (Ph.D. diss., UCLA, 1976), 352–68.

113. *J&L*, 2:156; Haskins, Journal, vol. 2, 12 November 1782.

114. Haskins, Journal, vol. 2, 7 November–6 December 1782.

115. Harry Dorsey Gough, Inv., 24 August 1808, BA Invs., 1808, bk. 25, fols. 447–63, MDSA. As was common in the eighteenth century, preachers also slept two to a bed: see *J&L*, 1:91–92. See also Bull, "John Wesley Bond's Reminiscences." Robert Coleman points out that circuits tended to be laid out geograpically rather than by population, giving more work to those on the more populated circuits: "Factors in the Expansion of the Methodist Episcopal Church from 1784 to 1812" (Ph.D. diss., State University of Iowa, 1954).

116. Lyell, Autobiographical Manuscript, vol. 2, n.p. Benjamin Abbott noted that two societies in the Salem Circuit had not seen an itinerant for eighteen months in early 1790s: *Experience*, 167–68.

117. Haskins, Journal, vol. 2, 30 December 1782 and 3 January 1783.

118. Amos G. Thompson to Daniel Fidler, 10 September 1791, DUL. See also Thompson to Fidler, 23 February 1791, DUL, on "Economical Rules for a Preacher."

119. Stith Mead to John Kobler, 1 March 1795, Stith Mead Letterbook, 1792–1795, Virginia Historical Society in Richmond. Christine Leigh Heyrman draws the same conclusion regarding this correspondence: see *Southern Cross: The Beginnings of the Bible Belt* (New York, 1997), 298n.

120. William Watters, *A Short Account of the Christian Experience and Ministereal Labours of William Watters Drawn Up By Himself* (Alexandria, VA, 1806), 127.

121. Lee, *Short History*, 316–39. On specific preachers, see ibid., 316–19, and *J&L*, 1:76n, 138n, 554–55n, and 669–70n. For the method of suspending preachers, see *D&D* (1798), 109–10.

122. Vasey later returned to the English Methodist connection. On these preachers, see John Lednum, *A History of the Rise of Methodism in America, Containing Sketches of Methodist Itinerant Preachers, from 1736 to 1785* (Philadelphia, 1859), 404; Robert Ayres, Journal, 5 vols. (1785–1845), vol. 5 (1788–1789), 7 June 1789, microfilm, DUL; *J&L*, 1:69; Robert Lowell Arends, "Early American Methodism and the Church of England" (Ph.D. diss., Yale University, 1948), 172–76; and *J&L*, 2:205n. Dresbeck cites sixteen Methodists who left the connection for the Protestant Episcopal Church between 1784 and 1805 in Maryland: "Episcopalian Clergy," 286–87.

123. Lee, *Short History*, 317–30: numbers are through 1809. On Glendinning, see *J&L*, 2:663.

124. Schell, "Methodist Traveling Preachers," 53–67. One of these, William Jessop, died of consumption in 1795: at his last sermon, "[h]e was reduced almost to a skeleton; his face was pale, his eye sunken and glassy, his voice sepulchral, his countenance grave, and his manner solemn as eternity": Boehm, *Reminiscences*, 27–28.

125. Hatch, *Democratization*, table 1, p. 88; Noah Fidler, Journal (1801–1807), 28 February 1802, typescript, UMHS.

126. The rules for local preachers were standardized at the 1796 general conference: Lee, *Short History*, 246–47.

127. FA to Jasper Winscom, 23 January 1796, typescript, UMHS. Conversely, Thomas Morrell converted at age thirty-eight and gave up a merchanting business to preach (Atkinson, *Memorials of Methodism*, 318–20); Thomas Haskins forsook a career in law (Lednum, *History*, 356); and William Penn Chandler was studying dentistry with Benjamin Rush when he entered the itinerancy (Ware, *Sketches*, 226–27).

128. Watters, *Short Account*, 116.

129. *J&L*, 2:474.

130. NY Annual Conference Journal, 22 June 1801. In 1787, the amount paid to preachers with children was reduced with the consensus that *"many of our Preachers and people [are] dissatisfied with the salaries allowed our married preachers, who have children"*: *Minutes* (1795), 104. See also TC's secret plan to pay married preachers bonuses: TC to EC, 6 December 1797, EC Collection, GTS.

131. In debt from its inception in 1785 on land purchased from Josias Dallam in Abingdon, Maryland, the college was a losing proposition: see accounts and description in *Arminian Magazine* (PH) 1 (1789), 589–91. The first building burned down, possibly by arson, in December 1795. The replacement also burned, along with the Light Street Methodist Church, exactly a year later in December 1796: Baker, *From Wesley*, 153–55, Douglas R. Chandler, "A New Church in a New Nation, 1784–1800," in *Those Incredible Methodists: A History of the Baltimore Conference of the United Methodist Church*, ed. Gordon Pratt Baker (Baltimore, 1972), 67–71, and *J&L*, 1:490n. FA never favored the college. As he wrote: "Dr. Coke in his bigness printed and nominated it a college. It was never agreeable to the public mind of Methodists, they did not willingly support it. . . . I wanted nothing but a Kingswood School": FA to Jasper Winscom, 23 January 1796.

132. See correspondence between Robert Lindsay and Edward Dromgoole, 1783–1788, in Edward Dromgoole Papers, microfilm, no. 1, SHC/UNC. After his marriage, although just starting out "as a house-keeper," William Watters continued to travel: *Short Account*,

99. The preachers occasionally if rarely make oblique references to their sexual urges, as when Thomas Haskins wrote, "Arose in the morning and found I had had a severe and very bold assault by my fleshly enemy," and again, "Arose early & sought the Lord, found myself to have been much buffetted by my enemies. Oh Lord, Cleanse me from secret Sins & keep me from presumptuous sins": Journal, vol. 2, 19 January and 2 May 1783.

133. John Dickins to EC, 10 April 1794, EC Collection, GTS.

134. Cornelius Cook, Will, 13 June 1789, DUL.

135. Haskins, Journal, vol. 2, 8–9 July 1783; vol. 6 (1782–1785), 8–9, 15–17 December 1784, and 13 May 1785, LCMD.

136. John Littlejohn, Journal, 10 vols. (1776–1832), vol. 4 (1778–1789), 11 August 1778, KWC.

137. MEC, *Journals of the General Conference*, 34, 36, 33.

138. Ibid., 33.

CHAPTER EIGHT
THE GREAT REVIVAL AND BEYOND

1. MEC, *Minutes of the Methodist Conferences, Annually Held in America; From 1773 to 1813, Inclusive* (New York, 1813), 232–39, 240–43. The total does not include the circuits for Upper Canada. Exact figures for individual regions are: 5,839 for New England; 22,562 for the greater Middle Atlantic; 35,730 members in the South and West; 4,975 blacks in the Greater Middle Atlantic; 6,470 blacks in the South and West combined. The northern Maryland circuits included in the tally for the greater Middle Atlantic are: Annapolis, BA Circuit, BA Town and Point, Cecil, Federal, Frederick, Harford, Kent, Montgomery, Prince-George's, and Queen-Ann's.

2. C. C. Goss, *Statistical History of the First Century of American Methodism With A Summary of the Origin and Present Operations of Other Denominations* (New York, 1866), 104, 109–11.

3. The term originally used was "epoch." Cf. overviews in C. C. Goen, "The 'Methodist Age' in American Church History," *Religion in Life* 34 (1965): 562–72, and Winthrop S. Hudson, "The Methodist Age in America," *MH* 12 (1974): 1–15.

4. Nathan O. Hatch, *The Democratization of American Christianity* (New Haven, 1989), 6–7, 89, 93. See also idem, "Mormon and Methodist: Popular Religion in the Crucible of the Free Market," *Journal of Mormon History* 20 (1994): 24–44, for more explicit use of the "free market" concept.

5. Gordon S. Wood, *The Radicalism of the American Revolution* (New York, 1991), 232.

6. George Roberts to Paul Hick, 18 November 1799, DUL; *J&L*, ed. Elmer T. Clark, J. Manning Potts, and Jacob S. Payton, 3 vols. (London and Nashville, 1958), 2:202.

7. Thomas Morrell, Journal [May 1801], NJSL; *J&L*, 2:234–35.

8. The revivals has been assisted by the regularly scheduled general conference, where 116 preachers attended and 50 participants, mostly young people, claimed to be converted: Morrell, Journal [May 1800]; see also EC, Journal, 13 vols. (1784–1802), vol. 13 (1798–1802), 1 July 1800, EC Collection, GTS; and CLG to Margaret Tillotson, 19 March 1800, DUL.

9. George Roberts to Paul Hick, 10 November 1800, DUL.

10. *J&L*, 2:296, The revivals attracted both blacks and whites: see Richard Bassett to EC, 1 June 1801, EC Collections, GTS.

11. See recent assessments of political, territorial, demographic, and economic developments in Joyce Appleby, *Capitalism and a New Social Order: The Republican Vision of the 1790s* (New York, 1984); Wood, *Radicalism*, 229–369; Joseph J. Ellis, *American Sphinx: The Character of Thomas Jefferson* (New York, 1996), 200–272; Peter S. Onuf, "Thomas Jefferson, Missouri, and the 'Empire of Liberty,' " in *Thomas Jefferson and the Changing West: From Conquest to Conservation*, ed. James P. Ronda (Albuquerque, NM, 1997), 111–53. Also cf. implications of economic change, in James A. Henretta, *The Evolution of American Society, 1700–1815: An Interdisciplinary Analysis* (Lexington, KY, 1973), 187–223, and Wood, *Radicalism*, 325–47. On the Middle Atlantic economy, see esp. Joyce Appleby, "Commercial Farming and the 'Agrarian Myth' in the Early Republic," *JAH* 68 (1982): 833–49. Population statistics appear in George Brown Tindall, *America: A Narrative History*, 3d ed. (New York, 1992), A35.

12. On upstate NY, see esp. Paul E. Johnson, *A Shopkeeper's Millennium: Society and Revivals in Rochester, New York, 1815–1837* (New York, 1978), and Mary P. Ryan, *Cradle of the Middle Class: The Family in Oneida County, New York, 1790–1865* (New York, 1981), 60–104.

13. Jon Butler, *Awash in a Sea of Faith: Christianizing the American People* (Cambridge, MA, 1990), 224.

14. For an overview, see Ronald G. Walters, *American Reformers, 1815–1860*, reprint ed. (1978; New York, 1997), 21–60. See also Butler, *Awash in a Sea of Faith*, 225–36, 252–55, and Hatch, *Democratization*, 40–43.

15. Hatch, *Democratization*, 67–122; Butler, *Awash in a Sea of Faith*, 225–56, 250.

16. *Aurora, and General Advertiser* (PH), 5 August 1803, reprinted in John Ffirth, *A Friendly Reply to "A Few Remarks" on the Subject of the Present and Past State of Religion in the United States* (Burlington, NJ, 1803), 9–10; [Anon.], *A Few Remarks on the Subject of the Present and Past State of Religion in the United States* ([n.p.], NJ, 1803), 2.

17. Ffirth, *Friendly Reply*, 5–6.

18. On Delaware, see chap. 7 above. On New England, see George C. Baker, *An Introduction to the History of Early New England Methodism, 1789–1839* (Durham, NC, 1941), 45.

19. Philip Gatch, Autobiography, Gatch Microfilm Group I, pp. 31, 40–44, MTSO; idem to Benjamin Gatch, 11 February 1802, Gatch Microfilm Group IV, MTSO. On Jeffersonian Indian policy, see Anthony F. C. Wallace, " 'The Obtaining Lands': Thomas Jefferson and the Native Americans," in Ronda, *Thomas Jefferson*, 25–41.

20. William B. Sprague, *Annals of the American Pulpit; or Commemorative Notices of Distinguished American Clergymen of Various Denominations*, vol. 7, *The Methodists* (New York, 1859), s.v. "McKendree, William."

21. Bruce David Forbes, " 'And Obey God, Etc.': Methodism and American Indians," in *Perspectives on American Methodism: Interpretive Essays*, ed. Russell E. Richey, Kenneth E. Rowe, and Jean Miller Schmidt (Nashville, 1993), 209–27. On the early-nineteenth-century revival among the Seneca, see Anthony F. C. Wallace, *The Death and Rebirth of the Seneca* (1969; New York, 1972).

22. See, for example, Ronald Schultz, "God and Workingmen: Popular Religion and the Formation of Philadelphia's Working Class, 1790–1830," in *Religion in a Revolutionary Age*, ed. Ronald Hoffman and Peter J. Albert (Charlottesville, VA, 1994), 125–55, and Carroll Smith-Rosenberg, "The Cross and the Pedestal: Women, Anti-Ritualism, and the Emergence of the American Bourgeoisie," in idem, *Disorderly Conduct: Visions of Gender in Victorian America* (New York, 1985), 129–64.

23. William S. McFeely, *Frederick Douglass* (New York, 1991), 67–68; Frederick Douglass, *Narrative of the Life of Frederick Douglass, An American Slave, Written By Himself*, reprint ed. (1845; New York, 1982), 153–59. Douglass later purchased the Strawberry Alley Chapel and converted it into dwellings called Douglass's Place: James A. Handy, *Scraps of African Methodist Episcopal History* (Philadelphia, [ca. 1901]), 16.

24. Charles Grandison Finney, *Lectures on Revivals of Religion*, ed. William G. McLoughlin (1835; Cambridge, MA, 1960), 273; 9. See also Goen, "Methodist Age," 565, and Hatch, *Democratization*, 196–201.

25. John B. Boles, *The Great Revival, 1787–1805: The Origins of the Southern Evangelical Mind* (Lexington, KY, 1972), 63. The advantage of camp meetings for the Methodists' competitors is evidenced by a gathering in Warren County, South Carolina, where 3 Presbyterian and 5 Baptist ministers joined 18 Methodist ministers to lead a meeting of some 7,000 people in 1803: Stith Mead to [TC], 4 January 1803, in *Methodist Magazine* (London) 26 (1803): 418–19.

26. Kirk Mariner, "William Penn Chandler and Revivalism in the East, 1797–1811," *MH* 25 (1987): 135–40.

27. Mr. W. to Editor of *Methodist Magazine*, ca. 1805, in EC Collection, GTS. See also descriptions in William Penn Chandler to [FA], excerpted in *J&L*, 3:327–31; William Morgan, "Morgan's Memoir of his own life and time," 37–40, DSA; Mariner, "William Penn Chandler," 141–42; and William H. Williams, *The Garden of American Methodism: The Delmarva Peninsula, 1769–1820* (Wilmington, DE, 1984), 82–84.

28. Mr. W. to Editor.

29. *J&L*, 3:330–31.

30. Morgan, "Morgan's Memoir," 40. See also Williams, *Garden*, 83–84.

31. Morgan, "Morgan's Memoir," 41; G. A. Raybold, *Annals of Methodism; or Sketches of the Origin and Progress of Methodism in Various Portions of West Jersey; derived from the most authentic sources. First series. Camden and Vicinity* (Philadelphia, 1847), 139–40.

32. Mariner, "William Penn Chandler," 141–42.

33. Mr. W. to Editor; William P. Chandler to FA, 5 August 1805, in *J&L*, 3:327–31; Morgan, "Morgan's Memoir," 39.

34. Mariner, "William Penn Chandler," 144–45; Morgan, "Morgan's Memoir," 42.

35. Robert Drew Simpson, "Lost Letters of Bishop Asbury," *MH* 32 (1994): 103.

36. Morgan, "Morgan's Memoir," 38–39.

37. Peter Cartwright, *Autobiography of Peter Cartwright, The Backwoods Preacher*, ed. W. P. Strickland (New York, 1857), 2, 23, 37–38, 49, 63, 65–66, 72, 341. See also Charles L. Wallis, introduction to *Autobiography of Peter Cartwright*, reprint ed. (Nashville, 1984), 5–9: Running as a Democrat, Cartwright lost to Lincoln in the 1846 congressional race.

38. Christine Leigh Heyrman, *Southern Cross: The Beginnings of the Bible Belt* (New York, 1997), 206–52, 248; Cartwright, *Autobiography*, 63. See also Susan Juster, *Disorderly Women: Sexual Politics and Evangelicalism in Revolutionary New England* (Ithaca, NY, 1994).

39. Richard Carwardine, "Methodist Ministers and the Second Party System," in Richey, Rowe, and Schmidt, *Perspectives*, 163, 167.

40. Hatch, *Democratization*, 204, 297n, 201–4; William R. Cannon, "Education, Publication, Benevolent Work, and Missions," in *The History of American Methodism*, ed. Emory Stevens Bucke et al., 3 vols. (New York and Nashville, 1964), 1:576–78.

41. Cannon, "Education," 1:552, 553–60, 583–85.

42. Hatch, *Democratization*, 202. The first of these new structures may well have been the chapel erected by the Philadelphia Academy Church on Tenth Street in 1811, called "City Road" by FA after JW's leading chapel in London; an early Methodist historian described it as "much the best church edifice that the Methodists then had in the nation," and it too suffered the loss of members unhappy with symbolic departure from Wesleyan simplicity: John Lednum, *A History of the Rise of Methodism in America, Containing Sketches of Methodist Itinerant Preachers, From 1736 to 1785* (Philadelphia, 1859), 430.

43. A. Gregory Schneider, *The Way of the Cross Leads Home: The Domestication of American Methodism* (Bloomington, IN, 1993), 74–75; see also full discussion on women, 169–95.

44. *The Methodist Magazine* (NY) 1 (1818) 9 (1826), passim; Joanna Bowen Gillespie, "The Emerging Voice of the Methodist Woman: *The Ladies' Repository*, 1841–61," in Richey, Rowe, and Schmidt, *Perspectives*, 248–64.

45. Cannon, "Education," 1:581, 560; Gillespie, "Emerging Voice," 252.

46. Lorenzo Dow, *The Life and Travels of Lorenzo Dow, Written By Himself: In Which Are Contained Some Singular Providences of God* (Hartford, CT, 1804), 170–88, 219–21; Nicholas Snethen to Matthias Joyce, 16 November 1805, quoted in Lorenzo Dow, *History of Cosmopolite; or the Four Volumes of Lorenzo's Journal. Concentrated in One*, 3d ed., corr. and enl. (Philadelphia, 1816), 578; see also Richard Carwardine, *Trans-Atlantic Revivalism: Popular Evangelicalism in Britain and America, 1790–1865* (Westport, CT, 1978), 103–7. On women preachers leaving the MEC, see Catherine A. Brekus, *Strangers and Pilgrims: Female Preaching in America, 1740–1845* (Chapel Hill, NC, 1998), 294–95.

47. Hatch, *Democratization*, 132; see also 36–40, 130–33. Among Dow's titles are *A Chain, With Its Concomitants: Or, Polemical Reflections* (Poughkeepsie, NY, 1809), *Cosmopolite Interrogated: Or, A Dialogue Between the Curious and Singular!*, 5th ed. (New York, 1813), and *Lorenzo's Thoughts on the Progress of Light and Liberty* (Philadelphia, 1817).

48. Carwardine, *Trans-atlantic Revivalism*, 106–7, Julia Stewart Werner, *The Primitive Methodist Connexion: Its Background and Early History* (Madison, WI, 1984), 45–50, and Frederick E. Maser and George A. Singleton, "Further Branches of Methodism Are Founded," in Bucke, *History of American Methodism*, 1:630–35; on English women especially, see Deborah Valenze, *Prophetic Sons and Daughters: Female Preaching and Popular Religion in Industrial England* (Princeton, 1985).

49. See Peggy Dow, *Vicissitudes; or the Journey of Life*, reprinted in Dow, *History of Cosmopolite*, 593–700; Lorenzo Dow, preface to Nancy Towle, *Vicissitudes Illustrated, in the Experience of Nancy Towle, in Europe and America*, 2d ed. (Portsmouth, NH, 1833), 16, the title of Towle's book apparently inspired by Peggy Dow's autobiography.

50. "African Supplement," reprinted in RA, *The Life Experience and Gospel Labours of the Rt. Rev. Richard Allen*, ed. George A. Singleton, reprint ed. (New York, 1960), 37–41. On these developments, see Will B. Gravely, "African Methodisms and the Rise of Black Denominationalism," in Richey, Rowe, and Schmidt, *Perspectives*, 110–17, and Gary B. Nash, *Forging Freedom: The Formation of Philadelphia's Black Community, 1720–1840* (Cambridge, MA, 1988), 198.

51. Gravely, "African Methodisms," 116; Nash, *Forging Freedom*, 193, 228–31.

52. Will B. Gravely, "The Rise of African Churches in America (1786–1822): Re-Examining the Contexts," *Journal of Religious Thought* 41 (1984): 71; idem, "African Methodisms," 117–20.

53. RA had had an uneasy relationship with FA. Lorenzo Dow, an associate of RA's, claimed that FA had "embargoed" RA to settle in Philadelphia to avoid competition from the black evangelist: see "On Church Government, Etc.," dated 10th mo. 9th 1816, in *History of Cosmopolite* (1816), 558–59. Dow refers to the exact size of RA's first society— forty-two members—as also reported by *RA* in his *Life*, suggesting that RA was in the process of writing his undated memoir in this year, and that he was the source of Dow's information. FA, however, was far more conciliatory toward black independence than were the southern preachers.

54. David Smith, *Biography of Rev. David Smith of the A.M.E. Church*, facsimile ed. (1881; Freeport, NY, 1971), 134–35. On the founding meetings, see Handy, *Scraps of African Methodist Episcopal History*, 26, Maser and Singleton, "Further Branches," 1:606– 9, and Nash, *Forging Freedom*, 230–33. On subsequent years, see Christopher Phillips, *The African American Community of Baltimore, 1790–1860* (Urbana, IL, 1997), 133–44.

55. Gravely, "African Methodisms," 122–24; Maser and Singleton, "Further Branches," 1:611–14. Peter Spencer's Wilmington Union Methodists remained independent of both the MEC and AME churches, while loosely affiliated with congregations in Connecticut, New York, New Jersey, Pennsylvania, and Canada: Maser and Singleton, "Further Branches," 1:616.

56. Albert J. Raboteau, *Slave Religion: The "Invisible Institution" in the Antebellum South* (Oxford, 1978), 163; Clarence Walker, *A Rock in a Weary Land: The African Methodist Episcopal Churches during the Civil War and Reconstruction* (Baton Rouge, LA, 1982), 19–20.

57. Cannon, "Education," 1:592; Raboteau, *Slave Religion*, 176.

58. Jarena Lee, *The Life and Religious Experience of Jarena Lee, A Coloured Lady, Giving an Account of Her Call to Preach the Gospel . . . Written by Herself* (1836), reprinted in *Sisters of the Spirit: Three Black Women's Autobiographies of the Nineteenth Century*, ed. William L. Andrews (Bloomington, IN, 1986), 36; introduction to ibid., 4–7, 36.

59. Zilpha Elaw, *Memoirs of the Life, Religious Experience, Ministeral Travels and Labours of Mrs. Zilpha Elaw, An American Female of Colour* (1846), reprinted in Andrews, *Sisters of the Spirit*, 61–62, 124.

60. Douglas R. Chandler, "The Formation of the Methodist Protestant Church," in Bucke, *History of American Methodism*, 1:638–54.

61. Ibid., 650.

62. Ibid., 654–65. An earlier group of Reformed Methodists left in 1814 over some of the same issues, although also holding to faith healing, pacifism, and antislavery: Maser and Singleton, "Further Branches," 1:622–24.

63. Quoted in Donald G. Mathews, *Slavery and Methodism: A Chapter in American Morality, 1780–1845* (Princeton, 1965), 126; see also 112–24, 88–92.

64. Quoted in ibid., 231; see also 216–32; and Timothy L. Smith, *Revivalism and Social Reform: American Protestantism on the Eve of the Civil War*, reprint ed. (1957; New York, 1965), 114–34.

65. Mathews, *Slavery and Methodism*, 254; see full discussion of the 1844 general conference, 246–69.

66. Ibid., 255–67, 272.

67. Smith, *Revivalism*, 129–34; Donald W. Dayton, "From 'Christian Perfection' to the Baptism of the Holy Ghost,' " in Richey, Rowe, and Schmidt, *Perspectives*, 289–97.

68. Smith, *Revivalism*, 20; Goss, *Statistical History*, 109–14. The precise numbers, from Smith for 1855, and from Goss for 1865, are as follows:

Branch	1855	1865
MEC North	783,358	929,259
Methodist Church, South	579,525	708,949
Methodist Protestant Church	70,015	105,120
The Evangelical Association (an independent Wesleyan church)	21,076	51,185
AME Church	21,237	53,670
AME(Z) Church	6,203	30,600
Wesleyan Methodist Church	23,000	25,620
Free Methodist Church	—	3,655
Primitive Methodist Church	1,100	1,805
Total	*1,505,514**	*1,909,863*

*The total cited in Smith (1,577,014) includes 67,000 United Brethren and 4,500 Calvinistic Methodists.

In 1865, the various Baptist churches tallied 1,399,637 communicants within their ranks; Presbyterians, also split into southern and northern halves, altogether counted 609,977. See extended discussion of the secularization of Methodism and rising strength of the Baptists after the Civil War in Roger Finke and Rodney Stark, *The Churching of America, 1776–1990: Winners and Losers in Our Religious Economy* (New Brunswick, NJ, 1992), 145–98. For a provocative sampling of the varieties of American religious experience before and after the Civil War, see Harold Bloom, *The American Religion: The Emergence of the Post-Christian Nation* (New York, 1992). Bloom does not discuss the most important of these new options, at the center of American immigrant life: the Roman Catholic Church.

As of 1998, close to 8,500,000 Americans belong to the United Methodist Church, and another 7,000,000 to its historical offspring. Current statistics for inclusive membership, dating from various years, appear in Eileen W. Lindner, ed., *Yearbook of American and Canadian Churches* (Nashville, 1998), 304–11. Besides the United Methodist Church, denominational memberships tallied here include those for the African Methodist Episcopal Church, the African Methodist Episcopal Zion Church, the Allegheny Wesleyan Methodist Connection, the Christian Methodist Episcopal Church, the Church of God (Anderson, Indiana), the Church of the Nazarene, the Evangelical Methodist Church, the Free Methodist Church of North America, the Fundamental Methodist Church, Inc., the Primitive Methodist Church in the U.S.A., the Salvation Army, the Southern Methodist Church, Inc., and the Wesleyan Church. The AME and AMEZ denominations, with 3,500,000 and 1,252,369 inclusive memberships respectively, are by far the largest of these Wesleyan descendants. For a summary of Methodist denominational splinterings, see *Dictionary of Christianity in America*, ed. Daniel G. Reid (Downers Grove, IL, 1990), s.v. "Methodist Churches."

69. James Sowden, *An Inquiry into the Cause of the Prosperity of the Methodist Episcopal Church in the United States* (Sag Harbor, NY, 1809), 3, 11–21, 29–41.

70. *J&L*, 3:415.

71. Emphasis added: ibid., 476.

72. Ibid., 491–92.

73. Sowden, *Inquiry*, 38.

CONCLUSION: A PLAIN GOSPEL FOR A PLAIN PEOPLE

1. *Methodism delineated, or a Discourse Taken in Short Hand, As lately delivered in the Academy in Norwich, by G.P. one of that Sectary, With some brief Remarks thereon annexed* (Norwich, [CT], 1795), 5, 7–8, 10–12.

2. William Colbert, Journal (1790–1833), 10 vols., vol. 2 (1794–1798), 21 September 1794, p. 21, GTS.

3. David Campbell to [Rev. James P. Carrell], 27 February 1850, Campbell Family Papers, Box (1850–1851), DU.

APPENDIX D

1. *D&D* (1798), 78.

2. Christine Leigh Heyrman, *Southern Cross: The Beginnings of the Bible Belt* (New York, 1997), 261. See also 323n.

3. Jesse Lee, *A Short History of the Methodists, in the United States of America: beginning in 1766, and continued till 1809* (Baltimore, 1810), 163.

4. TC to William White, 24 April 1791, microfilm, NYHS.

5. Lee, *Short History*, 371–40. Lee also set the stage for what Kenneth Rowe describes as "focusing on how the Methodists kept pace with the nation's march": "Counting the Converts: Progress Reports as Church History," in *Rethinking Methodist History: A Bicentennial Historical Consultation*, ed. Russell E. Richey and idem (Nashville, 1985), 12.

6. Peter Cartwright, *Autobiography of Peter Cartwright, the Backwoods Preacher*, ed. W. P. Strickland (New York, 1857), 521–23.

7. Frank Lambert, *"Pedlar in Divinity": George Whitefield and the Transatlantic Revivals, 1737–1770* (Princeton, 1994), 63.

INDEX

Names of American Methodists, including immigrants, appear in italics.

Abbott, Benjamin, 56, 59, 80–84, 110, 134, 138, 141, 159, 174, 195, 217, 290n.4, 295n.66; conversion of, 86–87, 89–90, 92; and preaching, 82, 84, 156–58, 208–9, 294n.56

Abbott, David, 56, 306n.102

abolitionism. *See* antislavery, Methodist

Abraham, Ann, 306n.102

Academy Church (Phila.), 176–77, 260, 330nn.128 and 135, 346n.42

Adam Bede (the novel, 1859), xii

Adams, John, 52, 193, 195

African Americans. *See* black Methodists

African Methodist Episcopal Churches. *See* AME Churches.

African Methodist societies, 138–39, 153. *See also* AME; Fish St. African Methodist Society; Sharp St. African Methodist Society

African Methodists. *See* black Methodists

age: of preachers, 64, 89–90, 203, 207–9, 218; of women members, 114–15

Age of Reason, The (1794), 187, 191–92

Airey, Henry, 104, 159

Airey, Thomas Hill, 57, 130

Allen, Beverly, 217

Allen, Flora, 149, 319n.122

Allen, John, 88, 140–41, 149, 319n.122

Allen, Richard, xii, 8, 171, 180, 234, 316n.85; and African union church, 144–47; and AME (1816), 232, 234; AME (Phila.), 148–50; and Bethel Chapel, 319n.122; conversion of, 86, 88–92, 140–41; early life of, 88–89, 140–41, 316n.86; elected as bishop of AME (1816), 234; emancipation of, 89–90, 140–41; entrepreneurship and wealth of, 147, 316n.91, 318nn.115 and 116; and FAS, 144–45; and Francis Asbury, 142, 148, 347n.53; itinerancy of, 141–42; Methodist identity of, 146–48; ordained as local deacon, 150; portrait of, 142 fig. 8; and promotion of black preachers, 139–50; and relationship to white preachers, 140–42, 146–48, 173–74

Allen, Sarah (neé Bass), 149

altar call, 226.

AME Church (1816), 222, 232, 234, 237, 348n.68

AME Church (Ezion), 152. *See also* Union Church of African Members

AME Church (Phila.), xii, 8, 168, 175, 177, 257, 291; and African Supplement, 232; and antislavery, 150, 320n.133; founding of, 148–50, 318n.111, 319n.122; members of, 149–50, 319n.127, 320n.132, table 10 in appendix

AME Church (Zion), 151–52, 163, 222, 234, 237, 321nn.142 and 144, 348n.68

AME Churches. *See* AME Church (1816); AME Church (Ezion); AME Church (Phila.); AME Church (Zion)

American colonies, 13–14, 29–31, 38–47, 49, 123. *See also* Middle Atlantic

American Revolution, xi-xiii, 8–9, 47–72, 81, 106, 124–25, 129–30, 145, 190–91, 204–5, 230, 241, 267n.10

Americanization, of Methodism, 3–9, 220, 237–44

Anderson, Mary, 118, 167

Anderson, James, 160

Anderson, William, 152

Anglican Church. *See* Anglicans; Church of England

Anglican reforming societies, 13–18, 62. *See also* Bray, Thomas; SPCK; SPG

Anglicans, 95, 241, 243; in American colonies, 34, 37–38; evangelicals among, 34–37, 41–42, 47, 66, 125, 144–50, 168, 177, 190–91; and founding of MEC, 70, 289n.177; after Revolutionary War, 62–63, 65, 69, 162, 179, 240, 290n.4. *See also* Anglican reforming societies; Church of England

Annapolis (MD), 8, 101, 109, 129, 132, 223

antifederalism, 187–88, 203, 204

Anti-Federalists 188–89

antislavery, Methodist, 46, 71, 125–32, 165, 181–82, 191, 310–11n.14, 320n.133; after 1800, 235–36, 347n.62. *See also* First Emancipation; Pennsylvania Abolition Society

Arcularius, Elizabeth, 116

Arcularius, Philip Jacob, 164–66, 326n.60

Armat, Thomas, 74, 85, 130, 171, 328n.105

Arminian Magazine (Phila.), 196

Arminianism. *See* Wesleyan theology

Armstrong, James, 171

Armstrong, John, 182

Armstrong, Robert, 280n.27

Armstrong, Thomas, 280n.27